Alexander Runciman, *The Blind Ossian Singing and Accompanying Himself on the Harp*, 1772. The National Galleries of Scotland, Edinburgh, D 299. Reproduced with permission.

Beyond Fingal's Cave

Ossian in the Musical Imagination

James Porter

UNIVERSITY OF ROCHESTER PRESS

The University of Rochester Press and the author gratefully acknowledge generous support from the Otto Kinkeldey Endowment of the American Musicological Society, funded in part by the National Endowment for the Humanities and the Andrew W. Mellon Foundation.

Copyright © 2019 by James Porter

All rights reserved. Except as permitted under current legislation, no part of this work may be photocopied, stored in a retrieval system, published, performed in public, adapted, broadcast, transmitted, recorded, or reproduced in any form or by any means, without the prior permission of the copyright owner.

First published 2019
Reprinted in paperback 2022

University of Rochester Press
668 Mt. Hope Avenue, Rochester, NY 14620, USA
www.urpress.com
and Boydell & Brewer Limited
PO Box 9, Woodbridge, Suffolk IP12 3DF, UK
www.boydellandbrewer.com

ISBN-13: 978-1-58046-945-6 hardcover
ISBN-13: 978-1-64825-034-7 paperback
ISSN: 1071-9989

Library of Congress Cataloging-in-Publication Data

Names: Porter, James, 1937– author.
Title: Beyond Fingal's cave : Ossian in the musical imagination / James Porter.
Other titles: Eastman studies in music ; v. 158.
Description: Rochester : University of Rochester Press, 2019. | Series: Eastman studies in music ; v. 158 | Includes bibliographical references and index.
Identifiers: LCCN 2019020021 | ISBN 9781580469456 (hardcover : alk. paper)
Subjects: LCSH: Music—19th century—History and criticism. | Music—20th century—History and criticism. | Ossian, active 3rd century. | Romanticism in music.
Classification: LCC ML196 .P67 2019 | DDC 780.9/034—dc23 LC record available at https://lccn.loc.gov/2019020021

This publication is printed on acid-free paper.
Printed in the United States of America.

To my family: Christina and James

Toi qui chantais l'amour et les héros,
Toi d'Ossian la compagne assidue,
Harpe plaintive, en ce triste repos
Ne reste pas plus longtemps suspendue!
Du vent du soir j'entends les sifflements;
L'obscur brouillard se promène à pas lents;
Porté vers nous sur des nuages sombres,
Je vois venir le peuple heureux des ombres:
Chante! ta voix saura les arrêter.
De leurs exploits recueille la mémoire.
Sans doute encore elles aiment leur gloire;
Oui, je le vois, elles vont t'écouter!

(Thou who hast sung of love and heroes,
Thou diligent companion of Ossian,
Mournful harp, in thy sad repose
Do not any longer stay suspended!
I hear the whistling of the evening wind,
The gloomy mist advances slowly;
Brought down upon us by darkling clouds
I see, nearing, the blissful folk of the shades:
Sing! Thy voice will know how to stop them.
Gather the memory of their feats,
Without doubt they still love their glory.
Yes, I see now, to thee they will listen!

—Alphonse de Lamartine, 1808

Translated by James Porter and Jehane Zouyene

Contents

	Preface	xiii
	Acknowledgments	xvii
	Note to the Reader	xxi
1	Battling Critics, Engaging Composers: Ossian's Spell	1
2	On Macpherson's Native Heath: Primary Sources	18
3	A Culture without Writing, Settings without a Score, Haydn without Copyright, and Two *Oscar*s on Stage	32
4	"A Musical Piece": Harriet Wainewright's opera *Comàla* (1792)	45
5	Between Gluck and Berlioz: Méhul's *Uthal* (1806)	57
6	*Fingallo e Comala* (1805) and *Ardano e Dartula* (1825): The Ossianic Operas of Stefano Pavesi	72
7	From Venice to Lisbon and St. Petersburg: *Calto*, *Clato*, *Aganadeca*, *Gaulo ed Oitona*, and Two *Fingal*s	87
8	Beethoven's Ossianic Manner, or Where Scholars Fear to Tread	102
	❧ ❧ ❧	
	Excursus: Mendelssohn Waives the Rules: "Overture to the Isles of Fingal" (1832) and an "Unfinished" Coda	113
	❧ ❧ ❧	
9	The Maiden Bereft: "Colma" from Rust (1780) to Schubert (1816)	123
10	*Scènes lyriques sans frontières*: Louis Théodore Gouvy's *Le dernier Hymne d'Ossian* (1858) and Lucien Hillemacher's *Fingal* (1880)	146

11 Ossian in Symbolic Conflict: Bernhard Hopffer's *Darthula's Grabesgesang* (1878), Jules Bordier's *Un rêve d'Ossian* (1885), and Paul Umlauft's *Agandecca* (1884) 171

12 The Musical Stages of "Darthula": From Thomas Linley the Younger (ca. 1776) to Arnold Schoenberg (1903) and Armin Knab (1906) 194

13 The Cantata as Drama: Joseph Jongen's *Comala* (1897), Jørgen Malling's *Kyvala* (1902), and Liza Lehmann's *Leaves from Ossian* (1909) 216

14 Symphonic Poem and Orchestral Fantasy: Alexandre Levy's *Comala* (1890) and Charles Villiers Stanford's *Irish Rhapsody No. 2: Lament for the Son of Ossian* (1903) 238

15 Neo-Romanticism in Britain and America: John Laurence Seymour's "Shilric's Song" (from *Six Ossianic Odes*) and Cedric Thorpe Davie's *Dirge for Cuthullin* (both 1936) 257

16 Modernity, Modernism, and Ossian: Erik Chisholm's *Night Song of the Bards* (1944–51), James MacMillan's *The Death of Oscar* (2013), and Jean Guillou's *Ballade Ossianique, No. 2: Les chants de Selma* (1971, rev. 2005) 274

Afterword: The "Half-Viewless Harp"—Secondary Resonances of Ossian 293

Appendix 1: Title Page and Dedication of Harriet Wainewright's *Comàla* 305

Appendix 2: French and German Texts of Louis Théodore Gouvy's *Le dernier Hymne d'Ossian* 307

Appendix 3: Texts of Erik Chisholm's *Night Song of the Bards* 310

Appendix 4: Provisional List of Musical Compositions Based on the Poems of Ossian 313

Notes 323

Selected Bibliography 387

Index 389

Preface

James Macpherson published his *Fragments of Ancient Poetry, collected in the Highlands of Scotland and translated from the Galic or Erse Language* in Edinburgh in 1760. The success of this work was followed by the publication in London of *Fingal* (1762) and *Temora* (1763). Together with the later editions, *The Works of Ossian* (1765) and the revised *The Poems of Ossian* (1773), this poetry was hugely influential on the course of European Romanticism. With their novel emphasis on heroic ideals, noble behavior, and feeling rather than the formal elegance of Enlightenment verse, these prose poems impressed personalities such as Thomas Jefferson and Napoleon as well as literary giants from Goethe and Schiller to Byron and Pushkin. Composers such as Franz Schubert and Johannes Brahms set the poems that Macpherson (and others, including the Irishman Edmund de Harold) had rendered, sometimes very freely, from oral and written Gaelic sources attributed to the legendary third-century bard Ossian (the anglicized version of the Gaelic name Oisín). While the English-language versions, principally those of Macpherson, were met with enthusiasm and also skepticism as to their authenticity, they inspired translations into most European tongues. In turn, the translations as well as the English-language originals provided the basis for a remarkable number of music settings. Over three hundred compositions (monodramas, operas, cantatas, pieces for solo instrument, symphonic poems) poured forth, from the late eighteenth century even into the twenty-first—works that are largely unknown or obscure but at times astounding in their originality and inventiveness. This book is chiefly about them.

The period that receives most attention here is the flowering of "musical Osssianism" just before, during, and for some time after the Romantic era, from about 1780 to 1900. My mainly chronological examination of this long century is buttressed near the outset by discussion of "traditional" sources of music and their role in the genesis of the poems (chapter 2) and towards the end by a brief exploration of "modernity" (chapter 16). We can view modernity here not just as a convenient term for an opaque time period but as a force that qualifies and modifies the dominantly "romantic" stance of composers in their emotional reaction to and realization of the poems. In the dialectic between feeling and structure, modernity can act for the latter as a counterbalance: it suggests the cumulative weighing of rationality, compositional skill, and awareness of public expectation as against the surge of inspiration. Equilibrium between the two forces is not always achieved satisfactorily, or even achieved at all. But sufficient masterpieces have emerged to prove the powerful impetus of the Ossian poems in the creation of original music.

One concept that is invoked throughout this study of musical works based on the poems ascribed to Ossian is that of *transmediation*, a term derived from semiotics. I use it in the sense of adaptation or transference from one medium to another in the creation of a different genre (that is, from poetry to a musical form, whether monodrama, opera, cantata, symphonic poem, or work for solo instrument). I outline this process of transmediation, the thread that connects the book's chapters, in more detail in chapter 1. With this concept in mind I decided to deal relatively briefly with the most celebrated (and analyzed) piece of abstract music associated with Ossian, Mendelssohn's overture *Die Hebriden* (the "Hebrides" overture, 1832; also called *Die Fingals-Höhle* or Fingal's Cave), in an excursus, outside the standard chapters, because of the extraordinary physical as well as psychic effect on the composer of his voyage to the island of Staffa in 1829.

On the other hand, I have chosen not to treat here the two Ossian-derived works by Mendelssohn's Danish friend and contemporary Niels W. Gade, namely the overture "Echoes of Ossian" (1841) and the cantata *Comala* (1846), since a number of commentaries on these works already exist. Nor have I elected to discuss Jean-François Le Sueur's epochal and sensational opera *Ossian, ou les Bardes* (1804), which has likewise undergone descriptive analysis at other hands.[1] Many musical works influenced by Ossian are accessible in published form while others, catalogued in library manuscript holdings, are normally available for study. Less fortuitously, published lists of composers' works often lack those directly inspired by Ossian. My decisions on which compositions to select for discussion in this book were based partly on ease of access, partly on personal judgment.

The chapter organization here is largely chronological (from late classical through Romantic to modern) because the gradual progression from opera to cantata and purely instrumental pieces, as well as the persistence of solo song, signifies the developing way in which composers perceived and realized the poetry of Ossian in the long nineteenth century. Chapters 7 and 12, however, depart from this progression by pausing to consider in detail first the thematic grouping of certain opera plots and their dissemination throughout Europe (chapter 7), and second, genre development and variety in the multiple settings of one outstanding poem ("Dar-thula") from the late eighteenth to the twentieth century (chapter 12). Following chapter 4, and again after chapter 8, the discussion assumes some knowledge of musical terminology and analytical method in the reader. But this book, though part of a well-established series of music monographs, is a work of musical historiography rather than of abstract theory. It is intended as much for a broadly-informed readership as for specialists in music, simply because the central topic is of extensive literary and cultural interest. It aims at clarity of exposition, and readability.

While the early Ossian lieder of Schubert, Mendelssohn's "Hebrides" overture, Brahms's two cantatas "Gesang von Ossian" (op. 17) and "Darthulas Grabesgesang" (op. 42, no. 3), and Massenet's Ossian-derived aria "Pourquoi me réveiller, ô souffle du printemps?" in his opera *Werther* are relatively familiar, it is heartening that lesser-known works inspired by the poems have lately been revived, both in live performances and recordings: Friedrich Wilhelm Rust's astounding monodrama *Colma* (1780), for instance, and Étienne Méhul's dark one-act opera *Uthal* (1806), each a masterpiece. Pietro Morandi's groundbreaking opera in pre-Romantic style, *Comala* (1780), was staged in Vadstena, Sweden, in 2015. Commercial recordings of Romantic and, especially, modernist works inspired by Ossian, such those by Erik Chisholm or Jean Guillou, are readily available in recordings and scores.

Although this book is concerned chiefly with concert music, I also consider (chapter 2) the traditional oral culture in which Macpherson located his sources for Ossian's poems. It has long been shown that the poet drew the subject matter from personal knowledge of his native Gaelic-language tradition as well as from manuscript sources such as the sixteenth-century "Book of the Dean of Lismore," an important compilation whose survival we owe to Macpherson. In the Scottish Highlands traditional forms of communication such as tales and songs were a dominant cultural fact. Thematic novelty played a much less prominent role; repetition and standard epithets represented a world of steely but vulnerable warriors, beauteous and valiant women, both set against a brooding landscape of mountains, storms, torrents, with the occasional armed foray through perilous seas; the names of known personages and locations were resonant.[2] Stories about the bard Ossian, and songs reputedly by him about his father, Fionn (Macpherson's Fingal), and the Fenian warriors as defenders of Erin (Ireland), were recorded in Gaelic-speaking areas of the Scottish Highlands and from emigrant Gaels well into the twentieth century. Whatever the quality of Macpherson's English-language poems, their long-term influence on representational art and literature is by now well attested, but their influence on music is much less so. This book may, I hope, go some way toward redressing that gap.

Finally, some critics may feel that Ossian symbolizes the attempt by Anglophone Europeans to dominate and colonize the world, militarily, economically, and culturally (and perhaps ideologically as well). Macpherson, after all, was for a time an agent of the British administration in Florida and became, in the wake of his literary success, an apologist for state domination of the American colonies. This domination, after independence, morphed into racism, giving continued support to slavery and, later, to race-based segregation and exclusion in the United States and elsewhere. But one answer to the charge of cultural appropriation by the forces of domination is that the poems also powerfully appealed to and encouraged aspiring nations of the Romantic era as they sought to break away from imperial suppression.

The accusation of racism in Ossian is troubling; that of sexism less so. How did the poems, and the music they inspired, embody domination when their narrative was so often one of heroic struggle, frequently by women, or moral behavior toward antagonists? Many readers esteemed the Ossian poems for their generosity toward enemies, unlike the mutual savagery of combatants in Homer. Women are admired not just for their beauty but also as part of a sophisticated view of gender, for assuming male roles in armed conflict, at the same time that their male warrior counterparts display "feminine" traits such as weeping and consolation. It is not surprising, then, that a female composer in the latter part of the nineteenth century, Marie Jaëll, should compose a symphonic cantata in which Ossian has become a woman.[3]

Edmund Burke's twin concepts of The Sublime and The Beautiful (1757) penetrated deeply into the consciousness of eighteenth-century readers, preparing the way for a new landscape of feeling, and with it, poetry of sensibility, prime among which was the poetry of Ossian. Ossian has endured because the Romanticism it fostered powered its way into the twentieth century (despite fierce resistance) partly through the resonance of its names and the poetic narratives associated with them. For some composers, the fashion of modernity (making present the new, and also as a more generalized concept than modernism) was not wholly able to counter the appeal of Romanticism as they came to grips in their music with questions of style and appropriateness. But I suggest that while Romanticism tended to give way, from World War I, to varieties of modernity, it is surprising that more composers have not exploited the episodic structure of the poems to devise a musical narrative that is more authentically true to the texts. For such work, we must turn to Rust's monodrama *Colma* (1780) and to pieces written much later: Erik Chisholm's virtuosic piano nocturnes *Night Song of the Bards* (1941–44) and Jean Guillou's rhapsodic *Ballade Ossianique, No. 2: Les chants de Selma* for organ (1971, rev. 2005).[4]

As I reflect on the motives that drew me into this work of some years, I should confess to an involvement with European traditional music and its links with composition, performance, and reception. The complex character of traditional expressive genres has been a major source of engagement, just as it has been for all those who found in the poems of Ossian, as in European folk ballads, a lost world of heroes, bards, and warrior women, along with descriptions of nature that conjure up the ferocity of the elements but also their gentler side. As in the folk ballads, there are no moral judgments, no Christian God, only a stoicism, a retrospective on an aging bard, familiar in popular tradition: "Ossian after the Fenians" is a title well known in Gaelic folk narrative. The narrative style of the poetry of Ossian, with its unconnected leaps (parataxis) similar to those in the folk ballads, appealed to no less a pioneering culture theorist than Johann Gottfried Herder. The episodic nature of both Ossian and ballad poetry led Herder to consider the distinctiveness of a popular expressive style, practiced and loved by generations of performers, good, bad, and indifferent, throughout the course of European oral tradition. Composers, too, caught between Romanticism and modernity, have tried to capture the manifold but elusive qualities of Ossian, even into the new millennium.

Acknowledgments

I am beholden to very many friends, colleagues, archivists, and professional librarians for their assistance in my research. Among those who have inspired me to write this ambitious book, I would mention especially Brenno Boccadoro, University of Geneva, in whose hospitable home in 2012 it was first conceived. His knowledge of musical aesthetics and our conversations as he completed his edition of Rousseau's classic *Dictionnaire de musique* were a direct stimulus for an early draft of my book; for sharing his thoughts with me, and for his generosity of mind and spirit, I owe him a huge debt. Similarly, I pay tribute to my colleague Steve Loza, until recently chair of the Department of Ethnomusicology at UCLA, for hosting me at his apartment in Los Angeles on several occasions and allowing me to stay at his desert retreat, where I drafted chapters of this book. I appreciate his public support, and that of my former colleague Joseph Nagy (now at Harvard University), and also that of Ray Knapp, former chair of the Musicology Department at UCLA, who invited me to lead a seminar there on April 3, 2015, on the topic of music inspired by Ossian. Likewise, I thank Dan Melia of Celtic Studies, UC Berkeley, who arranged my lecture there on Ossian and music on April 15, 2015. That same year, Magnus Tessing Schneider, University of Stockholm, kindly invited me to give a paper at the conference on Ossian and opera that he had organized at Vadstena, Sweden, for August 2016; he deserves special commendation for promoting, as part of the conference, a fully staged performance of Pietro Morandi's pioneering opera *Comala* (1780), which boasts a libretto by Ranieri de' Calzabigi, the renowned collaborator of Gluck in his "reform" operas. This significant event ought to result in the revival of meritorious operas (and, indeed, other musical genres) based on Ossian. And I must put on record the generous hospitality of my friend Mike Fergus, whose Oslo home served as a welcome break on my research travels between Europe and North America.

At another level of indebtedness, my esteemed former colleague Izaly Zemtsovsky promptly answered my questions on music in pre-Soviet Russia, especially for chapter 7. Rob Dunbar, University of Edinburgh, commented helpfully on the Gaelic references in chapter 2. Edward Welch, University of Aberdeen, willingly found a native speaker in his department, Jehane Zouyene, to check the French of chapters 5, 10, 11, and 13 and to discuss with me issues of translation in the prefatory poem by Lamartine. Enrico Mattioda, University of Turin, readily consented to read and make suggestions for correction and improvement in the chapters on opera in Italy, while Gerald Bär kept me straight on the usage of Brazilian Portuguese in chapter 14. And for technical expertise in compiling the musical examples, often from my wretched pencil manuscript, I am most grateful to Nathalie Vanballenberghe, who has thereby contributed hugely to the completion of this book. Last but by no means least, I express my gratitude to Howard Gaskill, doyen of contemporary Ossian scholars, who answered my endless queries promptly and read several chapters in draft. Without the benefit of his encouragement and his unrivaled knowledge, especially of German sources, I doubt this study would ever have seen the light of day.

For permission to use specific material I am especially indebted to the following (in alphabetical order): Annalisa Bini, Bibliotecamedia, Accademia Nazionale di Santa Cecilia, Rome, for quotations from Harriet Wainewright's opera *Comàla* and Antonio Leonardi's song "Dartula"; Iben Brodersen, Royal Library, Copenhagen, Denmark, for the short score of Jørgen Malling's *Kyvala*; Marina Dorigo, Teatro La Fenice Archives, Venice, for the use of material from the MS of Stefano Pavesi's opera *Ardano e Dartula;* S. Victor Fleischer, University of Akron Archives, for citation from the score of Alexandre Levy's symphonic poem *Comala*; Maria Fátima Gomes, Biblioteca da Ajuda, Lisbon, for a music example from the MS of Francesco Bianchi's opera *Calto;* Simon Groot, Special Collections, University of Amsterdam, for the microfilm short score MS of Simon van Milligen's opera *Darthula* and Selma Kogenhop-Schreuders, University of Utrecht Library, for the libretto of that opera; Andrea Harrandt, Music Collection, National Library, Vienna, for the autograph MS of Friedrich Neumann's song "Darthulas Grabesgesang"; Gunter Hägele, University of Augsburg, Germany, for a short extract from the MS of Francesco Sampieri's opera *Oscar e Malvina;* Mika Jantunen, University of the Arts, Helsinki, for the MS score of "Darthulas gravsång" by Erkki Melartin, and for the published copy of the song by Selim Palmgren; Aygün Lausch, Universal Edition, for permission to reproduce a page from Schoenberg's *Darthulas Grabgesang*; Hugh Macdonald, chairman of the Erik Chisholm Trust, for use of the composer's *Night Song of the Bards*; Michael Mullen, Royal College of Music, London, for quotations from the MS of Charles Villiers Stanford's *Irish Rhapsody No. 2: Lament for the Son of Ossian*; Olivia Wahnon de Oliveira, Bibliothèque, Conservatoire royal de Bruxelles, for extracts from the MS score of Joseph Jongen's cantata *Comala*; Sean Rippington, University of St. Andrews Archives, for permission to use material relating to Cedric Thorpe Davie; Andreas Roloff, Landesbibliothek Mecklenburg-Vorpommern, Schwerin, Germany, for material from the MS of Pietro Generali's *Gaulo ed Oitona*; Jürgen Schaarwächter, Max Reger Institute, Karlsruhe, Germany, for providing a microfilm of Adolf Busch's *Darthulas Grabgesang;* Licia Sirch, Conservatorio Giuseppe Verdi, Milan, for MS material from Luigi Caruso's *Duntalmo*. Portions of chapters 1, 10, and 11 were published as "Beyond Fingal's Cave: The Undercurrent of Cantata Settings of Ossian between Mendelssohn's 'Hebrides' Overture (1832) and Massenet's Opera *Werther* (1892)," *Journal of Musicological Research* 37, no. 4 (2018), 317–59, https://doi.org/10.1080/01411896.2018.1524696, reprinted by permission of Taylor & Francis Ltd (http://www.tandfonline.com).

In a research undertaking of this geographical and historical scope that inevitably involves knowledgeable cooperation, I would like to recognize the following (in alphabetical order): Heinrich Aerni, Central Library, Zürich; Jeppe Plum Andersen and Claus Røllum-Larsen, Royal Library, Copenhagen; Stuart Bedford, London; Cindy Brightenburg, Special Collections, Brigham Young University, Provo, Utah; Gale Burrow and Tanya Kato, Claremont Colleges Library, California; Morag Chisholm, Erik Chisholm Trust, Isle of Wight; Annarita Colturato, University of Turin, Italy; Steve Cork, Christopher Scobie, and Claire Witherspoon, British Library, London; Emma Darbyshire, Fitzwilliam Museum, Cambridge, England; Nadine Englert, Herder Institute, Marburg, Germany; Manuel Erviti and John Shepard, Music Library, UC Berkeley, California; Emily Ferrigno and Suzanne Lovejoy, Music Library, Yale University, New Haven, Connecticut; Elke Fess, Arnold Schoenberg Center, Vienna; Jean Christoph Gero, Berlin State Library; Jason Gibbs, San Francisco Public Library; Gottfried Heinz-Kronberger, Bavarian State Library, Munich; Rik Hendriks, Music Institute, The Hague; Kerstin Herzog, Carolin Rawein, and Sabine Seybold, University Library, Augsburg, Germany; Martin Holmes, Bodleian Library, Oxford, England; Peter Horton, Royal College of Music, London; Caroline Kane, Schott Music Publishers, New York; Clive Kirkwood, Special Collections, University of Cape Town, South Africa; Aygün Lausch, Universal Edition, Vienna; Lisa Lazar and David Prochazka, University Archives, University of Akron, Ohio; Laura Feliu Lloberas, National Gallery of Scotland, Edinburgh; Murdo Macdonald, University of Dundee, Scotland; Jennifer MacLeod, Edinburgh; Isabelle Mattart, Royal Conservatoire of Music, Brussels; Enrico Mattioda, University of Turin, Italy; Brian McMillan, University of Western Ontario, London, Ontario, Canada; Cristina Meisner, Harry Ransom Center, University of Texas, Austin; Angelika Neumann, Prussian Mansions and Gardens, Potsdam, Germany; Ines Pampel, State and University Library, Dresden; Andreas Pernpeintner, University of Munich; Alasdair Pettinger, Scottish Music Centre, Glasgow; Federica Riva, Luigi Cherubini Conservatoire, Florence; Bart Schuurman, State Archives, Amsterdam; Matthew Vest, Music Library, UCLA, California; Robert Wein, Stadtmuseum, Berlin; Mike Williams, Boosey & Hawkes Music Publishers, London. I am further indebted to the staff of the National Library of Scotland; to Special Collections personnel at the universities of Edinburgh, Glasgow, and St. Andrews; and to Cordula Grewe, Indiana University, Bloomington, concerning the provenance of the painting of Anna Milder-Hauptmann in chapter 5.

Finally, I want to express my gratitude to the staff at the University of Rochester Press, particularly Julia Cook and Sonia Kane, for their skill and patience in facilitating the technical aspects of my book; and to Ralph Locke, senior editor of the Eastman Studies in Music series, for his enthusiasm and erudition throughout the process of revision, especially when I needed to fill important gaps in the text. His warm encouragement was a principal factor in my desire to complete the book to the high standards of the series.

Note to the Reader

In citing musical works, I have placed shorter examples such as individual vocal or instrumental works in quotation marks but larger compositions like cantatas, song cycles, symphonic poems, suites, and so on (but not sonatas or symphonies, by convention) in italics. Thus, songs such as Beethoven's "Trocknet nicht" are set in quotes whereas a cycle of instrumental pieces has its title in italics (e.g., Chisholm's *Night Song of the Bards*). Exceptions to this general plan are works with a nickname, such as Beethoven's Symphony No. 3 ("Eroica") and Schubert's Symphony No. 8 ("Unfinished").

Another difference is in the interpretation of a particular episode such as that of Colma from "The Songs of Selma." The extensive settings of the poem by Rust, Zumsteeg, and Zelter are conceived and built in contrasting, through-composed sections. Somewhat like Rust's monodrama, which contains within it recitatives, spoken interpolations, and arias, these settings resemble a solo cantata rather than a single song. I have therefore placed the titles of these compositions in italics but the ostensibly simpler, strophic settings by Reichardt and Schubert in quotation marks.

A minor point concerns the occasional use of the apostrophe in German titles such as *Kolma's Klage* in chapter 9 or *Darthula's Grab[es]gesang* in chapter 12. Johann Gottfried Herder's original poem on Macpherson's "Dar-thula," published in his *Volkslieder* (1778), does in fact use the apostrophe, and some composers setting the poem have followed his example in the title, while others omit it. The older usage is often found until the twentieth century, when the form of German plural nouns was standardized (without the apostrophe). I have retained the apostrophe in those few settings that use it in the title. Similarly, I retain the comma before "e" in Italian texts and titles (chapters 6, 7) when it appears in the original source, even though that usage is no longer observed. For the Italian libretto texts, which are full of other inconsistencies (such as "dio/Dio" and so on), I have generally kept the original forms even when they are, in modern terms, faulty.

The music examples largely follow the notational practices of the time, including spelling and syllabification.

Chapter One

Battling Critics, Engaging Composers

Ossian's Spell

In 1763, Europe was full of ghosts, of military dead. That year saw the end of the disastrous Seven Years' War—involving all the great powers, Austria, Britain, France, Prussia, and Russia, and with around one million fatalities—in the Treaty of Paris and the Treaty of Hubertusburg. Britain was one of the victors, though at a cost of perhaps 20,000 combatants. But it was ultimately from an earlier, smaller, but significant local conflict in Britain, the Jacobite Uprising of 1745–46—in essence a dynastic quarrel between supporters of the Stuarts and the Hanoverians over the succession to the throne—that there emerged a poet who caught Europe's imagination in celebrating its ancient hero-warriors and *their* ghosts. A Gaelic bard apart, a rival to Homer, James Macpherson's Ossian seduced a continent. Napoleon, an enthusiast for Ossian, and his battlefield opponents alike carried the poems in their saddlebags, despite heated accusations among literary critics of the time that they were literary forgeries.[1]

As a young boy, however, Macpherson had experienced the savage reprisals of Hanoverian troops against his fellow-Highlanders in the aftermath of the Battle of Culloden (1746) that ended the Stuart claim to the British throne. Exposed from birth to the oral traditions of the Gaelic-speaking Highlands, he later attended the lectures of the noted Homer scholar Thomas Blackwell at the University of Aberdeen. Struck by the stirring episodes of the Homeric epics, and with encouragement from Edinburgh intellectuals such as Hugh Blair (1718–1800), professor of rhetoric and belles lettres at the University of Edinburgh, who contributed an important and influential "dissertation" to the 1765 edition, he claimed that the poems he published were "translations" from Gaelic. The tone of the poems, with their dwelling on feeling, heroism, and transitoriness, appealed to readers tired of clever but arid neoclassical verse. But critics such as David Hume and Samuel Johnson, tied to the classical world of literature and current French literary fashion—at the same time ignorant of the Highlands and Gaelic poetic traditions—demanded that Macpherson produce the "originals" from which he had made these. Although Macpherson drew from both oral and written sources, he was clumsy and defensive in the explanation of his methods; oral tradition was not, at that time, considered a trustworthy source of literature by urban intellectuals. Their skeptical view has tended to persist in the debate over the "authenticity" of the poems. Macpherson himself, it appears, began to believe that the "fragments" were part of a larger "epic" creation and increasingly began to believe in his own destiny as the "bard" who had reconstituted the epics of *Fingal* and *Temora* (the equivalents to the *Iliad* and *Odyssey*).

The twenty-two poetic creations of Macpherson that comprise the poems of Ossian, including the *Fragments, Fingal, Temora* and others that are shorter and possibly less well known, are constructed, for the longer poems, in "books" (or *duans*, episodes) and in a kind of rhetorical prose that is anything but prosaic. They conjure up the majesty, ecstasy, and casual horror of a world akin to that of Homer with, however, two important motifs: the honorable treatment of vanquished enemies, and heroic female participation in battle. These motifs were valued by readers across the boundaries of translation. But the overall feeling of the poems is one of lament. A typical scene at the conclusion of *Fingal* Book III captures the pervasive tone of regret for a lost heroic world:

> Many a voice and many a harp, in tuneful sounds arose. Of Fingal's
> noble deeds they sung; of Fingal's noble race. And sometimes, on
> the lovely sound, was heard the name of Ossian. I often fought, and
> often won, in battles of the spear. But blind, and tearful, and forlorn,
> I walk with little men! O Fingal, with thy race of war I now behold
> thee not! The wild roes feed on the green tomb of the mighty king
> of Morven! Blest be thy soul, thou king of swords, thou most
> renowned on the hills of Cona!

It is only lately that a challenge to the conventional disparagement of Macpherson's work, a view qualified already in the nineteenth century by authorities such as Matthew Arnold,[2] has begun to filter into the ken of music historians, whose knowledge of the poems is often secondhand or displays accumulated prejudice in their constant use of the damning terms "forgery" or "fraud."[3] Few seem to have actually read the poems or to be aware of current studies that assess their inherent qualities and, just as decisive, their enduring international impact.[4] Current books and essays by musicologists that mention Ossian tend to use epithets such as "half-faked," "pseudo-Celtic," "purported translation," "counterfeit," and "fabrication" without further comment, as if the poems are presumed worthless, while their influence on Thomas Jefferson, Napoleon, and generations of poets and writers from Coleridge to Walt Whitman and composers from Schubert to Schoenberg is brushed aside. But the powerful effect of Ossian in German-speaking lands, for instance, arguably more profound than in any other area of Europe, has been well documented.[5] Skepticism, not only in English-speaking lands, appears to have affected those who have absorbed the criticism of anti-Ossian propagandists from Samuel Johnson to Hugh Trevor-Roper.[6] Macpherson may not be a great poet, but he has his visionary moments, especially in poems like "Comala," "The Songs of Selma," and parts of *Fingal*. These are the poems that appealed most strongly to composers.[7]

In her insightful biographical study, Fiona Stafford, briskly rejecting the charges of fraudulence or forgery against Macpherson, asks what it was about the poems of Ossian that caused such a furor during the late eighteenth century and the Romantic period. Neither emerging nationalism nor antiquarianism can account for the fact that the poems were read, reprinted, and translated, during the half century following their appearance, into Italian, French, German, Polish, Russian, Danish, Spanish, Dutch, Bohemian, and Hungarian, even influencing Japanese writers.[8] It was, indeed, the inspirational quality of the poems that elicited reaction across linguistic boundaries. Two of the main conduits for the poems on the European continent were the Swiss writer Mme. de Staël, who referred to Ossian as "the Homer of the North" and "the mother of Romanticism" (1800), and Johann Gottfried Herder, whose influence as a poet, essayist and cultural historian spread his enthusiasm for the poems throughout German-speaking lands and beyond.[9] While writers in Britain, Ireland, France, Italy and elsewhere were powerfully influenced by the poems, it was in Germany that they had possibly their greatest impact, through figures such as Goethe, Schiller, and Herder. The translation made by Michael Denis (1768–69), a Jesuit priest living in Vienna, had been cast in hexameters and for that reason was strongly attacked by Herder, who felt that the poetic language of Ossian required a more fitting and sensitive linguistic transference. But it is a well-attested fact that every poet of consequence in Germany proclaimed their debt to Ossian.[10]

These inspirational poems of Macpherson display the conflicted aims of their author, as "translator" on the one hand and "poet" on the other. They have one foot in Gaelic tradition, the other in the world of modern literature, with its turn toward sensibility and feeling, the "fragment" being the means of bridging the two.[11] A further implication of "fragment" is that of an early modern world in fragmentation, one that was already in danger of losing its smaller, more fragile cultures and attempting to rescue what is deemed of value to an urban world of consumption. But as Stafford notes, the poems offer readers of different cultural sensibilities "the opportunity to enter the text and begin creating their own imaginative worlds."[12]

Major Topics in the Poems

The musical response to Ossian over the two and a half centuries since the poems' publication has been constant and prolonged, if at times spasmodic.

Composers, librettists, and stagers of musical drama, of differing national traditions, social classes, and technical skills, reacted to four major aspects of the poetry. First is the gentle melancholy that suffuses the texts: Ossian is the singer of "the joy of grief," a species of emotional ambivalence that releases the subject from despair and instead conveys a kind of dignity, as suggested in a short passage from "Carrick-Thura:[13]

> Pleasant is the joy of grief: it is like the shower of spring, when it
> softens the branch of the oak, and the young leaf rears its green head.

Second is the loneliness of the artist: Ossian is the last of the bards, grieving for the spirits of dead warriors as echoes of a Golden Age. In "The Songs of Selma" the poet concludes,

> I hear the call of years! They say, as they pass along, why does
> Ossian sing? Soon shall he lie in the narrow house, and no bard
> shall raise his fame!

Third is the dramatic opposition of characters as they conform to Edmund Burke's gendered categories of the Sublime and the Beautiful (1757) in their qualities of bravery, justice, and wisdom (male), on the one hand, and on the other hand, forbearance, kindness, and liberality (female). But the poems, significantly, allow gender roles to overlap: heroic males weep and are compassionate, while females take up arms on behalf of their beloved. Finally, the background of a wild, untamed Nature acts as a counterpart to human action; sun, moon, stars, lightning, meteors, precipices, torrents, waves, and gloomy moors all contribute to the atmospheric deployment of the "pathetic fallacy" in Ossian.

Against this tumultuous landscape, Ossian, the last of the bards, is invariably portrayed bearing a harp, and composers often highlight the "bardic" instrument in rippling piano figuration alongside French horns as symbols of heroism in battle and also the hunt for wild animals. Several times the harp is described in the original poems as "half-viewless"—dimly perceived, barely visible. The stage action is set in extreme or liminal areas: remote beaches, dense forests, underground caverns. Storms often accompany or preside over the progress of the plot. A small army of ingenious librettists, especially in Italy, found ways to soften the deadly conflicts in the original poems and provide a comfortable ending to the drama in which the romantically linked characters are paired off in conventional fashion and the threat to their happiness, usually from a tyrant-father figure, is dispelled. These strategies of plot, however, could be read as political by audiences of the time. In the poems, the hero (Fingal or Ossian) is poised against the ancient enemy, often the pagan Scandinavians. But in Romantic times, the foe ranged against the heroic Caledonians—the localized defenders of both Alba and Erin—was seen as symbolizing the dominant imperial power, whether Austria, France, or Sweden.

Musical Responses to Ossian

The Ossian poems that composers fastened on for their settings are primarily "Fingal," "Berrathon," "Comala," "Dar-thula," and episodes such as that of "Colma" from "The Songs of Selma," although at least one composition (Liza Lehmann's *Leaves from Ossian*, 1909) draws on multiple poems. Among the poems' characters, composers found Fingal, and Comala, daughter of Sarno, chieftain of Inistore, far and away the figures most attractive for musical treatment. From the very beginning, these two inspired operas, cantatas, ballets, and lyric scenes (increasingly, toward 1900, symphonic poems) because of their tragic relationship, recounted in the tales. The huntress Comala, for instance, dies in the mistaken belief that her beloved, Fingal, whom she has followed to Morven in disguise, has been slain in battle. The fair-haired Agandecca, another love interest of his, is killed by her father, Starno, for warning Fingal of a plot to assassinate him under cover of hospitality. Composers chose the lonely, lamenting Colma (from "The Songs of Selma") and the warrior maiden Darthula almost as often as Comala and Agandecca: again, both have lost their beloved. Then there is King Toscar's daughter Malvina, the lover of Ossian's son, Oscar, who is left desolate when he is killed.

The characters and their narratives, often rather static in the poems, have in general been better served in cantatas than on the operatic stage, at least insofar as fidelity to the source is concerned. Librettists often felt they had to revise the plots (such as they were) to provide a dramatic edge to the stories. It is hardly surprising that these liberties taken in giving operatic form to a disjunct narrative were most assiduously cultivated in Italy. But the mere names of main characters in the poems of Ossian had the power and resonance to trigger rhythmic and tonal motifs even in abstract symphonic works.

The musical response to Ossian thus slots aptly into Stafford's notion of composers creating their imaginative worlds. Beginning first with settings of the prose poems themselves, the trajectory of compositions over the century and a half following Macpherson's publication runs from monodramas, songs, and stage works to cantatas, symphonic poems, and solo instrumental pieces. Almost every musical genre was exploited, and the works flowed in an unbroken stream, from before Schubert to Brahms, from Mendelssohn to Massenet, Saint-Saëns to Schoenberg, up to the twentieth century and beyond. This stream carries not only the flotsam and jetsam of mediocre compositions but a few major and some minor masterpieces that have been ignored or are relatively unknown.

Text settings were produced not only in English, in Britain, but in a dozen other languages, mainly French, German, or Italian. Even composers whose native language was English still had to decide how the language of the poems was to be handled. The genre they chose was predominantly the cantata rather than opera, which, for cogent cultural and historical reasons, came to be the preferred medium in Italy. The German counterpart of the Italian opera was the *Singspiel* with its spoken

Figure 1.1. Friedrich Georg Weitsch (1758–1828), *Klage um Comala* (Lament over Comala), 1802. GK I 3220. Photograph of lost painting. Stiftung Preußische Schlösser und Gärten Berlin-Brandenburg/Photographer: Oberhofmarschallamt/Verwaltung der Staatlichen Schlösser und Gärten (1927–45).

dialogue, a genre that culminated in Mozart's two brilliant examples.[14] Writing an opera on Ossian topics presented a serious challenge, for the "epic" or "heroic" qualities of the poems often had to be adapted, not only for reasons of internal dramatic action but also to accord with the tastes of the audience. The cantata, on the other hand, because it avoided the bizarre plot interventions by librettists and the hazards of awkward dramaturgy, was taken up intermittently all over Europe, as early as the 1770s and increasingly after 1850.

The much-favored poem "Comala" has a plot of sorts. Even though it is written in dialogue form it was well suited to both opera treatment and cantata. Most composers stuck by the original narrative, in which Fingal's affianced, Comala, is falsely informed by Fingal's jealous lieutenant, Hidallan, that her betrothed has been slain. She then commits suicide (or dies of grief).[15] Whereas the lament of "Colma" for her brother and her fiancé (who slay each other in combat) was mostly set as a solo song in Germany, "Dar-thula" there received numerous settings, both solo and choral, between 1850 and 1900 using the verses of Johann Gottfried Herder.[16] The figure of Oithóna, like Darthula a warrior woman who dies with her beloved in battle, inspired four operas, including the very first attempt to set the drama for the musical stage, in 1768.

In the period 1780–1815 Macpherson's reconstructed epic *Fingal* was mined for metropolitan glees, madrigal-like settings for the small singing groups that flourished in London and elsewhere in Britain. These settings, in their choice of text, were powerfully influenced by the war with France and, ironically, Napoleon Bonaparte, Ossian's stoutest champion. The poem "Berrathon," or episodes adapted from it, was especially attractive to Napoleonic composers such as Méhul (his one-act opera *Uthal*, 1806), while "Calthon and Colmal," a tale of lovers united against paternal interdict, found favor as the basis of opera plots, notably in Peter von Winter's *Colmal* (1809). After Napoleon's defeat at Waterloo, composers began to view the relationships of Fingal and Ossian with women (particularly Agandecca, Comala, and Malvina) as more suitable for cantata treatment than for opera. The tender dialogue between Shilric and Vinvela in the poem "Carric-Thura" and its appearance in other versions of Ossian, such as the "translations" of the Irish Edmund de (or von) Harold, served as material for composers, notably Franz Schubert.[17]

The Relevance of Transmediation

The concept of transmediation, as I use it here, is the process by which an agent (the composer) adapts a plot as evidenced in a poetic text or its translation to a musical form, attempting at the same time to crystallize the import or meaning through devices of tonal shaping, color, texture, and, occasionally, motifs or topics extraneous to the style, so as to create referential meanings beyond the musical score.[18] The process of transmediation from plot or poetry to a musical genre or genres involves three main types or orders: first, *convergent*, in which a song or cantata, chiefly, remains closely bound to the poem and its narrative, emotionally as well as structurally; second, *divergent*, whereby an opera or parody departs, sometimes sharply, from the original, affecting the nature of the musical genre and setting; and third, *symbolic*, in which the work is purely instrumental and becomes thereby a meditation on the original poem; this last type is the most difficult to interpret, and can sometimes assume aspects of the first two types in the degree of adaptation.

The categories of transmediation, in other words, are not hard and fast, or mutually exclusive. With the second type, *divergent*, Italian librettists thought nothing of changing names and plots from Ossian to suit their imagination and their audience's idea of how the operatic plot should proceed onstage: for instance, in Francesco Bianchi's three-act opera *Calto* (1788), the plot is from Macpherson's poem "Calthon and Colmal," which has "Calthon" for its hero. But the opera's librettist, Giuseppe Foppa, adjusted the plot to suit the prevailing Venetian taste for dramatic action, removing Ossian, as well as the murder of Calthon's brother, Colmar, by Duntalmo, from the action and introducing a happy ending. The transmediation of the plot to operatic form aligns with the libretto, but in doing so diverges from the basic narrative, and in terms of the music from the drama and emotional import of the poetic original.

The same plot was used in the stage work *La disfatta di Duntalmo* (1789) with music by Luigi Caruso, performed in Rome a year after the Venetian *Calto*. As with several other proper names in the poems, a somewhat later work was titled, confusingly, with a similar name, in this case *Clato* (adapted from the name of Fingal's second wife, Clatho)—this second *Clato* was Pietro Generali's "dramma serio in musica con cori" (1816). Pietro Raimondi's two-act "tragedia lirica" of the same name followed in 1832.[19]

These works for staged action with music—"azione teatrale," "dramma serio per musica," "tragedia lirica," and so on—signify a search for an appropriate designation in a genre that did not conform to accepted ideas of how opera should be constructed: the search for an appropriate named type was the result of an evolving perception among librettists and composers of how episodic poetry like that of Ossian might be molded into something resembling a coherent opera plot.

These ploys of the operatic stage, however, can be set aside in the face of two transmediated works of the third type affected by *The Poems of Ossian*: Mendelssohn's concert overture "The Hebrides" (or "Fingal's Cave"), op. 26 (1832), and, less patently, Beethoven's "Eroica" Symphony, op. 55 (1804). While the relationship of Mendelssohn to the poems and to the Highland seascape is well documented, that of Beethoven to Ossian at the time he completed his Third Symphony is more problematic, although I argue that Ossian is a contributory factor in Beethoven's conception of heroism and thus his motivation behind his composition of the work.[20] In the mass of commentaries the "Eroica" has provoked since it first appeared, many writers do not mention Ossian at all, preferring to dwell on, for example, the Napoleonic dimension, especially in the first movement, or the Promethean aspect of the work as it unfolds in the finale. All this is discussed in chapter 8 below.

Four Stylistic Phases

Composers' responses to *The Poems of Ossian* fall into four broad periods; these cannot be strictly delimited because chronology and periodicity are not always in alignment. In terms of music historiography, chronology tends to promote the idea of a temporal unfolding of styles, each of these successively built on its predecessor, and with an assumption of greater complexity. But that is an illusion, especially in the twentieth century, when heterogeneous styles of composition proliferated in the wake of the information explosion. The emphasis on set periods, on the other hand, supplies a different kind of illusion, namely that of delimited time periods in which a common style crystallized. But even in so-called stable periods such as those following the Congress of Vienna in 1815 or the 1848 revolutions, composers could be found groping for an individual style as the poeticizing of content and fragmentation of form proceeded apace.

Yet we can discern four broad periods of composition based on Ossian. For convenience these are as follows: from approximately 1780 to 1815, from 1816 to 1880, from 1880 to 1918, and from 1918 to the present. Opera dominates the first of these periods, the cantata the second, and the symphonic poem and instrumental works the third and fourth phases. The evolution of musical responses traces a path of increasing abstraction as the persons and events in the poems recede into the aesthetic and temporal distance. In later compositions the "voices" of Ossian's characters give way to the "instruments" of his bards: the undulating harp or plangent *cor anglais* gradually assumes the narrative that heroes and maidens once enunciated in operatic or cantata form.

This does not mean that vocal expression of the narrative was suppressed or denied; rather, a receding emotional reality and gradual relinquishing of "heroic" situations and dated language meant a sharper focus on symbolic gestures, on orphic penetration to the essence of the poems to retrieve their meaning. Macpherson, after all, believed himself to be to Ossian as Homer had been to Orpheus; the turn to nature and to antiquity as the sources of musical creativity had, around the same time as the publication of the Ossian poems, manifested itself in Gluck's renowned version of the Orpheus myth, *Orfeo ed Euridice* (Vienna 1762, Paris 1774).[21] While Méhul's Ossianic opera *Uthal* (1806), with its motif of the hero's search for the beloved in the forest, displays influence from Gluck's masterpiece, works such as Liszt's symphonic poem *Orpheus* (1854) allowed contemplation of these relationships in light of the conflict and social tension in Europe after 1848.[22]

First Phase: Proto-Romanticism (ca. 1780–1815)

The first phase of Ossian composition stems from around 1780 to the early songs of Franz Schubert (1815–16), a stretch of time that has been termed "pre-" or "proto-Romantic." The classical norms of balance and harmoniousness in music such as Haydn's and Mozart's were giving way to a freer, more questing style prone to upheaval in its dynamic, emotional, and harmonic language. In Germany, the period between roughly 1765 and 1785 is known as *Sturm und Drang* (Storm and Stress), the early stage of Romanticism. Its features include a predilection for the natural, rustic, or primitive; revolt against authority; individualism that borders at times on extremism; and a rejection of the class equilibrium, manners, and good taste valued by the Enlightenment. Ossian was congruent with this general movement in the arts—indeed, helped it along from around 1780 until the Romantic movement found its feet at the turn of the century.

This restlessness affected those composers who went searching not only for new sources of employment outside their own country but for fresh sources of inspiration.[23] That it should be a French immigrant in London who composed the first musical work based on Ossian is, in this context of greater migration, both unsurprising and prophetic when we consider the later, post-Revolutionary enthusiasm for the poems. François-Hippolyte Barthélémon, encouraged to settle in London by Thomas Erskine, earl of Kellie, whom he met in Paris, composed his opera *Oithóna* in 1768.[24] This can claim to be the first musical work of cosmopolitan urban taste to be based on the poems of Ossian, except that only the libretto survives.

Within this earliest phase of Ossianic composition, the work that excited public attention in the British capital was not *Oithóna* but the picturesque "ballet-pantomime" entitled *Oscar and Malvina, or, The Hall of Fingal* (1791), a work cobbled together by William Reeve and William Shield.[25] The connection of *Oscar and Malvina* with the Ossian poems, while fugitive and superficial, was acceptable to a London theater audience by then relieved that the Highlands were safe from Jacobite aggression.

As audiences in Paris would discover, parody was never far away from the attempt to put Ossian on the stage.[26] In London, parodies of the poems, in pamphlets by Charles Churchill and John Wilkes, were in fact coded attacks on the current prime minister, John Stuart, third earl of Bute, Macpherson's patron. Scots were felt by some to have been unfairly favored and to constitute a threat to metropolitan judgment and political stability.[27] But versifications and adaptations of the poems continued to multiply, and dramatic versions of Ossian had wide appeal. David Erskine Baker's *The Muse of Ossian: A Dramatic Poem in Three Acts*, performed in Edinburgh in 1763, for example, wove together passages from Macpherson's prose poems "Comala" and "The War of Caros."[28]

Unlike the pantomimic *Oscar and Malvina*, the opera *Comàla* was, like *Oithóna*, "a dramatic poem." "Set to music by Miss Harriet Wainewright," it was performed at the Hanover Square Rooms on January 26, 1792, and constituted a landmark in concert programs of the time, produced during Joseph Haydn's first visit to London. Although the composer herself always referred to the work as an opera she had encountered difficulty in getting it staged at any of the theaters; audiences, she was told, wanted lighter, comedic distractions. *Comàla* was therefore given as a concert piece with assistance from prominent figures in London musical life such as Samuel Arnold. Haydn, of course, was far too famous and busy with his own composing to attend an opera by an unknown female, even if he knew of its existence. This unique event and Harriet Wainewright's composition of the work merit separate discussion below.[29]

This first phase of the musical response to Ossian falls within a context of dissatisfaction with neoclassical formalism (particularly of a French kind) in literature and philosophy; the seeds of the movement were contained in a firm rejection of Enlightenment rationalism. Haydn, however, had actually prefigured this shift to some extent in his middle-period symphonies and string quartets.[30] In Germany, the poet Friedrich Gottlieb Klopstock (1724–1803) began to free his country's literature from the tyranny of the French alexandrine and introduce into German poetry a new emotionalism, derived largely from his encounter with Ossian. Goethe, the central personality in the *Sturm und Drang* period, came under the influence of the poet and philosopher Herder, who had been taught by the anti-Enlightenment philosopher Johann Georg Hamann (1730–88), now seen as the true prophet of the movement in German-speaking lands. Eventually it was Herder, even more than Goethe, who spread the word about Ossian and stoked the poetry's influence in Germany and other parts of Europe.[31]

The power of Ossian's surge was evident by 1780, when Friedrich Wilhelm Rust (1739–96) produced his masterly *Colma, ein Monodrama mit Prolog nach Ossian*, for soloist and orchestra, which alternated solo arias and monologue with instrumental accompaniment.[32] The writing of songs on Ossianic themes increased in the final decades of the eighteenth century and the first years of the new nineteenth. It had already begun in the 1770s with such composers as Beethoven's first teacher, Christian Gottlob Neefe (1748–98), and his contemporaries in Germany. This paralleled technical improvements in piano construction, and the expanding repertoire of the instrument found its way into domestic life. Ossian had a foothold even in the United States, where the harpsichord still had its uses: Francis Hopkinson, born in Philadelphia in 1737, composed his "Ode on Ossian's Poems" for voice and harpsichord in 1788, shortly after Thomas Jefferson had proclaimed Ossian "the greatest poet that ever existed."[33] Meanwhile, Johann Friedrich Reichardt (1752–1814) had energetically cultivated the *Singspiel*, and the song with spoken interpolations multiplied in such works after Ossian as Bernard Anselm Weber's duodrama, *Sulmalle* (1802), Franz Cramer's *Hidalan* (1813), and Peter von Winter's *Colmal* (1809), a stylistic intermediary between Mozart and Carl Maria von Weber. Winter, indeed, thought *Colmal* his best work.

The fateful year of 1792 in Europe heralded the post-Revolutionary wars, the advent of Napoleon, and the founding in Britain of the radical Society of the Friends of the People that agitated for reform of Parliament, as well as one event of political significance in Ireland, namely the Belfast Harp Festival, held in July to coincide with the third anniversary of the fall of the Bastille. The harp thus became a kind of totem in claims by the Celtic world to ownership of Ossian, while to the Friends of the People in Ireland the instrument signified a desire for political independence from Britain. Shortly afterward, from 1796, Jean-François Le Sueur began work on his epochal five-act opera *Ossian, ou les Bardes*, which was finally staged in Paris in 1804, to Napoleon's delight.[34] Etienne Nicolas Méhul's atmospheric one-act opera *Uthal* followed, in 1806.[35] Both operas immediately drew mockery in stage works parodying their pretensions to accurate historical dramaturgy.

After the Revolution, the craze for Ossian on the Continent—not only in France—was the consequence of the enthusiasm of one man: Napoleon Bonaparte, whose intimate acquaintance with the poems was already under way by 1790. One witness to Napoleon's early taste for Ossian was Victorine de Chastenay (1771–1855), who had a four-hour conversation with him about the poems at Châtillon-sur-Seine at the end of May 1795.[36] The later 1790s was the beginning of, as Van Tieghem describes it, the "mode ossianique" that was to inspire authors and poets in France such as Chateaubriand and Lamartine or painters like Gérard, Girodet, and Ingres at the moment when Napoleon swept to power, first as consul, then later as emperor. As is well known, Beethoven was profoundly affected.[37]

This period was to last until just after the final defeat of Bonaparte at Waterloo in 1815. Le Sueur's opera, with its eight harps as part of the orchestration, was staged for the final time in 1817.[38] The sensational effect of this work spread to Russia, where, in the hands of the dramatist Vladislav Ozerov, the stage tragedy *Fingal* (1805), with incidental music by the Polish-Russian composer Osip Kozlowski (1757–1831), was performed to great success.[39] In the meantime, ballets based on Ossian were flourishing, such as those by Antonio Landini (*Oscar e Malvina*, 1801), Armand Vestris (*Calto e Colama*, 1822, music by Carlo Romani), and Antonio Monticini (*Clato*, 1833). These often bore subtitles such as "ballo eroico-tragico" or "ballo tragico pantomimo."

Comparable developments had been afoot in the Italian *melodrama* (sometimes subtitled *dramma per musica*) and the German *Singspiel*, as both moved toward a more "operatic" style, with formal recitatives and arias. This was evident ever since Pietro Morandi's *Comala*, Francesco Bianchi's *Calto* (1788), and Ettore Romagnoli's *Comala* (1798) had emerged around the same time as Rust's monodrama *Colma* (1780). William Bach's *Colma* (1791), composed at the court of Frederick II of Prussia in Berlin and entitled "an episode from Ossian," has no spoken narrative for its characters and therefore is not a *Singspiel*; unfortunately, its music is untraced.[40] F. L. Æ. Kunzen's three-act *Singspiel Ossians Harfe* was completed in 1799, published in 1802, and performed in Vienna and Hamburg in 1806. From the turn of the nineteenth century, operas proliferated in Italian theaters: Stefano Pavesi's two examples, the successful *Fingallo, e Comala* (1805) influenced by Le Sueur's *Ossian, ou les Bardes*, and the less-applauded *Ardano e Dartula* (1825), were first staged at La Fenice in Venice.[41] They rode a wave of operatic productions based on Ossian: Morandi's early *Comala* (1780) with a libretto by Gluck's master collaborator, Ranieri de' Calzabigi, and others with texts by Salvatore Cammarano, who was later to provide librettos for Donizetti (*Lucia di Lammermoor*, 1835), Verdi (*Luisa Miller*, 1849), and Giovanni Pacini (*Malvina di Scozia*, 1851).

Second Phase: Romanticism (1815–80)

The defeat of Napoleon at Waterloo in 1815 may have brought the French love affair with Ossian to a temporary halt, but it had little or no effect on the culture change in Europe as a whole that was already well under way before 1800. Full-fledged Romanticism in German-speaking lands did not in any case begin with Schubert, for the remnants of *Sturm und Drang* emotionalism found their way into his group of Ossian settings through the influence of songs by Reichardt and Zumsteeg: Schubert's "Kolma's Klage" (1815) is known to have been influenced by Zumsteeg's setting in particular.

But within a decade there was composed the most frequently performed piece with Ossian associations, Felix Mendelssohn's "Hebrides" overture, op. 26 (1832), which might more accurately be entitled "Fingal's Cave" because of its stormy climax at the close of the exposition.[42] Mendelssohn's techniques in the overture were imitated to some extent by his Danish contemporary Niels W. Gade (1817–90), whose prize-winning, folk-inspired overture *Efterklange af Ossian* (Echoes of Ossian, op. 1), composed in 1840, was performed by the Royal Danish Orchestra in November 1841 and later throughout Germany.[43] Gade's cantata *Comala* (op. 12, 1846) was often held by reviewers to exude "Nordic character," with its use of minor keys and modal or folk-like melodies, somber orchestration, and harp interludes.

The revolutions of 1848 marked a significant break, as composers came to terms with the settlement imposed by the Congress of Vienna in 1815, one that restored the old order through the repressive regimes of statesmen such as Prince Metternich in Austria-Hungary. Indeed, Ossian, as an exercise in the recovery of orally transmitted narratives, can be said to have inspired the discovery (and invention) of "foundational" epics that endowed smaller nations eager to cast off the yoke of imperialism with cultural energy as well as political identity. The ideology of linguistic and narrative dispersal from a hypothetical original, an *Ur*-form, motivated antiquarian field collectors such as Elias Lönnrot, whose reconstruction of the Finnish national epic, *Kalevala* (1849), owes a great deal to the example of Macpherson.[44]

As noted above, Herder had a huge influence on the reception of Ossian, especially in Germany but also throughout central and northern Europe. His poem on the fate of the warrior maiden Darthula, based on Michael Denis's translation of

1768–69, was written about 1770 and published in his *Volkslieder* of 1773; it gave rise to settings by composers, mainly in Germany, that multiplied from mid-century.[45] Choral music saw the rise of the *Männerchor* (male voice choir) in this time of incipient national aspiration. Herder's "Darthula's [sic] Grabesgesang," with its stirring evocation of spring ("Wach auf, Darthula, Frühling ist draussen!"), offered, furthermore, the hope of spiritual resurrection.

The desire for political unification gathered momentum in cantata settings by Brahms and his associates such as Carl Reinthaler (*Das Mädchen von Kola*, ca. 1865), the influential teacher and conductor Carl Reinecke (*Fingal und Ossian*, 1876), and the ailing Berlin composer Bernhard Hopffer (*Darthula's Grabesgesang*, 1878).[46] Paul Umlauft (1853–1934), who had studied with Reinecke, composed a Wagner-influenced cantata for soloists and male voices on the episode of the unhappy *Agandecca* (1890).[47] Another pupil of Reinecke, Arnold Krug (1849–1904), whose cantata *Fingal*, for soloist, male choir, and orchestra, appeared in 1891, displays again the potent influence of Brahms in positioning the cantata form as an alternative to Wagnerian opera.

A preference for Fingal as musical protagonist in the second half of the nineteenth century resulted in some sixteen or more works involving the epic hero: for instance, Edmond Membrée's *Fingal*, scored for reciters, chorus, and orchestra, premiered in 1861. A concern for the clarity of text is evident, in this as in other French settings of Ossian. A lesser-known topic from the poems gave rise to Ferdinand Heinrich Thieriot's opera *Armor e Daura* (1869, described as a "tragische Episode aus dem Schottischen auf Ossian") with a libretto by the German feminist poet Louise Otto-Peters (1819–95), who was also librettist for the opera *Leyer und Schwert* (Lyre and Sword, 1863).[48] Thieriot (1838–1919) established a firm reputation for well-crafted symphonies, cantatas, and chamber works, with some influence from Mendelssohn and more immediately again from Brahms, in whose circle he moved.[49]

A gifted composer who emerged from cultural borderlands, Louis Théodore Gouvy, divided in his cultural heritage between France and Prussia, drew the admiration of both Berlioz and Brahms. The genre of the *scène lyrique* that Gouvy helped develop (*Le dernier Hymne d'Ossian*, op. 15, for bass voice and orchestra, 1858) was originally conceived for voice and piano at the beginning of the century. Later, in 1880, the *Fingal* of Lucien Hillemacher (a Parisian, but of Belgian ancestry) carried off the Prix de Rome of the Académie des Beaux-Arts.[50] Another work of the same title (also entered for the Prix de Rome that year) was by Raymond Bonheur, a confidant of Debussy.[51] Around this time Jules-August Bordier, a native of Angers, composed an impressive *scène lyrique*, his *Un rêve d'Ossian* (1885) for soli, chorus, and orchestra; this opens with a recitation that underscores the French concern, noted above, for clarity of text. These last three works were created during a period of economic depression in France, one that lasted from the collapse of the Paris Bourse in 1882 to the end of the century. Some have argued that this situation stemmed from the reparations imposed on France after the Franco-Prussian war of 1870–71.[52]

Indeed, the echoes of that conflict, and the tragedy of the Paris Commune, are vividly present in Bordier's dramatic fresco.

Operas and cantatas on the subject of Fingal and Comala continued to appear in Italy. By 1847 the melodrama *Fingal*, to a libretto by Gaetano Solito and with music by Pietro Antonio Coppola, had been produced in Palermo; it was staged in Lisbon, in 1851 and again in 1864.[53] Another opera, *Komala*, premiered by Franz Liszt in Weimar in October 1858, came from the pen of the Polish-American Frydryk Eduard Sobolewski who, born in Königsberg, had studied with Zelter in Berlin and with Carl Maria von Weber in Dresden. Liszt had already conducted the premiere of Sobolewski's Ossianic cantata, *Vinvela*, for soli, string quartet, and harp, in Weimar in April 1853.[54] Emigrating from Germany to the United States in 1859, the composer promoted opera and symphony concerts in Milwaukee and later founded the Philharmonic Society in St. Louis. A native of New Orleans, Louis Moreau Gottschalk (1829–69) was not merely an international-level virtuoso but also the composer of several atmospheric Chopin-influenced piano pieces: his Ossian *Ballades*, op. 4 (1843), *Danse ossianique*, op. 12 (1850–51), and the popular *Marche de nuit* with its catchy rhythm (1855).[55]

Third Phase: Late Romanticism (1880–1918)

As the century wore on, operas on texts from Ossian gave way to cantatas and symphonic poems, largely because of a dearth of compelling librettos and, in many countries, lack of resources for the costly genre of opera. Two Greek composers revived the drama of *Oithóna*, the neglected subject of Barthélemon's 1768 attempt. The operas by Dionisio Rodoteato (1876) and Dionisio Carradi (1891) may have had limited time spans and audiences, but they, like the Lisbon performances of Coppola's *Fingal* in 1851 and 1864, show how far Ossian had penetrated into southern European culture.

In more northerly climes, Massenet's opera *Werther*, premiered in Vienna in 1892, is one of his most inspired works, and contains the famous scene in which the tenor "reads" (sings) from a translation of the Ossian poem "Berrathon" ("Pourquoi me réveiller, o souffle du printemps?"). In contrast, the opera *Darthula* by Simon van Milligen, which premiered in Amsterdam in 1901, marks a minor strand of musical Ossianism, a sideshow to the Bayreuth bandwagon. Milligen had studied with Franck and d'Indy in Paris, but the main influence in his opera is patently that of Wagner.[56] In the New World, the Mexican composer Julián Carillo Trujillo, trained partly in Europe, composed a one-act opera on the unusual topic of Macpherson's poem "Oina-Morul" (1903). Apart from Massenet's *Werther*, many of these operas were never published and remain in manuscript.

A fair number of Ossian settings in the later nineteenth century fell under Brahms's spell: several German composers of the time who wrote Ossian-derived pieces knew him personally. As German nationalism intensified after 1848, choral compositions were given impetus as singing societies, especially male ensembles, proliferated in northern as well as central Europe. Choral works on Ossian came out of the Finnish north—for instance, those by Erkki Melartin (1897) and Selim Palmgren (1913), both composed on a Swedish translation of Herder's "Dar-thula" poem. The year 1903 marked, significantly, the emergence of a draft by Arnold Schoenberg on the subject of Darthula, a large-scale cantata for chorus and orchestra on the same verses by Herder.[57]

Cantatas and symphonic poems were by now in the ascendant. Some cantatas began to approach an operatic conception, with quasi–stage directions: those, for instance, on the subject of Comala by Joseph Jongen (1897) and Jørgen Malling (1902).[58] At the same time, composers accelerated the drive toward abstract orchestral works. Symphonic poems by the French composer Arthur Coquard (*Ossian*, 1882) and the Belgians Sylvain Dupuis (*Moina*, 1884) and Adolphe Biarent (*Fingal*, 1894, and *Trenmor*, 1905), for example, with their coded allusions to the Franco-Prussian hostilities of 1870–71, evince anxiety over Prussian militarism and the threat of a larger European conflict. Concurrent works drawn from Ossian include the Brazilian Alexandre Levy's tone poem *Comala* (1890), the Italian composer Nicolò Celega's *Il cuore di Fingal* (undated, but ca. 1895), and Charles Villiers Stanford's *Irish Rhapsody No. 2: Lament for the Son of Ossian* (1903), written at the climax of the Second Boer War.[59]

This period of "crepuscular" Ossianism, with the backdrop of the Franco-Prussian conflict and German unification as a threatening prelude to continental involvement, has a parallel in the "Celtic twilight" researches of field explorers such as Marjory Kennedy-Fraser around the time of World War I. She arranged, in voice and piano versions intended essentially for drawing-room consumption, Gaelic-language lays that she had recovered from Highland oral tradition. For composers, the heroism of the early Romantic passion for Ossian was waning in the light of the human cost of armed antagonism, just as European powers braced themselves for an even greater conflict.

Fourth Phase (1918–Present)

British composers working between the two world wars turned again to Ossian, among them the prolific Granville Bantock (1868–1946) and the Yorkshire bandmaster Joseph Weston Nicholl (1875–1925), whose opera *Comala* (1920) illustrated the battle between a Celtic heroine and her Germanic adversaries.[60] The libretto of Nicholl's opera, by Reginald Buckley, began as a one-act lyric tragedy, "Comala," which appeared in the *Poetry Review* in the summer of 1915. The plot is nationalistic: Comala is a Dark Age Celtic princess receiving shelter from Christian Britons on a Northern Isle. She symbolizes the spirit of Celtic-Christian Britain, while the invading Norse rovers represent the light and dark sides of "Teutonism."[61]

Nor was Nicholl the only composer to rediscover Ossian after World War I. In Russia Mikhail Ippolitov-Ivanov (1859–1935), a pupil of Rimsky-Korsakov, completed his *Three Musical Tableaux from Ossian*, op. 56, in 1925, although it was published only in 1938.[62] Russia had long celebrated the poems, mainly in the 1792 translation by Ermil Ivanovich Kostrov (1755–96) that drew on Le Tourneur's French version of 1777. But the Soviet Revolution, in suppressing individualism, was ambivalent about the heroic characters portrayed in epics of the past (*byliny*, *stariny*) and wished to portray them (in the newer genre of *noviny*) as representations of the spirit of the people as a whole.[63]

The composer John Laurence Seymour is one of the few Americans to write songs based on Ossian. Around the same time as Seymour's *Six Ossianic Odes* (1936), the Scottish composer Cedric Thorpe Davie completed his cantata *Dirge for Cuthullin*.[64] Twenty years later the prolific André Ameller (1912–90) produced what may be the last opera on an Ossianic theme, the one-act *La lance de Fingal*, op. 50 (1957). Around this time the French musical appetite for Ossian surfaced again. Jean Guillou (b. 1930) devised two technically challenging pieces for organ, *Ballade Ossianique, No. 1* (*Temora*), op. 8 (1962, rev. 2005), and *Ballade Ossianique, No. 2* (*Les chants de Selma*), op. 23 (1971, rev. 2005); these rhapsodic, tumultuous works are among solo items inspired by the poems.[65]

A few works for other solo instruments exist, some from the Romantic period: for guitar, by Johann Kaspar Mertz (1806–56), "An Malvina" and "Fingals-Höhle" (1847); for piano, Gottschalk's pieces referred to above, Wilhelm Fritze's *Bilder aus Ossian: Fünf Stücke*, op. 7 (1866),[66] Erik Chisholm's *Night Song of the Bards* (1941),[67] and Carlo Alfredo Piatti's *Ossian's Song*, for cello and piano, undated. The Ukrainian composer Valery Kikta's stylish, Ravel-like four pieces, *Ossian, Suite for Harp* (1968), show how far away in time and space European modernity found inspiration in the bardic images of Ossian. Oddly, however, the urge to musical modernity was evidently in conflict with Michael Denis's remark, at the time he completed his complete translation (1768–69), that the poems were very *un-modern*, thus raising the question for composers of aesthetic appropriateness.[68]

Chapter Two

On Macpherson's Native Heath: Primary Sources

The poet Robert Burns, owning himself a great admirer of Ossian, remarked that the poetry was "one of the glorious models after which I endeavour to form my conduct."[1] Burns was a major contributor to James Johnson's collection *The Scots Musical Museum* (1787–1802), which includes songs related to Ossian. Commenting on the song "The Maid of Selma," number 116 in the poet's interleaved copy of the second volume of the *Museum*, the antiquarian Robert Riddell (1755–94) refers first of all to the tune attributed to James Oswald,[2] then describes some "Fingallian" airs he had come across in John Bowie's *A Collection of Strathspey Reels & Country Dances* (1789):

> This air began to be admired at Edinburgh about the year 1770. The words are a little alter'd, from the original, in the Poems of Ossian, and I am doubtfull whether the tune has any pretensions to antiquity. That very valuable Collection of Highland, and Western Island Music published by the Revd Mr McDonald of Kilmore, which is the ancient and undoubted oldest Scottish music existing, is different from this air—which breathes more of an Italian, than an old Ergadian Composition [i.e., from the districts of Argyll, Lochaber, and Wester Ross]. —RR. Since I wrote the above I have met with a Collection of Strathspeys &c by John Bowie of Perth—In the end of this collection are three airs, (said) [to be] by Fingal and the following note precedes them—"The following pieces of ancient music were furnished to the editors by a gentle-man of note in the Highlands of Scotland—were composed originally for the Harp, and which were handed down to him by his ancestors, who learned them from the celebrated Harper Rory Daul, who flourished in the Highlands in the reign of Queen Ann—this air here called the Maid of Selma seems to be taken from these ancient Fingallian ones.[3]

On the "The Maid of Selma," with its text adapted from Macpherson's "Oina-Morul," Riddell remarked further: "Here is another Fingallian air said to be—But the moment a Tune suffers the smallest alteration, it loses its prominent features, its Costume, its everything—Music, like a fine painting, can admit of no alteration, no retouching by any other hand, after it has come from that, of the original composer. RR."

This remark reveals the very different attitudes toward melody as codified in print and music as orally transmitted. It suggests that there is an identifiable composer, even for popular folk songs; it is not surprising that the Lowland tunes, at a time when Scottish identity was in danger of being overcome by conceptions of "North Britain" and imperial expansion, often were assigned to living persons who had supposedly composed them. These native "compositions" often were reworkings of known songs or tunes—a task at which Burns was adept. The acknowledgment that a tune might be "traditional," however, without a known author, would have been Riddell's escape from too restricted a view of how oral transmission was "authenticated" only when it was committed to writing or print. The episode of the desolate Colma in "The Songs of Selma" shows how composers such as Oswald could adapt the text of Ossian, by using melodic progressions like the 5–6–1 cadence, evident also in "The Maid of Selma," to cobble together tunes that sounded "Fingalian."[4]

In the Highlands, oral tradition was much more fluid than in the Lowlands. It often operated in families or local townships rather than in the order of bards, which had already disintegrated by the early eighteenth century. Melodic formulas, aurally absorbed and largely pentatonic, could be manipulated at will in varying contexts and were well known to musicians, whether singers or instrumentalists. Thus, the "alterations" Riddell refers to were normal in a tradition where literacy existed and was valued but where oral communication retained a vitally important social function. This was evident in the Highland *ceilidhs* (evening social gatherings) in Highland townships recorded by students of tradition in the later nineteenth century and even into the twentieth. These cultural events have been well described for the Scottish, Irish, and New World contexts.[5]

David Hume, Samuel Johnson, and other eighteenth-century literati located authority in the writing down of orally transmitted songs and tales: script and print embodied authenticity and, increasingly, legality as well as legitimacy. But unlike these gentlemen, Burns recognized the vitality of oral tradition and its importance to the culture of both Highlands and Lowlands. In any case, the two cultures were never entirely separate, despite the language difference, as the instrumental and song collections of the period clearly show. Preparing his collection of airs "peculiar to the Highlands" (1816–19), Capt. Simon Fraser (1773–1852) articulated this melodic consanguinity by listing in his preface some twenty-five tunes common to both traditional repertoires—and there were certainly many more as contact between Highlands and Lowlands increased during the later eighteenth century with the opening up of communications.[6]

But Fraser also intimated that he had entered his collection of tunes into Stationers' Hall, so that "no other may assume the right of publishing them without consent." The authority of written tunes was now being tied to personal ownership,

Example 2.1. John Bowie, "Air by Fingal," *Collection*, p. 32

to intellectual property, something that would have been possible in a song tradition formally sustained by specialist bards with a precise repertoire, but which latterly, with the demise of their order, had become an oral one communally shared. As eighteenth-century antiquarians became interested in "older" or "fragile" traditions, it was not so much "the tune" that was owned but the "version" published by the collector: essentially what Fraser was claiming. Nevertheless, with songs or tunes that were rare, the version recovered and printed was often considered the only "authentic" existence it had. This clearly matters in the case of Ossian.[7]

In his note on "The Maid of Selma," Riddell refers to the Rev. Patrick McDonald (1729–1824), minister of Kilmore (Argyll), who had published his *Collection of Highland Vocal Airs* (1784). One of his "Argyleshire airs" is "Ossian 'am deigh nam Fion" (Ossian after the Fianna), the poet's soliloquy on the death of his contemporaries the Fenian warriors, a prose narrative and also an associated air well known in Highland tradition. McDonald included the melodies of eight heroic lays, including that of *Laoidh Mhanuis* (The lay of Manus).[8] A version of this Ossianic tale of Magnus [Manus], similar in substance to that of Fingal, was included by John Francis

Example 2.2. Anon., "The Maid of Selma," *The Scots Musical Museum*, p. 119

Example 2.3. Rev. Patrick McDonald, "Ossian an déigh nam Fion," *Collection*, p. 117

Campbell in his important *Leabhar na Feinne*,[9] and was recorded from oral tradition as late as 1968. In 1870–71 the knowledgeable collector Frances Tolmie (1840–1926), born in Skye, noted five of these lays, including *Laoidh Dhiarmaid* (The lay of Diarmid), from a cottar, Margaret Macleod, at Portree on the Isle of Skye.[10]

Before 1700 these heroic lays were part of the repertoire of trained, specialist poets attached to a particular clan chieftain. Such poets composed in a literary language, in meters based on the number of syllables to a line, a technique some scholars believe stems from early Christian hymns in Latin.[11] When the special institution of clan bard in Ireland disintegrated after the Battle of Kinsale in 1601, their repertoire was taken over by the lower rank of bard, who came to use different kinds of meter with measured stresses rather than syllables, and a harp might often have accompanied

Example 2.4. Frances Tolmie, collector, "Laoidh Dhiarmid" (The Lay of Diarmid), *Journal of the Folk Song Society* 4 (1910–13): 245

the singer. Harpers in Scotland, too, such as Roderick Morison (1656–ca. 1714), were known to compose poetry in the more informal style known as *amhran*, and would have sung their songs indoors, for the upper ranks of society. In other words, this was the drawing-room music of the period, even in the "remote" Highlands.[12] On the other hand, the late-modern vernacular art of singing practiced among ordinary people, as remarked above, was an individual art learned and communicated within families or a local township.[13]

The Recovery of Gaelic Lays

The lays from the Fenian Cycle deal with the adventures of the band of warriors led by Fionn or Finn (Macpherson's renamed "Fingal"). They were popular in both Ireland and Scotland from the late medieval period. The scholar of Gaelic narrative John Francis Campbell, in publishing a list of Irish lays compiled by James Goodman in 1858, noted, "It appears from this list that Heroic Ballads current in the South of Ireland in manuscript are very similar to those which are now current in the Scotch Islands orally preserved, which have been current here ever since Dean MacGregor wrote Text A." This reference is to the highly significant early sixteenth-century *Book of the Dean of Lismore*,[14] which has its counterpart of manuscript tradition in the Irish *Duanaire Finn*. In his edition of the latter, Gerard Murphy suggested that the heroic lays probably took their metrical shape in the twelfth, thirteenth, and succeeding centuries.[15] The lays were in syllabic meter, and the oldest written sources are manuscripts of the medieval period. To what extent oral and manuscript versions interacted is a complex question that continued to vex Macpherson as he scrambled to locate the manuscripts that Johnson and others held to be the "authentic" versions of Ossianic poems. Where, they demanded, are the manuscripts? For them, the only credible evidence was written documents.

But the heroic lays, orally transmitted, were also remote from mainstream western European culture, however that is defined.[16] In 1789 Charlotte Brooke included

Fenian lays in her *Reliques of Irish Poetry*, but without tunes. The young Edward Bunting (1773–1843) published two tunes without words in his 1840 collection, airs he had evidently obtained much earlier, at the time of the celebrated Harp Festival held in Belfast in 1792.[17] He also included an "Ossianic Air" sent to him by Sir John Sinclair, who, writing to him in 1808, declared, "It was recently transmitted to me by the Rev. Mr. Cameron, Minister of Halkirk, in the county of Caithness, North Britain, who learned it many years ago from a very old man, a farmer on my estate, who was accustomed to sing some of Ossian's poems to that air, with infinite delight and enthusiasm."[18] Another air printed by Bunting, "The Battle of Arganmore," from "Murloch" (now Murlough in County Antrim), is similarly notated in $\frac{4}{4}$ with a B♭ key signature (indicating F major, although the tune has no fourth degree), in this regard like many of the attempts to capture in conventional notation what was essentially a freewheeling word-based, syllabic rhythm.[19]

Further, transcriptions made from sound recordings in recent times have shown that melodic variation recurs from verse to verse in a way that differentiates it from lyric song. The comparison of airs from the Irish tradition, for example, makes clear their strongly pentatonic character, their rhythmic freedom, and an overarching structure of balanced phrases.[20] The character of the melodic line as sung is thus not easily described, and traditional notation gives only an approximate idea of its declamatory style.

When writing his *Historical Memoirs of the Irish Bards* (ca. 1784–85)—around the same time Patrick McDonald published his *Highland Vocal Airs*—Joseph Walker described the singing of Cormac Common, an eighty-year-old blind singer from

Example 2.5. Ossian air sung in the highlands of Scotland

Example 2.6. Edward Bunting, ed., "The Battle of Argan More"

Mayo living in Galway: "He did not ... chant his tales in an uninterrupted even tone: the monotony of his modulation was frequently broken by cadences introduced with taste at the close of each stanza. "In rehearsing any of Oisin's poems, or any composition in verse," says Mr. Ousley, "he chants them pretty much in the manner of our cathedral-service.'"[21] In her autobiography, Marjory Kennedy-Fraser (1857–1930) describes a similar style in the singing of Calum MacMillan of Benbecula in the Outer Hebrides: "He chanted many lays, some on a monotone, the phrases defined by cadences, some on a gradually descending scale within the compass of a sixth, and among them a well-defined air to which he sang the lay of Aillte."[22]

The use of repeated couplets in recorded lays gives the impression that they may have been founded at one time on a call-and-response pattern. At any rate, the lays, as evident from both poorly notated pre-1900 versions and later recordings made with wax cylinder, wire, or magnetic tape, were often freely sung in a chant-like fashion, at other times with a marked regularity of rhythm. The so-called double tonic—melodic phrases repeated a tone higher or lower—is a common characteristic of Scottish music, both Highland and Lowland, with the occasional octave leap to counteract any sense of monotony in the vocal line.

By the end of the nineteenth century, the controversy over Ossian, as well as its presumed merits, was stoking the fires of curiosity among professional and amateur musicians. Partly in response to this demand, Marjory Kennedy-Fraser, the best-known arranger of such music for an urban audience, published her three-volume *Songs of the Hebrides*, with the collaboration of the collector Kenneth MacLeod, in 1909, 1917, and 1921, with a further volume in 1925.[23] Two Ossianic lays appeared in volume 2: "Cuchulainn 's a Mhac" (Cuchullan and his son), and "Aillte" (subtitled "Heroic Ossianic Chant").[24] MacLeod recovered the air and words of the first from Duncan Maclellan of the Isle of Eigg, Inner Hebrides, and Kennedy-Fraser arranged the lay for voice and piano in the by-now "exotic" and lugubrious key of E-flat minor, relying mostly on solemn chords, occasionally in arpeggios, to convey the dirge-like quality of the melody.[25]

Kennedy-Fraser recounted their meeting on the island of Benbecula with the singer of "Aillte":

> Driving across the ford early next morning, we had to tramp five miles (and a bittock) in drenching rain and driving wind to the cosy fireside of a crofter, Calum Barraich, the last apparently of the race of Ossianic singers, a type even then supposed to have long passed away.... At eighty-seven, still bright and active, he was to be seen daily out on the Machair herding his cattle. And in the clean white-sanded kitchen of his thatched cottage he sang, but not before he had set everything in perfect order for the ceremony—these old pagan tales were sacred to the Isleman.[26]

The ritual aspect of this performance was important, for it reflected the traditional respect felt by the practitioners of Fenian lore, whether performing prose tales or

Example 2.7. Marjory Kennedy-Fraser, arr., "Cuchullan's Lament for his Son," bars 37–57

heroic lays. Men were known to doff their caps before a performance of the songs or tales, in memory of the hero: the Rev. Alexander Pope, collecting heroic lays in his parish of Reay, Caithness, in 1739, tells of just such a singer, "that very gravely takes off his bonnet as often as he sings 'Duan Dermot.'"[27]

Kennedy-Fraser does not mention this particular aspect of the formal preparation for singing heroic lays, but it was a practice widely noted in Gaelic-speaking areas of Ireland and Scotland. Her arrangement of "Aillte" as printed in Volume 2 of *Songs of the Hebrides* is cast in A minor, with repeated notes in the voice and harp-like figurations in the piano part interspersed, again, with "modal" chords. This heroic lay was "collected in the Island of Benbecula from CALUM MACMILLAN" (the capitals indicating a welcome respect for the source). No doubt well-meaning in making the song public, Kennedy-Fraser nevertheless subjects the vigor of the original vocal line, as in "Cuchullan's Lament," to a vapid series of piano chords in a foursquare rhythm, transferring the song content and context of performance from the rural cottage to an Edwardian parlor.

These pieces were published during the Great War and convey an aura that was perhaps intended to console and encourage, the first sinking to a *pianissimo* conclusion on the tonic E-flat minor, the second ending with triumphant C-major chords. But the general effect of both arrangements is of awkward accommodation of the original Gaelic to an English translation replete with archaisms ("a-seeking Cuchullan," "malisons be on thee," "there were that wounded fell") and vocal rhythms constricted by the rigidity of the bar lines. This entire move was part of the "Celtic Revival" that surged into prominence in the late nineteenth and early twentieth centuries as Queen Victoria embraced the Highlands, a region now safe for tourists, while rich landowners cleared the land for sheep and crofters were forced to migrate from their treasured glens and straths (valleys) to the New World.[28] The influence of Kennedy-Fraser was still considerable in the interwar years. But examples of this kind were the last gasp of a fashion dating from just before 1900—a sentimental, distanced, quasi-Victorian view of the Highlands and its music that had been very largely set in motion by the fame of *The Poems of Ossian*.

Heroic Lays in Oral Tradition after World War II

The continuity of oral tradition in the Highlands has been amply demonstrated ever since the invention of mechanical recording devices in the late nineteenth century. Even as these aids were just coming into use by ethnologists, musicians became eager to capture the "authentic" voice of orally transmitted material. Remarkably—a tribute to the power of oral tradition—a dozen or so Ossianic lays were recorded even in the twentieth century: these include the *Laoidh Mhanuis* (Lay of Manus), a melody published by Patrick McDonald in 1784. A late version was recorded from Donald Sinclair in 1968. Hebridean islanders have been the most fertile source of lays: in 1953 Duncan MacLeod of South Uist sang a version of *Laoidh Fhraoich* (The lay of Fraoch), a tale that has been recorded in Mull, Skye, South Uist, and Tiree.[29]

Other lays captured in versions from oral tradition include *Duan na Muilgheartaigh* (Song of the sea hag), *Laoidh Chaoilte* (Lay of Caoilte), *Duan na Ceárdaich* (Lay of the smithy), *Laoidh a' Choin Duibh* (Lay of the black dog), and *Laoidh Dhiarmaid* (Lay of Diarmid). *Laoi na mná móire* (Lay of the big woman) was found in County Waterford in Ireland in 1936, and is documented from elsewhere, including Donegal, where Séamus Ó híghne of Glencolumcille was recorded singing a version in 1945 and Micheál Ó highne again in 1949.[30] It would be tiresome to list every example of a heroic lay recovered since the advent of recording devices, except to note that such songs have been found even in the New World: in 1953 the Gaelic scholar John Lorne Campbell made a wire recording of a Fenian lay, *Teanntachd Mhór na Féinne* (The greatest difficulty of the Fiann), from seventy-eight-year-old Angus MacIsaac of Antigonish, Nova Scotia, the son of an immigrant from Moidart.[31] The song recounts how, in the course of conversing on the relative merits of paganism and Christianity, St. Patrick asks Oisín to tell him of the hardest battle fought by the Fiann. Eighty years earlier John Francis Campbell had published versions of the song, with many more verses.[32]

The Gaelic lays that recall the days of heroism by Fionn and his warriors were, therefore, not concocted or "forged" by Macpherson ("forgery" being a strongly emotive term connected with illegality): they were simply the basis for his self-conscious extension of them, adapted, remodeled, and transformed, into the wider world of European literature. That even Highland-born scholars such as John Francis Campbell and Alexander Carmichael could disagree profoundly about his methods and results is neither here nor there when one considers the long-lasting impact of *The Poems of Ossian* abroad, in other languages as well as English.[33] Continental critics were not naive; they knew all about the controversy but, like Herder, they tended to see the traditional elements, the anatomy behind Macpherson's fleshed-out poesy.[34] Composers, young and old, were no different in their view of the poems as inspiration for musical invention.

Public Consciousness of Vernacular Harp Traditions

In the notes to her collection, Frances Tolmie of Skye suggested that the singing of such lays was confined to a solo voice.[35] In the days of specialist poets, a harper might have accompanied the recitation of praise poetry, as in John Derricke's famous illustration of the *reacaire* (reciter) and harper in late sixteenth-century Ireland.[36] Praise poetry, of course, and "'dis-praise' poetry," or satire, was a function of the clan bard, and should be distinguished from heroic lays. But later, with the clan system breaking down, these functions gave way as itinerant harpers sought patronage. Harpers such as the renowned Turlough O'Carolan (1670–1738) composed tunes with variations in a style influenced by composers such as Francesco Geminiani or Handel.[37] Singing with the harp was a specialized skill, and Irish harpers often sought patrons in Scotland because of the shared Gaelic-language tradition, even though their repertoire was much more varied than simply heroic lays.[38] One of these Irish harpers, Echlin O'Catháin (1729–ca. 1790), is said to have sung to his own accompaniment. But once patronage declined, the itinerant harper began to fade from the scene.[39]

In Scotland, the *clarsach*, or Highland harp, had fallen into complete neglect by the end of the eighteenth century.[40] Despite the songs of the blind harper Roderick Morison (Ruaidhri MacMhuirich) of Bragar in Lewis (ca. 1656–ca. 1714) or Sileas MacDonald of Keppoch in the 1720s, the art of singing verse to harp accompaniment (the genre of *amhran* or *óran*) was on the wane in the Highlands as the eighteenth century progressed.[41] Irish harpers, though, as composers mainly of recorded tunes, are known to have traveled in Scotland in the later seventeenth century; they included the blind Ruari Dall Ó Catháin (with whom Roderick Morison is often confused), Echlin Ó Cathain (1729–ca. 1790), Denis Ó Hampsey (ca. 1695–1807), and Pádraig Ó Beirn (ca. 1794–1863). Around the same time, in the 1680s, the Dukes of Hamilton were employing an Irish harper, Jago McFlahertie.[42] But a century later, when Patrick McDonald, in his *Highland Vocal Airs* (1784), wrote, "The taste for that style of performance seems now, however to be declining. . . . [T]he native harpers are not much encouraged," he was reflecting a widespread perception that the older world of harp performance in Ireland and Scotland was about to disappear—hence the urban interest in a style that had been kept alive by the patronage of rural gentry.

John Gunn's *An Historical Enquiry Respecting the Performance on the Harp . . . Until it was discontinued, about the Year 1734* (Edinburgh, 1807) traces this neglect, referring, at the same time, to a "Mr Wood, an ingenious mechanic, and a manufacturer of the harp and other musical instruments" in Edinburgh, which signified the contemporary attempt to develop a modern instrument. But at the instigation of the Highland Society of Scotland, this same Mr. Wood had already restrung with wire strings the famous "Queen Mary" instrument (Clàrsach na Banrìgh Màiri) belonging to the Robertson family of Lude, in Perthshire. This Highland harp was played for members of the society on two occasions by the Swiss composer and musician Joseph Jean (or John) Elouis (ca. 1752–ca. 1827), "the celebrated performer on the Pedal Harp," who had settled in England by 1794 but moved to Scotland by 1805; there, in February, he gave a concert on the Pedal Harp at the Assembly Rooms in George Street, and Edinburgh this seems to have led to the invitation, later that year, to play the Queen Mary instrument.[43]

In Ireland, the harp had long served as a national emblem and its social function was not unconnected with political movements of the day. The instrument was explicitly adopted as the insignia of the United Irishmen in October 1791, with a motto that announced a new beginning for the nation: "It is new strung and shall be heard."[44] This resulted in the renowned four-day-long Belfast Harp Festival of 1792, in which Bunting, then an assistant organist at St. Anne's Church in Belfast, gathered together a group of ten older harpers as the last remaining exponents of the traditional style of playing. Assiduously, he noted down the music they played as well as the general style of execution. These transcriptions and commentary by Bunting were published in two key documents of the period: *Ancient Irish Music* (1796, 1809) and *Ancient Music of Ireland* (1840). Arthur O'Neill (1737–1816), a harper at the Belfast event, recalled in his *Memoirs* how there had been annual harp festivals held at Granard from 1781 to 1785, with up to eleven performers, prize money of seven, five, three, and two guineas, and in the last one, subscriptions for all the players whether they had won a prize or not. This newer enthusiasm for the older harp music occurred, of course, at a time when its very existence was threatened.[45]

The most celebrated of the Irish harpers in the earlier part of the eighteenth century was, of course, Turlough O'Carolan (1670–1738), whose musical talent spurred Oliver Goldsmith to proclaim: "Of all the bards this country has ever produced, the last and greatest was Carolan the blind." Yet even Carolan molded many of his compositions, which are usually cast in the form of theme and variations, and his performance style to some degree, after the classical procedures of European composers of the day. Moreover, he was playing the strings of his instrument with his fingertips rather than plucking with the fingernails like the ninety-seven-year old Denis Hempson (or Ó Hampsey), the only harper at the Belfast Harp Festival to have retained this ancient technique, one associated with the wire-strung harp.[46] A little later, Charles and John Egan devised a portable Irish harp that employed a mechanism in the pillar that allowed the player to change the harp's tuning. Instead of foot pedals, the player could use small buttons, known as "ditals," to activate a mechanism in the pillar whereby linkages there turned small discs with pins that pressed up against specific strings to retune the harp.[47]

The latter-day exponents of the harp tradition were, however, nothing like the ancient Greek rhapsodes imagined by Ossian enthusiasts of the late eighteenth and nineteenth centuries. By the time of the later Middle Ages and Renaissance, the functions of the bard and the harper had become distinct. To English government officials in sixteenth-century Ireland, for instance, the "harpers, rhymers, Irish chroniclers, bards, etc. were seditious and dangerous persons" although the music could be agreeable even to "gentlemen in the English Pale." The diplomat Thomas Smith, one of these English agents, provides a sour description of a praise poem to a chieftain who had just carried out a successful cattle raid. The portrait contrasts clearly the function of the *reacaire* with that of the harper.[48]

The picture of the Ossianic bard, then, as some kind of latter-day Homeric figure who chanted his epic songs to the accompaniment of the triangular harp (or quadrilateral lyre, the two never being clearly differentiated in literary accounts) in no way corresponded to the historical reality in Ireland, Scotland, or Wales. The classical world of Homer that the harp or lyre evoked for continental literati appears in Mme. de Staël's *Corinne, ou L'Italie* (1807), where the heroine accompanies herself on a lyre as she improvises verses on the Capitol in Rome: "Sa lyre, instrument de son choix, qui resemblait beaucoup à la harpe, mais était cependant plus antique par la forme, et plus simple dans les sons."[49] Representations of the lyre on Greek pottery were beginning to impose themselves on notions of Ossianic "epic song" and lament, as well as on the iconography of the harp.

Figure 2.1. Anne-Louis Girodet de Roucy-Trioson (1767–1824), Untitled (Bards calm the anxious Malvina, scene from the opera *Uthal*). Oil on panel, 1802. The National Galleries of Scotland, Edinburgh, NG 2761. Reproduced with permission.

The literary image of the harper, usually blind, persisted in the eighteenth century even after a technological breakthrough in harp construction with the new pedaling system patented by the French firm Érard. Sebastien Érard, after much experiment, had devised a single-action harp in London in 1794 using a unique fork mechanism that, when engaged with the pedal, brought two forked pins into contact with the strings, shortening them by a semitone. By 1801 he patented a harp with three semitones per string, and then, in 1811, perfected his double-action mechanism based on the fork principle, again in London. Tuned in C-flat, this harp could be played in any key, and Érard's principles are used by harp-makers of today with little modification. By 1820 no fewer than 3,500 of these forty-three-string "Grecian' harps"—so called because of their ornamentation—had been sold. Later, Pierre Érard developed his uncle's instrument into the forty-six-string "Gothic" model produced from 1835 until it was expanded, in about 1900. We should remember in this context, then, that the opera by Le Sueur (1760–1837), *Ossian, ou les Bardes*, first performed in Paris on July 10, 1804, employed eight harps (although the composer had asked for twelve) to provide an overwhelming effect as the bards hymn the rising sun.[50] Méhul turned this idea on its head in his rival opera, *Uthal* (1806), by having the harp (and flute) gently accompany the four bards as they sing the atmospheric hymn to sleep ("Hymne au sommeil").

It was undoubtedly an Érard instrument that the harpist mentioned above, Jean Elouis, used in tutoring the princess of Wales, the duke of Kent, and Princess Sophia of Gloucester, as he remarks in his "Advertisement" to his *Second Volume of a Selection of Scots Songs, with Accompaniments for the Harp or Pianoforte* (London, Dublin, and Edinburgh, 1808; first vol., 1806). This work is important for its rejection of the elaborate "graces" and "symphonies" (introductions and codas) used by previous composers, including Haydn, and for its attempt to embrace a simpler, more authentic style of accompaniment for Scots songs (whose occasionally "unsuitable" or "impolite" texts were amended by Mrs. Elouis). Elouis decided to remain in Edinburgh as a teacher of harp, the fashion of the time being especially conducive to young ladies' taking up of the instrument, and by all accounts he made a decent living as a teacher and performer. But there is no sign, in any accounts of his concert repertoire, of items connected to Ossian: rather, descriptions mention concertos by continental composers and items from popular operas such as Mozart's *Don Giovanni*.[51] The craze for Ossian on the Continent appears to have left Elouis untouched; he no doubt felt safer dealing with Lowland music and its appeal for genteel ladies in the post-Burns Regency and Walter-Scott-land of early nineteenth-century Britain.[52]

Chapter Three

A Culture without Writing, Settings without a Score, Haydn without Copyright, and Two *Oscars* on Stage

The philosopher David Hume, already celebrated in his day as the author of *Treatise of Human Nature* (1739–40) and *Inquiry Concerning Human Understanding* (1748), was at first an enthusiast for the Ossian prose poems but increasingly had doubts: he declared to James Boswell that "if fifty barea--ed highlanders should say that *Fingal* was an ancient Poem, he would not believe them." He could not credit that a people who were forever concerned to keep themselves from starving or being hanged should preserve in their memories a poem in six books. In other words, the Highlanders were hopelessly illiterate, a Lowland view that had persisted at least from the days of King James VI, who had proclaimed Gaelic-speaking Highlanders "utterly barbarous"—that is, they did not behave according to the civilized manners of the time.[1]

Dining at David Garrick's in London, Hume met Edmund Burke, who told him that the Irish protested they knew all these Ossian poems, but he could never find anyone able to repeat the original verses.[2] Burke, at least, had been exposed in his youth to Irish Gaelic, but Hume and many other Lowland Scottish literati were not at all familiar with the contiguous Celtic language and rich oral tradition of their own Highlands.[3] Even in his own lifetime that tradition was producing, at midcentury, poets of the quality of Dugald Buchanan (1716–68), Rob Donn (Robert Mackay, 1714–78), Alexander MacDonald (ca. 1698–1770), and Duncan Ban MacIntyre (1724–1812). The last of these moved to Edinburgh in 1767, serving as a constable in the City Guard from then until 1806, and his poems were published there in 1768. In 1769 Hume himself finally settled in Edinburgh, living in the city until his death seven years later. In any case, the pull of literature and aesthetics in "North Britain" at the time was toward the classical world, and to France.

The effect of Macpherson's poems, for one astute critic of the time, was of "personal intonations" rather than "literal translations"—what we might call a kind of literary ventriloquism.[4] This was sensational, because a European educated class, bored by clever or sterile neoclassical verse, was ready for a new fashion, a poetry of "feeling" consonant with but developing separately from the philosophy of Jean-Jacques Rousseau: a return to nature, meaning not only a retreat from formality in manners but, more profoundly, a social and cultural revolution based on education and moral consistency. The prose poems Macpherson conjured out of Gaelic oral and manuscript tradition astonished literary circles of the time, beyond Britain and across the European continent; translations into French, German, and Italian, as well as critical works and original compositions based on the poems, followed rapidly. The poems were saturated with just such natural images and consistency of behavior as Rousseau was advocating, even though he and Macpherson were poles apart in their literary purposes and methods.

The *Oithóna* of François-Hippolyte Barthélémon (1768)

And so it came about that, just a few years after the original publication of the poems in Edinburgh, a young French musician serving in the Irish brigade in France, François-Hippolyte Barthélémon (1741–1808, later anglicized to "Barthelemon"), came to London and designed a concert that was to include acts 1 and 2 of a three-act "dramatic poem" based on the poems of Ossian.[5] This premiered on March 3, 1768.[6] The work amounted to a hybrid form of oratorio-opera, "with grand Chorusses" that were not part of normal London opera at the time.[7]

The plot given in the libretto, and promised to be continued at a second concert, is straightforward. It explores relations between the sexes, and sexual morality. Oithóna, the wife of Gaul (an ally of Fingal), is forcibly abducted by Dunrommath, lord of Uthal, while her husband is away fighting for Fingal; raped by the man she had formerly rejected, she is hidden in a cave on a desert island. Gaul and his men return and seek revenge, but in the course of battle Oithóna, having armed herself, rushes into the fray and is killed.

The story sticks fairly close to the original plot, the language being converted from prose to blank verse. The protagonist is just one of a number of "female warriors" (among them, Crimora, Utha, Colmal, Inibaca, Darthula, and Morna) that appear in the poems.[8] The plangent imagery drawn from nature ("mossy towers") and epithets reminiscent of Homer (Oithóna's "snow-white arm") are essential features in the paraphrase. The unnamed librettist of *Oithóna*, who adapted the text fairly closely from Macpherson's original plot, built its three acts around the classical strophe and antistrophe, with arias, recitatives, choruses, duets, and instrumental music. This last was to be played, in the intervals between the acts, by Barthelemon himself on the "viola d'amour" or by Signor Gervasio on the mandolin.[9]

The "chorus" is specified in the libretto as "sometimes of one Voice, sometimes of more, and consisting of two Bands, Strophè and Antistrophè." The music is, unfortunately, untraced, and we can only guess from the composer's surviving compositions at the character of the "symphonies" that precede acts 2 and 3, or of the "Short Symphony" in act 2 following Oithóna's lament, a *recitativo* in blank verse not far removed from the original of Macpherson:

> He took me in my Grief, amidst my Tears,
> And raised the Sail. —For, ah, the Traitor fear'd
> LATHMON with Strength, returning from the War,
> LATHMON, OITHÓNA'S Brother, hapless Maid![10]

There was no spoken dialogue. The words "strophè" and "antistrophè" in the "Persons of the Drama" suggest that the author or authors were aiming at a kind of Greek tragedy, emphasizing this aspect by describing the work as a "dramatic poem." The first few pages cast the recitatives, arias, and choruses in iambic pentameter, and this meter dominates. It is not until Gaul's air, "Perdition on the Ravisher/The Villain I'll pursue," that the metrical scheme changes to the ballad meter (8.6.8.6), and this in turn gives way to the trochees of the semi-chorus (male) as the act begins to wind down, interpolating banal sentiments (not in Macpherson's text) on the role of women:

> Lovely females, form'd for Pleasure,
> Source of highest human Joy,
> Oft you cause, in equal Measure,
> Griefs that all our Peace destroy.

Ballad meter occurs just once in act 2, again with an air by Gaul, "No more a prey to black Despair, / But for future Bliss prepare." Overall, the dominance of iambic pentameter creates a certain monotony of poetic rhythm, but Barthelemon may have found musical solutions to this problem. In the libretto, act 2 ends with Dunrommath's warriors feasting and singing "in full harmony":

> The Toils of War suspending,
> We'll give the day to Joy,
> Love *Shells and Music blending,
> Our Feast can never cloy.
> To the Harp's enliv'ning Sound,
> O'er the Turf we'll lightly bound,
> Far from Danger, free from Care,
> All for Love and Joy prepare.

An amusing footnote explains the asterisk: "Their drinking cups were made of Sea Shells; what their liquor was, is unknown to us" (by all accounts it was the honey-based mead).

Act 3 was intended to open with a "Warlike Symphony, or Dunrommath's March," with a counterpart for Gaul when he appears in order to rescue Oithóna. And there is a "Discord of Horror" at the moment Oithóna, in disguise, is fatally wounded. The opera was to end with a choral Epode: "Conscious of her guiltless Shame, / Martyr to her Virgin Fame, / As she fell, all free from Blame, / Glory celebrates her Name." Only two of the three acts were given at the premiere. The reason for this is unclear, but perhaps there were problems of staging, musical or personnel issues. Subsequent performances, entire or in part, never materialized, and there is no sign of the music in Barthelemon's surviving manuscripts.

Because of his unique role as the first professional composer to set an Ossianic piece, Barthelemon deserves some attention. Born in Bordeaux to a French father and an Irish mother, he had lessons in violin and composition in Paris shortly after the famous "querelle des Bouffons," the dispute between supporters of French as against Italian opera (1751–54). Rousseau famously supported the cause of the Italians. The reverberations of this affair must have made an impression on Barthelemon, and he would have been familiar with the recitatives and arias of Rousseau's *Le devin du village* (1752) as well as, after arrival in London, with Burney's doctored English version.[11] On the advice of the composer Thomas Erskine, sixth earl of Kellie (1732–81), who met him in the French capital (where he was playing in the orchestra of the Comedie-Italienne), he moved to London in 1764.[12] There, he was a soloist at a benefit concert for Mozart and his sister at the Great Room, Spring Garden, St. James's Park (June 1764), and performed a violin concerto at Hickford's Room during the concert given there by the Mozart family on May 13, 1765.

Barthelemon eventually succeeded Felice de Giardini as leader of the band at the King's Theatre, Haymarket. Assisted by David Garrick, whose paternal grandfather had migrated to Britain from Bordeaux, he contributed music for Garrick's *Orpheus: an English burletta, introduced in the Farce called 'A New Rehearsal, or A Peep behind the Curtain'* (premiered on October 23, 1767, following dinner with Samuel Johnson). Six months later he was able to offer *Oithóna*, his interest in the subject aroused not just by his Irish ancestry, perhaps, but also by catching sight of the "Mémoire au sujet des Poëmes de M. Macpherson" by John O'Brien, Bishop of Cloyne, published in the May 1764 number of the influential Parisian review *Journal des Sçavans*.[13]

Somewhat later, Barthelemon and his family welcomed the visits of Haydn to London in 1791–92 and 1794–95. In a concert in May 1792 the celebrated composer accompanied Mrs. Barthelemon at the piano in airs by Handel and Antonio Sacchini (1730–86). Barthelemon adapted three of Haydn's quartets—presumably with Haydn's agreement—by composing adagios and finales based, respectively, on

Scots airs and reels (ca. 1796, and later, in 1815). William Napier published his quartets, opus 9, about 1785.[14]

Adapting Haydn

Parenthetically, and more appositely for Ossian, an unnamed editor had, a few years earlier, adapted the melody from the second movement of Haydn's Symphony No. 76 (1782) to a passage from the poem "Carric-thura" and published the music as Ballad VIII in the *Second Sett of Twelve Ballads* (1787?).[15] Ballad VIII is preceded by a quotation from the poem, which curtails "fountain" to "fount" for musical purposes and repeats several phrases ("above me," "is troubled," "sad sad are my thoughts," "my love," "thy Father's house") to fit the melodic line and its harmonic underpinning. The anonymous editor had no qualms about tailoring the original structure

Example 3.1. Haydn, Symphony No. 76, opening of second movement

Example 3.2. Anon., Haydn-adapted setting, "I sit by the mossy fount," *Second Sett of Ballads*, pp. 16–17

by foreshortening Haydn's first fourteen bars to twelve. Ironically, the conventional, neoclassical poetry of Ballad VII preceding this setting is by Samuel Johnson, a sly joke, no doubt, on the part of the editor of these ballads given the well-known animosity between Johnson and Macpherson. In the same volume, moreover, a poem by Charlotte Smith (Ballad IV, "Werter's Sonnet"), set to the *poco adagio* melody in B-flat of Haydn's String Quartet, op. 9 (1771), reveals the profound effect that Goethe's novel *The Sorrows of Young Werther* (1774) was having on the educated English public of the time, with its segment in which the protagonist quotes extensively from Ossian's "The Songs of Selma" and a short passage from "Berrathon."

If Haydn knew about the pirated "I sit by the mossy fount" he made no protest. It entered the public domain under his name, even though the English words and phrase-lengths sit oddly with his *Adagio, ma non troppo* melody. The publisher, Preston, recognized that Haydn's popularity as well as that of Ossian could be used to profit from a middle-class clientele eager to perform the work of an acknowledged master in a domestic context. The textual and musical liberties taken by the arranger (e.g., "fount" for the original "fountain," or the orchestral texture reduced to a bare keyboard part) were tolerated in an age when plagiarism was rife. The dispute between Haydn and his pupil Ignaz Pleyel at this time over who had written certain trios is only the best known of the contemporary controversies over copyright.[16]

To return to the Barthelemon family: the visit of Haydn did not push their connection with Ossian into obscurity, for Mrs. Barthelemon was a soloist in Harriet Wainewright's sensational opera *Comàla*, performed in the Hanover Square Rooms on January 26, 1792.[17] Whether her husband played in the orchestra under the direction of Mr. [William] Cramer is uncertain. The family's fortunes, however, declined somewhat in the 1780s, and they became more involved in spiritual matters. Barthelemon, friendly with the chaplain of the Asylum for Female Orphans in St. George's Fields, wrote hymn tunes such as the well-known "Awake my soul" ("Morning Hymn"). In 1782 this turn to spirituality led him and his wife to become founder members of the society dedicated to the works and vision of Emanuel Swedenborg, who had died in London ten years earlier. Barthelemon was baptized as an adult at the Swedenborgian chapel in Blackfriars, and passed away at his house in Hatfield Street, Southwark, on July 20, 1808. The subject of Oithóna, the pure but wronged heroine, was to appear again as a central figure for the specifically operatic stage only spasmodically, like Agandecca less popular for librettists and composers than Comala, Colma, Darthula, or Malvina.[18]

The *Colma* of William Bach (1791)

Another "dramatic poem with music" may appear surprising in its link with the illustrious Bach family of musicians. In the same year that saw the premiere of Mozart's *Die Zauberflöte* in Vienna (1791), a concert piece to a text based on Ossian, namely the musical drama *Colma* (subtitled "Eine Episode aus den Gedichten Ossians"), was performed in Berlin. The composer was William Bach (1759–1845), chamber musician (*Kammermusikus*) to Frederick Wilhelm II of Prussia.[19] The son of Johann Christoph Friedrich Bach and grandson of Johann Sebastian, Wilhelm Friedrich Ernst (his birth name) studied with the composer sons of J. S. Bach, Carl Philipp Emanuel and Johann Christian Bach. He had spent time in London and was there when his uncle Johann Christian died in 1782. At that point he adopted the English form of his name; thus "William Bach" appears as the author of *Colma*.[20]

The work is neither a melodrama nor a *Singspiel*, for there are no spoken interludes. It shares the fate of Barthelemon's opera of 1768 in that the music is untraced. But because the composer was the last scion of a renowned musical family the drama is of more than just curiosity value. William Bach was born just one year before the publication of Macpherson's *Fragments of Ancient Poetry, Collected in the Scottish Highlands* (1760). Although the volume was translated early in Germany (in 1764 and 1765), it was probably the complete translation of Ossian by Michael Denis (1768–69) that Bach encountered.[21]

Conceived in two acts to a libretto by the composer himself, the anguish of Colma over the death of her brother and her lover follows the original prose poem, but in verse form. The text is principally divided into recitatives and arias, the former in free verse, the latter in varieties of the octosyllabic or, less prominently, the hendecasyllabic line, normally with alternating rhymes (ABAB or AABB). The *dramatis personae* are three soloists: Colma, beloved of Salgar; Minona, Colma's friend; and

Marlo, Minona's brother.[22] A chorus of ghosts and a mourning song of bards supply a conclusion to the action. There is no indication in the libretto as to the range or vocal type (soprano, mezzo, tenor, baritone, bass) of the three characters.

Act 1 is almost wholly taken up with Colma's four recitatives and two arias, broken by a "Rondo," whose text reads, "Hier ist der Felsen, hier der Baum / Und hier des Silberbaches Schaum. / Du sagtest: dort kam ich zu dir, / Ach! Ach! wo geht mein Salgar irr?" (Here the rock, and the tree, and here the foaming silver stream. Thou hast spoken: there I came to thee. Oh, where has my Salgar strayed?). Without the music it is uncertain what the term rondo signifies here, but perhaps it is meant in the operatic sense common in the late eighteenth century, as "slow-fast." Thus the composer intended the first two lines to be sung relatively slowly, the second distich in a livelier tempo. After Colma's cry for Salgar, in separate recitatives and arias (Minona's is a *da capo* aria) Minona and Marlo tell Colma that Salgar and her brother will not return. In his recitative, Marlo addresses Colma as "erste der Mädchen von Selma" (first of the maidens in Selma), a description that echoes Herder's portrayal of Darthula, adapted about 1770 from the translation of Denis (1768–9), as "schönste der Mädchen in Erin" (loveliest of maidens in Erin).

Act 2 begins with Colma's recitative "Ha! nun bricht der Mond durch die Wolken" (now the moon breaks through the clouds) and proceeds with her *ariosa* "O du, mein Bruder, ach, warum / Kam Salgar durch sein Eisen um?" (Oh my dear brother, how did Salgar fall by his sword?). A *terzet* follows as the trio sing separately, then a final distich together:

[Dich] Alles was mich sonst vergnüget [Minona, Marlo]
[Dein] Ich mein Salgar ist nicht mehr. [Colma]

The chorus of ghosts reply that they have heard her plea ("Wir haben dein Gebet vernommen"), and Colma continues with her farewell aria, "Zum letzten lebe wohl, um diesen Abschiedskuss, Minona" (At the last farewell, with this parting kiss), and finally, in recitative mode, sings, "Ich höre Salgars Stimme im Winde" (I hear Salgar's voice in the wind), and throws herself to her death from the rocks.

The ensemble of bards then adds its threnody with "Zu diesem Lager kommt die Sonne nimmer," an echo, again, of Herder's version of Darthula: "Nimmer, O nimmer kommet die Sonne" (Never more comes the sun). A duet with Minona and Marlo mourning Colma's passing precedes a final repeat of the chorus of bards. To all intents and purposes, *Colma* is a compact piece that would stand up well in performance, but without the music it is impossible to guess its true worth. Bach's versification exhibits striking features of syllabic variety and adjectival coloring, based as it was on a variety of sources ranging from Michael Denis's comprehensive translation of Ossian to poetry by Goethe and Herder with which Bach was obviously familiar.

Two Versions of *Oscar and Malvina* on Stage, with Music

By this time, twenty years after their publication, Ossian's poems and the characters in them were attracting impresarios and choreographers as well as composers. A theatrical work derived from Ossian premiered in London as the outlandish *Oscar and Malvina, or, The Hall of Fingal* (1791). This was billed as a ballet pantomime "taken from Ossian" with "the new Music composed, and the ancient Scots Music selected and adapted, by Mr. Shield. The Overture by Mr. Reeve."[23] In fact, when William Shield (1748–1829) left suddenly (probably pursued by creditors) Reeve took over the task of arranging and composing the music.[24] William Reeve (1757–1815), a Londoner by birth, was elected to the Royal Society of Musicians in 1787 but had also worked as an actor at the Haymarket and Covent Garden theaters.

In general, *Oscar and Malvina* seems to have been a choreographer's and composer's bizarre metropolitan notion of what a London audience would expect to see and hear in the distant Scottish Highlands: Oscar's betrothal to Malvina is threatened by the visiting chieftain, Carrol, who, in love with her, treacherously contrives to have Oscar thrown into a prison tower; in the end, however, Carrol's plan is revealed; rescued by Fingal, his grandsire, Oscar leaps to safety, Carrol is dispatched by Malvina, and all ends happily. The work approaches parody, a *burlesca* rather than a *burletta*,[25] presenting a caricature of the cultural landscape of Ossian with Fingal's castle, stubble fields, bards, and the inevitable bagpipers. There was no speaking, and all the action was mimed.[26] The huge success of *Oscar and Malvina* at Covent Garden on October 20, 1791, resulted in some forty performances until the season ended on May 31, 1792, while the published libretto sold like hotcakes, reaching a third edition in 1791.[27] The ballet was revived from time to time over the next thirty years, not only in Britain but also in Germany, Ireland, and the United States.[28]

An Irish dancing master, James Byrn or Byrne, choreographed the production and danced the role of Oscar. The imported French ballerina, Mme. St. Amand, took on the role of Malvina. An itinerant Irish bagpiper, Dennis Courtney (1760–94), who had achieved some success in helping the Highland Society of London (founded in 1778 to promote Gaelic culture in the capital), provided much of the music onstage. Somewhat incongruously kitted out in Highland dress, Courtney (or Courtenay) played Scots tunes on his Irish "union" bagpipes, accompanied at first by a German harpist turned harper, Charles Meyer, and later by Meyer's compatriot John Erhardt Weippert (1766–1823).[29]

After Courtney's death, Patrick O'Farrell took over the role of piper.[30] A "Mr Murphy" (probably John Murphy) also played "union" bagpipes at a performance on May 5, 1799, returning on May 18 to play a solo accompanied by Weippert on the harp.[31] The pair teamed up for the last time at Covent Garden on March 2, 1800, for Reeve's overture to *Oscar and Malvina*. Like Courtney, Murphy had played for the Highland Society of London in 1788, but was less talented than Courtney. It appears, however, that both piper and harper joined the orchestra for the overture in the manner of concertante soloists, but with instruments that could blend with the standard intonation, unlike the Highland bagpipe with its idiosyncratic scale and tuning. An observer at the time ridiculed Courtney's Highland garb, which included a "Scotch bonnet," and pointed out the absurdity of bellows-blown Irish bagpipes playing Scottish melodies, though the quite different tuning and limited range of the Great Highland bagpipe prevented its being adapted to common harmony–based songs for the theater. But when one considers the debates on provenance over the next century (that is, the shared inheritance of Ossianic tales in Gaelic-speaking areas), these Irish-Scottish musical and dramaturgical connections were not altogether inappropriate.[32]

Apart from the excited if unremarkable overture, the music was mostly "Scotch tunes" (i.e., melodies in a Scottish style) concocted by Shield or Reeve. These took the form of the traditional Highland strathspey (slow dance) and reel, which were played by the piper and harpist, or were "battle pieces" with flourishes by the orchestra.[33] In her memoirs, the actress Mrs. Crouch (sometime mistress of George, Prince of Wales) gushed, "Lovers of Ossian felt a kind of enthusiastic rapture when they beheld the guests seated and the bards arranged in the flower-decked hall of Fingal; when they heard the sweet harmony of the harps and Union pipes (bagpipes), and the songs of the bards—they heard, also, the warlike sound of the shield of the Hall of Fingal."[34] This account seems to confirm that, as James Boswell told David Hume some years earlier, many in London were already captivated by Macpherson's epic; clearly, universal skepticism had not yet set in by the time of *Oscar and Malvina*.[35]

A pupil of Byrne, Maria de Caro, staged *Oscar e Malvina* as prima ballerina at the Teatro Venier in San Benedetto during the Carnival season in Venice in 1797. It was billed as a "ballo eroico pantomimo in cinque atti," with music ("tutta nuova") by Giuseppe Nucci, an opera composer later engaged at the Regio Theatre in Turin. Caro herself interpreted the role of Malvina at this performance, and Cairbar (the villain and Oscar's nemesis) was danced by Antonio Landini, a noted choreographer who would go on to produce *Oscar e Malvina* during Carnival in Turin in 1801.[36] Derived, ultimately, from the London production, the thematic connection of *Oscar e Malvina* to the Ossian poems is already fugitive and superficial, even embarrassingly so, and nowhere near the fidelity of Barthelemon's libretto for *Oithóna* or, for that matter, the text of Harriet Wainewright's opera *Comàla*.

By this time in Britain, the Highlands had become the fashionable locale for extraordinary operatic events, mainly through Sir Walter Scott's works such as the poem "The Lady of the Lake" (1810), from which Rossini and his librettist were to forge the two-act melodrama *La donna del lago* (1819).[37] But Milan's Teatro Re had already staged a work with authentic Ossian credentials, namely *Oscar e Malvina: Dramma serio per musica da rappresentarsi nel Teatro Re il carnevale del 1816*. The libretto was by Leopoldo Fidanza, who had penned the text for Stefano Pavesi's *Fingallo e Comala*, a hit opera presented in provincial theaters of northern Italy between its premiere in Venice (1805) and staging in Milan (1814).[38] The music was

Example 3.3. William Reeve, *Oscar and Malvina*, rondo for union pipes and harp

Example 3.4. *Oscar and Malvina*, skirmish, battle piece,

by Marchese Francesco Sampieri, director of music in Bologna's Casino and member of its Philharmonic Society.

Sampieri (1790–1863) had a circle of artistic friends, among them, indeed, Rossini, whom he entertained at his villa. As a musician and composer Sampieri was an accomplished amateur, with seven operas and other compositions, mainly vocal, to his credit, although after 1827 he gave up composing, perhaps aware that his friend's star quality had eclipsed his own modest talents. The libretto for *Oscar e Malvina*, at any rate, was published in three versions according to the performance locations: at Bologna, 1816; in Milan the same year; and at Florence, 1817. The first performance took place at Sampieri's villa at Casalecchio di Reno in the summer of 1816. The title page of the libretto published in Florence announces that the performance during Carnival 1817 was under the protection of Ferdinand III, grand duke of Tuscany.[39]

The plot of Fidanza's libretto for *Oscar e Malvina* involves Caroso, a Romano-British king, who has abducted Malvina (the betrothed of Ossian's son Oscar, a Caledonian warrior, and daughter of Toscar, king of one of the Orkney Islands). The action takes place in Caroso's domain and vicinity, and there is a sense that a greater realization of historical reality has begun to permeate Italian perceptions of British history (although in the *argomento* the walls of Hadrian and Antonine are attributed to the earlier invasion of Agricola). While the wall in Caroso's kingdom is being restored for defensive purposes, Toscar and Oscar attack in order to rescue Malvina.

The structure of the libretto for Sampieri's Milan performance and the later public staging in Florence is compact in its two acts, but Fidanza imported much of his text from Pietro Generali's *Gaulo ed Oitona* (1813). For instance, the opening chorus of the operas are identical: "Vieni a gioir con noi, / Duce Trionfator. / Fuggon da te gli Eroi, / O figlio del valor" (Come, rejoice with us, triumphant leader. Heroes flee from you, son of valor). It is not entirely surprising that Fidanza simply copied chunks of earlier libretti into *Oscar e Malvina*; after all, composers were doing the same thing, importing arias and ensembles from earlier works, especially where they had been effective. The process of transmediation in these cases points to the key role of the librettist, although we must take into account the degree of collaboration between librettist and composer in shaping the final text.

The libretto for act 1 of *Oscar e Malvina* in both locations, Milan and Florence, is similar, but in act 2 composer and librettist cut the first two scenes so that the action takes on a more urgent cast. Fidanza repeats the irascible exchange between Dunromath and Gaulo of act 2, scene 2 of Generali's opera in act 2, scene 5 (scene 3 in the Florence version) for Oscar and Caroso: "Geloso lo sdegno / Nel petto si asconde: / Do smanie profondo / Straziato e il mio cor" (Jealous disdain rises in my breast and a deep yearning lacerates my heart). The gripping but by now stylized scene 9,[40] influenced by Le Sueur's opera, is set in an "orrido oscuro carcere" (dismal and dark prison), where Oscar, incarcerated, sits on a rock exclaiming, "Oh albergo della morte! / In te mai splende il giorno" (Oh lodging of death, in you the day never shines).[41] But after this recitative, Oscar's followers eventually rescue him, and as he is reunited with Malvina, all ends well. The final chorus repeats the quatrain of *Gaulo ed Oitona*: "La goija, ed il piacere / Echeggino d'intorno. / Coroni un si bel giorno / La fede, ed i valor" (Joy and pleasure echo around, / Crowning a beautiful day are faith and courage). Sampieri's opera contains thematic echoes of earlier works by other composers: the young lovers, the threat from a tyrannical figure, a harrowing scene for the hero in a grotto or prison, the final rescue and reconciliation.

Competently written if lacking something of the flair evident in the Ossian-based operas of Generali and Pavesi, this *Oscar e Malvina* may not have achieved the fame and influence in Italy as Pavesi's *Fingallo e Comala*, yet it provided a context for Rossini's absorption of the dramatic elements that the poems of Ossian could provide, in his case through the medium of Scott's "Lady of the Lake," and Rossini enjoyed the triumph of *La donna del lago* almost a decade later. Critical opinion now

Example 3.5. Francesco Sampieri, *Oscar e Malvina*, *scena* (recitative): "Oh, albergo della morte"

sees Rossini's work as the first flush of Romantic opera, and it is no surprise that the librettist, Andrea Leone Tottola, was moved to introduce into his text fashionable Ossianic features such as a chorus of bards and the appearance of a meteor, neither of which are in Scott's poem. Some of the names, too, are from Ossian: Morve, Inibaca, and Tremmor.

It appears that Tottola was not only familiar with the poem through Cesarotti's translation of 1763 or later editions; he was also aware of the five-act Ossianic opera *Aganadeca*, with a libretto by Vincenzo de Ritis and music by Carlo Saccenti, performed at the Teatro San Carlo in February 1817.[42] The story of Agandecca from Macpherson's *Fingal* Book III was to attract—perhaps oddly, given the number of tragedies on the poem from Italian dramatists—only one other opera, *Fingal* (1847), by the Sicilian composer Pietro Antonio Coppola (1793–1877).[43] Written some forty years later, the final works on the hero's romantic adventure include two notable compositions: the dramatic cantata *Agandecca* by Paul Umlauft (1853–1934), for soli, male chorus, and orchestra (1890), and the *Fingal*, op. 43, of Arnold Krug (1839–1904), published a year later.[44] These works testify to the blossoming of the *Männerchor* movement in central Europe and North America. More significantly, they confirm the rise of the quasi-operatic cantata in late Romantic works based on the poems of Ossian.

Chapter Four

"A Musical Piece"

Harriet Wainewright's Opera *Comàla* (1792)

The advertisement of January 25, 1792, reads: "Hanover Square Rooms. — Tomorrow, January the 26th, will be performed COMALA, a musical piece; consisting of Recitative, Airs, Duets, and Choruses, the entire composition of Miss Harriet Wainewright. The words taken from a dramatic Poem of Ossian. Leader of the Band, Mr. Cramer. Principal Vocal Performers: Mr. Page, Mr. Bartleman, Mrs. Barthelemon, Miss Hagley, and Miss Corri. The doors to be opened a quarter before eight. Performance to begin a quarter before nine. Tickets half-a-guinea; to be had at Messrs. Ransom, Moreland, and Hammersley's, Bankers, Pall Mall, and also, for convenience, at Longman and Broderip's, No. 26, Cheapside, and No. 13, Haymarket. No person can be admitted without a ticket. Books of the Performance at the Rooms on the evening."

Thus was described an event of some importance in the musical life of London, a dramatic work for the stage based on Ossian, by a woman, publicly performed some twenty-four years after François-Hippolyte Barthelemon's desultory attempt with his *Oithóna* of 1768.[1] Although the composer's autobiography does not reveal a motive for choosing this particular poem, it appears to have appealed to her as the tragic tale of a noble huntress. It relates how Comala, daughter of Sarno ruler of Inistore (the Orkney islands), falls in love with Fingal, chieftain of Morven, and follows him disguised as a youth when Fingal marches to resist the army of the invading Caracul. Having spurned Hydallan, Fingal's warrior lieutenant who is enamored of her, Comala throws herself from a rock when Hydallan falsely tells her Fingal has fallen in battle.[2] Fingal, however, returning victorious, laments her passing with his bards.[3]

The title page of the score published by William Napier in 1803 reads: "Comàla/ A Dramatic Poem/from/Ossian/As performed at the/Hanover Square Rooms/Set to Music by/Miss Harriet Wainewright/Dedicated with Permission to the/Most Noble Marquis Wellesley./London/Printed for the Author by William Napier,/Musician in ordinary to his Majesty/Lisle Street, Leicester Square." The dedication page is dated "Calcutta, August, 1803," and signed "Harriet Stewart" (Wainewright's married name). Beneath the formal dedication there follows the usual fulsome address to a patron. The list of some 248 subscribers includes the "Right Honourable Lord Clive (four copies)" and Major General Baird, the hero of Seringapatam.[4] An appreciation of the work by that patron, Richard, marquis of Wellesley, governor of India, appeared in *The Calcutta Post* for Friday, April 27, 1804:

> We take great pleasure in announcing the reception of Comàla, a Musical performance by the accomplished and ingenious Mrs. Stewart, late Miss Wainwright [sic]. The subject is happily chosen; the splendid imagery and language of Ossian have acquired a degree of pathos and energy, which they (wonderful as they are) never possessed, until they were modulated and chaunted by the inspiring genius of Mrs. Stewart. The Scottish Bard astonishes—we read his lines, and "tremble when we read"; but to pour the full tide of his ecstacising [sic] song on the ear, was a privilege reserved by the kindred muse of Ossian for our sublime minstrel; and her name, and her musical version of the noblest of Caledonian poets, will exist, and be admired, until the most excellent works and productions of human ingenuity shall be consumed by the Vandal torch of expiring Time.[5]

Not every budding composer, even if male, could expect such a flowery compliment from a minister of state—at that, the governor of India. It is quite extraordinary that the most noble marquis should go to the lengths he did to praise so generously both the composer and the source of the libretto. The opera was performed at the Hanover Square Rooms, on Thursday, January 26, 1792.[6]

The composer later recounted the reception of the work in the press. The *Morning Chronicle* of January 27, for instance, enthused, "Miss Wainewright, by this happy effort, will clearly be placed in the front rank of musical ladies. The performance was deserving of the highest praise. Mr. Cramer led the band. The principal vocal part was sustained by the fascinating Miss Corri."[7] The *World*, February 2, observed likewise: "The modulation in many parts was extremely fine, and, though uncommon, seemed easy and natural. There were, indeed, some wonderful strokes of genius, which would have done honor to the greatest masters."[8] And the *Morning Post* of February 4 commented:

> . . . where a profound knowledge of the science (the consequence of many years' study), is happily aided by a surprising natural genius, such as is visible in all the works of those two great modern composers, Haydn and Pleyell, such a coalition is truly desirable. The candour with which the latter of these was heard to deliver his sentiments, during the performance last Thursday evening, does him real honour, and convinces us that he has generosity enough to give merit its due, and sense sufficient to listen to the effusions of genius with unprejudiced ears. Indeed, the whole audience seemed to have heard something so much beyond their expectations, that we think Miss Harriet Wainewright cannot refuse the public the gratification of a second performance, the first having so wonderfully escaped the fiery trial of criticism.[9]

The composer clearly felt encouraged by these reviews, and perhaps even got wind of the favorable comments of Ignaz Pleyel. She went on to compose songs and church music, some of which has survived. But after attempts failed to have both *Comàla* and her earlier opera on Don Quixote staged in London, she left for India in 1796, taking with her both scores.[10] *Comàla* was performed there with some success, Wainewright singing the main role herself with amateur singers taking up the other parts. Her fame was established in India, as she wrote, both as a singer and as a composer. Setting up a subscription list, she had *Comàla* published in London by William Napier, and proofs arrived in India in the spring of 1804, shortly after she had married a Colonel Stewart. Eventually several hundred copies, she wrote, were delivered to the subscribers.[11]

After some fifteen years Wainewright returned to England, a country whose climate affected her singing voice adversely.[12] In India her voice had responded positively to the climate, and she was solicited to sing Handel ("I know that my Redeemer liveth") at an oratorio performance, finding herself compared thereafter with the famous Madame Mara.[13] In November 1831 she presented a copy of *Comàla*, "handsomely bound in three volumes," to Queen Adelaide at the Pavilion, Brighton, "which was graciously received." Yet she ruefully recollected that, without patronage (especially royal patronage) the piece would have little chance of public performance.[14] The last we hear of the composer and singer is some nine years later, when "A NOVEL CONCERT is announced to take place at the Hanover-Square Rooms tomorrow morning, for the benefit of the Chelsea Benevolent Loan Society, *the whole of the music* to be performed is the composition of Mrs. Colonel Stewart."[15]

Harriet Wainewright Stewart

Who, then, was Harriet Wainewright, later "Mrs. Colonel Stewart"? Her autobiographical narrative, published in 1836, tells little of her early life. But she seems to have been the daughter of a Liverpool musician, Robert Wainwright (1747–82), organist of St. Peter's. She gives no date for her birth. David Baptie, in his *Handbook of Musical Biography*,[16] states that "she is said by some to have been a pupil of Dr. Richard Woodward," the organist of Christ Church, Dublin, who died in 1777 at the age of thirty-four. In her narrative she claims only that she has reached the legendary limit of "three score years and ten," which suggests that she was born about 1766. In that case, she would probably have been a pupil of Woodward when she was about ten or eleven years old.[17]

"In my childhood," she writes, "I was generally allowed to be what is called a musical genius; my voice possessed compass, sweetness, uncommon flexibility, and great power, when occasion required its being called forth; but unfortunately my lungs were weak, and consequently would not admit of my practicing long at a time.... The love of harmony, however, displayed itself in me at a very early age

... whenever I was allowed to go to bed early ... not for the purpose of sleeping, but to indulge my inventive musical faculties." Traveling in the city, walking the London streets, led to similar musical sensations and a kind of musical reverie. Having received no other musical instruction "than such is to be found at boarding schools," she became the pupil of John Worgan (1724–90), a London organist known for his performances at Vauxhall Gardens, who instructed her in thorough bass and counterpoint, as well as in singing arias by Handel and Purcell in the appropriate style.[18] Although she had a range of up to D in *alt*, he advised her to confine herself to the middle register, an admonition that left her voice strong in later life when contemporary sopranos had lost theirs.

Moving to London and getting, through contacts, the right sort of social introductions (including one to the music historian Charles Burney) led her to experience opera, in particular the singing of the renowned castrati Gaspare Pacchierotti (1740–1821) and Luigi Marchesi (1754–1829). She particularly liked to imitate the vocal style of Pacchierotti before he left England; afterwards, she found Marchesi equally persuasive as a model.[19] But soon, composition began to obsess her:

> About this time [she resumes] the mania for composition possessed me. The excitement was occasioned by my perusal of Ossian's Poems, where, among the wars of Fingal, I met with the dramatic episode of Comàla, which I resolved on setting to music; and, in the spirit of enthusiasm, almost amounting to inspiration, I spent whole days, weeks, nay months, in this arduous yet delightful employ; scarcely allowing myself time to eat, drink, or sleep—for Comàla was the theme of my thoughts by night and by day ... At the expiration of a twelvemonth I had completed my opera. I composed it, in the first instance, with only a pianoforte accompaniment for the voices; but after acquiring some knowledge of the different instruments which form an orchestra, I wrote the opera out in score, and happily succeeded in the attempt. The music was universally admired. ... Dr Burney was also an admirer of my opera, and warmly expressed his opinion that 'in it was combined the sublimity of Handel, with the taste and elegance of the Italian school; and that he considered the composition to be truly original.'[20]

At the London premiere of the opera, Sophia Corri (1775–ca. 1831), making her first appearance as a soloist, sang the main role of Comàla, while James Bartleman (1769–1821), who sang Hydallan, also made his debut, complimenting the composer on writing songs that "could not have suited his voice better." Dr. Benjamin Cooke (1734–93), organist of Westminster Abbey, coached the six boys of the abbey's choir in the choruses. According to the composer, the concert was well attended by the fashionable world and by some of the leading nobility: the Duke of Leeds, Lord and Lady Dartmouth, Lord and Lady Eardley, and others. "The music," Wainewright wrote later, "both vocal and instrumental, was exceedingly well performed, and met with the greatest applause." Indisposition, apparently, prevented the Prince of Wales from attending.[21]

Harriet Wainewright's account is valuable in showing how she came to realize her musical talent. That a woman should, in the late eighteenth century, compose an opera was remarkable enough in the eyes of many; detailing how she came to write it, how it was performed and received, and what the subsequent fate was of an opera based on an Ossianic theme make for instructive reading. But what is missing from her narrative would have been just as revealing. Where was she born? Who were her parents, and what role did they play in her life? What schools did she attend? How did she gain her entry into society, and into London's musical life? Although she mentions getting to know Lady Brudnell, an amateur singer who took her under her wing, and Charles Burney, the process by which she established relations with them is unclear.

All this is masked in her account, as is the matter of her marriage to Colonel Stewart in India.[22] According to traceable records, she married John Stewart at Bhaugulpore [Bhagalpur], Bengal, on October 23, 1801.[23] The lengthy episode of her sojourn in India, included in her autobiographical narrative, is admittedly useful in its description of how "the English at Calcutta were very musical," and of how, in singing the main role in her opera there, she came to be called "Comàla, the white-handed daughter of Sarno."[24] A chorus she composed on the victory at Seringapatam (1799) was performed in the presence of the Governor-General and later published by William Napier in London in 1805. Burney, though slightly condescending, had some warm words for her concerning this work: "I know of no female contrapuntist ... who could surpass, if equal, the merit of the composition."[25] Returning to London, Wainewright contrived to have published a collection of pieces she had presumably composed in India.[26] A number of her manuscripts, submitted between March and June 1829, are in the British Library.[27]

In her account of her life, Wainewright mentions the difficulties she experienced in trying to get both *Comàla* and her opera on Don Quixote staged, difficulties not unconnected with contemporary prejudice toward "women composers," as Burney's comment implies. Nevertheless, Wainewright's narrative of her life still leaves the reader with a sense of frustration: we have valuable information about her musical taste and ability as well as her feelings on composing, but less than we would like about the decisive context of these for her, the critical facts of her childhood, adolescence, and married life. Her will, dated December 5, 1843, might suggest that she died a widow that year or shortly afterward, at St. Marylebone, London.

The *Comàla* Scores

Two copies of the score published by William Napier in 1803 are extant in the British Library, one bound as a single volume (H.90), the other a presentation copy in three handsome red leather-bound volumes with gold tooling, one for each of the three acts (R.M.13.c.1.).[28] The pagination in both copies is identical. A libretto was also published at the time.²⁹ But a document of equal importance, now in the library of the Accademia di Santa Cecilia in Rome, appears to be a fair copy of the score prepared by the composer for the publisher (A.MS.3693). Bound in leather with gold lettering, the cover bears the legend COMALA: A DRAMATIC POEM/ FROM OSSIAN/SET TO MUSIC BY/HARRIET WAINEWRIGHT, and this is repeated on an ornamental title page (to which has been added in pencil "Italian hand," and on the verso page, "Printer 1803").³⁰ There is handwritten double pagination that is very confused, with frequent deletions: the numbering of set pieces is crossed out and renumbered in all three acts. Up to page 52 the pagination is in ink, but, beginning at 53, pages also bear penciled page numbers beginning with 39, this double pagination ending at page 328 (for the ink numbers) and at 350 (pencil numbers). The final score printed by Napier has 406 pages.

In the British Library copy of the libretto published shortly after the first performance, the singers are identified as "Mr Page, Mr Bartleman, Miss Corri, Miss Davies Inglesina, Miss Hagley, with chorus singers." The name of Miss Davies, however, has been struck out and "Mrs Barthelemon" substituted.³¹ The *dramatis personae* (Comàla, Fingal, Hydallan, Dersagrena, Melilcoma, and a chorus of bards) are named as on the second page of the published score, with musical *incipits* for all three acts that identify the recitatives and airs of the main characters.³² The instrumentation is listed, the instruments being arranged in the current fashion, with the bassoon below the violas: "Timpani in D, Trombe in D, Corni in D, Flauti, Oboi, Violino primo, Violino secondo, Viole, Fagotti (col basso), Cembalo, Basso." The harpsichord part appears only in the published score, and was clearly added between correction of the fair copy and publication. This perhaps marks again the conservative, Handel-influenced nature of Wainewright's orchestral style, since the developing style of the classical period tended to make the harmonic and textural presence of the harpsichord seem old-fashioned.

The overture begins with a sturdy first segment of sixty-eight bars (*allegro*) in D major and common time, a second section that moves to D minor (*andante*) leading to a pause at bar 80 on the dominant A, and finishing with a reprise of the *andante* section. From the opening D major, the tonality in act 1 ranges through to B-flat major for Dersagrena's first recitative ("The chace is over"), to C minor for her aria ("Rise, rise, Comàla from thy rocks"), to A-flat major for Melilcoma's accompanied recitative ("There Comàla sits forlorn"). The tonal and rhythmic resources the composer employs to enliven the poetic drama in this first scene are varied and full of interest, and the flavor of the original Ossian text is captured in the subsequent airs and recitatives.

The scenario of act 1 is announced in the libretto as "Scene in Scotland / A sun set. —A cave, with rocks in the foreground. —A view of the river Carun, and a distant camp." The text of the opera, with stage directions as in the libretto, keeps close to the original poem: Comàla, passionately in love with Fingal, is preparing a feast with Dersagrena and Melilcoma for his return from battle: Dersagrena opens with a recitative in B-flat, "The chace is over," which in turn leads to a striking passage in E-flat and slow tempo with staccato strings, "Lay down the bow and take the harp." Melilcoma's aria in C major ("I saw a deer at Crona's stream") follows, with full orchestral accompaniment, clearing the way for a *fioritura* passage on "soon he bounded away." Comàla, her introductory recitative cast in a melancholy F minor for "O Carun of the streams! Why do I behold thy waters rolling in blood?," switches to A-flat for her aria in an *allegro*, and this leads to a touching episode in F major (marked *affetuoso*) with a prominent flute part, "Rise moon, thou daughter of the sky."

Hydallan, one of Fingal's chiefs, also in love with Comàla, enters as a storm breaks with the (false) news that Fingal has been slain: "Roll thou mist of gloomy Crona.... The bands of battle are scatter'd, and no crowding steps are around the noise of his steel." At the entry of Hydallan and soldiers, the strings scramble along in a *presto* until at a graver *Largo* Hydallan sings, "Oh Carun! Roll thy streams of blood, for the chief of the people fell." The gentle $\frac{6}{8}$ *siciliana* in B minor then frames Comàla's solo "Who fell on Carun's grassy banks, son of the gloomy [libretto: "Cloudy"] night." Hydallan responds with a recitative in B major and an aria in E major, "Blow, thou gentle breeze, and lift the heavy locks of the maid, that I may behold her white arm, and lovely cheek of her sorrow." The finale moves to a *maestoso* (majestic) section for Comàla's aria in G major with busy strings and tremolos in the bass parts as she sings, "The thunder rolls on the hill, the lightning flies on wings of fire, but they frighten not Comàla, for her Fingal fell." The *fioritura* must have exercised the composer, reminding her of her own training as a singer as well as the brilliance of Pachierotti and Marchesi.

Act 2 (page 138, pencil in the fair copy) begins without change of scene, the storm having ceased and the moon rising, as Comàla finally realizes that Hydallan has deceived her and Fingal is alive. The music opens with Comàla's recitative in G minor, "Say, chief of the mournful tale, fell the breaker of shields?" This is followed by Hydallan's $\frac{2}{4}$ air in E-flat (*andantino*), "The nations are scattered on their hills, for they shall hear the voice of the chief no more!" An agitated passage in C minor captures the tension between Comàla and Hydallan, whose air with solo cello "Look on them, O Moon!" is succeeded by an interlude of a *siciliana* in $\frac{6}{8}$ and F major, sung by Melilcoma and accompanied by flutes: ("What is that sound on Ardven? Who is that bright in the vale? Who comes like the strength of rivers, when their crowded waters glitter to the moon?") Comàla, seeing Fingal return, thinks it is his ghost: her aria in B-flat and $\frac{2}{4}$ time ("Ghost of Fingal! Do thou, from thy cloud, direct Comàla's bow") opens with a bassoon solo. Fingal, having triumphed in the field, at first confines himself to an announcement of victory in his *maestoso* E-flat aria, "Raise, raise ye bards of song," which gives way to the lively "Caracul has fled from my arms."

Fingal then becomes aware of Comàla, poised on a rock, fearful she is seeing only his specter. She rejoices (F major) in "He is returned with his fame ... but I must

Example 4.1. Harriet Wainewright, *Comala*, aria: "Rise moon, thou daughter of the sky!"

Example 4.2. Wainewright, *Comala*, aria: "That I may behold her white arm"

Example 4.3. Wainewright, *Comala*, aria: "The thunder rolls on the hill, the lightning flies on wings of fire"

rest beside the rock, till my soul settle from fear. Let the harp be near, and raise the song, ye daughters of Morni" and with *pizzicato* strings the harps of Melilcoma and Dersagrena are evoked, while Dersagrena concludes act 2 with her F major air "Comàla has slain three deer on Ardven, and the fire ascends to the rock; go to the feast of Comàla, king of the woody Morven." At this point (bars 20–21 in the fair copy), a red pencil has been used to score bar lines in the working copy, perhaps to emphasize the rhythmic stress. After a heartfelt exchange with Fingal, Comàla sings "Take me to the cave of thy rest!" and falls to her death from the rock. As the two

Example 4.4. Wainewright, *Comala*, aria: "Take me to the cave of thy rest"

main characters sing, pencil strokes in the fair copy of the manuscript appear to indicate a break: at bar 45 "Begin here" has been added in pencil. Numerous bars at this point are marked with "x," including the final measure; their meaning is not entirely clear.

In act 3 the scene changes to the interior of a cave, where Fingal and his chiefs are at an entertainment, with bards attending. This section begins (page 240, pencil numeration in the fair copy) with Fingal's "Raise, ye sons of the song, roll in joy" and continues in an *allegretto* duple time for chorus in B-flat, "Roll, streamy Carun, roll in joy; the sons of battle fled" for sixty-three bars, ending in F major. The music then shifts to an *andantino* (G minor), Melilcoma pursuing the idea of mourning for Comàla in "Descend, ye light mists, from high; ye moonbeams, lift her soul. Pale lies the maid at the rock; Comàla is no more." Fingal's sorrowful recitative "Is the daughter of Sarno dead?," which moves from *affetuoso* to *vivace*, then *dolce* ("Meet me Comàla on my Heaths") is answered by Hydallan's "Ceas'd the voice of the huntress of Galmal? Why did I trouble the soul of the maid?" For Fingal, conscious now of Hydallan's treachery, this confrontation merges into his dismissal of the latter in the commanding C-major aria, "Youth of the gloomy brow, no more shalt thou feast in my halls."

After the scene change, Comàla is discovered dead at the foot of the rock, with Dersagrena standing by the body. Then, in B-flat tonality, Fingal pleads for Comàla to meet him with the accompanied recitative, "Lead me to the place of her rest, that I might behold her beauty" which clouds into B-flat minor for "Pale she lies at the rock, and the cold winds lift her hair" with a conclusion on an F-major cadence. The chorus of bards, accompanied by horns, proclaim (in D minor) "See, meteors roll round the maid, and moon-beams lift her soul." This final section is varied by interspersing choral comments with what the composer terms in the libretto "canto solo," "canto duet," and "canto for four voices." This lament-like sequence oscillates between major and minor, until a sixteen-bar *allegro* in F major strikes up at the canto duet, "And they shall think with joy on the dreams of their rest." At this point

Example 4.5. Wainewright, *Comala*, aria: "Youth of the gloomy brow, no more shalt thou feast in my halls"

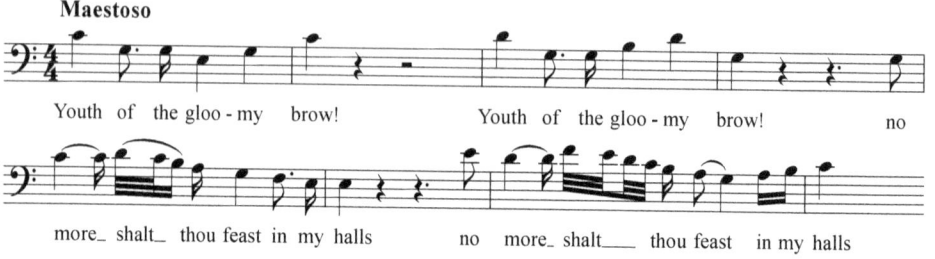

Example 4.6. Wainewright, *Comala*, chorus: "See! See! Meteors roll round the maid!"

there is a note in the score, "Add a line for the Horns—insert them with the violin." The harmony then turns to D minor, a *larghetto* in $\frac{6}{8}$, for a repeat of "See, meteors roll round the maid . . ." This in turn yields to an *allegro moderato* in D major that, lively for some forty-four bars, ends for the chorus of bards with the poetic injunction of Macpherson's poem, "See, meteors roll round the maid, and moonbeams lift her soul!"

What, then, is the significance of this opera? First of all, the composer has kept close to the action and text of the original poem (a relatively rare case in opera of convergent transmediation). She has also developed a finely tuned sense of key contrast and tempo as instruments of musical drama. The framing tonal conception is cyclic, setting out in D major and returning to that key at the end of the opera. The number of recitatives is carefully structured. Recitatives in the three acts are also arranged in a symmetrical fashion: five are accompanied in act 1, five are unaccompanied in act 3; and in act 2 both types number four each. The airs follow a contrasting pattern of seven in act 1; six plus the duet between Comàla and Fingal in act 2; and just three plus the choral numbers in act 3 (which is essentially a lament for the heroine and has little action apart from the exposure and banishment of Hydallan). In all three acts the tonalities are astutely employed and varied so as reinforce the dramatic situation while suiting the characters involved. The composer also harnesses standard harmonic effects such as a bass that rises or drops by step to indicate growing tension or a darkening of the emotional atmosphere: for example, in act 1, Dersagrena's recitative has a sinking bass, A♭–G–F, to indicate "These are the signs of Fingal's death," but later, this turns into a bass line that rises from A♭ to A♮, B♭, B♮, and, finally, C, to pause on its dominant, G. Reprises in the arias are always varied, usually by intensifying the string parts with livelier rhythms.[33]

While the style is fundamentally Handelian insofar as any English composer writing in the later eighteenth century was bound to feel that master's influence, Wainewright's conception of the poetry as inherently dramatic allowed her a great deal of latitude in the tonal structure of the three acts, with their more Haydn-flavored recitatives, arias, and ensembles. The panoply of keys ensures that the colors and shading of the characters as they play out their roles are sharply drawn and contrasted. Her experience of Italian opera and renowned singers in London, along with her advantage of an introduction into polite society, must have encouraged her determination to compose an opera herself—not as an amateur, for she did not regard herself as such, having taken lessons in harmony and counterpoint from John Worgan, though to some extent her understanding of operatic convention was gathered through observation and diligent application of her musical talents to the task of composition. On the other hand, her firsthand experience of the vocal technique of stellar castrati such as Pacchierotti and Marchesi must have been significant in her molding of vocal lines in her opera. She does not mention as an influence the most popular English *opera seria* in London at the time, Thomas Arne's *Artaxerxes* (1762), which was performed more than any other until the 1830s. Yet knowledge of its success must have been a spur to her ambition to find a text of "classical" content for which she could compose music of a similar quality.[34]

The fact of Wainewright's gender is clearly a central issue in the matter of recognition by critics who troubled to attend the opera premiere. It has been accepted without question by some music historians that after Handel's *Alcina* (1732) there were no historically important opera premieres in London, but the success of Arne's *Artaxerxes* alone renders this claim groundless.[35] Even though commentators refer to the work as an oratorio, Wainewright herself always referred to it as an opera, and had conceived it as such. The performance at the Hanover Square Rooms, a concert venue, presumably led to the assumption that *Comàla* must have been a non-operatic work, but Wainewright outlined clearly in her autobiography the problems she had getting impresarios to stage it: Sheridan at Drury Lane, for example, wanted only comic operas like *The Duenna* (1775), which was stuffed with popular tunes harmonized by Thomas Linley the Younger. In the magazine *Belle Assemblée* for September 1823, a note on "English Music" remarked on the opera's being composed by a "female amateur," but adjudged the author to possess "talent and originality of taste for musical composition . . . which would do credit to a professor."[36]

The social barrier to acceptance and respect for woman composers was still in place, even though a number of female composers were productive at the time: the singer-composers Harriet Abrams (1758–1821) and Cecilia Maria Barthelemon (1767–1859), for instance. And despite the later praise for *Comàla* by the Governor-General of India, Richard Wellesley, it is easy to see why Wainewright despaired of any fully staged performance in London. Haydn, moreover, was in town, and the idea that a new opera by a woman could somehow attract the interest of (never mind upstage) a celebrated master as he brought forth a stream of new works for the Salomon concerts that began on February 17, 1792, must have seemed highly unlikely, even preposterous.[37]

Nevertheless, William Napier, to his credit, took it upon himself to print the score, and in light of his work for the generous Haydn (who employed him when he had become bankrupt in 1791), intelligence about the opera may well have reached the master's ears; there is, however, no mention of it in his letters. Be that as it may, a possible connecting thread might well have been Haydn's friendship with the Barthelemons, whose residence at 8 Kennington Place, Vauxhall, he visited often: Mrs. Barthelemon, of course, sang in the premiere of *Comàla*. The influence of Haydn in the opera overtakes that of Handel on many counts, his presence in London at the time of its premiere a touchstone for the taste of the period. Some more "progressive" critics may have seen *Comàla* as conservative in conception, methods and techniques despite its undoubted professionalism. Today, however, more than two centuries later, with plentiful evidence of exceptional musical composition by other women during her lifetime, Harriet Wainewright's opera *Comàla* is due for a fresh appraisal.

Chapter Five

Between Gluck and Berlioz

Méhul's *Uthal* (1806)

"A wonderful masterpiece," wrote Donald Francis Tovey on his copy of the score of Étienne-Nicolas Méhul's opera, *Uthal*, adding rather acidly, "within the limits of its dry clichés."[1] What Tovey meant by "dry clichés" were those associated with French opéra comique of the period, notably in the works of André Grétry (1741–1813), the most influential and popular French composer of the day: that is, music interspersed with spoken dialogue, the latter often overlong.[2] He was no doubt referring to a limitation of the genre, namely the breaking off of musical development in order to advance the plot with dialogue. But Tovey was enthusiastic about the orchestration and tonal resources that Méhul devised for a one-act opera that lasts less than an hour. Famously, the composer omitted violins from his scoring in order to suggest the darker color of the story's origins in the poems of Ossian. Some critics objected to this as tending to produce monotony: Grétry is notoriously recorded as remarking, "Je donnerais un louis pour entendre une chanterelle!" (I'd give a ducat to hear an E string). Berlioz thought the effect of violas and cellos would be a "monotonie plus fatigante que poétique de la continuité de ce timbre clair-obscur" (a monotony more tiring than poetic with the prolongation of that light-dark coloration).[3] Tovey was right, however, in noting that the brevity of the opera would counteract such criticisms.[4]

Uthal is a work by Méhul (1763–1817), the most important opera composer of the age in France, composed in his later maturity. But this opera has had few performances since it was written. It was first performed at the Opéra-Comique on May 17, 1806, two years after Le Sueur's more famous opera *Ossian, ou les Bardes* (1804). Le Sueur's work had caused a sensation: Napoleon was enthusiastic, rewarding the composer with the Légion d'honneur (instituted on May 19, 1802), and accounts of it stirred audiences and composers as far as Italy and Russia.[5] Apart from the use of multiple harps and the tam-tam (the latter to represent shields being struck), Le

Sueur was acclaimed for the musical scenario of act 4: Ossian is imprisoned and has a vision of ancestor spirits, a scene that impressed Berlioz.[6] Reputedly, as no friend of Le Sueur, Méhul wanted to create something much more authentic in terms of the subject matter.[7]

The genesis of Le Sueur's opera goes as far back as June 2, 1796, when the first stage play on Ossian, *Oscar, fils d'Ossian*, by A. V. Arnault, was staged at the Théâtre de la République. But the first French *romance* on the topic of Ossian, "Oscar et Dermide," with words by Arnault and music by Méhul, had been published in February of that year.[8] Around the same time, it may have been Méhul who supplied the gentle, A-minor accompaniment of a string quartet for Marie-Joseph Chenier's "Colma," a *romance* taken again from Ossian.[9] Thus, some rivalry existed between Le Sueur and Méhul as regards the poetic content of Macpherson's works and their musical potential. Pierre Le Tourneur had published his translation of the Ossian poems in their entirety in 1777, and Pierre Baour-Lormian had produced his edition in 1801 (rev. ed. 1804); an educated public in France, therefore, was already familiar with them.[10] With Le Sueur's opera, critics began to detect a new kind of musical drama: the presence of bards, warriors, spirits of ancestors, and so on was prefiguring how opera would develop in the next decades, namely toward a "grand" conception that was both epic and lyric in its portrayal of a third-century society. It appears that Méhul began to write his opera late in 1803 and certainly most of it was ready in 1804, but it may have been the illness of Mme. Scio-Messié, for whom the role of Malvina was written, that prevented the staging in that year.[11]

Méhul's librettist for *Uthal* was Jacques Maximilien Benjamin Bins de Saint-Victor (1772–1858), who drew his plot (with considerable freedom) from Macpherson's poem "Berrathon," and more distantly, from Pierre Baour-Lormain's already very free version in rhyming alexandrines.[12] He also defended, in his preface, his choice of an Ossianic subject against the critics who thought the subject uninteresting.[13] But the librettist made some radical changes to both characters and plot, and thus the process of transmediation from one genre (lyric poetry) to another (dramatic opera libretto) is, in this case, palpably divergent. The changes include Larmor (Macpherson's Larthmor),[14] chief of Dunthalmon (a place name the composer and librettist presumably felt to be more singable than Baour-Lormain's "Dunlathmon"); Malvina, his daughter (for Macpherson's "Nina-thoma"); Uthal, Malvina's husband (a role changed from that in Macpherson's poem); Ullin, Larmor's main bard (usually, in Macpherson, Fingal's bard); and the addition of a chorus of bards and another of Morven warriors. The libretto differs in some minor respects from the published score: its description of the dramaturgy is more elaborate, as in the opening staging of the forest, which specifies pines and other trees, foreshore for ships (*vaisseaux*), and several large rocks that act as a platform for the bards, whereas the music score simply states that the staging represents a forest, with rocks at intervals along the shore.[15]

The plot of the opera tells of Uthal's seizing of the lordship of Dunthalmon by deposing his father-in-law, Larmor, whom he accuses of being too old and unable

Figure 5.1. Wilhelm von Schadow (1789–1862), portrait of Pauline Anna Milder-Hauptmann (1785–1838) as Malvina in the opera *Uthal*. Oil on canvas, 1818. Stadtmuseum Berlin. Reproduction: Oliver Ziebe, Berlin. Reproduced with permission.

to rule his kingdom effectively. Uthal's wife, Malvina, daughter of Larmor, is dismayed to find that her father has summoned Fingal, chief of neighboring Morven, to help him regain his throne. She fears that Uthal may come to harm. Larmor's bard Ullin, dispatched to Fingal for assistance, returns to announce that Fingal and his army are near and ready to engage Uthal's men. Ullin suggests a night of rest before the conflict; four bards sing of the glory of Selma while the soldiers sleep. But Malvina is prey to anguish because of conflicting loyalties; distressed, she wanders into the forest, only to come upon Uthal, whom she does not recognize because he is wearing armor.[16] He confesses that he regrets his actions that have caused unhappiness. Larmor and Ullin discover the pair, and Uthal commands Malvina to choose between him and her father. As she reluctantly chooses the latter, battle is inevitable. Ultimately, in the conflict Larmor's allies prevail and Uthal is taken prisoner. When he is brought before Larmor, Malvina pleads for his life. Uthal, preferring execution to life as a subject chieftain, demands to be sent into exile. At this, Malvina declares that she will join him. Her generosity of spirit moves Uthal to beg forgiveness from Larmor, who pardons him, and this act ensures a happy ending to the opera. All this is quite different from Macpherson's "Berrathon," in which Uthal is killed by Ossian for seizing the throne of Larthmor, ally of Fingal. Larthmor's daughter, Nina-thoma, in love with the handsome Uthal, dies of grief when he is slain.

Saint-Victor's libretto is cast in lines of seven, eight, ten, and the familiar twelve-syllable alexandrines, with alternating rhymes, not only in the sung numbers but also in the spoken lines (e.g., rapide/déserts/perfide/la perds). In vocal terms, the main characters are imagined as follows: Malvina (soprano), Larmor (baritone), Uthal and Ullin (*hautes-contre*, or high tenor voices). The chorus of bards sings at first in three (two tenors, one bass) and later in four parts. The orchestration is for first and second violas, flutes, oboes, clarinets, bassoons, four horns, harp, lower strings, and percussion.[17] The story of the opera is set at night, in a forest "of the North." The overture depicts a storm, with "meteors, glowing oak trees, mists, harps, and spirits seated on clouds."[18]

The music begins, *pianissimo*, in the bass strings, *andante poco adagio* in $\frac{3}{4}$ and ostensibly in C major (but really veering toward F minor), to establish the mood of gloom, before the violas enter, still softly, at bar 8. Following an oscillation between C and G that hovers around the edge of F minor, the tempo changes to *allegro*, maintaining *piano* in volume, and duple time (bar 42). Developing around a progression in the bass via E♭, E♮, and F,[19] with passages of increasingly agitated sixteenth notes in the violas, the music drives the tonality toward B-flat minor (bar 120), when before the curtain rises Malvina is heard calling her father: "Larmor!" (D♭/F).[20] The call is repeated two bars later, on a diminished chord that is followed by a chromatic shiver of the orchestra (strings tremolo and timpani rolling) as it descends from a C♯ to a quasi-cadence on A.[21]

The first scene introduces Malvina and her father, who speak their affection for each other and lament the actions of Uthal, as Larmor, in the "Air et Duo No. 1,"

Example 5.1. Étienne Méhul, *Uthal* (1806), overture, p. 13 (Malvina)

sings his dignified E-flat aria "Ombres de mes ayeux" (Spirits of my ancestors) with its arching arpeggio in the home key. After some fifty-six bars Malvina responds with her gently moving, C-major reassurance of "Pour soulager tes maux, pour calmer ta souffrance" (To relieve your aching and calm your suffering). They then join in the livelier duet, cast in $\frac{4}{4}$ and F major, of "Je te revois; quel charme a la nature!" (I meet with you again; what charm nature contains). The melody is characterized by a dropping seventh at "revois" and a *forte-piano* on the second syllable. The spoken dialogue resumes; Larmor advises Malvina that he has requested aid from Fingal and the forces of Morven to help him reclaim his dominion.

This leads to "No. 2, Morceau d'Ensemble," in which horns, clarinets, bassoons, and harp announce the approach of the bards and warriors in a bold C-major march. The men are heard in the distance declaring that Fingal has set sail and will punish the rebels. Gradually, as they come nearer, the C major often turns to D minor as Larmor welcomes them with "Au son des harpes éclatantes / Se mêlent les cris des rameurs" (The brilliant sound of the harps mingles with the cries of the rowers),[22] and indeed, the harp has a prominent part in this ensemble. Malvina, however, is anguished about her husband's future: "O malheureux époux! O fatales querelles! / Ce jour va combler tous mes maux" (O unfortunate husband, these fatal quarrels! / for this day completes my troubles). But Larmor is implacable: he wants revenge, to Malvina's distress. The warriors sing a short three-voice chorus in a stormily assertive C minor, stating they have braved the tempest and are ready for combat. Here, the oscillating bass (C–B) of the overture returns, speeded up. After a brief final exchange with Malvina, Larmor praises the warriors of Morven as they arrive with flambeaux, condemning Uthal as a traitor. A longer chorus ensues as the warriors comment on the misfortune of Larmor and Malvina: "Vers le palais de tes nobles ancêtres" begins in A minor and after seventy-six bars reaches A major with Larmor declaring "suivez mes pas dans ces sombres forêt," (follow my path through this dark forest), but they decide, on Ullin's advice, to wait until sunrise before joining combat.

After Larmor leads the warriors into the forest, Malvina, left alone, sadly ponders her fate in a short recitative ("Quoi! ce combat affreux est donc inévitable!") that becomes ever more anguished until, as she envisions the coming carnage, a dotted eighth-note figure in the violas captures her horror. While she is musing, the bards slowly wend their way on to the higher rocks; four sing of the glory of Selma,[23] the tonality turning from G minor to D major with flutes, harp, and horns in a celebrated *andante* in $\frac{3}{4}$, the "Hymne au sommeil." Malvina, meanwhile, continues with her recitative accompanied by a short, reiterated figure in the strings. Distraught, she continues to hear the soft murmur of harps as she moves into the forest. Uthal then appears, clad in armor, his head covered with a helmet and launches into his recitative, desperate to find Malvina. He reminisces on their earlier happiness and his ambition in seizing Larmor's lordship, blaming the older man for his impetuous nature. Opening with a dramatic descending two-octave scale in the basses in G minor ($\frac{4}{4}$), his recitative ponders the torment he has suffered at being separated

Example 5.2. Méhul, *Uthal*, chorus: "Hymne au sommeil"

Example 5.3. Méhul, *Uthal*, romance: "Tel que l'on voit"

from Malvina. The descending string figure and stabbing *forte-piano* chords of the woodwinds effectively suggest Uthal's depressed condition, his distress at Malvina's preferring her father in her conflicting loyalties. When this subsides, he launches into his *romance*, "Tel que l'on voit sur nos montagnes / Croître un lys, l'amour du Zéphyr," the first part of which is accompanied by the cellos in long-held notes.[24] The *romance* progresses with simple chords accompanying the voice, still in G-minor and in an *andante* tempo ($\frac{2}{4}$), but the second half is accompanied by flowing, insinuating sixteenth notes in the violas, the clarinet imitating the held notes of the cello in the first half: "Pour prix d'un bien si plein de charmes, / J'ai de Larmor troublé les jours. . . . Et dans mon palais solitaire, / Chants et bonheur, tout a cessé." This brings the *romance* to a close, as Uthal then decides he is not to blame for the situation. He ascends a rock, from which he can see the ships, the bards, and the bronze armor of warriors.

At this point Uthal encounters Malvina, who does not recognize him. Each wonders, in asides, about the identity of the other. She asks him for assistance, and after some increasingly nervous self-questioning by both, he removes his helmet and is revealed as her husband. This relatively lengthy scene is designed as a $\frac{4}{4}$ *allegro vivace* in B minor, characterized by a jagged motif of three eighth-note upbeats followed by two plus a quarter note. Agitated figures in the violas and basses that hover around E minor reach a cadence in that key as Uthal intones the name "Malvin-A" (the misplaced accent in names from Ossian occurs in several cases of French or German adaptation).[25] After some 120 bars of further heated exchanges between the two, Larmor and the bards arrive. The key switches to E major for just thirty-two bars in increased tempo as Larmor feels his anger at Uthal renewed, the latter defiant. The final fourteen bars contain some remarkable harmonic touches: after a stretch of pedal harmony on E, the bass line twice moves through the sequence C–G–B♭–F–A, to B as the dominant before resolving on a final E major as Malvina urges Uthal to stop the potentially fatal quarrel.

Scene 6 involves all the principals, along with the bards and warriors. "I was born violent," says Uthal, "perhaps ambitious, but you know very well that I am not a coward." Larmor insists he must pay for his crime of usurpation, but Uthal prefers to die in battle, and leaves the stage. Scene 7 then brings a trio of Larmor, Malvina, and Ullin together with the bardic and warrior choruses. Larmor, in his recitative, urges on the warriors and asks the bards to sing the fatal hymn as he hears the sounds of Uthal's shields. The bards and warriors then proclaim, "Vole aux combats, troupe guerrière, / Vole, attaque, poursuis!" This *allegro vivace* is accompanied by a slashing thirty-second-note figure in the strings to drive home the image of armed conflict between the forces of Morven and Uthal. The chorus sings at first in F major, moving to C major for "Nous bravons les tempêtes" (from no. 3 earlier) while Malvina laments on the sidelines. The action continues into scene 8 as she praises the bards but is sad that their voices are powerless to calm her sorrow; the chief bard tells her of Hidallan, who experienced a fate worse than hers: he was slain by his father for assumed cowardice in war. An *andante*-paced "Chant des Bardes" in $\frac{2}{4}$ highlights the voice of the chief bard.[26] During the narrative the chorus of bards, hearing the noise of the conflict, interject their vision of two spirits seated on a cloud near the stream of Balva in Larmor's kingdom (from the poem "The War of Caros").[27] Malvina interrupts them, claiming from atop a rock that she can see the forces of Dunthalmon in trouble and fretting about the fate of her husband ("ah, mon époux n'est plus"). The tonality suddenly turns to A minor, with jagged dotted motifs that come to a half-close, as Larmor and Ullin join her and the bards.

In the ensuing scene 9, Larmor confirms to Malvina that Uthal has been defeated, and she urges her father to pardon his enemies. The rapidly following scene 10 introduces a victorious march (some 100 bars long) in duple time and in D major, beginning behind the stage *pianissimo*, but gradually growing in volume as the warrior chorus sings, "Réjouis-toi, Morven, une noble victoire / Couronne encore ta valeur." After sixty-four bars the tonality is diverted to B-flat for a half dozen bars before returning to the dominant of D major, a wrench typical of Méhul's mastery of dramatic devices. A barque at the foot of the stage brings the captive Uthal before Larmor, and the latter insists on severe justice for the rebel; Uthal for his part claims that he would have preferred to die in combat. Larmor imposes the penalty of exile,

Example 5.4. Méhul, *Uthal*, aria: "Près de Balva sur le nuage je vois deux fantômes"

Example 5.5. Méhul, *Uthal*, final chorus, no. 9: "Doux moment"

which Uthal refuses, wishing rather to be executed. Malvina intercedes with Larmor and tells Uthal that she will come with him, pleading that otherwise she would perish. At this expression of conjugal love Larmor relents and pardons Uthal. A final chorus of bards and warriors, in a bright F-major tonality, rejoices that peace has displaced armed conflict.

Méhul, in avoiding the sensationalism of Le Sueur's *Ossian* for a "more authentic" *Uthal*, was clearly intent on capturing the darker atmosphere of the plot. He achieved this despite the substitution of a happy ending for an audience that was possibly unprepared for the harrowing drama that precedes the resolution. The structuring of scenes, ensembles, and choruses, moreover, could be confusing for an audience, as these overlap at times: for instance, the No. 2 ensemble with the bards and warriors singing in the distance precedes the formal change to scene 2; No. 5, Uthal's recitative and *romance*, occurs at the beginning of scene 4; while No. 8, a chorus of warriors, opens the final scene, 10. One point of musical criticism not raised by reviewers is the composer's overreliance on common time, whether in two or four. Triple time (as $\frac{3}{4}$) appears only twice, at the beginning of the overture and in the "Hymne au sommeil" (a parallel to Le Sueur's chorus of spirits, heroes, and bards in act 4, scene 3, of *Ossian, ou les Bardes*). But Méhul finds other ingenious ways with which to create rhythmic variety.

We should also consider the plot's technical features, for Saint-Victor drastically altered the narrative core and linguistic style of his source, causing, as noted above, a divergent transmediation in Méhul's apprehension and realization of change from the original (Macpherson's "Berrathon"). This was to be the fate of other operas culled from Ossian, especially in Italy in the years following the success of Le Sueur's *Ossian, ou les Bardes*, whose librettists, Dercy and Deschamps, also took a free hand with the story line. Because the narrative of the poems was often more lyric or epic in character than dramatic, librettists had to devise ways of plotting and introducing action within the aura of Northern mists and heroic endeavor. The forest in *Uthal* stands as a symbol of mystery that corresponds to the anguish and mental confusion of the main characters: Larmor's over his loss of power, Malvina's over the conflict between filial piety and conjugal loyalty, Uthal's over his lust for power and abandonment of Malvina.

Musically, the opera is convincing in its pacing of the action and in its characters and their emotions. The three soloists interact as distinctive figures in the drama, their vocal lines sharply differentiated in each scene. Uthal's *romance* is a highlight of the genre that Méhul had initiated a decade earlier. The *haut-contre* is traditionally a high tenor part (written in the alto clef) with the ability to sing falsetto. Uthal's initial recitative is in the lower reaches of the voice, but later climbs up as far as A. The other tenor part, that of the bard Ullin, could have been confused with that of Uthal. But Méhul ensures that the two *haut-contre* voices are kept apart. The two tenors do sing together in the final scene, but along with the entire cast. The choruses, too, are inserted at key moments: the hymn to sleep and the song of the bards capture the moments of repose needed to mark a lull in the emotional turmoil of the principals.

The voices are skillfully imagined in terms of contrast. Malvina as a soprano (written in the C1 clef) and Larmor as a baritone are cast appropriately. The rising E-flat arpeggio motif in the lower strings that introduces Larmor's aria demonstrates Méhul's ability to portray the essence of the chieftain's character. Larmor's melodic lines are often conceived around this arpeggio idea, for instance in No. 4 as he tries to justify his actions to his daughter. In contrast, the gentle, lilting melody in $\frac{2}{4}$ with which Malvina seeks to calm her father's disquiet creates a sense of her filial piety.

Uthal's *romance*, also in $\frac{2}{4}$, is a counterpart to Malvina's aria. The soft G-minor chords that accompany his melody are transformed after 40 bars into sixteenth notes that circle around the tonic, suggesting feelings of conflict over his treatment of Larmor. Uthal's *romance* reaches a climax with an octave leap at the word "solitaire" as he laments his separation from Malvina. The three main characters in the opera are thus differentiated in musical terms, and the final chorus (No. 9) allows their reconciliation to bring the drama to a fitting conclusion, with "malheur" (misfortune) outweighed by the rhyming "douceur" (gentleness) and "valeur" (courage).

Méhul pays particular attention to the recitatives, conceiving these carefully in terms of the declamatory effect.[28] This care is especially noticeable in Malvina's recitative "Quoi! ce combat affreux est donc inévitable!," as she becomes more and more distraught, the tonality moving from D minor in preparation for the stark contrast with the bardic chorus in D major that follows immediately ("O de Selma! la joie et l'espérance"). Malvina resumes her quasi-recitative with the rippling accompaniment of the harp and violas as she contemplates the sleeping warriors. The chorus gradually draws to a close while she sings ("Ou chercher un appui dans ma douleur amère? Parcourons de ces bois le profondeur sauvage. / Amour et pieté, soutenez mon courage" [where to find support in my bitter grief? Traversing the earthy depth of this wood, love and compassion, bolster my courage]). As Malvina plunges into the forest, the murmur of harps prepares the way for the entrance of Uthal. The scoring for his *romance* is for violas, woodwinds, horns, string bass, and timpani. Along with the "Hymne au sommeil" (No. 4), both the recitative and the *romance* were later extracted from the opera in various arrangements.[29]

The pacing of the action is cleverly matched by the orchestration, which is always varied in rhythm and texture. Berlioz, who at first, like Grétry, thought the violas alone as melody instruments in *Uthal* tiring on the ear, had words of admiration for Méhul's assured use of the orchestra.[30] The instrumental coloring is evident in the overture, with its striking melodic motifs and tempestuous dynamics, all carefully calculated to arouse interest in the drama to come. The influences on Méhul at this time were no longer Gluck, but Haydn and Mozart. And perhaps Beethoven was an influence, too, for his first symphony had been performed in Paris in 1800. But influence certainly flowed the other way, for Beethoven's *Fidelio* (1806–14) is the only example of French Revolutionary "rescue opera" to remain in the active repertory, its text adapted from Bouilly's *Léonore ou l'amour conjugal, fait historique espagnol*, with music by Pierre Gaveaux (1798).[31] *Uthal* was composed at a time when Méhul's orchestral thinking was maturing; his first symphony was to appear in 1808.

A dramatic opera score without violins, trumpets, or trombones may appear to lack brightness and weight, but Méhul's clever use of orchestral technique creates excitement throughout the work. Despite dispensing with violins, he takes pains over the string parts in terms of rhythmic attack, variety of bowing, sustained notes, tremolo or staccato passages. Likewise, he has an instinctive feel for the character of woodwinds and horns, which he uses effectively in quieter lyric scenes as well as in grander scenarios. A striking feature is the dynamic level: much of the score is marked *piano* or *pianissimo* in order to create a sense of mystery and exotic distance. The stabbing *forte-piano* chords in the winds and horns prefigure the drama to come. In the march-like No. 8, notably, the orchestra is instructed to begin *pianissimo* and gradually increase in volume to the end, a difficult feat to bring off in the space of a hundred bars. In "Hymne au sommeil," the accompanying flute, horns, and harp are directed to play onstage, an effective way of deploying instruments in a dramatic stage work. With suitable foreboding, the tam-tam sounds three times in No. 7 as Malvina sings, "Quels sons affreux!" and the bards announce, "Vole aux combats, troupe guerrière."[32]

Uthal had only nine performances at its first staging, although it went on to more than a dozen performances outside France.[33] That would seem to compare unfavorably with the seventy performances Le Sueur's *Ossian* enjoyed over the twelve years after its first performance in 1804. But the fewer performances of *Uthal* are not hard to explain: the opera's title was not a name that would have registered immediately with the Parisian opera-going public even though it was based, however loosely, on a fashionable literary work. Further, a one-act opera, while not a rarity, may have been problematic to stage on its own.[34] Another factor was perhaps the music itself, in its serious purpose and darker coloring. The theme of the apostate hero who deserts his wife and unseats his father-in-law, but is defeated and captured, even if forgiven and reconciled at the last, may not have appealed to the current elite. Parodists, as they had in the case of Le Sueur's *Ossian*, did not take long to exploit the exotic dramaturgy of Méhul's *Uthal*.[35] The new, heroic warrior ethos of the Consulate and Empire was not to everyone's taste.

Professional reviewers commented on the "impression de gravité mélancholique et sombre qui se dégage d'Ossian." The journal *Mercure* pronounced the poetry fine, while the *Décade* thought that *Uthal* was a "genre ennuyeux" and the subject matter too severe, offering little in the way of variety. The *Magasin Encyclopédique* was hardly less critical, deeming the poetry "tiresome and monotonous." The *Journal de l'Empire*, however, paid tribute to the music, with its well-constructed arias and effective ensembles; the overture's somber coloring produced a melancholy atmosphere, and Uthal's *romance* was affecting. Altogether it amounted, the author thought, to a meritorious work.[36] The Parisian critic F. R. de Toreinx (Eugène Ronteix) remarked in 1829 that Méhul's "vigorous imagination is at its best in a quartet or a finale, but it allows itself to be imprisoned within the narrow confines of a romance or couplet for two voices (a duo, as it is called)."[37] This seems harsh in light of the public success of Uthal's *romance* and the composer's ensemble pieces. Around the same time, Louis Désiré Véron, writing in the *Revue de Paris* (1834), praised much about the opera and singled out the "Hymne au sommeil" for special mention.[38] These mixed reactions gave the impression that critics deemed *Uthal* a serious effort by a recognized composer, but also that the work was not one geared to popular taste. One effect of the Revolution had been to popularize the theater and encourage composers to write for less sophisticated audiences. Contributing to this popularity were the laws easing restrictions on the theaters, exploitation by the authorities of opera as a propaganda weapon, and the ideals of the Revolution itself.[39] In the longer term, however, nineteenth-century critics like Rockstro found Méhul "remarkable for his inexhaustible vein of Melody, and for the beauty and dramatic power of his ever-varied instrumentation."[40] If *Uthal* is a masterpiece, as Tovey asserted, then it must be shown anew, through sympathetic staging and performance, to be exactly that.

Chapter Six

Fingallo e Comala (1805) and *Ardano e Dartula* (1825)

The Ossianic Operas of Stefano Pavesi

Today, the auditorium of the Teatro La Fenice in Venice glows with a golden luminescence, much as it would have for operas staged during the Carnival season in the late eighteenth and early nineteenth centuries. Even today, after the disastrous fire of 1996 and the restoration in 2003 to a design by the architect Aldo Rossi, modern lighting recreates all the burnished splendor that gilt embellishment, ceiling frescoes, and chandeliers offered to the impresarios, stage designers, composers, singers, and orchestral musicians of Romantic opera and their audiences.[1] These planners and executants demanded and enjoyed an enviable lightness and radiance in their performance spaces even before the revolutionary gas lighting was introduced in 1826. Sophisticated techniques of illumination for stage performances had been developed from the sixteenth century.[2] But by 1825 the authorities in Venice had "repeatedly expressed their displeasure with the way the decoration of the theater auditorium had deteriorated on account of the smoke from the oil-lamps."[3]

The history of performance and staging at La Fenice is remarkable, not least because, during the period of Carnival from December to March, the operas produced there in the early nineteenth century included two on themes from Ossian, namely *Fingallo e Comala* (1805) and *Ardano e Dartula* (1825) by Stefano Pavesi, a productive composer who completed over sixty operas.[4] His most conspicuous triumph, the two-act opera buffa *Ser Marcantonio*, with a libretto by Angelo Anelli, which was first staged at La Scala, Milan, on September 26, 1810, attained no fewer than fifty-four performances, and subsequent engagements in other theaters followed up to 1831.[5] But his first notable success was *Fingallo e Comala*, premiered at La Fenice on December 26, 1804, St. Stephen's Day, as the inaugural production of the Carnival season.[6] Pavesi is important because of the political and artistic influences that bore on his career in Venice: first, the rise of Napoleon, and second, the effect on him of the opera by Jean-François Le Sueur *Ossian, ou les Bardes* (1804).[7]

Pavesi was not the first Italian composer to be drawn to the Ossian poems as a source for the musical stage. That distinction belongs to Pietro Morandi (1745–1815), a pupil of Padre Martini, who composed his *Comala* for a wedding in Senigallia as early as 1780. Described as "azione teatrale," it was graced with a libretto by Ranieri de' Calzabigi (1714–95), already famous for his collaboration with Gluck in Vienna.[8] Significantly, the opera announced a return to the ideals that had launched the reform of *opera seria* by Gluck and Calzabigi with the performance of *Orfeo ed Euridice* in Vienna in 1762.[9] These ideals asserted that the music should serve the poetry without interrupting the action; that excessive ornamentation should be removed from the arias; that arias should be structured in relation to development of the drama rather than as a vehicle for the vocal talents of the singer; and that the overture should prepare the audience for what would follow.[10] Morandi's *Comala* was the first of a procession of around twenty stage productions in Italy alone, including ballet as well as opera, drawn from Ossian.[11] Notable in this regard, and again preceding Pavesi's first Ossian opera, was Francesco Bianchi's *Calto*, produced at the Teatro San Benedetto in January 1788.[12]

It was in this context of opera reform, and the fever for Ossian created by the translations of Melchiorre Cesarotti,[13] that Pavesi was able to absorb the elements of stage composition as he forged a career in the municipal theaters of northern Italy. Born in the small village of Casaletto Vaprio, near Crema, in Lombardy, on January 22, 1779, he undertook his early studies in Varese, where he had lessons from the organist Giovanni Domenico Zucchinetti. After returning to Crema, he completed his training with the composer Giuseppe Gazzaniga. Aided by generous patrons, he went on, in 1795, to study at the Naples Conservatory of San Onofrio with Niccolò Piccinni (1728–1800) and, later, Fedele Fenaroli.[14] The arrival of French forces in Naples in January 1799, however, and the establishment of the new Parthenope Republic interrupted his time there. In July of that year the Bourbons imprisoned Pavesi, who was a fervid supporter of the Republic, when they ousted the French and the Republic fell. Deported, he took ship to Marseilles, where he joined other exiles and went on to Dijon. There, with some friends from his conservatory years, he joined a pro-French Italian military band, playing the serpent. The repertory of marches he learned as the band toured cities like Geneva may well have remained a spectral presence in the Ossianic operas he was later to compose.[15]

After the Battle of Marengo (June 14, 1800), Pavesi went to Venice in 1802 and got to know the prolific Venetian librettist Giuseppe Foppa, who proposed working with the then-unknown composer at the San Benedetto theater.[16] This collaboration resulted in the one-act *farsa Un avvertimento ai gelosi* (A warning to the jealous), staged at the San Benedetto on August 7, 1803, and its success was a positive sign for the young Pavesi's career: it was performed in both Italian and foreign theaters for some thirty years thereafter.[17]

Another influential figure who touched Pavesi's career at this point was the official censor of the Venetian theater from 1801 to 1805, Giuseppe Carpani (1751–1825), who, reviewing *Fingallo e Comala* in a letter dated December 12, 1804, declared that Pavesi "has contrived a [musical] language that attempts to express the text whereby, in reducing the richness of his instrumentation, which is otherwise outstanding, he contrives to polish and soften the vocal line in such a way as to come pretty close to perfection."[18] Carpani, well connected in Vienna, was also a significant figure in the introduction of French opera libretti into Italy as a result of his translating activity.[19] Deeply conservative, he admired French music but detested French politics, and was an informer in Venice almost throughout his tenure as censor.[20]

The libretto for *Fingallo e Comala* was supplied by Leopoldo Fidanza, who said of the "Comala" of Ossian in the libretto's preface, "This poem is of great worth for the light it casts on the antiquity of Ossian's compositions, and in the words of the immortal Cesarotti is one of the best subjects for serious drama. It has been necessary in part to relate the story by adjusting it to the present taste of Italian drama by adhering to the prescribed decorum of theatrical presentation."[21] This "decorum" may refer partly to the social rules relating to appropriate language and subject matter, and partly to the role of Fingal being sung by a woman, the mezzo-soprano Camilla Balsamini (or Balzamini), who assumed the character again in Piacenza in 1808.[22]

The plot of the opera differs from the original poem, in which Comala, passionately in love with Fingal, is deceived by Hidallan, Fingal's henchman, when he falsely tells her Fingal has been slain in battle; she subsequently dies after a brief reunion with Fingal, who has returned alive. In Fidanza's adaptation, Fingal is in love with Comala, daughter of Sarno, king of Inistor and the Orkney Islands. Morval, king of Caledonia and Fingal's father, wants his son to marry Morna, a princess of Selma. Meanwhile, Comala escapes from the Orkneys and arrives in Morven. Morval then declares war on Sarno, imprisons Comala, and confines Fingal, chained, in a grotto[23] used as a temple to ancestor heroes of the Caledonians. Sarno lays siege to Morven and is about to fight a duel with Morval when Fingal and Comala (now released) arrive and, pleading their love, stop them. The two fathers relent and agree to the marriage of Fingal and Comala. At the conclusion of the opera, the characters sing "Trionfi l'imene, / Tronfi il valor" (Marriage triumphs, courage triumphs), echoing the final chorus of Gluck's *Orfeo ed Euridice*, "Trionfi Amore!" (Love triumphs!).

But the inspiration for the sensational grotto scene in which the imprisoned Fingal has his dream is clearly derived from Le Sueur's *Ossian* and its scene in which Ossian is confined—not least because the Paris opera was widely commented on by journals of the time in Venice.[24] In any case, by then Venetian librettists had departed from the old rules of opera seria to devise fluid, dramatic constructions better suited to the stark realism of revolutionary Europe.[25] The evolving structure of libretti can be seen by comparing those for Venice (1805), Reggio Emilia (1810), and Milan (1814): the scenes for Milan in particular are compressed or deleted, the text adjusted or rewritten, and one character, Idarto, is dispensed with.[26]

These variations signal more serious changes than the minor revisions evident in the Reggio libretto of 1810. The revisions, while keeping the most effective scenes of the original, may well have been partially based on the availability of specific singers for the main roles, but they may also have been designed to meet local taste. The full scores now in Milan and Florence display additional variations of scene structure.[27] In the nine years between premiere of *Fingallo e Comala* at La Fenice and the production in Milan, both Fidanza and Pavesi no doubt reflected on what changes could enhance the effectiveness of their *dramma serio per musica*.

Table 6.1. Pavesi's *Fingallo e Comala*: structural variation, act 1

Venice 1805	**Reggio Emilia 1810**	**Milan 1814**
Act 1, scene 1	*Act 1, scene 1*	*Act 1, scene 1*
[Ridentissima Valle con grande caduta d'Acqua, sedili erbosi.. Caledoni, e Bardi sparsi quà e là con arpe, ed istrumenti bellici. Spunta il sole.]	[Spiaggia di Mare presso la Regia di Morven]	[Ridentissima valle con grande caduta d'acqua, e sedili erbosi. Caledoni sparsi qua e là con arpe ed istrumenti bellici. Spunta il Sole]
Morvallo, e Lamor; Coro di Caledoni, e Bardi	Morvallo, e Lamor; Coro di Caledoni, e Bardi	Morvallo, e Lamor. Coro di Caledoni.
Scene 2	*Scene 2*	*Scene 2*
[Durante il Coro Fingal seguito da Idarto, e dalle sue schiere che recano palme, e trofei si presenta al Rè]	[Durante il Coro Fingallo seguito da Idarto, e dale sue schiere che recano palme, e trofei si presenta al Re]	[Durante il Coro Fingal seguito dalle sue schiere, che recano palme e trofei, si presenta al Re]
[Fingal, Morval, Coro]	[Fingal, Morval, Coro]	Fingallo, Morna e detti
Scene 3	*Scene 3*	*Scene 3*
Lamor, e Idarto	Lamor, e Idarto	Morna sola
Scene 4	*Scene 4*	*Scene 4*
Morna sola	Morna sola	Fingallo solo
Scene 5	*Scene 5*	*Scene 5*
Fingallo, poi Idarto	Fingallo, poi Idarto	Lamor e Fingallo

(continued)

Table 6.1.—*(continued)*

Venice 1805	**Reggio Emilia 1810**	**Milan 1814**
Scene 6	*Scene 6*	*Scene 6*
Lamor, e detti	Lamor, e detti	[Spiaggia di mare presso la Regia di Morven. Montagna praticabile da un lato con un antro spazioso. Il mare agitatissimo; da lungi alcune navi fieramente battute dall' onde. La musica spiega gradatamente l'orror della tempesta. In mezzo a questo escono i Caledoni cantando il CORO] Comala sola
Scene 7	*Scene 7*	*Scene 7*
(Scenario as Milan, scene 6)	[A gradi a gradi, il mare diviene agitatissimo. Da lungi vedesi una nave fieramente battuta dall' onde. La musica spiega gradatamente l'orror della tempesta; in mezzo a questo sortono i Caledoni cantando in seguente CORO] Comala sola	Fingal, indi Comala

[Duetto: "Piaceri dell' anima"] |
Scene 8	*Scene 8*	*Scene 8*
Fingal, Idarto, Lamor, con alcuni Orcadi salvati	Fingal, Idarto, Lamor, con alcuni Orcadi salvati	Lamor solo
Scene 9	*Scene 9*	*Scene 9*
Fingallo, indi Comala

[Duetto: "Piaceri dell' anima"] | Fingallo, indi Comala

[Duetto: "Piaceri dell' anima"] | [Magnifica Sala nella Reggia di Morval adornata di trofei militari, e dell' armi di Tremmor, e di Tratai] Morval e Lamor |
| *Scene 10* | *Scene 10* | *Scene 10* |
| Lamor solo | [Magnifica Sala nella Regia di Morval addornata di Trofei militari] Morval, e Idarto | Fingal, Comala, gli Orcadi salvati e detti |

Table 6.1.—*(concluded)*

Venice 1805	Reggio Emilia 1810	Milan 1814
Scene 11 (Scenario as in Milan, Scene 9) Morval, e Idarto	*Scene 11* Fingallo, Comala, Lamor, gli Orcadi salvati, e detti	*Scene 11* Morna sola
Scene 12 Fingal, Comala, Lamor, gli Orcadi salvati, e detti	*Scene 12* Idarto, e Morna	*Scene 12* [Giardini Reali] Fingallo, e Comala
Scene 13 Idarto, indi Morna	*Scene 13* Fingallo, e Comala	*Scene 13* Morval, Morna, Lamor, Caledoni, detti [Fin.: "Cessate, oh dio, cessate"]
Scene 14 Morna sola	*Scene 14* Morval, Morna, Idarto, Lamor, Caledoni, e detti [Fin.: "Cessate, oh Dio, cessate"]	**Fine dell' Atto primo**
Scene 15 [Giardini Reali] Fingallo, e Comala	**Fine dell' Atto primo**	
Scene 16 Morval, Morna, Idarto, Lamor, Caledoni, detti [Fin.: "Cessate, oh dio, cessate"]		
Fine dell' Atto primo		

Fingallo e Comala was an immediate success, and after its Venice premiere was presented in Padua (Nuovo Teatro, 1806), Trieste (Teatro-Nuovo, 1806), Vicenza (Teatro Eretenio, 1806), Piacenza (Nuovo Teatro, 1808), Reggio Emilia (Teatro Communale, 1810), Brescia (Teatro Grande, 1813), and Milan (Teatro Re, 1814).[28] The opera was also performed at the Kärntnertortheater, Vienna, on January 28, 29 and February 4, 1812, although by this time Italian *opera seria* in general did not suit the Viennese taste.[29] The staging had been preceded a few years earlier, in 1808, by the production of a single scene (Fingal's dream sequence) at the academy of the Theater an der Wien, with a happier critical outcome.[30] Indeed, over its performance life the opera became notable for several set pieces, some of which exist in separate manuscripts, including the Sinfonia (Overture) in C major with its trumpet fanfares, and the duet for Fingal and Comala in act 1, scene 9 ("Piaceri dell' anima"), a

Example 6.1. Stefano Pavesi, *Fingallo e Comala*, duet: "Piaceri dell' anima"

celebrated and much copied piece preceded by a short recitativo exchange ("Ah, quanto mesta io la lasciai").[31] By such means, Pavesi builds a melodic shape for his accompanied recitatives and creates expectation for the soothing quality of the aria with its string accompaniment.[32] Other set pieces include the duet for Fingal and Morval in act 2, scene 4, "Se padre mi sei" (You are my father), with its concluding passionate exchange as Fingal pleads for his father to listen to his sentiments of tenderness for Comala, in "M'ascolte, [oh Dio]."[33] Further highlights are the hero's passionate outburst "Cessate, oh Dio" in scene 16 (which Carpani found "di grande effetto"),[34] and in act 2, scene 10 (Venice), the dream sequence of Fingal often referred to as "*il sogno,*" beginning with the recitative "Quale orror mi circonda!"

Example 6.2. Pavesi, *Fingallo e Comala*, duet: "Se padre mi sei"

to the accompaniment of throbbing strings, and continuing with the aria "Dono del ciel clemente sonno,"[35] while the hero is confined in chains by Morval in the gloomy grotto that serves as a temple of the Caledonians to their ancestors.[36]

In the hothouse of political activity in Venice as the figure of Napoleon loomed large, it is worth posing the question of whether *Fingallo e Comala* was in any sense a political statement.[37] With Carpani as imperial censor keeping a watchful eye on artistic events, radical sentiments could not be expressed openly. Pavesi was, after all, an enthusiast for the Revolution, and given his close collaboration with Fidanza, a passionate republican, it would not be surprising if undercurrents in the opera suggested the clash of opposing forces: not only a contrast between personal feelings

Example 6.3. Pavesi, *Fingallo e Comala*, aria: "Dono del ciel clemente sonno"

and family solidarity in the arias and ensembles, or between the Caledonian and Orkney combatants (the "All' armi" of the final scene), but also in the relationship between orchestra and singers.[38] Especially remarkable in this regard is the *a cappella* quartet that immediately precedes the confrontation of the two forces, "Qual di pietade assalto / M'accende il sen m'invade.... L'opra coroni amor" (What pity stuns me and invades my breast.... We wish love would complete and crown the action), an effect which, according to Carpani, if not entirely novel (some thought it reminiscent of Palestrina) was much more telling than earlier uses of the technique.[39] Pavesi's accompaniments to critical cavatinas or arias, in capturing the sense of the

Example 6.4. Pavesi, *Fingallo e Comala*, quartet: "Qual di pietade"

text, are also keyed as far as possible to the range and abilities of a particular singer, such as Camilla Balsamini, who sang the role of Fingal in Venice and Piacenza.

Exactly one year after the premiere of *Fingallo* at La Fenice, on December 26, 1805, Napoleon and Francis II signed the Treaty of Pressburg by which Venice was taken from Austria and became part of Napoleon's Kingdom of Italy. Pavesi's pro-French sympathies must have been fostered when on May 1, 1806, Venice was united with the kingdom, an event solemnized by a cantata at La Fenice through the initiative of the Società filarmonica. Then on the emperor's birthday, August 15, 1807, there followed, again in La Fenice, the cantata entitled "Napoleon il grande al tempio dell' immortalità: omaggi della città di Venezia ricorrendo il de lui felecissimo giorno nomastico Venezia 1806."[40] The verses were by Giuseppe Foppa, and Pavesi composed the music. This piece must have gratified those who accepted and admired Napoleon's projection of himself as a Caesar or Alexander the Great of the "modern," post-Revolution age.

Festivities in Venice continued until the end of 1807, when Napoleon visited the city (November 28 to December 7). It was at this time that a decision was made to redecorate La Fenice, now functioning as a state theater, in blue and silver in accordance with the fashionable imperial style, and Napoleon duly visited the theater on December 1. As a further sign of honoring the emperor, Pavesi's "dramma eroica" *Aristodemo*, was performed at the San Carlo Theatre in Naples on Napoleon's birthday, as noted above. By 1810, at least Pavesi was established as an opera composer of special flair, and his *Ser Marcantonio* (1810) assured his engagement at La Scala and other houses in Europe as a master of opera buffa (sometimes entitled "melodramma comico," as with *La festa della rosa*, 1808). His two-act opera seria *Nitetti*, with a libretto based on Metastasio, was played at the Teatro Regio, Turin, on December 26, 1811.[41] But Pavesi was also intent on evolving the genre of the "dramma eroico" or "melodramma serio," as with *Tancredi* and *Teodoro* (both 1812). These varieties of opera seria led, in time, to his second opera on an Ossianic theme.

In the wake of Napoleon's abdication, Venice was returned to Austria and became part of the Kingdom of Lombardy-Venetia. As a consequence, Pavesi was compelled to tone down his republican sympathies. He continued, nevertheless, to compose energetically, although occasionally troubled by health problems. Twenty or so operas between 1812 and 1825 testify to his productivity; these were staged not only in Venice (La Fenice, Teatro San Moise, Teatro San Benedetto) but also in Milan (Teatro alla Scala), Naples (Teatro del Fondo, Teatro Nuovo), Turin (Teatro Regio), and Paris (Théâtre-Italien), as well as smaller houses at Bergamo and Florence. In 1818, Pavesi was nominated *maestro di cappella* for Crema Cathedral, a position he held for the rest of his life. After further productions of his work at La Fenice, Milan, and Naples (1821–22), he composed his second opera based on Ossian, *Ardano e Dartula*.[42]

Ardano e Dartula is something of a mystery.[43] First staged on March 5, 1825, it received six further performances, on March 8, 9, 10, 12, 16, and 17. But no subsequent productions have been recorded. The *Allgemeine Musikalische Zeitung*, which had earlier acclaimed Pavesi as one of the five best composers in Italy, reported that the opera "fand eine laue Aufnahme" (had a lukewarm reception).[44] The autograph score of 362 pages, the only copy in existence, has a modern foliation in pencil, and several pages have been excised at the end of act 1. With a libretto by Paolo Pola, the opera has a picturesque forested and castellated design by Francesco Bagnara.[45] Pavesi's work is in two acts, and the narrative, while ostensibly drawn from Ossian's tale of Darthula, departs radically from the original. Macpherson's poem, taken from oral sources, relates the destiny of Darthula, daughter of the Ulster chieftain Colla: she falls in love with the youth Nathos, sent from the Highlands to reclaim the Irish throne, but dies with him and his two brothers, Althos and Ardan, in the armed struggle against Cairbar, usurper of the throne.

Pola's libretto recasts the story root and branch by making Ardano the son of Cairba (the final *r* is omitted), who has killed Clessamore, lord of Balclutha, a township of the Britons on the River Clyde, and usurped his position. The bard Carilo has saved Clessamore's son Gaulo (sung, like Fingal in the earlier opera, by a woman), and sent him to be reared by Fingal, while Dartula, Clessamore's daughter, was raised by Cairba.[46] The opera begins with Dartula about to marry Ardano (like Gaulo, sung by a woman); Gaulo appears, looking to revenge his father's death, but is imprisoned. Set free by his father's allies, Gaulo then challenges Ardano to a duel. They are about to fight when Dartula finds Cairba, who, suffering from remorse for the death of Clessamore, relinquishes power to save his son's life, and the two combatants desist from their duel. From this moment, Gaulo can rule Balclutha along with his sister Dartula, now Ardano's wife, and the cast signal all is well by singing "Amor, natura arridano / Al nostro giubilar" (Love and nature favor our jubilation).

Many of the elements that made *Fingallo e Comala* a success twenty years earlier are present: the tyrant-father, the thwarted lovers of the title, the prison scene (act 2, scene 6), the duel, the final intervention by the two young lovers. Yet Pola's plot is much less convincing than that of Fidanza, and the asymmetry of the ending (Gaulo left to govern Balclutha with his sister Dartula, who is married to Ardano) must have puzzled the audience at La Fenice. This lack of a neat, coherent finale with male and female protagonists paired off may well have led to general discontent, for instance at the finale of act 1, which Pavesi may have decided was in need of shortening or revision—hence the removal of some pages from the score.[47] The political context, too, had changed: the excitement republicans like Pavesi had felt with the rise of Napoleon and the proclamation of empire in 1804 contrasted sharply with the depressed atmosphere under imperial Austrian rule in Venice, particularly in the years 1814 to 1818.[48]

Compared with his lively music for *Fingallo e Comala*, Pavesi's score for *Ardano e Dartula* could still display melodic invention and an astute tailoring of the arias and choruses to dramatic effect. The first act opens with a desolate scene by the seashore at dawn, the towers of Balclutha in the distance. Carilo and the chorus of "cantori" (presumably minor bards) enter and are joined by warriors lamenting the death of

Example 6.5. Pavesi, *Ardano e Dartula*, aria, "Se nel silenzio della notte"

Clessamore, whose tomb is nearby. The omens of conflict are announced, and Gaulo hails the grave of his father. In scene 2 the drama switches to a room in the ancient castle, where Dartula sings of her love for Ardano in an affecting recitative and cavatina with harp and flute accompaniment: "Torna il mio bene? / Come mi batte il cor! Recami l'arpa, / Ch'io cantar voglio la canzone usata / Dell' amor mio . . . Se nel silenzio de la notte io sento" (Has my well-being returned? How my heart is beating! Bring me my harp, that I would sing of my love that I feel in the silence of the night).[49]

In the final scene of act 1, at the point where the chorus murmurs "Qual mai novello orror (words that in the libretto are assigned to Ardano), an unknown hand has removed several pages. It may have been that of Pavesi himself if he was dissatisfied with his original ending.

Act 2 opens in a grotto (*sottoraneo*) designed by Bagnara, rather like that in *Fingallo e Comala*. Pola must have been aware of the *sogno* scene's effectiveness in the earlier opera and consciously modeled his scenario here after it, with an opportunity for Gaulo to lament his circumstances. Scene 2 allows Dartula to return to the B-minor tonality of her earlier cavatina for "Infelice ch'io son!" Scenes 5 to 10 of the libretto are rearranged by Pavesi to omit scene 6 and go straight from scene 5 to scene 7, which concludes with a martial chorus in a resounding E-flat, "Sacro e di Guerra il cantico / Ai figli dell' acciar / Che vengono a pugnar / Con alma intrepida" (the song of war is sacred to the sons who come to battle with a fearless soul).

In scene 9, in the castle of Barluta, Pavesi makes the tonality veer off into the relatively distant B-flat minor for Dartula's dialogue with Bresilla, "Lassa, dove m'aggiro" (weary, where I wander). This is followed a little later by her cabaletta in D major (*un poco allegro*), "Non posso esprimere/In tal momento / Quanto sia il giubilo" (I can't express at this moment how great is my rejoicing). Cairba's anguished confession in scene 10, begging forgiveness from the shade of Clessamore, is preceded at "Ombra terribile, / Pietà, pietà" by a harp interjection, and the instrument may be said to play a vital part in Pavesi's imagining of local color. His harmonic juxtaposition and vivid instrumentation apt for the dramatic situation is one of his gifts. This quality shows him to be one of the most confident and talented opera composers in the years that precede and overlap the career of the masterful Rossini who, in *Eduardo e Cristina* (1819), indeed owed something to his predecessor.[50]

Pavesi's awareness, however, of the success of Rossini's *La donna del lago* in its Milan performance (1821) and elsewhere may have led him to abandon any attempt to revise *Ardano e Dartula*: Dartula's opening cavatina, "Se nel silenzio de la notte," would pale beside Elena's famous aria "Oh mattutini albori / vi ha preceduti Amor" (Love has preceded you, to awake me again from my slumbers), which begins Rossini's opera.[51] The relative failure of *Ardano e Dartula* to recapture the excitement of *Fingallo e Comala* may also have resulted from waning public interest in Ossianic subjects. The process of transmediation is not divergent merely because of the libretto's shortcomings (although that must be accounted a factor), but also because of the composer's hesitant and intermittent inspiration. The opera as a whole lacks the coherence, inventiveness, and critical approval that constitute modernity.

Shortly after the production of *Ardano e Dartula* in March 1825, Pavesi was appointed to succeed Salieri as director of the Italian opera in Vienna, a position he filled from 1826 to 1830 with a commitment to live there for six months a year; this permitted him to fulfill his obligations at Crema Cathedral. His Vienna appointment allowed him to revise his comic opera, *La festa della rosa* (1808) in a German-language version (*Maienfest*, 1829); to write the two-act melodramma comico *La donna Bianca d'Avenello* (based on the same plot as Boieldieu's wildly successful *La*

Dame Blanche, 1825) for Milan in 1830; and to complete what was to be his last work, an *opera seria* on the same subject as Auber's *La muette de Portici* (1828), his *Fenella, ossia, La muta di Portici*, for La Fenice in 1831. Retiring to Crema to live with his sister, he wrote only sacred music for the remaining years of his life, and died on July 28, 1850. But at his death, the appeal of Ossian in Italy as a rich source of theatrical inspiration was by no means over.

Chapter Seven

From Venice to Lisbon and St. Petersburg

Calto, Clato, Aganadeca, Gaulo ed Oitona, and Two *Fingals*

Well before Pavesi created his *Fingallo e Comala* in Venice, other Italian composers had found in Ossian a basis for composition. Francesco Bianchi (1752–1810), for example, produced his *Calto*, which was first performed at the Teatro Grimani di San Benedetto in Venice on January 23, 1788, some seventeen years before Pavesi's first Ossian opera. *Calto*'s libretto was by Giuseppe Foppa who, reinventing the plot for popular consumption on the lyric stage, concocted a narrative from the poem "Calthon and Colmal," removing the violence and substituting a happy ending.[1] Bianchi was the first to work with Foppa in embracing the newer style of libretto that treated non-classical subjects, introduced duets for two males, added ballets and choruses, and evolved a newer range of orchestral colors. These transmediation trends were already evident in Bianchi's *Alonso e Cora* (1786).

The plot of *Calto*, which is only partly from Ossian, is set in the region of Theuta between the Roman walls of Hadrian and Antonine, where the ruler of the Britons, Sirmo, has been killed by his vassal Duntalmo, who has usurped the throne. The latter takes Calto, the only child of Sirmo, under his protection, but Calto secretly marries Corimba, Duntalmo's daughter, and has two children with her. Duntalmo, enraged, tries to have them put to death, and when Calto discovers from his friend Sinveno that Duntalmo killed his father, he vows revenge. Act 1, scene 6, in a darkly forested setting, introduces Calto's encounter with a chorus of ghosts, leading him to sing his two E-flat cavatinas: "Ombre pallidi dolente" (*andante sostenuto*) with strings and woodwind, and a little later, "Nel mirarti o Padre amato" (*larghetto*),

Example 7.1. Francesco Bianchi, *Calto*, cavatina: "Nel mirarti o Padre mio"

accompanied by strings, bassoon, horn, and the pathos of a *cor inglese*. With Sinveno, his ally, Calto manages to escape Duntalmo's clutches and regain the throne; finally, he disarms the usurper and spares his life, so all ends joyfully: Calto and Corimba are able to declare their spousal relationship. The chorus sings, "Viva, e regni il prode il forte, / Viva sempre il nostro Re." It is worth noting that act 2, scene 6, takes place in a vast *souterrain* containing the tomb of Sirmo, a scenario involving the spirits of ancestors that will be repeated in a number of operas, most notably Pavesi's *Fingallo e Comala*.[2] Act 3 of *Calto*, set in the royal apartments, is short, with just three scenes, in which the lovers are united.

Example 7.2. Luigi Caruso, *La disfatta di Duntalmo*, duet: "Che fatal momento è questo!"

La Disfatta di Duntalmo, Re di Theuta, by Luigi Caruso (1754–1822), was presented in Rome at Carnival a year after *Calto*. It uses virtually the same libretto and characters, but with adjustments to the text and scenic action.³ Bianchi's three-act drama is condensed into two acts, and this remains the structural model for future operas on Ossianic texts. The eight scenes of act 1 mirror those of Bianchi's *Calto*, and act 2, with thirteen scenes as against *Calto*'s twelve, moves from the royal palace garden to the graves of the royal family, a mausoleum to Sirmo.⁴ Calto, in a "fearful wood" complete with ancient ruins, sings his aria "Ombra del Genitore" (shade of our ancestor). Joined by Corimba, he announces their duet "Ah, se l'avverso fato," which includes a joyous cascade of *fioriture* at "Che fatal momento è questo! / Lacerar mi sento il core. / Ah tu poi pietoso amore / Le nostr' alme consolar" (What a fateful moment this is! I feel my heart torn, then, merciful love consoles our souls). The action follows that of the Bianchi opera, including the pathetic addition of the two children of Calto and Corimba. Again, the chorus proclaims the happy resolution. Indeed, Foppa's plot served as the basis of several ballets between 1801 and 1822.⁵

These ballets included *Oscar e Malvina* by the choreographer Antonio Landini, which was staged during Carnival in Turin in 1801, with music by Pietro Romani. Landini had already danced the part of Cairbar when Maria de Caro exported *Oscar and Malvina* from London to Venice in 1797.⁶ The plot of these ballets revolves around the usual tyrannical father figure—in these cases, Duntalmo, who, as the father of Colama, is opposed to the relationship between her and Calto, son of the murdered Ratmor. It is left to Ossian, Fingal's son, to resolve the situation. The scenic designs for these ballets often tended toward classical models rather than the more rugged appurtenances of the Ossian operas. This was true of Antonio Monticini's *Clato*, produced in Milan in 1830 (when the libretto was published) and in Turin three years later.⁷ The music seems to have been a selection from the hands of various composers, including Giuseppe Gabetti (1796–1862), director of the orchestra at the Teatro Reggio in Turin from 1831 to 1848. Another Ossian ballet staged at the Teatro alla Scala in Milan around this time, *Toscar* (1831), was devised by Antonio Cortesi, with music by the Valletta-born Vincenzo Schira (1802–57).⁸

Meanwhile, between the triumph of Pavesi's *Fingallo e Comala* and his completion of *Ardano e Dartula* twenty years later, other opera composers were mining the Ossianic lode. One who produced two works on themes from the poems was Pietro Generali, born in Masserano, near Biella, Piedmont, on October 4, 1773, and credited with the composition of some fifty-six operas. With a libretto by Leopoldo Fidanza, his dramma serio *Gaulo ed Oitona*, was performed at the Teatro Real di San Carlo, Naples, for the Carnival season of 1813.⁹ Three years later his opera *Clato* (libretto by Adriano Lorenzoni) premiered at the Teatro Comunale, Bologna, on December 26, 1816, with the brilliant international tenor Giuseppe Siboni in the role of Clessamore.¹⁰ Generali, like Pavesi, used both Giuseppe Foppa and Gaetano Rossi as librettists, and while his main locus of operatic activity was Naples, a number of his operas were staged in Venice through 1816: his successful farce *Pamela nubile*, for instance, was performed at the Teatro San Benedetto in April 1804. He died in Novara, on November 8, 1832. His early comic operas with their brilliant orchestration were well received, but serious operas such as the disastrous *Francesca da Rimini* (1828) betrayed, according to one critic, a triviality of style and laziness in construction, and a leaning on convention that came perhaps from completing operas during rehearsal.[11] This last failing (if such it is) must have been a common result of the pressure under which composers in Italian opera houses often had to work.[12]

The libretto of *Gaulo ed Oitona* tells how Dunromath, lord of Cuthal, an island in the Orkneys (where the action takes place), took advantage of the absence of Fingal's warrior Gaulo on an expedition to take the beauteous Oithóna by force when she refused his advances. Gaulo, the betrothed of Oithóna, returns to rescue her along with Nuath, her father, and Lathmon, her brother. In act 2, scene 2, Gaulo, confronting Dunromath, agrees to a duel as they sing a duet, "Geloso lo sdegno," in which the separate and rather sinister asides of the initial *allegro* give way to a *larghetto* with impassioned ornamentation in both voices, "Qual pena nell' alma / Che smania mi sento! / Più fiero tormento / La morte non ha!" (what pain in my soul, and restlessness I feel! Death does not have a torment more fierce) before returning to the *allegro*. This displays, at least, Generali's knowledge of voice technique and decorative possibilities, even when the vocal line is cast against a throbbing if conventional tonic-dominant accompaniment:

Eventually, Dunromath is defeated and disarmed. The bardic chorus, Caledonians, and Orcadian servants, as well as soldiers from the opposing sides, proclaim the happy ending. Scene 7 of act 2, which takes place in a vast *souterrain* with Gaulo alone, sees him agonizing over Oitona ("Qual orror mi circonda"), a casual rehash of the effective scene from Pavesi's *Fingallo e Comala* (1805) in which Fingal has his dream, itself derived from that in Le Sueur's *Ossian, ou les Bardes* (1804). Fidanza later incorporated whole pages of the libretto for *Gaulo ed Oitona* into Sampieri's *Oscar e Malvina*, staged in Milan (1816) and Florence (1817).

In Generali's *Clato*, the scenic background for the opera is on the banks of the River Clyde and in the ancient city of Barcluta, situated near the wall built by Agricola; the time is the reign of the emperor Caracalla. Clato is the daughter of Reutamiro, lord of Barcluta, and wife of Classamore, a Caledonian driven by a storm into the territory of Reutamiro, who received him hospitably. But Reuda, a British aristocrat at court, falls in love with Clato, wounds Classamore in a duel such that he is thought dead, and becomes Clato's second husband, resulting in a child by him (in addition to that which she has by Classamore).

In scene 6 of the first act the township of Barcluta is seen in the distance. Reuda enters with his warriors and bards, the former "alla percussione degle scudi" (the clattering of shields providing a novel coloring in the orchestral score). The seventh scene ends as a blood-red meteor soars through the sky and the cast announce, "Splende in Cielo cometa sanguigna; Che maigna—minaccia la morte" (The blood-red comet

Example 7.3. Pietro Generali, *Gaulo ed Oitona*, duet, "Qual pena nell' alma"

shines in the sky, and threatens death)[13] But Classamore revives, and Clato and the children present a pathetic sight as she snatches a dagger from a nearby soldier and commits suicide, allowing Generali to coin some expressive music for the final chorus of warriors and "cantori," who hail the emotional ending.

The transformation of the happy ending to a somber one is a new departure in the annals of Ossianic opera, and served as a model for Pietro Raimondi's subsequent two-act *Clato* of 1832, with a libretto by Ferdinando Livini.[14] The plot is more or less the same, but with the addition of Comala as a confidante of Clato, and Carilo as an equerry to Reuda, and Alpino, the old bard, to the cast of characters. Act 1 has eleven scenes, act 2 ten. In the opera's opening scene Raimondi calls on atmospheric orchestration for the array of bards with harps at the tomb of Classamore. The composer was fortunate to have, again, Giovanni David sing the role of Classamore in the Naples production. In act 2, scene 5, his soliloquy echoes that of Fingal in the grotto. As for the unhappy ending, Clato embraces her children then perishes by leaping from a rock, rather than by cold steel as in the Generali-Lorenzoni version. What might have been appropriate for Bologna was clearly a step too far for a Naples audience, at least at this stage of genre development in the "tragedia lirica" and its unhappy ending. The concluding scene has no chorus, only the principals, with Classamore proclaiming, "O rimorso" and the cast, "O terrore!" The audiences at San Carlo, a theater that was the scene of many innovative examples of opera seria, could be notorious for its raucous behavior, as Rossini had found when *La donna del lago* was premiered there on October 24, 1819.[15]

Two final works in this panoply of Italian operas based on Ossian may be mentioned: *Aganadeca* [sic], with a libretto by Vincenzo de Ritis and music by Carlo Saccenti, performed at the Teatro San Carlo in 1817;[16] and Antonio Coppola's three-act *Fingal*, premiered thirty years later at the R. Teatro Carolino, Palermo, in October 1847, while Raimondi was teaching at the conservatory there.[17] Both operas are based on the episode from *Fingal* Book III (1773 edition): Starno, chieftain of Lochlin, sends a message to Fingal, offering him his daughter, Agandecca, as a bride. Fingal and his warriors journey to Lochlin, where Starno welcomes them but at the same time plots to have them killed. Agandecca, having fallen in love with Fingal and discovering her father's designs, warns Fingal. When Starno finds out Agandecca has foiled his plot, he fatally stabs her.[18] In his autobiography, Louis Spohr (1784–1859) gives a cheerfully dismissive account of Saccenti's *Aganadeca*:

> Another opera, also by a dilettant, Signor Carlo Saccenti, was given a week ago, after a three month's study and rehearsal. . . .[At the premiere] the opera was booed in *optima forma*. It had the same fate on following occasions, without a single friend of the composer's daring to clap. Following this second performance, at which I was present, the opera was for ever consigned to the grave. It is called 'Aganadeca,' the author is a Signor *Vincenzo de Ritis*. The subject, from Ossian, is said not to be without merit, and it is a pity that it did not fall into the hands of a better musician. The composer, however, is not sensible of his own deficiency: he attributes the failure to the limited musical judgment of the Neapolitan public, and wants to send the work to Germany. May Apollo and the muses bestow their blessings upon it![19]

Despite the presence of stellar singers in the staging such as Isabella Colbran, later Rossini's wife, and the tenor Giovanni David; the fact that the music for the third act was specially composed by the "signor conte di Gallenberg" (the Viennese ballet composer Robert Graf von Gallenberg, who had written music for Joseph Bonaparte in Naples between 1806 and 1808);[20] and the publication of a libretto with a dedication of the work to Ferdinand I, king of the two Sicilies, *Aganadeca* disappeared from the repertory. Spohr may well have been right in his judgment, and even the music of the experienced Gallenberg in the third act could not rescue what seems to have been an ill-fated collaboration.[21]

Coppola's much more successful effort found its way to Lisbon after the composer moved there to be director of the Royal Theatre Sao Carlos, from 1839 to

Example 7.4. Antonio Coppola, *Fingal*, duet: "Ah! ricevi in questo amplesso"

1842 and from 1850 to 1871. The work was repeated nine times following its premiere on April 21, 1851, and staged again twice in 1864.[22] The libretto by Gaetano Solito is based, like that of the Naples opera, on Caesarotti's version of Fingal's love story with the Scandinavian princess Agandecca; it was published in a bilingual edition, with the Italian and Portuguese on facing pages.[23] Clearly, its three acts rather than five concentrated the narrative events and dramatic focus more tightly. Act 1 allows the sonorous sound of harps to ring out as the townspeople enter with bards to greet Fingal as he arrives at the court of Starno, king of Loclin [sic]. The sound of the horn, in contrast, is heard in act 2, set in the forest of Gormallo, while act 3 takes place in a temple with an image of the Scandinavian god Odin. The best-known piece in the opera is the duet between Fingal and Starno from act 1, scene 2, when they embrace as a pledge of friendship: "Ah! ricevi in questo amplesso . . . sacro pegno d'amistà" (with this embrace receive a sacred pledge of friendship), an emotive phrase set earlier by Rossini and others.[24] The catch here is, of course, that Starno intends to have Fingal slain during a hunting expedition. The duet is prefaced by strident fanfares that parallel the more famous ones of Verdi, who, like Coppola, saw the possibility of their ironic use in certain dramatic situations.[25]

Kozlowski's Music for Ozerov's *Fingal*

On December 8, 1805, three days after the Battle of Austerlitz in which Napoleon defeated the forces of Austria, Sweden, Great Britain, and Russia, and some eighteen months after the premiere of Le Sueur's opera *Ossian, ou les Bardes* in Paris, the tragedy *Fingal*, by Vladislav Ozerov (1769–1816), with incidental music by the composer of Belorussian origin Osip Kozlowski (1757–1831), opened in the Bolshoi Theatre in St. Petersburg.[26] According to reviewers the audience applauded the premiere enthusiastically, shouted for encores, and some of them even wept openly. Ozerov had already tasted success with stage works set in early Kievan Rus and classical Greece. *Fingal* marked a new departure for the playwright and his audience in that it was set not in old Russia or ancient Athens, but in third-century Scotland. Based on an episode in Book III of Macpherson's *Fingal*, it was cast in three rather than the conventional five acts.[27] Ozerov appears to have used Ermil Kostrov's 1792 translation of Le Tourneur's French version (1777) of *The Works of Ossian* (1765).[28]

The composer had moved to Russia in 1786, joining the army as aide-de-camp to Prince Dolgoruky. There, he caught the attention of Prince Grigory Potemkin, the de facto prime minister, who, impressed by Kozlowski's musical talent, introduced him to the court. In 1791 Kozlowski contributed the music for the unofficial Russian anthem of the late eighteenth and early nineteenth centuries, "Grom pobedy, razdavaysya" (Let the thunder of victory sound). Tchaikovsky later cited the second part of this polonaise in the final ballroom scene of his opera *The Queen of Spades* (1890). Between 1799 and 1819 Kozlowski supervised the theater orchestras at St. Petersburg and contributed stage music for *Edip v Afinakh* (Oedipus in Athens, 1804), *Fingal* (1805), and *Tsar Edip* (Oedipus Rex, 1816). His incidental music for Ozerov's *Fingal*, melodically and harmonically progressive, marks him as an accomplished composer. He had mastered the idioms of Russian melody, and in employing the techniques of melodrama he displayed his experience of stagecraft, a critical component in a play by Russia's greatest tragedian of the first half of the nineteenth century. The influence in Russia of a Venetian musician such as Baldassare Galuppi (1706–85), appointed court composer in St. Petersburg (1765–68) by Catherine the Great, had an impact on court opera, as he composed two while in her service: *Il re pastore* (1766) and *Ifigenia in Tauride* (1768). Other Italians, such as the prolific Giuseppe Sarti (1729–1802), invited to St. Petersburg by the empress in 1785, influenced the direction of court music.

The poetry of Ossian, too, was already well known by this time in Russia. Gavrila Derzhavin (1743–1816), Vasily Zhukovsky (1783–1852), and Nicolay Karamzin (1766–1826) all quoted or translated Macpherson's poems.[29] Later, Pushkin begins and ends his "Ruslan and Liudmila" (1820) with a quotation from "Carthon" (in Karamzin's translation); and Mikhail Lermontov, claiming Scottish ancestry through the family of Learmonth, wrote the short, wistful poem "Grob Ossiana" (The Grave of Ossian, 1834).[30] Ossian also had political overtones: the poet Vilgel'm Kiukhel'becker (1797–1846), imprisoned for his part in the Decembrist rising of 1825, identified his defeated generation with the blind bard of Morven in his poem "Ossian" (1835).[31] The Russian generals Aleksey Yermolov and Alexander Ivanovich Kutaisov were reading *Fingal* to each other on the eve of the battle of Borodino (September 7, 1812), in which Kutaisov was to meet his death.[32]

Ozerov's plot in his play revolves around Fingal's desire to woo the daughter of Starno, king of Lochlin, whose son Toskar he has killed in combat. Starno secretly plots revenge, planning to assassinate Fingal during a hunt, but his proud daughter (named Moina here, another Ossianic name, substituted for the "Agandecca" of the original, no doubt for reasons of singability) returns Fingal's passion. She warns him of her father's plot and rallies Fingal's men to rescue him. An additional character, Karill, a Scandinavian warrior whom Fingal had treated well when he was his prisoner, refuses to participate in the plot to kill Fingal. Starno, however, takes Moina's life and his own, while as the curtain falls Fingal laments over the body of his beloved. Here, the obvious difficulty for both dramatist and composer was how to make a three-act drama out of this material.[33] Effective staging was the answer, with authentic sets, costumes, music, choruses, and ballet. The spoken dialogue is in lines of twelve syllables similar to the French alexandrine, and the text in the 1808 edition is in both French and Russian.

The first act takes place in a palace in Lochlin, where windows look out on a garden, with a temple of Odin and a burial mound in the distance. Fingal arrives at the court in the final scene. The second act takes place in a temple open to the sky, but with the audience able to see through an arch of rocks both the palace and the mound of act 1: a statue of the god stands in the middle, a smoking sacrifice in front of it. The priest of Odin disrupts the proposed wedding ceremony, insisting Fingal make amends for the death of Toskar at his tomb. In the final act, the view is from the tumulus, from which we can see the temple of Odin and the seashore in the distance. The burial place of Toskar is in the middle of a "wild forest with scattered rocks," while the grave itself is, by custom, marked by four large rocks and by the shield, sword, and armor of the departed. The palace of classical antiquity is thus gradually left behind for the world of Celtic antiquity.[34]

The staging was lavish: soloists and chorus were decked out in Empire costumes, Gothic armor, Roman helmets, oriental turbans, Roman togas, Russian cloaks, and Scottish tartan capes. This combination offered a set of historical and cultural layers to which the music added the critical dimension of feeling. The illustrious singer V. M. Samoilov took the important role of the bard, Ullin, while S. V. Samoilova headed the chorus of Lochlin maidens. The famous soprano Ekaterina Semenova took the role of Moina, and her success was so great that she was invited to sing Moina's plangent arias in the salons of St. Petersburg. Alexander Pushkin wrote of Semenova, "She adorned the imperfect creations of unhappy Ozerov and created the role of Antigone and Moina. . . . Semenova has no rivals." And in his famous work *Evgenii Onegin* (1825–32) he wrote, "Ozerov shared the unwilling tribute / Of the people's tears and applause / With the young Semenova."[35] This refers to the mysterious death of the playwright in the Russian countryside and his alleged mental instability. Ozerov's tragedies, however, remained in the repertoire of the Russian theater into the 1860s.

The music for the tragedy comprises ten numbers: no. 1, orchestra, chorus, and solo ("un jeune fille," namely Moina, as is clear from the separately printed text);[36] no. 2, melodrama (Ullin, orchestra, chorus); no. 3, march and chorus; no. 4, entr'acte; no. 5, orchestra, chorus; no. 6, orchestra, "Pas de trois pantomime"; no. 7, orchestra, "Pas seul"; no. 8, orchestra, entr'acte; no. 9, chorus; no. 10, orchestra, march. The opening scene of act 1, with a chorus singing in iambic tetrameters praising love, harks back to the world of seventeenth-century opera: "Kakoe sil'no darovan'e / Vo vlasti, krasota, tvoei?" (How strong a gift is in your power, O beauty?).

The unanimous view of critics was that Kozlowski's music added emotional richness to the drama. An overture and two entr'actes created thematic units that the composer repeats in incidental songs and music throughout the play.[37] The orchestration is for horns in F, woodwinds, trumpets, timpani, strings, and harp. Following the overture, act 1 introduces Moina's solo part with the accompaniment of bards and Lochlin maidens. But it is the second number that is striking with its use of melodrama and arioso in a continuous passage of music divided into sections: an *andante* in F, in $\frac{2}{4}$ (melodrama, with harp and strings): "Let all be silent in the sublunar land," announces Ullin, "that the voices of the gold-stringed harp may carry over the distant hills and roar out in the deserts," as the violins and violas play a short curving triplet figure alongside harp arpeggios.[38] "I sing the miraculous wars of Fingal," Ullin continues, "the pastimes of his youthful days. And you, warriors laid to rest, covered with damp earth, arise from your silent tombs, appear on the mountain tops."[39] Moving from F to the relative minor, then D major, a recitative in common time ensues, with *tremolando* strings, and Ullin sings how he wants to celebrate the deeds of Fingal. The harmony moves to G minor, then E-flat, for a short *allegro* of three bars as Ullin asks the heroes in the clouds above the vast universe to lend their eyes and ears to "nos concerts."

At this point in the drama, the tam-tam, employed by Le Sueur in *Ossian, ou les Bardes*, sounds loudly along with assertive trumpets and timpani for an *allegro vivace* in E-flat and $\frac{3}{4}$, in which the chorus sings (I quote the French text here) in a strongly marked rhythm, "Deja l'airain a résonné, les braves ont repris leurs armes, pour eux le combat" (Already the brass resounded, the brave resumed their weapons, for them the battle). This section of thirty-two bars sways through D-flat to a cadence in C minor, the *diminuendo* suddenly interrupted by an *allegro furioso*, again bolstered by strident brass and busy string figuration. Ullin begins his E-flat arioso segment, "Fingal le plus vaillant des rois . . ." Fingal, the most valiant of chiefs, is armed with his lance and other weapons, his arrows in the quiver, his buckler shining on his chest. Veering between E-flat and C minor, Ullin's soliloquy lasts a further thirty-six bars; all the while, rushing scale passages in the strings are paired with horns, trumpets, and woodwinds, but wind down eventually with another *diminuendo* and pause on C minor.

The return of the *allegro* heralds another choral episode, this time in F major, *risoluto*: "Tout tombe, tout périt," a motif captured in the strings with descending eighth-note figures. This sixteen-bar segment recalls the deer that manages to escape his pursuers ("comme le cerf échape au trait qui le poursuit"). Finally, an inventive *andante* of fifteen bars, with muted strings pizzicato and two solo cellos playing mostly in thirds and sixths, prepares the chorus for a softly intoned meditation on the lamenting soul overwhelmed by armed struggle. Ullin then returns with his melodrama (F minor), "Comme un éclair on t'a vu disparaître, digne héritier du trone de Loclin" (like lightning we saw you disappear, worthy heir to the throne of Lochlin), a reference to Toskar, whom Fingal has killed. Loclin celebrated his bravery, Ullin proclaims, as harp chords lead to *tremolando* strings in a short E-flat minor *andante*. The ensuing *allegro furioso*, still in E-flat minor, leads back to a melodrama with Ullin's "et les échos à ton heure dernière ont répeté les chants de douleur." This entire section of thirty-two bars represents Kozlowski's intensification of Ozerov's text, the tonality, orchestration, and vocal parts cleverly varied to lend emotional weight to the drama.

Music historians have adjudged *Fingal* the height of musical tragedy in Russian theater, and Kozlowski's score is an inseparable part of its effectiveness. With the defeat at Austerlitz so fresh, the audience could empathize even with Moina's grief on hearing Ullin's song, as they remembered the Russian soldiers who fell in battle, leaving widows and orphans, and at the same time responded to the death of the brave

Example 7.5. Vladislav Ozerov, *Fingal*, recitative: "Héros, qui du sein des nuages"

Example 7.6. Ozerov, *Fingal*, chorus: "La plus ténébreuse vallée"

young Toskar, Fingal's opponent. Kozlowski's music supplies the sentiment that the text alone is unable to muster. While it is uncertain whether Ozerov or Kozlowski witnessed Le Sueur's Paris opera, the parallels are obvious: the pagan Scandinavians are the enemy for the French in Le Sueur's *Ossian*, the French for the Russians in *Fingal*.

Le Sueur's dedication of his opera to Napoleon had created a justification of the Napoleonic imperial project.[40] The composer adapted "Calthon and Colmal" from Macpherson for *Ossian, ou les Bardes*, where the conflict is between the brutal Scandinavian chief Duntalmo and the heroic Celt Ossian. Finding themselves subject to the Scandinavians in their own land, the ancient Caledonians have to defeat Duntalmo in order to rescue Ossian and his bride, Rozmala. They accomplish this after a notable scene in which Ossian, imprisoned and bound, has a visionary dream, and the opera ends on a happy note. In *Fingal*, by contrast, Moina receives the dagger thrust by Starno intended for Fingal, and after the suicide of Starno the curtain comes down on a lamenting hero who is warned by Ullin the bard not to follow these deaths with his own. In creating a subtext, Ozerov is drawing a parallel between the Ossian/Napoleon symbolism of Le Sueur and that of Fingal/Alexander I—the czar would appeal to a Russian audience as less militaristic than Bonaparte, and be a patriotic symbol in the wake of Austerlitz. Similarly, the Odin-worshipping Duntalmo and Starno represent enemies of the pious Celts (and by association, Russians). The ideological undertow to the tragedy is clear. But it was Kozlowski's music that contributed decisively not only to the plot of the tragedy but also to the emotional atmosphere of St. Petersburg in a time of war, suffering, and foreboding.

The spell of Ossian for the Russian stage was not over: the Venetian-born Caterino Cavos (1775–1840), a pupil of Francesco Bianchi, had moved to St. Petersburg in 1797.[41] There, he provided the music for another poetic drama, the three-act *Fingal i Rozkrana* (Fingal and Roskrana, 1828), by the prolific author and playwright Aleksandr Aleksandrovich Shakhovskoi (1777–1846), director of the Imperial Theatres.[42] The latter had already collaborated with Cavos on *Ivan Susanin* (1815), often termed the first Russian opera, composed twenty years before Glinka's more famous operatic version of the tale.[43] The performance of *Fingal i Rozkrana* had music not only by Cavos, but also by the French composer Charles-Simon Catel (1773–1830). Possibly Cavos adapted music by Catel as part of the drama, although this is speculative.[44] In any case, Kozlowski's earlier music for *Fingal* had confirmed the appeal of *The Poems of Ossian* for a deeply patriotic audience.

Chapter Eight

Beethoven's Ossianic Manner,

or Where Scholars Fear to Tread

On October 1, 1837, the composer and folk song enthusiast Friedrich Silcher (1789–1860) wrote to Robert Schumann: "I have long entertained the idea of making comparisons between Beethoven's music and Ossian's poetry . . . I would very much like to know *if Beethoven really took Ossian to heart,* because all his music sounds Ossianic."[1] From this it appears the impact of *The Poems of Ossian* on Beethoven has very likely been underplayed by music historians, either because they believed the poems to be unimportant, of dubious ontology, or because the documented reference by the composer is solitary and can safely be ignored in comparison with the known quantities of other writers, such as Goethe and Schiller, whose poetry the composer set to music. Beethoven (1770–1827), after all, lived at the height of Ossian's influence on German poets and writers. In the light of works such as the "Eroica" Symphony, however, and the composer's confession some six years after completing it that Ossian was one of his favorite authors, the link cannot easily be dismissed. While the "Eroica" occupies a special position in Beethoven's life and work, this chapter will also refer to other compositions in which a variety of influences from Ossian is detectable.

As for the "Eroica," what new can be said about a renowned work that has provoked a deluge of commentaries since it was written? Anything that might be added here cannot claim special attention among influences affecting its genesis; there are simply too many factors bearing upon its conception, and also its finalizing in the autumn of 1803.[2] Beethoven's generally reliable biographer Alexander Thayer recorded in his notebook that of all his symphonies, the composer preferred the "Eroica."[3] Whether or not this anecdote is true, the symphony has stimulated a variety of interpretations, but few of these mention the poems of Ossian; if they do, it is merely offhand or in passing. This is distinctly odd, when the composer explicitly referred to Ossian. After all, the poems had a profound effect on German writers and poets of consequence in Beethoven's lifetime and after: Goethe, Herder, Schiller, Hölderlin, Lenz, Tieck, Novalis, Kleist, Arnim, and "virtually the whole of German Romanticism proper."[4]

From its first performance, critics were obsessed with the breadth, originality, and grandeur of the "Eroica" Symphony, seeing its significance in Beethoven's output as it forged a "new path" for the composer in a time of personal crisis, with his approaching deafness. The attention from scholars to this "second period" of his style arises from two factors: the social context of composition and the expansion of the symphonic form.[5] The title Beethoven eventually gave to the symphony in 1806 was "Sinfonia eroica . . . composta per festeggiare il sovvenire di un grand Uomo," a title that recalls Hölderlin's unfinished "Ode to Napoleon" (1797).[6] Because of the proximity of the work's genesis to the rise of Napoleon as First Consul and the name of "Bonaparte" (which Beethoven relayed to his publisher, Breitkopf & Härtel, in a letter of August 26, 1804), critics, adducing literary or philosophical models, have advanced occasionally daring interpretations. By the outset of the nineteenth century the educated public in Europe was increasingly captivated by the ancient and classical worlds, by epic poetry, and by the poetry of sensibility. In these decades following the French Revolution, the works of Homer and those of his Highland counterpart Ossian were among the dominant forces.[7]

Beethoven's sole documented remark concerning Ossian occurs in a letter from Vienna to his publishers on August 8, 1809. In the letter, he requested copies of the complete works of Goethe and Schiller, confessing that "these two poets are my favorites, as are Ossian and Homer, though unfortunately I can read the latter only in translation."[8] Breitkopf & Härtel did not oblige with copies but merely quoted the purchase price. Beethoven did not request copies of Homer or Ossian, which presumably he had read much earlier in enlightened Bonn, where new editions of Rousseau, Herder, Klopstock, Goethe, and Schiller had been readily available.[9] His letter was written six years after the composition of the "Eroica," about the same time as his negotiations with George Thomson, the Edinburgh antiquarian and musical amateur, regarding the arrangement of Lowland folksongs. The circumstances suggest that Beethoven was to some extent still under the spell of Ossian. Just as significant, perhaps, is that Beethoven tended in the years 1808–9 to compose important works in the same E-flat key as the "Eroica" Symphony: the Trio, op. 70, no. 2; the "Emperor" Piano Concerto, op. 73; the "Harp" String Quartet, op. 74; and the "Les Adieux" Piano Sonata, op. 81a.[10]

Thomson had written to Beethoven on July 20, 1803, requesting arrangements of Scottish poetry and music.[11] Beethoven replied (in French) on October 5, 1803, that he was willing to compose six sonatas.[12] The date of this letter is just a year after his crisis of the *Heiligenstadt Testament*, at the time of the completion of the "Eroica." It has, therefore, more than just momentary interest. Emerging from the immense creative effort of finalizing the symphony, Beethoven showed a mundane interest in earning money for Thomson's project, one that had already engaged composers such as Haydn and Pleyel. Further, Beethoven's stipulation, on more than one occasion, that Thomson supply the words of the songs is evident in a subsequent letter of February 29, 1812, in which he chides Thomson for not doing so.

But the composer's first encounter with the poems of Ossian would have occurred much earlier, during his studies in Bonn with Christian Gottlob Neefe (1748–98). Neefe had set three odes of Friedrich Gottlieb Klopstock (1727–1803) to music, adapted by the poet from Michael Denis's German translation of Ossian (1768–69), which was the first complete version of Macpherson's poems into any language and one widely disseminated throughout the German-speaking world. Klopstock, in a letter to Denis of August 4, 1767, expressed his love for Ossian, but Denis, familiar with Cesarotti's partial version in Italian (1763), was already well advanced with his own translation into German. For his part, Klopstock had not only freed poetry from the influence of the French alexandrine, but he was also a notable conduit for the reception of Ossian even while "Germanizing" his poetry.[13] If, for Beethoven, Ossian was indeed "one of his favorites," he would most probably have read the poems at that time in the translation of Denis but also, at second hand, as it were, through the medium of Klopstock.[14]

It is likely, then, that Beethoven was familiar with the settings of Klopstock's odes by his teacher Neefe, among which are the paired "Selma und Selmar" and "Selmar und Selma, Eine Elegie" as well as "Ullin zum tapfern Carthon," nos. 9, 12, and 13, respectively, in the collection.[15] The names Selma, Ullin, and Carthon come directly, of course, from *The Poems of Ossian*. In one of his letters from Vienna, the critic Johann Friedrich Rochlitz (1769–1842) relates an anecdote concerning Beethoven's humorous assessment of Klopstock. While he was much taken with the poet's works that he had carried around with him while he walked, finding them both great and uplifting, he felt they had a flaw: "If only he did not always want to die!"[16] This gloomy and rather melancholy coloring in Klopstock's poems was an immediate legacy from Ossian. Beethoven later was to refer to Klopstock as "one of the immortals, along with Homer and Schiller."[17]

If Beethoven went to Denis's translation of Ossian at around the time of his studies with Neefe, he would have found there the plangent term *Wonne der Wehmuth* (joy of grief) that was adopted by Goethe as the title for his poem of 1775 (published in 1789) even though the topic is not associated with Ossian: "Trocknet nicht, Thränen der ewigen Liebe!" (Dry not, tears of eternal love).[18] Nevertheless, although the English term "joy of grief" originated in the first book of Macpherson's *Fingal*, it was only with Denis's version of the poem "Carric-Thura," in the third volume of his translation, that the term *Wonne der Wehmuth* is used as the translation of "joy of grief." Goethe would of course have been familiar with Denis's term. Yet commentators on Beethoven's setting have missed the link with Ossian: the composer set Goethe's verses as the first song of his opus 83 in the late summer of 1810, freely adapting the words to his expressive purpose.[19] In due course the heavily revised manuscript of the song came into the possession of Goethe (possibly through

Example 8.1. Beethoven, "Trocknet nicht," bars 1–10

Rochlitz), who showed it to the young Felix Mendelssohn in October 1821.[20] The latter delighted Goethe with his skillful playing through of the manuscript and his transcription.

For music enthusiasts such as Silcher in the early nineteenth century, the idea that an Ossian-influenced program might lie behind the mighty structure of the "Eroica" Symphony, or perhaps might inform unspecified elements in Beethoven's compositions, was probably not uncommon. Similar reactions were current during the early Romantic period as the political storms of the *Vormärz* social unrest (from

1830) began to color much of Beethoven's production.[21] By this time the image of the composer was taking on a portentous cast. Max Maria von Weber, in his biography of his father, refers to Sir Julius Benedict's description of Beethoven as resembling "King Lear or the Ossianic bards."[22] The artist August Karl Friedrich von Klöber (1793–1864) is reported to have remarked about his sitter Beethoven in 1818 that "when his hair was tossed about by the wind he had something absolutely Ossian-like and demoniacal about him."[23] Goethe had, after all, in his earlier, *Werther* period produced his ode on Prometheus (1774), which was, with its defiance of Zeus in the opening stanza, inspired by Fingal's injunction to the Spirit of Loda (in "Cath-Loda") not to meddle in human affairs. Later, he characterized the daemonic type in his *Faust* (1808), viewing the *daemon* as a kind of inner energy that challenged the moral order.[24] E. T. A. Hoffmann (1776–1822) was to popularize this aspect of the composer. But Beethoven, contrary to his image in the public imagination as a kind of Promethean creator urging opposition to tyranny, remains resistant to such easy stereotyping because of contradictions in his character that were part of his creative persona.[25]

The effect of Ossian on Beethoven may at first appear epiphenomenal. While it would be a mistake to emphasize the effect of any single literary or philosophical work on Beethoven's compositional method in the "Eroica," the role of Ossian as part of an inspirational background has been underrated in comparison with, say, Homer. The "heroic" quality of the symphony's first movement, in particular, identified as such by its composer, and its association with Napoleon (himself a famed devotee of Ossian) is sufficient warrant to look more closely at the effect of the poems. The names Beethoven passed along to his publisher as his favorites—Goethe, Schiller, Ossian, and Homer—seem important enough to suggest a residue of both memory and signification.

Nevertheless, Beethoven reaffirmed the title of the work when he offered it to Breitkopf & Härtel on August 26, 1804: "The Symphony is really entitled *Bonaparte*, and in addition to the usual instrumentation there are, specially, three obbligato horns."[26] Whether the composer intended these horns in the Scherzo to evoke the battlefield or the hunt (the latter being associated with Ossian) is immaterial since the ideal rather than the real was always before his eyes. As for the harp, symbol of the "bardic" instrument in other settings of Ossian,[27] the instrument was not part of Beethoven's conception apart from its appearance in the ballet *Die Geschöpfe des Prometheus* (The Creatures of Prometheus), op. 43, composed in 1801 and performed between 1801 and 1802. Some critics have seen in the ballet a significant link to the "Eroica," in particular to the final movement.[28]

Indeed, interpreters have sometimes seen the entire conception, not just the finale, dominated by the idea of Bonaparte as Prometheus, or Napoleon as the liberator of humanity from tyranny. As shown from a study of the sketchbooks, an evident link with the ballet exists in theme and musical motif, particularly in sections 8 through 10 (the first a "danza eroica," the second a "tragica scena," and the last a "giucoso scena"). These incorporate the idea of struggle against tyranny, death, and rebirth, and this process can be seen as a trope for the symphony as a whole. But Beethoven's admiration for Napoleon did not last, and consequently he carried the idea of "heroism" into a deliberately more abstract form, as "a commemoration of a great man." If, moreover, Prometheus's agony in the ballet version leads, not only to his death and rebirth but also to misunderstanding and the "plight of the misunderstood artist," then we are dealing with some complex, perhaps even contradictory interpretations of how the Prometheus myth is absorbed into Beethoven's conception of the symphony as a whole.[29] There is always the danger of reductionism in analyzing a work that defies simple attribution.

Regarding the Funeral March in the symphony, Beethoven, when told about Napoleon's death, is said to have boasted that, without having intended it, he had already composed the music as a prediction seventeen years earlier.[30] If this was a characteristic quip, it did not go down well with the redoubtable A. B. Marx, who considered the search for a program in symphonic music a very serious matter.[31] The question of the Funeral March is troublesome, and many critics have asked why Beethoven buries his hero so early in the work. The issue is not so much about the structure, which is worked out in a persuasive way with the double fugue, but who might be commemorated here, and how this affects the overall conception. Again, the answer must be, most probably, an idealized hero, a personage more imagined than real. And this even though benefactors of Beethoven such as the elector Max Franz or Prince Louis Ferdinand had both recently died.[32] Arnold Schering believed that Hector, the Trojan hero slain by Achilles in the *Iliad*, was the central ghost of the *Eroica*, ignoring the unfortunate fact that Homer's focus is actually on Achilles; he also thought the Scherzo represented funeral games for fallen heroes.[33] Nonetheless, Schering held that poetic ideas animated many of Beethoven's works; he strenuously opposed the polemic of Hans Pfitzner, who, attacking Paul Bekker's interpretation of a poetic background to Beethoven's inspiration, insisted that purely musical ideas were at the heart of the composer's compositions.[34]

Beethoven, as Schering maintained, was known to refer to literary works in relation to his compositions.[35] Is there some echo here of legendary warriors not only in Homer but also from Ossian, where there is a constant theme of heroic death: that of Cuchullin, for example, or of Ossian's son, Oscar? In "The Songs of Selma" (translated by Goethe in *Werther*), the tone is one of lament, of mourning for those who have passed away; Ossian, however, survives to a sorrowful old age. In native Celtic tradition, with which Macpherson was familiar, Fingal (or Fionn) the prototypical hero and Ossian's father, does not die but sleeps, deathless, in a cave surrounded by his warriors, ready to return to defend his country against invaders.[36] For a reader without this knowledge of oral sources, the presumption of Fingal's immortality might still make plausible the onward, life-affirming progress of the "Eroica" after the Funeral March, when the idea of Prometheus begins to take over.[37] The final movement has its roots in Beethoven's Fifteen Variations and Fugue in E-flat, op. 35, the so-called "Eroica" or "Prometheus" Variations, a work that is itself linked to the ballet music composed around the same time (1802).[38] Even here it is certain that Beethoven would have known Goethe's poem "Prometheus" (1774), which, besides the inspiration from "Cath-Loda" referred to above, contains imagery such as the young boy topping thistles, with its obvious links to Ossian.[39] To grasp the complexity of the literary influences and how they are intertwined in Beethoven's consciousness and creative use, we should begin with Goethe, his foremost literary hero.

Goethe was profoundly affected by the poems of Ossian in his early phase as a writer—that is, from as early as the 1760s—even before he had seen the original English of Macpherson. That did not happen until 1771, when he returned to Frankfurt after his extended meeting with Herder in Strasbourg in September 1770, at which time mutual enthusiasm for Ossian had occupied both men. The epochal novel *Die Leiden des jungen Werthers* (1774), read and admired by Napoleon, was (in Goethe's own account) written by the twenty-four-year-old in four weeks and contains, toward the end, a skillful translation into German of "The Songs of Selma" and a short passage from "Berrathon," both in Macpherson's *Poems of Ossian*.[40]

Goethe's translation takes up roughly seven percent of the entire novel, and is placed at a critical point in the tale of Werther's anguish over his love for Lotte, who is engaged to another man, and his impending suicide.[41] The protagonist announces in a letter of October 12, 1772: "Ossian has displaced Homer in my heart. What a world that exalted soul leads me into!"[42] The novel introduced Ossian to a whole generation of young writers and composers. Neefe, Beethoven's first teacher, paid tribute to Goethe by composing a series of songs headed "An Werther's Lotte," in which he set his own texts.[43] His pupil could not have failed to sense the novel's impact.

The novel certainly helped to spread the mania for Ossian on the Continent and "to create a cult of melancholic, blue-coated Ossian readers."[44] But Goethe later came to regret the influence of the poems in his own work: the novel draws on his real-life experience with Charlotte Buff and her fiancé, Christian Kestner, in the summer of 1772, and the suicide of Goethe's friend Karl Wilhelm Jerusalem in October of that year.[45] In his later years Goethe affected to have left behind the enthusiasm for Ossian he had shared with Herder in Strasbourg. He created, in the novel, a semiautobiographical character that lives out destructive tendencies he saw in his own artistic and emotional life. As Thomas Mann noted about his predecessor as a young artist, "Goethe did not kill himself, because he still had *Werther* to write."[46]

This episode has a dramatic parallel in Beethoven's life. Undergoing a well-documented emotional crisis at the time of his *Heiligenstadt Testament*, he wrote to his brothers Carl and Johann on October 6, 1802: "I would have ended my life—it was only *my art* that held me back!" and "Thanks to [virtue] and to my art I did not end my life by suicide."[47] Passages in the *Testament* seem to paraphrase *The Sorrows of Young Werther*.[48] Beethoven's "imagined death" has something in common with Goethe's procedures in his novel, in that the composer was struggling to come to terms with his "new path" and "completely new manner" that would result in "rebirth." In the postscript to the document dated October 10, 1802, Beethoven refers to his forlorn hope for a cure for his oncoming deafness in a phrase reminiscent of the language of Ossian: "That beloved hope ... I must wholly abandon, as the leaves of autumn fall and are withered so hope has been blighted," a simile that resonates with Herder's portrayal of Ossian's poems.[49] Written at the time of the *Testament*, the oratorio *Christus am Oelberge* (Christ on the Mount of Olives), op. 85, involves notions of intense struggle, undeserved suffering, terror, imminent death, love of mankind, and eventual triumph over adversity.[50]

Beethoven's lament in the *Marcia funèbre* of the "Eroica" is of a universal kind that embraces not only the death of those known to him but also a vision of his own mortality. The "heroic" qualities it embodies are amassed from various sources, including the composer's own psyche. This has some bearing on the notion of a "heroic type," whether male or female, and suggests a Jungian archetype.[51] In his reading of Ossian, the young Beethoven would have come across not only heroic male protagonists but also female figures such as Comala, Darthula, and Oithóna, women warriors who sacrifice themselves on behalf of their beloved, donning armor and entering the fray.[52] But in continental Europe in 1800, conquest and killing on land, at least, was a male preserve. For Beethoven's transformation of heroism into a female attribute, we must turn to the figure of Leonora in his opera *Fidelio*, op. 72 (1805–1814), the model for which seems to have been Schiller's play on Joan of Arc, *Die Jungfrau von Orleans* (1801). The parallels to Ossian are not difficult to see: a heroine who reveals herself at the critical moment, having donned a male disguise as "Fidelio," to confront and depose the tyrant Pizarro.[53]

All these real and legendary heroic figures, and real or imagined deaths, may have contributed to Beethoven's inspiration for the Funeral March as well as for the entire symphony. To narrow the conception to a single rationale for the work, or to specific persons for this movement, is unduly selective. As for any sedimentation from Ossian, the ethical core of Beethoven's composition mirrors to some extent the mores embedded in the poems, the nobility and generosity that readers came to admire in Ossianic heroes, in contrast to the heartlessness of warriors pictured in the *Iliad* and *Odyssey*—this despite Schering's bold interpretation, in 1933, of the symphony as enclosing scenes from Homer's *Iliad*.[54] In his enthusiasm for a symbolic reading of the "Eroica," Schering unwisely used the term from the Eucharist ("transubstantiation") to indicate "nothing other than the transformation of every kind of impression into a tonal event."[55] This process would now in semiotic terms be better rendered as "transmediation," the transposition from one sign system to another.

While Goethe looms large for Beethoven, the huge influence of Herder (1744–1803) must be considered. He was, after all, the philosopher of the *Sturm und Drang* par excellence, and Beethoven knew his writings, for citations from them appear in his *Tagebuch*.[56] Relatively late in life, Herder supported the French

Revolution. His seminal essay published in 1772/73 (written in 1771), "Auszug aus einem Briefwechsel über Oßian und die Lieder alter Völker" (Extract from a correspondence on Ossian and the songs of ancient peoples), encouraged his countrymen to read Ossian not as an exercise in nostalgia but as an inspiration for the future, a model for national regeneration that would embody a spirit of liberty and independence.[57] His famous collection, *Volkslieder* (1778/79) contains his poem, written around 1770, on the fate of the comely warrior maiden "Dar-thula" as registered in Denis's translation, even before Herder had seen Macpherson's original. Later, a fair number of composers, including Brahms and Schoenberg, were to set this poem entitled "Darthula's Grabesgesang" (Grave Song).[58]

The third literary figure influential in Beethoven's creative life was Friedrich Schiller, whose "Ode to Joy" forms the text for the Symphony No. 9.[59] Schiller's enthusiasm for the Ossian poems had begun as early as the end of 1776.[60] In January 1779, aged just nineteen, he was called on to deliver a formal oration in the presence of Duke Karl Eugen of Swabia. On this occasion, he drew from the first book of *Temora* for an example of high-minded modesty: "The light of heaven was in the bosom of Cathmor. . . . But Cathmor dwelt in the wood, to shun the voice of praise."[61] To Schiller, as a friend in Stuttgart of the song composer Johan Rudolf Zumsteeg (1760–1802), whose settings of Ossian were to influence Schubert, the poems were no mere passing phase. During his courtship of Charlotte von Lengefeld, he discovered she too was a devotee of Ossian and had translated "The Death of Cuchullin," which she announced to him in a letter of August 14, 1788. In that year and the following one she also translated the poems "Calthon and Colmal" and "Dar-thula," probably from the pirated *Works of Ossian* in four volumes (1773–77) published by Johann Heinrich Merck with Goethe's participation.[62]

Schiller endorsed these translations, not just because he had a romantic attachment to the translator but also because he was fascinated by the poems. He was affected, too, by the widely read *Allgemeine Theorie der schönen Künste* (General theory of the fine arts, 1771–74) by Johann Georg Sulzer (1720–1779), which lauded the heroes of Ossian over those of Homer because of their generosity to enemies. In treating Ossian, Sulzer speaks of the sublime as arousing our astonishment and admiration. He claims that "the sublime (*Erhaben*) should be resorted to only when the psyche is to be attacked with hammer-blows, when admiration, awe, powerful longing, high courage, or even fear or terror are to be aroused, whenever the aim is to intensify the powers of the soul or violently to curb them."[63] If Beethoven read this in his student days, it would assuredly have made an impression.[64]

In his *Über naïve und sentimentalische Dichtung* (1795–96), Schiller outlines what is now known as "Romantic literature." Invoking the shade of Ossian, he holds the poems up as a model of elegiac poetry, exemplifying this by reference, again, to "that excellent poem, *Carthon*." Referring to Goethe's novel *Die Leiden des jungen Werthers*, he writes: "It is interesting to observe with what happy instinctive skill everything that fosters the romantic character is blended in *Werther*: ecstatic and unhappy love, a feeling for nature, religious emotions, the spirit of philosophical contemplation, and finally—so as not to leave out anything—the gloomy, formless, melancholy Ossianic world."[65]

The poems of Ossian are not naive, Schiller maintains, but imbued with feeling because they mourn the loss of an ideal; they are elegiac because the love of nature is stronger than reality.[66] If Beethoven read this passage it would surely have impressed itself on him:

> The elegiac poet seeks nature, but as an idea and in perfection in which she has never existed, even if he mourns her as something having existed and now lost. When Ossian tells of the days that are no more, and of the heroes who have disappeared, his poetic power has long since transformed those images of recollection into ideals, and those heroes into gods. The experience of a particular loss has been broadened into the idea of universal evanescence and the bard, affected and pursued by the image of omnipresent ruin, elevates himself to the skies to find there, in the cycle of the sun, an image of the immutable.[67]

Furthermore, in a later essay (1794) on the landscape poetry of Friedrich von Matthisson (1761–1831, whose best-known poem, "Adelaide," was set to music by Beethoven), Schiller explains that music translates into notes insights gained from acts of introspection: studying human thought and feeling, the composer creates an analogue in sound.[68] Music can become a symbol of the human. The great strength of instrumental music arises from its lack of fixed content. Composers might guide the listener's imagination but must avoid anything that blocks its free play. Music, in other words, is a model for the other arts because its potential meanings are unlimited but not arbitrary.[69] Some critics have doubted Beethoven's ability to read such works of aesthetics and philosophy critically, although at a broader level the authors he most admired formed a kind of model for cultural greatness.[70]

Finally, much of the debate about musical meaning that involves a program in the early Romantic period originated with the writer Jean Paul ([Richter], 1763–1825), a copy of whose work *Die Flegeljahre* (Adolescent Years, 1804–5) Mendelssohn took with him on his Scottish journey.[71] Already aware of Ossian, both from Goethe's *Werther* (1774) and from his time studying theology in Leipzig (1781), Richter happened also to meet, later in 1798, the Rev. James Macdonald (1772–1810), a friend of Hugh Blair, Ossian's enthusiastic promoter in Edinburgh), who assisted Herder on issues surrounding the poems because his father, a bearer of Ossianic oral tradition, had been one of Macpherson's contacts.[72] Jean Paul was on friendly terms with Herder in Weimar, and Macdonald was a regular visitor at the Sunday evening gatherings at Herder's house.[73]

Goethe and Schiller were notoriously out of sympathy with Jean Paul's mentality and literary style.[74] Robert Schumann, however, remarked about Jean Paul that "he could possibly contribute more to the understanding of a Beethoven symphony or fantasia through a poetic counterpart . . . than a dozen critics who lean their ladders against the colossus to take his exact measurements."⁷⁵ Comparisons have even been drawn between Jean Paul's capricious style and Beethoven's music: "Beethoven, finally, may be compared to Jean Paul because of his all-encompassing humor—and still better, in view of his dramatic nature, he might be compared to Shakespeare."⁷⁶ Jean Paul's conception of "annihilating humor" in Haydn's music (violent contrasts of key and tempo) embodies "a kind of psychic vertigo" that he found in masters such as Beethoven and Shakespeare.⁷⁷ The famous E-minor episode from the development section of the "Eroica" (first movement) has been described as typical of this quality of "humor."⁷⁸ For the influential E. T. A. (Ernst Theodor Amadeus) Hoffman (1776–1822), in contrast, Beethoven's music "stirs the mists of fear, or horror, of terror, of grief, and awakens that endless longing which is the very essence of romanticism."⁷⁹

Hoffmann's commentary on Beethoven's instrumental music includes the declaration that "music discloses to man an unknown realm, a world that has nothing in common with the external sensual world that surrounds him, a world in which he leaves behind all *definite* feelings to surrender himself to an inexpressible longing."⁸⁰ That longing (*Sehnsucht*) was closely associated with the "sentimental" poetry to which Schiller referred and to which, he insisted, Ossian poems belong. But the ethical and social complexion of Beethoven's art cannot be subjugated to purely literary or purely musical considerations, as Adorno has insisted.⁸¹ The qualities of honor and truthfulness that emerge from Ossian must have appealed greatly to Beethoven, whatever Goethe in middle life came to think of the poems. He and Beethoven, after all, did not agree about social conventions, as their encounter with passing royalty in Teplice in July 1812 attests, Goethe bowing deeply while Beethoven stood aloof and scornful.⁸² We will never know to what extent Beethoven internalized the poetry of Ossian he read in translation and which formed part of his pantheon of favorite writers But we can be sure, from his own declaration, that it was, like the works of Goethe, Schiller, and Homer, imprinted on his mind and a presence throughout his life.

Excursus

Mendelssohn Waives the Rules: "Overture to the Isles of Fingal" (1832) and an "Unfinished" Coda

Felix Mendelssohn was seasick. The composer, during his visit to the isle of Staffa in the Inner Hebrides on August 8, 1829, was "under the weather," so to speak, on the steamer *Ben Lomond*. Unusually, he made no recorded reference later, in his letters or sketchbook, to the island's renowned Fingal's Cave, only to "the most fearful sickness" on the voyage.[1] However, his companion, Karl Klingemann, cheerfully unaffected by the Hebridean swell, did provide a vivid description of the island and the cave, likening the pillars of the latter to "the inside of an immense organ, black and resounding, absolutely without purpose, and utterly isolated, the wide grey sea within and without."[2] The day before Mendelssohn's visit to Staffa, the composer had written to his family in Berlin, "In order to make you realize how extraordinarily the Hebrides have affected me, the following came into my mind there," and followed this with a twenty-one-bar outline of the opening of his *Die Hebriden* (the "Hebrides" overture, op. 26, also titled "Overture to the Isles of Fingal" and "Fingal's Cave") in short score.[3]

Vividly, the orchestration of the piece evokes the Ossianic seascape by means of unusual melodic and harmonic devices as well as clarity of instrumental color; these together create a memorable procession of dovetailed tonal frescoes, the opening theme in B minor and its many repetitions capturing the swell of the sea and salty air, while later in the work trumpets recall the ghostly clamor of ancient battles as they unfold in the poems.

The experience must have unnerved the young composer, brought up as he had been in a cultivated, bourgeois environment in Berlin. That he made no record or account of his floating visit other than the overture itself is highly significant. Seeing the great cave from close up, as his companion described, arguably affected his physical being, engulfing him with an unforgettable impression of grandeur and the

Figure E.1. Joseph Mallord William Turner, *Staffa: Fingal's Cave*. Oil on canvas, 1832. Courtesy of the Center for British Art, Yale University. Reproduced with permission.

sublimity identified by Edmund Burke in his famous essay: the basalt pillars evoked for the sensitive nineteen-year-old, perhaps, the vision of Fingal's warriors, captured in the climactic brass and woodwind fanfares (in the eighteen bars from rehearsal letter B to four bars after rehearsal letter C in the score).[4] Is there any doubt that this *tutti* passage with its rolling timpani and brass fanfares signifies not, as some would have it, a vague Hebridean panorama but the momentous effect that witnessing the cave had on Mendelssohn? The strident, repeated half notes, sixteenth notes, and quarter notes proclaim as much in miming, perhaps, the silent cry of "Fin-gals Höhle!"[5]

The subsequent section, which includes the staccato march of phantom warriors from bar 149 where the instruments are marked *pianissimo*, moves from B-flat minor through D minor and A minor to the rising tide of a chromatic scale to rehearsal letter F as the waters convulse and then subside for the recapitulation (from bar 180) in what is essentially the return journey, accompanied briefly by the flute's soft birdcall (bars 182–83).[6] Just as remarkable is the writing for strings in capturing the incessant swell of the waves: the triplets in the lower strings against the melodic movement in the upper strings (from bar 33) and again in the woodwinds (from bar 72); the cello and bass sixteenth notes at the important climax of the exposition (bars 77–87); the perpetual sixteenth-note oscillation on F♯ and G, and that around D,

Example E.1. Mendelssohn, "Fingal's Cave," bars 180–94

E♭, and C♯ with *sforzando* markings in the *tutti*, create a sense of menace, an image of seething forces that underlie the wildness of the scene. The preliminary fanfares at rehearsal letter B anticipate the sighting of the cave, increasing the tension by the chromatic move D–D♯–E–E♯–F♯: the full impact of the phenomenon only comes upon the senses at bars 88–95, with the *fortissimo* brass and woodwind fanfares in D major, underlined by these turbulent sixteenth notes in the strings.

The depiction of heaving swell has been subjected to ingenious interpretations: some of these make heavy weather of the content, ascribing "spiritual" or "emotional turbulence," for example, to the initial theme.[7] It is just as likely that it was Mendelssohn's physical reaction at the time, his lack of sea legs, as it were, in a totally strange environment that bore the unexpected and indelible impression upon him and remained with him long afterward: an experience that he could only describe in musical terms, and certainly not in a drawing or a chatty epistle to his family. This factor, what we might call the "psycho-physiological disturbance factor," must also have contributed to his difficulties in revising the score—and not only that score,

Example E.2. Mendelssohn, "Fingal's Cave," bars 85–90

but those of his "Scottish" and "Italian" symphonies as well. His Staffa experience haunted him for years as he worked on these compositions.[8]

The transfer from Ossian's poetic prose to an operatic conception is one thing, but the transference of feelings aroused by poetry and landscape into a textless, abstract instrumental piece opens up a debate not only about symbolic transmediation but also the neurologically based phenomenon of synesthesia: that is, intersensory association through which one sensory impression triggers a different one, for instance visual, aural, or melodic. This is especially relevant in the case of the "Hebrides" overture, with its evocation of heaving waves and spume-laden air. It is, of course, the most performed work with explicit associations of Ossian, one of its alternative titles being "Fingal's Cave" (*Die Fingals-Höhle*), with its quite specific reference to the poems.[9] The masterpiece has attracted commentary ever since it was first performed at a Philharmonic concert in London on May 14, 1832, and has done so increasingly from the 1940s on, as critics scrutinize the complexities of its genesis.[10]

The questions surrounding its composition, in fact, crowd in: why do so many versions of the score exist? Why was he so dissatisfied with his first drafts? How far, if at all, did Mendelssohn, encouraged by his teacher Carl Zelter, enquire into the indigenous music of the Highlands? It seems very unlikely that he knew, or knew about, local composer John Gow's traditional fiddle tune with the title "Fingal's Cave," which had been published nearly thirty years earlier.[11] How far did the composer anticipate the pictorial image of Fingal's Cave in his sketches for the overture, before he actually saw it? Representations of it were available to him, even as he toyed with his original title of "Die einsame Insel."[12] And in the process of transmediation, did this German title, with its six pregnant syllables, somehow mimic the six notes of the opening theme? Or was it the other way around? Could the syllables of "Die Fingals-Höhle" have been a factor in this mimetic, melody-shaping process?[13]

The score of "The Hebrides" was completed on December 16, 1830, with this title, and Mendelssohn gave the version to his friend Ignaz Moscheles at the beginning of May 1832. Yet the composer also completed a piano duet arrangement (June 19, 1832) that he entitled "Overture to the Isles of Fingal," and this preceded the final version of the score, which is dated a day later, June 20, 1832.[14] These multiple versions hint at the composer's tendency toward abstraction, a way of covering his emotional tracks, and a preference for musical content and meaning that was not dependent on the kind of denotative program developed at the same time by Berlioz in his *Symphonie Fantastique* (1830).[15] But they also reflect a struggle to grasp the sense of desolate seascape and heroic background of the Ossian poems, a struggle that in a comfortable life would seldom be repeated as the composer found ever greater favor with the good and great in Berlin, Leipzig, and London. The flair with which he was gifted was, in this piece, tested to the limit. He would strive in later years to equal the skill he displayed in the "Hebrides" overture.

A tension exists in the overture between the concept of "program music" and that of "absolute music," just as there is between notions of "classic" and "romantic" in

Mendelssohn's output.[16] In light of the talent for drawing and sketching that he displayed during his travels, the link between the visual and the aural in Mendelssohn's artistic personality has readily been recognized.[17] To what extent this amounts to synesthesia in terms of precise coordination or interaction between or among mental faculties is difficult to tell, but his own references in correspondence to the development section of the overture as "very stupid . . . tast[ing] more of counterpoint than of train oil, gulls, and salt cod" suggests an acute multisensory interaction, a synesthesia that he attempted to conjure into the score.[18]

At the same time, the "Hebrides" overture is revolutionary in its musical development and proceeds in terms of colorful episodes, almost as if Mendelssohn were trying to imitate the structure of the Ossian poems.[19] In that sense the structure is not so much one principally couched in narrative terms but rather one that resembles a series of tonal juxtapositions calculated to replicate to some extent the poetic form, thus "waiving the rules" of conventional sonata development.[20] While one music historian describes the structure as a "relatively uncomplicated ternary sonata form,"[21] another calls it "a complex sonata structure such as many a fanatically 'absolute' musician would have been proud of."[22] Further, the overture is not obviously "bardic" in terms of narrative style as there are no harp or harp-like imitations in the orchestral texture—a sign of the composer's aversion, like Beethoven, to obvious "programmatic" elements.

What is more, the first theme, pervasive and almost obsessive throughout, is pentatonic, dividing the plagal octave (F♯s in the key of B minor) with six notes that give off an "unfinished" air by ending on the dominant note of F♯; even the magical flute solo in the final bars, which evaporates into the salt air, is pentatonic, a gesture toward a thumbprint of native Scottish melody. If there is any weakness in the melodic lines, it is in the cadence of the secondary theme in the cello and bassoon (bars 56–57), where concluding the melody on the tonic D seems altogether tame; it might have been better to end with a 6-7-5 (B/C♯/A) or 6-4-5 (B/G/A) cadence in order to dovetail more smoothly with the subsequent repetition in the upper strings (and sound more "Hebridean"). In subsequent appearances of the theme, however, Mendelssohn develops the cadence with greater assurance.[23]

This secondary D-major theme is in fact all the more surprising in its attempt to dispel the melancholy; instead of a dramatic contrast, as one might expect in Viennese classicism, it contributes to the monothematic character of the work. One commentator believes it betokens "hope," the promise perhaps of a more authentic existence, as Herder might have put it when referring to folk culture as a whole, and that may be partly true.[24] But it is also the formal demands of sonata form that made for a contrasting tonality and character in this second theme. Tovey may have thought it the most memorable theme the composer ever wrote, but still, the cadence that comes to rest on the tonic at its first appearance lets it down. It is too final, too settled, too reminiscent of the less convincing items in the *Songs without Words* and the "religious kitsch" that some detect in Mendelssohn's subsequent, more comfortable compositions.[25] Later in the overture, of course, the composer makes amends by developing and extending the theme in the thirds of the clarinets (bars 207–10). Mendelssohn, in his wrestling with the dilemma of what to do with sonata structure after Beethoven, may well be, as one writer puts it, the "first composer of modernity."[26]

An inveterate reviser of his work, Mendelssohn made a number of changes to the orchestral score between the first London performances in May and June 1832 and two in Berlin in January and February 1833. He also completed an arrangement of the piece for piano (four hands) entitled "Overture to the Isles of Fingal" and dated June 19, 1832.[27] As for the finished orchestral score, he returned the proof copies of these to his publisher, Breitkopf & Härtel, two years later, on November 15, 1834. The complexity of these multiple versions of "The Hebrides" involves an important copy of the autograph orchestral score dated June 20, 1832, that went missing after being owned privately; it only turned up again at auction in London on May 17, 2002.[28]

The "Hebrides" or "Fingal's Cave" overture offers an example of how complex the issue of cultural and generic medium-transference becomes. The composer's arm's-length view of folk music and his use of unusual techniques in the overture makes us wonder just how closely he observed, or absorbed, the native musical and pictorial idioms during his 1828 sojourn in Ossian-land. Yet the sense of geographical and historical distancing is achieved by a unique interrelationship of the two main themes in a free sonata-form movement: they are arguably derived from the same basic thematic and tonal conception, while at the same time their ingenious structure and the atmospheric orchestration capture a feeling of exoticism appropriate to Ossian.[29] This technique appears again in Mendelssohn's unpublished *scena* for bass solo and orchestra, "On Lena's Gloomy Heath" (1846), based on an extract from *Fingal* Book IV: "On Lena's gloomy heath, the voice of music died away." The aria was performed in London in March 1847, a week after Mendelssohn's death. Judging by the number of surviving manuscript copies, the *scena* enjoyed some popularity in subsequent decades.[30]

The conviction that abstract music such as "The Hebrides" embeds a narrative, a program, is one that appealed increasingly to listeners during the Romantic period, and audiences certainly believed it of Mendelssohn's overture. The existence of multiple versions of the work, whether for keyboard or in orchestral score, suggests that each of these has some validity as a concept in the creative process of working toward a final, definitive form. Unlike the setting of words, purely instrumental music raises a very different issue of meaning, one that Mendelssohn was pushed to answer by admirers of his works, especially in relation to the popular *Lieder ohne Worte* (*Songs without Words*, eight volumes, 1829–45). The usual complaint people make, Mendelssohn replied, is that music is so ambiguous, so unclear, while everyone can understand words. But it is words that are too indefinite, he famously objected, since they call up different associations in everyone who uses them: "What the music I love expresses to me are thoughts not too *indefinite* for words, but rather too *definite*."[31]

In a review of the *Songs without Words* in 1835, Schumann suggested that Mendelssohn could have had specific poems in mind when composing them, though what these poems might be is hard to tell.[32] Twenty years later, Liszt commented that Mendelssohn had only himself to blame for the flood of instrumental works that appeared soon after, with figurative titles, accompanying poems, epigrams, and the like.[33] Textless, abstract music such as "The Hebrides" or "Fingal's Cave" progresses toward its goal, however, by intimating a purposeful thematic and tonal direction. It proceeds by analogy rather than narrative in some kind of literary directedness: it draws on allusion and association even while, in its originality, it thwarts expectation of conventional sonata form with a truncated recapitulation. The overture is not merely a procession of vivid tonal pictures with a distinctive orchestration. Its personality, atmosphere, and architecture represent a moment of lived but distinctly traumatic experience that the composer struggled manfully to recapture, and become reconciled to, in his versions. He had to conquer, as it were, his remembered distress by making difficult compositional decisions.

Mendelssohn's compositional techniques in "The Hebrides" came to be shared to some extent by his Danish contemporary Niels W. Gade (1817–90), whose prize-winning folk-inspired overture, *Efterklange af Ossian* (Echoes of Ossian, op. 1), composed in 1840, was performed by the Royal Danish Orchestra on November 19, 1841, and later throughout Germany.[34] Gade's later Ossianic cantata, *Comala* (op. 12, 1846), was often taken by reviewers and audiences to exude a "Nordic character" in its use of minor keys and modal or folk-like melodies, somber orchestration, and harp interludes. These evocations of Ossian had an effect on Robert Schumann through his personal friendship with Gade and admiration of his work.[35] The Nordic aspect of Gade's compositional style filtered into Schumann's consciousness, no doubt as an alternative to Mendelssohn's Hebridean adventure, making its way into piano pieces of his such as the "Nordisches Lied" of the *Album für die Jugend*, op. 68 (1848), and his settings of the poet Ludwig Uhland (1787–1860), whom Heine dubbed the "Ossian des Mittelalters" (the medieval Ossian).[36] Uhland was himself a keen admirer of the Ossian poems. Schumann, however, was evidently drawn more to the straightforward versification of traditional ballads or the folk-like poetry of Robert Burns than to the sprawling lyric-epic worlds of Macpherson's prose poems. He apprehended Ossian largely through Gade, whose influence is perceptible in the cycle of four ballades for soloists, chorus, and orchestra that Schumann composed to poems by Uhland and Emanuel Geibel in Düsseldorf between 1851 and 1853.[37]

Finally, it may be useful to consider that other striking work composed in the key of B-minor, a decade earlier than the overture, namely Schubert's Symphony No. 8 (D.759), which is dated October 20, 1822, on the manuscript. This key, well known in the Baroque era, is relatively rare in late classical or early Romantic music, and Schubert's use of it for the dark opening of the first movement in the lower strings, along with its sunny D-major secondary theme, in parallel with Mendelssohn's two main themes in the overture, must lead to some speculation as to the two composers' choice of keys at this particular time.[38] The young Mendelssohn, who was on his Scottish visit at the beginning of August 1829, nine months after Schubert's death on November 19, 1828, could not have known of the symphony, which was not premiered until 1865, even though Mendelssohn may at times have used Schubert's techniques of development as a model in his own works. His familiarity with the younger composer's compositions is evident, and he was certainly involved in conducting Schubert's "Great" C-major symphony, at Schumann's request, on March 21, 1839, in Leipzig.

But the mystery of the key of B minor remains. A study of Schubert's songs finds B minor (and B major) as representing the center of the composer's ambivalent emotional world: passionate attachment to and interest in the human condition, mental and physical suffering, loneliness, alienation, and derangement.[39] Among Schubert's works only the song "Der Unglückliche" (The Forlorn One), D713, written in this key in January 1821, is an apposite example of the emotional atmosphere of alienation. And even allowing for Schubert's readiness to transpose the key of a song for a singer, his original conception of mood, of tonality, of a particular key as representing and embodying the textual essence, remains primary. Chronologically, Schubert's Ossian songs of 1815–16 and the "Unfinished" B-minor Symphony are separated by only a few years: could the opening theme of the symphony in the clarinet and oboe be distilling the loneliness and despair of "Kolma's Klage"?

Mendelssohn's view of B minor in his overture is not all that different from Schubert, as he seeks to express feelings not only of desolation and melancholy but also of grandeur that the poems of Ossian had aroused in him as well—again, as the physical effect of being confronted at last with Fingal's Cave after seeing only picture-book representations of it.[40] Perhaps, though, his feeling of anticipation was already present in the gently swaying theme he wrote down before he even saw the cave: the implicit melancholy of B minor materialized as the appropriate key for the dramatic land- and seascape he and his companion were about to experience as they gazed at the reality of Ossian in the Melodious Cave with, as Klingemann put it, its enormous pillars that resembled organ-pipes. But they may not have been fully prepared, as we can tell from his account, for the sights and sounds that greeted them.

They both knew, already, the mood of the poems from their cultured family upbringing in Berlin, the "joy of grief" that Michael Denis's translation of Ossian in 1768–69 had rendered as "Wonne der Wehmut." The precocious twelve-year-old Mendelssohn may well have made the connection between that plangent phrase and Goethe's poem of that title when the now celebrated author placed Beethoven's setting in front of him in October 1821. Seven years later, as the world of Ossian and that imposing cavern materialized, he may have remembered the connection with Denis, with Goethe, and with Beethoven.[41] The "ethereal" quality sometimes attributed to Beethoven's use of E major in "Wonne der Wehmut" has become, here, in Mendelssohn's transformational psychology, the B minor of brooding melancholy, the minor dominant reverse of the calm, reflective, almost religious E major. In this case it is not, as C. F. D. Schubart would have it, the key of patience while awaiting one's fate or divine dispensation.[42] There is altogether too much of the storm-tossed turbulence for that.

But the key was unusual enough at the time for two young composers, born just twelve years apart as the nineteenth century dawned, to associate it with a certain mood that the novel poems of Ossian, the sensation and touchstone of the times, aroused in them and which, in Mendelssohn's case, remained with him long afterward. The "Scottish" and "Italian" symphonies, both intimately bound up with this period of the composer's life, cost him trouble. The continued impress of Ossian can be detected not only in the tolling fanfares of these works and the 1846 concert aria "On Lena's Gloomy Heath," but also in the finale of the "Scottish" Symphony. Until recently the *maestoso* conclusion to the symphony troubled some critics and conductors who felt that its A-major melody was inappropriate, whereas thematically it has been shown to be integral to the composer's conception of cyclic form.[43] Most of all, perhaps, the memory of Ossian is evident in Mendelssohn's attempt symbolically to transmediate the heroism of Ossian—in the male voice choir style of the symphony's finale—to the cultural chrysalis and masculine voices of his youthful Germany.[44]

Chapter Nine

The Maiden Bereft

"Colma" from Rust (1780) to Schubert (1816)

The figure of Colma appeared first in "Fragment X" of Macpherson's anonymously published *Fragments of Ancient Poetry* (1760). Unnamed there, she is the lover of Salgar (or Shalgar), slain along with her brother in their mortal combat with each other, and the poem opens with her famous declaration, "It is night; and I am alone, forlorn on the hill of storms." In "The Songs of Selma," she is introduced and named by Minona, daughter of Torman and sister of Morar: "Colma left alone on the hill, with all her voice of music! Salgar promised to come: but the night descended around.[1] Hear the voice of Colma, when she sat alone on the hill!" Colma repeats her lament, and concludes, "I sit in my grief. I wait for morning in my tears. Rear the tomb, ye friends of the dead; but close it not till Colma come. My life flies away like a dream: why should I stay behind?" An extension of her original song in the *Fragments* adds, "Our tears descended for Colma, and our souls were sad." The general atmosphere of mourning led by Ullin, Fingal's chief bard, and Ossian himself, is intensified with the lament for Alpin and Ryno, two of their fellow bards.

This tale of Colma appealed to both French and German composers, the latter more searching in their approach: nine German-language settings of Colma appeared between 1791 and 1873. The number in itself is not especially impressive, but one of the settings, "Kolma's Klage," is by Franz Schubert, and apart from the wide diffusion of his music in German-speaking lands, his influence on the development of both the *mélodie* and the *romance* in France after 1830 or so was considerable. The French settings of "Colma" were restricted, however, to the period roughly between 1800 and 1817 when Ossian fever in France was at its height. The music for M.-J. Chenier's versification of "Colma" (possibly by Méhul, ca. 1800) was followed by settings by Jean-Baptiste Bouffet (1809), Camille Pleyel (1815), and Henri-Montan

Berton (1815–17). Because of the influence the German-language settings before 1815 had on the young Schubert, this chapter treats these in relation to song genres, from monodrama to the lied.

Rust's *Colma* (1780)

The earliest setting of "Colma" to a German text is a monodrama by Friedrich Wilhelm Rust (1739–96).[2] Rust, born in Wörlitz, near Dessau, was a musical prodigy in his youth: he studied music first with Wilhelm Friedemann Bach, then in Berlin and Potsdam with Carl Philipp Emanuel Bach and Franz Benda. During a visit to Italy in 1765–66, Rust pursued his studies with, among others, Franz's younger brother, Georg Benda (1722–95), famous for his development of the melodrama or monodrama, a quasi-operatic conception for solo voice with music, gesture, pantomime, and spoken dialogue. Jean-Jacques Rousseau had initiated the genre with his *Pygmalion* (1762), first performed in Lyon in 1770 with music by Horace Coignet.[3] Benda, kapellmeister to the duke of Gotha, took up the form and created several German-language melodramas, the most successful being his duodrama (as a counterpart for two singing actors), *Ariadne auf Naxos* (1775). Rust's *Colma*, therefore, came hard on the heels of a developing, popular form of music drama. Its full title, *Colma: ein Monodrama mit Prolog, nach Ossian*, suggests that Rust had become familiar with Benda's work, and his meeting with the twenty-six-year-old Goethe in 1776 no doubt increased his awareness of the latter's translation of "The Songs of Selma" in *Die Leiden des jungen Werthers*, published in Leipzig in 1774 (a revised edition appeared in 1787).[4]

Rust's composition of 128 pages, completed in 1780, is not confined to spoken monologue. Indeed, it includes two central arias as well as the normal spoken commentaries and interpolations.[5] The overall structure has four main sections: prologue; access to the monodrama ("Eingang zum Monodrama"); Aria 1, followed by further spoken and musical interludes; and Aria 2, followed by a short spoken and musical conclusion. The vocal part is for soprano with a tessitura stretching from low C♯ to A above the staff, and the orchestration includes flutes, oboes, clarinets, bassoons, horns, timpani, strings, and harp. These instrumental forces are varied depending on the drift of the poetic narrative: for instance, in the opening prologue Rust employs flutes, clarinets, horns, harp, and strings, but in the "Eingang" he draws on the different coloring of flutes, oboes, bassoons, horns, and strings (without harp, which only appears again with the first aria). After the prologue, Rust dispenses with the clarinets, no doubt to emphasize the pathetic quality of Colma's position by the use of double-reed woodwind, namely oboes and bassoons. He also reserves use of the timpani to the shorter second aria, with its description of wind on the heath and ghosts, as the monodrama approaches its conclusion.

Table 9.1. Rust's *Colma*: simplified structure

Section	Tonality	Time signature	Marking	Orchestration
Prolog (9–137)	E♭ major	2/2	un poco lento	fls, clars, hns, harp, str
Eingang (138–89)	C minor	4/4	poco largo	fls, obs, bsns, hns, str
Monodrama (190–251)				
Aria 1 "Vertrauter meiner Liebe" (252–310)	E major–minor–major	3/4 4/4 3/4	andante con moto–andantino–larghetto–allegro	fls, hns, harp, str
Monodrama (311–526)				
Aria 2 "Vom Felsenhügel" (527–658)	D minor	4/4 3/4 4/4	allegro–larghetto–allegro	fls, obs, hns, bsns, timp, str

The tonal resources inhabit a wide spectrum of keys, with a dramatic shift from E-flat and C minor to E major for the first aria, returning thereafter to D minor for the second aria and conclusion.

Opening in E-flat, the prologue of 116 bars ranges within the tonal centers of B-flat, C minor, and A-flat, returning afterward to E-flat as the speaking part announces the drama. The orchestral introduction, rooted in C minor, introduces an upward-rushing figure spanning an octave in the violins at bar 14 (and more intensively from bar 52) that will become an important motif in the emotional turmoil surrounding Colma, and later be a cliché in full-fledged Romantic instrumentation. The monodrama proceeds with Colma reiterating her loneliness until a significant key change occurs, to E major, with solo horns (bar 227) that refer to the hunting prowess of Salgar, her dead lover. The upward-rushing string motif reappears in the *andante moderato* passage that follows Colma's desperate cry of "Salgar," until a pause signals the first aria, in E major and $\frac{3}{4}$ time, "Vertrauter meiner Liebe, O Mond, verweile nicht" (confidant of my love, Oh moon, do not linger). Prominent in this aria is the role of the harp, doubled by solo violin, which together provide a counterweight to the highlighted flute and horn parts; the strings are directed to play *con sordino*, and the bass *pizzicato*. The overall effect is carefully calculated, evoking the entreaty of Colma to the moon:

After the reprise of the main theme in E major, the tempo slows to *adagio*, and Colma cries "Warum zaudert meiner Salgar?" (Why does my Salgar delay?). The passage then darkens to a dotted motif in E minor for the violins. This section turns enharmonically toward F minor for an *allegro moderato* in $\frac{4}{4}$ that reintroduces the upward-sweeping string figure in the violins (twice). The monodrama then returns in spoken passages in which Colma refers to "the rock and the tree" with orchestral commentary and pauses for effect, and finally, in a climax at "Wir sind keine Feinde, O Salgar" (We are not enemies, Salgar). At this point an *andantino* passage in C major with an oboe solo marks the heroine's realization that she is dealing only with imaginary shades, or ghosts. In a *larghetto* section ($\frac{3}{4}$, F major), with a reiteration of the horn motifs, she repeats her cry for her lover as the music merges into a final *maestoso* passage in E major and common time. Increasingly restless, the orchestral texture incorporates the upward-rushing figure as Colma murmurs, "Redet, meine Freunde" (Speak to me, my friends), and "Die antworten nicht" (they do not answer).

A final segment culminates with Colma's cry, "O mein Salgar, warum hast du meinen Bruder erschlagen?" (O Salgar, why hast thou slain my brother?), with the counterpart, "O my brother, why hast thou slain my Salgar?" This draws a reply from the orchestra with B♭/A repetitions in the bass and the upward-rushing motif in the violins, the true climax of this long section. Following a cadence in B-flat the tonality turns, in an introductory twenty-eight bars, toward D minor for the second aria, "Vom Felsenhügel, auf der Winde Flügel" (From the rocky height, on the wings of the wind) with its rising triad of D-F-A in the violins and the voice together, with

Example 9.1a. Friedrich Wilhelm Rust, rising motif, *Colma*: bars 14–15

Example 9.1b. Rust, rising motif, *Colma*: bars 312–13

Example 9.2. Rust, *Colma*, aria 1: "Vertrauter meiner Liebe"

undulating eighth-note thirds in the bass. The timpani enter at bar 7 of the aria to suggest, perhaps, the windy mountain from which Colma pleads with the ghosts to speak. The tonality in this passage gradually moves toward A minor until, after some 65 bars, the impetus comes to a pause with a *larghetto* section in $\frac{3}{4}$ time, still in D minor, with syncopated repeated notes in the violins. Thereupon the music launches, after a brief cadence, into the initial *allegro* of the aria, Colma invoking the ghosts of the dead ("Kommt, ihr Geister der Todten"), and after just thirty-nine bars of a reprise the work draws to its close, to end in D minor.[6]

Example 9.3. Rust, *Colma*, aria 2: "Vom Felsenhügel"

The conclusion consolidates a key relationship reflecting the overall drama in the four main sections of the work, from E-flat (Prologue) to C minor (Access), and from E major (aria 1) to D minor (aria 2). The general effect of these key relationships is to draw the tonality firmly toward the drama inherent in Colma's narrative of loss, but with a central section (aria 1) that makes for dramatic key contrast before returning to the relatively bleak D minor of aria 2. In doing so, "Colma" masterfully merges the influence of Goethe, whose translation of "The Songs of Selma" was known almost immediately throughout the German-speaking world, with the pioneering work of Georg Benda in his development of the monodrama and duodrama.[7] Melodically, it creates shapely figures for the vocal part, and orchestral writing that is both varied and idiomatic. The sparing use of clarinets, harp, and timpani helps to color the spoken monologue as well as the arias at appropriate points. In summary, "Colma" is perhaps Rust's most ambitious and successful work.[8]

Ossian-Lieder by Zumsteeg, Reichardt, and Zelter

These three composers have often been considered only as precursors of Schubert in the development of the lied as a distinctive musical form.[9] Each came from a different part of German lands: Johan Rudolf Zumsteeg (1760–1802) from Baden-Württemberg; Carl Friedrich Zelter (1758–1832) from Berlin; and Johann Friedrich Reichardt (1752–1814) from Königsberg, in Prussia. Yet each had something to say in the setting of Ossian texts. It is well known that Schubert, though in distant Vienna, was influenced by the settings of Zumsteeg and Reichardt in particular. According to his friend Josef von Spaun, Schubert was deeply affected by Zumsteeg's *Lieder und Balladen* and this current shaped not only his early songs but also his later, fully mature style. Until 1815, the strophic song modelled after Zumsteeg became the rule for the young Schubert, and it was at this time he began to compose his Ossian settings. Zumsteeg, for his part, had made a setting entitled *Colma: Ein Gesang Ossians, von Goethe*, published in 1793 or 1794, for voice and piano.[10] Schubert, greatly taken by Zumsteeg's songs since 1811, collared his friend Spaun one day and said, "Listen to the song I've got here," then sang *Colma* with a half-breaking voice ("und dann sang er mit schon halb brechende Stimme *Kolma*").[11]

As the title page of his *Colma* setting proclaims, Zumsteeg had turned to Goethe's translation of "The Songs of Selma" for a setting that is through-composed rather than strophic, and in fact a mixture of arioso and recitative sections and styles amounting to 516 bars in length.[12] Even more than Rust, Zumsteeg's frequent oscillation between modes of response to the text in terms of tempo and rhythm makes it difficult to reduce his setting to a simple chart. This is partly, too, because his setting includes the passage that precedes Colma's lament. Choosing the key of E-flat, with a calm opening keyboard motif of four bars in a moderately slow $\frac{3}{4}$ rhythm, the composer invokes the famous opening line of Goethe's translation of the prologue, "Stern der dämmernden Nacht" (Star of the fading night), in a descending vocal line with tonic-dominant harmony.[13] Gradually, from bar 10, restless sixteenth notes in the piano guide the voice upward to E♭ as it then imagines the star descending a full octave in stately eighth notes to its first cadence (bar 16).

After three bars of subdominant-dominant thirds in the piano, the voice enters with an ornamented melody line that refers to the stormy winds on the heath. At this point the accompaniment launches into rippling thirty-second notes in the right hand to capture the murmur of the torrent and the hum of evening flies, modulating toward the dominant with chords that underpin the vocal line as it plunges toward its cadence and the short interpolation in the voice, "Wornach siehst du, schönes Licht?" (What dost thou behold, fair light?). Moving into a moderately slow $\frac{2}{4}$ time, based firmly but gently in the dominant key of B-flat, the song celebrates the departure of the evening star, returning to E-flat for the next slower section, while the voice lingers over the words "Lebe wohl, ruhiger Strahl" (Farewell, silent beam). After six bars of piano interlude that veer toward A-flat major, this passage leads to

Example 9.4. Johan Rudolf Zumsteeg, *Colma*, bars 1–16

Example 9.5. Zumsteeg, *Colma*: "Erscheine du, herrliches Licht von Ossians Seele!"

Example 9.6. Zumsteeg, *Colma*: "Salgar versprach zu kommen"

the first of several recitatives: "Erscheine du, herrliches Licht von Ossians Seele!" (Let the light of Ossian's soul arise!).

Marked (in translation) "majestically, and rather fast," this entire section moves dramatically to C major, the voice documenting Colma's departed friends in thirty-four bars of recitative and arioso. The following section begins in F major and $\frac{2}{2}$ rhythm until it reaches a slow, plangent D-flat major passage in common time as the text announces, "Da trat Minona hervor in ihrer Schönheit" (Minona came forth in

Example 9.7. Zumsteeg, *Colma*: "Tritt, o Mond, aus deinen Wölken"

her beauty). A short section that moves from A minor to D minor is succeeded by a faster passage as Colma finds herself alone on the hill: "Salgar versprach zu kommen, aber ringsum zog sich die Nacht" (Salgar promised to come: but the night descended around), and at the word "Nacht" (night) Zumsteeg makes a characteristically bold statement by following a G-minor chord with dotted chords in A-flat major.

Colma's lament begins at this juncture, with "Es ist Nacht; ich bin allein" and an impassioned vocal line that moves largely through E-flat major and C minor with forty-three bars of stormy piano accompaniment which conclude the passage in emphatic G major chords. The succeeding $\frac{3}{4}$ section in E-flat incorporates Colma's address to the moon, opening with a melodic motif that recalls Gluck's famous melody from act 3 of *Orfeo ed Euridice* (Italian version 1762, French version 1774), "Che farò senza Euridice / J'ai perdue mon Eurydice." The entire passage reaches a climax at Colma's "aber wir sind keine Feinde, Salgar!" (but we are not foes, Salgar!). As this declaration ends in E-flat, Zumsteeg plunges the piano part into a passionate D minor with rapid sixteenth-note figuration until Colma commands this representation of the wind to stop as she calls on the ghost of Salgar.

The final section of Zumsteeg's setting alternates between recitatives with piano commentary and desperate appeals by Colma to the spirit of Salgar. The $\frac{6}{8}$ section in C major that begins "Sieh, der Mond erscheint" (Lo! the calm moon comes forth) offers some relief, and after a short break, this rhythm returns in A-flat major for some ten bars, only to be followed by another stormy session of piano figuration, with downward, offbeat arpeggios in F minor. Here, the sequence of Colma's rhetorical questions unfolds in a prolonged recitative, asking why her brother and Salgar have killed each other. The tonality sinks calmly toward E-flat minor (*forte* then *piano* in the score) as Colma murmurs, "Kalt wie die Erde ist ihr Busen" (cold are their breasts of clay). In an enharmonic twist, Zumsteeg guides the tonality to chords of B major leading to E minor, whereby Colma appeals to the ghosts of the dead ancestors to speak to her ("redet Geister der Todten").

As the piece draws to a close with Colma's resigned "Ich sitze in meinem Jammer" (I sit in my grief), the tonality grounded in A-flat major, Zumsteeg introduces a figure in the piano part (bars 10, 12), a chromatic upward sweep of a fifth to repeated notes that recalls a similar motif in Rust's setting. The conclusion involves several slower passages, with F minor the dominant tonality: "Das war dein Gesang, o Minona, Tormanns sanfte erröthende Tochter" (Such was thy song, softly blushing daughter of Torman). A descending group of sixteenth notes marks the tears that fall for Colma, and the composer injects an F♭ and a G into the chord that dissolves into A-flat major in the final cadence to complete the pathos of Colma's fate. It is no wonder that Schubert was impressed by Zumsteeg's ability to capture the mood of a poem and vary the musical texture so as to extract the reverberations of meaning that lie under the surface.

Example 9.8. Zumsteeg, *Colma*: "Wühlet das Grab"

Zelter's *Colma: ein altschottisches Fragment* (1810)

In his capacity as director of the Sing-Akademie in Berlin, the city in which he was born and died, Zelter taught a number of celebrated students, among them Felix and Fanny Mendelssohn, Giacomo Meyerbeer, and Otto Nicolai. Composer of some 210 lieder, he occupies a worthy place in the development of the lied more because of his influence as a pedagogue than any outstanding intellectual or musical ability of his own.[14] Moreover, his extensive correspondence with Goethe between 1799 and 1832 includes a letter (September 14, 1812) containing the famous remark about Beethoven.[15]

Despite his friendship with Goethe, Zelter's choice of text for his setting of *Colma, ein altschottisches Fragment aus den Liedern der Selma des Ossian* (1803) was not Goethe's translation but a paraphrase from 1767 by Ludwig Gottlieb Crome

(1742–94).[16] Zelter most likely was familiar with the settings of "Colma" by Rust and Zumsteeg. His own version was published in his *Sämmtliche Lieder, Balladen und Romanzen für das Pianoforte* (1810–12).[17] Like that of Zumsteeg it is through-composed, almost in the manner of a dramatic *scena*, with direction to the soloist to stand up, come forward, and so on. The title of the keyboard part ("fortepiano") suggests that the instrument could impart the kind of "antique" sound appropriate to an "altschottisches Fragment."

Some 380 measures in length, the piece falls into six main sections. Setting out with short *pianissimo* C-minor chords in ¾ (*lento ma con moto*) to establish a dramatic mood, the keyboard introduction becomes more impassioned after eight bars with a Beethoven-like passage in double octave chords that proceed through D-flat major to a quiet cadence on a unison C. The voice then enters alone in a descending phrase, "Um mich ist Nacht!" (It is night!).[18] The broken chords return to accompany Colma's phrases that reach up to and fall from a high G with a downward rush of sixteenth notes from A♭ to B♮ at "Verirret steh' ich hier am stürm'schen Hügel" (I am alone, forlorn on the hill of storms).

Gentle staccato chords in the piano guide the voice as it seeks to break free of the B-flat tonality and return to E-flat at "Warum, warum, mein Salgar, warum?" The mention of the tree and the rock precipitates a climactic high B♭ in the voice at "der Strom" (the flood) as the piano plunges from a high D♭ to middle C and then elaborates in thirty-second notes for two bars, at which point the singer is instructed to stand, agitated (*unruhig*). A faster section in C minor ensues, as Colma entreats the wind to cease so that her call to her beloved can be heard. A curious episode in B-flat and ⁶⁄₈ (*andantino*) follows, with the direction, "Sehr sanft und leicht" (very gently and lightly). Marked *pianissimo*, the keyboard preamble resembles a folk-like dance, its eight bars modulating in conventional fashion to the dominant before resuming in B-flat with the voice's entry, "Dort glänzt der Mond hervor" (Lo! the calm moon comes forth). Zelter, in this section of forty-five bars (167–211), appears to intend an interlude of calm relief (the singer is seated) after the anguish of the preceding passages, but its jogging ⁶⁄₈ rhythm and foursquare tonic-dominant tonality, even when played *pianissimo*, seem quite inappropriate to the sentiments expressed in the text: earthbound when, in fact, Colma's mood is one of anxious ecstasy—a patent miscalculation on the composer's part.

Closing with tonic-dominant chords in B-flat, the tonal impetus now moves back, with an E-flat key signature, to a recitative-like passage as Colma laments Salgar and her brother, with dramatic chords interrupting her desperate pleas to them to be heard, and to receive from them an answer: "Ach! ihre Schwerdter sind gefärbt mit Blut" (Ah! their swords are covered with blood). The piano sinks chromatically with unison notes on C, C♭, and B♭, then G, G♭, and F (also in the voice) at "Wie? erschlugst du meinen Bruder, Salgar, du?" (Why, O Salgar? Hast thou slain my brother?). Two extended keyboard passages of right-hand sixteenth notes in a spirited *allegro*, built around C minor, G minor, and F minor, follow

Table 9.2. Zelter's *Colma*: structure

Section	Key signature	Time signature	Marking
"Um mich ist Nacht" (bars 1–67)	C minor	3/4	lento ma con moto
"Du Strom, du Wind" (68–85)	B♭	2/4	allegretto ("mit Wehmuth u. Unwillen")
"Warum verweilst du" (86–166)	E♭ (B♭ minor)	3/4	andante—etwas lebhaft wie allegro—langsam wie vorhin
"Dort glänzt der Mond hervor" (167–211)	B♭	6/8	andantino (sehr sanft und leicht)
"Aber wer sind die, die auf der Heide liegen" (212–81)	B♭–E♭	4/4	(schnell u. heftig)
"Ach Jammer" (282–end)	C minor	2/4	allegretto (heftig u. jammernd)

Example 9.9. Carl Friedrich Zelter, *Colma*: "Hier ist der Fels . . ."

for some eighteen bars each; these passages, intended to comment on the terrifying aspect of Salgar in battle, are punctuated by descending $^6_3$ eighth-note chords (bars 238–39, 273–74).

Uncertain tonally, the piece dwells for a moment in G minor then suggests a fresh approach to the relative major, B-flat, as the voice intones, "Ach! Ihr war't mir beyde theuer" (Ah, you both were dear to me!). The song then closes in C minor with the words "Er war schrecklich in der Feldschlacht" (he was terrifying in battle). The sixteenth-note section resumes in the keyboard, this time in C minor, with the $^6_3$ chords delayed to bar 15 as the sixteenth notes scurry downward to a unison cadence on C. The vocal part has two descending phrases at "O!" and "hört meine Stimme" (Oh speak to me, hear my voice), as simple chords lead back to E-flat.

With eighth-note chords, each of three notes in the keyboard, the text announces the final segment of Colma's tale: "Ich sitz' in meinem Gram und warte nur der

Example 9.10. Zelter, *Colma*: "Dort glänzt der Mond hervor"

Morgenroth' in meiner Thränen Fluth. Mein Leben flieht gleich einem Traum dahin, was soll ich länger leben?" (I sit in my grief, I wait for morning in my tears; my life flies away like a dream, why should I stay behind). As the piano continues in C minor to match this pathos in the voice, the cadence returns again, rather surprisingly, to E-flat major. Indeed, Zelter's proclivity for this key often weakens the drama with which he began, offering a more comfortable tonality than the text demands: for example, at the beginning of the *andante* ("warum verweilt mein Salgar?"), at "wir sind nicht Feind'" (we are not enemies), or in the final section, at "was soll ich länger leben?" (why should I live any longer?).

Like Reichardt, Zelter uses the flattened seventh of E-flat (D♭) to continue the atmosphere of tearful resignation: "Hier will ich bey meinen Freunden schlafen" (here shall I rest with my friends). Sparsely accompanied by the piano, the vocal part grasps at shorter and shorter phrases, broken only by twofold chord interjections in the piano, until the words (referring to Colma's voice heard only in the wind) "und klagen." The first syllable of "klagen" (lament) is prolonged for six bars, moving from A♭ to B♭ to C as the dominant note of F minor, then a high G and A♭ on the words "jammern laut" (loud grieving). In addition, the rest of the phrase, "um meiner Freunde Tod," receives a relatively elaborate treatment: a melisma from a high G on "Freunde" before settling on the C of the home key, now finally, again, anticipating C minor (but ending with a major third). Ambitious, but stilted and mundane in its sensitivity to the pathos of the text, Zelter's setting has remained, perhaps for these reasons, relatively unknown, despite his prominence as a pedagogue and establishment figure in the musical world of early nineteenth-century Berlin.[19]

Example 9.11. Zelter, *Colma*: ". . . und klagen, jammern laut um meiner Freunde Tod"

Reichardt's "Kolma's Klage" (1804)

A passionate disciple of Rousseau, the restless Johann Friedrich Reichardt believed that the expression of sentiment was the true purpose of music, and that of all the arts song was the closest to nature. The influence of the French *vaudeville* led him to complete examples of the *Singspiel* or *Liederspiel* (the latter conceived for singing actors rather than professional singers) at the National Theatre in Berlin before publishing his major collection of songs. When Schubert came to set his "Kolma's Klage" on June 22, 1815, he did not follow Zumsteeg's example but rather chose the lyric paraphrase, in unrhymed strophes, of Goethe's text that he found in volume 2 of Reichardt's *Lieder der Liebe und der Einsamkeit, zur Harfe und zum Klavier zu singen* (Leipzig [1804]).[20] Three of the songs in this collection, subtitled *Lieder nach Ossian*, include a setting of "Kolma's Klage" in three strophic verses.[21] Reichardt directs these to be sung in immediate succession (the note "gleich weiter" is appended to the first and second songs).

The first of the three-part setting, "Rund um mich Nacht," relates the loneliness of Colma in the storm as she sits alone on the hill and calls for Salgar, her lover. Marked *langsam* (slow), in common time, and again in E-flat tonality, as are many of the Ossian settings, the seven-line, unrhymed strophe observes the syllabic form 8.9.6.7.7.9.4. Reichardt's vocal line is simpler in style, as one might expect with a strophic melody; it remains within the ambit of an octave, and as a consequence is more folk-like. The regularity of the phrase-lengths displays this calculated simplicity of structure, a well-known hallmark of this period of German song. The harmonic pattern (I–V–VI–III) that opens each of the three settings provides a unifying element. The accompaniment, cast in arpeggios evenly distributed between the hands, moves briefly through B-flat, skirting the darker E-flat minor, to come to rest in the original E-flat major.

The second part, "Doch sieh, der Mond erscheint," is somewhat more narrative in character, as Colma laments the deaths of Salgar and her brother. Reichardt directs it to be sung in a "rather lively" (*etwas lebhaft*) tempo. In $^6_8$ time and C major, the song extends the vocal range, from low C to high F, while the divided triplets in the two hands subtly vary the arpeggio quintuplets of the first song. After a brief move to the dominant key of G, the tonality gradually slides toward C minor and ends with the piano preparing, at the end of the third stanza, for the third song with a dominant seventh (D-flat) cadence on E♭. The eight-syllable lines extend those of the first song and follow the pattern of 6.7.6.7.7.7.7.6.6, the final quatrain addressing the dead Salgar: "Ach sprecht noch holde Worte! / Ach höret meine Klagen! / Doch ewig schweigt ihr Mund! / Eiskalt ist ihre Brust!" (Oh, speak some noble words, listen to my lamenting; but ever silent is their mouth, and ice-cold is their breast!).

The concluding part, in A-flat major, is a prayerful address by Colma to the spirits of the dead. Reichardt conceived this as a slower version of the strophic,

Example 9.12. Johann Friedrich Reichardt, "Kolma's Klage," part 1, bars 1–8

eight-syllable line, shortening the syllable count to a 6.6.6.5.6.6.6.5 pattern. Cast in $\frac{3}{4}$ time, with a gentle accompaniment in half notes and eighth notes, the melodic curve captures the plea of Colma, resigned to her fate. In an era in which the poetic interpretation and association of particular keys was still current, the writer C. F. D. Schubart would designate the key of A-flat as associated with death and burial.[22] Although Reichardt could well have been aware of such views, the tendency by composers, especially German ones, to cast the musical settings of "Colma" largely in E-flat or associated flat keys cannot be an accident.

In any case, Reichardt had been attracted to the French Revolution and its progressive ideals and this caused him to fall out with Goethe, whose tendency to conservative views led him to oppose Napoleon even though he was later to meet the emperor, in Erfurt, on October 2, 1808.[23] The break with Goethe, around 1804,

Example 9.13. Reichardt, "Kolma's Klage," part 3, bars 1–16

when Zelter replaced Reichardt as Goethe's musical adviser, may explain Reichardt's choice of text for his setting of *Kolma's Klage*: though he had set a number of Goethe's poems, the souring of their relationship could well have led to his choosing another translator of Ossian for his *Kolma*. Nevertheless, it is worth remarking that Reichardt and Goethe had earlier planned an opera on the subject of Ossian, a project that fell by the wayside as their political views diverged.

Mendelssohn regarded Reichardt as a major figure in developing the lied, valuing him over his teacher Zelter, and even above Schubert, because he had written, after all, some 1,500 songs over his sixty-two years. Reichardt's astonishing output continued after his marriage in 1776 to Juliane Benda (1752–83), youngest of Franz Benda's six daughters and a composer herself. His letters from Vienna during 1808 and 1809 were published in Amsterdam in 1810, five years before Schubert began to compose his first lieder.[24] Reichardt's contribution to the development of the lied is undeniable.[25]

Reichardt and Schubert

The settings by Zumsteeg and Reichardt of "Colma" had an immediate influence on Schubert. His version of "Kolma's Klage" is strophic in using the same text as Reichardt, not through-composed like those of Rust, Zumsteeg, and Zelter.[26] At this early stage in his career, Schubert was searching for the simplicity that Reichardt was manifestly striving for in his tripartite strophic setting.[27] Nevertheless, the emotional impact of Zumsteeg's *Colma*, with its drama-infused mixture of arioso and recitative, remained with Schubert for his Ossian settings such as "Lodas Gespenst" (D150), "Cronnan" (D282), and "Shilric und Vinvela" (D293). The key selection is also relevant: Schubert employed C minor, Schubart's key of unhappy or tragic love, for three more of these songs besides "Kolma's Klage": "Cronnan," "Das Mädchen von Inistore" (D281), and "Der Tod Oskars" (D375).

"Kolma's Klage" is the best of these early songs in its strongly etched rhythms and harmonic depth reminiscent of "Erlkönig" (D328, composed in the same year but not published until 1821). The rising octave triplets in the left hand of the piano in part 1 (bars 8, 10, 25, 27, 42, 44) are related to those in the better-known song, though to be played at a much slower pace. In the vocal part, Schubert is clearly moving toward a more declamatory style, with irregular phrase lengths that are perceptibly different from Reichardt's folk-like pattern.[28]

The transition to part 2 in A-flat major and $\frac{6}{8}$ rhythm (marked, as in Reichardt, "gleich weiter") throws into relief the gesture of Colma to the moon ("Doch sieh, der Mond erscheint") and her question about her lover's resting place ("Doch wer sind jene dort"); Schubert, however, omits verse 6 with its appeal to Salgar to answer ("Du warst der schönste mir"). Part 3 then moves into a gentle F minor in $\frac{2}{4}$ to reflect Colma's prayer to the spirits of the dead and her grief for her brother and her lover ("Geister meiner Todten" and "Hier in tiefem Grame"). Schubert dispenses with the final verse (verse 9), ending instead with "Mit den lieben Freunden / Will ich ewig ruhn" (I shall rest eternally with my dear friends), thereby tightening the structure. The main relationships between verse and music in the two settings can be seen in table 9.3:

Table 9.3. Kolmas Klage (Reichardt, Schubert)

	Reichardt				Schubert		
Key signature	Time signature	Marking	Syllables	Key signature	Time signature	Marking
E♭	4/4	langsam	8.9.6.7.7.9.4	C minor	2/2	ziemlich langsam
C major–minor	6/8	etwas lebhaft	6.7.6.7 (bis) S. omits v.6	A♭	6/8	etwas langsam
A♭	3/4	langsam	6.6.6.5 (bis) S. omits v.9	F minor	2/4	langsam, trauernd

The key relationships that Reichardt and Schubert employ in their strophic settings call for brief comment. While Reichardt's tonal trajectory for parts 1–3 of the setting is E-flat major–C major/minor–A-flat major, Schubert's arrangement is C minor–A-flat major–F minor, a parallel but fundamentally reconceived version of a relationship among the tonic, mediant, and dominant keys to capture more affectingly the pathos in the text. Both settings are effective, but in quite different ways: Reichardt's A-flat major close conveys a calm if sorrowful resignation, Schubert's F-minor ending a more tragic atmosphere. There is no need to belabor the point, for Schubert's setting has been discussed many times. His "Kolma's Klage" owes a great deal to Zumsteeg in its emotional colouring as well as to Reichardt for its structure, and perhaps also, less immediately, to the settings of Rust and Zelter. It is timely, though, to draw greater attention again to precursors of Schubert, the impact that the poems of Ossian had on both him and them, and their contribution to the development of German poetry and song in the years 1780 to 1815.

Chapter Ten

Scènes lyriques sans frontières

Louis Théodore Gouvy's *Le dernier Hymne d'Ossian* (1858) and Lucien Hillemacher's *Fingal* (1880)

The *scène lyrique* has a continuous if mottled history in France. Stemming from Rousseau's *Pygmalion* (1762), the genre became progressively more dramatic in character and was often identified with the *mélodrame* on the one hand and the *drame lyrique* on the other. It remained more akin to the Italian cantata, however, with a soloist or soloists, instruments, and sometimes chorus as well, performed as a concert piece rather than a full-fledged *tragédie en musique*, the form of opera initiated by Lully in the second half of the seventeenth century. Lully's successor Rameau subsequently created other related genres, such as his *opéra-ballets*, *pastorales héroïques*, and *comédies lyriques*, bringing them to a high degree of sophistication.

It was Jean-Frédéric Edelmann (1749–94) and his better-known pupil Étienne Méhul who took up the form of the *scène lyrique* and developed it in such a way that Hector Berlioz, a few years later, was able to complete works which included *Herminie* (1828) and *La mort de Cléopâtre* (1829) as effective, cantata-like compositions.[1] These were written for soprano and orchestra, and *Herminie* won second prize in the Prix de Rome competition. But it was on his fourth attempt, *Sardanapale* for tenor, chorus and orchestra (1830), that Berlioz finally won joint first prize. In due course almost every major French composer from Berlioz to Debussy (*L'Enfant Prodigue*, 1884) undertook to compose a *scène lyrique*, from simple voice and piano works to more ambitious choral-orchestral compositions.

Always one for promoting French musicians, Berlioz referred to Théodore Louis Gouvy (1819–98) in the *Journal des débats* (1851) as an important composer, one who should be known in Parisian musical circles. But the public at that time in the capital was only interested in opera, and Gouvy's extensive instrumental works, many of which were published during his lifetime, had to wait for universal recognition until the twentieth century.[2] He produced over two hundred substantial compositions, including symphonies, cantatas, and religious works, but his industry, poetic sensitivity, and skill are all apparent in the single composition he based on Ossian: the *scène lyrique*, *Le dernier Hymne d'Ossian*, op. 15, published in 1858.[3] Its full score of 72 pages is redolent of a mind acutely responsive to nuances in the chosen text, which is based on Macpherson's prose poem "Berrathon."

Gouvy was born into a French-speaking family, in the Sarre, on the Franco-Prussian border, four years after the Battle of Waterloo (the surname is from a municipality in Belgium). Because Prussia took over administration of his birthplace in his youth, he was unable to assume French citizenship until 1851. Moving to Paris in 1837 to study law, he made friends there with the prominent composer Adolphe Adam. But musical studies in Berlin introduced influence from Mendelssohn and Schumann into his compositions, to a much greater degree than that from French composers such as Charles Gounod. Drawn to instrumental music rather than opera, he assumed the difficult role of symphonist in an opera-mad Paris. But in Germany, Brahms, the violinist Joseph Joachim, the conductor Hermann Levi, and Carl Reinecke all recognized the worth of Gouvy's compositions, especially the chamber music, a great deal of which was performed in his lifetime.[4] By the mid-1850s, when Gouvy began to write *Le dernier Hymne d'Ossian*, he was already an established composer.[5] This was not, as in so many cases of enthusiastic settings of Ossian, the work of a young man.

Louis Théodore Gouvy's *Le dernier Hymne d'Ossian* (1858)

The cantata is devised for low male voice (*voix de basse*) and orchestra. The text of thirty-seven lines, couched in the standard alexandrine of twelve syllable lines, comes mainly from *Ossian, barde du troisième siècle: poésies galliques* by Pierre-Marie-Joseph Baour-Lormian (1770–1854), a work that went into four editions after its first edition of 1801 (1804, 1809, 1822, 1827) and was more influential in France, as a free version of Ossian, than Pierre Le Tourneur's more accurate translation of 1777.[6] Reflecting Gouvy's dual cultural heritage, the poetic text is printed under the solo voice line in both French and German (*Ossian's letzter Gesang*).[7] The composer has set the first thirteen lines of Baour-Lormian's French text faithfully for the soloist, but the succeeding lines vary in some respects from the text edition of 1822.[8] Seventeen lines in Baour-Lormian's later editions, including that of 1827, are omitted in the present setting, and the final couplet seems to be an addition of the composer.[9] Otherwise, the texts agree up to "Ossian va dormir, ne le réveillez pas"

Gouvy has conceived the vocal part for a low male voice, with a tessitura from a low G to a high E. While the former note occurs only once (two bars before rehearsal letter B), there are frequent high Ds and Es that make the range a testing one for the singer and recall the role of Larmor in Méhul's *Uthal*. The orchestra is a large one, with double woodwinds, horns, and trumpets, three trombones, timpani, harp, and strings. The Adagio ($\frac{3}{4}$, E major, *pianissimo*) sets a somber tone in the first half dozen bars with low Es in the strings and second horn, while the first horn sounds a gentle upward-curving five-bar melody against a rising bass line in the cellos; the solo horn motif is repeated, with an expressive, chromatically descending line in the cellos that lends a quiet air of lament.

A melodic flurry in the violins for three bars followed by a "Scotch snap" figure is accompanied by soft horn calls, and this leads to a new, slower passage in $\frac{9}{8}$ and the key of E minor (bar 22). Here, the cellos usher in a rustling upward-moving chromatic phrase in sixteenth notes, joined by bassoons with a short melodic motif. Ten bars later the full orchestra, in a sumptuous *pianissimo* E-minor chord, with *tremolando* strings, announces the entry of the soloist: "Conduis, o fils d'Alpin, le vieillard dans ses bois" (Lead, son of Alpin, lead the aged to his woods, bar 33). In his imaginative instrumentation Gouvy seems to have absorbed some of Méhul's skill, particularly in his writing for woodwinds and brass, as well as Mendelssohn's facility in string writing. Tracked by the ascending cello motif, the bass line rises to a D against repeated low octave Es in the horns at "l'aquilon" (the North Wind), then sinks to a low B for "Retombent à grand bruit sur la rive écumante" (the final adjective seems to mean "foaming"). At this point (rehearsal letter A in the score) the cello motif is taken over by the upper strings, crescendo, while the woodwinds play a short, excited motif of thirds and sixths, the horns holding a pedal B. Accelerating, the tempo and dynamic reaches a climax with the entrance of the trumpets and timpani, with trombones holding an F-major first inversion chord as the cellos and bassoons sound a D (bar 55). This last note is soon released in an upward octave rush to herald the voice of Ossian with its high repeated Ds for "Le Barde va chanter pour la dernière fois," all against a sinking bass line, from D to low E.

Meanwhile, trumpets and trombones offer short interjections off the beat. In this work Gouvy uses trumpets and trombones sparingly but effectively: *pianissimo* chords in the brass accompany the phrase "Le Barde va chanter pour la dernière fois" (the bard would sing for the last time), and the phrase is repeated as the tempo slows and the strings are silenced. The voice holds on to a B accompanied by the bassoons, trumpets with repeated Bs, and the trombones with a succession of sixth chords, from C major to E minor. The woodwinds and brass, with timpani, then signal a cadence in the latter key, with a *pianissimo* chord.

A return to the initial *adagio*, with the violin melisma interspersed against a sinking bass, lasts for a mere nine bars. This passage acts as a short transition to a longer, main *moderato* section in G major and $\frac{9}{8}$, the strings articulating a continuous pattern of sixteenth notes as accompaniment to solos by the two horns in turn. The bass voice then enters with "Sur le torrent se balance un vieux chêne, / Que d'un souffle de glace ont blanchi les hivers" (An aged oak that the winters have bleached with

Table 10.1. Gouvy's *Le dernier Hymne d'Ossian*: structure

Section	Bars	Key signature	Time signature	Marking	Orchestra
[intro]	1–21	E major	3/4	adagio	str, horns
"Conduis, ô fils d'Alpin" (bar 32)	22–74	E minor	9/8	piu mosso	str, ww, brass (55–)
[transition]	75–83	[fluid]	3/4	(adagio)	harp, ww
"Sur le torrent se balance un vieux chêne" (bar 92)	84–140	G major	9/8	moderato	horns soli, str
"Que transport m'agite et m'enflamme!" (bar 145)	141–277	E minor	2/2	allegro assai	str, ww, harp (156–/228–)
[transition]	278–83	[fluid]	2/2	adagio	fl, clar, harp horn solo
"Quand ta colère est apaisée" (bar 292)	284–351	B major	6/8	allegretto	str, ww, horn solos
"Ô toi que j'ai chéri" (bar 364)	352–401	E major	2/2	allegro spiritoso	str, ww, harp (364–) oboe (402)
"Ah! Vents orageux du soir" (bar 402)	402–41	E major	2/2	[allegro spiritoso]	str, ww, harp (406–)
"Je l'entends! Il m'appelle, c'est lui!" (bar 42)	442–95	E major	2/2	andante maestoso (quasi recit.) vivace assai	trpt, tromb, timp, full orch

Example 10.1. Louis Théodore Gouvy, *Le dernier Hymne d'Ossian*, bars 32–40

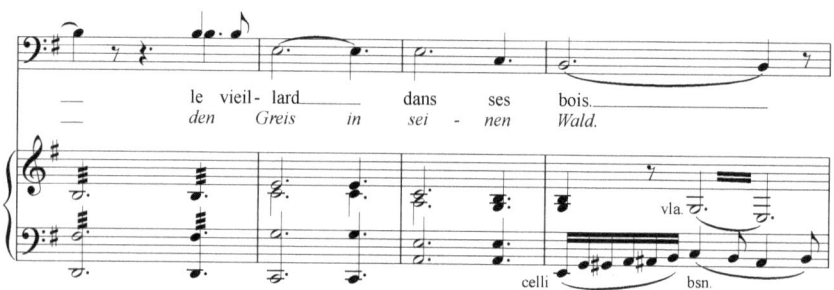

their icy breath) as the tonality veers between G and E minor (at "hivers," the vocal part ends on a low G). With "Ma harpe est suspendue à sa branche prochaine" (My harp hangs on a blasted branch), chords from the harp punctuate the orchestral texture. A sudden *pianissimo* rustling of the strings on a sixth chord of C major *tremolando* ushers in the words "Est-ce le vent, ma harpe, ou bien quel qu'ombre vaine / Qui t'arrache, en passant, ces funèbres concerts?" (Does the wind touch thee, oh harp, or is it some passing ghost that offers, in passing, these funeral concerts?). Flute and oboe provide a melodic backdrop for this brief section while the bass repeats, again with high Es at "qu'ombre vaine" (empty shadow) and "ces funèbres concerts," with somber bassoon, horn, and cello accompaniment. This entire section of fifty-six bars subsides in G major, with gentle pizzicato chords in the horns and strings.

Here, the tone switches. Harmonically, the composer has molded the opening of the new development section to suggest uncertain tonality. The work moves quickly into *allegro assai* in duple time with syncopated octave repetitions in the second violins doubled by a held G♯ in the bassoons, a swaying figure in the clarinet, and a gradually rising bass line. The voice murmurs, "Quel transport m'agite et m'en

Figure 10.1. Christian Gottlieb Kratzenstein-Stub (1783–1816), *Ossian and the Son of Alpin Hear the Spirit of Malvina Grasping the Strings of the Harp. Illustrating Ossian's Swansong*. Oil on canvas, ca. 1818. Hirschsprung Collection, Copenhagen. Reproduced with permission.

Example 10.2. Gouvy, *Le dernier Hymne d'Ossian*: "Est-ce le vent," bars 126–34

flamme! / Approche, fils d'Alpin!" (What is it that moves and inflames me! Come close, son of Alpin!). At these last words, fifteen bars later, the harp makes a prominent entrance with triplet figuration on a dominant seventh chord of E minor. Two bars later the voice of Ossian reaches a high D♯ for "Ô mes chants, dans les airs / Accompagnez le départ de mon âme" (Oh my songs, in the melodies accompany the farewell of my soul), with these words attaining a *forte-piano* cadence in E major (rehearsal letter D). With mounting volume and successive appoggiaturas around F-sharp minor, the woodwinds and strings frame the vocal cry, "La mort va mettre

Example 10.3. Gouvy, *Le dernier Hymne d'Ossian*: "La tonnerre à ta voix," bars 238–52

un terme à mes longues douleurs" as the horns and trumpets move the *tremolando* strings to a *fortissimo* E-minor cadence.

Reference to the North Wind drives the bass line's upward chromatic surge, while the violins imitate Mendelssohn's seascape in precipitate but controlled sixteenth notes. Again, with a bass rising by semitones, the tonality turns toward E-flat minor with Ossian's "Portez jusqu'à Fingal mes plaintes solennelles," which ends on a high E♭ before the tonality returns to E minor, the syncopated string figures, the harp temporarily silent. But soon the harp enters again with its triplets (rehearsal letter F). The vision of Fingal controlling the storms, and the thunderous sound of his voice (ex. 3), takes the tonality into B-flat minor territory, then, with a series of diminished chords and *fortissimo* climax (rehearsal letter G), to the relative haven of D major and the now-placid syncopation of the violins and violas. In gentler tones the voice, with repetition on the note D, intones, "Et des clartés du jour tu prives nos climats" as the music slows, *pianissimo*, before reaching a transitional *adagio* of six bars, with mildly dissonant flute and clarinet chords poised against staccato harp arpeggios, first on E♭ and then, a bar later, on a dominant seventh on F♯, preparing the way for the next section.

Gouvy's fastidiousness is most evident in his orchestral coloring, mastery evident in his gauging of the precise effect of an instrumental or vocal sound. A solo horn introduces the new $\frac{6}{8}$ *allegretto* in B major, with quietly ticking woodwind chords offset by brief interjections by violin and clarinet. This novel texture prepares for the hushed entry of the voice, "Quand ta colère est apaisée, le zephyr du matin caresse les ruisseaux" (When your anger is appeased, the morning breeze caresses the streams). The instrumentation then changes with ten bars of rustling strings, until (rehearsal letter H) the strings articulate softly an E-major chord for "Le soleil du printemps se couronne de feux." At this point E major is displaced, *fortissimo*, by a D-major chord a tone lower: a "Scottish" modulation? This segment then draws softly to a close with descending horn chords (soli, *a piacere*), and a new section, now in E major and $\frac{2}{2}$, enlivens the tempo.

The *allegro spiritoso* begins in muted fashion, with a horn and viola melody accompanied by rapid string figuration in triplets and quiet chording in the clarinets and bassoons. After twelve bars (rehearsal letter K), the harp, too, enters with a motif in triplets, again in E major. Its entrance heralds the voice, with the plea of Ossian, "Ô toi que j'ai chéri, ô toi que j'ai pleuré / Ô mon père, ô mon roi, je vais te voir encore / Et gouter le repos si souvent désiré" (O you whom I have loved, for whom I weep, my father and king, I would see you once more and taste the rest so often wished for). The clarinet then repeats the horn and viola melody over a pedal B and a crescendo until the voice utters its "Ah, vents orageux du soir" (Ah, stormy winds of evening) on B with a background of a jagged oboe entry against descending clarinet chords for the prolonged sign of "Ah." Still in E major, the harp again supplies its triplet accompaniment for "Ma bouche vous implore" (My lips implore you) and a cadence in E is reached, finally, at "De vos bruyantes voix retenez les éclats" (Keep

Example 10.4. Gouvy, *Le dernier Hymne d'Ossian*: "Quand ta colère est apaisée": bars 292–301

Example 10.5. Gouvy, *Le dernier Hymne d'Ossian*: "Ah! Vents orageux du soir," bars 402–12

Example 10.6. Gouvy, *Le dernier Hymne d'Ossian*: "Je l'entends! Il m'appelle, c'est lui!," bars 442–58

the brilliance of your voices), as Ossian again invokes the stormy winds of evening (rehearsal letter M).

Gouvy's use of the harp in this work is especially notable. The instrument provides a tranquil accompaniment to "O vents du soir" as the harmony oscillates between tonic and dominant of E major, up to "Ossian va dormir, ne le réveillez pas" (Ossian wants to sleep, do not wake him), at which point the winds and strings enunciate briefly and effectively a C-major chord. The voice then returns the harmony to E major for the final *andante maestoso*: a brass and oboe fanfare over soft timpani rolling introduces a "quasi recitativo" passage for Ossian, *vivace assai*, in *alla breve* time: "Je l'entends! Il m'appelle, c'est lui!" (I hear him, he calls me, it is he!). Clarinets, bassoons, and *tremolando* violins and violas accompany the soloist's ecstatic "c'est Fingal! mon père adoré, je viens à toi!" (It is Fingal, my adored father, I come to you!). After ten bars the directions *più animato* and *crescendo* include a prominent D♮ placed among the half-note chords. The expected A-major harmony is immediately contradicted by a resumption of E major in brisk *fortissimo* chords, the harp now symbolically silent. At the *a tempo* marking, in the final fifteen bars, the violins again inflect their uprushing scales with a D♮, but sharpen the D before the final *tutti*.[10]

What is remarkable about Gouvy's composition is the sophisticated handling of the orchestral texture in framing the vocal part. In this he anticipates Ravel. By offering grateful if testing lines to the solo voice, he has at the same time supplied much more than a conventional accompaniment: formally the composition is as much a symphonic concept as it is a solo cantata. Framed by a slow introduction and a lively coda, the work simulates a sonata structure: *più mosso* (E minor), *moderato* (G major), *allegro* assai (development), *allegretto* (B major), *allegro spiritoso* (E major). In his transmediation, the composer has not only devised the shape of the work carefully to match the mood of the Ossian text, with finely judged changes of tempo and dynamics, he has planned the design in such a way that, in terms of dramatic key contrast (E minor, G major, B major, and E major in sequence), the overall structure has a musical life of its own. The work is a highly significant contribution to the development of the *scène lyrique* as a crucial genre in the nineteenth century, and is a persuasive masterpiece.

Lucien Hillemacher's *Fingal*

An equally impressive *scène lyrique* is *Fingal*, by the twenty-year-old Lucien-Joseph-Édouard Hillemacher (1860–1909), to a text in alexandrines by Charles Darcours; it was of sufficient quality to win the Prix de Rome in 1880.[11] It is dedicated to "mon cher Maître, J. Massenet." Hillemacher worked closely in collaboration with his brother, Paul (1852–1933), who had also won the Prix de Rome, with his *scène lyrique, Judith* (1876). They were sons of the prolific French history and genre painter Eugène-Ernest Hillemacher (1818–87), noted for his academic style. It is probable that the family name originally came from North Rhine-Westphalia, close to the border with the Netherlands, although this particular branch of the Hillemachers settled in Paris. For their collaborative work, the brothers devised the authorial name Paul-Lucien Hillemacher, and this suggests that they benefited from each other's ideas and criticism, both for individual works and for those they completed together. Their intellectual and artistic frontiers often merged.[12]

In the catalogue of the Bibliothèque Nationale, the date of publication of the voice and piano reduction is given as 1880 and the publisher as the firm of Alphonse Leduc (which brought out other works by the brothers).[13] The history of the work after its first outing is obscure. A performance of the prize composition was certainly given on October 10, 1880, by the executants named in the score: M. Talazac ("Fingal, Roi de Morven," tenor); Mlle. Fouquet ("Comalha, Fiancée de Fingal," soprano); M. Hermann-Léon ("Hidallan, Jeune Guerrier," baritone). The work is cast in four scenes, and the action, following Macpherson's note on the poem "Comala," supposedly takes place in Scotland in the third century AD, during a war between the Caledonians and the Romans. Hillemacher seems to have originally envisaged the work as a staged operatic scene rather than a cantata.[14]

A "Table des Morceaux" lists the main musical pieces in the four scenes: in scene 1, the recitative "La bataille est finie" and air "Reviens, la nuit est commencée"; in scene 2, the recitative "Nuit de crime"; in scene 3, the duo "Ah, les regards inquiets" and "Marche"; in scene 4, the recitative "Bardes, prenez vos harpes" and trio "Ô fleur qui vient d'éclor." A striking contrast to Gouvy's symphonic conception in *Le dernier Hymne d'Ossian*, Hillemacher's vision is chamber-like, the orchestration of the four scenes more akin to the movements of a string trio or wind quartet. In the tradition of French writing for woodwind instruments since Méhul, the flute and bassoon parts are particularly effective in their solo and collective sonority.

Scene 1 is conceived against a background of mountains, crags ("rochers"), and forest, and the time is evening. The *andante* introduction, in E-flat and $\frac{9}{8}$, contains a motto theme, played by the horn ("doux et mysterieux"), that pervades the entire scene.[15] After thirty bars Comalha begins her recitative, *pianissimo*, against an E-flat sixth chord, "La bataille est finie.... L'ombre tombant des monts" and proceeds with the motto theme, "Fingal, chef glorieux des fiers enfants de la Calédonie!" Modulating to C major, the recitative is followed by the *allegretto* air in $\frac{2}{4}$, "Reviens, la nuit est commencée" (to be sung "avec mélancholie"), accompanied by gentle chords in the treble clef. "Reviens," sings Comalha, "Ô mon amant," but *tremolando* and jagged octave chords in the bass instruments change the mood as she becomes aware of disaster looming: "Le ciel s'est voilé, la terre a tremblé, bruits redoutés, sombres nuages!" She asks, "Where are you, son of Trenmor?" as the bass line hovers around B-flat minor. The music returns to the introductory movement of $\frac{9}{8}$, with wistful harmonies framing Comalha's sadly enunciated "Il ne vient pas!," and she beseeches the spirits of Loda to watch over Fingal ("Ô spectres de Lodas sur lui veillez et dirigez ses pas!") as the motto theme quietly ushers her from the scene.

Example 10.7. Hillemacher, *Fingal*, bars 4–11

The short scene 2 sets off with a brisk $\frac{4}{4}$ *allegro (ma non troppo vivo)* in C minor as the dominant of F minor. A growling trill in the bass, a syncopated motif emphasizing the tonality, and a brief chromatic oboe solo introduce an agitated Hidallan with his recitative, "Nuit de crime, nuit d'épouvante." The night shows no star in the sky, the pale features of wild phantoms appear from the edge of the clouds: it is the moment, he sings, when the souls of the dead leave their graves. A storm rages, much as it did for Méhul in *Uthal*. Here, an F-minor chord tumbles down chromatically as Hidallan continues, "Et vont sillonner l'air en livides flambeaux," a fiery sky that denotes a time of weeping and wailing. As the accompaniment continues with staccato thirds, his line ascends to a high E♭ at the word *abîme* (abyss) as he contemplates his love for Comalha: nothing can prevent your fate, he declares, or my transgressions ("ton sort ni mes forfaits"), the vocal line at "mes forfaits" reaching a high G (or E♭ as alternate) and F. The storm abates, the music slows, and a few bars move enharmonically toward F-sharp minor as Comalha approaches and scene 2 ends.

Scene 3 begins with an *adagio maestoso* in $\frac{3}{4}$. A forceful figure rises from the bass with dotted eighth-notes and thirty-second notes indicating the pair's emotional turmoil as Hidallan tells Comalha how Fingal's battle is near. A rapid repeated motif like a fanfare at the *a tempo* becomes a sign of doom: "Le torrent de Carron roule des flots de sang." Comalha, terrified, asks about Fingal. The fanfare-doom motif is paired with upward steps in the bass as Hidallan tells Comalha that Fingal has fallen ("Il n'est plus"), until at an *allegro vivace* she pours out her cry of vengeance accompanied by a rising torrent of eighth-notes. The ensuing *allegro giusto* releases a jagged

Table 10.2. Hillemacher's *Fingal*: structure of scene 1

Section	Bars	Key signature	Time signature	Marking	Voice
Intro	1–30	E♭	9/8	andante	
"La bataille est fini!"	31–40, 41–60, 61–69	E♭	4/4, 3/4, 2/2	stesso tempo	Comalha recit.
"Reviens!"	70–121	C major	2/4	allegretto poco andante	air
"Mais, funeste presage"	122–37	C major	4/4	lo stesso tempo	recit.
"Où donc es-tu, fils de Trenmor?"	138–42	C major / B♭ minor	[4/4]	le double plus lent	recit.
"Reviens!"	143–70	C major	2/4	allegretto	air
"Il ne vient pas!"	171–88	E♭	3/4 (voice) 9/8 (acc)	andante (movement de l'intro)	

Table 10.3. Hillemacher's *Fingal*: structure of scene 2

Section	Bars	Key signature	Time signature	Marking	Voice
"Nuit de crime"	1–62	F minor	4/4	allegro non troppo vivo	Hidallan recit.
"C'est elle"	63–65	D♭	(4/4)	piu lento	recit.

Example 10.8. Hillemacher, *Fingal*, aria: "Comalha! désormais rien ne peut conjurer," bars 235–44

dotted rhythm, repeated on a single note (from bar 131), expressing her resolve. The music is then transformed to an urgent F-sharp major as Hidallan justifies his action as motivated by his passion for Comalha ("En mon coeur un fol amour régne!"). When he tells her she will be his alone, she does not listen, repeating her cry for retribution.

The ensuing duet becomes a case of two people caught in the throes of Hidallan's falsehood. The music expresses their anguish in a tied half-note motif followed by three eighth notes: "Oui,'" sings Hidallan, "tu seras mon seul bien," as Comalha cries out again for vengeance, both voices reaching a climax with a combined F-sharp (Hidallan) and A(Comalha) over a diminished chord based on G♯. The succeeding chord of a minor ninth on C♯, *fortissimo*, prefaces a tremulous F-sharp major cadence. Comalha then engages in a short recitative, asking Hidallan why he told her that Fingal was dead. This leads to a change of key (B-flat) for a reprise of the air in scene 1 ("Reviens"). She dreams of seeing her love appear from the mountain nearby. The tempo enlivens as she asks Hidallan to lead her so that she can see Fingal again. With the return of the fanfare motif and rising bass, for a short interlude the tempo again assumes a quicker pace. Accompanied by the ascending sixteenth-note motif first heard at the beginning of scene 3, Comalha declares, in a muted voice ("d'une voix sourde"), that since Fingal is dead she will seek vengeance. She and Hidallan then reprise their duet in F-sharp major, she crying for revenge, he singing of his *fol amour*. More than double the length at its first appearance, the developed duet is the high point of the entire work, and something of a tour de force for the singers.

The march that the critic from the journal *La Fantaisie artistique et littéraire* called pretentious and banal is in fact an effective bridge to scene 4, as Comalha tries to discern Fingal among the souls of the dead when they leave their resting place "sous le noir feuillage." Repeated fanfares on D are interspersed with arpeggio harp chords a tone apart (a Celtic reference?) at bars 212–15. As with Gouvy, are we hearing an echo of Mendelssohn's brass flourishes in "Fingal's Cave"? The greatly elaborated scene in this version of the Comala story opens with a striding *Poco più largo* in G major. This broader tempo allows the tenor voice of Fingal, entering surrounded by his generals, to instruct his followers: "Bardes! Prenez vos harpes, et chantez / Des fils d'Erin célébrez la victoire." In the third and fourth bars (550–51) of his *moderato poco andante*, the melodic turn is Wagnerian at "que vos accents illustrent leur mémoire." At this point, Hillemacher has the tenor sing "Et dans ce jour, Morven nos armes valoreuses / Souvent la liberté, ton sol et les enfants" with, in succession, a high A♭, an A♮, and a B♭ at the words "liberté, ton sol et les enfants." This last note is sustained for two bars as his victory panegyric concludes in a broadening tempo and B-flat major.

Comalha, meanwhile, thinks she is seeing the ghost of her love; as Fingal suddenly recognizes her, she falls into his arms. With abrupt chords, the music moves to E major for a trio, at which juncture Hidallan joins them. The trio lasts for seventy-five bars, even though the *Fantaisie* critic thought the charm of the opening phrase

Example 10.9. Hillemacher, *Fingal*, duet: "Car j'ai poussé le cri de haine," bars 346–50

underdeveloped ("Le trio débute par une phrase empreinte d'un certain charme, qui n'est malheureusement pas assez dévelopée"). Comalha sings of her joy at Fingal's return ("heure pleine de charmes"); he in turn declares his love for her, while Hidallan regrets that "mon amour, flamme impure, / Pour elle est une injure . . . guerrier traître . . . je quitte ces bords à jamais . . . je suis seul hélas!" The bass harmony slides upward chromatically to a dominant B-flat for the climax and a pause on an E-flat chord before resuming again (*ppp*) in E major for the hushed ending of the trio.

Comalha and Fingal sing tenderly of their love; Hidallan confesses his crime and asks Fingal to dispatch him with his sword. Fingal however, urged to be merciful by Comalha, announces their marriage at the palace of Selma. But Comalha suddenly feels weak; the tension has been too much for her to bear; the death she feared for Fingal has descended on her. This passage, an *allegro moderato* in B minor with

Table 10.4. Hillemacher's *Fingal*: structure of scene 3

Section	Bars	Key signature	Time signature	Marking	Voice
"Ah! Ses regards inquiets"	1–32	F♯ minor	3/4	adagio maestoso	duo (Comalha, Hidallan)
"Ah j'ai poussé le cri de haine"	33–59	F♯ minor	4/4	allegro vivace	duo (Comalha)
"En mon coeur un fol amour regne"	60–97	F♯ major	(4/4)	(allegro vivace)	duo (Hidallan)
"Toi qui n'as pas su le defender"	98–108	B minor	(4/4)	(cédez un peu)	duo (Comalha)
"J'ai souvent rêve"	109–30	B♭	2/4	mouvement de l'air	
"Hidallan!"	131–43	F♯ minor	4/4	a tempo	
"Conduis-moi"	144–50	F♯ minor	3/4	andante non troppo lento	
"Viens!" "Comalha!"	151–67	F♯ minor	4/4	allegro giusto	
"Car j'ai poussé le cri de haine"	168–203	F♯ major	(4/4)	(allegro giusto)	
"Mais, quel bruit!"	204–16	B♭	4/4	allegro moderato	marche
"Que vois-je, c'est l'image de Fingal!"	217–69	G minor	4/4, 2/4	meno presto	marche

Table 10.5. Hillemacher's *Fingal*: structure of scene 4

Section	Bars	Key	Time	Marking	Voice
Intro	1–15	G major	4/4	poco più largo	
"Bardes! prenez vos harpes"	16–24	G minor	4/4	très largement	Fingal recit.
"Des fils d'Erin célébrez la victoire"	25–56	G minor	4/4	moderato poco andante	air
"L'image de Fingal dans le séjour"	57–68	B minor	4/4	(moderato poco andante)	Comalha, Fingal recit.
"Vivant!" "Malheur!"	69–72	E major	4/4	(moderato poco andante)	Comalha/ Hidallan recit.
"Ma bien aimée"	73–77	E major	4/4	andantino	Fingal recit.
"O fleur qui viens"	78–134	E major	4/4	andante	trio
"C'est toi"	135–40	A minor	4/4	(andante)	Comalha, Fingal recit.
"Hidallan est un traître"	141–53	A minor	3/4	très modéré	Hidallan recit.
"Infâme!" "Sois clement"	154–61	A minor	4/4	allegro	Comalha, Fingal recit.
"Et vous!"	162–64	A minor	4/4	allegro moderato	Fingal recit.
"Mes compagnons fidèles partons"	165–74	G minor	4/4	(allegro moderato)	
"Mais, je ne sais, en mes sens en va bis"	175–99	B minor	2/2	allegro moderato	trio
"Je vais au séjour immortel"	200–232	B minor	2/2	un poco più lento	Comalha, Fingal duo
"Laisse ma rête en tes bras reposer"	233–47	B minor	2/2	mouvement de l'ensemble du trio	duo
"Sur nous malheur!"	248–60	B minor	2/2	l'istesso tempo	Fingal, Hidallan duo

Example 10.10. Hillemacher, *Fingal*, arioso: "Les fils d'Erin célébrez la victoire," bars 547–56

with chromatic shifts, accompanies her solo with eighth-note appoggiaturas on the first and third beats of the bar, inserting rests that separate the eighth notes to suggest her failing strength. As the melancholy mood persists with *tremolando* chords and the same appoggiaturas, the final slowly moving passage (*un poco più lento*) sees Comalha sing of her eternal love for Fingal. In the tempo of the trio, she asks him if she can rest her head on his arm, "je mourrai sous tes derniers baisers . . ."; in place of a wedding march, she sings, lead me to the tomb where I shall lie. The eighth-note appoggiaturas in the bass recur, but less and less often as Comalha bids Fingal farewell, while the latter and Hidallan lament her passing ("sur nous malheur") and the work ends in the desolate B-minor key that half a century earlier had plangent associations for Schubert and Mendelssohn.

The critic of the journal *La Fantaisie artistique et littéraire*, Georges Servières, writing in the issue of November 13, 1880, praised the work of the twenty-year-old composer, noting at the same time "certaines coupes rythmiques et mélodiques,

Example 10.11. Hillemacher, *Fingal*, trio: "Heure pleine de charme," bars 645–54

certaines successions harmoniques, certaines formes d'orchestration" that recalled the stylistic traits of Hillemacher's teacher, Massenet. Nevertheless, he found the aria "Reviens, la nuit is commencée" to be "une des bonnes pages de la partition." He did not care much for the *Marche* in the final scene, which he termed pretentious, but thought the entry of Fingal had grandeur, and that his recitative on returning victorious was "très large" (very spacious).[16] The composer and critic Victorin Joncières, on the other hand, considered the final scene the best: "Il y a d'abord une marche guerrière puis l'air d'entrée de Fingal, d'un caractère et d'une expression bien appropriés au sujet."[17] The conclusion of contemporary critics appears fair and balanced even though, for them, the influence of Massenet was a little too obvious. But if the imprint of Hillemacher's teacher is certainly present (and, occasionally, that of Wagner) the overall conception is individualistic and structurally sound, with its own personality struggling to be heard.[18] And the question in turn may be asked: how far did Hillemacher's setting of *Fingal* influence Massenet's choice of subject in *Werther*? After all, the final scene in act 3, with its famous tenor aria "Pourquoi me réveiller," involves a quotation from Ossian.[19]

Lucien Hillemacher's *Fingal* is a meritorious work for a twenty-year old composer, well deserving of its prize-winning status. Like *Le dernier Hymne d'Ossian* of Gouvy, the composer's imaginative treatment of the text realizes the possibilities of the *scène lyrique* as a flexible form for the setting of librettos based on Ossian. The directions in the score suggest that Hillemacher envisaged the work as a semi-opera, even though there are only three characters. At the outset of scene 4, for instance, the victorious Fingal appears, surrounded by his generals ("paraît entouré de ses chefs de son armée"), bards, and followers. How this *mise-en-scène* was expected be realized is unclear, but the composer may have wanted a modicum of naturalism to color the work, even without a chorus.[20]

The composition is brilliantly conceived in terms of the characters and their corresponding voices (soprano, tenor, baritone), and is testing in terms of range: the soprano part reaches to a high B, the tenor to a B♭, the baritone to a G. The tempi and rhythms ebb and flow frequently, almost too much so, in parallel with the emotional tension. The melodic lines are underpinned by both stable and shifting harmonies depending on the degree of repose or tension in the text: a quiet C major for Comalha's air in scene 1, an adroit use of a rising chromatic bass and pedal points in the trio of scene 4. Harmonically, the music is at its boldest in the trio of scene 4 and in the urgent, spasmodic appoggiaturas that accompany Comalha's "la force m'abandonne," a succession of intermittent eighth notes and rests on the first and third beats of the bar that capture her increasing frailty.

The timing of the scenes and characters is finely contrived in relation to the presence of the latter onstage: Comalha in the first scene, Hidallan in the second, their duet in the third, and the trio with Fingal in the final scene. If anything, scene 2 is on the short side: 65 bars as against 188 for scene 1, 269 for scene 3, and 260 for scene 4. Presumably, the reason for the brevity of scene 2 is that Hillemacher did not want to assign too much prominence to Hidallan in view of Comalha's and Fingal's love relationship: he is just the pivot, an important one admittedly, on which the drama turns. The late entrance of Fingal allows Hillemacher to reserve the climax of the entire work to scene 4, in which the three characters confess their desires or regrets in a convincing ensemble. Despite the use of effects that would now be regarded as clichés, such as *tremolandos*, running chromatic scales, and shifting angular harmonies over a pedal bass, Hillemacher's *Fingal* succeeds as a dramatic conception. Aesthetically accomplished, it is an entirely original contribution to the development of the *scène lyrique*.

Chapter Eleven

Ossian in Symbolic Conflict

Bernhard Hopffer's *Darthula's Grabesgesang* (1878), Jules Bordier's *Un rêve d'Ossian* (1885), and Paul Umlauft's *Agandecca* (1884)

Otto Bismarck concluded the unification of Germany at Versailles on January 18, 1871.[1] Praise of the Hohenzollern dynasty accompanied the elation felt in Germany at the defeat of France, and no less a composer than Johannes Brahms was caught up in the surge of national feeling with the writing of his *Triumphlied*, op. 55, which he dedicated to Wilhelm I.[2] Bernhard Hopffer (1840–77), as a young composer, was inevitably drawn into writing patriotic works of this kind. The year 1871 was an auspicious one for him: his opera *Frithjof*, written when he was just 21, had its premiere on April 11 in Berlin, receiving ten performances.[3]

At the beginning of 1872, however, Hopffer contracted a lung ailment that forced him to live in spa towns in Switzerland and Italy. He finally settled in Wiesbaden in the autumn of 1876. His brother Emil, who had also studied music and to whom he was very close, joined him there in the spring of 1877.[4] Despite his poor health Hopffer completed another opera, *Sakuntala*, on a text by his brother who, also ailing, passed away in July of that same year.[5] Bernhard, deeply upset by Emil's death, sought physical and spiritual relief in the curative spa, the former Jagdschloss (Hunting Lodge) Niederwald, at Rüdesheim, where, after a short illness, he died on August 20, 1877.[6] Among his papers were the scores of *Sakuntala*, the comic operas *Der lustige Capitän* and *Der Student von Prag* (his first composition), lieder, cantatas, and other works that remain unperformed.[7]

Hopffer seems to have composed his cantata *Darthula's Grabesgesang*, op. 23, during his time in Rüdesheim; Robert Lienau published the work posthumously, in 1878. It is dedicated to Louis Ehlert.[8] The story of Darthula made an early impact in German-speaking lands: Michael Denis (1729–1800), a Jesuit priest in Vienna, had produced the first complete translation of the Ossian poems in 1768–69.[9] "Darthula" was greatly admired by Friedrich Schiller, who believed the poem to be one of the most beautiful in Ossian.[10] About 1769 or 1770, Johann Gottfried Herder drew on Denis's version to compose his poem on Darthula's fate as a gift for his future wife, Caroline Flachsland. Later composers sometimes entitled these verses "Das Mädchen von Kola" (from the name of Colla, Darthula's father):

Darthula's Grabesgesang
Aus Ossian

Mädchen von Kola, du schläfst!
Um dich schweigen die blauen Ströme Selma's![11]
Sie trauren um dich, den letzten Zweig
Von Thrutils Stamm!
Wenn erstehst du wieder in deiner Schöne?
Schönste der Mädchen in Erin!
Du schläfst im Grabe langen Schlaf,
Dein Morgenroth ist ferne!
Nimmer, o nimmer kommet mehr die Sonne
Weckend an deine Ruhestätte: "wach auf!
Wach auf, Darthula!
Frühling ist draussen,
Die Lüfte säuseln
Auf grünen Hügeln, holdseliges Mädchen
Weben die Blumen! im Hain wallt spriessendes Laub!"
Auf immer, auf immer, so weiche denn, Sonne,
Dem Mädchen von Kola, sie schläft.
Nie ersteht sie wieder in ihrer Schöne!
Nie siehst du sie lieblich wandeln mehr.[12]

Bernhard Hopffer's *Darthula's Grabesgesang*

Hopffer's setting is scored for double woodwinds and horns, timpani, harp, and strings, for first and second sopranos and first and second altos, and for soprano solo. The central tonality of the work is F-sharp minor. The piece begins *pianissimo* with a three-bar phrase in a slow tempo ($\frac{2}{2}$ *adagio*). This phrase is imitated at various levels for some seventeen bars until the chorus, prompted by a horn call, enters singing softly, *divisi* in three parts: "Mädchen von Kola, du schläfst" and imitatively in canon at the second, at "Um dich schweigen die blauen Ströme Selma's!"

The voices then take up the text in homophony for "Sie trauren um dich," coming to rest on the dominant C-sharp at "den letzten Zweig / Von Thrutil's Stamm!" At this point, the strings and harp initiate a triplet rhythm that, after six bars, enters

Example 11.1. Bernhard Hopffer, *Darthula's Grabesgesang*, chorus: "Mädchen von Kola, du schläfst!" bars 17–25

a *più animato* section with regular eighth notes and a descending bass line for "Wann erstehst du wieder in deiner Schöne?/ Schönste der Mädchen in Erin!" At "Du schläfst" there occurs a notable discord between the two sets of voices: F♯/D in the sopranos, B♭/G in the altos. The discord turns into a diminished seventh for "im Grabe langen Schlaf," and sidles through G major, with harp commentary, back to F-sharp minor for the phrase "Dein Morgenroth ist ferne!" At this the triplet rhythm returns for a short four bars. Then, unaccompanied, the voices reverse the opening dominant-tonic incipit for "Nimmer, o nimmer kommet mehr die Sonne," and at "weckend an deine Ruhestätte!" a loud interjection of an F-sharp minor chord in the woodwinds prefaces a vocal cadence in the home key.

Example 11.2. Hopffer, *Darthula's Grabesgesang*, chorus: "Du schläfst im Grabe langen Schlaf," bars 49–57

But now a new section begins, with a change of key and time signature to D major and $^6_8$. This *allegretto* section introduces the soprano soloist's "Wach auf!" in rippling string figuration, harp arpeggios, and the initial three-bar phrase in the bassoon. Dutifully, the voices repeat, "Wach auf, Darthula!" The subdominant G major provides the soprano solo with a high G at "Frühling ist draussen" (Spring is out there). The tonality switches to E minor, then B minor. Four more bars of a rising bass, from C♯ to G♯, prefaces a $^2_4$ change (for four bars), with an assertive chord on the dominant A, the woodwinds recalling the original three-bar phrase, the harp contributing another arpeggio.

A new musical idea then surfaces for the green landscape conjured by Herder, with trills in the first violins (later, in the flutes and oboes) and triplet reminiscences

Example 11.3. Hopffer, *Darthula's Grabesgesang*, solo, chorus: "…auf grünen Hügeln, holdseliges Mädchen," bars 102–16

Table 11.1. Hopffer, *Darthula's Grabesgesang*: structure

Bars	Key signature	Time signature	Marking	Solo/chor	Orchestra
1–17	F♯ minor	2/2	adagio	n/a	bassoons, lower str, harp, timp.
18–40				chor: "Mädchen von Kola, du schläfst!"	ww, str.
41–68			più animato	chor: "Wann erstehst du wieder . . ."	ww, harp, str
69–123	D major	6/8 2/4	allegretto	solo/chor: "Wach auf, Darthula!"	ww, harp, str, timp
124–end	F♯ minor	2/2	tempo primo	chor: "Auf immer . . ."	full orch

of the original phrase in the cellos. The voices repeat their appeal to awake as the eighth-note figuration and timpani rolls subside, returning via the horn call to the opening F-sharp minor, but with the harmony of a minor ninth, the top G of the sopranos against the F♯ bass. At "auf immer, so weiche denn, Sonne" the sopranos and altos descend in thirds to "dem Mädchen von Kola, sie schläft." The soft thirds are repeated in the woodwinds, *dolce*, for the voices, again singing in thirds that she will never arise again in her beauty.

The final bars rely on the rising bass line from tonic to dominant for "Nie siehst du sie lieblich wandeln mehr," and for the appended "Nie mehr!" the voices repeat their cadence to a brief recollection, in the violins, of the original three-bar phrase. As the voices fade, the first violins, climbing unaccompanied from a low C♯ for two octaves via an F-sharp minor to a high C♯–A–F♯, are imitated by the hushed entry of the flute with a falling triad to F♯ and *pianissimo* chords in the full orchestra and harp. And here these closing chords form an effective and gentle conclusion to Herder's poem.

The work exudes the spirit of Brahms and his orchestral writing. A relatively short setting, it displays Hopffer's competence in shaping melodious if somewhat unadventurous lines. The harmony is stable and "correct," using devices such as diminished sevenths and enharmonic changes to create tension and variety within a limited circle of keys. But there are felicitous touches: for instance, the way in which the original three-bar phrase provides a unifying element. The cantata shows a composer working within well-defined stylistic limits; captivated by national enthusiasm at the time of German unification, he was absorbed into the stream of musical sensibility, one in which ideology became a major factor in building a musical style. But the illness he developed shortly after the premiere of his opera *Frithjof* in 1871, may have been brought on, to some extent, by sensitivity to the criticism his work received.

How he came to Herder's poem is uncertain, and it is unclear whether he composed it before or after the death of his brother. The mood of the piece, with its images of the stricken Darthula, the call to awaken, the regeneration of nature in spring, may reflect personal sorrow at his plight, or possibly a lament for his brother but with hope of a brighter tomorrow. He may well have known settings of the poem for voice and piano by contemporaries, especially that in F-sharp minor, the same key as his own setting, by Wilhelm Hill, in his "Das Mädchen von Kola," op. 13, published in 1867.[13] It is probable that he knew the settings by Brahms (1861, published 1872) and by Carl Reinthaler (1865). Nevertheless, Hopffer devised his own means of transmediating the Herder poem in a relatively short but effective setting.

Jules-Auguste Bordier's *Un rêve d'Ossian* (1885)

From an affluent background like that of Hopffer, in his case a family of bankers, Jules-Auguste Bordier (1846–96) was born and died in Angers. There, he was co-founder of the Association artistique d'Angers and conductor of its concerts between

1877 and 1893. Honorary presidents of the association included Gounod, Massenet, and Saint-Saëns, who dedicated to Bordier the cadenza he devised for Mozart's Piano Concerto in E-flat (K449).[14] Lack of municipal support in 1893 caused Bordier to leave for Paris for a few months, and on his return he reconstituted the association as the Société des concerts populaires d'Angers, which has led to the present-day Orchestre National des Pays de la Loire.[15] As a composer, Bordier wrote songs, instrumental music, and several operas: one of these last, *Nadia*, a one-act *opéra-comique*, was performed at the Opéra-Populaire in Paris on May 25, 1887, and again at Le Monnaie in Brussels on January 18, 1889.

Bordier published his *Un rêve d'Ossian* in 1885.[16] It was written at a difficult time economically for France, during a worldwide depression caused by the collapse of the Vienna Stock Market in May 1873. The reparations France was obliged to pay to Germany following its defeat in the Franco-Prussian War meant that the country was already reeling financially. The Union Générale bank failed at the same time as the Paris Bourse, in 1882, and French national output declined for a decade between 1882 and 1892. The depression lasted longer in France and was more severe than in other European countries. It was against this gloomy backdrop that musicians such as Bordier had to work, and his championing of the Association artistique must be seen as a heroic effort at a time of great national difficulty.

The work is dedicated to A. Guillot de Sainbris.[17] The dedication is not without significance, for Sainbris was a noted singing teacher, and Bordier may well have consulted him on technical points. The overall conception is a work for chorus with orchestral accompaniment. The text, by the writer, librettist, and composer Henry Moreau (1864–1936), is in alternate rhyming ten- and twelve-syllable lines. As noted above, it contains echoes of Christian Pitois's and Baour-Lormian's immensely popular editions of Ossian in France. The title of the composition was probably suggested by the celebrated artwork *Le Songe d'Ossian* (Ossian's Dream) that Jean-Auguste-Dominique Ingres painted in 1811 for a commission from Napoleon, a painting to be installed in the ceiling of the emperor's bedroom at the Palais Quirinal.[18]

As a *scène lyrique*, *Un rêve d'Ossian* includes verbal and visual components, with short speaking parts at the beginning and the end, and stage directions, as well as a normal-sized orchestra with two harps and the addition of a harmonium. The opening *andante*, in F minor and common time, has a simple string motif that begins in the basses, then is taken up by the lower strings and finally the violins. The personage of Ossian is envisaged, dreaming, on an otherwise deserted heath. After eight bars the harps execute arpeggios as a preface to the violins' more agitated sixteenth notes. As this passage stills, Ossian recites, "Ombre des temps passés, pourquoi venir encore / De mes yeux fatigués éloigner le sommeil? Pourquoi faire vibrer mon bouclier sonore? Laissez moi m'endormir et rêver du soleil?" (Shade of the past, why do you come again and remove the sleep from my tired eyes? Why vibrate my resounding shield? Let me sleep and dream of the sun). The key and time change to F major and $\frac{6}{8}$ as the shades surround Ossian for an *andantino*, tinted by a soft melody from the horns. Scenes of the past are revived: Fingal stands alone, pensive, on the heath.

Figure 11.1. Jean-Auguste-Dominique Ingres (1780–1867), *Le songe d'Ossian* (The dream of Ossian). Pencil, black and white chalk on paper, 1811. The National Galleries of Scotland, Edinburgh, D 5369. Reproduced with permission.

Table 11.2. Bordier, *Un Rêve d'Ossian*: structure

Section	Bars	Key signature	Time signature	Marking	Orchestra
Intro	1–18	F minor	4/4	andante	str, brass, harps
(spoken) "Ombre des temps passés"	19–29	F minor	4/4		lower str.
	30–56	F major	3/4	andantino	horns, str harps
(Les Guerriers) "Quel vent soufflé sur la colline?"	57–78	D minor	4/4	andante	str
"Tu chantes"	79–82	G minor	4/4	a tempo	fl, cl, str, harp
""Tu chantes et ta lyre a résonné dans l'ombre"	82–89	G major	4/4		str, harp
(Fingal) "Trois fois le cri des morts"	90–123	D minor	2/4	energico–più moderato	tutti
(Les ombres) "Tourne les yeux vers la colline"	124–40	C major	6/8	largo	str harm.
(Fingal) "Debout! du sommeil secouez les voiles!"	141–55	F minor	2/4	energico	cl, horn
(Les ombres) "Venez, esprits des morts . . . " "Glissez vers nous, sous le regard de Dieu!"	156–202	B♭	2/4	andante	str. (mute) harp, hns, cymbals
(Les Guerriers) "O nuit d'horreur! O nuit sanglante!"	203–30	D minor	3/4	maestoso	tutti
(Les femmes et les enfants dans Tura): "Le feu! Le feu! C'est le feu!"	231–50	B minor	2/4	maestoso	tutti

(Fingal): "Quels sanglots, quells appels funèbres"	251–59	B minor	$\frac{4}{4}$	allegro	str.
"Écroulez-vous, murs glorieux"	260–74	G major	$\frac{4}{4}$	più moderato	str.
	275–83	C♯ minor	$\frac{3}{4}$	maestoso	tutti
(Double chorus): Les femmes et les enfants dans Tura; "Le feu!" Les Guerriers: "O nuit d'horreur!"	284–304	C♯ minor	$\frac{3}{2}$	maestoso	tutti, brass, vns
	305–10	C♯ minor	$\frac{3}{2}$		tpts, str.
	311–18	B♭	$\frac{3}{4}$	andantino	harm, str (pizz)
(all voices except the children): "Lumières de Morven"	319–45	F major	$\frac{3}{4}$	andantino	hns, str
(Ossian, spoken) "Versez encor . . ."	346–49	[F minor]	$\frac{3}{4}$		basses
(Chor): "Éveille toi ma bien aimée, voici le jour"	350–57	F major	$\frac{3}{4}-\frac{4}{4}$ (353)		hns, str, cellos, harps

After twenty-three bars, the time changes back to 4/4 as from the printed score we discern warriors appearing in the distance, troubled by omens, at which point the tonality shifts to D minor. The harps and strings announce the first chorus of warriors in that key. Just as Hopffer divided his female chorus into first and second sopranos and altos, so Bordier divides his tenors and basses into firsts and seconds. Accompanied by a D-minor *ostinato* in the orchestra, they begin in a slightly increased tempo, *mezza voce*: "Quel vent souffle sur la colline?" (What wind blows on the hill?), the basses at the same time enunciating their text with closed lips (*bouche fermée*). This effect may well have been one on which Bordier consulted Sainbris. This phrase, "Ou la biche frissonne et l'arbre s'incline" (The deer shivers and the tree bends), is followed by "Quel présage a troublé les cieux? O Barde, que ta voix est sombre!" (What omen troubles the heavens? Bard, your voice is gloomy). At this the tonality moves to G minor, but only for four bars, then arrives at a G-major cadence: "Tu chantes et ta lyre a résonné dans l'ombre, et des pleurs ont obscurci tes yeux" (You sing and your lyre resounds in the darkness, tears have obscured your eyes).[19]

An energetic, speedier orchestral *tutti* in 2/4, still in the key of D minor, allows Fingal to declaim, "Trois fois le cri des morts a frappé mon oreille" (Three times the cry of the dead has hit my ear), and at this, while the spirits of dead warriors approach the hero, the sopranos (first and second) and altos, twelve voices in all, sing, in a slower *largo* (6/8) in C major, "Turn your eyes to the valley, to your beloved town, that resounds with joyful songs that, in the night, were funeral cries, down there, to tear away the darkness. The flame gushed towards the heavens." As the dominant C major melts into F minor, Fingal cries, "Debout! La ville est en feu!" (Get up! The city is on fire!). The female voices then turn the tonality to B-flat over a pedal F in the horns, the sound of cymbals combining with the harp, while the spirits recede: "Glissez vers nous, venez au séjour des étoiles, glissez sous le regard de Dieu!" (Glide toward us, come to an abode in the stars, slide under the gaze of God!). The mention of God here is rare, and presumably an interpolation by Moreau, for Ossian's world is notoriously godless.[20] The hushed sound of cymbals and harp draw this extended section of forty-seven bars to a close with the plea, enunciated *pianissimo*, "Glissez."

A new 3/4 passage in D minor has the harps introduce the male chorus of warriors with plangent, arpeggio chords of D minor, A minor, B-flat major, and F major that amount to a ground bass: "O nuit d'horreur! O nuit sanglante!" (Oh night of horror! night of blood!). The sequence of chords is repeated shortly afterward. The earth, the voices sing, is full of fear at these omens. This choral peroration surely recalls the terrible events of the Paris Commune some dozen years before, the *semaine sanglante* of May 21–28, 1871, when upwards of 5,000 communards were killed in a rising against the government.[21] Eighteen thousand Parisians were killed, and 25,000 imprisoned, while thousands were executed later. This notorious event followed the defeat of France in the war with Prussia, and ended the Second Empire of Napoleon III (1852–70).

Example 11.4. Jules-August Bordier, *Un rêve d'Ossian*, chorus: "Quel vent souffle sur la colline?" bars 62–68

As a twenty-five-year-old living in Angers, Bordier must have been appalled at the chaos in Paris at that time, and remembered the events in these anguished choral declamations. With the despair of the "cri de mort" at night, the orchestra forces the harmony away from its D-minor roots to a series of dominant chords of B minor, again in $\frac{3}{4}$, and with an agitated sequence of discords, contrived by pitting a chromatically rising bass against descending octaves, the chorus of female and children's voices (in Tura) crying out in a series of triplet repeated notes, "Le feu, c'est le feu! Sous nos pieds bouillonne / Un fleuve de feu partout répandu, La flamme s'élance et nous environne! Fingal! où donc est-tu?" (The fire boils under our feet, a flood of fire is everywhere, flames surround us! Fingal, where are you?) Fingal is seen as the savior from the waves of flame boiling around their feet.[22]

These twenty bars are succeeded by an *allegro* section in B minor in which Fingal continues the horrendous vision: "What sobs and funereal cries fly through the air of dread." Coursing through the tonalities of B minor, G-flat, and its relative minor, eventually, at "Et quels guerriers vivaient dans ces palais dé-truits" (And what warriors have lived in these ruined palaces), the passage reaches a *maestoso* in C-sharp minor that reiterates the arpeggio chords and leads to a double chorus in $\frac{3}{2}$ of sopranos, altos, tenors, basses, and children, who repeat the phrases "Le feu!," "O nuit d'horreur!," and "O nuit sanglante!" with calls to Fingal, the entire time accompanied by running thirty-second-note scales in the violins. This passage subsides into a short orchestral interlude in $\frac{3}{4}$, *andantino*, in B-flat major as before, but *pianissimo*. This slows to introduce the final chorus for all the voices except those of the children, with horns providing the main melodic accompaniment: "Lumières de Morven, O rayon plus doux que les nuits d'été" (Heroes of Morven, O sweetest beam of summer nights). Tenors and basses, in F minor, declare softly, "Et vous glissez déjà dans la brise embaumée" (and you glide already in the balmy breeze). Then, a tempo, "Eveille toi, ma bien aimée, voici le jour" (Awake, my beloved, here is the day) as clarinet and flute climb up a chord of F major. At this Ossian speaks, as in the beginning, "Versez, versez encore votre sainte lumière" (Pour, again, your sacred light), accompanied by slow descending octaves F–E♭–D♭–A♭ to a six-four chord,

Example 11.5. Bordier, *Un rêve d'Ossian*, chorus: "Le feu! O nuit d'horreur!" bars 284–85

Example 11.6. Bordier, *Un rêve d'Ossian*, chorus: "Eveille toi, ma bien aimée, voici le jour," bars 350–57

at which the chorus repeats, "Awake, my beloved, here is the day," the sound dying away on an F-major chord.

This ending recalls that of "Darthula," in which the poet apostrophizes the blossoms of spring outside as a call to awaken from deadly slumber. All of this is a trope for France's woes since the end of the Second Empire. By combining a vision of the Paris Commune's *semaine sanglante* with the promise of a new beginning ("voici le jour"), Bordier was injecting a ray of hope into a dark period in French history. To that extent the work has both artistic merit and historical significance; its transmediation is not merely convergent with the text but also symbolic, in that it expresses in music feelings about the past and the future of France that are not always explicit in Moreau's graphic scenario.

Paul Umlauft's *Agandecca* (1892)

The story of Agandecca comes originally from a lay describing Fingal's visit to Lochlin. In Macpherson's version (Book III of the epic poem *Fingal*), Starno, king of Lochlin, sends a messenger to Fingal offering his daughter, Agandecca, as a bride, and Fingal and his men set off for Starno's kingdom. This episode from *Fingal* might conceivably have appealed to more composers, for the narrative is sufficiently dramatic: the dastardly plot to kill the hero, the comely maiden (in love with the hero) who discovers the plan, her father's wrath, her murder, and the hero's retribution. But apart from the incidental music by Kozlowski for Ozerov's 1805 play and the feeble opera by Carlo Saccenti in 1817, the tale has appealed more to writers of tragedy than of opera, especially in Italy, where Agandecca was the most popular subject after 1830.[23]

It was a different situation in German-speaking lands, where male choral societies were a growing phenomenon. With varying sobriquets these groups formed their identities in names such as "Liederkranz," "Germania," even "Ossian." The influence of such singing groups on neighboring countries like The Netherlands, and large-scale German emigration that created similar groups in North America and Australia, made for a significant transnational development.[24] The growth of patriotic sentiment in Germany and the unification of 1871 spurred the founding of such groups into the 1870s and 1880s. From the beginning the male choral repertoire celebrated national sentiment, nature, manly pursuits such as hunting, ancient drinking songs, and the like. By the early 1880s, when *Agandecca* was completed, Umlauft had a number of experienced vocal groups at hand.

It is no surprise, then, that the story of Agandecca could lend itself to a score by a German composer in which male-voice harmony played a major role. Paul Umlauft (1853–1934), whose family was involved in the famous Meissen porcelain factory, studied philosophy and philology at the University of Leipzig and was a pupil of

Carl Reinecke at the conservatoire. From 1879 to 1883 he received a stipend at the Mozart-Stiftung in Frankfurt, an honor accorded to other composers such as Max Bruch, Engelbert Humperdinck, and Arnold Krug. Having composed songs, choruses, and chamber works, and his cantata *Agandecca*, Umlauft later submitted an opera, *Evanthia*, which in 1893 won a prize in the competition sponsored by Duke Ernst II of Saxe-Coburg-Gotha.[25] In *Agandecca* Umlauft seized the possibilities for a cantata on the tale by incorporating a male voice chorus.[26] Why he chose Agandecca is unclear, but the poems of Ossian were by that time well known in Germany. Furthermore, his teacher, Reinecke, had composed a work for male chorus based on the poems, *Fingal und Ossian*, in 1876.[27]

In his conception of *Agandecca* Umlauft combines a number of themes: the romantic love between Fingal and the heroine; celebration of a warrior ethos; unforgivable treachery by a host; death of a maiden for subverting her father's will; and the remorse of the hero for being unable to rescue his beloved. Two themes get special attention: the passion of Fingal for Agandecca, and the warrior ethos. The latter receives weighty treatment because Germany was in the 1870s and 1880s suffering from large-scale emigration; as a sign of active musicality and patriotic spirit, maintaining the male voice choirs was becoming a serious cultural necessity. It is significant that the composer dedicated the work to a choir in Frankfurt, where he served his apprenticeship at the Mozart-Stiftung.

Umlauft's harnessing of a male chorus brings a suitably heroic warrior ethos to life as background to the solo parts of Starno, king of Lochlin (bass or baritone); Agandecca, his daughter (soprano); Fingal, chieftain of Morven (tenor); Snivan, Starno's bard (tenor); Ullin, Fingal's bard (baritone or mezzo-soprano); and a chorus of bards and warriors. The action takes place in the hall of Starno's castle (parts 1 and 3), and in the meadow outside (part 2). The orchestra is a moderately large one: double woodwinds; two horns in E-flat and two in B-flat (high); two trumpets in E-flat; alto, tenor, and bass trombones; timpani; and strings. The choral parts are divided among first and second tenor and first and second bass.[28]

The work opens, *maestoso*, with eighteen bars in common time and E-flat, a tonality by this time very common in German settings of Ossian. The choral voices then enter with "Erhebet die Becher, das Fest der Schalen zu feiern in tönender Halle!" (Raise the cups to celebrate the feast of shells in the resounding hall), a phrase that conjures up the legacy of drinking songs (apart from the reference to shells, which was a Celtic custom).[29] Reaching the dominant of B-flat, the warriors instruct the bards to conjure the heroic song of jubilation from the strings (of their harps). Moving to a C-minor harmony, they ask the bards to tell of kings famed in their country, of heroes long gone. As the harmony switches to A-flat major, the voices exclaim, "Youths arise, begin the dance, show us the play of weapons, and with the sound of swords and heroic songs, let us enjoy the foaming draught of mead!"

Example 11.7. Paul Umlauft, *Agandecca*, chorus: "Jünglinge auf, beginnet den Tanz," bars 78–95

A sudden change to C-sharp minor and a slower tempo marks a recitative by Starno, commanding them to cease their singing. Responding in B minor, the warriors proclaim, "Let us board the dark ships, sail on the wings of the wind to conquer the youth of Morven!" In a gentler tone, Starno tells them that he has offered his daughter Agandecca to Fingal for his wife. After three days of feasting, and three days hunting deer in the woods, he declares that Fingal, exhausted from tracking the wild boar, will fall by his, Starno's, hand in the darkness of the woods. His bards, with a hearty E major in $\frac{3}{4}$, sing a song of greeting for the approaching Fingal in an extended chorus of ninety-six bars: "Hail Fingal, the first of men, breaker of shields! Men tremble at the sound of his steel!"

Starno goes on to welcome Fingal, who replies in a majestic A major arioso, thanking him and saying how pleased he was to accept the invitation. Starno's greeting describes the glorious deeds of Fingal, and he invites his bard, Snivan, to sing of these. The bard complies, and with harp arpeggios in E minor, A minor, and D minor he evokes the heroic world of Fingal and Loda's ghost.[30] Fingal in turn asks Ullin, his bard, to celebrate the beauty of Agandecca by striking the strings of his harp: "Du aber, Ullin, mein Barde" (or, if sung by a female, "mein Knabe"), "auf, greife in die Saiten, Agandecca zu feiern, die Schönste der Mädchen." Ullin then launches into an *andantino* in common time, comparing her beauty to a beam of moonlight in the silence of night. The male chorus takes up this theme until Agandecca herself appears to sing, in A-major, how the wondrous singing in the hall caught her ear. The scene then ends (in F major) with another chorus addressing both Fingal and Agandecca.

Scene 2 makes for a dramatic contrast in its vocal resources, as the action is mostly confined to the nocturnal meeting of Fingal and Agandecca during which she warns him of her father's treachery. At the outset Fingal is in the meadow, alone, musing. His $\frac{3}{4}$ *andante* in E major describes the calmness and beauty of the night and quotes Herder's poem, "O komm, Agandecca, Frühling ist draussen, holdseliges Mädchen, die Lüfte säuseln, auf grünen Hügeln weben die Blumen, im Hain wallt spriessendes Laub," adding, to the accompaniment of gently swaying triplets in the orchestra, "Do you not hear the warbling nightingale; love stirs her song in the blossoming thickets!"[31] Agandecca and Fingal sing a passionate duet that culminates in a kiss, and Fingal's pledge in D-flat major, "Süssestes Weib, wonnigste Maid, dir schwör' ich Treue in Ewigkeit!," is met with a similar promise of eternal love by Agandecca. Eventually she confides that her father is plotting to kill him. In a passage in duple time marked "fiery and passionate," she asks Fingal to remember her when he returns home. The initial C-major triplets travel through keys, in true Wagnerian style, for some eighty-eight bars, to a dominant of F minor. Fingal, shocked and angered, sounds his shield and calls up his men, while Agandecca bids him farewell. "Wir hören tönen den rasselnden Schild," the chorus sings in an agitated F-sharp minor, and Fingal commands them to prepare for battle. "We will follow thee, Fingal," a lively section in $\frac{3}{4}$ surges to a majestic B major that lasts for eighty-four bars, "Hail to our chieftain, the king of Morven."

Example 11.8. Umlauft, *Agandecca*, aria: "Dich preise mein Lied," bars 699–704

Ullin: Dich prei-se mein Lied, A-gan-dec-ca, hold-se-li-ges Mäd - chen, de-ren Schön - heit strahlt gleich dem Mond in der schwei-gen-den Nacht!

Scene 3 opens with preparations for the hunt; "Trarah, wir ziehen hinaus!" exclaims the chorus in a confident E major. But an anguished Agandecca then sings a gentle *larghetto* in B major praising Fingal's beauty and speech; her anxiety continues, but the memory of Fingal brings back tender feelings in a warm A-flat melody. The mood changes with an *allegro vivace* as she contemplates signs in nature: evening shadows on the meadow, gray figures shrouded in mist, thunder and lightning. Spirit of our ancestors, she asks, have you come from your seat in the clouds to proclaim disaster for me? Her fears are assuaged when Snivan, her father's bard, tells her that Fingal and his men have routed the men of Lochlin, and in a short G-flat section she gives thanks to the spirits of the ancestors that have protected Fingal. Now, warns Snivan, she should flee her father's wrath because he is intent on revenge. Starno enters, demanding, where is the traitor so that I can punish her?

The final part of scene 3 imparts Agandecca's call on her brother and Fingal to rescue her, and her pledge of faithfulness to the latter in a short aria that recalls their D-flat duet in scene 2. As the orchestra launches into an *allegro assai*, Starno stabs her to death. Fingal takes revenge, however, and in the ensuing duel kills Starno. His remorse over Agandecca's death leads to his lament over her body. Apostrophizing,

Example 11.9. Umlauft, *Agandecca*, duet, scene 2: "Süssestes Weib, wonigstes Maid," bars 246–53

he repeats Herder's poem along with the chorus, extending it with "O Agandecca, der Sturm ist hin, die Sonne strahlt ... du, Licht meiner Seele, du liegst und schlummerst trüb' in der Kluft!" (the storm is over, the sun is shining, thou, light of my soul, you slumber, laid in the earth). The voices echo this in their final comment, "Strahlen der Sonne trugen die Seele der lieblichen Jungfrau zu Wolken empor" (Sunbeams, carry the soul of the maiden to the heavens) in a prolonged E-major conclusion.

Reviews of Umlauft's cantata at the time were generally favorable. The *Neue Zeitschrift für Musik* noted that the work had a number of well-received performances shortly after it was published.[32] The critic for the *Musikalisches Wochenblatt*, citing a performance in Chemnitz, pointed to influence from Mendelssohn, Schumann, and Wagner. Umlauft was at his best, the critic felt, in matters of emotional impact, as in the love duet in scene 2. The monumental song of farewell at the end was an extravagant outpouring of emotion; experienced at writing for choral forces, Umlauft

Example 11.10. Umlauft, *Agandecca*, aria, scene 3: "Du kamst, O Fingal, schön unter den Schönen der Haide," bars 82–95

offered worthy material, if not always on a similarly high level.[33] The correspondent for *The Musical Times* noted of *Evanthia* that it showed "the careful student of Wagner, who uses the Leitmotive and the 'endless melody' with great success, his themes are generally noble, expressive, and interesting, and the whole is the work of a musician of unquestionable talent, high ideals and refined taste."[34]

This assessment could apply to *Agandecca*, with some reservations. The enharmonic shifts and kaleidoscopic orchestration certainly suggest Wagner as the main influence on the overall style; the score is likewise replete with dominant ninths and extensions of chromatic harmony. The transmediation of *Agandecca* is, in effect, beholden in style to an identifiable master. There are certainly fine moments of melodic invention in the ariettas of the heroine and her duet with Fingal in scene 2. The choral writing, if foursquare and predominantly homophonic, shows the voices to advantage. The orchestration is on the heavy side, especially with the trumpets and trombones: a lighter touch might have made for a subtler aesthetic balance in relation to the vocal parts. Nevertheless, as a work of dramatic power and lyric sensibility, Umlauft's *Agandecca* deserves recognition of its virtues.

Chapter Twelve

The Musical Stages of "Darthula"

From Thomas Linley the Younger (ca. 1776) to Arnold Schoenberg (1903) and Armin Knab (1906)

The prose poem "Dar-thula" was first published as one of the companion pieces to the epic poem *Fingal* (1762).[1] Among the longer items in the volume, it combines features of the extended epic with those of the shorter lyrical and dramatic fragments. The poem, which opens with Ossian's famous address to the moon ("Daughter of heaven, fair art thou"), relates the love and death of Darthula, daughter of the chieftain Colla. She falls in love with the youth, Nathos, but dies with him and his two brothers in armed struggle with Cairbar, usurper of the throne of Ireland, who was also in love with her. A remarkable feature of the original poem is its interplay of present, past, and future as Ossian, serving as narrator, comments on the fate of Darthula and her beloved Nathos.[2]

Macpherson, who keeps close to traditional Gaelic accounts,[3] commented in his notes that the heroine's name means "a woman with fine eyes" and that Darthula "was the most famous beauty of antiquity." Her counterpart in Irish tradition is Deirdre, who remains alive to lament the death of her brothers, while Darthula, after witnessing her brothers' fate, dies when an arrow pierces her side, and she falls on the body of Nathos. Even when this original narrative was modified (as in Herder's versification of the final scene) or drastically altered for local conventions (as on the Italian stage), the story of the beautiful Darthula drew a response from composers who recognized its universal appeal. Those who set "Dar-thula" over a span of two centuries inevitably faced the problem of having to negotiate between personal understanding of the poem's content and prevailing compositional standards.

In terms of period, the musical settings of "Dar-thula" fall into three main groups. The first, a "pre-Romantic" or early Romantic cluster, runs from a manuscript song by Karl Siegmund von Seckendorff (1774) to Stefano Pavesi's opera *Ardano e Dartula* (1825). Second is a full-fledged Romantic group stretching from Otto Ernst Lindner's *Lied* (1855) to a fragment by the German-American composer Hermann Hans Wetzler (1888). The third group includes late-Romantic and modern works, from an unaccompanied choral setting by the Finnish composer Erkki Melartin (1897) and an unfinished cantata by Arnold Schoenberg (1903) to a short setting for voice and piano by the Austrian composer Friedrich Neumann (ca. 1950).

First Group of Settings (1774–1816)

Settings of "Dar-thula" include the lied by Seckendorff, a cantata by Thomas Linley the Younger (ca. 1775), a glee for five voices by R. J. S. Stevens (1790), a fragmentary vocal line in manuscript (again of Herder) by the influential Swiss composer Hans Georg Nägeli (ca. 1795), and a curiosity by Carl Ditters von Dittersdorf (1739–99), namely a plagiarized version of Seckendorff's published setting of 1782.[4] Dittersdorf's setting of 1795 is ascribed to him as composer.[5] But Seckendorff's setting can be traced back to a manuscript version of around 1774.[6] Born in 1744, Seckendorff died in 1785, and perhaps Dittersdorf thought he could pass off the setting as his own since the originator was now dead. The musical typography is different, but in all other respects the setting is identical. Understandably, there is no mention of Seckendorff in Dittersdorf's autobiography.[7] Plagiarism, certainly, was not uncommon at the time; the Johann Friedrich Christmann appropriation (1785) of Johan Rudolf Zumsteeg's setting of "Ossians Sonnengesang" (1782) is another example.[8]

Seckendorff's setting, the earliest, is cast in a gently swaying $\frac{3}{8}$ rhythm in the key of E-flat, a tonality later favored by R. J. S. Stevens in his Ossianic glee for five voices, "Some of my heroes are low" (A2T2B).[9] The treatment of the injunction "Wach auf" (Awake!) by Seckendorff moves the tonality to the dominant B-flat, and the melody to the G clef, common time, *andante*, and a three-line stave, with rippling arpeggios in the right hand accompaniment. For the final stanza, he slides the tonality back into E-flat and $\frac{3}{8}$, with a more decorated right-hand part in sixteenth notes, the bass alternating between E♭ and B♭ until the last few bars, marked *pianissimo* to follow the final line of text, "Nie siehst du sie lieblich wandeln mehr" (never more will you see her move in her loveliness). Oddly, he parses the name "Darthula" with the stress on the final syllable (i.e., the first beat of bar 4 in the middle section of $\frac{4}{4}$ time): Darthu-LA. Later in the song, he places the stress on the first syllable: DAR-thula.[10] Reportedly, Goethe may not have thought much of Seckendorff's

Table 12.1. Pre- and early Romantic settings of "Dar-thula"

Title	Composer	Year	Setting	Key signature	Time signature
"Das Mädchen von Kola"	Seckendorff	1774	v [MS]	E♭	$\frac{3}{8}$
"Darthula"	T. Linley Jr	ca. 1775	2 vv, orch	A major–E major– D major–A minor	$\frac{4}{4}$–$\frac{3}{4}$ allegro–affetuoso–adagio
"Darthulas Grabes-Gesang"	Seckendorff	1782	v, kbd	E♭	$\frac{3}{8}$ traurig–sanft–andante– largho sssai
"Some of my heroes are low"	Stevens	1790	alt, 2 ten, 2 bass	E♭	$\frac{4}{4}$ largo–andante–allegro con dignita– $\frac{3}{2}$ largo
"Das Mädchen von Kola"	Dittersdorf	1795	v, kbd	E♭	$\frac{3}{8}$
["Darthulas Grabgesang"]	Nägeli	ca. 1795	v, [kbd] [MS]	E♭	$\frac{3}{8}$
"Ossians Lied nach dem Falle Nathos"	Schubert [Harold]	1815	v. pf	E major	$\frac{4}{4}$ ruhig
"Ardano e Dartula" [opera]	Pavesi [Fidanza]	1825	soli, chor, orch [MS]	n/a	n/a

musical ability, but the setting of "Darthulas Grabes-Gesang" is touchingly simple and dramatically effective.

The glee by R. J. S. Stevens (1757–1837), "Some of my heroes are low," is unusual in having only altos, tenors, and basses to convey a darker sense of mourning.[11] Stevens's setting, adapted from the words proclaimed by Fingal and Ossian as Darthula and her brothers prepare for the final conflict, sets off at a measured *largo* in $\frac{4}{4}$ time, but soon becomes *andante* at "Bid the sorrow rise," then *allegro con dignita* for "Lay by the red terror of your course." Following a short *lento* passage for "Receive the falling chief," the song adopts *allegro* again for "whether he comes from a distant land," up to the final section in $\frac{3}{2}$ time, then *largo e espressivo* for "And oh! Let his countenance be lovely . . ." The setting, late in the century, by the influential Swiss composer and publisher Hans Georg Nägeli (1773–1836), exists only in manuscript, and the keyboard part is missing.

The cantata *Darthula* by Thomas Linley the Younger (1756–78), written for the composer's eldest sister around 1775, was published posthumously in 1824.[12] Accounts of an original performance are lacking, although the composer himself may have participated since he was an orchestral player at Drury Lane between 1773 and 1778. Between 1768 and 1770, Linley had studied in Livorno and Florence with Pietro Nardini (1722–93), pupil of the renowned Giuseppe Tartini and friend of Leopold Mozart. After he returned to England in 1771, he led performances of concertos and oratorios in Bath from 1773 to 1776. His music thus displays not only an Italianate flavor but also the influence of Handel. *Darthula* is the most successful of his six published cantatas, the young composer evidently inspired by the Ossian poem to confident vocal and orchestral writing (perhaps completed with the genial criticism and advice of his father, also a composer).[13]

The work takes the form of four recitatives and three arias, with Ossian himself as narrator. The versification of the arias, without attribution but possibly by the composer, is cast in hexameters. Darthula's first recitative ("Daughter of Heav'n") is followed by her aria ("But why dost thou retire / Why round thee shadows grow?"). Marked *andante* and in the key of E major, it displays the clever use of two French horns to suggest the pairing of lovers and, later, to provide martial coloring for the main *da capo* aria, "My arm shall lift the spear / And ev'ry danger fly / Like night at op'ning day / Before the morning's Eye." Preceded by Ossian's recitative, in which the orchestra strings (*tutti furioso*) conjure up the "roaring of his [Nathos's] mountain streams" in sweeping sixteenth notes, this *maestoso* aria in D major is a tour de force for Darthula, with extensive embellishment on the words "ev'ry," "danger," and, especially, "night," its forty-eight sixteenth notes suggesting the forced dispersal of darkness. The orchestral palette then draws an upward rush of notes from the violins at "a thousand arrows fly" as the lovers perish. A gentle rondeau in A-minor reflects on the fate of Darthula, while the concluding *adagio*, moving to A major, ends on a bare fifth to conjure the idea of emptiness. Linley's cantata is an astonishing work for a young man of twenty-two, his handling of the vocal lines and orchestral texture the sign of an assured and sensitive composer.

Example 12.1. Thomas Linley the Younger, *Darthula*, aria: "My arm shall lift the spear," bars 33–38

Twenty years later, Franz Schubert's "Ossians Lied nach dem Falle Nathos" (D278) is one of a dozen settings of Ossian material made by the composer in the years 1815–16, using a "translation" in the rather pedestrian German of Edmund von Harold.[14] At the time, the eighteen-year-old Schubert was enthused about the poems.[15] An early draft of this setting outlines a conception realized more fully later. The chosen text suggests that it was the demise of Nathos, rather than that of Darthula, that caught Schubert's imagination. The song opens with a simple chordal accompaniment in E-major for "beugt euch aus euren Wolken nieder, ihr Geister meiner Väter, beuget euch!" (bend thou from the clouds, spirits of my fathers!), then veers toward a C-sharp minor cadence at "oder er steig' aus dem tobenden Meer" (or whether he rises from the rolling sea).

As Ossian's vision of the fallen but resurgent chieftain and his weapons takes hold, Schubert intensifies the accompaniment: in particular, through the eighth-note motifs and their inversion that animate the right-hand treble part, and a rising chromatic bass line that finds a dominant pedal for four bars at "und ach, sein Gesicht sei lieblich, dass seine Freunde frohlocken in seiner Gegenwart" (and O, may his countenance be comely, so that his friends may rejoice in his presence). The song closes with a repeat of the first line, the voice and piano sinking to a conclusion, the latter with a *crescendo* and two chords (marked *fp* [*fortepiano*]). While this song of thirty-eight bars is not the most inspired of his Ossian settings, Schubert

Example 12.2. Franz Schubert, "Lied nach dem Falle Nathos," bars 24–29

was careful to convey the central vision of the fallen chieftain, contrasting the stolidity of the opening and final E-major chords with the restless chromaticism of the central section. To that extent the setting is both apt and compelling, and begins to approach the high level of his "Kolma's Klage."[16]

Second Group of Settings (1855–ca. 1890)

The cluster of vocal settings in the second half of the century includes a half dozen for voice with piano, and four for voices unaccompanied or with orchestral accompaniment. The relative hiatus between 1815 and 1850 may be put down, in part, to the results of the Battle of Waterloo and the need for political stability in France and central Europe. Yet the continuing survival of the *ancien regime*, and suppression by those in power such as Metternich in Austria, was no barrier to creative output such as that of Beethoven, Schubert or Mendelssohn.

The half dozen settings of Herder's poem "Darthula's Grabesgesang" on the death of the heroine are lieder with piano accompaniment: by Wilhelm Taubert (1811–91), Carl Grädener (1812–83), Otto Ernst Lindner (1820–67), Constantin Bürgel (1837–1909), Adolf Jensen (1837–1902), and Wilhelm Hill (1838–1902). Together,

Example 12.3. Simon van Milligen, *Darthula*, act 1, trio of brothers

these represent a high point in German-language musical apprehension of Ossian in the mid-nineteenth century. Structurally, within the compass of sixty to eighty measures, almost every setting follows the pattern of the poem. A slow incipit, often with repeated notes, suggests the "sleeping" Darthula. Animation increases from "Wann erstehst du wieder in deiner Schöne?" to "Wach auf, Darthula, Frühling ist draussen!" Lindner, for example, directs *allegro*, and Hill, *bewegter* (moving along), thereafter subsiding for "nie siehst du sie lieblich wandeln mehr," as in Seckendorff's setting. The vocal tessitura is medium or low, either baritone or low female voice, doubtless to convey the mood and character of the poetic address.[17] The tonality of most settings is in a minor key: Lindner (B-flat minor), Bürgel and Taubert (A minor), and Hill (F-sharp minor). Grädener begins with slow D-major eighth notes in the left-hand accompaniment but soon turns the harmony through flat keys and ultimately B major toward, at "den letzten Zweig von Thrutil's Stamm," a decisive E-minor climax.[18]

Table 12.2. Romantic period settings of "Dar-thula"

Title	Composer	Year	Setting	Key	Time signature
"Ossian's Mädchen von Kola"	Lindner	1855	v, pf	B♭ minor	$\frac{4}{4}$ adagio
"Darthulas Grabgesang"	Brahms	1861 [publ. 1872]	chor (2 alt, ten, 2 bass)	G minor–G major–G minor	$\frac{2}{2}$–$\frac{3}{2}$ moderato, ma non troppo—poco animato
"Das Mädchen von Kola"	Bürgel	1865	v (alto or bar), pf	A minor	$\frac{4}{4}$ langsam
"Das Mädchen von Kola"	Reinthaler	1865	chor, orch	D minor	$\frac{3}{4}$ andante—allegro moderato $\frac{4}{4}$ [allegro]—andante sostenuto
"Das Mädchen von Kola"	Hill	1867	v, pf	F♯ minor	$\frac{4}{4}$ andante
"Darthula's Grabgesang"	Taubert	1867	low v, pf	A minor	$\frac{4}{4}$ andante lugubre
"Darthula"	Grädener	1874–79	v (bar/low sop), pf	D major	$\frac{2}{2}$ sehr langsam
"Darthula's Grabgesang"	Jensen	1875–76 [1904]	med v, pf	E minor	$\frac{4}{4}$ andante sostenuto—animato–largo
"Darthula's Grabgesang"	Hopffer	1878	sop. solo, fem chor, orch	F♯ minor	$\frac{2}{2}$–$\frac{6}{8}$ adagio—allegretto
"Dartula"	Leonardi	ca. 1880	v, pf	B minor	$\frac{3}{4}$ [largo]
"Darthulas Grabgesang"	Wetzler	1888	2 sop, alt, 2 hns, hp [fragment]	A minor	$\frac{4}{4}$ moderato

Example 12.4. Adolf Jensen, "Darthulas Grabgesang," bars 44–48

Usually in common time, the tempo of the settings is mainly slow (*adagio* or [*sehr*] *langsam*). Hill prescribes *andante*, and Taubert, *andante lugubre*. Taubert's setting, unlike the others, allows no change of tempo, triplet eighth notes maintaining the rhythmic pulse up to "auf grünen Hugeln . . . weben die Blumen! Im Hain wallt spriessendes Laub" for calming half notes; at this point an elaborate pianism would be superfluous. Jensen, too, in his setting, op. 58, no. 2, uses triplet figuration to elegant effect, especially in his animated middle section where the vocal line seems Schumann-like for the phrase "holdseliges Mädchen." Jensen, after all, has been seen as the bridge between Schumann and Hugo Wolf.[19]

Finally, some special effects can be noted: Lindner's use of *tremolando* in the right-hand part at "Frühling ist draussen"; agitated triplet eighth notes by Bürgel and Hill at the same critical point; and Taubert's play of G♯ in the treble triplets against G♮ in the slowly sinking bass line. The settings by Bürgel and Hill pay detailed attention to the course of the text, even when, as with Hill, the complex rhythm of the accompaniment threatens to steal the show. Skillfully, both composers bring the vocal part to a close on the dominant, as if the whole import of the poem was a lack of finality.

Arresting, as a rare Ossianic work of this period by an Italian composer, "Dartula" is a setting for soprano or tenor and piano from about 1880 by the Italian

Example 12.5a. Constantin Bürgel, "Das Mädchen von Kola," bars 39–42

Example 12.5b. Wilhelm Hill, "Das Mädchen von Kola," bars 33–35

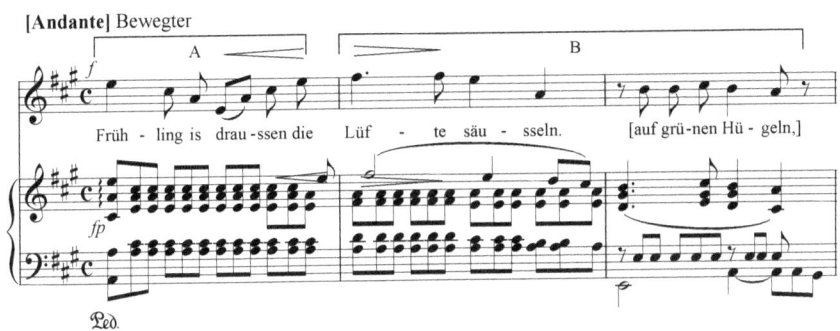

composer Antonio Leonardi (1852–90).[20] Inscribed to the Russian princess Nadine Shakhovskoi Helbig (1847–1922), who had studied piano with Clara Schumann and was a friend of Liszt, it was probably composed for a musical soirée when the princess and her archaeologist husband, Wolfgang Helbig, were living at the Villa Lante, Rome, in the 1880s.[21] The manuscript setting in the form of a *romanza* for soprano or tenor is apparently to verses by the composer himself: "Come fantasmi nella fredda notte / Stavan le quercie. Della luna ai vai / Lampeggiava uno scudo, e il forte braccio / Del giovine guerriero" (Like phantoms in the chilly night stood the oak trees; in the moonlight there flashed a shield and the strong arm of the young warrior).[22] Beginning without tempo direction, in B minor and $\frac{3}{4}$ throughout, dominated by its obsessive rhythm, the piece progresses through a succession of keys that include the remote D-flat, only to break off on a diminished-fifth chord at "Dartula, oh quanto io t'amo." The final page is untraced.

Example 12.6. Antonio Leonardi, "Dartula," bars 7–14

Some composers employ larger forces: Carl Reinthaler (1822–96), Bernhard Hopffer, Hermann Wetzler (1870–1943), and Brahms, whose setting of "Darthulas Grabesgesang" followed his earlier "Gesang aus Fingal" (1862).[23] Reinthaler's setting for "Das Mädchen von Kola" (1865) is subtitled "Elegie für Chor und Orchester nach Ossians 'Darthula' . . . Op. 16." This extended piece of some 368 measures is cast in D minor and $\frac{3}{4}$ with a *dolce* section at "wann erstehst du wieder in deiner Schöne?" while rippling eighth notes in the orchestra accompany the mixed chorus. Somewhat conventional, it is less impressive than Hopffer's use of similar forces in his "Darthula's Grabesgesang."[24] The concurrent setting by Hermann Wetzler, begun under the influence of Brahms's opus 17, is an incomplete sketch of just twenty-six bars, in A minor and $\frac{4}{4}$, marked *Moderato*.[25]

Two points may be made about the Brahms setting of "Darthulas Grabesgesang." In its six-part choral texture (SAATBB), with higher and lower voices responding antiphonally, the piece has been likened stylistically to a motet of the sixteenth century, although it has a contrasting central section cast in a lied-like manner. The opening melody in G minor and duple time gently curves in on itself, gradually expanding in antiphonal exchange until, at "Wann erstehst du wieder in deiner Schöne," the male voices, repeating the opening alto statement, answer with a striking modification of Herder's text: from "Schönste der Mädchen in Erin!" (Most beautiful of the girls in Erin!) to "Schönste der Schönen in Erin!" (Most beautiful of the beautiful in Erin!).[26] This change stems, perhaps, from the fact that around this time (1864) Brahms was also working on a setting of a poem by Paul Flemming (1609–40), "O liebliche Wangen" (O lovely cheeks), as the fourth of the Five Songs, op. 47 (1868). There, stanza 3 reads, "O Schönste der Schönen / benimm mir dies Sehnen / Komm, eile, komm, du süße, du fromme" (O fairest of the fair / ease my longing, / come, make haste, come, sweet, faithful one). The phrase no doubt stuck in Brahms's head, and perhaps the euphony appealed to him such that he made the change in "Darthula."

The other point involves Brahms's stressing of the final syllable of the name: Dar-thu-LA; along with Seckendorff, he accentuates the third rather than the normative second syllable.[27] He does this not just once but four times in the *poco animato* middle section, in all six voice parts. The temptation of the open *a* syllable may well have been hard to resist. In his biography of the composer, Karl Geiringer claims that Brahms was not a good linguist outside the German cultural area. He sidestepped the offer of an honorary degree from Cambridge, for instance, partly out of cultural loyalty to German-speaking lands.[28] While his library contained poetic and musical books of all kinds, and in different languages, his acquaintance with Ossian was largely through the medium of German.[29] Although Brahms's contemporaries readily grasped the normative pronunciation of "Dar-THU-la" in their settings, it appears to have eluded him.[30] This is odd when it is well known that Brahms devoted enormous care and effort to his works.[31]

Third Group of Settings (1897–ca. 1950)

The majority of the settings in this group harness choral and instrumental resources, usually mixed voices with orchestra, although two are for male voices only. In contrast to the settings in table 12.2, only two are for voice and piano accompaniment. The settings for chorus and orchestra include two from the year 1903: those by Wilhelm Koehler-Wümbach (op. 32) and Schoenberg. The former uses male voices within a lush Romantic harmony, brimming with emphases and diminished chords, that takes the first tenors to a high B♭ at "Wann erstehst du."

The Dutch composer Simon van Milligen (1849–1929) completed his two-act opera *Darthula* in 1899, to a published libretto by Emil Coenders (1879–1938).[32] Its premiere took place in Amsterdam's Stadsschouwburg on January 14, 1902.[33] A full score and piano reduction by the composer survive in manuscript.[34] Van Milligen conducted some of the opera (it is uncertain how much) at a festival in The Hague held on June 26–27, 1900, to mark the twenty-fifth anniversary of the Dutch Musicians Union.[35] A music critic and teacher as well as a composer and conductor, Van Milligen left his post as director of the music school at Gouda in 1888 to make the acquaintance of Franck and d'Indy in Paris. Influence from these composers is detectable in the melodic lines, while the more potent presence of Wagner is evident in the harmony and orchestral writing.

Table 12.3. Late and post-Romantic settings of "Dar-thula"

Title	Composer	Year	Setting	Key	Time signature
"Darthulas grafsäng"	Melartin [Runeberg]	1897	mixed chor [MS]	B♭ minor	$\frac{4}{4}-\frac{6}{4}$ langsam
Darthula [opera]	Van Milligen	1899	soli, chor, orch [MS]	n/a	n/a
Darthulas Grabgesang	Schoenberg	1903	soli, chor, orch [MS]	E♭ minor [E major]	$\frac{6}{4}$ mäßig langsam
"Das Mädchen von Kola"	Koehler-Wümbach	1903	male chor, orch	D minor	$\frac{4}{4}$ lento–mäßig schnell
"Darthulas Grabgesang"	Knab	1906 [publ. 1929]	high v, pf	A minor–D major–A minor [poly-tonal]	$\frac{4}{4}-\frac{2}{4}$ $\frac{3}{4}-\frac{4}{4}$ langsam, aber nicht schleppen
Darthulas Grabgesang nach Ossian	Busch	1911	chor, small orch [MS]	D major–B major–D major	$\frac{3}{4}-\frac{4}{4}$ andante (con moto moderato)
"Darthulas gravsäng"	Palmgren [Runeberg]	ca. 1919	male chor	F♯ minor	$\frac{4}{4}$ grave
Darthula aus Ossian	Fleischmann	"after 1910"	mixed chor, orch [MS red.]	G minor–E♭ minor–E minor–G minor	$\frac{6}{8}$ gravamente–andante lacrimoso–animato
"Darthulas Grabesgesang"	Neumann	1950?	v, pf [MS]	E minor [poly-tonal]	$\frac{6}{8}\frac{9}{8}$ zart bewegt

The opera is for soloists, female chorus, and an orchestra of woodwinds, brass, timpani, and harp, this last instrument with an increasingly prominent role toward the end. The plot sticks quite closely to the original tale. The action opens by the castle of Seláma on the coast of Ireland, whose king, Cormac, has recently been slain. It is evening, the moon rising behind clouds. Darthula sits by a cliff, deep in contemplation, with other women on a terrace behind her.[36] The mood is set in the sedate introduction of thirty-eight bars in the key of G minor in $\frac{6}{8}$ time, with low, rising woodwinds and timpani softly reverberating. Darthula then sings a short recitative-like aria and the chorus follows, commenting on the plight of "Colla's daughter" as the tempo enlivens and the rhythm moves to common time. Ithorna, Cairbar's mother, maintains to Darthula that her son, from whose unrequited passion Darthula has fled, is now the rightful king of the realm.[37]

The music gradually illustrates its debt to Wagner in triadic triplet flourishes and striding bass lines. At the halfway stage, the tonality shifts to E minor for an aria by Nathos; this is "his" key. By the end of the first act, however, as the ship carrying Darthula and her brothers vanishes in a storm, the tonality has moved to E-flat minor. It is in this key that the brothers, in a homophonic trio, begin their address to the moon, but there is an abrupt shift to E-flat major for "O dochter des hemels, laat vol uw glans / Neerdalen van der wolken trans, / Doe storm en nacht verdwijnen! / O red ons, red ons, reine!" (O daughter of heaven, let your glory shine through the clouds to make the storm and night vanish! / O save us, save us, pure one!). After Ithorna pronounces a short, violent curse on the voyage, dramatic chords in the minor key conclude the act. The second act propels the narrative to its destined end, with the deaths of Darthula and Nathos in conflict with Cairbar's forces while Ossian, accompanied by pulsating harp arpeggios, comments on the sad fate of the lovers. The opera's critical and public reception is obscure. It appears to have joined the host of late Romantic works overshadowed by Wagner's achievement.

The composition by Schoenberg, an extensive manuscript sketch of 138 measures, is conceived for soloists, mixed voices, and a large orchestra. Written in a late Romantic style close to that of his cantata *Gurrelieder* (1900–1911), it has been published with a detailed commentary asserting that it is the composer's most important fragment.[38] At this time Schoenberg was still under the influence of Wagner and Mahler but not yet at the point of abandoning conventional tonality. Like *Gurrelieder*, the work is conceptually grandiose, perhaps excessive for the succinct Ossianic narrative of Herder. Why then did he abandon it? It is possible that the grandeur of Gurre appealed more to his sense of the gargantuan. This much is uncertain, but the question of aesthetic balance may well have been implicated.

The German-born Aloys Fleischmann (1880–1964), who emigrated from Dachau to Ireland in 1906 and became choirmaster at North Cork Cathedral, completed his cantata for mixed chorus and orchestra, *Dartula aus Ossian*, in Ireland. The autograph score is fairly complete, the text being Herder's poem in both English and the original German.[39] The date of the unpublished setting is uncertain, but it

Figure 12.1. Arnold Schoenberg, page from unfinished cantata, *Darthulas Grabgesang* (1903). From *Chorwerke 1: Fragmente und Skizzen*, edited by Tadeusz Okuljar and Martina Sichardt (Mainz, Vienna: Universal Edition, 1991), 33. Reproduced with kind permission by UNIVERSAL EDITION A. G., Wien. Courtesy of Musiksammlung der Österreichischen Nationalbibliothek.

Example 12.7. Aloys Fleischmann, *Darthula aus Ossian*, bars 84–93

is "after 1910."⁴⁰ Announced gravely by horn calls, the opening G-minor tonality in $\frac{6}{8}$ has those parameters in common with the opera of Simon van Milligen, especially when both works veer, later on, toward the "distant" key of E-flat minor (a key prominent in Schoenberg's setting). This might be termed the tonality of "Ossianic distance," exotic and remote from workaday keys based on C, G, or F.⁴¹ It is also the obverse of the E-flat settings of Ossian, well known by this time in German-speaking lands. The choral writing displays a mastery of chromatic harmony and, significantly, in its freely parsed "Erin arise again" when the original German has "wann erstehst du wieder" (when will you arise again?), an identification of Darthula with Ireland (Erin).⁴²

Opposed to Schoenberg's radicalism, the energetic Adolf Busch (1891–1952) adopted a conservative stance in his chamber cantata, *Darthula's Grabgesang*, op. 1. Renowned for his founding of the long-lived Busch Quartet after World War I, on leaving Germany in April 1933 Busch spent much of his life elsewhere in Europe and in the United States. His unpublished setting, composed in June 1911, was written for chorus (SATB) and a small orchestra of flutes, oboes, bassoons, horns, and strings.[43] Premiered on January 24, 1912, with the Bonn City Choral Society in the Beethovenhalle, it was conducted by Hugo Grüters, director of music for the city of Bonn and Busch's future father-in-law. The work was apparently offered to the publishers Breitkopf & Härtel who, while interested in other compositions by Busch, turned it down.[44]

Some 219 bars long, the piece displays the influence of the prolific Max Reger. The elaborate string writing, dense and concentrated, reflects Busch's already formidable grasp of idiomatic orchestration. The choral writing is mainly homophonic, diatonic, and imitative between the upper and lower parts. Cast in $\frac{3}{4}$ time and *andante (con moto moderato)*, the music opens in A-minor but moves eventually to establish D major as its root key, at which point the voices enter. Unison horn and flute soli an octave apart preface the continuation, "dein Morgenroth ist ferne" (your dawn is far-off). The piece then modulates through various keys to a climax in B major, the key of contrast selected by Busch, with agitated eighth-note triplets in $\frac{4}{4}$ at "Nimmer kommt dir die Sonne," returning subsequently to a quiet resolution in D major and the triple time of the opening. Despite the judgment of his publishers, like the Ossian setting of Gouvy half a century earlier Busch's *Darthula* could claim to be an undiscovered gem.

The two settings in Swedish that address Herder's poem present a striking contrast: that by Erkki Melartin (1875–1937), "Darthulas gravsång" (dated 1897) is for mixed voices (SATB), whereas the other, by Selim Palmgren (1878–1951), is for male voices only. These settings attest to the rise of the choral movement in central and northern Europe during the second half of the nineteenth century as lands formerly part of imperial states strove to encourage national consciousness through communal singing. The translation of the Herder text for both settings is by Johan Ludvig Runeberg (1804–77), who made a partial account in the early 1830s.[45] The setting for mixed chorus, composed while the twenty-two-year old Melartin was still studying in Helsinki, bears the influence of Mahler rather than of Sibelius, Melartin's celebrated compatriot. The B-flat minor tonality and common time ($\frac{4}{4}$) of the opening "Flicka från Kola, du sover" give way after thirty-two bars to a middle section in B-flat and $\frac{6}{4}$ time, only to return in twenty-two bars to the initial gloom of the minor key. Except for the segment from bars 14 to 32 the texture is homophonic throughout.

The setting for male choir by Palmgren is an altogether bolder affair. Composed in 1906 when he was conductor of the Helsinki University Chorus, it won a prize sponsored by the Viipurin Laula-Veikot choir, but a printed edition appeared (in

Example 12.8. Adolf Busch, *Darthulas Grabgesang*, bars 13–17

Example 12.9. Busch, *Darthulas Grabgesang*, bars 147–52

Sweden) only in 1913.[46] Challenging technically and laid out on two staves, the setting for six-part male voices is in F-sharp minor and common time, marked *Grave*. It opens with striding *pianissimo* octaves in the lower voices and, in the three upper parts, softly intoned B-minor chords on the name "Darthula." As the lower octaves become more insistent in their repetition of the heroine's name, the texture intensifies at "Aldrig, aldrig nalkas väl solen mer din bädd" (Never will the sun return to your place of rest) as the voices exclaim, "Stå upp, Darthula!" (Awake, Darthula!).

Example 12.10. Selim Palmgren, "Darthulas Gravsång," bars 16–20

The tempo becomes more agitated until a climax on a *fortissimo* B-minor chord with an added A in the bass harmony. Returning to the opening, unison octaves lead to the home key of F-sharp minor, with some plangent G-major harmony, sung *pianissimo*, before the final cadence.

The manuscript arrangement of Herder's poem for voice and piano by Friedrich Neumann (1915–89) is a more "modern" conception, using intervals of the fourth, fifth, and ninth in the accompaniment, rather in the manner of Hindemith, to underpin a declamatory voice part. Of uncertain date (probably around 1950), it was never published.[47] Marked *Zart bewegt* (with tender movement), its forty-one bars oscillate between $\frac{6}{8}$ and $\frac{9}{8}$:

Example 12.11. Friedrich Neumann, "Darthulas Grabgesang," bars 18–28

Example 12.12. Armin Knab, "Darthulas Grabgesang," bars 1–12

Although the setting by Armin Knab (1881–1951) is less declamatory than that of Neumann, the harmonic language and varied rhythm anticipate the latter's by almost a half century, with fourths, fifths, and sevenths for harmonic astringency. The setting is one of Knab's first compositions: the manuscript is dated "15–20 Aug., 1906."[48] Setting himself the task of abandoning late Romanticism, he asserted that the voice part should express the essence of the lied; and it should do this more readily than the accompaniment that earlier, with its rich harmony, had dominated the genre. The vigor of the lied lay in melody, and he turned to folk song for a model rather than the sentimental "folk-like" song of the early twentieth century.[49]

Example 12.13. Knab, "Darthulas Grabgesang," bars 59–66

Knab's setting of the Herder poem (mistakenly, as in the attribution of Hopffer, subtitled "Goethe-Ossian"), is mainly in common time and marked *Langsam, aber nicht schleppen* (slow, but not dragging).[50] The piano's opening A-minor eighth notes in the right hand are set against consecutive fifths in the bass, as if to emphasize the folk-like nature of his setting. After the first two bars of piano introduction, the voice part enters quietly in a gentle pentatonic descent. Triplet chords take the voice forward to "dein Morgenrot ist ferne," where the key and tempo change to D major and $\frac{3}{4}$. Rippling piano quintuplets and sextuplets around F major, D major, and E-minor/seventh chords gradually urge the voice to a climax at "Auf immer so weiche denn, Sonne / dem Mädchen von Kola" until the music subsides for the final lines of the poem as the voice, accompanied by chords, returns the tonality to A minor. Of all the settings of Herder's poem, Knab's is the most ambitious and persuasive in its conception and execution.

Among these settings, several stand out for their accomplishment (for instance, the Linley cantata, Schubert's "Nathos," arrangements by Busch, Fleischmann, Jensen, and Palmgren). The predominance of the Herder verses confirms that these were well known in central and northern Europe. As the century progressed, the use of major keys like E-flat often moved, not to the relative minor (C minor) but to the minor equivalent (E-flat minor). In the context of enlarged, more grandiose settings, this could be interpreted as a late Romantic disenchantment with armed strife in Europe as well as a search for musical horizons that would keep cultural history intact but break free from a stifling conventionality. But periodicity, cultural memory, aesthetic sensibility, and compositional skill do not run parallel to one another, as major differences among the settings attest. The transmediation into opera, cantata, and solo song, however, reflects the continuing spell of the poems of Ossian, even into the "modernist" twentieth century.

Chapter Thirteen

The Cantata as Drama

Joseph Jongen's *Comala* (1897), Jørgen Malling's *Kyvala* (1902), and Liza Lehmann's *Leaves from Ossian* (1909)

Increasingly, as the focus on Ossian after the mid-nineteenth century shifted from south to north in Europe, the cantata began to take on features of the operatic stage, with occasional directions for scenery and action. An example of this trend is *Comala, poème dramatique*, by Joseph Jongen (1873–1953), written in 1897. Marie-Alphonse-Nicolas-Joseph Jongen was born on December 14, 1873, in Liège. Aged seventeen when Cesar Franck died, he has been described as a follower of that composer. But after studying in Germany (a condition of the Grand Concours in composition) he began to forge his own individual style. His first musical education was from his father, and thereafter he studied at the Conservatoire royal de musique in his native city. At the time he obtained his diploma, he was taking lessons in composition from the director of the conservatoire, Jean-Theodore Radoux, and won a prize for piano and organ performance in 1895. Participating in another competition of the Beaux-Arts de l'Académie royale de Belgique, he won second prize for a trio for piano, violin and cello, first prize going to François Rasse.[1]

Discouraged by this relative failure, Jongen wanted to withdraw from the Prix de Rome competition but was persuaded to enter by Radoux, his father, and friends. Finally, he gained the coveted prize at the age of twenty-four, winning for his cantata, *Comala* (1897).[2] After studying abroad as a condition of his award, Jongen taught harmony for more than two decades at the Liège Conservatoire, from 1898 until 1920 (with the exception of a stay in England during World War I), and at the Brussels Conservatoire from 1920 to 1933. In the summer months he composed mainly at his country house in the Ardennes, near the area called "Balmoral" because of the many British who visited during the nineteenth century. It was there that he died on July 12, 1953. With over 240 works to his credit, in almost every genre except opera, he showed a predilection for organ, piano, and chamber music.[3]

Joseph Jongen's *Comala* (1897)

Tucked away in the top right-hand corner of the title page of his cantata, *Comala*, is the notation by Jongen: "J'ai été laborieux" (I've labored).[4] This is a variation of Johann Nicolaus Forkel's remark that he attributed to Johann Sebastian Bach: "Ich habe fleißig seyn müssen."[5] The cantata is a composition into which Jongen, spurred on by the prospect of the Prix de Rome and his rivalry with François Rasse (1873–1955), poured a great deal of work. One hundred and ninety-five pages long, it comprises the two musical parts of a three-part composition, the third part being spoken or recited. Paul Gilson (1865–1942), himself a composer, provided the libretto.[6] The final page of the autograph score bears the legend "Bruxelles, Août 1897." The work is scored for three soloists: Comala (soprano), Hidallan (tenor), and Fingal (baritone); chorus; and a large orchestra: two separate choral groups represent Comala's companions (sopranos, altos) and Fingal's warriors (tenors, basses). The orchestra has double woodwinds with piccolo, cor anglais, bass clarinet in B-flat, four horns in F, three trumpets in F, three tenor trombones and bass trombone, timpani, cymbals and bass drum, harp, and strings.

The work is semi-staged, set up for either concert performance or a dramatic scenario. The two parts amount to 495 and 428 bars, respectively. Part 1 opens with Comala, pensive, seated on a rock with Hidallan nearby: he is listening to the distant sound of Fingal's warriors getting ready for combat. An unaccompanied melody of A-minor in the first violins suggests Comala's anxious plight, awaiting the outcome of Fingal's battle.

This slow opening soon gives way to an *allegro poco agitato*, with a rising bass, trumpets, and horns, and warriors are heard singing, "Fingal, conduis nous au combat." Hidallan then addresses Comala (D major), and here Jongen, like Brahms with "Darthula," accents Comala's name on the last syllable, Co-ma-LA.[7] "Proche est le combat," Hidallan announces, to which she replies, accompanied by the harp, "Proche est le jour de la gloire radicale" (Near is the day of total victory); he replies, darkly, "and for many, death" (le trépas).

Hidallan draws her attention to the menacing hordes of the enemy below as the hills tremble at their advance. Horns signal a sustained *andante* as Comala sings, in G minor, that Fingal, her lover, is unconquerable: "Son bras est la mort des heros!" Hidallan looks at her with emotion, and in the key of D-flat declares his love for her: "Comala, femme héroique . . . ta voix impérieuse est sembable au du cri guerrier de Fingal lui-même. . . . O Comala, je t'aime!"

Example 13.1. Joseph Jongen, *Comala*, bars 1–6

Example 13.2. Jongen, *Comala*: "Proche est le jour de la gloire," bars 50–55

Warriors materialize, and as the tempo reaches an *allegro molto* in $\frac{3}{4}$, a *maestoso molto* ensues as Fingal himself appears, to the enthusiasm of his warriors and fanfares from the brass. The soldiers hail Fingal in a bright A major: "Fingal, roi de Morven, conduis nous!" Their cries of "a ho ha" (reminiscent of *Die Walküre*) gradually subside, allowing Fingal to speak in G minor, then *agitato*; "Follow me," he says, "like the torrent that floods from the top of Cromla." He then asks the horns to sound the signal for combat. Before leaving again for the field of battle, Fingal sits by Comala and speaks tenderly to her: "Et toi douce fleur d'Inistore. . . ." He declares that she gives his army heart to win the victory. Comala herself expresses misgivings, but, to the sound of a brief $\frac{2}{4}$ march in G-flat major and triumphant fanfares, Fingal and his troops depart. This brings part 1 to a close.

Example 13.3. Jongen, *Comala*: "O Comala, femme heroïque!" bars 94–102

At the beginning of part 2, Comala sits brooding with her companions as a D-minor strain murmurs in the lower strings and timpani. A plangent four-bar cor anglais solo captures Comala's mood. Accompanied by clarinets, the melody is repeated with different harmony and shape until the chorus sings, "La nuit étend son voile sombre dans la plaine." Comala has a vision of the river swollen and the color of blood: "Ô Fingal, où donc est-tu?" Here, she launches into her famous address to the moon, in a moving *andante sostenuto* in F major and $\frac{3}{4}$.

Example 13.4. Jongen, *Comala*, part 2: "Ô lune, lève-toi," bars 68–74

Table 13.2. Jongen's *Comala*: structure of part 2

Section	Bars	Key signature	Time signature	Marking	Orchestra
"La nuit étend son voile sombre"	1–50	D minor	4/4	non troppo lento	str, clar, timpani chor.
"Lointain torrent"	51–68	D minor	4/4	agitato	ww, str. (trem.) cor anglais [Comala]
"Astre blanc de la nuit"	69–86	F major/minor	3/4	andante sostenuto	str (trem), harp, fl, clar
"Ou toi feu follet"	87–97	dimin.	3/4 (9/8)	[même mouvement]	ww, str. (trem)
"Fingal, ou donc est-tu?"	98–119	C major/A minor	4/4	sostenuto	cor anglais str.
"Voyez, des guerriers"	120–202	B♭ major (minor)	2/2	allegro non troppo	hn, timp, str. chor.
"Fuyons"	203–23	F major	3/4	vivace	lower str chor.
"Victoire . . . il est tombé, le roi de Morven"	224–46	C minor (F minor)	4/4	allegro molto moderato	hns, str [Hidallan] chor.
"Tombé, dites-vous?"	247–81	C minor	4/4	[allegro]	ww, str. [Comala]
"O roi du monde"	282–99	F minor	4/4	plus largement	brass, hns
"Oh! Que ne suis-je au bord du Carron"	300–20	E minor	4/4	moderato molto	cor anglais, str. bass clar.
"O lune, pâle lune . . ."	321–38	A major	3/4	andante sostenuto	harp, ww, str. (trem.) [Hidallan]
"C'est sur l'Ardven glacé"	339–59	C major/D minor	4/4	moderato molto (misterioso)	clar, celli, str. [Comala]
"Avant la fin du jour la victoire"	360–78	A minor	2/4	allegro sostenuto–lento–très lent	str. hns. [Comala]
"Gloire à Fingal"	379–427	F major	4/4	allegro molto–maestoso	hns, str full orch. chorus of warriors

The tonality quickly turns to F minor, then D-flat major at "páles rayons." Comala asks the moon to dispel the clouds and shine on the glorious army of Morven. A soft trumpet call announces a change of orchestral color, with woodwind triplets in piccolo, flutes, and clarinets. A mirage entices her ("conduis moi sur le champ de bataille"). The time changes to $\frac{4}{4}$ as the cor anglais melody is heard again. This is followed by an *allegro* in which Comala's companions, restless, assert, "Look, our warriors are fighting invisible forces." They fear defeat and say Comala should flee: "Fuyons," they urge in G-minor. But Comala insists, "Je reste."

Accompanied by a soaring horn (then oboe and violin), Hidallan sings of victory: the combatants are dispersed, but Fingal has fallen. To restless sixteenth notes, the maidens repeat the news, "O douleur," over a falling bass. Comala sings, "Tombé, dites-vous?" Was it Fingal in battle, terrifying like the lightning? Strings and wind rush upward while the fanfares ring out: tell us, the chorus sings, which hero fell on the banks of Carron? Passionately, Hidallan persists in his lie: the up-rushing motto in the strings allows him to brave it out: "Mort, Fingal est mort . . ." while the chorus despairingly sings, "Il n'est plus le chef glorieux du Morven!"

A slightly broader section in F minor allows Comala, backed by sustained trumpet chords that turn funereal, to cry "O roi du monde, meurtrier de Fingal, que le malheur te poursuive dans les plaines." She laments as the tonality moves toward E minor. Hidallan addresses the moon, asking it to hide its rays falling on Fingal's breast. The woodwinds quiver and the bass line droops as he mourns the commander. The orchestra calms for Comala to interject, as if she is dreaming, that Fingal has his tomb in icy Ardven. "But wait," she says, "I must see my hero once more." A slow section in A-flat with quiet chords in the strings provides a harmonic background for a recitative-like meditation: "Victory before day's end. . . . Fingal doesn't come, the king of the world has slain him." She sinks down, and expires. Gradually, the strings pick up their pace, and horn calls announce that the soldiers are not far off. Gathering speed over a C bass (F major), the warriors give triumphant cries ("Ha-oho!"), along with trumpets, trombones, and woodwinds. "Gloire à Fingal le roi des épées . . ." With multiple flourishes, the full orchestra brings the cantata to an end in a brisk F-major cadence.

Why Jongen's cantata was never published is puzzling, for it is an accomplished piece of transmediation for a twenty-four-year-old. We must presume that the text was that given to competitors for the Belgian Prix de Rome, since François Rasse also set "Comala" in Gilson's adaptation. Unlike Jongen, Rasse had one extract published later.[8] Perhaps, at home or in his travels, Jongen came across the literary controversy around Ossian; his time in England during World War I may have convinced him that his work was a youthful *jeu d'esprit*. But whatever faults he saw in his cantata pale in comparison with its strengths: it is pleasingly set for the voices; the instrumentation is confident and sophisticated; and the dramatic force of the scenes is convincing, especially in the rapid fluctuations of tempo, dynamics, and the variety of tonal centers around which the plot development is built. Jongen has inserted some clichés, certainly, such as the bass line that falls by semitones, *tremolando* strings, and the like. But the work as a whole emanates a strong sense of musical imagination, as well as of devoted application.

A critic writing for the Brussels journal *Le Guide Musical* found the premiere remarkable among works recently presented under the auspices of the Académie.[9] Jongen himself had conducted. Although the critic thought the pastiche of the original poem banal, he found the composer to have an advanced sense of proportion, musical taste, and an unusual mastery of orchestral technique. A minor criticism was that the music was almost too ponderous for the subject matter. Still, the setting was well adapted to the text, he felt, clothing it with charm. The writer was particularly impressed by Hidallan's aria at the point when he proclaims his love for Comala, pronouncing it a "grand morceau lyrique" with an attractive freshness in the coloring and emotion. The introduction to the second part, with its melancholy tone, was at the same time, he thought, not lacking in grandeur. The positive tone of this review, at least, must have given Jongen some satisfaction.

Jørgen Malling's *Kyvala* (1902)

Malling's *Kyvala*, to give it its Danish title, embodies a similar trend in the dramatic cantata. In the autograph score the composer has written a note stating that "Kyvala" (or Küwala, in German) reflects the Gaelic pronunciation of the name Caomhmala, which Macpherson, and others, following him, had anglicized to "Comala."[10] Malling (1836–1905), significantly, took care over the correct pronunciation of her name, with the accent fallling on the second syllable.[11] The work is dedicated to "Hendes Majestaet/ Kejserinde Dagmar af Rusland."[12] Jørgen, an organist and a musical pedagogue, was the brother of the composer Otto Malling (1848–1915). Like him, Jørgen was at one time a pupil of Niels W. Gade, and it was perhaps in the spirit of Gade's cantata *Comala* (1846) that he came to write *Kyvala*—though with some important differences in the overall conception.

In 1861 Malling was the first composer to receive a stipend from the Anckerste Legat, a foundation instituted in 1857 by Carl Andreas Ancker to make it possible for poets, musicians, and painters to study abroad.[13] Malling's studies took him first to Paris, then Vienna and Klagenfurt. He then worked in Munich and Zürich as a music teacher, choral director, and composer, before being appointed *dozent* for music theory and musical aesthetics at the University of Munich.[14] Around 1900 he returned to Denmark to teach at the Matthisson-Hansen Music Conservatoire. He composed an opera on the subject of Frithjof, chamber works, and arrangements of folk songs. *Kyvala* (completed in 1901) is described in Danish as a "concert drama" and includes stage directions for the participants. The score is in the composer's hand: "Jørgen Malling scr." appears at the end.[15] That the work resembles a one-act opera is confirmed not only by a prelude ("Vorspiel") but also by a final curtain following a choral version of Herder's poem "Der Vorhang fällt" (The curtain falls).[16]

The work has a bilingual text in Danish and German by Severin Sørensen.[17] The plot follows the prose poem, with one significant difference: in the original account, Hidallan is banished for falsely telling Comala that Fingal has been killed in battle with Caracul; here, the jealous Hidallan slays Comala as she rests in a cave after Fingal's return. Thus, musical transmediation involves a novel dramatic impulse at a critical point in the action.

The *dramatis personae* are Fingal, king of Morven (tenor); Hidallan, a chieftain (baritone); Kyvala, daughter of Sarno, king of Inistore (soprano); and two friends of the heroine, Culma and Malwina (both mezzo-soprano). In Macpherson's poem, the two companions are called Dersagrena and Melilcoma; as in some other adaptations, the original names have been changed for reasons of euphony or singability. Culma ("Colma") and Malwina would have been relatively familiar characters to anyone who had read Ossian, even though they appear in different poems. Two choruses, one female (sopranos, altos) the other male (tenors, basses) represent young maidens and bards, respectively. The orchestra is standard for the turn of the century: double woodwinds, two horns and two trumpets in F, three trombones, harp, timpani, side drum, triangle, and strings.[18] The action takes place in Ardven, an area in Morven, Fingal's kingdom in western Scotland; the time is around the third century.

The work's prelude opens with a slow march-like motif in E minor announced by bassoons, horns, trombones, and lower strings, interspersed with harp arpeggios. After twenty-four bars this turns into an *allegro* in G major with a fragmentary theme that, after migrations into D minor, E minor and F-sharp minor, relaxes into a $\frac{12}{8}$ *larghetto* with a short but plangent clarinet motif concluded by the strings. This brief section, tinged with pathos and suggestive of Kyvala's anxiety about Fingal's fate, recurs. The collection of relatively short themes in the prelude portrays the main characters: Kyvala in the slower passages, Fingal or Hidallan in the brisker ones (the latter represented by a sinister B-minor/E-minor *allegro*).

The action takes place on a hilly plateau, mountains in the distance. The time is late evening, and the moon is rising. The river Carun is nearby. Large rocks are positioned stage left; a path runs through them. Smaller rocks serve as a table and chairs; a cave is at stage right. Kyvala sits on one of the large boulders, her head in her hands. Behind her are maidens, some preparing a fire to roast a deer on a spit. Bows, arrows, and spears lie on the ground. This scenario suggests that composer and librettist envisaged the work as a theatrical drama with scenery, costumes, and all the trappings of full-blown staging.

"Still ist die Jagd," sing the maidens in three-part harmony, "kein Laut in Ardven," echoing the original words of Dersagrena: "The chace is over. No noise on Ardven [but the torrent's roar!]." Grounded in E minor and $\frac{12}{8}$, the chorus in this *larghetto* is mindful of Fingal: when will he return? The tempo increases and the music modulates to G major for "Come, prepare the feast; with the coming of night there will be songs and joy on the mountains of Morven!" In an *allegro* in D-minor (marked "II" in the score) Culma and Malwina then take up their vision of the deer around whose

Example 13.5. Jørgen Malling, *Kyvala*: "Vorspiel," bars 66–74

horns a meteor plays, signaling disaster. This introduces Kyvala's aria, an *andante* in $\frac{3}{4}$ and the plangent key of C minor, accompanied at first only by bassoons and timpani. As a tearful Kyvala asks when her Fingal will return, the tempo broadens in a return to E-minor for the chorus's original *larghetto* in $\frac{12}{8}$ (IV).[19] This presages the entrance of Hidallan, jealous of Fingal's prowess and of his love for Kyvala. Darkly, his F-sharp minor aria declares, "Your pain will be my rejoicing." With an accelerated *allegro*, Hidallan pushes the pair aside and calls to Kyvala that he has a message for her, accompanied by rustling diminished seventh chords.

Fearing the worst, Kyvala sings an F-minor *arietta* until Hidallan brings her the news that Fingal has fallen, his army destroyed. Kyvala's impassioned B-minor turns eventually to a gentler G-major/D-major plea reminiscent of Colma in "The Songs of Selma": why does her lover not return as he promised? Gradually, her anguish brings the tonality back to B minor, as Hidallan tells her that Fingal's body has already been interred. At this, the chorus of maidens asks who the victor in battle is, Caracul or Fingal? Hidallan entreats Kyvala to flee with him as the conflict draws near. But perceiving that Fingal is alive, he makes for the cave.

Fingal appears, followed by his bards, armed and carrying their harps on their back. As he tries to embrace Kyvala, she retreats, asking if he is a ghost. In a $\frac{3}{4}$ *andante* that begins with quiet horn calls in E-flat minor/B-flat minor, she pleads, "Take me to your grave, where my spirit can meet yours." In an *allegro molto* in F major (IX), accompanied by the full orchestra, Fingal stoutly asserts that he is no ghost. Again, he asks her to speak to him: "I am listening, gladden the heart of your warrior with the sweet sound of your voice." "Is it really you?" says Kyvala (X). They embrace, but she feels her strength leave her, her joy is so great: fainting, she is supported by her

Table 13.3. Malling's *Kyvala*: structure of scenes and setting

Section	Key signature	Time signature	Marking	Solo/chorus	Orchestra
1	G minor	12/8	larghetto	chor, "Still ist die Jagd…"	str, ww
2	D minor	4/4	allegro	Malw/Culma: "Sahst du?"	ob, bassoon, str, ww
3	C minor	3/4	andante–poco più lento–largo	Küwala: "O Karun, du trübster"	bassoons, timp, str, ww
4	E minor	12/8	larghetto	chor, "Still ist die Jagd…"	str, ww
5	F# minor	4/4	allegro–allegro molto	Hidallan: "Ruhet, Nebel und Grau'n…"	ww, trpt tromb, str
6	F minor–E minor–B minor	4/4	andantino	Küwala: "Wessen Stimme?"	celli, fl, clar, full
7	B minor	2/4	allegro–più lento–allegro–poco più allegro–presto	chor, "Welch Geräusch ertönt dem Ohr?"	hn, trpt, clar, str
8	G minor	3/4	andante	Küwala: "Ha Fingal"	str (pizz), ww
9	F major	4/4	allegro molto	Fingal: "Kein Geist bin ich"	bassoons, hns, str
10	F major–A minor	4/4	l'istesso tempo–più lento	Küwala: "Bist Fingal du?"	ww (piccolo) str.
11	G minor	4/4	allegro–andante–lento	Fingal: "Sie sinkt! Ihr Jungfrauen, herbei!"	ww, str, trpt, hn
12	B♭	12/8–9/8	andantino	chor, "Drei der Hirsche…"	str (pizz), triangle

13	G minor	4/4	allegro	Fingal: "Zum Mahle denn"	ww, trpt, str
14	E♭ major	3/4	moderato	chor, "Ströme Karun . . ."	chor, harp, lower str.
15	G minor	4/4	allegro	Hidallan: "Fingal, du stolzer Fürst!"	ww, str
16	G minor	4/4	maestoso	Hidallan: "Haltet ein!"	trpt, trmb, ww
17	G minor	4/4	allegro molto	Fingal: "Kyvala! Meine Wonne!"	ww, str
18	C minor	4/4	adagio	Fingal: "O lass mich schauen . . ."	hn, timp, ww, str
19	F minor	4/4	grave—un poco più vivo—tempo primo	chor, "Holde, Küwala, du schläfst!"	harp, clar, ww, str

Example 13.6. Malling, *Kyvala*, aria: "O Karun, du trübster der Ströme!"

Example 13.7. Malling, *Kyvala*, aria: "Fingal, du stolzer Fürst!"

Example 13.8. Malling, *Kyvala*, aria: "O lasst mich schauen"

maidens, as Fingal entreats her to rest in the cave (XI). As she does so, the chorus urges the warriors, bards, and maidens to feast on the deer Kyvala has slain (XII). In a vigorous *allegro* (XIII) beginning in G minor, Fingal, inviting the bards to the feast, asks them to calm Kyvala with their song as she sleeps. Harp arpeggios signal an ode by the bards, who sing in praise of Fingal (XIV).

To the sound of a semi-tonal clash, Hidallan appears from the cave, and is accused by Fingal of treachery (XV). Hidallan confesses his passion for Kyvala (XVI). In a G-minor aria resembling a funeral march, he tells how he has pierced Kyvala's heart in the cave, then commits suicide (XVII); Malling conveys this act with a rising chromatic line, A♭–A–B♭–C, culminating in a *fortissimo* $^6_3$ chord of G minor with a high E♭ in the voice at *entseelt* (lifeless), then silence. Hidallan's body is slowly borne away by the bards. Fingal has the corpse of Kyvala brought from the cave and laid gently on the ground. In a stately *largo* in C minor (XVIII), he laments her death: "O let me see the picture of loveliness."

There follows an epilogue (XIX), a chorus of maidens and bards who sing an adaptation, interspersed with harp arpeggios, of Herder's familiar poem on Darthula. Malling sets the six-voice chorus in the key of F minor, with excursions into B-flat minor via A♮s and a reversion to the home key for the concluding quatrain.

According to a penciled note in the autograph score, also naming the soloists, *Kyvala* was performed only twice, on February 14 and 15, 1901. But as a one-act music drama it has some minor significance: first, the aim of accurately representing the heroine's Gaelic name; second, variations in the *dramatis personae*; and last, in the ending, the radical adaptation of Macpherson's plot. The dedication to the Danish-born empress suggests that her influence might have led to more performances in Denmark and perhaps even in Russia; yet it appears that impresarios declined to sponsor the work.

The dramatic and musical design of *Kyvala* is well constructed: the nineteen sections are proportionate in contrast and pacing. The solo and chorus parts are carefully calculated in terms of vocal range and dynamics; the musical resources, however, are rather conventional. Despite a modal flavor in the melodic lines (for example, bars 49–57) as an attempt to capture a "northern" atmosphere, Malling relies too readily on diminished chords and *tremolando* effects as part of the stock-in-trade of late Romanticism. While the work is not on the level of Jongen's *Comala*, it is competently written and effective. One wonders what the dedicatee, the empress, thought of it.

Liza Lehmann's *Leaves from Ossian* (1909)

The cantata by Liza Lehmann (1862–1918) is a composite of episodes from different poems.[20] This displays the composer's powers of literary analysis as much as her musical imagination. She selected the nine scenes herself, stitching verses together as suited her purpose for narrative effect and ease of articulation, and assigning varied forces to each section. She was proud of a critical sense: "Perhaps," she wrote, "the press notice that gave me the most pleasure of all is one . . . that dwelt on the fact that . . . I chose my lyrics with literary discrimination."[21] Neglected in England, the work was received warmly in North America, where it was performed up to the 1930s.[22]

In the vocal score the composer noted: "Ossian's remarkable 'word-pictures' depict vividly for all times the primitive joys and sorrows of his noble race, whose chief characteristics were bravery in battle, tenderness in love, and veneration of their forefathers. The ghosts of the dead were believed still to inhabit this earth, holding communication with their descendants and often appealing to them in hours of peril." She does not detail how she came to choose the poems of Ossian. The *fin-de-siècle* atmosphere had enticed a number of British composers to pen works around topics from Ossian. The success of Lehmann's *In a Persian Garden* cycle (1896) probably encouraged her to attempt the more ambitious setting.

Lehmann was born Elisabetha Nina Mary Frederica Lehmann, in London, the daughter of a German painter, Rudolf Lehmann, and a Scottish mother, Amelia Chambers (1838–1903), a music teacher, composer, and arranger, daughter of the

Table 13.4. Lehmann's *Leaves from Ossian*: settings and sources

No.	Title	Setting	Source
1	"A tale of the times of old!"	chorus, solo quartet	"Carthon"
2	"In the days of Fingal"	a. We sat and heard the sprightly harp (quartet) b. Who is that so dark and terrible? (chorus) c. They fought on the heath of Lena (scene: tenor, baritone) d. Spread the feast on Lena (chorus)	*Fingal*, Book IV; *Fingal*, Book I, "The War of Caros," "Carric-Thura"; *Temora*, Book I; *Fingal*, Book VI; *Fingal*, Book III
3	"Pleasant are the words"	contralto solo (with contralto chorus)	*Fingal*, Book III
4	"The daughter of Conloch" (ballad)	soprano solo with chorus	*Fingal*, Book II
5	"Episode of the chase"	a. Morning trembles (baritone solo) b. But one deer fell at the tomb of Ryno (contralto recit.) c. Our youth is like a dream (quartet)	*Fingal*, Book VI, "The War of Inisthona"
6	"Cuchullin's Love-Song"	tenor solo	*Fingal*, Book I
7	"Ode to the Sun"	chorus	"Carthon"
8	"Shilric and Vinvéla" (A fragment)	contralto and tenor	"Carric-Thura"
9	"Scene of Ossian's Death"	a. Star of descending night (sop. solo with male chorus) b. The death of Ossian (baritone solo) c. The chiefs of other times are gone (chorus, with tenor solo)	"The Songs of Selma," "Oithóna," "The War of Caros," "Berrathon"

antiquarian writer and publisher Robert Chambers.[23] In her childhood the family lived in France, Germany, and Italy because of her mother's delicate constitution. The wide circle of artistic friends and acquaintances of the family included Liszt, Anton Rubinstein, Verdi, Gounod, Clara Schumann, Brahms, and Stanford. When in London, Lehmann studied singing with Jenny Lind and composition with the Scottish composer Hamish MacCunn. Abroad, she took lessons from Niels Ravnkilde (1823–90), a Danish pianist and composer living in Rome, and Wilhelm Freudenberg (1838–1924), conductor of the Singakademie in Wiesbaden.

Lehmann knew very well the obstacles that English women composers could encounter.[24] The barriers to performance for *Leaves from Ossian* are comparable to those that prevented staging of Harriet Wainewright's opera *Comàla* a century earlier. But unlike Wainewright, who had to work hard to cultivate the custom of aristocrats and impresarios, Lehmann was well connected: her upbringing allowed her to meet influential personalities in London's music world. Yet after writing *Leaves from Ossian* she was still unable to get a performance in the capital.[25] In her autobiography (1919), Lehmann refers briefly to the work and its composition, adding that Chappell & Co had commissioned it. What is more, she remarked that it was "the scoring of *Leaves of Ossian* during the winter months, by electric light, that almost ruined [her] eye-sight," necessitating the use of glasses to read small print. In an interview for an American journal, she noted, "My latest work has been a cantata, a musical setting of some poems of Ossian ... if Macpherson was the author, there was no reason for his concealing his identity, as many famous English literary authorities have praised the poems highly. However, the uncertainty as to their identity adds to the interest in them."[26]

In her tour of North America in 1910, she was often billed as "Liza Lehmann the great" (or "world famous composer").[27] Her stay in the United States made for a reception of *Leaves from Ossian* quite different from that in England.[28] The work was given in the Temple Auditorium, Los Angeles, on May 25, 1911, with the Los Angeles Oratorio Society (126 members) and Orchestra (63 personnel) led by Harley Hamilton, with four soloists: Mrs. C. E. Bernard (soprano), Leah Pratt (alto), J. P. Dupuy (tenor), and Fred Ellis (baritone).[29] Another performance, by the Orpheus Club led by Dupuy, was advertised for November 29, 1911, at the Simpson Auditorium. Brigham Cecil Gates and the music department of the Latter Day Saints University also gave performances, in Salt Lake City in the spring of 1919[30] and in the College Amphitheatre, Logan, on May 26, 1927, the latter event before an audience of more than four thousand.[31] This performance, part of the "Sunset Festival" there, involved a full orchestra and choral forces from Utah Agricultural College and the Imperial Glee Club, conducted again by B. Cecil Gates.[32] Another performance was announced for Brigham Young University in Provo, Utah, on Monday, April 9, 1934.[33]

Leaves from Ossian is cast in nine sections with subdivisions. Following an introduction, a repeated two-bar phrase precedes the first choral and solo quartet number,

"A Tale of the Times of Old," in common time and A-major. As it concludes, an instrumental continuation is built on chords of the seventh until the tenor repeats the choral theme of the opening, now in $^6_8$. This pensive reflection, with its interval of a falling sixth, recalls the chorus in E-major from *In a Persian Garden* ("Alas! that spring should vanish with the rose"). A short section in $^6_8$ in F-sharp minor for the solo baritone ("Dost thou not behold Malvina?") ensues. In the related harmony of C-sharp minor, the soprano, accompanied by harp septuplets, continues the poem with "There the flow'r of the mountain grows." The chorus takes up the image of the thistle shedding its ancient beard as the harmony glides through a pedal dominant of F major, changing enharmonically to E minor for a *più lento*. This is the cue for the contralto and tenor solo voices to return to common time and intone, "Two stones half sunk in the ground / show their heads of moss."[34]

Scene 2 is in four parts. The soprano leads off with "We sat and heard the sprightly harp / By Lubar's gentle stream" in staccato vein, to be quelled by the direction *subito legato*, as the other soloists join in over a pedal D. Scene 2b retains the D-minor tonality and duple time in a series of trills on A, B♭, and C♯, when the chorus take up the words: "Who is that so dark and terrible / Coming in thunderous course?" Scene 2c is a duet for tenor and baritone, with a *moderato quasi allegretto* in G minor for "They fought on the heath of Lena." The final scene, 2d, has the chorus return with "Spread the feast on Lena" in a slightly faster B major. The short scene 3 is for contralto solo and contralto chorus, in a slow, tranquil meditation in D-flat major. When the voices get to "When the sun is faint on its side," they are unaccompanied, and the falling bass, E♭–D♭–C–C♭–B♭, conveys succinctly the image of a failing sun.

"The Daughter of Conloch" (scene 4) extends its opening decorative phrases for the soprano soloist to begin in the key of A minor and *in modo di ballata*, that is, following a quasi-strophic form. The tragic ballad, during which the young woman, in love with Comàl, puts on armor and is slain by him unknowingly, includes a slower central section in E major, *cantabile*, when Comàl tenderly asks her to rest in the cave: "Rest here, he said, my love, Galvina, thou light of the cave of Ronan." At "he thought it was his foe," the tonality veers to E minor, preparing for a return to A minor at the *ritenuto* (grave) section. At this, Comàl converses with the dying maiden over a pedal A. The solo voice, prompted by a $^6_4$ chord in C minor, engages in a coloratura flourish from B♮ to a high B♭ as an arrow ends Comàl's life.

Scene 5, "Episode of the Chase," is for baritone solo, contralto recitative, and solo quartet. The baritone solo, "Morning trembles," is cast in E-flat, and begins with a reminiscence of the opening motto theme. Gradually the music grows livelier, as Fingal calls for his hunting dogs, with a series of D-major chords decorated by *appoggiaturas*, until "that the joy of the king might be great." Scene 6 is the tenor solo, "Cuchullin's Love-Song," a setting of a poem known from countless glee settings: "O strike the harp in praise of my love." Scene 7 pictures the equally famous "Ode to the Sun": a long *tremolando* pedal on G♯, *pianissimo*, underlines a chromatic series

Example 13.9. Liza Lehmann, *Leaves from Ossian*, aria: "The murmur of thy streams, O Lora"

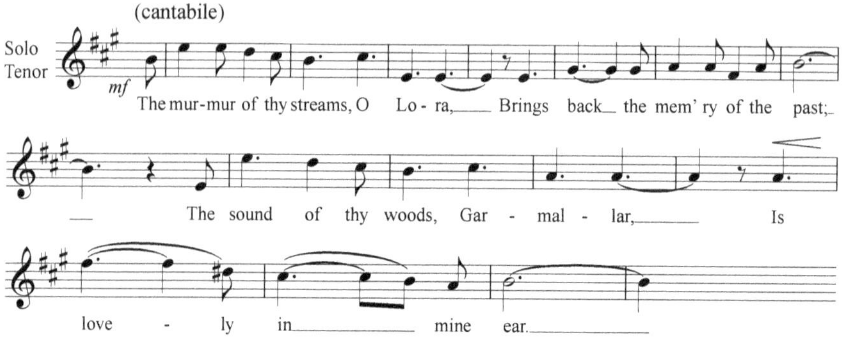

Example 13.10. Lehmann, *Leaves from Ossian*, recitative: "Two stones half sunk in the ground"

Example 13.11. Lehmann, *Leaves from Ossian*, recitative: "He threw away his dark brown shield"

of rippling triplet eighth notes in fifths and sixths until, after twenty bars, the chorus enters in C-sharp minor with "O, thou that rollest above."[35] At "the moon, cold and pale sinks in the Western wave," the key collapses to E-flat minor, the key of gloom or apocalypse. By the end the tonality has changed to E-flat, and for the majestic "thou lookest forth in thy beauty" the key switches abruptly to E major, carefully managed by an eighth note tied over from the preceding whole note. Chromatic sixteenth-note runs conjure the image of the storm, to end on an emphatic C-sharp major chord. The composer has set scene 8, "Shilric and Vinvéla," from the poem "Carric-thura," for contralto and tenor, in the key of F major. After a dozen bars of the final scene, 9, the tonality settles into a Schumann-like E-flat major for the soprano solo, "Star of descending night," in which the *tessitura* soars to a high C at "what dost thou behold, fair light?" Tenors and basses continue in duple time and C minor with a couplet adapted from another Ossian poem, "Oithóna": "The daughter of night turns her eyes away; / She beholds the grief that is coming"—prophetic, perhaps, of Lehmann's loss of her son a few years later.

A baritone solo returns to the opening motif, with "Bring, daughter of Toscar, bring the harp." Moving abruptly to B minor, Ossian muses on the death of his son,

Example 13.12. Lehmann, *Leaves from Ossian*, chorus: "The moon, cold and pale"

Oscar. Beseeching Malvina to lead him to the woods and streams he frequented of old, he confesses that his life is failing. The chorus continues the mood with solemn chords in C minor derived from scene 2 but with more frequent chromatic shifts, until the final *lento* is reached. The chorus then concludes by returning to the opening motto theme, now in A-major, with a line adapted from "Berrathon": "Ossian, thy fame shall remain / And grow like the oak of Morven / Which spreads its broad head to the storm / And rejoices in the course of the wind." This last phrase is effectively realized as the harmony switches to B-flat major in a dramatic gesture for the tenor solo, before the final cadence in the home key.

Example 13.13. Lehmann, *Leaves from Ossian*, chorus: "The daughter of night turns her eyes away"

Composing just a few years after Stanford's *Irish Rhapsody No. 2: Lament for the Son of Ossian* (1903), Lehmann may well have been moved by that work to turn to the poems. Without the orchestral score, which is untraced, it is difficult to judge *Leaves from Ossian* conclusively. Its reflective, nostalgic tone tells against it, even though there are imaginative touches in the vocal lines and flashes of instrumental inspiration, as in the vision of sunrise. The work, however, tends too often to rely on the effective but conventional gestures of the composer's *Rubáiyát* settings that were so impressive in 1896.[36] She seems to have reached this conclusion herself and thus discounted further mention of the work in her autobiography.[37] Uneven though *Leaves* may be, had the composer and metropolitan critics witnessed its effect in America, she—and they—might have reconsidered their judgment.

Chapter Fourteen

Symphonic Poem and Orchestral Fantasy

Alexandre Levy's *Comala* (1890) and Charles Villiers Stanford's *Irish Rhapsody No. 2: Lament for the Son of Ossian* (1903)

Alexandre Levy's composition *Comala*, his opus 11, written in 1890, advertises itself as a *Poema sinfonico para grande orquestra*. It is both an evocative response to the Ossianic poem of that name and a highly accomplished work for a twenty-six-year-old.[1] Less typical than other pieces of the composer that incorporate elements of Brazilian popular music, its antecedents are in the symphonic tradition of illustrative or program music such as the concert overtures of Mendelssohn or tone poems of Franz Liszt. His life spanned the musical period between Offenbach's opéra bouffe *La Belle Helène* (1864) and Debussy's "L'après-midi d'un faune" (1892). Born in São Paulo, Alexandre (1864–92) and his three siblings were children of the French clarinetist Henrique Louis Levy, originally from Dehlingen in Alsace, and Anne Marie Teodoreth, a Swiss from Treyvaux in the Fribourg canton.[2] Henrique had fled to Switzerland at the time of anti-Semitic riots in February 1848.[3] Later that same year, the couple emigrated to Brazil, settling first in Campinas, the city of the renowned opera composer Carlos Gomes (1836–96). Eventually they moved to São Paulo, where in 1860 they founded the Casa Levy, a piano and sheet music store that was also an important outlet for concerts and informal music-making. It still exists.[4]

Alexandre received his first piano lessons from his brother Luiz (1861–1935) and had further musical training from the French pianist Gabriel Giraudon.[5] With his brother he set up the Clube Haydn in 1883 to encourage musical culture in São

Paulo, and two years later, in 1885, he conducted an orchestra of twenty-six players in a performance of Haydn's Symphony No. 1. In 1887 he went to Europe, spending nine months in Milan and Paris in order to take lessons from Emile Durand, Debussy's teacher, and from Vincenzo Ferroni, who had studied with Massenet. A number of Levy's compositions had been published in the early 1880s and by this time his work was entering a mature phase: he drew particularly on native urban music, in works such as the *Variations sur un thème populaire brésilien* (1887), which uses a Brazilian children's song.

The language of the title is significant: French was the language of Levy's family and of his student days in Paris. It was only later that Portuguese titles of works indicate Levy's greater absorption of native motifs; the piano piece *Tango Brasileiro* (1890), for instance, shows the influence of the *maxixe*, or Brazilian tango, its syncopations derived from Afro-Brazilian dances. The other main impact on his style, however, was that of the early Romantic composers: Chopin (*Mazurcas*, op. 6), Mendelssohn (*Romance sans paroles*, op. 4), and more especially Robert Schumann (*Schumanniana*, op. 16, and the tone poem *Werther*). Levy's symphonic language was primarily shaped, on the one hand, by exposure to French and German idioms of the half century between 1830 and 1880, and on the other, by the urban idioms he encountered in São Paulo.[6]

Levy's awareness of Ossian probably came, first, from the translation of Christian Pitois, by far the bestselling version of the poems in the French-speaking world.[7] He may also have read the classic translation by Le Tourneur (1776/77). Although no complete Portuguese translation of *The Poems of Ossian* was available, Levy may well have known of Antonio Coppola's lauded opera *Fingal*, performed at the Theatre São Carlos in Lisbon on April 21, 1851, and again in 1864.[8] The libretto (text by Gaetano Solito), published in 1851, gave the Italian original and the Portuguese translation on facing pages.[9] While Levy was studying in Paris, the setting of *Fingal* by Lucien Hillemacher (1880) and its prize-winning status may have come to his notice. Yet another source of Ossian's literary influence must have been Goethe's novel *Werther*, for Levy composed a tone poem with that title in 1888, after his return to Brazil.

Alexandre Levy's *Comala* (1890)

Levy's *Comala*, completed two years later, is a more mature work, one less dependent on the influence of Schumann. It is cast in two main sections, with subdivisions. First, a Lento of 148 bars (*um poco più*, rehearsal letter D) represents Comala and her anxiety over the fortunes of Fingal, her betrothed, in his battle with Caracul. The second main section, marked *allegro molto tempestuoso*, reflects the treacherous intelligence of the lovestruck Hidallan as he tells Comala that Fingal has fallen, her reaction to the news, and her vision of Fingal's ghost. Last, the music reverts to the slow

Table 14.1. Levy's *Comala*: manuscript and published sources

	2-piano reduction (1892)	Eduardo Dohmen copy (1937)	BdeP publication (2002)
bar 37 [D]	andante maestoso	lento	lento
41		um poco piu [*sic*]–pp e legato	um poco più–pp legato
61	cantabile	cant. e express.	cantabile e espressivo
79 [G]	espress.	molto express. e legatiss.	molto espressivo e legatissimo
87	p cantabile	pp cresc.	pp cresc.
94 [I]	espress.	express.	espressivo
96		sfz on last beat	sfz on last beat
100		sfz on last beat	sfz on last beat
116-17 [K]	fff espress.	fff oboe: A♭, C♭ missing	fff
122			bass tromb. flat sign missing (D♭)
124 [L]		decresc.–ff	decresc.–ff
136 [M]	un poco più mosso	um poco più vivo	um poco più vivo
149	allegro tempestoso	allegro molto tempestuoso	allegro molto tempestuoso
13			clar. 1, third note is F♯ (nor G♯)
14		Fl. 1, ♯ sign missing	bassoon 2, E♮
17	bass, E♮	bass, E♭–E♮, errors in clars, horns	bass, E♭–E♮, errors in clars, horns
22		fff	fff
30			tromb. 1–2, F♯/A (not E♯/G)

41		tromb. 1–2, tenor clef missing
45		tromb. 4: B♭ (not A)
50		tromb 2–4, ♮ missing
65	marcatissimo sempre	marcatissimo sempre
67		cello, second note of triplet is B♭ (not C)
97	fff e marcato molto	fff e marcato molto
105–6	C♮ in treble, C♯ in bass	C♮ in treble, C♯ in bass
119	decresc	
132–3	allarg.	
134 [AA]	pp marcato il canto	ppp (sempre)
148 [BB]	molt' espressivo	espressivo
183	lo stesso movimento	largo
190	decresc. poco a poco	
193–94		dim.
203	ben marcato il canto	
212 [GG]	dolcissime espessivo	bem expressivo
214		horn, second minim E (not D)
220 [HH]	pp e dolce	pp espressivo [*sic*]
223–25		cello, tenor clef missing
229		bsn, second minim is F♯ (not E♯)
234 [II]	dolce	pp espressivo
	express.	

(*continued*)

Table 14.1.—*(concluded)*

	2-piano reduction (1892)	*Eduardo Dohmen copy (1937)*	*BdeP publication (2002)*
247 [JJ]–	sempre più piano	sempre ppp	sempre ppp
263 [KK]		ppp	tromb. 2, F (nor G)
264	f	sfz (fp)	sfz (fp)
270		vla. A♮ (not A♭)	vla. A♮ (not A♭)
283–8	pp	ppp (tpt, trom. pppp)	ppp (tpt/trom. pppp)
298		lento	lento
318[OO]	pp espressivo	um poco più (ppp)	um poco più (ppp)
322		cantabile e express.	bene legato (horns), cantabile e express. [*sic*]
374			tromb. 1–2, E♭, G
378			tromb. 1, A
379	Largo	Lento (fff)	Lento (fff)
383			tromb. D♭ missing
398	Allargan.	alargando cresc molto	alargando cresc molto
398	marcato per em?		
400		pp e legatissimo	pp e legatissimo
401	lunga rallentan.		clar. 1, second note = C♯ (nor D)
402			oboe 2, B♭ (not B)
405–6	harp arpeggios written out	harp arpeggios not written out	harp arpeggios not written out

tempo for Fingal's return and Comala's demise.¹⁰ The composer has devised figures and motifs that appear to follow the story quite closely: the harps, for example, are associated with Comala, and enter at critical points in the orchestral narrative. The orchestra is one of double woodwinds (with piccolo and cor anglais), four horns (in F), two trumpets (in B-flat), three trombones, bass trombone (*trombone baixo*) and tuba (used alternately), timpani, bass drum and cymbals, two harps, and strings.¹¹

Levy's symphonic poem is a sensitive representation of events in the tale of Comala. The transmediation conjures up effectively the presence, and the dialogue, of both major and minor characters (Comala, Fingal, Hidallan; Dersagrena, Melilcoma).

The work opens in slow $\frac{3}{4}$ time with a sequence of three quiet chords, perhaps echoing Comala's name: D minor, C major, B-flat major, with parallel fifths in the bassoons. The distant sound of a horn is heard at rehearsal letter A in the score (*um poco più*), an eight-bar phrase oscillating between three notes, A, B♭, and G. (This motif—the voice, perhaps, of Comala's companions, Melilcoma or Dersagrena—will emerge again, much later, in the trumpet part.) The three chords of the opening are repeated three times. At rehearsal letter D the two harps, with arpeggios, accompany a soft B-flat melody of sixteen bars in the first violins that seems to signify Comala's tender relationship with Fingal. After a brief harp interlude the melody is taken up and developed, this time with the three sequential chords of the opening in the clarinets and bassoons as they turn the harmony toward G minor. Rehearsal letter F sees the harps' arpeggios turn to the key of B-flat minor as Comala's anxieties increase. Her volatile emotions are conveyed through the rapid harmonic changes for these instruments: F major, B-flat major, A major, B-flat/E-flat major (with that added seventh), D major.

At rehearsal letter H a ten-bar theme with dipping sixths and sevenths (derived from and merging with the B-flat melody) arises in the violins and oboe. The theme is briefly concluded by woodwind, flute, and oboe in a way that suggests Comala and Fingal's love. Then *pianissimo* fanfares of the trombones (B-flat minor, then B-flat major) and timpani, backed by woodwind chords, mirror the far-off sound of battle. Comala's apprehension increases as the harp arpeggios accumulate into sextuplets for twelve bars, moving through the key of G-flat as the trombones utter quiet fanfares. The instruction in the score, *um poco più vivo* (rehearsal letter M), heralds a repeat of the tender love motif. This extends for twelve bars, with *sforzando* markings indicating, possibly, the approach of Hidallan, and leads to a dominant seventh chord on F as the section ends with a linking *crescendo* flourish of the timpani.

The second main section of the work, *allegro molto tempestuoso*, begins with a change to common time and a sharply accented diminished chord, sixteenth notes in the lower strings injecting a restless string passage into the texture. A rising chromatic bass line leads to a quieter clarinet melody in the low *chalumeau* range of the instrument, a jagged motif over two bars that is repeated a semitone higher (bars 18–21). The climax of this subsection at rehearsal letter R is a double *fortissimo*

Table 14.2. Levy's *Comala*: structure

Section	Key signature	Time signature	Orchestration	Marking
bars 1–36	B♭	3/4	str, ww, hns	lento
37–82	B♭	3/4	(+ harps)	um poço più
83–123	B♭	3/4	(+ tr, tromb, timp)	
124–35	B♭ (B♭ minor)	3/4	(+ harps)	
136–48	B♭	3/4	str, ww, hns	um poço più vivo
1–28	(G minor)	4/4	str, ww, hns, tromb, timp. percussion	allegro molto tempestuoso
29–63	B♭	4/4	(+ trpts)	
64–119	B♭	4/4	full orch. (trem str.)	
120–33	B♭	4/4	str, ww, (trb)	
134–82	A major	4/4	(+ harps, trpt, trb, perc)	
183–219	B♭ (G minor)	3/2 2/2	full orch. (–harps)	(largo)/ tempo primo
220–317	B♭	2/2	str, ww, tpt	
318–75	B♭	2/2	str, hns, hrps, trpt, trmb, timp	
376–406	B♭	4/4 3/4	str, ww, hrps	largo–lento

Example 14.1. Levy, *Comala*, opening section, *lento* (two-piano score), bars 37–43

D-minor chord in the full orchestra, the trombones, *tremolando* violins, and violas descending chromatically against a rising chromatic bass as if to symbolize Fingal in danger (bars 41–44). Fanfares on ninth chords in the four trombones, with bass drum and timpani, lead to a restatement of the chromatic descending strings motif. Scurrying strings usher in a new scalic group of uprushing sixteenth notes (rehearsal letter U) that, with fanfares in the horns and a spiky trumpet motif reinforced by timpani and a clashing cymbal, suggests Hidallan's desperate cry, "the nations are scattered on their hills; they shall hear the voice of the king no more." This desperation is further evoked by *fortissimo* D-minor chords in the strings, alternating with uprushing sixteenth notes in the strings and woodwinds, until, with the spiky brass

Example 14.2. Levy, *Comala*, ten-bar theme with love motif, bars 87–96

motto, the tumult subsides at rehearsal letter Z. Quiet *tremolando* strings are offset by repeats, in the woodwinds, of the brass triplet figure.

The key signature now changes from the two flats of G minor to the three sharps of A major (rehearsal letter AA). The entry of harp arpeggios, *pianissimo*, against high *tremolando* As in the violins, recalls Comala, and her plea: "Stop, ye sons of the grave, till I behold my love!" Brass fanfares, and a rising chromatic bass from E to B, lead to anguished dissonant half note chords (rehearsal letter DD). Insistent trumpet and trombone fanfares reach a *fortissimo* climax at a *largo* bar in $\frac{3}{2}$ time before the narrative returns to the initial tempo, the uprushing sixteenth notes, and spiky brass motif. A diminution in both dynamics ensues, with solo trumpets, and then horns, sounding fanfares in succession, *mezzo-forte*, then gradually to *pianissimo*.

A hushed solo cor anglais, partnered by a horn against a pedal D, announces the love motif (*bem expressivo*). The motif is repeated in the strings and by the clarinet, and suggests Comala's delusion that she is seeing Fingal's ghost. A new, tender countermelody in the bassoon and two cellos, and the trumpet's expressive repeat of the motif, impart the return of Fingal. At rehearsal letter KK haunting diminished chords in the four trombones are doubled by shimmering lower strings.[12] The effect is striking.[13]

Following this the lower strings, clarinets, and bassoons provide a hushed background for swaying clarinet and trumpet half notes (rehearsal letter LL). The entire section is perhaps Levy's attempt to convey Comala's delusion that she is seeing Fingal's ghost. At rehearsal letter MM offstage trumpets and trombones play a short, three-bar phrase (*pppp*), repeated a semitone lower two bars later.[14] The sonority is reduced, with only lower strings, clarinets, and bassoons, as the time changes to a slow $\frac{3}{4}$ for repetitions of the three chords that opened the work. At this the harps return with their arpeggios, in a secure B-flat tonality, with Comala's theme (rehearsal letter OO), developed through an excursion to B-flat minor as before: "He is returned with his fame," as she declares in the poem, "but I must rest beside the rock till my soul returns from my fear! O let the harp be near! Raise the song, ye daughters of Morni!" By this time the musical narrative (rehearsal letter RR) has reached a six-four chord of B-flat, where the trombones give out a confident fanfare to prove that indeed Fingal has returned alive and victorious. But Comala,

Example 14.3. Levy, *Comala*, second section, *allegro tempestuoso*, bars 64–69

Example 14.4. Levy, *Comala*, trombone chords, bars 263–69

trembling, stricken by her fears and the treachery of Hidallan (a repeated triplet figure *pianissimo* in the horns succeeded by *fortissimo* trumpets), expires.

A new brass motif, a rising triad on E♭, leads to a final *largo* section that captures Fingal's instruction to his bards: "Raise, ye sons of song, the wars of the streamy Carun; that my white-handed maid may rejoice: while I behold the feast of my love." Divided cellos and the cor anglais return to the short love theme while triplets in the flutes and oboes, and subsequently in the final *largo* section, perhaps refer to the bardic pronouncement, "See! meteors gleam around the maid! See! moonbeams lift her soul!" Soft G♭ triplets in the horns, succeeded by assertive B♭s in the trumpets, broaden out to accompany the violin melody with a crescendo to reach repose in the home key of B-flat. Whispered arpeggios in the harps, *pianissimo* and *staccato*, bring the piece to a close.

Comala is an ambitious work that attests to Levy's close acquaintance with the original poem, even if in translation. The episodes into which the narrative falls (the anxiety of Comala, the falsehood of Hidallan, Comala's vision of Fingal's ghost, Fingal's return, and the final reunion before her death) are perceptible in the musical events that reflect them. Without tying passages of the music to very specific elements in the poem, the composer has devised melodic figurations and tonal motifs that can be associated with the three main characters, Comala, Fingal, and Hidallan. The first, extended section is almost entirely a portrait of the heroine, not only in the use of the harp but also in the main theme (ex. 14.1) and the short love motif that recurs throughout the piece.

The overall proportions show a sure-footedness of characterization and dramatic juxtaposition, with instances of both regular and irregular barring of themes and subsections as well as, in dynamic contrast, *crescendo* and *diminuendo*, accentuation, and dynamic extremes such as *fff* and *ppp*. The circular structure concentrates the focus on the hapless heroine, the harp parts evoking her emotions as Fingal battles his enemies. The tonal contrasts are well conceived, with major segments in B-flat, D minor, E-flat, G-flat, B-flat minor, and F major. Harmonic originality is evident in the diminished and augmented trombone chords that precede what may be the ghostly return of Fingal from the battlefield (rehearsal letter KK). Major chords with an added seventh are evident in the harp chording. Minor thirds appear often, both melodically and harmonically. These feed into the orchestral colouring, which is original in its instrumentation, especially the brass. The brass, in fact, tends to

Example 14.5. Levy, *Comala*, brass fanfares, bars 375–78, 382–86

dominate the piece, and not just with fanfares: at times the weight of four trombones is barely offset by the rest of the orchestra. Levy could not shake off the ghost of Schumann entirely: the trombone sonorities of the Third Symphony ("Rhenish") may well have impressed him.

But the presence of the cor anglais and piccolo at key moments (providing pathos, or critical emphasis) attest to the composer's restraint. Some segments attain a chamber-like quality, especially those in the final scene, at the tragic end of Comala and what may be construed as Fingal's mood mirroring the poem's "Lead me to the place of her rest, that I may behold her beauty." The final quiet chords in the cellos and woodwinds (*pp e legatissimo*) summarize the harmonic range of the work: B-flat, E-flat minor, D-flat major, dissonant G/B in the oboes against B♭/E♭ in the cellos and basses, dominant seventh on A♭, and finally a return to B-flat major for the conclusion, marked by the gentle, staccato arpeggios of the harps. *Comala* is a mature work that shows both imagination and flair in its symbolic transmediation of the celebrated poem.

Charles Villiers Stanford's *Irish Rhapsody No. 2*: *Lament for the Son of Ossian* (op. 84)

At the beginning of the twentieth century, Willem Mengelberg, conductor of the Concertgebouw Orchestra in Amsterdam from 1895 to 1945, commissioned a work from the Dublin-born Charles Villiers Stanford (1852–1924), professor of music at Cambridge University since 1887 and already an established composer. Stanford had also taught at the Royal College of Music from its establishment in 1883: among his pupils were Gustav Holst and Ralph Vaughan Williams. He himself had studied in Leipzig with Carl Reinecke, teacher of the composers Albéniz, Bruch, Busoni, Grieg, Janáček, and many others. Although Stanford found the conservative and caustic Reinecke uninspiring as a pedagogue, his compositional idiom by 1900 owed much to the style, through Reinecke's instruction, of Schumann, Mendelssohn, and Brahms.[15]

The work that Mengelberg commissioned from Stanford was the *Irish Rhapsody No. 2*, subtitled *The Lament for the Son of Ossian*. In 1889 the critics had praised the composer's *Irish Symphony* (1887), and the *Irish Rhapsody No. 1* (1901) achieved a popular success, partly because of its arrangement of the well-known "Air from County Derry." Stanford would go on to complete six Irish rhapsodies, the rhapsody as a genre offering the composer some freedom in design: it not only released him from the constraints of conventional sonata form but also signified to him the unfettered character of his traditional material. The rhapsody, further, was a mark of deep cultural commitment to his origins, although politically he was unsympathetic to the idea of Irish independence. The score of the Second Rhapsody is dated February 23, 1903, but Stanford had begun work on it in March 1902, six months before the First Rhapsody was performed.

The Second Rhapsody is dedicated to Mengelberg, who led its premiere in Amsterdam on May 25, 1903. The first performance in the United Kingdom took place at St. James's Hall, on June 8, 1903, with the same conductor and the Concertgebouw Orchestra, who were in London as part of a Richard Strauss Festival.[16] Another performance took place in Bournemouth on October 26 of that year with Stanford himself conducting, and the work was heard again in a Philharmonic Society concert in the Queen's Hall, London, on March 15, 1906, directed by the composer Fredric Cowen, who like Stanford had studied with Reinecke in Leipzig. The performance that Stanford conducted with the Queen's Hall Orchestra in February 1907 was its last until the Ulster Orchestra recorded the piece in 1991.[17] The score was never published, and the lament-like character of the work may have contributed to its subsequent neglect.

The autograph score of forty pages and 345 bars is deposited in the Royal College of Music.[18] Its title page is headed, "To Willem Mengelberg," with the designation below: "Irish Rhapsody/No. 2/'The Lament for the Son of Ossian'/for/Full Orchestra/composed by/Charles Villiers Stanford/Op. 84." Also below, a hand, possibly that of Stanford himself, has scribbled in blue pencil, "This score to be returned to CV Stanford, Kensington, London." In paginating the score the composer has mistakenly numbered page 35 as "36"—that is, there are two pages numbered 36. Several pages have a line drawn through them (3, 9, 10, 37), though what this signifies is uncertain. The score has numerous blue and black pencil markings, some apparently in Mengelberg's hand: for example the abbreviation "pos," i.e., *Posaune* (German for "trombone," bar 204) and other insertions indicating tempo and dynamics, along with the instruction *halten* (German for "steady" tempo: bars 113, 125–26, 215, 217). Numbers in blue pencil, probably again in Mengelberg's hand, mark off the thematic sections of the score. A few red pencil markings mainly relate to dynamic levels (bars 86, 104–7, 139–40).

The programmatic matter of the Second Rhapsody evokes the death of Ossian's son Oscar, his burial, and Ossian's quest for vengeance. The composer draws on traditional Irish tunes to express the feelings associated with this material, writing on the score: "Strike the harp, and raise the song: be near, with all your wings, ye winds. Bear the mournful sound away to Fingal's airy hall. Bear it to Fingal's hall, that he may hear the voice of his son: the voice of him that praised the mighty. —Ossian." The quotation comes from Macpherson's "Berrathon" and is part of a general lament by Ossian on his predicament as the last of Selma's heroes. We can speculate how deeply Stanford, in writing the rhapsody, was affected by the results of the Boer War that had recently ended, for the Royal Irish Regiment had been prominent in the conflict.[19]

Musically, the Second Rhapsody is scored for full orchestra (with harp). Stanford used three traditional Irish melodies as building material: "The Lament for Owen Roe O'Neill," "Awake Fianna," and "Lay his Sword by his Side."[20] A melody for "The Lament for Owen Roe O'Neill" is attributed to the seventeenth-century harper Turlough O'Carolan (1670–1738), who is supposed to have composed the tune at the request of Charles O'Conor of Belanagare. Beethoven, notably, made an arrangement for piano trio of Carolan's melody in his *Seven British Songs* (WoO 158b), no. 7: "Lament for Owen Roe O'Neill (Irish)," with the text included.[21] Grattan Flood, however, in his *History of Irish Music* (1905), claims that the lament was composed soon after Owen Roe's death in 1649, when tradition relates that he was poisoned by a woman who placed a toxin in his shoes.[22] Owen Roe O'Neill (1582–1649), a member of the aristocratic O'Neill family of County Tyrone, left Ireland to fight on behalf of the Spanish in the Netherlands but returned to lead a rebellion against the Stuart regime. Three years after his victory at the Battle of Benburb in 1646 he died at Cloughouter, Co. Cavan.[23]

The tune that Stanford uses in his rhapsody, however, is one taken down by the folk song collector of Scottish ancestry George Petrie (1790–1866), from the fiddler Frank Keane of Co. Clare, then living in Dublin, who had learned it from the singing of women in Clare;[24] Keane could not remember the words. This melody now appears to have been sidelined by Carolan's version. Because the Carolan tune was arranged by Beethoven, is strongly associated with its Irish composer, and has an instrumental character, it is not surprising that it has found its way into the repertoire of groups specializing in the performance of traditional Irish music. But the distinctive lamenting shape of Stanford's melody indicates its vocal origins, and it is in all probability for this reason that the composer intended it to dominate the piece.[25]

Table 14.3. Stanford's *Irish Rhapsody No. 2*: structure

Section	Key	Theme	Time	Marking
1-87	F minor	"Lament for Owen Roe O'Neill"	3/4	adagio
88-101	D♭ major	"Awake Fianna"	3/4 | 9/8	allegretto moderato
102-25		["Awake Fianna"]	[3/4 | 9/8]	allegro moderato
126-91	C minor	"Lament"	[3/4 | 9/8]	
192-235		"Lament"/"Awake"	[3/4 | 9/8]	
236-67	A♭/F minor	"Lament"/"Awake"	3/4	adagio
268-304	F major	"Lay his sword by his side"	4/4	lento e solenne
305-24	B♭ minor/ F minor	"Lament"	3/4	molto adagio
306-end	F major	"Lay his sword by his side"	4/4	lento e solenne (alla marcia)

The primary tonality of the work suggests that Stanford may have chosen F minor as a reminiscence of Schubert's "Kolma's Klage," whose third and final part ends in that key. Furthermore, the piece is almost entirely in $\frac{3}{4}$ apart from the final slow march segment. Certainly the marking "$\frac{3}{4}$ ($\frac{9}{8}$)" at the *allegretto moderato* allows the lively central section to evolve in variegated triplets such that the ternary rhythm is never stilted.

The opening *adagio* in $\frac{3}{4}$ with its rapid, rising sixteenth-note anacrusis in the lower strings leads to a solemn brass chord in F minor. The violas and second violins continue their impassioned keening for some ten bars until the *pianissimo* entrance of the timpani's gently rolling background.[26] A hastening of the pace allows the first violins to take up the lament melody for twelve bars, embellishing the six jagged eighth notes with upbeats. Subsequently, a solo horn and the cellos sound a warm, Brahms-like version of the melody, the harp interweaving the texture with broken chords and arpeggios.

The tempo gradually gathers speed until an *allegretto moderato* in $\frac{3}{4}$ ($\frac{9}{8}$) introduces the second melody, "Awake Fianna," otherwise known as "The Monks of the Screw" (or "When Saint Patrick our order created"), enunciated here by the horns:[27] this section, scored for full orchestra (from bar 88), gains in intensity with triplet figuration in the strings and leads back to a dramatic restatement of the first lament theme in the clarinets and horns, with the restless accompaniment of dotted eighth notes in the strings (from bar 126). In this development Stanford combines both the first and second themes, gradually slowing the tempo and stilling the volume of the full orchestra. The development returns to *adagio*, the first F-minor theme played by oboe and clarinet while accompanied by harp arpeggios and soft chords in the strings. The melodic line is taken up by the violins in a passionate statement that varies the initial keening melody, moves to a climax, then draws down via a chromatic

Example 14.6. Charles Villiers Stanford, *Irish Rhapsody No. 2: Lament for the Son of Ossian*, "Lament for Owen Roe O'Neill," bars 25–36

Example 14.7. Stanford, *Irish Rhapsody No. 2*, scoring of "Awake Fianna," bars 88–95

descent to a slow section (from bar 268) marked *lento e solenne* (*alla marcia*) in common time.[28]

Here, the violins come into their own again with a lengthy passage of high-pitched, mainly pentatonic melody in F major, "Lay his Sword by his Side," against a background of offbeat chords, *piano* and *pianissimo*, in the harp and woodwinds. This gradually rises to a *fortissimo* climax in the full orchestra (bar 290). The violins eventually subside for the final *molto adagio* (306). But almost immediately they pour out the lament theme in a rhapsodic repeat of the initial keening against a *fortissimo* background, the G♭s in the melody clashing with the pedal F in a B-flat minor tonality. This string cantilena gradually moves to a final *molto adagio* (with *"ed appassionato"* added in pencil, in the composer's hand) whereby the violins accentuate the dotted figure at the end of the first, lamenting theme. The bassoons and cellos take up a final, truncated statement of the "Lay his Sword by his Side" theme, and the rhapsody draws to a hushed close.

Example 14.8. Stanford, *Irish Rhapsody No. 2*, scoring of "Lay his sword by his side," bars 271–89

Despite, or perhaps because of, its episodic character, the rhapsody gives an impression of sharply differentiated material that achieves a convincing unity toward the end of the piece, when the first theme ("Lament for Owen Roe O'Neill") is continued by a statement of the third melody ("Lay his Sword"). The second theme ("Awake Fianna") supplies a dramatic tonal contrast for the middle section: its D-flat major enunciation in the horns gives way to a stirring development by the full orchestra. The *Irish Rhapsody No. 2* has been criticized for its episodic structure, but Stanford has managed to develop and bring together three traditional tunes in a convincing combination that eschews grandiose sonorities in favor of a gently calculated conclusion. The material that Stanford used in this work may appear divergent in terms of its relationship to Macpherson's Ossian when we focus on the transposition of the thematic matter to a patriotic Irish context. But it is convergent structurally and emotionally, its episodic character mirroring the fragmentary nature of the poems. As an example of symbolic transmediation, it provides, in its skillful blend of known airs that bring it into alignment with contemporary armed conflict, a striking contrast to Levy's symphonic poem.

Chapter Fifteen

Neo-Romanticism in Britain and America

John Laurence Seymour's "Shilric's Song" (from *Six Ossianic Odes*) and Cedric Thorpe Davie's *Dirge for Cuthullin* (both 1936)

Sporadically, as the nineteenth century progressed, the poems of Ossian continued to inspire musical works in Britain: a ballet, *Mora's Love, or The Enchanted Harp* (1809), and an unfinished opera, *Fingallo* (ca. 1810), by Henry Bishop; a ballad opera, *Malvina*, with music by the Irish composer Thomas Simpson Cooke (1826); an overture, *Ossian* (1882), written and performed in 1882 by the London-born composer Frederick Corder (1852–1932), curator of the Royal Academy of Music from 1889 (his planned opera on the topic, ca. 1905, was apparently never performed); and William Augustus Barratt's cantata *The Death of Cuthullin* (1897).[1] As tensions mounted over colonial wars and European unrest at the beginning of the twentieth century, the association with loss of compatriots in battle found ready expression in works such as Stanford's *Irish Rhapsody No. 2: Lament for the Son of Ossian* (1903) and Liza Lehmann's cantata *Leaves from Ossian*, its disquiet and longing conveyed by solo voices, chorus, and orchestra (1909).[2]

A handful of works based on Ossian survived the Great War, including Edgar Bainton's opera *Oithóna* (1915), revisiting the protagonist of Barthelemon's effort in 1768. Bainton (1880–1956) wrote the work for the Glastonbury Festival of 1915, although at the time of production he was in a civilian detention camp in Ruhleben, Germany, where he was held from 1914 to 1918. The work received four performances at Glastonbury, along with the second act of Wagner's *Tristan*. The critic for *The Times*, writing on August 12, 1915, noted that "the composer has gone to early British legend for his subject, and that type of subject has unfortunately earned a reputation for unreality in opera . . . Of the two scenes, the second, which begins with the lament of Oithóna and ends with her self-sought death in the battle between her two lovers, is the better, because the emotion of the drama is stronger and the music rises to its opportunities."

Ossian was much in the air at this time. For the second of a series of War Emergency Concerts in London, the promoter Isidore de Lara asked the composer Eugene Goossens (1893–1962) if he could supply an orchestral work at short notice. Goossens gives a disarming account of how he came to compose a symphonic prelude based on Ossian:

> For the second of these War Emergency Concerts, until the middle of November [1915] Mary Garden had been especially engaged, and only six weeks before the actual date de Lara asked me whether I had something ready, or nearly ready, for inclusion in the programme . . . I immediately cast around for a subject, and lit upon a fragment from one of the poems of Ossian. It was an apocalyptic thing, full of thunder, earthquakes, and disaster, but I thought it appropriate to the times, and immediately set to work on the sketch. This was completed in eight days, and the orchestration three weeks later. The Symphonic Prelude, which lasted about quarter of an hour, employed a very large orchestra, an organ, and the enormous mushroom-bells of Queen's Hall up in the organ gallery, likewise a thunder-machine. I used such a big orchestra that near the finish Lara, looking at the score, remarked, 'Are you quite sure you haven't forgotten something?' The din of the climax created a great effect, and while the musical content of the piece didn't bear too close a scrutiny . . . the public seemed enraptured. . . . I was still a member of the Queen's Hall Orchestra at the time of the concert, and, as had often previously been the case, left my seat among the first violins to conduct my piece, and returned to it at the finish.[3]

By the turn of the twentieth century, a decrease in musical works based on the poems—in metropolitan-dominated England at least—was partly a consequence of attacks on Ossian, partly a result of changing fashion in European artistic and literary circles—the powerful association of Ossian with Romanticism, on the one hand, and continued carping about the poems' authenticity, on the other.[4]

In any case, by 1900 a significant link to Gaelic oral tradition had emerged with the "Celtic recovery" project of Marjory Kennedy-Fraser, undertaken with encouragement from the critic Ernest Newman and the composer Granville Bantock (1868–1946), one of Corder's former students. Bantock endorsed Kennedy-Fraser's *Songs of the Hebrides* as "a classic work, unique in its knowledge and expression of the peculiar characteristics of Gaelic Music," and went on to compose his "Hebridean" Symphony (1913) and "The Death of Morar" (1917), a setting for mixed voices on a text from "The Songs of Selma."[5] Toward the end of a career powerfully influenced by this strand of revivalist Celtic folklore, Bantock produced not only his "Celtic

Symphony" (1940, which asks for six harps) but also two short orchestral pieces, "Cuchullan's Lament: A Heroic Ballad for Orchestra" and "Kishmul's Galley" (1944). Bantock's works are often, like the "Hebridean" Symphony, built on pentatonic fragments of melody that closely resemble Highland airs. From the 1950s, ethnomusicologists using digital tape recorders have captured orally transmitted Ossianic lays in the Outer Hebrides that owe little or nothing to Macpherson's poems.[6]

Further along in time, the Ossian poems periodically inspired orchestral, choral, and operatic works that were to leave late Romanticism behind in order to embrace leaner textures and a fresh interpretation of the poems. Opera, one of the main forms for continental expression of Ossian, had seemed to defeat native composers: the lack of an operatic tradition or suitable librettos and the expense of staging told against the form. This was true, for instance, for Corder and for John Blackwood McEwen (1868–1948), later principal of the Royal Academy of Music in London from 1924 to 1936, who began an opera on the subject of Comala ("about 1889," according to the MS) in the wake of his symphonic poem of the same name (also 1889).[7] Both of these works McEwen left unfinished, although the score of the symphonic poem is well over three hundred bars in length.

A similar fate overtook the attempt by the prolific composer and conductor of the BBC Scottish Symphony, Ian Whyte (1901–60), to fashion an opera on the theme of Comala (1929).[8] Headed "Comala, an opera (words from Ossian)," this draft remains in short score, though two of the three acts are fairly complete in a piano arrangement. An unusual feature of the overture, which was apparently performed, is the frequent change of time signature: after four bars in $\frac{4}{4}$ time, the sequence of changes is: $\frac{2}{4}$ (1 bar), $\frac{3}{4}$ (2 bars), $\frac{4}{4}$ (3 bars), then $\frac{6}{8}, \frac{4}{4}, \frac{3}{4}, \frac{7}{8}$, and $\frac{9}{8}$ in rapid succession. The tonality hovers around B-flat in acts 1 and 2, while act 3 conducts an adventurous foray into G-flat major.[9] It is unclear why Whyte never completed the opera, for the sketches suggest an intimate involvement with the subject matter.

Although in America Louis Moreau Gottschalk had written his pianistic *Ossian: Deux Ballades*, op. 4 (1843), "Danse ossianique," op. 12 (1850–51), and the popular "Marche de nuit," op. 17 (1855),[10] it was the tour of North America by Liza Lehmann and her ensemble in 1910 that enchanted audiences with her compositions, among them *Leaves from Ossian* (1909).[11] The later performances of that work in Utah, in 1919, 1927, and 1934, may have caught the attention of the composer John Laurence Seymour (1893–1986) who, born in Los Angeles and educated in Sacramento, later settled in Cedar City, Utah. In 1922 he traveled to Europe and from 1923 to 1928 studied music in Rome with Pizzetti, in Florence with Felice Boghen, and in Paris with d'Indy. During these years he composed no fewer than 22 operas, as well as operettas, musical plays, and a fair amount of chamber music, including songs for voice and piano such as the *Six Ossianic Odes*, op. 23.[12] The influence of Henry David Thoreau and Walt Whitman, great admirers of Ossian, was at this time strong in the United States. In his literary taste and college teaching Seymour may well have felt empathy especially with Whitman's admiration for the poems.[13]

John Lawrence Seymour's "Shilric's Song" (1936)

Seymour's *Six Ossianic Odes*, op. 23, seem to have been written just after his one-act opera, *In the Pasha's Garden*, op. 17, was premiered at the Metropolitan Opera in New York, on January 24, 1935.[14] While it earned the composer the Bispham Memorial Medal Award, the opera was not a success, receiving only three performances.[15] The *Odes*, with their strong current of lament, may well reflect Seymour's feelings at the opera's fate. The six songs are entitled: (1) Shilric's Song, (2) The Poet's Prayer, (3) A Dirge for Ryno, (4) Bend thy Blue Course, O Stream, (5) Malvina, Where Art Thou?, and (6) Thou Has Left Us. Only the first three were published.[16] The text of the first ode is based on the poem "Carric-Thura," that of the second on "Dar-thula," and that of the third on Book V of *Fingal*; the text of odes 4, 5, and 6 is based on "Berrathon."

The first setting, "Shilric's Song," is for low voice, with a range from A (below middle C) to E♭ an octave and a diminished fifth higher.[17] The text is, apart from a very few minor differences (such as "descend" rather than "descends"), that of Macpherson's poem "I sit by the mossy fountain, on the top of the hill of winds."

Marked *andante triste* and in $\frac{6}{8}$ time, the G-minor opening with a hypnotic syncopated motif involving a prominent A♭–G shift in the bass helps establish the mood of lament. Rhythmic subtlety accompanies throughout a dynamic level that, apart from the short central section, varies from *piano* to double *pianissimo*. From bar 14, at "Sad are my thoughts alone," the harmony turns toward F minor, and with the return of the initial *ostinato* motif at "thy hair floating on the wind" (bar 20), the keyboard figuration develops into passionate sixteenth notes in the key of G-flat major for "thine eyes full of tears for thy friends." As this outburst calms, in a new, more lively section ("But is it she that there appears like a beam of light"), the voice is supported by soft *tremolando* motifs in the upper range of the piano. With a return to the G minor of the opening, the music's *pianissimo* ending, with a prominent G–A♭ motif in the bass against the thirds of the right-hand part, sinks to an open fifth in the home key.

This first ode is more convincing in its inspiration and workmanship than, for instance, no. 3, the "Dirge for Ryno," whose text Seymour adapted from *Fingal*.[18] His verse adaptation of the episode seems jejune in literary terms, although the third ode is musically adventurous, passing through D minor, A minor, G major, B minor, B-flat minor, and F major before its return to the opening key. The cadences involve modal shifts to a key a tone higher or lower and liberal use of flattened sevenths, inflections that suggest an "antique" or "Celtic" flavor in line with the verses. In the wake of criticism of his opera, Seymour may have felt a personal identification with the fallen hero Ryno: the foray into B-flat minor at "His bosom broad and fair / Is gash'd by livid scars untold" may reflect his feelings of disappointment. That the *Odes* were published one year later seems to place in doubt the claim that he did not compose for long afterward.[19] Rather, it seems probable that the *Odes* were an

Example 15.1. John Laurence Seymour, "Shilric's Song," bars 1–3

Example 15.2. Seymour, "Shilric's Song," bars 21–24

Example 15.3. Seymour, "Shilric's Song," bars 35–41

immediate and brave reaction to the opera's fate. As the only published music based on Ossian at this time in North America, these odes seem to continue the style of Liza Lehmann's *Leaves*, with their obvious debt to Schumann as model. It seems possible that Seymour could have attended the performance of that work in Provo on April 9, 1934, or read reviews of it.[20] He may also have studied or possessed the vocal score.

Cedric Thorpe Davie's *Dirge for Cuthullin* (1936)

While the political struggles in Europe during the 1930s might have appeared fertile ground for inspiration from Ossian, only a few British musicians found the poems apt for setting. Composers under the Ossian spell at the time of World War II included Ronald Center (1913–73), whose tone poem *The Coming of Cuchulain* (now untraced) was broadcast in 1944; the London-born Cedric Thorpe Davie (1913–83), who composed two orchestral works based on the poems; and the energetic and uncompromising Erik Chisholm (1904–65), who completed his Symphony No. 2 ("Ossian") in 1939 but then arranged it for a ballet, *The Earth Shapers*, with a scenario he devised from Celtic sources.[21] Between them, Chisholm and Thorpe Davie resurrect the Ossian ghost with some verve: the former found his brand of modernity in Bartók, the latter in Sibelius and Vaughan Williams. The four movements of Chisholm's symphony also show the influence of Sibelius, a composer prominent in British musical life at the time; his shadow is also perceptible in Thorpe Davie's first orchestral essay, the *Elegy for an Ossianic Warrior* (1932), written at the age of nineteen.[22] But while Chisholm might be described as a "modernist" in that his life and work fall into the half century between 1910 and 1960, Thorpe Davie's idiom is more traditional, welded to that modal-tonal ground between late romanticism and the radical modern.

Thorpe Davie's ambitious and skillfully conceived cantata *Dirge for Cuthullin* (1935–36, published in 1937) was composed while studying with Vaughan Williams at the Royal College of Music, although the extent of his teacher's influence must be qualified, as the young composer's correspondence reveals.[23] The cantata represents his first mature composition; completed when he was in his early twenties, the piece is scored for full orchestra and chorus, is some 208 bars in length, and lasts about fifteen minutes.[24] The composer excerpted the text from Macpherson's "The Death of Cuthullin," on which the author had noted: "This is the song of the bards over Cuthullin's tomb. Every stanza closes with some remarkable title of the hero, which was always the custom in funeral elegies." While Macpherson's text is in poetic prose, Thorpe Davie arranged it in stanzas, remaining faithful to the words and with only minor differences in punctuation:

Dirge for Cuthullin

Blest be thy soul, Son of Semo!
Thou wert mighty in battle,
Thy strength was like the strength of a stream,
Thy speed like the eagle's wing;
Thy path in battle was terrible!
The steps of death were behind thy sword.
Blest be thy soul, son of Semo,
Car-borne chief of Dunscaith!
Thou hast not fallen by the sword of the mighty,
Neither was thy blood on the spear of the brave.
The arrow came like the sting of death in a blast,
Nor did the feeble hand which drew the bow perceive it.
Peace to thy soul in thy cave,
Chief of the isle of mist.
The mighty are dispersed at Temora;
There is none in Cormac's hall.
The king mourns in his youth,
He does not behold thy return.
The sound of thy shield is ceased,
His foes are gathering round.
Soft be thy rest in thy cave,
Chief of Erin's wars.
Bragela will not hope for thy return,
Or see thy sails in ocean's foam.
Her steps are not on the shore
Nor her ear open to the voice of thy rowers.
She sits in the hall of shells;
She sees the arms of him that is no more.
Thine eyes are full of tears,
Daughter of car-borne Sorglan.
Blest be thy soul in death,
O chief of Shady Tura![25]

The Meta-Narrative of Composition

How Thorpe Davie came to be interested in the poems of Ossian is unclear, but he had already found inspiration therein for *Elegy for an Ossianic Warrior*, a work he preferred to regard as an apprentice piece. He noted in a letter of May 17, 1935, to his family that he found the words of "The Death of Cuthullin" to be "most inspiring." Writing of the work's progress, he remarked that his teacher Vaughan Williams "was very pleased with old Cuthullin, especially the second half, and who has made a variety of suggestions for improvement of details in the first half, which I am at the moment considering."[26] A month later he observed,

I am full of excitement as Cuthullin draws to a close. I think now that it will be finished today or tomorrow, and details of the score ready for my lesson with V.W. on Wednesday next. It turns out not to be a very long work; I should say ten minutes at a guess; and I am hoping against hope that it has not fallen into any of the wayside pits that beset the paths of such works. To wit, scrappiness of construction, sloppiness (i.e. Celtic Twilight), and last but not least effectiveness. . . . [V.W.] confined himself chiefly to matters of balance and scoring, in which several important details were altered by his advice, definitely for the better.[27]

It is possible, even probable, that Thorpe Davie knew of J. B. McEwen's (1889) and Ian Whyte's (1929) attempts on Ossian topics, as well as Stanford's second orchestral rhapsody. Thorpe Davie admitted to his parents that he had a strain of romanticism in his character, but he made it quite clear that works of the "Celtic Twilight" were not the kind of artistic expression from which he wanted to feel influence.[28]

Studying in Budapest later that year, Thorpe Davie showed the score of his cantata to Kodály: "His manner [was] anything but friendly. However, I have got his permission to show him a work or two, and if he likes them, he may thaw . . . And today I met Dohnányi—in manner he was the complete reverse. . . . On Monday I go to hear Kodály's "Psalmus Hungaricus" and Honegger's "King David.""[29] A week later he was able to report that he had seen Kodály twice and that "his manners had improved." Thorpe Davie had given the *Cuthullin* score to Kodály and the cello fantasia (for which he had won the Cobbett Prize at the academy) to Dohnányi. Kodály still had said nothing by the end of the first week of November, but promised to do so on the coming Friday. By November 13, Kodály was "quite complimentary regarding Cuthullin."[30] The composer and musicologist Howard Ferguson, writing to Thorpe Davie a little later, remarked, "I am so glad that Kodály approves of Cuthullin; though his strictures on the Brangäne [Bragela] bit leave some doubts in my mind as to the reliability of his judgments."[31]

Vaughan Williams, meanwhile, had continued to correspond with Thorpe Davie while the latter was in Budapest, and when his former student moved to Finland to study with Kilpinen, Vaughan Williams wrote to him there: "Listened to Cuthullin, it is very good—Waddington [S. P. Waddington, a friend of Vaughan Williams] likes it. Give my profound respects to Kilpinen & to the GREAT MAN [Sibelius] if he remembers having once met me."[32] Thorpe Davie sent a copy of the score to Vaughan Williams, who replied: "Thank you so much for Cuthullin—I am glad it is printed—I will certainly write to Warrell [the conductor Arthur Warrell, 1882–1939] & see if I can interest any one else . . ."[33]

The work, dedicated to the composer's wife, received its first performance on April 15, 1936, in a broadcast from the London Region by the BBC Chorus and Orchestra conducted by Leslie Heward. The BBC Scottish Orchestra and Singers conducted by Ian Whyte gave a further broadcast performance on December 10, 1937. In the interim, on February 26, 1937, students at the Royal Scottish National

Table 15.1. Thorpe Davie's *Dirge for Cuthullin*: structure.

Bars	Time signature	Marking	Orchestra	Text
1–32 [intro]	$\frac{4}{4}\frac{3}{4}$ (bar 15)	lento, poco più mosso (bar 15)	fls, clar, hns, harp, str.	(chor. tacet)
33–53	$\frac{4}{4}$		strings, trumpets	"Blest be thy soul, son of Semo!"
53–69	$\frac{4}{4}$	poco meno mosso	full	"Thou hast not fallen"
71–75	$\frac{4}{4}$	poco ritenuto (bar 72)	solo strings, woodwind	"Peace to thy soul in the cave"
76–91	$\frac{4}{4}$	poco più mosso	strings trem. harp	"The mighty are dispers'd at Temora"
92–101	$\frac{4}{4}$	meno mosso	ww, strings	"The sound of thy shield"
102–11	$\frac{4}{4}$	ancora meno mosso	full orch.	(chor. tacet)
112–44	$\frac{4}{4}$	poco più mosso, tempo giusto		(basses entry) "Bragela will not hope for thy return"
145–50	$\frac{4}{4}$		(contralto solo) (+chor, orch. tacet)	"Thine eyes are full of tears"
151–59	$\frac{4}{4}\frac{5}{4}\frac{3}{4}$ (bar 158)	pochetto più mosso	flutes, oboe, str.	(chor. tacet)
160–82	$\frac{3}{4}$	a tempo–largamente	celli, ww, str. (brass, perc.)	(chor. tacet)
183–90	$\frac{3}{4}\frac{4}{4}$ (bar 191)		full orch. (+ harp)	"Ah!"
191–208	$\frac{4}{4}\frac{3}{4}$ (bar 199)	tranquillo	horns, flutes	"Blest be thy soul in death"

Academy of Music performed an arrangement of the work for choir, two pianos, and timpani.[34] No further performances of the work are on record.

Thorpe Davie's cantata is cast in four main sections corresponding to the text, with orchestral interpolations that vary from two to thirty-two bars in length. Because of the multimodal harmonic structure, there is no key signature: section 1 (bars 1–61); section 2 (bars 62–102); section 3 (bars 103–86); final section (bars 187–203). The instruction on the score reads: "Except between figures 12 and 16, the tempo must be very elastic throughout."

The score of *Cuthullin* opens with three slow, softly contrasting chords (horns) of A-flat minor, E minor, and A-flat major, marked *misterioso*. The tonal effect, if not the dynamics, resembles the opening of Vaughan Williams's *Sea Symphony*, where the composer juxtaposes chords a third apart (B-flat minor, D major) for the choral entry: here, Thorpe Davie alternates his chords to produce an effect of "faery lands forlorn," a poetic gesture doubtless intended to conjure up an aura of Celtic legend.[35] This is succeeded by oscillating, syncopated E major–C minor chords for flutes. The metaphor of "faery lands forlorn" (from John Keats's poem "Ode to a Nightingale") is not entirely random, for Keats also was overcome by his visit to Staffa in 1818, comparing "Fingal's Cave," like Joseph Banks before him, to a cathedral of the sea "architected thus / By the great Oceanus" (a name that echoes Ossian).[36]

In terms of overall harmonic structure, the work is dominated by the juxtaposition or agglomeration of major and minor chords (for example, A-flat major, E minor), together with striding bass octaves that create an overall effect of purposeful drama. The debt to Vaughan Williams is obvious, but for all that, the work exudes a sense of solid, individual commitment to realizing the poetic text by means of multimodal techniques. The commitment is also evident in the careful choice of orchestral coloring. As in his apprentice "Elegy for an Ossianic Warrior," Thorpe Davie employs a harp as part of the orchestral texture, though here much more effectively.

After thirty-two bars of orchestral introduction, the voices (SATB) enter on a unison G that moves toward a C-minor tinge for "Blest be thy soul" but quickly subsumes chords of the seventh and ninth, which dominate Thorpe Davie's harmonic language in this setting. Veering suddenly away to A-flat at "son of Semo," the tension between the opening chords of A-flat minor and E minor fuses in the words "Thou wert mighty in battle, Thy strength was like the strength of a stream" with a dotted rhetorical motif that turns on itself, rising to a climax in the triplet figuration of "Thy path in battle was terrible" on clashing E♭ (alto) and D (bass) against high A♮s in the soprano and tenor.

A quieter collision ensues at the words "The steps of death were behind thy sword," as the voices enunciate a bare fifth on F and B♭. Following two bars of orchestral interpolation, the voices reprise the opening harmonies for "Blest be thy soul, son of Semo, car-borne chief of Dunscaith!" A slightly slower eight-bar interlude then reprises some of the orchestral introduction, moving to E-flat minor for "Thou hast not fallen by the sword of the mighty," but then, after two bars, changing

Example 15.4. Cedric Thorpe Davie, *Dirge for Cuthullin*, bars 1–9

meter to 3/2 (6/4) and a chord of G-sharp minor (enharmonically, A-flat minor of the opening) for "Neither was thy blood on the spear of the brave." This shortly gravitates, via a reversion to common time, into B minor for "The arrow came like the sting of Death," with a rising crescendo to a C-minor ninth chord ("in a blast") that drifts toward the key of F minor for "Nor did the feeble hand perceive it," whereupon the strings revert to the rhetorical F–E♭–D♭–F that turns upon itself. A slower section, *pianissimo*, of four bars ensues for "Peace to thy soul in thy cave, Chief of the isle of mist" and leads briefly to a quicker section whereby G-minor lines switch to E minor, then E-flat, B-flat minor, E-flat minor, and back again to C-minor tonality for "The mighty are dispersed at Temora" as the separate vocal lines are broken up. Prominent harp arpeggios (between figures 8 and 9) color this passage.

Thorpe Davie's kaleidoscopic array of minor keys is a notable feature of his construction. These keys, and their interrelationship with both minor and major tonalities, effectively create a mood of fierce regret. Their contrast, and conflict, also captures the varied images in the text, such as the arrow that is seen as the sting of death, the mighty scattered in Temora, or Bragela in the hall of shells. The voices are again broken up for the lines "His foes are gathering round, the sound of thy shield is ceased, Soft be thy rest in thy cave" with an F-major chord over a low C♯ bass that

Example 15.5. Thorpe Davie, *Dirge for Cuthullin*, chorus: "Thou hast not fallen," bars 62–65

suggests, then realizes, an F♯ chording in the voices for "Chief of Erin's wars." Ten bars of solemn interlude bring back the syncopated chords of the opening against a measured bass line, until chords of E major against G minor recall the first bars. An enlivened section introduces the lines for basses only, in G minor.

The succeeding passage may have been the one about which Kodály had some misgivings, and to which Howard Ferguson referred in his letter to Thorpe Davie. Presumably the composer took these strictures to heart in his final version: "Bragela will not hope for thy return, Or see thy sails" (progressions from E major to C-sharp minor to B minor to G-sharp minor) as the remaining voices join in, then

Example 15.6. Thorpe Davie, *Dirge for Cuthullin*, harp arpeggios, bars 77–83

harmonically moving to E minor, C minor, then E-flat minor for "Her steps are not on the shore, Nor her ear open to the voice of thy rowers," with a further shift of keys from F minor to B minor to D-sharp minor, and finally to a $^6_4$ chord on F♯ that melts via B minor for "She sits in the hall of shells."

At this point the tenors, underpinned by the E-flat minor chord, oscillate to E minor for "She sees the arms of him that is no more," the other voices repeating "no more" in chords of B minor. A contralto solo sighs in a slow, descending line as the voices announce, still in that key, "Thine eyes are full of tears, Daughter of car-borne Sorglan." The closing orchestral section picks up speed and returns to the solemn chords of a steadily moving bass line for nine bars, to a new section with a prominently positioned harp part in a melody that develops, with sixteenth-note accompaniment of some twenty-three bars, to an interpolated, exclamatory *fortissimo* "Ah" octave unison on G♯ in the soprano, alto, and tenor voices with an F-minor harmony against a C♯ and an A♮, for four bars. A pedal point on the note A sustains a plaintive oboe melody of ten bars, leading to a final three-bar statement by the voices on an octave unison E, "Blest be thy soul in death." This is followed by the oboe solo, underpinned by chords of B-flat minor, for a final choral line of "O chief of shady Tura," the sopranos and tenors holding an octave unison F while the altos and basses move downward, E♭, D♭, C, B♭, to A♭ (altos) and F (basses), and come to rest on a plangent chord of F minor. As the oboe confirms this tonality in a held high F, the horns take over with the soft opening of a B-flat-minor chord. The flutes articulate the interval of a seventh on D (D–F–C as quasi-dominant of E minor), alternating with an E-minor chord in syncopated eighth and sixteenth notes, these dying away to *pppp* without slowing down as the horns' sustained chord finally breaks off.

The *Dirge for Cuthullin* is a remarkable work for a composer still in his early twenties. Unlike Chisholm, Thorpe Davie tends toward the traditional in his models; he is less politically engaged, but nevertheless admiring, like his radical contemporary, of the poems of Ossian. While in terms of musical craft Thorpe Davie came under some limited influence from Vaughan Williams, he was bold enough to choose what was an unfashionable text for the late 1930s, at least in the London where he was trained. Nevertheless, composers' interest in the Ossian poems was beginning to reemerge, in works by Granville Bantock and others. As the achievement of a twenty-two-year-old, Thorpe Davie's cantata parades itself as a work in which unity of purpose is evident—in its workmanship and passion, it is more than just a youthful *jeu d'esprit*. In terms of transmediation, it is an instance of close and positive convergence with the feeling and import of the poem.

Thorpe Davie must have concluded later, like many colleagues, that the text source might not satisfy those who thought Macpherson a charlatan despite passages of imaginative power. Yet, echoing the rhetorical declarations of the text, there is a certain grandeur in the young composer's composition, despite the gloomy aura of "dirge" in the title. The music surges back and forth convincingly as sense and feeling merge in the rhetoric of the vocal lines, multi-modal harmonic construction

Example 15.7. Thorpe Davie, *Dirge for Cuthullin*, contralto solo and chorus: "Thine eyes are full of tears," bars 145–57

often based on the piling up of thirds, and the subtle use of instrumentation. It is one characteristic of his style that may explain his approach to Alban Berg while in Europe.[37] The influence of Berg's early works, notably his Piano Sonata (op. 1, published in 1911), is apparent. The cantata prefaced for Thorpe Davie a career notable for skilled writing of dramatic, workmanlike music for plays and feature films.[38] The metanarrative in his letters to his parents reveals much about his compositional process and the reception of the work by leading composers.

To what extent Thorpe Davie's sojourn in Europe affected his sense of the political context of his cantata is difficult to tell. Again, if he had met Bartók or Berg in person, having written to them, he might have been influenced to take a different artistic direction. Compared to Erik Chisholm, Thorpe Davie seems less interested in political realities or in taking an ideological position; a cheerful skepticism seems to have been part of his persona and his attitude toward politics.[39] He may have seen the domestic toll that a committed socialism took on his energetic colleague. Moderately prolific as a composer, he avoided the radical language of his contemporaries, concentrating on workmanlike music for films and the theater. He does not appear to have revived his Cuthullin cantata, perhaps because he felt the subject was passé in a London-dominated Britain. Nevertheless, with the current revival of interest in Ossian, his inspired, driven, and sturdy *Dirge for Cuthullin* merits renewed appraisal and performance.

Chapter Sixteen

Modernity, Modernism, and Ossian

Erik Chisholm's *Night Song of the Bards* (1944–51), James MacMillan's *The Death of Oscar* (2013), and Jean Guillou's *Ballade Ossianique, No. 2: Les chants de Selma* (1971, rev. 2005)

Modernity, the advent of "the new" in social life, has also been a recurring phenomenon in the history of Western classical music. Influential composers have framed modernity in their visions of artistic change: Monteverdi, Gluck, and Beethoven are notable examples in a recurrent if discontinuous aesthetic program. When the poems of Ossian appeared, they were themselves modern in departing from Augustan classicism to create a style based on heroic ideals, noble behavior, and sentiment (feeling). By translating these notions into musical terms following the French Revolution, Beethoven became the most modern composer of all, and with his successors in the later nineteenth century, modernity was condensed into its artistic agency, namely modernism.[1] Recently, both Wagner and Brahms have been proposed as the precursors of a musical modernism.[2] Composers of the twentieth century were only freed from overripe Romanticism by such as Scriabin and Debussy, who evolved complex harmonies that could be relished for their own sake, for the resonance of their overtones.[3] Debussy's *L'après-midi d'un faune* (1894), Schoenberg's *Five Pieces for Orchestra* (1912), and Stravinsky's *Rite of Spring* (1913) marked the rupture with the Romantic past. The Soviet Revolution of 1917 then created a radically new context for composers who fell under its influence.

At the time, Schoenberg had broken with the past by rethinking tonal architecture, but did so only after he had shaken off the influence of Wagner, Mahler, and Strauss (though not that of Brahms).[4] Before he had reached that point, he was sufficiently captivated by Herder's "Darthula's Grabesgesang" to draft an extensive sketch for a cantata (1903) on these Ossian-inspired verses, which were, by that time, well known in the German-speaking world. He left the work unfinished to complete his grandiose cantata on a "Nordic" theme, the *Gurrelieder*, begun in 1901.[5] Perhaps the forces of modernity, in relation to his Herder cantata, were more demanding than he had anticipated. At any rate, by the time the *Gurrelieder* had reached performance in 1913, Schoenberg's idiom had changed radically, abandoning late Romanticism to embrace new pitch concepts in works such as the *Five Orchestral Pieces* and *Pierrot Lunaire*, op. 20 (also 1912).

Schoenberg's contemporaries Béla Bartók and Leoš Janáček, however, sidestepped his Viennese experimentalism by mining the heritage of music and song they found in east-central Europe, transforming for the stage and concert platform the vital intonation of a peasant music threatened by the artistic and political conflicts of the early twentieth century.[6] At one level, then, "modernism" emerged as a particular stage in a historicist view of music, one in which styles succeed one another in a "progressive" way: an unfolding, as it were, of the inevitable advance of complexity, of a more refined and systematic view of aural horizons.[7] This view was typical of much Austro-German musical philosophy. On another level, one rooted in ahistorical, communal idioms, it became a search for novel expression by drawing from the authentic songs and dances of an age-old, productive, but endangered way of life.[8] The use of folk elements, however, particularly in Bartók's case, did not signify his support for political nationalism: it was an attempt to radicalize urban audiences to awareness of an imperiled musical heritage.[9]

Erik Chisholm's *Night Song of the Bards* (1944–51)

Britain was not immune from these European developments.[10] Of composers born before World War I, two stand out for their substantial works based on the poems of Ossian: Erik William Chisholm (1904–65) and Cedric Thorpe Davie.[11] Both emphatically rejected the "Celtic twilight" interpretation of the poems.[12] Both were immersed in Scottish literature and folk music, but Thorpe Davie inclined in his composing to the more traditional tonal idiom of first Sibelius and then his teacher Vaughan Williams, while Chisholm, more radical and wide-ranging in his tastes, found his modernist ideal in the atonal structures of Bartók. Chisholm created his six piano nocturnes, *Night Song of the Bards*, between 1944 and 1951.[13] This composition was inspired by an episode Macpherson related in a footnote to the poem

"Croma," in which five bards and their chief pass an October evening by extemporizing descriptions of night. Introducing the poem, Macpherson claims it was the only bardic composition he had found that was worthy of translation.[14] Chisholm, influenced by both Indian techniques of raga (melodic mode) improvisation and Bartók's method of using small cells to construct larger building blocks, devised a set of textures in his *Night Song* that approach the ruggedness of Beethoven's later piano sonatas, with elaborate trills, jagged harmonies over a drone bass, and textural references to his own one-act opera composed at the same time, *The Inland Woman* (1950), whose music he scored for a small orchestra with horns and harp.[15]

Chisholm, also enthused by Janáček's work, completed a book on the composer's operas (1971). Moreover, he invited Bartók to Glasgow in February 1932 and November 1933 to perform his works. Not only that, he conducted the British premiere of Bartók's opera, *Duke Bluebeard's Castle*, in London on January 16, 1957, followed by performances a week later in Glasgow.[16] Chisholm is therefore a key figure in the late modern apprehension of Ossian as a source for composition in Britain. This is especially the case with his Second Symphony of 1939 (subtitled "Ossian") and *Night Song of the Bards*.[17] In the structure of the latter work, Chisholm switched his settings of the "Third Bard" and "Fourth Bard" so that the music more readily accorded with its predecessor or successor. Further, the second and fifth pieces (Second Bard, Fifth Bard) absorb the poem's images in all their vitality, and it is these two (the longest and shortest) that will be discussed here.

In light of Chisholm's acquaintance with Bartók, the shaping influence might appear to be the latter's *Piano Sonata* or the *Out of Doors Suite* (both 1926) with their rhythmic seconds, tone-clusters, and microtonal clashes, especially in the "Night Music" movement of the suite. The *Three Studies* (*Etüdök*), op. 18 (1918, published in 1920), is possibly a more direct model. Chisholm's facility as a pianist is likely to have drawn him to these pieces, with their novel effects and formidable technical demands. He had already composed a spiky, virtuosic piano sonata in four movements (1939), based partly on the classical music of the Highland bagpipe.[18]

Recently, musicologists have seen the use of interval cycles as the basic source for the harmonic and linear fabric of the *Three Studies* and other works of Bartók. These interval cycles include one of minor seconds, two of whole tones, three of minor thirds, four of major thirds, one of perfect fourths, and six of tritones.[19] Interaction between interval cycles and the pentatonic or modal elements of folk music is fundamental to the organic development of Bartók's composition.[20] The composer himself referred to this interlocking as "extension in range," in which chromatic material is expanded into diatonic themes, or the reverse, which he referred to as "chromatic compression." Both variety and unity will be achieved because of this hidden relationship between the interval cycles and the folk music elements.[21]

The same could be said for Chisholm's construction in *Night Song of the Bards*. Here he uses a sequence of six notes closely resembling the raga Sohani, from the much-reprinted book on the music of Hindustan by A. H. Fox Strangways, familiar to him because of his interest in Hindustani music.²² He chose the raga Sohani because of its associations with performance after midnight and before dawn, and it was thus an appropriate stimulus for the atmosphere of *Night Song*.²³ It was also an appealing frame for a set of pieces based on a lesser-known poem from the well-thumbed Ossian sheaf. This six-note cell (minus the additional A♯ and B of the instrument tuning) is similar to the interval cycle Bartók used in *Three Studies*: in Chisholm's case, the cell B–C–D♯–E–F–G♯ is the basis for free organic development of the ratios contained within it: minor seconds (B–C, D♯–E, E–F), a whole tone (D♯–F), minor thirds (C–D♯, F–G♯), major thirds (B–D♯, E–G♯), perfect fourths (B–E, D♯–G♯), and a tritone (B–F).

The potential of the cell structure is set out in the "Second Bard." The *allegro tempestoso* in $\frac{6}{4}$ outlines the cell from the very start (E–F–G♯–A–B–D♯) in ascending and then descending sixteenth notes in both hands an octave apart. This torrent of notes brings out the image of the poem: wind, rain, roaring rivers, the storm "driving the horse from the hill." After sixteen bars a transitional passage leads to a slower segment in which the potential of the perfect and augmented fourth is exploited in a right-hand melody (containing a "Scotch snap") set against a murmuring bass with the instruction, "play on top of the keys as lightly as possible" (bar 22). Is this, perhaps, in the poem's vision, the hunter starting from his sleep, as his "wet dogs smoke around him"? After two bars the music returns to the first *allegro*, but only briefly, for a second statement of the right-hand melody, now developed from its original two bars into an eight-bar peroration, until a broadening *fortissimo* brings together (bar 37) the chordal complex A–D♯–A (LH) and G♯–D♯–G♯ (RH). This resembles the bichordal construction that closes Bartók's Study No. 1, a fused G major (LH) and F-sharp major (RH) chord.

More menacingly, the chord in bar 39 of "Second Bard," namely B–E♯–B (LH) and G–C♯–F♯–G (RH), ushers in a developmental passage whose right-hand figuration in sextuplets at the higher end of the keyboard (bars 41–44) is reminiscent of the pianistic technique of Chopin's *Ballade No. 4*, which involves rapid sixteenth-note chords in the right-hand part. This complex figuration seems to conjure the image from the poem: "Ghosts ride on the storm tonight . . . their songs are of other worlds." In this section, the main theme with its snap is carried by the left hand, ornamented by sixteenth notes. Gradually the music reaches a *fortissimo* climax (bar 45) that touches a tonal base with F major and B-flat major dominant chords, though always qualified by chromatic alterations. The tolling, downbeat chords in the right-hand part, interspersed with rapid figuration, continue for five emphatic bars.

This leads, through a bar of rippling sixty-fourth notes, to a *molto più mosso* passage (bar 51) and the opening divided-octave, sixteenth-note statement of the cell. A further eight bars moves the music back to the "Scotch snap" melody (bar 67), which itself dies out as the eighth notes of the left-hand part become more fragmented. "The rain is past," says the poem, "I see the starry sky. But the shower

Example 16.1. Erik Chisholm, *Night Song of the Bards*, "Second Bard," bars 1–3

gathers again. The west is gloomy and dark. Night is stormy and dismal; receive me, my friends, from night." A final few bars, *adagio* in $^6_4$, identify the tonal cadence as C major, but with a *pianissimo* chord superimposed that consists of E♭–F♯–A♯–B: in fact, it is the cell with two notes, F–G♯, rearranged as F♯ and G♮, a minor second substituted for the original minor third (B–C–D♯–E/F♯–G–A♯).

In the fifth bard's piece, just forty-seven bars long, Chisholm captures the "calm, but dreary" night in the *lento tranquillo* of the $^3_2$ opening. The suggestion of the moon behind a cloud emerges in a right-hand C♯–G♯ chord, qualified by F♯ appoggiaturas and a G♮ in the left-hand part. After four bars a G♯-G♮ oscillation begins in the higher reaches of the keyboard, accompanied by chords of the seventh and ninth rooted on F. Is this "the distant wave [that] is heard," while sixteenth notes introduce the idea of the torrent murmuring on the rock (bar 10)? The crowing cockerel is heard in the right-hand leaps of the initial tempo as they skirt a B-flat minor tonal shape. At the change of time ($^3_4$) the atmosphere darkens again as "the housewife . . .

Example 16.2. Chisholm, *Night Song of the Bards*, "Second Bard," bar 37

Example 16.3. Chisholm, *Night Song of the Bards*, "Second Bard," bar 45

Example 16.4. Chisholm, *Night Song of the Bards*, "Second Bard," bars 77–79

Example 16.5. Chisholm, *Night Song of the Bards*, "Fifth Bard," bars 1–4

Example 16.6. Chisholm, *Night Song of the Bards*, "Fifth Bard," bars 15–19

re-kindles the settled fire." Heavy half note plus quarter note motifs of sevenths and ninths in the bass are set against an obsessive, syncopated octave F/F in the right hand.

The hunter, as day approaches, calls his bounding dogs as the *tessitura* moves up from bass to treble, again in syncopated chords, the top line leaping in octaves on A♯. This note becomes its enharmonic equivalent, B♭, which serves as the counterpart to the chords rooted earlier in F. "A blast removes the cloud" at the *forte* chord of bar 41, so that the hunter sees the "starry plough of the north" in a series of syncopated dotted eight notes. Then, at the marking of *adagio*, trills in both hands evoke "the whirlwind . . . in the wood" and "the mighty army of the dead returning from the air." This effect, marked "quasi trill," seems to be derived from Bartók's usage in the second study of opus 18 (bar 19 and later).[24] In four gentle closing bars with continuing trills in the right-hand part, Chisholm concludes the movement, *pianissimo*, with notes both high and at the bottom of the keyboard, subsiding in an F-minor chord with a supertonic G imposed.

The essentials of Chisholm's nocturnes are: the use of cell structure to unify the composition; free development of the cell in terms of interval extension and compression; reliance on reinforced octaves, often embellished with a perfect or diminished fifth in the middle; closures that often involve a major or minor chord (E major chord in "First Bard"; a qualified C major in "Second Bard"; D major in "Third Bard"; E-flat major/minor in "Fourth Bard"; a qualified F minor in "Fifth Bard"; and an open-fifth F garnished with a D♭ at the close of "The Chief"); filigree decoration of melodic content; accented use of appoggiaturas; oscillating figures and scale tracery (bars 33–40 of "Third Bard" closely resemble a similar texture in the second of Bartók's *Three Studies*, op. 18); contrast among textures; left-hand and right-hand differentiation in keyboard technique; and finally, attention to the mood and images of the poem. The fusion of poetic image and dazzling piano writing makes *Night Song* a powerful symbolic testament to the imaginative transmediation of its creator.[25]

Example 16.7. Chisholm, *Night Song of the Bards*, "Fifth Bard," bars 41–47

James MacMillan's *The Death of Oscar* (2013)

MacMillan's symphonic essay, written in 2012 and published in 2013, is dedicated to Stéphane Denève and Alexander Stoddart, the former a noted conductor,[26] the latter a distinguished sculptor.[27] The work was inspired by Stoddart's project to sculpt an amphitheater to be given the name "Oscar" into the rock in the Highlands as a tribute to Ossian, somewhat akin to the heads of US presidents carved into Mt. Rushmore, South Dakota. MacMillan's work is for a large orchestra: three flutes, two oboes (the second doubling cor anglais), three B-flat clarinets, two bassoons and contrabassoon, four horns in F, three trumpets in C, three trombones, tuba, timpani, percussion (two players) that includes glockenspiel, triangle, bass drum, and tubular bells, snare drum, and large tam-tam, with harp and strings. The piece is 168 bars in length and falls into seven sections with an A-B-A¹ frame.[28]

A slow and somber tread in common time (♩ = 46) opens with a low C♯ in the bassoons, cellos, and basses, the timpani and harp adding a G♯ while the bass drum and tam-tam suggest funereal steps. After three bars the horn and cellos take

Example 16.8. James MacMillan, *The Death of Oscar*, bars 15–25. Copyright 2013 by Boosey & Hawkes Music Publishers Ltd. Reproduced by permission.

up a lament-like fragment marked *brooding*. Drifting in and out of minor tonalities around C♯, F♯, and B, the horn, cello, and harp pick up speed, the first of these moving into sixteenth-note leaps of a fourth and fifth. The first oboe then enters (bar 15) in unison with the first violins to articulate the important A-minor melody (marked *sadly* at bar 18) for ten bars, the second violins and violas imitating the melodic line at the half bar. The horns, contrabassoon, and tuba, meanwhile, continue their oscillation around D♯, E♯, and G♯, while the woodwind engage in modal tracery around A minor and D minor.

This episode continues in the first violins with a development of the A-minor melody, the divided second violins again imitating the first violins at the half bar. The oboe joins the keening, again in unison with the violins, until the horns wind down the tension in parallel sixth chords.[29]

A *pianissimo* unison on F♯, swelling to a *fortissimo*, introduces the central section with *staccato* chords of B minor in the strings. The three trumpets overtake these with two-bar phrases consisting of repeated eighth notes and jagged semitones, still in B minor. This paean continues for a further twelve bars. The trumpeters are granted a one-bar rest before rehearsal letter D (bar 74), when they resume their staccato figuration, this time in E minor, again with brief chords in the strings on each beat. Two groups of five bars, with a silent bar in between, lead to a further ten bars of fanfare-like statements, the snare drum and triangle adding punctuation to the momentum. This segment reaches a climax three bars after rehearsal letter E, where the trombones assert their presence in upward striving chromatic triplets accompanied by timpani, bass drum, and tam-tam. The horns interject a commanding melody that descends from an accented A–B♭ toward D minor.

Fortissimo, the bassoons, trombones, tuba, cellos, and basses announce a surging motif in fourths from C♯, then from C♮, then B. After five bars, as the upper

Example 16.9. MacMillan, *The Death of Oscar*, bars 61–62. Copyright 2013 by Boosey & Hawkes Music Publishers Ltd. Reproduced by permission.

Example 16.10. MacMillan, *The Death of Oscar*, bar 104. Copyright 2013 by Boosey & Hawkes Music Publishers Ltd. Reproduced by permission.

strings soar to a high E over a bass C♯, the tubular bells now appear prominently with an entrance marked *ecstatic*. This instrument makes itself felt for no fewer than eighteen bars, along with bass drum and timpani. Meanwhile, the upper woodwinds have taken over the leaping motif of the horns (bars 10–12), and the bassoons and trombones continue to fragment their upward triplet motif, accompanied by the bass drum. At rehearsal letter F the horns repeat their descending melodic curve, this time toward A minor. A secondary motif that turns out to be an important development appears in the trumpets, one derived from the leaping motif of the horns.

The insistent B minor reasserts itself from bar 117, when the horns and first violins double one another, and a high violin motif with appoggiaturas finally brings the tubular bells to a halt, and even the trumpets, still toying with the repeated motif and the leaping figure, bring their peroration to a close. With a new tempo of ♩ = 60, the muted and divided strings play a chord (from the bass, E♭, B♭, G♭, D, F, C♯, A, E) that is enriched by a trumpet chord of E major. The string chord, reinforced by trilling flutes and oboes, moves upward chromatically to rehearsal letter G (bar 129) and introduces the reverberant sound of the cor anglais (marked *languid*) for thirty-three bars, now securely in the key of A minor, recalling the famous solo in Sibelius's *Swan of Tuonela* (also in that key). The instrument signals the third and final part by repeating the first oboe-plus-violin melody (see ex. 8). The long solo is accompanied by alternately short and sustained figuration in the strings, woodwind, and the harp, an instrument that has had little to do since the opening. With a long-held chord of

Example 16.11. MacMillan, *The Death of Oscar*, bars 125–29. Copyright 2013 by Boosey & Hawkes Music Publishers Ltd. Reproduced by permission.

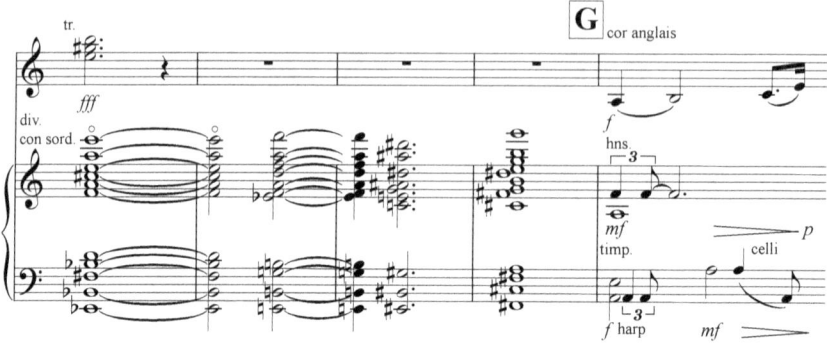

C♯–F♯–G♯ in the strings, the timpani interject a triplet leaping motif as the orchestra, expanding to *fortissimo*, draws the work to a close.

Several features of this composition can be noted: the link to the legendary world of Macpherson's Ossian poems through the medium of the sculpture project; reference to the battle in which Ossian's son, Oscar, meets his death; the idea of lament in musical terms, using the cor anglais to express this emotion; the A-B-A arch form in which material announced at the outset is recapitulated toward the end. But there are also unusual features: the prolonged sequences for three trumpets, for example, or the use of tubular bells. Bells in particular are often part of this composer's imagination, suggesting religious overtones: has St. Patrick already arrived, perhaps, to converse with Ossian, to Christianize his godless world, as is known from traditional accounts? In these, Ossian is the last of his line, living into the early Christian period to relate the past glory of Fionn's (Fingal's) warriors.

If this is the point of the bells, with their eighteen bars of D major in the middle of the battle music, it creates a question of appropriateness. Why would bells ring out "ecstatically" and *fortissimo* in a depiction of the Battle of Gabhra between the Fianna and the forces of the high king Cairbre, in which Oscar and the latter slay each other? The world of Fionn, Ossian, and Oscar was notoriously a godless one in the tales. If the purpose was to create a sense of Christian intervention in the battle and its music, tubular bells could certainly act as symbols for the smaller hand-bells used by early Christian saints. But is this really the composer's intention? Is the presence of St. Patrick, and the dawning Christian era, conveyed by these tubular bells? Or are they just part of MacMillan's orchestral texture, like the little-used glockenspiel (three notes) and harp? The artistic effect is arresting, but ambiguous.

The softening of unresolved dissonance in *The Death of Oscar* marks a continuing move on the composer's part toward tonally based structures, just as his desire to write for amateur singers has resulted in a retreat from the harsher, uncompromising gestures of purely orchestral works.³⁰ Despite the main melody's acknowledgment of both Gaelic keening and the psalm-singing of Calvinist congregations in the Hebrides, pain is not evident in this piece: the tonal clashes when they occur resemble those of Chisholm and Thorpe Davie more than those of Schoenberg or Messiaen, whose compositions MacMillan admires. The influence of psalm-singing in congregational worship in the Hebrides, grave and unmetered in its liturgical context, is captured here in simple imitation at the half bar.

Like Chisholm in *Night Song of the Bards*, MacMillan finds consolation in tonal endings of fourths and fifths. The melodic interest is wholly tonal, based on traditional folk models, while the harmony relies on groupings of fourths, fifths, and seconds. The final effect is one of quiescence, of comforted (and even comfortable) fatalism.³¹ It is not a religious work in the narrow sense of burning zeal or sectarian affiliation; nor is it one concerned with transcendence. As a hybrid in the stylistic no-man's land between the Stravinsky of *Le rossignol* (1914) and Sibelius, its formal shape looks back to nineteenth century principles of tonal organization.

Jean Guillou's *Ballade Ossianique, No. 2 (Les chants de Selma)*, op. 23

There is nothing relaxed or ambiguous about Jean Guillou's *Ballade Ossianique, No. 2* for organ, written in 1971 and revised in 2005. It follows a companion work, the *Ballade Ossianique, No. 1: Temora*, op. 8, which was written in 1962 and revised, like the *Ballade No. 2*, in 2005. The composer's prefatory note provides an explanation of second ballade's genesis:

> The present composition, recast several times, represents the final version of what was originally, like some of the Sagas, one of my recorded improvisations. After the ongoing growth of a note from *pianissimo* to the *fortissimo* of a chord thrust out like a cutting sword, undulating phrases conjure up a landscape shrouded in mist. The ongoing note appears, and soon isolated notes, falling like drops of rain in a cave, seem to constitute the outline of a melodic figure in embryo. This latter, after numerous episodes of expectancy and sometimes menacing solitude, gradually takes shape, as though feeling its way through the darkness. Periodically, developmental passages are interrupted by the insistent note, which each time seems keen to push back the hostile forces. The thematic cell, the sole cell constituting the constructional element of the whole work, now flares up and breaks through the innumerable shifting forces. At last a kind of transfiguration takes place in this torment, giving way to a concluding hymn full of enthusiasm and jubilation.³²

The piece, some 316 bars in length, is technically challenging for the performer. It uses the cell structure now familiar from Bartók, and also Messiaen, whose influence permeates the work. But the improvisatory mood of the piece means that the cell structure is freely expanded and developed. The work begins with a single high B (Bourdon 8 ft), *lento* and *pianissimo*, that grows in volume to a commanding *fortissimo* chord with pedal: C♯–D–F, G♯–E–A♯–B–D♯. Is this, for the composer, the star of descending night? This high note is repeated, with a transitional bar to an emphatic octave figure, A♯–F♯, in the right-hand upper area of the staff, which then generates accelerating eighth notes for eight bars to a restatement of the first swelling, *pianissimo* B (and a different chord at the *fortissimo*). Are these "the flies of evening on their feeble wings"? The twenty-four bars are succeeded by a series of

Example 16.12. Jean Guillou, *Ballade ossianique no. 2*: "Les chants de Selma," bars 1–4, 10–15

Example 16.13. Guillou, "Les chants de Selma," bars 25–40

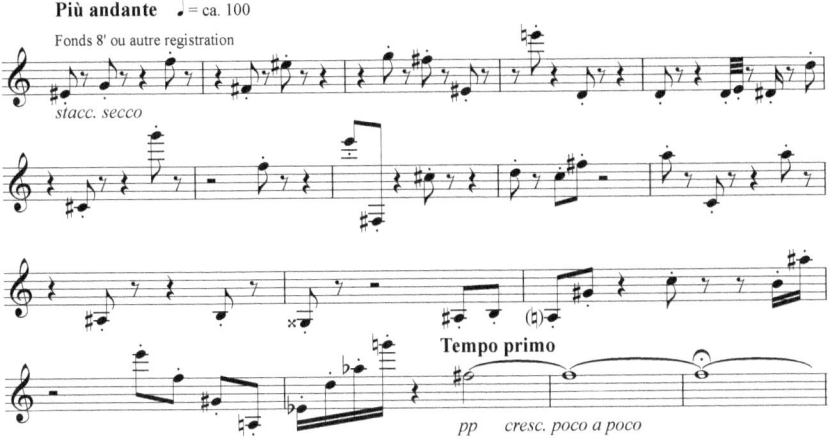

single notes, *più andante* and *staccato secco* (quarter note = 100), until a prolonged crescendo on F♯ replaces the B as the signal for that recurring, disruptive *fortissimo* chord. Chains of seconds and fourths lead to a reiteration of the high A♯ and F♯ in bar 10, and their insistence is underpinned by an octave G–A motif in the pedal (bars 46–47). Is F♯ a symbol for Fingal, and the torrent of notes for his heroes gathering around him? These notes indicate a looming conclusion on the high F♯ (bar 66), which is held for eight bars against an oscillating flute motif of six bars close by, circling *pianissimo* around the sustained note.

Starkly contrasting, a solo ("Régale 8′ ou Voix humaine") emerges in a left-hand motif rooted on B, with single-note Fs and F♯s marking the rhythm. This is perhaps an image of Minona, who "came forth in her beauty; with down-cast look and tearful eye." A portrait of the lonely Colma "on the hill of storms" ensues, with gloomy night suggested by a long-held seven-note chord (C♯, D, E♭, F♯, G, A, B♭) in the left-hand bass register. Clarinet or bassoon stops articulate a short motif that circles round the interval of a third and then a fourth and sixth. After eighteen bars the pedal enters with a low C that quickly becomes a repeated D in eighth notes, while at the high end of the keyboard ("cornet" stop) an important new melodic fragment descends, A♭, G, G♭, to F, then B, A♯, G, E, D♭, to C, a fierce, shuddering lament.

A silent bar (141) prefaces a prolonged episode of Bartókian rhythmic intensity that involves complex chords in the keyboard part and pedal part alike: the pedal part includes six-note chords. The chord of night reappears in the left hand (C–E–F–B♭–D♭; four bars later as D–F–B–E♭) while fragmented thirty-second notes seem to echo the phrase of Colma: "I sit in my grief . . . my life flies away like a dream." This extended episode lasts for some thirty bars. A three-bar melody in octaves appears

Example 16.14. Guillou, "Les chants de Selma," bars 105–14

in the upper keyboard: C–D♭–B♭–D♮–B♭–E–F–D (bars 189–91). At bar 200 the right hand engages in multiple trills, joined by the pedal in a peroration that lasts fully ten bars, to climax in a *fortissimo*, the single note G.

This returns to the image of Minona, possibly, or the laments of the bards Ryno and Albin. A gentler atmosphere, at any rate, is created at the outset of this passage, with a crucially poised C–E♮ on a flute stop. Moving to a much higher pitch, the flute stop reiterates an E♭ and F above a series of staccato chords (B, E, C) and this prolonged F leads back to, as it were, the Berlioz-like *idée fixe* of the high held note, this time C♯. At the change of tempo to *allegro giusto* we seem to be at the point in the poem at which "the grief of all arose, but most the bursting sigh of Armin" as he remembers the death of his son.

Thereupon the music echoes the cry, "Arise, winds of autumn, arise; blow along the heath! Streams of the mountains roar! Roar, tempests, in the groves of my oaks!" and the music ("sans 16′″") turns the time changes ($\frac{2}{4}, \frac{3}{4}, \frac{4}{4}, \frac{7}{8}$) into a vehicle for an extended rhythmic series of chords that culminates (bar 252) in a doubled tetrachord (F♯, G♯, B, D♯), high up in the keyboard, the pedal part tracking it with descending sixteenth notes in intervals of a ninth.

This tetrachord launches a ferocious tirade of sixteenth notes in both hands, first against sixteenth notes in the pedal and then sextuplets in the hands against pedal sixteenth notes: "Alone, on the sea-beat rock, my daughter was heard to complain. Frequent and loud were her cries. . . . Loud was the wind; the rain beat hard on the hill. . . . Spent with grief she expired; and left thee, Armin, alone." The climactic

Figure 16.1. Anne-Louis Girodet de Roucy-Trioson, *The Song of Armin Mourning His Children*. Drawing on paper, 1816. Harvard Art Museums. Reproduced with permission.

four-note chord acts as a kind of focal point for the coda, the pedal contributing a glissando and further sixteenth notes until, at bar 306, both hands career upward in alternated chords for a repeat of the tetrachord, now a paean to the idea of "my voice remains, like a blast, that roars, lonely, on a sea-surrounded rock after the winds are laid. The dark moss whistles there; the distant mariner sees the waving trees!"

Jean Victor Arthur Guillou (1930–2019) was born in Angers, of Breton ancestry.[33] He studied music at the Paris Conservatoire with Marcel Dupré, Maurice Duruflé, and Olivier Messiaen. In 1955 he was appointed professor of organ at the Instituto di Musica Sacra in Lisbon, then spent five years in Berlin beginning in 1958, returning to Paris to become titular organist at the church of Saint-Eustache in 1963. Like Messiaen, with his sixty years at La Trinité, he is one of the longest-serving organists in a major Parisian church.[34] As in his *Ballade Ossianique, No. 1, Temora*, op. 8 (1962, rev. 2005), Guillou's technique of composition is strongly conditioned by his talents as an organist, pianist, and pedagogue as well as his considerable expertise in improvisation.

His creative idiom, derived primarily from Messiaen, relies on the development of cells, rhythmic motifs, and contrasting colors rather than contrapuntal or

Example 16.15. Guillou, "Les chants de Selma," bars 252–55

Example 16.16. Guillou, "Les chants de Selma," bars 311–16

imitative devices. In this respect he is closer to Chisholm's pianistic tone-painting. There is little concession to conventional tonality in either of his Ossian pieces, even though the *Ballade No. 1* opens with a fanfare in major thirds and ends in a qualified D minor (bar 239), while the conclusion of the *Ballade No. 2* involves a chord of B major second inversion (bars 297–312). Such tonal references are few and far between, however, and are almost always qualified by, or accompanied by, references to a different tonality or none: in these same bars the pedal, following a glissando, articulates a Bach-like sixteenth-note oscillation in C major against the B major chord (plus the G-sharp sixth).

The performer of this music is faced with formidable hurdles, with frequent chords of six notes in either hand, multiple chords in the pedals, rapidly moving clusters of seconds, sevenths and ninths, *tremolando* figures in both keyboard and pedals, changes of tempo and registration. These go into the making of the prism through which Guillou realizes his multileveled vision of "The Songs of Selma." The episodes of the poem are captured in a discourse of dense harmonic structures and rhythmic drive, the overall effect being remote from earlier accounts of Macpherson's poem. The work is a tribute to the long-standing involvement of French culture with that of both Ossian and the Nordic sagas, as the latter also feature in Guillou's œuvre.[35]

Modernism is only useful as a term when it is qualified by reference to particular composers working in specific contexts of learning, performing, and reception. Erik Chisholm can only be described as a modernist with reference to his artistic models, his love of folk and Asian music as well as his debt to Bartók, Janáček, and Szymanowski. Politically, he was radically socialist, and this is evident elsewhere in his work. The ruggedness of means in *Night Song of the Bards* shows not only his absorption of these artistic models but also a readiness to embrace progressive techniques of composition based on variegated tonal and atonal structures.

James MacMillan's *The Death of Oscar*, composed sixty years later than Chisholm's "Night Song," seems conservative, even neo-romantic in comparison. While MacMillan's deployment of the orchestra is skillful, the symbolic transmediation also appears divergent in relation to the original poem, the composer choosing to follow his own path in thematic development. Of the three composers, Chisholm and Guillou could be said to have earned the "modernist" tag, for the continuous and brilliant transformation of pitch collections and cells for their chosen instrument. Only at the very end of pieces do they venture into traditional tonal territory, Guillou here with a climax on the second inversion of a B-major chord that, in context, seems entirely convincing even when qualified by interpolations in another key. While indebted to the example of Messiaen on more than one level, Guillou has forged his own visionary language. The process of revision through which the work has gone since its first version of 1971, like that of its predecessor the *Ballade No. 1* (1962, rev. 2005) can only, at the moment, be guessed at.

But as with Chisholm, Guillou's technical accomplishment has allowed him to develop a freely rhapsodic interpretation of Ossian's famous poem. In its transmediation of the poem his style is consistent, even though the brand of modernism is no longer "modern." With that final added sixth chord, perhaps both Guillou and MacMillan are admitting that they have been forced, for reasons of narrative drama, to re-explore standard tonal territory without opting for a thoroughgoing postmodernism: that is, one in which discontinuities of style are the aesthetic goal, or where composition based on wholly tonal or atonal resources is avoided.[36] Reared in an atmosphere of conventional modernism, both appear to feel bound by its serious limitations (chiefly, a long history of arcane musical language and communication with a specialist audience). The conclusion of both pieces suggests a flirtation with postmodern musical ideas, as if traditional means (no matter how "ancient" or "modern") still exert a decisive pull in terms of structure, texture, and individual "voice." But in any case, other ways of perceiving the natural world, hearing its poetry, and transmediating it into music genres, have supplanted a neurotic modernism and a narcissistic postmodernism. Eclectic styles now mirror cross-cultural influences as well as a confusing globalism dominated by market forces. Fragmentary, episodic, and ambiguous, the poems of Ossian may still offer a channel for composers in these tumultuous, unsettling times.

Afterword

The "Half-Viewless Harp"— Secondary Resonances of Ossian

James Macpherson's *The Poems of Ossian* (1760–63) employ a memorable musical image twice: first, in the prose poem "Berrathon," in which the bard Ullin is pictured in the palace of Fingal, striking "the half-viewless harp," and again in the second book of the epic poem *Temora*, when Ossian is mourning for his son, Oscar: "Open thou thy stormy halls. Let the bards of old be near. Let them draw near with songs and their half-viewless harps." This notion of "half-viewless" suggests something dimly perceived, visually and aurally. The idea appears again, with a somewhat different application, in "The Songs of Selma," as Ossian says, "Often by the setting moon, I see the ghosts of my children. Half viewless, they walk in mournful conference together." The trope of an indistinct harp, however, barely perceived but nevertheless resonant, seems appropriate for the way in which the musical response to Ossian has been largely ignored or downplayed. Few know that in addition to a few pieces by Schubert, Mendelssohn, and Brahms, the poems of Ossian, since their appearance in the third quarter of the eighteenth century, have stimulated forty or so operas and scores of cantatas, songs, and symphonic works.

From the preceding chapters, we can glimpse the long-acting effect of Ossian on composers. Apart from the recognized works of masters such as those cited above (and, as I have argued, the more problematic case of Beethoven), perhaps a dozen or more of those discussed here, about one-fifth of the total number of musical compositions based on Ossian, stand out as reaching an elevated level of inspiration and craftsmanship. While this is a personal selection, I would maintain that these works show a magisterial blend of Romanticism and modernity in their melodic invention, harmonic language, and instrumental texture, or any combination of these factors. That is, the composers have not only realized their individual feelings but also created something new—and in reaching out to others, something "modern." In the process of transmediation they have achieved a delicate balance between Romanticism and modernity, and as a result this mastery is found at many levels in each work.

It is certain, at any rate, that an appreciation of a musical work's novel qualities (even when these display apparently conflicting elements) and unity must come from an understanding of the nature of creative thought, which in music is not discursive but integrative and convergent, in molding a cohesive sound world from contrasting elements. That world, while it may contain disparate components, must be perceived as a totality, not just for itself but also for the impact that it makes on the social context for which it is intended. These works have what we might call "presence." I have chosen the following, therefore, not only because of their mastery but also their integrated vision in transmediating the poems of Ossian that are often themselves, of course, episodic.

The outstanding compositions include Thomas Linley the Younger's cantata, *Darthula* (ca. 1775), F. W. Rust's monodrama, *Colma* (1780), the opera *Comala* by Pietro Morandi (1780), the opera *Calto* by Francesco Bianchi (1788), J. R. Zumsteeg's setting of *Colma* for voice and keyboard (1794), Stefano Pavesi's opera *Fingallo e Comala* (1805), Étienne Méhul's one-act opera, *Uthal* (1806), Louis Théodore Gouvy's solo cantata, *Le dernier Hymne d'Ossian* (1858), Lucien Hillemacher's lyric scene *Fingal* (1880), Jules Bordier's choral cantata *Un rêve d'Ossian* (1885), Alexandre Levy's symphonic poem *Comala* (1890), Joseph Jongen's cantata *Comala* (1897), Armin Knab's *Darthulas Grabgesang* (1906) for voice and piano, Selim Palmgren's *Darthula's Gravsång* (1906) for male chorus, Adolf Busch's cantata, *Darthula's Grabgesang* (ca. 1912) for chorus and chamber orchestra, Erik Chisholm's *Night Song of the Bards* for piano (1941), and the *Ballades ossianiques* of Jean Guillou for organ (1962, 1971, rev. 2005).

A second group, inventive but less inherently brilliant, might include the operas by Harriet Wainewright (1792), Pietro Generali (1813, 1815), and Antonio Coppola (1847); the *Singspiel* by Peter von Winter (1809); the settings for voice and keyboard by J. F. Reichardt (1804) and Adolf Jensen (1875); the cantatas by Bernhard Hopffer (1878), Paul Umlauft (1884), Jørgen Malling (1900), and Cedric Thorpe Davie (1936); and the symphonic poems of C. V. Stanford (1903), Mikhail Ippolitov-Ivanov (1925), and James MacMillan (2013). In all of these, influence from the late classical period onward is perceptible, though not to the extent that it overpowers originality and invention. The remaining settings of Ossian, in which the romantic element dominates any achievement of modernity, or any new aesthetic, lack the flair or novelty of the two groups above and sit more or less comfortably within stylistic convention.[1]

But beyond these limits of style and taste there is also an argument for the influence of Ossian on composers not directly stimulated by the poems, at least in making actual settings of them: the songs of Robert Schumann, for example, betray indirect influence.[2] The following assesses how, in works by other composers that are not explicitly tied to the poems, the same influence may be detected: the "half-viewless harp" of the title that suggests objects dimly perceived or understood. There is always the danger, in arguing for secondary influence, of appearing to make bricks without straw. But the poems of Ossian were so pervasive in all the arts that their resonance seeped into the minds of very diverse creative personalities, sometimes even at a subconscious level.

The following argument, then, deals with broader influences of Ossian, those that are not as obvious on the surface. This has become familiar territory in the past few decades in the writing of musical history, particularly with the notion of "the musical topic," a concept that has given rise to much theoretical writing.[3] Rather than formal analysis, this perspective draws on ideas from semiotics and related fields to build a picture of style and expression with powerful contextual connections in the understanding of musical topics: military or hunting motifs, for example, that carry meanings beyond the purely musical structure. The concept of transmediation, as I use it here, falls readily into this notion of semiotic theory that is not tied to the written notes but moves into the wider area of cultural signification, including elements that belong to "exotic" or "extraneous" cultures (from the perspective of Western classical music).[4] The transfer of meanings from words into a musical genre often involves a process of acute cultural adjustment when the source is, as it was for most continental composers, foreign. Ossian in translation, for them, was not always understood as Macpherson had intended, and the range of understandings (and also misunderstandings) of the poems by composers needs more penetrating analysis than can be undertaken here. Inevitably, composers would map their emotional and cultural concerns onto their apprehension of the poetry. And increasingly, under the pressure of external events, individual works such as cantatas and tone poems began to adopt an ideological or political tone. As a result, the echoes or resonances often tended to look to the past, to medieval or Renaissance times, for inspiration and legitimacy.[5]

Literature and Opera

Ossian's agency extended into literature and the pictorial arts to an equal or greater degree, even, to its reach in music. Writing from Venice to the Abbé Michele Leoni in Florence on May 30, 1818, for example, George Gordon, Lord Byron, devoted a large part of a letter to discussing Leoni's translation of Ossian: this work was not in fact a translation of Macpherson but of John Smith's *Galic Antiquities* (1780), styled *Nuovi Canti di Ossian, pubblicati in Inglese da Giovanni Smith e recati in Italiano da Michele Leoni* (1813). A third edition of the *Nuovi Canti* was published in 1818, and this was the edition that Byron bought. As has been recently shown, Leoni's "creative" translation had a potent influence not only on Byron but also on the *Canti* of Giacomo Leopardi (1798–1837), a major poet and one of the intellectual lights of nineteenth-century Europe. The stream of influence from Ossian, on important poets as well as composers, is thus often indirect or at second hand.[6]

Byron had his own contribution to make in his startlingly homoerotic imitation of Ossian, "The Death of Calmar and Orla": two warrior friends go off to war together, the female of Macpherson's Ossian replaced by Calmar, and when he and Orla are killed and fall together, their blood mingles freely.[7] With greater relevance for music, Byron's unfinished novella, "Fragment of a Novel," which appeared in the collection *Mazeppa*, in 1819, followed on the heels of the 1816 Gothic novel *Glenarvon* by Lady Caroline Lamb, Byron's former mistress. Byron's tale was the earliest to feature a vampire. John William Polidori then adapted Byron's narrative for his own short story, *The Vampyre* (1819), whose vampire character, Lord Ruthven (a Scottish aristocrat), was modeled on Byron himself. All of this displays the confluence, if not the fusion, of Ossianic and Gothic motifs in English fiction writing of the first decades of the nineteenth century.

But music was not far behind. In 1828 Wilhelm August Wohlbrück fashioned a libretto for the composer Wolfgang Marschner's two-act opera *Der Vampyr*, basing his text on the play *Der Vampyr oder die Totenbraut* (1821) by Heinrich Ludwig Ritter, itself based on the Polidori version of the story. A new element introduced into this latest plot rehash was the character Malwina (Malvina), a name already well known in continental Europe not only from Ossian but also from the 1801 novel by Sophie Cottin (1770–1807).[8] Marschner's opera has been recognized as a key transitional work between Weber's *Der Freischütz* (1821) and Wagner's *Der fliegende Holländer* (1843). Here we begin to move further away from Ossian as even an indirect source. Still, the lack of admission, by the majority of scholars in German-speaking lands, of the poems' pervasive influence on Romantic poets has been interpreted as ignorance rather than deliberate suppression for nationalistic reasons.[9]

Goethe's *Werther*

A major literary source of musical composition in this secondary stream of influence is, of course, Goethe's *Die Leiden des jungen Werthers*—that is, the stage and solo vocal works derived from his epochal novel of 1774.[10] Massenet's opera *Werther* (written in 1887 and premiered in Vienna in 1892) is well enough known, in particular its tenor aria in act 3, a French translation of a section from Macpherson's poem "Berrathon."[11] But a century earlier, by 1790, the novel had impressed itself on several composers: Rodolphe Kreutzer (1766–1831), with his *Charlotte et Werther* (1791–92), produced at the Comédie-Italienne, Paris, on February 1, 1792; and Gaetano Pugnani (1731–98), the Turin violinist, who penned a melodrama, *Werter* (1795), which premiered at Vienna's Burgtheater on March 22, 1796.[12] A few years later Vincenzo Pucitta (1778–1861), had his *Werter e Carlotta* (1802), staged in Venice.

Around the same time, in the late 1790s, the Bavarian Johann Simon Mayr (1763–1845), working in Bergamo, composed a lyric opera (*farsa*) with the title *Werter e Carlotta*.[13] Mayr took his cue from the five-act *commedia* of the same title by Antonio Simon Sografi (1759–1818). The playwright, born and raised in Padua but working in Venice, drew his inspiration in turn from the first Italian translation of Goethe's novel, by Gaetano Grassi, published in Poschiavo in 1782.[14] Because Catholic dogma opposed the notion of suicide, Mayr's *Werter* was premiered only in July 2001, at the "Rossini in Wildbad" Festival in Baden-Württemberg.

Following Grassi, Mayr retains the idea of a suicide that is avoided in order to achieve a happy ending: in Italy, Goethe's novel had a less than favorable reputation because of the Catholic Church's teaching. Grassi, however, did not consider Goethe's novel dangerous to public morals; it served, rather, as a lesson on how to deal with dangerous passions. The Enlightenment, and Goethe's novel in particular, inspired other literary and musical efforts: Charlotte Smith, a British admirer, penned a poem, "Werter's Sonnet (Make there my Tomb beneath the Lime trees Shade)," that was set, like "I sit by the mossy fount" (from Ossian's "Carric-Thura") in the same volume, to a Haydn melody by an anonymous editor: in this case the first movement of the String Quartet, op. 9, no. 5, a B-flat melody (*poco adagio*) in $\frac{2}{4}$.[15] Around the same time the glee composer Stephen Paxton (1734–87) set the Smith poem for alto, two tenors, and bass.[16] J. W. Callcott, likewise, composed two glees on the Werther theme.[17] The Milanese musician Pietro Urbani, who settled in Edinburgh, set the text for "Charlotte at the Tomb of Werter" (ca. 1795).

Schumann, Chopin, Rossini

We have seen the agency of the Ossian poems through the influence of Klopstock, Goethe, and Schiller on Beethoven, as well as their more direct impact on Schubert and Mendelssohn, partly through Edmund von Harold and Herder. These evocations of Ossian also had an effect on Robert Schumann, through his personal friendship with Niels W. Gade and admiration of his work.[18] The Nordic aspect of Gade's compositional style filtered into Schumann's consciousness, no doubt as an alternative to Mendelssohn's Hebridean adventure, in piano pieces such as the "Nordisches Lied" of the *Album für die Jugend*, op. 68 (1848), or his settings of the poet Ludwig Uhland (1787–1860), whom Heine dubbed the "Ossian des Mittelalters"(the medieval Ossian).[19] Uhland was himself a keen admirer of the Ossian poems. Drawn, evidently, to the more straightforward versification of traditional ballads or the folk-like poetry of Robert Burns than to the sprawling lyric-epic worlds of Macpherson's prose poems, Schumann apprehended Ossian largely through Gade, whose influence is perceptible in the cycle of four ballades for soloists, chorus, and orchestra that Schumann composed to poems by Uhland and Emanuel Geibel in Düsseldorf between 1851 and 1853.[20]

About the influence of Ossian on Chopin, little can be said except that direct evidence is even sparser than for its influence on Schumann.[21] Unlike the recorded confessions of Beethoven and Mendelssohn, nothing survives in the composer's correspondence to suggest a close acquaintance with the poems. And so, with Chopin and Ossian, we enter a world of conjectural osmosis and contingent parallels. Yet the evolution of Chopin's four Ballades reflects the composer's appreciation of

Adam Mickiewicz's poetry, especially his *Ballady i romanse* (Ballads and romances, 1822). The essentially narrative nature of the ballade genre and Chopin's development of it has received considerable critical attention.[22] The composer mentioned to Schumann in 1836 that "some poems of Mickiewicz" had inspired his first two ballades, and scholars have discussed Chopin's awareness of the emotional content or association of certain keys.[23] Indirect influence of Ossian may also have filtered through to him because of his admiration for Mickiewicz, who was enthusiastic about Johann Georg Sulzer's *Allgemeine Theorie der schönen Künste* (General Theory of the Fine Arts, 1771–74), in Chopin's youth one of the main critical channels through which Ossian fever reached Poland.[24] Like Mendelssohn, Chopin visited Scotland, in 1848, at a time when he was desperately ill, but was exasperated by the solicitousness of his hosts, the family of his pupil Jane Stirling, who had taken lessons from him in Paris. He dedicated two nocturnes to her (op. 55, 1842–44), and the story of her attention to his subsequent well-being has often been described. Chopin, on the other hand, while appreciating the Highland landscape had at the same time acid comments to make about his hosts.[25]

While it would be hazardous to speculate on a link to specific compositions, extended pieces such as the Fantasy in F minor, op. 49 (1841), parallel to some extent the episodic nature of the Ossian poems. In a sense, the improvisatory quality of the composition results in a freedom of form strangely analogous to the shape of the poems, but now, eighty years or so after their publication, in full Romantic mode. The associations of a particular key may likewise be relevant. The spectral tread of the dotted rhythm in F minor that announces the Fantasy surfaces again in the first of the two nocturnes that Chopin dedicated to Jane a few years later, at roughly the same time as the composition of the structurally intricate Ballade no. 4, also in F minor.[26] In light of his health and mental state in the later 1840s, the fanciful assigning of a lugubrious quality to this key (notably by C. F. D. Schubart) cannot be entirely dismissed.[27]

It is well known that Chopin admired melodic invention in the operas of Bellini and indeed contributed his Variations in E minor to the volume of compositions in memory of Bellini sponsored by Liszt.[28] Bellini's renowned opera *Norma* (1831) shows the contemporary mining of Celtic-Roman history for topics for the stage: the librettist Felice Romani (1788–1865) adapted the tragedy of infanticide from the French poet Alexandre Soumet (1788–1845), a fervent admirer of Klopstock and Schiller—both, of course, authors powerfully influenced by Ossian.

Ossian's influence on *bel canto* opera in Italy, however, came mostly through the poems of Sir Walter Scott, such as the bestselling *The Lady of the Lake* (1810), or through his novels like *The Bride of Lammermoor* (1819).[29] These gave rise to, respectively, Rossini's opera *La donna del lago* (1819), in Andrea Leone Tottola's Ossian-redolent libretto; Schubert's song "Ave Maria, Jungfrau mild" (1825) in a German translation of Scott's poem by Adam Storck (1780–1822); and Donizetti's opera *Lucia di Lammermoor* (1835) with, in act 3, its opening storm, mad scene, and final burial ground setting.³⁰ The last of these scenes, which features Edgardo's brooding aria "Tombe degl'avi miei" (Graves of my forebears) recalls similar graveyard settings in Bianchi's *Calto* (1788) and Caruso's *Duntalmo* (1789), as well as Pavesi's *Fingallo e Comala* (1805) and *Ardano e Dartula* (1825).³¹ All of these appurtenances of the Romantic imagination (storms, distraught women, graveyards of ancestors) had their roots in the poems of Ossian.

Berlioz, Smetana, Wagner

Some might imagine that Hector Berlioz (1803–69) was the typical Romantic artist, wildly temperamental in his Gallic tastes and behavior, yet the impress of Ossian on him came, rather, from secondary sources such as Byron and Scott, in works such as the early "Waverley" overture (1828) and *"Harold in Italy"* (1834). The *Symphonie fantastique* (1830), while Ossianic in its general mood, was more directly inspired by works such as Thomas de Quincy's *Confessions of an English Opium-Eater* (1822) and Goethe's *Werther* and, more obviously, *Faust* (part 1), which Berlioz read in Gérard de Nerval's translation in 1828. Berlioz's tutelage under Le Sueur no doubt affected his view of Ossian, and there is but a single reference to the poems in his *Mémoires*.³² Still, Berlioz was clearly familiar with the poems but was quite possibly diverted from setting them directly not only because of their apotheosis in his teacher's *Ossian, ou les Bardes* but also by their controversial history.³³

Appropriating the idea of the bard as a key element for a musical work can result in a composer's becoming a conscious agent of bardic ideology. A prominent instance of this is Bedřich Smetana (1824–84), in a case I have detailed elsewhere.³⁴ The phenomenon of bardism came to Smetana through German sources such as Klopstock, for German was his first language: he only learned Czech later, writing his letters in German up to the beginning of the 1860s. The discovery of allegedly ancient manuscripts in 1817–18 by Czech nationalists had set in motion the composer's interest in the story of the Bohemian princess Libuše as the founder of the city of Prague.

Of his opera *Libuše* (1872), which is performed to this day on all state occasions, he wrote, "I want [*Libuše*] to serve the celebrations of the whole Czech nation." The image of the bard found its way into his own description of his tone poem *Vyšehrad*. "The harps of the bards begin; the song of the bards of the happenings on Vyšehrad, of the glory and brilliance, the tournaments and battles up to the final fall and decay. The work ends on an *elegiac note*."³⁵ The idea of the bards, harps, and an elegiac tone can only have come from literary and operatic sources such as Denis and Klopstock or Le Sueur's renowned Ossianic opera.³⁶ It was already present in Mozart's unfinished "Bardengesang auf Gibraltar'" (1782) on a pretentious text by Denis, and Schubert's "Bardengesang" with its text from Ossian's "Comala" (1816).

The concept of "bard" was also known in Hungary, as in other parts of central-eastern Europe, through Klopstock and German translations of Ossian such as those by Ahlwardt and Rhode.³⁷ Liszt refers on several occasions to Ossian; in a letter to Marie d'Agoult of October 8, 1846, he described Hungarian melodies as "half Ossian" and "half Gypsy."[38] His son-in-law Richard Wagner (1813–83) was certainly aware of the Ossian poems, and adapted the name Arindal (from "The Songs of Selma") for the protagonist in his unfinished opera, *Die Hochzeit* (The Wedding, 1832).[39] His overture to *The Flying Dutchman* follows the "seascape" images of Mendelssohn's "Hebrides" overture by using horn calls and frenzied strings to announce the first theme of the Dutchman, and in contrast, a cor anglais melody to capture the tenderness of Senta, a counterpart to the song-like second theme in "The Hebrides." The overture to the opera, which premiered on January 2, 1843, in Dresden, replicates the atmosphere that Mendelssohn had portrayed a decade earlier, but now in a different context, as a stirring prelude to stage drama. The similarities of orchestral color in the overture are striking, as is the melodiousness of the second theme in both works.

The question of influences, from Ossian or not, on Wagner's conception of the work of "total art" (*Gesamtkunstwerk*) is too large a topic to be dealt with here. Developing his thoughts around this subject in two essays of 1849 and another two years later,[40] however, Wagner may have been influenced to some extent by the ideas of the artist Philipp Otto Runge (1777–1810), who had earlier devised an architectural space for showing his paintings, to be accompanied by music. Around the same time, Runge had also, in 1806, made a set of twelve drawings for an edition of Ossian in a translation by Friedrich Leopold Graf zu Stollberg. These drawings were never published, because Stollberg's conception that they should glorify Germanic heroes clashed with the artist's symbolic incarnation of God and nature: personages from the poems were assigned natural attributes, such as the sun, "the giver," for Fingal; Ossian is the earth, the receiver, the spirit of man, while Oscar is the moon, the messenger.[41]

Runge's anthropomorphic view of nature caught the attention of Goethe, who was, like him, developing a theory of color at the time. But in light of Goethe's championing of conservative Weimar classicism, it is not surprising that he eventually disapproved of the direction Runge was taking.[42] All of these ideas about the relationship of the arts were current at the time Wagner was formulating his notions of how to unify text, music, and visual staging for his operas, and he cannot have failed to note the conflict that had occurred earlier between reactionaries such as Goethe and younger, more radical artists such as Runge and Caspar David Friedrich. For his part, Runge can be understood as a precursor of Wagner in ideas of how the arts might be combined to create a complete, unified work.

After his two essays were published, Wagner had in 1851 found Karl Simrock's edition of the *Völsunga saga*, translated from the Old Norse, in the Royal Library in Dresden. Five years earlier, in 1846, he had remarked to Niels Gade, "I must study these Eddic poems of yours; they are far more profound than our medieval poems." From 1848 to 1852 he was occupied with completing his libretto for the Ring tetralogy, which is based much less on the South German *Nibelungenlied* than the *Poetic* (and *Prose*) *Edda*, a thirteenth-century Icelandic compilation. He was also evolving his novel conception of the *Leitmotiv*,[43] a musical phrase or phrases tied to specific characters, events, or ideas that would find expression in his tetralogy, *Der Ring des Nibelungen* (The ring of the Nibelungs, first perf., 1876).[44] Thus, while the influence of the Ossian poems on Wagner may not have been direct, it was one of the stimuli that, transmitted through Klopstock, Runge, and others, saw the "Germanizing" of many of the poems' heroic features. The work of the productive scholar Jakob Grimm undoubtedly played a part in Wagner's absorption of German history and legend, through publications such as the *Deutsche Sagen* (German legends, 1816–18), *Deutsche Grammatik* (2nd ed., 1822) and *Deutsche Mythologie* (1835).[45] With the growing impetus toward German unification after 1850, Wagner was to take this idea further than any of his predecessors or contemporaries.[46]

Sibelius, and Another Mendelssohn

Like Smetana, Jean Sibelius was bicultural (at least in his youth), learning Finnish only when his ethnically Swedish parents sent him to a school where Finnish was the everyday language. Exposed to the wider world of late Romantic music, he met Gustav Mahler in Helsinki in 1907 and later, on a visit to Berlin, was drawn to the music of Arnold Schoenberg. It is perhaps no accident that the short tone poem *Barden*, composed in 1913 and revised a year later, is written in the "remote" E-flat minor (that is, remote from the quotidian keys of C, F, or G), the same key used by Schoenberg in his extensive and important "Darthula'" sketch of 1903.[47] Was Sibelius trying, like others, to achieve a "northern" feeling in the use of that key? Many of his tone poems are based on episodes from the *Kalevala* (published 1835, expanded 1849), the Finnish national epic.[48]

It is tempting to assume that there is something vaguely northern about the key of E-flat minor, in that Russian composers from Tchaikovsky to Prokofiev and Shostakovich have inscribed music within its tonal space. But it is also true that earlier composers such as Reichardt and Zumsteeg, when setting "The Songs of Selma" or Colma's episode contained in it, sometimes switch from E-flat major into that emotionally dark tonal region.[49] The 115 bars of Sibelius's *Barden* include a prominent part for harp, an instrumental association that one could argue ultimately derives from Ossian by way of Elias Lönnrot's bard and sage, Väinämöinen, in the *Kalevala*.[50] Moreover, does the single appearance of the tam-tam in this piece echo Le Sueur's opera, *Ossian, ou les Bardes* (1804), Bellini's *Norma* (1831), or, more likely, Tchaikovsky's use of the instrument (1893) in his Symphony No. 6?

There are other tantalizing links in Sibelius's opaque relationship with Ossian: the tone poem, *The Swan of Tuonela* (1893, revised in 1897 and 1900, published in 1901) incorporates both the cor anglais and the harp, instruments associated with the works of Rust (1780), Bianchi (1788) and others such as Pugnani (1790) from a century earlier. Its direct ancestor, one could argue, is Mendelssohn's "Hebrides" overture, as the final rising cello line echoes the ending of the overture and mist envelops the muted string texture. The plangent sound of the cor anglais, suitable for a lament-like solo in a bleak landscape, more likely was brought to Sibelius's attention through its use by Berlioz and Russian composers such as Borodin or Rimsky-Korsakov.[51] Yet another, if superficial, connection to the name of Ossian is Sibelius's *Zwei ernste Melodien* (Two serious melodies), op. 77, comprising the *Cantique (Laetare anima mea)* and *Devotion (Ab imo pectore)*. Sibelius completed the first of these in 1914 for solo instrument and small orchestra, and dedicated it to the distinguished cellist Ossian Fohström (1870–1952), who premiered it under the composer's direction on March 30, 1916, in Helsinki.[52]

From the same period as these, and with rather different aesthetic effect, Arnold Mendelssohn's *Drei Madrigale nach Worten des jungen Werthers* (1912) demonstrates that the roots of the glee are in madrigals: the settings are for two sopranos, alto, tenor, and bass. The text of the third madrigal, "Warum weckst du mich, Frühlingsluft?" (Why dost thou awake me, O breeze?) is taken from "Berrathon" (as, too, with Massenet's *Werther*), the poem famously read aloud by the doomed hero of Goethe's novel toward the end. Marked "rather slow" in $\frac{4}{4}$ (punctuated by six bars in $\frac{12}{8}$), and in "Phrygian" mode with a key signature of two flats, the basic root is D. The first soprano articulates the first lines, which are then imitated by all the voices. The composer's express purpose was to use the church modes in his madrigals as they gravitate to basic tonality, for example, D-Dorian to C major, not like D minor to F major. In this way any "archaizing" tendency is subject to the way in which the church modes are related to modern standard tonal practice.[53]

Then what are we to say about Debussy's attraction to Celtic themes? There is undoubtedly an echo of the Napoleonic "mode ossianique" in the Celtic Revival of the late nineteenth century to which he was exposed: are not the mists ("brouillards") and heathery landscapes ("bruyères") of the *Preludes* (1910) for piano as well as "La fille au cheveux de lin" (girl with the flaxen hair) related to Celtic imaginings in terms of artistic representation and landscapes?[54] At this point the *mode ossianique* was becoming, rather, what I would call the "esprit celtique," a more generalized and collective view of sometimes quite disparate traditions, Gaelic or Breton. Borders between subcultures tended to dissolve in the creative imagination. Coeval with the growth of the antiquarian and literary movement in Ireland and Scotland, late Romanticism in francophone Europe was drawn to the "exotic" and "antique" character of Celtic music.[55] The popular "Clair de lune" from Debussy's *Suite Bergamasque* (1890), for example, could be termed a gloss on, or back-handed compliment to, Saint-Säens's "Le lever de la lune" (The rising of the moon), written in 1855 and published ten years later, with a text that pays homage to Ossian's "Darthula" and the famed address to the moon. In this regard, Debussy became the revolutionary he did partly by absorbing elements of myth and folklore from the resurgent wave of Celticism that flowed over France and Belgium after mid-century, transforming these elements into captivating musical images. Symbolist drama also imported Germanized concepts of this Celticism, as in Bartók's one-act opera *Bluebeard's Castle* (1911–21), where the spoken introduction by a "bard" is followed by a Hungarian old-style folk song-like strain, unison, in the lower strings as preface to the tortured vocal duologue between Bluebeard and his new wife.[56] Thus Bartók not only "Magyarizes" the action at the outset, but is also able, in the course of the opera, to explore his own psychological difficulties with women.[57]

Whose Music?

Finally, we may ask, with some twentieth-century writers, "whose music" is this, the music of Ossian? Composed, art-tradition music exists in a variety of genres: monodrama, opera, lieder, cantata, instrumental and solo works. These have appealed intermittently to the concertgoing public, principally but not exclusively the urban middle class in Europe and North America—the dominant social group, too, in the nineteenth century. But now, there is also the rural-based, vernacular tradition of Ireland and Scotland that, even in the twentieth century, has made its voice heard, mainly as a result of the efforts of music ethnologists and record companies that recognize the significance of a long-lived oral tradition. But the tradition also flourishes in the form of fiddle and harp music. This aspect, pursued not only by native instrumentalists but now by ones in continental Europe and North America, is closer to the original tradition as it was valued and transmitted by oral-aural means.[58] To that extent, vernacular music, as in early fiddle pieces such as Daniel Dow's "Ossian's Hall" (1773) or John Gow's "Fingal's Cave" (1802), has persisted in more muscular fashion, even, than the heroic song and the concert tradition, apart from the examples of Felix Mendelssohn's overture (and, as I have argued, Beethoven's "Eroica" Symphony).

The vernacular tradition, in other words, has appealed in late modern times to a large popular audience, broadly different in its economic structure and its age mix from the middle-class concertgoing public, since it tends to be kept vital by younger instrumentalists and an often participatory following. It now attracts an audience, in fact, that was formerly the preserve of fine art composers: festivals with "Celtic" connections are an umbrella for vernacular music from around the world and for the exchange of repertoire that was, in former, less mobile times, less possible.[59] That both "Ossian," as the name of a well-known folk group (1976–97), and its Irish counterpart, "Planxty" (possibly from Latin *planctus*, lament) (1972–2005), attracted huge audiences during their heyday is a testimony to the spirit evoked by the name; likewise the famed Irish group the Chieftains, who have recorded pieces from the ballet-pantomime *Oscar and Malvina* (1791); Alan Stivell and the "renaissance of the Celtic harp" in the 1970s; and the American band Golden Bough, founded in 1980, with a wider "Celtic traditional" repertoire. "Tradition" in this sense denotes a vast expansion of what was a shared cultural patrimony between Gaelic-speaking Ireland and Scotland, one that currently embraces audiences and cross-cultural practitioners from almost every part of the globe.[60] The culture that Ossian celebrated in the eighteenth century, hugely influential in Europe and America in terms of literature has, by virtue of its transmediation from poetry to music over almost three centuries, become international in a way that Macpherson could never have imagined.

Appendix One

Title Page and Dedication of Harriet Wainewright's *Comàla*

[*Leather-bound, gold tooling, gold leafing, three volumes, one for each act, the pagination the same as for the single volume.*]

COMALA,/A/Dramatic Poem/from/OSSIAN/As performed at the/Hanover Square Rooms/Set to Music by/MISS HARRIET WAINEWRIGHT/Dedicated with Permission to the/Most Noble Marquis Wellesley./LONDON/Printed for the Author by William Napier,/Musician in ordinary to his Majesty/Lisle Street, Leicester Square.

DEDICATION./TO HIS EXCELLENCY THE MOST NOBLE/RICHARD MARQUIS WELLESLEY, K.P./GOVERNOR GENERAL OF INDIA, CAPTAIN GENERAL, &c,&c,&c.

My Lord,

Without pretensions either to the Name or Talents of an Author, I yet presume to address an Epistle Dedicatory to your Lordship, trusting my Motive for so doing, will justify the Presumption of the Act.

Whatever Merit the indulgent Eye may ascribe to the musical Composition now offered to the Public, yet must I with heartfelt Gratitude acknowledge, that to your Lordship's kind Patronage and Example, I am greatly indebted for the Success attending my Publication.

The beautiful and sublime Poems of Ossian, from which I have selected the episode of Comala, for the subject of my Opera, are too generally known and admired by the Amateurs of Literature, among whom your lordship holds a distinguished Place, to require any comments on my Part.

Your Lordship's hereditary and acquired Taste for Music, exalted Character and distinguished Rank, were very powerful Incitements to my aspiring for the Honor of dedicating my Opera to your Lordship, whose condescending Acquiescence with my Request, has stampt an additional Value on the Work, and ushered it into the Musical World, with Credit and with Eclat.

I have the Honor to be,
My Lord,
With the most grateful Respect,
Your Lordship's
Much obliged, and most obedient humble Servant,
HARRIET STEWART.
Calcutta, August, 1803.

Appendix Two

French and German Texts of Louis Théodore Gouvy's *Le dernier Hymne d'Ossian*

French (*Le dernier Hymne d'Ossian*)

Conduis, ô fils d'Alpin, le vieillard dans ses bois,
Les sombres flots du lac, que l'aquilon tourmente,
Retombent à grand bruit sur la rive écumante:
Le Barde va chanter pour la dernière fois.
Sur le torrent se balance un vieux chêne,
Que d'un souffle de glace ont blanchi les hivers;
Ma harpe est suspendue à sa branche prochaine,
Je l'entends qui frémit au sein de ces déserts.
Est-ce le vent, ma harpe, ou bien quelqu'ombre vaine
Qui t'arrache, en passant, ces funèbres concerts?
Quel transport m'agite et m'enflamme?
Approche, fils d'Alpin . . . ô mes chants, dans les airs
Accompagnez le départ de mon âme;
La mort va mettre un terme à mes longues douleurs.
Rugissez, vents du Nord, et déployez vos âiles,
Portez jusqu'à Fingal mes plaintes solennelles.
Ô Fingal, je te vois assis sur des vapeurs,
Dans tes puissantes mains tu caches les tempêtes,
Et tu les sêmes sur tes pas.
Le tonnerre à ta voix éclate sur nos têtes,
Et des clartés du jour tu prives nos climats.
Quand ta colère est apaisée,
Le zéphir du matin caresse les ruisseaux,
Et sur le front des arbrisseaux
Frémit en gouttes d'or une humide rosée.
Le soleil du printems [sic] se couronne de feux,
Des parfums les plus doux la plaine est embaumée;

On voit bondir le chevreuil joyeux
Sur la verdure ranimée.

✤ ✤ ✤

Toi que j'ai tant chéri, toi que j'ai tant pleuré,
Ô mon père, ô mon roi, je vais te voir encore,
Et gôuter le repos si souvent désiré.
Vents orageux du soir, ma bouche vous implore:
De vos bruyantes voix retenez les éclats;
Ossian va dormir, ne le réveillez pas.
Je l'entends . . . il m'appelle . . . ô Fingal, ô mon roi!
Ô mon père adoré, me voici près de toi!

German (*Ossian's letzter Gesang*)

Geleite, Sohn Alpin's, den Greis in seinen Wald.
Des See's dunkle Fluth vom Sturmwind überflogen
Wirft brandend an den Strand die schaumumhüllten Wogen.
Des Helden letztes Lied verklingt hier und verhallt.
   Am Wildbach bebet dort er Stamm der altne Eiche,
Des eis'ge Windhauch hat das Laub ihr abgestreift,
Die Harfe zittert hoch an ihrem nackten Zweige,
Ich hör' ihr Klagelied, das durch die Öde schweift.
Ist's Sturm, ist's eine Hand aus schatt'gem Geisterreiche,
Die vorübereilt und in die Saiten greift?
   Welcher Muth, welche Gluth in mir entbrennet!
Komm näher, Sohn Alpin's . . . o mein Gesang, in Lüften
Geleite meinen Geist, der nun sich trennet,
Im Tode wird mein Loos, mein Schmerzensloos erfüllt.
Du Nordwind, heule laut, und deine Flügel schlage,
Und trag' zu Fingal hin die schmerzgeweihte Klage.
Ich sehe, Fingal, dich von Nebeln umgehüllt,
Du herrschest und befiehlst den grimmen Ungewittern,
   Und streust sie aus mit mächt'ger Hand.
Der Donner, auf dein Wort, macht unsre Häupter zittern,
Das heitre Tageslicht nimmst du von See und Land.
   Wenn friedlich blicket deine Braue,
Spielet kosend mit dem Bach des Morgens holder West;
   Und auf Zweigen und Geäst
Erbeben Tropfen von feuchtem, gold'nem Thau.
Des Lenzes Sonne krönet sich mit Feuerglanz,
Es stehen von süssem Duft die Fluren sanft beladen,
   Es springet und hüpfet in heit'rem Tanz
   Das Rehlein auf Frühlingspfaden.

✤ ✤ ✤

Den ich so heiss geliebt, den ich so heiss beweint,
O mein Vater, mein Fürst, dich werd' ich wiedersehn,
Es locket mich zu dir die langersehnte Ruh.
Du Sturm des Abendwinds, o hör', o hör' mein Flehn:
Halt ein der Stimme Schall, der wild aus Schluchten bricht,
Denn Ossian entschläft, o weck' ihn, weck' ihn nicht.
Ich hör' ihn . . . Fingal ist's . . . er ist's, er rufet mir!
Mein Vater, und mein Fürst, ich komm, ich bin bei dir.

Appendix Three

Texts of Erik Chisholm's
Night Song of the Bards

Five bards passing the night in the house of a chief, who was a poet himself, went severally to make their observations on, and returned with an extempore description of, night.

First Bard: Night is dull and dark. / The clouds rest on the hills. / No star with green trembling beam; / no moon looks from the sky. / I hear the blast in the wood, / but I hear it distant far. / The stream of the valley murmurs; / but its murmur is sullen and sad. / From the tree at the grave of the dead / the long-howling owl is heard. / I see a dim form on the plain! It is a ghost! / It fades, it flies. / Some funeral shall pass this way: the meteor marks the path. The distant dog is howling from the hut of the hill. / The stag lies on the mountain moss: / the hind is at his side. / She hears the wind in his branchy horns. / She starts, but lies again. The roe is in the cleft of the rock; / the heath-cock's head is beneath his wing. / No beast, no bird is abroad, / but the owl and the howling fox: / she on a leafless tree; / he in a cloud on the hill. Dark, panting, trembling, sad, / the traveller has lost his way. / Through shrubs, through thorns, / he goes along the gurgling rill. / He fears the rock and the fen. / He fears the ghost of night. / The old tree groans to the blast; / the falling branch resounds. / The wind drives the withered burrs, / clung together, along the grass. / It is the light tread of a ghost! / He trembles amidst the night. Dark, dusky, howling, is night, / cloudy, windy, and full of ghosts! / The dead are abroad! / My friends, receive me from the night.

Second Bard: *The wind is up, the shower descends. / The spirit of the mountain shrieks. / Woods fall from on high. Windows flap.*[1] */ The growing river roars. / The traveller attempts the ford. / Hark! that shriek! he dies! / The storm drives the horse from the hill, / the goat, the lowing cow. / They tremble as drives the shower, / beside the shouldering bank. The hunter starts from sleep, / in his lonely hut; / he wakes the fire decayed. /*

His wet dogs smoke around him. / He fills the chinks with heath. / Loud roar two mountain streams / which meet beside his booth.[2] *Sad on the side of a hill / the wandering shepherd sits. / The tree resounds above him. / The stream roars down the rock. / He waits for the rising moon to guide him to his home. Ghosts ride on the storm to-night. / Sweet is their voice between the squalls of wind. / Their songs are of other worlds. The rain is past. The dry wind blows. / Streams roar, and windows flap. / Cold drops fall from the roof. / I see the starry sky. / But the shower gathers again. / The west is gloomy and dark. / Night is stormy and dismal; / receive me, my friends, from night.*

THIRD BARD: The wind still sounds between the hills, / and whistles through the grass of the rock. / The firs fall from their place. / The turfy hut is torn. / The clouds, divided, fly over the sky, / and show the burning stars. / The meteor, token of death! / flies sparkling through the gloom. / It rests on the hill. I see the withered fern, / the darkbrowed rock, the fallen oak. / Who is that in his shroud beneath the tree, by the stream? The waves dark-tumble on the lake, / and lash its rocky sides. / The boat is brimful in the cove; / the oars on the rocking tide. / A maid sits sad beside the rock, / and eyes the rolling stream. / Her lover promised to come. / She saw his boat, / when yet it was light, on the lake. / Is this his broken boat on the shore? / Are these his groans on the wind? Hark! The hail rattles around. / The flaky snow descends. / The tops of the hills are white. / The stormy winds abate. / Various is the night and cold; / receive me, my friends, from night.

FOURTH BARD: Night is calm and fair; / blue, starry, settled is night. / The winds, with the clouds, are gone: / They sink behind the hill. / The moon is up on the mountain. / Trees glister, streams shine on the rock. / Bright rolls the settled lake; / bright the stream of the vale. I see the trees overturned; / the shocks of corn on the plain. / The wakeful hind rebuilds the shocks, / and whistles on the distant field. Calm, settled, fair is night! / Who comes from the place of the dead? / That form with the robe of snow, / white arms, and dark-brown hair! / It is the daughter of the chief of the people: / she that lately fell! / Come, let us view thee, O maid! / Thou that hast been the delight of heroes! / The blast drives the phantom away; / white, without form, it ascends the hill. The breezes drive the blue mist, / slowly, over the narrow vale / It rises on the hill, / and joins its head to heaven. / Night is settled, calm, blue, / starry, bright with the moon. / Receive me not, my friends, for lovely is the night.

FIFTH BARD: *Night is calm, but dreary. / The moon is in a cloud in the west. / Slow moves that pale beam along the shaded hill. / The distant wave is heard. / The torrent murmurs on the rock. / The cock is heard from the booth.*[3] */ More than half the night is past. / The house-wife, groping in the gloom, / re-kindles the settled fire. / The hunter thinks that day approaches, / and calls his bounding dogs. / He ascends the hill, and whistles on his way. / A blast removes the cloud. / He sees the starry plough of the north. /*

Much of the night is to pass. / He nods by the mossy rock. Hark! The whirlwind is in the wood! / A low murmur in the vale! / It is the mighty army of the dead returning from the air. The moon rests behind the hill. / The beam is still on that lofty rock. / Long are the shadows of the trees. / Now it is dark over all. / Night is dreary, silent, and dark; / receive me, my friends, from night.

THE CHIEF: Let clouds rest on the hills: / spirits fly, and travellers fear. / Let the winds of the woods arise, / the sounding storms descend. / Roar streams and windows flap, / and green-winged meteors fly! / Rise the pale moon from behind her hills, / or inclose her head in clouds! / Night is alike to me, blue, / stormy, or gloomy the sky. / Night flies before the beam, / when it is poured on the hill. / The young day returns / from his clouds, but we return no more. Where are our chiefs of old? / Where are our kings of mighty name? / The fields of their battles are silent. / Scarce their mossy tombs remain. / We shall also be forgot. / This lofty house shall fall. / Our sons shall not behold the ruins in grass. / They shall ask of the aged, / "Where stood the walls of our father?" / Raise the song, and strike the harp; / send round the shells of joy. / Suspend a hundred tapers on high. / Youths and maids begin the dance. / Let some grey bard be near me, / to tell the deeds of other times; / of kings renowned in our land; / of chiefs we behold no more /. Thus let the night pass until morning / shall appear in our halls. / Then let the bow be at hand, the dogs, / the youths of the chase. / We shall ascend the hill with day, / and awake the deer.

Appendix Four

Provisional List of Musical Compositions Based on the Poems of Ossian

Note: the abbreviations follow the forms in *Grove's Dictionary of Music and Musicians*. The dating is normally that of publication or, if unpublished, that of the manuscript. Bracketed entries signify that the material is not taken directly from Macpherson's poems.

Phase 1: ca. 1780–1815

Oithóna (op), François-Hippolyte Barthélémon, 1768
"Darthulas Grabes-Gesang" (v, acc) Karl Siegmund von Seckendorff, 1774 (MS; v, fp acc, 1782)
"Selmar und Selma" (v, kbd); "Selma und Selmar" (v, kbd); "Ullin zum tapfern Carthon" (v, kbd), Christian Gottlob Neefe, 1776
Darthula (2 vv, orch), Thomas Linley the Younger, ca. 1776
"Dauras Trauer" (v, kbd), Seckendorff, 1779
"Selma und Selmar" (v, pf), Johann Friedrich Reichardt, 1779
Comala (music drama), Pietro Morandi, 1780
"Selma" (v, pf), Reichardt, 1780
Colma (monodrama), Friedrich Wilhelm Rust, 1780
"Songs of Ardven, no. 2: Sung before Fingal, in the Hall of Selma" (S, A, B vv, 2 vns, fp or org), Anon., ca. 1780
"Ossians Sonnengesang" (v, kbd), Johann Rudolf Zumsteeg, 1782, 1803
"Darthulas Grabes-Gesang" (v, kbd), Seckendorff, 1782
Fingal in Lochlin (incid music), Rust, 1782
Inamorulla oder Ossians Grosmuth (incid music), Rust, 1783
"Address to the sun" (glee), John Wall Callcott, 1783
"Ossians Sonnengesang" (v, kbd), Johann Friedrich Christmann, 1785 [cf. Zumsteeg 1782]
"I sit by the mossy fount" (v, kbd), [melody from Franz Josef Haydn], 1787
Komala (Spl), Friedrich Boutterweck, 1788

Calto (music drama), Francesco Bianchi, 1788
"The Maid of Selma" (v, fig bass), James Oswald, 1788
"Song of Selma" (v, fig bass), Oswald, 1788
"Ode from Ossian's Poems" (v, harpd/pf), Francis Hopkinson, 1788
"Minonas Gesang" (v, kbd), Reichardt, 1788
Duntalmo (music drama), Luigi Caruso, 1789
"Ossian auf Slimora" (v, kbd), Zumsteeg, 1790, 1803
"Song of Selma" (duet, fig bass), Oswald, 1790
"Some of my heroes are low" (glee, 5 vv), R. J. S. Stevens, 1790
Colma (music drama), William Bach, 1791
Oscar and Malvina, or The Hall of Fingal (ballet-pantomime), William Reeve, collab. William Shield, 1791
Comàla (op), Harriet Wainewright, 1792
"Father of heroes" (glee, 5 vv), Callcott, 1792
"Fingal's Grand March" (instr), Thomas Brabazon Gray, 1793
"Colma, ein Gesang Ossians" (v, kbd), Zumsteeg, 1794
"Peace to the souls of heroes" (glee, 3 vv), Callcott, 1794
The Caledonian Frolic (pantomime), Benjamin Carr, 1794
"Minona lieblich und hold" (v, kbd), Christoph Willibald Gluck, 1795
"Das Mädchen von Kola: Ein Gesang Ossians" (v, kbd), Karl Ditters von Dittersdorf, 1795 [cf. Seckendorff, 1782]
"Darthulas Grabgesang" (v, kbd), Hans Georg Nägeli (ca. 1795) [sketch]
"Youth of the gloomy brow" (glee, 3 vv), Callcott, 1795
"Address to the sun" (glee), Legh Richmond, 1795
"Bragela" (glee, 2 S, B, acc), Stevens, 1795
"Half hid in the grove" (song, pf/hp), J. A. Stevenson, 1795
"Oscar et Dermide: Chant gallique imité d'Ossian" (v, kbd), Étienne Méhul, 1796
Oscar e Malvina (pantomime ballet), Giuseppe Nucci, 1797
"In the lonely vale of streams" (glee, also adapted pf), Callcott, 1798
Comala (dramatic poem), Ettore Romagnoli, 1798
"Retire my love" (glee, 4 vv), William Horsley, 1798
"Canto di Selma d'Ossian" (v, pf), Francesco Pollini, ca. 1798
"O strike the harp in praise of my love" (glee, 2 S, acc), Stevens
"Strike the harp" (glee, 5 vv), Stevens, 1798
"O strike the harp" (glee, 1, 2, or 3 vv, acc), Stephen Storace, 1798
"Oscar's Tomb" (v, pf), John Ross, 1798
"Desolate is the dwelling of Morna" (glee, acc), Callcott, 1799
"Strike the harp" (glee), "O thou that rollest above" (glee), Stevens, 1799
"Chief of windy Morven" (glee, 2 tr, B, acc), Callcott, 1799
"Who comes so dark from Ocean's roar" (glee), Callcott, 1799
Ossians Harfe (Spl), F. L. Æ. Kunzen, 1799
"It is night"; "Ghost of Carril" (glees), John Percy, ca. 1800
"Voice of echoing Cona" (glee), Thomas Welch, ca. 1800
Selmar und Selma (duodrama), Franz von Stubenvoll, ca. 1800
"O thou that rollest from above" (glee, 5 vv), Stevens, ca. 1800
"Les adieux d'Oscar et Malvina" (duet, hp/pf acc), Alphonse Butignot, ca. 1800

Ossian sur la tombe de Malvina, scène française, Jean-Baptiste Bouffet, n.d.
"Ossian an die untergehende Sonne" (v, vn, pf), Friedrich Heinrich Himmel, ca. 1800
"Oscar à Malvina" (v, pf/hp), François-Joseph Naderman, ca. 1800
"Chant imité d'Ossian: Colma" (v, orch), Anon., ca. 1800–1820
"Fingal's Lament, over the tomb of Ryno" (v, kbd), Anon., 1800
Scène tirée des Poesies d'Ossian (chor), Christian Kalkbrenner, 1800
"Descend ye light mist" (glee); "Where are our chiefs of old?" (glee), Joseph Kemp, 1800
"Raise the song and strike the harp" (glee, 2 Tr, B), Matthew Cooke, 1800
"It is night" (glee, A, T, B), Reginald Spofforth, 1800
"Hast thou left the blue course" (glee, A, T, B); "Song on the times of old" (glee); "Come on the light winged gale" (glee); "Green thorn of the hill of ghosts" (glee, A or CT, 2T, B), Callcott, 1801
Oscar e Malvina (ballet), Antonio Landini, 1801
"Rise winds of autumn"; "Morven" (glees), Callcott, 1802
"Alone on the sea-beaten rock" (glee, 5 vv); "Bards of the days of old" (glee, 3 vv); "Half hid in the grove" (glee), Stevenson, 1802
"Rise to the battle" (glee, 3 vv, acc), William Warren, 1802
Sulmalle (lyrical duodrama, chor), Bernhard Anselm Weber, 1802
"The clouds of night" (glee), Callcott, 1802
"Chant gallique" (v, kbd), Jean-François Le Sueur, 1802
"Calto e Comala" (2 vv), Francesco Gardi, 1803
"The harp of old Ossian, or Caledonia triumphant" [tune: "The Garb of Old Gaul"], Anon., 1803
Ossian, ou Les Bardes (op), Le Sueur, 1804
Bombarde, parodie d'Ossian, Alexis Daudet et al., 1804
Ossian cadet, parodie des bardes, E. Mercier Dupaty et al., 1804
Oh, Que c'est sçiant, ou Oxessian (burlesque imitation and vaudeville), M. A. M. Désaugiers and Francis, 1804
Fingallo e Comala (music drama), Stefano Pavesi, 1804
Ossian, ou les Bardes (pf arr.), Louis Alexandre Piccinni, ca. 1804
Fantaisie sur différents chants de l'opera des Bardes (pf arr.), Henri-Joseph Rigel, ca. 1804
Ossian, ou les bardes (ballet), Federigo Fiorillo, 1804
"Rise to the battle my thousands" (glee), Thomas Attwood, 1804
"Armins Klage um seine Kinder"; "Doch sieh der Mond erscheint; Geister meiner Toten; Kolma's Klage; Kolnadona" (v, pf), Reichardt, 1804
"Les adieux d'Ossian à Malvina"; "Ossian à Sulmala" (v, kbd), Jacques-Marie Beauvarlet-Charpentier, 1804
"Ullin, Carril and Ryno: Song of Selma from Ossian's poems" (v, kbd), Anon., 1805
"Scena Oskar umsonst!" (S, orch), Louis Spohr, 1805
"Come Ossian, come away" (glee); "Malvina's Lamentations" (glee); "When shall joy dwell in Selma?" (glee), John Clarke-Whitfield, ca. 1805
"Ossians Klage um Uthal und Oithóna" (v, pf), Friedrich Götzloff, ca. 1805
Fingal (incid music), Osip [Józef] Kozlowski, 1805
Uthal (op), Méhul, 1806
Brutal, ou il vaut mieux tard que jamais (parody), Marie-Joseph Pain et al., 1806
"Se vincitor ritorna" (aria with chor), from *Armira e Daura* (op), Nicola Giuliani, 1806

Calto e Colama (ballet), Pietro Angiolini, 1806

"Selmar und Selma" (duet, acc 2 vn, va, bass), Andreas Romberg, 1806

"Ossian, barde du III siècle, poésies galliques en vers français; Colma; Ossian à Sulmala" (v, pf), Bouffet, 1809

Colmal (Spl), Peter von Winter, 1809

Le Songe d'Ossian (ballet-pantomime), Josef Kinsky, 1809

Moras Love, or The Enchanted Harp (ballet), Henry Bishop, 1809

Malvina (op), Adalbert Gyrowetz, 1810 [recit, aria; duetto]

Fingallo (op [incomplete]), Bishop, ca. 1810

"Strike the harp in praise of Bragela" (glee); "When the storm aloft arise" (glee, A, T, B); "Where art thou beam of light" (glee, 2 S, T, B); "The harp of Ossian" (James Hogg), Bishop, ca. 1810

"Thy blue waves, O Carron" (glee), Thomas Hamley Butler, ca. 1810

"Thy blue waves, O Carron" (song, pf), Ross, 1802

"Le Chant d'Ossian" (chor, orch), Méhul, 1811

"Colma: ein altschottisches Fragment aus dem Liedern der Selma des Ossian" (v, fp), Carl Friedrich Zelter, 1813

Calto e Colama (ballet), Alessandro Fabbris, 1812

Hidalan (Spl), Franz Cramer, 1813

Gaulo ed Oitona (music drama), Pietro Generali, 1813

Ballade, op. 47, no. 3 ("Der Barde singt: Was stürmet die Haide auf?") (v, pf), Carl Maria von Weber, 1815

"La morte di Comala," recit and aria (S, orch), Georg Gerson, 1813

"On dit que je suis belle: Romance tirée du poème d'Ossian" (v, pf), Pierre Gaveaux, 1814

"Kolma's Klage"; "Shilrik und Vinvela"; "Ossians Lied nach dem Falle Nathos"; "Das Mädchen von Inistore"; "Cronnan"; "Lorma"; "Selma und Selmar" (Lieder: v, pf), Franz Schubert, 1815

"Comala is no more" (glee), Thomas Miles, 1815

"Ossian an die untergehende Sonne" (duet), Himmel, ca. 1815

"Colma, chant ossianique"; "Les Adieux d'Oscar et Malvina, chant ossianique" (v, pf), Camille Pleyel, 1815

"Songe d'amour" (v, guitar), Guillaume-Pierre-Antoine Gatayes, 1815

"Daughter of streamy Lutha" (glee, 3 vv), Frederick William Crouch, ca. 1815

Le Chef Écossais, ou La Caverne d'Ossian (pantomime), arr. M. Dreuil, 1815

Phase 2: 1815–80

"Bardengesang"; "Der Tod Oscars"; "Lodas Gespenst" (v, pf), Schubert, 1816

"Le Barde au tombeau de sa bien-aimée" (v, pf), Rigel, 1816

Oscar e Malvina (music drama), Francesco Sampieri, 1816

"Die Nacht" (v, pf), Schubert, 1817

"A Selma"; "Colma, ou le chant du barde"; "La plainte du barde, chant ossianique" (v, pf), Henri-Montan Berton, 1815–17

Malvina (op), N. Vaccai, 1816

Clato (music drama), Generali, 1817
Aganadeca (music drama), Carlo Saccenti, 1817
Ossian (ballet), arr. Kinsky, 1819
"The maid of Selma (In the hall I lay in night)" (v, vc acc), W. Crotch, 1820
"Oscar et Malvina" (v, pf/hp), Antonio Pacini, ca. 1820
Szene aus Ossians Comala (v, acc), Friedrich Kuhlau, ca. 1820
"Ossian, ou la harpe éolique" (v, acc.), Angelo Benincori, ca. 1820
"Chant ossianique sur le mort de Napoleon" (v, acc), Delphine Gay [Delphine de Girardin], 1821
Fingal (dramatic scene), Desiré-Alexandre Batton, 1822
Comala (op), Luigi Gordigiani, 1822
Calto e Colama (ballet), Pietro Romani, 1822
Fingal i Roskrana (op), Caterino Cavos, 1824
Ardano e Dartula (op), Pavesi, 1825
Malvina (ballad op), Thomas Simpson Cooke, 1826
Fantaisie sur les airs des bardes écossaises (pf, orch), Ignaz Moscheles, 1826
Clato (ballet pantomime), Antonio Monticini, 1829
"The Harp of Ossian" (v, pf), Bishop, 1829
Malvina (op), Michael Costa, 1829
"By the dark rolling waters" (glee, 4 vv), Joseph Macmurdie, ca. 1830
"Jeune Fingal, apporte-moi ma lyre" (*romance*), J. B. M. Braun, ca. 1830
Sinfonie dans le style d'Ossian (orch), Karl Borromeo Miltitz, 1831
Clato (lyric tragedy), Pietro Raimondi, 1832
Toscar (ballet), Francesco Schira, 1832
"Shades of heroes" (glee, 5 vv), T. S. Cooke, 1832
Die Hebriden (ov); *Overture to the Isles of Fingal* (pf duet), Felix Mendelssohn, 1832
"Ossian's hymn to the sun" (glee), John Goss, 1833
Oskars Tod (op), Johann Georg Kastner, ca. 1833
"Star of descending night" (glee, 4, 5 and 6 vv, acc), Richard Garbett, ca. 1835
"Chor aus Ossians Gesänge," Anon., 1839
Efterklang af Ossian (orch), Niels Wilhelm Gade, 1840
"Ossian's Glen" (male v, pf), George Loder, 1840 [words by Wordsworth]
"Chant d'Ossian, morceau fantastique" (pf), Theodor Kullak, 1840
Die Schlacht auf Lora (duet, female chor, pf), Josef Klein, ca. 1840
"Ossian 1"; "Ossian 2" (ballades, pf), Louis Moreau Gottschalk, 1843
"Malvina la bella" (v, pf), Gaetano Donizetti, 1843
"Alpins Klage um Morar," op. 95 (v, pf), Carl Loewe, 1844
Malvina, scène dramatique (v, pf), Donizetti, 1845
On Lena's Gloomy Heath (concert aria, orch), Mendelssohn, 1846
"Stimmen von Selma" (pf), *Vinvela* (solo, chor, hp, str quartet), Frydryk Eduard Sobolewski, ca. 1846
Comala (soli, chor, orch), Gade, 1846
Fingallo (op), Pietro Antonio Coppola, 1847
"Colma's Klage" (v, pf), August Walter, 1847
"An Malvina"; "Fingals-Höhle" (guitar), Johann Kaspar Mertz, 1847
[Ossian's Serenade (v, pf), Ossian Euclid Dodge, 1849]

Comala (orch), William Howard Glover, ca. 1850
"Danse ossianique" (pf), Gottschalk, 1850–51
"O thou whose beams [Ossian's hymne]" (glee, 5 vv), Goss, ca. 1852
"Le lever de la lune" (v, pf), Camille Saint-Saëns, 1855
Marche de nuit (pf), Gottschalk, 1855
"Das Mädchen von Kola" (v, pf), Ernst Otto Lindner, ca. 1855
"Le harpe ossianique" (pf), Wilhelm Krüger, 1855
Fingallo (op), Francesco Chiaromonte, 1855
Komala (op), Sobolewski, 1858
Le dernier Hymne d'Ossian, op. 15 (B, orch), Louis Théodore Gouvy, 1858
Gesang aus Fingal, op. 17, no. 4 (3 high vv, horn, hp), Johannes Brahms, 1859
Darthulas Grabgesang, op. 42, no. 3 (6-part chor), Brahms, 1861
Fingal (reciters, chor, orch), Edmond Membrée, 1861
Fingal (chor, orch), Wilhelm Fritze, ca. 1861
"Malvina, mélodie ossianique" (vn, pf), Eugene de C.p., 1862
"Das Mädchen von Kola" (A or Bar, pf), op. 12, Constantin Bürgel, 1865
"Malvina" (pf), Edouard Silas, ca. 1865
"Das Mädchen von Kola," op. 16 (chor, orch), Carl Reinthaler, 1865
Bilder aus Ossian: Fünf Stücke für Piano, op. 7: "Kolma's Klage"; "Fingal"; "Komala"; "Das Gespenst von Loda"; "Vinvela und Shilrik," Fritze, 1866
"Til Ossian"; "Ossians Sang til Aftenstjernen"; "Ossians Sang till Maanen" (v, pf), Peder Heise, 1866
Ossian (symph poem), Alarich Zahn, ca. 1866–69
"Das Mädchen von Kola" (v, pf), Wilhelm Hill, 1867
"Darthulas Grabgesang" (v, pf), Wilhelm Taubert, ca. 1867
"Stern der dämmernden Nacht" (A, 4 male vv), Hermann Zopff, 1868
Armor und Daura (op), Ferdinand Heinrich Thieriot, 1869

Phase 3: 1880–1918

Comala (op), Karl Hoffbauer, 1872
"Schön bist du, O Kind des Himmels" (4-part male chor, pf), Ernst Louis Meinhardt, 1871/72
"Colmas Todtenlied der Barden aus Ossian" (male chor, pf acc), Meinhardt, 1872
"Colma's Klage nach Ossian," op. 153, no. 3 (S, pf), Ferdinand Hiller, 1873
Die Klage der Kolma (Mez, orch), Vinzenz Lachner, 1874
"Das Mädchen von Kola" (v, pf), Karl Grädener, 1874–79
"Darthulas Grabgesang" (v, pf), Adolf Jensen, 1875
"Fingal und Ossian," op. 140 (male chor), Carl Reinecke, 1876
Oitona (op), Dionisio Rodoteato, 1876
Ossiane (symph poem, S, chor, orch), Marie Jaëll, 1879
Darthulas Grabgesang (S, fem chor, orch), Bernhard Hopffer, 1878
Mora (op), Luigi Vicini, 1880
"Fingal, poème dramatique" (3 vv, pf), André Gedalge, 1880

Fingal, lyric scene (v, orch, pf red), Raymond Bonheur, 1880
"Fingal" (v, pf), Louis-Charles-Bonaventure-Alfred Bruneau, 1880
"Ossian, Polka brillante" (pf), Nicolás Ruiz Espadero, ca. 1880
"Komm du Lichtstrahl: Gesang aus Ossian" (aria), J. Klenze, ca. 1880
Fingal, lyric scene (vv, pf) Lucien-Joseph-Édouard Hillemacher, 1880
"Dersagrenas Ballade"; "Fingals Klagegesang" (v, pf), Gade, ca. 1880
"Dartula" (v, pf), Antonio Leonardi, ca. 1880
Ossian (symph poem, hp), Arthur Coquard, 1882
Moina (symph poem), Sylvain Dupuis, 1884
Agandecca, dramatic poem (soli, male chor, orch), Paul Umlauft, 1884
"Ossians Lied" (soli, male chor), Benjamin Hamma, 1884
Un rêve d'Ossian, scène lyrique (soli, chor, orch), Jules-Auguste Bordier, 1885
Darthulas Grabgesang aus Ossian (2 S, A, 2 hns, hp), Hermann Hans Wetzler, 1888 [MS]
Comala (soli, chor, orch), Karl Emanuel Klitzsch, 1888
Comala (orch), John Blackwood McEwen, 1889 [MS]
Les noces de Fingal (lyric episode, soli, chor, orch), Blas-Maria Colomer, 1889
Les noces de Fingal (lyric episode), Georges Schmitt, 1889
Fingal (solo, male chor, orch), Arnold Krug, 1891
Oitona (op), Dionisio Carradi, 1891
Comala (symph poem), Alexandre Levy, 1890
Werther (op), Jules Massenet, 1892
Fingal (symph poem), Adolphe Biarent, 1894
The Death of Cuthullin (soli, chor, orch), William Augustus Barratt, 1897
Les noces de Fingal (op), Alix Fournier, 1897
Fingal (op), André Dulaurens, n.d. [MS]
"Darthulas gravsång" (mixed chor), Erkki Melartin, 1897 [MS]
"Le barde" (inc. "Le bouclier du grand Fingal"), Caroline Cresté, n.d.
Comala (soli, chor, orch), Joseph Jongen, 1897
"Comalas Sang paa Høien" (v, pf), Jørgen Malling, 1897
Darthula (op), Simon van Milligen, 1899
Kyvala (soli, chor, orch), Malling, 1902
Oina o Principe Ossian (op), Julián Carrillo(-Trujillo), 1903
Irish Rhapsody No. 2: Lament for the Son of Ossian (symph poem), Charles Villiers Stanford, 1903
Darthulas Grabgesang (soli, chor, orch), Arnold Schoenberg, 1903 [sketch]
Das Mädchen von Kola (male chor, orch), Wilhelm Koehler-Wümbach, 1903
Trenmor (symph poem), Biarent, 1905
Ossian (op, [incomplete]), Frederick Corder, 1905
"Darthulas Grabgesang" (v, pf), Armin Knab, 1906
"Darthulas Gravsång" (male chor), Selim Palmgren, 1906 [published 1913]
"Ossians Song" (cello, pf), Carlo Alfredo Piatti, n.d.
Leaves from Ossian (soli, chor, orch), Liza Lehmann, 1909
Darthula's Grabgesang (chor, cham orch), Adolf Busch, ca. 1912
Comala (S, orch or pf), François Rasse, ca. 1913
"An den Abendstern" (male chor), Robert Kahn, 1915 [MS]
Ossian (symph prelude), Eugene Goossens, 1915 [withdrawn]

"Cuchullin and his son"; "Aillte, an Ossianic lay" (v, pf), Marjory Kennedy-Fraser arr, 1917
"The Death of Morar" (chor), Granville Bantock, 1917
"An die untergehende Sonne" (chor), Kahn, 1918 [MS]

Phase 4: 1918–Present

Comala (op), Joseph Weston Nicholl, 1920
Three Musical Tableaux from Ossian (orch), Mikhail Ippolitov-Ivanov, 1925
Comala (ov), Ian Whyte, 1929
"Ossian und Malwina" (female chor), Arnold Mendelssohn, ca. 1930
Darthula (chor, orch/pf), Aloys Fleischmann, ca. 1930 [MS]
"Ossianic Processional" (chor), Hugh S. Roberton, 1933 (arr, org, Purcell J. Mansfield, 1939)
Elegy for an Ossianic Warrior (orch), Cedric Thorpe Davie, 1935 [MS]
Six Ossianic Odes: "Shilric's Song"; "The Poet's Prayer"; "A Dirge for Ryno"; ["Bend Thy Blue Course, O Stream"; "Malvina, Where Art Thou?"; "Thou Hast Left Us"] (v, pf), John Laurence Seymour, 1936
Dirge for Cuthullin (chor, orch), Thorpe Davie, 1936
Night Song of the Bards (six nocturnes, pf), Erik Chisholm, 1941–44
Cuchullin's Lament (orch), Bantock, 1944
"Darthulas Grabgesang" (v, pf), Friedrich Neumann, ca. 1950 [MS]
Le lance de Fingal (op), André Amellér, 1957
"Oiséan's Song" (v, pf), Chisholm, 1964
Ossian, Suite for Harp, Vladimir Kikta, 1965
"Szene aus Ossians Gesänge" (chor), Kurt Brüggemann, ca. 1981
"Oisean is Malmhine" (v), arr Heinrich Möller, ca. 1982
Ossian, concerto for flute (fl, str orch), George McIlwham, 1987 [MS]
Ballade ossianique, No. 1: Temora (org), Jean Guillou, 1962 (rev 2005)
Ballade Ossianique, No. 2: Les chants de Selma (org), Guillou, 1971 (rev. 2005)
The Death of Oscar (symph essay), James MacMillan, 2012

Untraced or lost works

Comala (incid music), F. G. Fletcher, late 18th century
Comala (op), Thomas Busby, 1799
La chasse d'Ossian (orch), Georges Bizet, 1860–61
Oithóna (op), Edgar Bainton, 1915
The Coming of Cuchulain (orch poem), Ronald Center, 1944

Traditional melodies

"Ossian's Hall" (vn), Daniel Dow, 1773

"Dàn Deirg"; "Laoidh Ghara 's nam ban"; "Ossian 'an déigh nam Fion"; "Laoidh an amadain mhòir"; "Tha sgeul beag agam air Fionn"; "Dàn Liughair"; "Dàn Fhraoich"; "Manus" (lays): publ. Patrick McDonald, 1784

"Three Fingalian airs" (harp): publ. John Bowie, 1789

"Fingal's Lamentation" (vn), Niel Gow, 1800

"Fingal's Cave" (vn), John Gow, 1802

"Specimen of Ossianic Music," in *An Account of the Highland Society of London*: publ. Sir John Sinclair, 1813

"Bàs Dhiarmaid" (The death of Diarmaid); "Duan Fhraoich" (The song of Fraoch); "Cath Mhanuis" (Manus's battle) (lays): Elizabeth Ross MS, 1815

"Fingalian Air" (vn): publ. Simon Fraser, 1816

"The Battle of Argan More (in the time of Ossian)": publ. Edward Bunting, *The Ancient Music of Ireland*, 1840

"Oisiansk melodi, in Oisians sånger efter gaeliska originalet": publ. Nils Arfwidsson, 1842 [cf. Sinclair, 1813]

"Mùr Oiseain or Ossian's Hall"; "Guil Fhinn, or Fingal's Lament": publ. William Gunn, *Caledonian Repository of Music Adapted for the Bagpipes*, 1848

"Laoidh Fhraoich" (lay): Frances Tolmie coll. 1870 [publ. *Journal of the Folk-Song Society*, 1911]

"Cumha Fhinn" (Ossian's lament for his father): James Logan, *The Scottish Gael*, 1876

"Fingal's Cave"; "Ossian Alone, The Last of the Fingalians": publ. J. F. Morison, *Highland Airs & Quicksteps*, 1882

"Laoidh Dhiarmaid"; "Laoidh Osgair"; "Fingal's Weeping"; "Cumha Dhiarmaid": publ. Keith Norman MacDonald, *Gesto Collection*, 1895

"Ossian's Lament": publ. Francis O'Neill, *The Music of Ireland*, 1903

"Ossian, An Elegy"; "Fingal's Dirk" (vn, pf), Scott Skinner, 1904

"Fingal's March"; "The Maid of Selma": publ. Francis Roche, *Roche Collection of Traditional Irish Music*, 1927

"The Dirge of Ossian and MacAnanty's Reel" (string orch), John Francis Larchet, 1943

Notes

Preface

1. "Descriptive" analysis is often understood in a pejorative sense by musicologists. Ludwig Wittgenstein, however, argued for (verbal) "description" over "explanation" in analytical philosophy, and a parallel might well be drawn with musicological discourse. See his *Philosophical Investigations*, trans. G. E. M. Anscombe, 2nd ed. (Oxford: Blackwell, 1958), 99: "Thinking of a description as a word-picture of the facts has something misleading about it: one tends to think only of such pictures as hang on our walls: which seem simply to portray how a thing looks, what it is like. (These pictures are as it were idle)." Wittgenstein was referring more to theory; he had no difficulty with "explanation" when it aimed at clarification of meaning. Thus, a music score in prescriptive notation is not a picture of the facts but a code that requires interpretation. In the analysis of music, such notation is merely a convenient shorthand to indicate structural and performative features that the composer has prescribed. To that extent it is, when supplemented by verbal commentary, still the most practical way of describing music (in the Western concert tradition) that is to be performed. On Wittgenstein's relationship with music, see Béla Szabados, *Wittgenstein as Philosophical Tone-Poet: Philosophy and Music in Dialogue* (Amsterdam: Rodopi, 2014), 59–86, 97–116, 142–50.
2. Aldo is a popular male first name in Italy; Malvina and Oscar are still common names for women and men, respectively, in Germany, Poland, Scandinavia, and the Baltic region. Ossian is favored in Wales as a first name for males. Morven is the first name of many women in Scotland. Place names from Ossian can likewise be found throughout the Anglophone world, especially where Scottish or Scots-Irish emigrants settled: for example, the US townships of Ossian in Indiana and Iowa, or in New York State, where there are settlements called Ossian and Burns (the latter named after the poet, an avowed admirer of Ossian; it was founded partly by residents from the former after fire destroyed many homes there in 1826).
3. On Marie (Trautmann) Jaëll, see the essay by Sébastien Troester, "A Passion for Composing," in the 3-CD set *Marie Jaëll: Musique Symphonique, Musique pour Piano* (Ediciones singulares, 2016).
4. For discussion of Rust's *Colma*, see chapter 9. We might also include Stanford's *Irish Rhapsody No. 2* (1903) among related works with an episodic character; see chapter 14. On the issue of narrative in music, see Byron Almén, *A Theory of Musical Narrative* (Bloomington: Indiana University Press, 2008).

Chapter One

1. See Derick S. Thomson, *The Gaelic Sources of Macpherson's Ossian* (Edinburgh: Oliver & Boyd for the University of Aberdeen, 1952). Further, Dafydd R. Moore, "The Critical Response to Ossian's Romantic Bequest," in *English Romanticism and the Celtic World*, ed. Gerard Carruthers and Alan Rawes (Cambridge: Cambridge University Press, 2003), 38–53.
2. Matthew Arnold, *The Study of Celtic Literature* (London: Smith, Elder & Co, 1891), 127–28.
3. For example, Derek Carew, in *The Cambridge History of Nineteenth-Century Music* (Cambridge: Cambridge University Press, 2001), 243, refers to "Macpherson's famous forgeries of the 1760s."
4. This applies even to prominent music studies such as that of R. Larry Todd, *Mendelssohn: A Life in Music* (Oxford: Oxford University Press, 2003), in which "the forgeries of Macpherson had long been exposed" (526). But critical studies of the poems had already been under way since the 1980s, with, for example, Fiona Stafford's important biography, *The Sublime Savage: James Macpherson and the Poems of Ossian* (Edinburgh: Edinburgh University Press, 1988), and Howard Gaskill's scrupulous edition of the poems, *The Poems of Ossian and Related Works* (Edinburgh: Edinburgh University Press, 1996).
5. Rudolf Tombo, *Ossian in Germany: Bibliography, General Survey, Ossian's Influence upon Klopstock and the Bards* (New York: AMS Press, 1966; orig. ed. 1901); Wolf Gerhard Schmidt, *"Homer des Nordens" und "Mutter der Romantik": James Macphersons Ossian und seine Rezeption in der deutschsprachigen Literatur*, 4 vols. (Berlin: de Gruyter, 2003).
6. Johnson was not free of prejudices himself; see Katie Trumpener, *Bardic Nationalism: The Romantic Novel and the British Empire* (Princeton, NJ: Princeton University Press, 1997). As for Trevor-Roper, he was the historian who initially authenticated the forged Hitler diaries, although he was later persuaded to change his mind; see Robert Harris, *Selling Hitler: The Story of the Hitler Diaries* (London: Faber & Faber, 1986).
7. *The Report of the Royal Highland Society* (1805) on the "authenticity" question suggested that Macpherson had failed, as a translator, to capture the beauty of his Gaelic originals. He, on the other hand, might have argued that it was the successful transposition into other languages that shows the English-language Ossian to be genuine poetry; see Howard Gaskill, "'Genuine poetry . . . like gold,'" introduction to *The Reception of Ossian in Europe*, ed. Howard Gaskill (London: Thoemmes Continuum, 2004), 9–10.
8. During his stay in London (1901–3), the poet and novelist Soseki Natsume (1867–1916) visited Dundarach House, Pitlochry, and its Japanese garden at the invitation of John Henry Dixon (1838–1926), a wealthy Englishman who had stayed in Japan from 1899. Much of the influence of Ossian on Japanese writers such as Soseki came through its arresting presence in Goethe's *Werther*.
9. Germaine de Staël, *De la littérature* (1800), ed. Axel Blaeschke (Paris: Classiques Garnier, 1998); Johann Gottfried Herder, "Auszug zu einem Briefwechsel über Oßian und die Lieder alter Völker" [Extract from a Correspondence on Ossian and the Songs of Ancient Peoples] in Hans Dietrich Irmscher ed., *Von deutscher Art und Kunst: Einige fliegende Blätter* (Stuttgart: Reclam, 1995), 7–62.

10. See Howard Gaskill, "German Ossianism: A Reappraisal?" *German Life and Letters* 42 (1989), 329–41.
11. See Susan Manning, "Henry Mackenzie and *Ossian*: Or, the Emotional Value of Asterisks," in *From Gaelic to Romantic*, ed. Fiona Stafford and Howard Gaskill, 136–52.
12. Fiona Stafford, *The Sublime Savage*, 4. See also her introduction to *The Poems of Ossian and Related Works*, ed. Howard Gaskill (Edinburgh: Edinburgh University Press, 1996), v–xxi.
13. In the poem *Croma*, Macpherson describes this key phrase: "there is joy in grief when peace dwells in the breast of the sad." Stafford, *The Sublime Savage*, 105, sees "a certain perverted quality" in the phrase, a "brooding indulgence of morbid eroticism." But note the impact of the German equivalent of "joy of grief" (*Wonne der Wehmut*) as rendered by Michael Denis in his translation of 1768–69 (the first complete translation of the Ossian poems). Beethoven set Goethe's poem of that title in 1810; see chapter 8.
14. *Die Entführung aus dem Serail* (1782) and *Die Zauberflöte* (1791).
15. But see chapter 13 for *Kyvala*, in which the Danish composer Jørgen Malling has Hidallan slay Comala in a cave.
16. Herder wrote his "Darthula's Grabesgesang" about 1770, before he had seen the original English of Macpherson. He was familiar only with the German translation of Ossian (into hexameters) by Michael Denis (1768–69). See chapter 11.
17. See chapter 9. Howard Gaskill identifies "Carric-Thura" as "perhaps the most popular and influential of all the Ossianic poems." See his introduction to *The Reception of Ossian in Europe*, 6. In musical works, the most commonly set poetic narrative has been "Comala," with "Dar-thula" (more often than not from Herder's poem), "Colma," and "Oithóna" some way behind.
18. Leonard G. Ratner introduced the concept of "musical topics" in *Classic Music: Expression, Form, and Style* (New York: Schirmer, 1980). On the notion of topics, see Raymond Monelle, *The Musical Topic: Hunt, Military, and Pastoral* (Bloomington: Indiana University Press, 2006). The significance of topics inheres in their semiotic relation to "affect" (feeling) and allusion in music rather than to the building blocks of harmony, melody, or rhythm. Topic theory grew out of studies of music theory in the eighteenth century, but it has implications for the interpretation of concert music of the Romantic period.
19. This group of operas is discussed more fully in chapter 7.
20. See chapter 8.
21. Gluck's duet from the ode of the same name by Klopstock, "Minona lieblich und hold haucht reine Liebe," was published in *Musikalisches Blumenlese* (Berlin, 1795), 18–19. See *Christoph Willibald Gluck, Oden und Lieder* (Complete Works, series 6, vol. 2), ed. Daniela Philippi and Heinrich W. Schwab (Kassel: Bärenreiter, 2011), 19.
22. Liszt composed his Symphonic Poem No. 4 as an introduction to the first performance of Gluck's opera in Weimar. The orchestration of *Orpheus* includes two harps and four horns, and these instruments dominate the first fourteen bars of a work that influenced Liszt's son-in-law Wagner; see Rainer Kleinertz, "Liszt, Wagner, and Unfolding Form: *Orpheus* and the Genesis of *Tristan und Isolde*," in *Franz Liszt and His World*, ed. Christopher H. Gibbs and Dana Gooley (Princeton, NJ: Princeton University Press, 2006), 231–54. The Orpheus-Ossian link is discussed in Jason R. D'Aoust, "The

Orpheus Figure: The Voice in Writing, Music and Media" (PhD diss., University of Western Ontario, 2013), 134–39.
23. The works of the Königsberg-born Johann Friedrich Reichardt are typical of this questing spirit: he travelled to Leipzig, Berlin, Paris, Vienna, London, and Italy. Despite this, he managed to write some 1,500 songs and a fair number of *Singspiele*.
24. See chapter 3 for a discussion of Barthelemon's opera libretto.
25. The plot is outlined in detail in *The European Magazine and London Review* (October 1791).
26. Both Jean-François Le Sueur's *Ossian* and Étienne Méhul's *Uthal* were parodied soon after their first performance. See appendix 4.
27. See Dafydd Moore, "The Reception of Ossian in England and Scotland," in *The Reception of Ossian in Europe*, 21–39; here, 24.
28. Moore, "The Reception of Ossian in England and Scotland," 35.
29. See chapter 4.
30. See H. C. Robbins Landon, "Crisis Years: *Sturm und Drang* and the Austrian Musical Crisis," in *Haydn: Chronicle and Works*, vol. 2 (London: Thames & Hudson, 1978), 266–393. Also Charles Rosen, *The Classical Style: Haydn, Mozart, Beethoven*, 3rd ed. (London: Faber & Faber, 2005); Carl Dahlhaus, *Foundations of Music History*, trans. J. B. Robinson (Cambridge: Cambridge University Press, 1983), 125.
31. Herder's essay on Ossian ("Auszug zu einem Briefwechsel"), first published in Hamburg in 1773, was an important contribution toward making Germans conscious of Ossian.
32. See chapter 9 for a discussion of the settings of "Colma" by Rust, Zumsteeg, Zelter, Reichardt, and Schubert. Rust's monodrama precedes both Berlioz's *Lélio* (1831) and Schoenberg's *Erwartung* (1909) as a striking example of the genre.
33. Letter to Charles McPherson, February 25, 1773: see *The Papers of Thomas Jefferson*, vol. 1, ed. Julian P. Boyd (Princeton, NJ: Princeton University Press, 1950).
34. Napoleon was probably familiar with both Cesarotti's Italian translation and Le Tourneur's French version. At the second performance of *Ossian, ou les Bardes*, Napoleon presented Le Sueur with a gold snuff box containing the Légion d'honneur and six banknotes, each worth 1,000 francs.
35. Méhul's opera was first given privately at Saint-Cloud. Famously, the composer scored for violas rather than violins in order to lend a somber coloring to the orchestration. See chapter 5.
36. *Mémoires de Madame de Chastenay*, vol. 1 (Paris: 1987; orig. ed. 1896), 284.
37. See chapter 8.
38. Van Tieghem, *Ossian en France*, 179.
39. See chapter 7.
40. See chapter 3.
41. See chapter 6.
42. See the Excursus below.
43. Breitkopf & Härtel published the full score in 1854; the autograph score is untraced. Gade himself made a four-hand piano version shortly after the first performance, in 1841.
44. See Joep Leersen, "Ossian and the Rise of Literary Historicism," in *The Reception of Ossian in Europe*, 109–25.

45. See n. 7 above and chapter 12. Brahms composed his now seldom-performed *Triumphlied*, op. 55 (1871), on the occasion of the German victory in the Franco-Prussian War, dedicating it "ehrfurchtsvoll" (reverently) to "seiner Majestät dem Deutschen Kaiser Wilhelm I." See also Daniel Beller-McKenna, *Brahms and the German Spirit* (Cambridge, MA: Harvard University Press, 2004), 98–132.
46. Hopffer (1840–77) was, like his brother (who predeceased him), prone to tuberculosis and spent much of his life in spa resorts.
47. For a discussion of the cantata, see chapter 11.
48. The four-act opera, by Wendelin Weißheimer (1838–1910), pupil of Liszt and erstwhile friend of Wagner, is based on the life of Theodor Körner (1791–1813), poet and soldier, whose collection of patriotic poems under the title *Leyer und Schwert* (Lyre and sword) was published in 1814. The opera was premiered with great success in Munich in 1872.
49. Thieriot's "Loch Lomond: Symphonisches Phantasiebild für Orchester," op. 13, is in B minor and shows the impress of Mendelssohn's "Hebrides" overture even though it ends, triumphantly, in B major.
50. See chapter 10. Six editions of Hillemacher's *Fingal* were published between 1880 and 1881.
51. On Bonheur, see Guillaume Labussière, *Raymond Bonheur, 1861–1939, parcours intellectuel et relations artistiques d'un musicien proche de la nature* (Paris: L'Harmattan, 2005).
52. On this period, see Jess Tyre, "Music in Paris During the Franco-Prussian War and the Commune," *Journal of Musicology* 22, no. 2 (2005), 173–202.
53. See Gerald Bär, "Ossian in Portugal," in *Reception of Ossian*, ed. Howard Gaskill, 370. The published 1864 libretto has Italian and Portuguese texts on facing pages.
54. Liszt, writing to Wagner from Venice (23 February 1859), notes that Sobolewski composed *Komala* at first in three acts for performance in Bremen, but afterwards added two more acts. In that form Liszt conducted the first performance in Weimar, but at the second omitted the additional acts and altered the finale, which was shaped after the finale of the second act of *Tannhäuser*. "In that manner," wrote Liszt, "the work will appear in its only true form, and may keep its place as a fine cloud-and-mist picture in perfect accord with Ossian's poem." See *Correspondence of Wagner and Liszt*, trans. Francis Hueffer, vol. 2 (New York: Vienna House 1973 [orig. ed. Scribner & Welford, 1897]), 259; also Robert T. Laudon, "Eduard Sobolewski, Frontier Kapellmeister: From Königsberg to St. Louis," *The Musical Quarterly* 73, no. 1 (1989), 94–118.
55. The ballade "Ossian" is prefaced by a quotation from P. Christian's *Ossian, barde du troisième siècle: poèmes gaélliques* (Paris: Lavigne, 1842), the most successful nineteenth-century translation into French; it was also popular in Spain.
56. The full score and piano reduction are still in manuscript. Chapter 12 discusses settings, from the mid-nineteenth to the mid-twentieth century, of the poem by Herder.
57. See chapter 12. Schoenberg left *Darthulas Grabgesang* on one side in order to finish his other cantata, *Gurrelieder*, the subject taken from a medieval Danish legend.
58. See chapter 13.
59. The Second Boer War ended on May 31, 1902; see chapter 14.
60. The situation in Britain is discussed in chapter 15. See also Roger Savage, *Masques, Mayings and Music-dramas: Vaughan Williams and the Early Twentieth Century Stage* (Woodbridge: Boydell, 2014), 124, which describes Nicholl as a forty-year old Yorkshire sergeant band master with the Twenty-First West Yorkshire Regiment in World War I.

61. The narrative of Nicholl's *Comala* continues with Norse sea rovers having set up images of Woden on the island. The Norsemen's violent leader, Hodbrod, has designs on Comala, but she loves the younger Norse rover Hakon, who respects the Christians. A henchman of Hodbrod's kills Hakon and Comala, witnessed by the spirit of Woden.
62. Both Pushkin and Lermontov knew them well: Lermontov's "Grob Ossiana" (Ossian's grave) mirrors to some extent knowledge of his own Scottish ancestry. For the incidental music by Osip Kozlowski for Ozerov's play *Fingal*, see chapter 7.
63. See Margaret Ziolkowski, *Soviet Heroic Poetry in Context: Folkore or Fakelore?* (Lanham, MD: University of Delaware Press, 2013), 2–12.
64. See chapter 15.
65. See chapter 16.
66. Fritze's suite is untraced. He had already composed a cantata, *Fingal*, for chorus and orchestra (1861), also untraced. See Robert Musiol, *Wilhelm Fritze (1844–1881): Ein musikalisches Charakterbild* (Demmin: Frantz, 1883), 34.
67. See chapter 16.
68. "Ossian ist viel zu sonderlich, viel zu *unmodern*, viel zu unterschieden von denen Dichtern, die man immer in den Händen hat" (Ossian is so very special, so very *unmodern*, much different from these poets that we are accustomed to read); see Tombo, *Ossian in Germany*, 48.

Chapter Two

1. Letter to John Murdoch, January 15, 1783. See *The Letters of Robert Burns*, ed. James De Lancey Ferguson and G. Ross Roy, 2 vols. (Oxford, 1985, 2nd ed.), 1, 17. That is, Ossian had a positive effect on Burns's art as a poet and not, clearly, as a model of upright behavior. Burns divided his poem "The Vision" into *duans* (verses) à la Macpherson, and one of the dogs in "The Twa Dogs" is named Luath, after Fingal's hound.
2. According to William Stenhouse, in his *Illustrations of the Lyric Poetry and Music of Scotland* (Edinburgh: W. Blackwood, 1853), p. 116, the melody of "The Maid of Selma" is a variant of the traditional tune, "Todlin' Hame," with variants and antecedents that include Oswald's "Lude's Lament." It is entirely possible that Oswald simply "arranged" the traditional tune, and this adaptation was later adopted by Johnson for vol. 2 of the *Museum* and printed with the new title, "The Maid of Selma." Oswald (1710–69) made many arrangements of Scots tunes for violin but did not live to see the publication of Johnson's important collection (*The Scots Musical Museum*, six vols, 1787–1803).
3. See James C. Dick, *The Songs of Robert Burns and Notes on Scottish Songs by Robert Burns* (Hatboro, PA: Folklore Associates, 1962), 63–64. Riddell omits the final sentence of Bowie's note, which reads: "These tunes are called in our language Ports, and were composed either for Religious Worship, or on Heroic Subjects." The embellishments of Oswald's tune that Riddell refers to are by Domenico Corri (1746–1825), native of Rome, composer, arranger, voice teacher, and publisher, who moved to Scotland in 1781 and then to London around 1790. Most of the arrangements for Johnson's collection were by Stephen Clarke (d. 1797).
4. "Song of Selma," no. 119 in Johnson, *The Scots Musical Museum*, vol. 1 (1787).

5. Alexander Carmichael, *Carmina Gadelica: Hymns and Incantations*, 6 vols. (Edinburgh: Constable, 1900), vol. 1, xxviii; John Dewar's account in John Francis Campbell, *Popular Tales of the West Highlands*, 4 vols. (Edinburgh: Edmonston & Douglas, 1860–62), vol. 1, li–liii; Seamus Delargy, "The Gaelic Storyteller," *Proc. British Academy*, xxxi (1945), 177–221, 187; also Margaret Fay Shaw, *Folksongs and Folklore of South Uist*, 3rd ed. (Aberdeen: Aberdeen University Press, 1999; orig. ed. London: Routledge & Kegan Paul, 1955), 1–18. For the New World, see Joe Neil MacNeil and John William Shaw, *Sgeul gu Latha: Tales until Dawn: The World of a Cape Breton Gaelic Story-Teller* (Kingston: McGill–Queen's University Press, 1987), 1–37.
6. Capt. Simon Fraser, *The Airs and Melodies Peculiar to the Highlands of Scotland and the Isles* (Printed and sold for the editor, Edinburgh, 1816; reprint Sydney, Nova Scotia, 1982).
7. Vol. 1 of *The Scots Musical Museum* contains a song entitled "Oscar's Ghost," the words of which were written by Walter Scott's acquaintance Anne Murray Keith, with a melody by Flora Touch, wife of Rev. Dr. John Touch, minister of St. Cuthbert's Chapel of Ease, Edinburgh, and sister of Rev. Patrick McDonald. See *The Scots Musical Museum*, vol. 1, 71; also John Glen, *Early Scottish Melodies* (Edinburgh, 1900), 80.
8. The heroic lay (*laoidh*) might also be known as *dàn* or *duan*.
9. No. 122 of John Francis Campbell ed, *Leabhar na Feinne: Heroic Gaelic Ballads collected in Scotland chiefly from 1512 to 1871* (London: Spottiswoode, 1872; reprint, with an introduction by Derick S. Thomson (Shannon: Irish University Press, 1972). See also "The Elizabeth Ross MS," ed. Peter Cooke, Morag MacLeod, and Colm Ó Baoill, nos. 55, 57, School of Scottish Studies, University of Edinburgh (online series, 2011); J. F. Campbell, *Popular Tales*, vol. 3.
10. See *Journal of the Folk-Song Society*, vol. 4 (1910–13; reprint, Ceredigion: Llanerch Press, 1997, and Burnham on Sea: Llanerch, 2018), 245. The extracted text in translation reads: "Green last night was the knoll, though it be red today with the blood of Diarmid, and grievous were this to the Feinn, had it not been the desire of Fionn." See further Ethel Bassin, *The Old Songs of Skye: Frances Tolmie and her Circle*, ed. Derek Bowman (London: Routledge & Kegan Paul, 1977; reprint, 2017), 48–52.
11. See W. J. Watson, *Bardachd Ghaidhlig: Specimens of Gaelic Poetry*, 1550–1900, 3rd ed. (Edinburgh, 1959; orig. ed. Stirling: Learmouth, 1932).
12. *The Blind Harper (An Clarsair Dall): The Songs of Roderick Morison and his Music*, ed. William Matheson (Edinburgh: Scottish Gaelic Texts Society, 1970).
13. Andrias Hirt, "The Connection between Fenian Lays, Fingalian Chant, Recitative and Dán Díreach: a Pre-Medieval Song Tradition," in *Language and Power in the Celtic World*, ed. Anders Ahlqvist and Pamela O'Neill (Sydney: Celtic Studies Foundation, University of Sydney, 2015), 123–58.
14. This manuscript is important as a source for James Macpherson; see Donald E. Meek, "The Gaelic Ballads of Scotland," in *Ossian Revisited*, ed. Howard Gaskill (Edinburgh: Edinburgh University Press, 1991), 19–48.
15. Gerard Murphy, *Duanaire Finn*, part 3 (London: Irish Texts Society, 1953).
16. In his essay published in 1776, "On Poetry and Music as They Affect the Mind . . . ," James Beattie (1735–1803), the Scottish poet, moralist, and philosopher (a Lowlander), wrote of these arts in Highland culture: "The wildest irregularity appears in its

composition: the expression is warlike, and melancholy, and approaches even to the terrible. —And that their poetry is almost uniformly mournful, and their views of nature dark and dreary, will be allowed, by all who admit the authenticity of Ossian; and not doubted by any who believe those fragments of highland poetry to be genuine, which many old people, now alive, of that country, remember to have heard in their youth, and were then taught to refer to a pretty high antiquity" (p. 186).

17. Edward Bunting, *The ancient music of Ireland: arranged for the pianoforte; to which is affixed a dissertation on the Irish harp and harpers, including an account of the old melodies of Ireland* (Dublin: Hodges and Smith, 1840).
18. Sir John Sinclair (1754–1835) supervised the compilation of the *Statistical Account of Scotland*, 21 vols. (1791–99).
19. In his introduction to *The ancient music of Ireland*, Bunting asserts that this tune is an Ossianic air, still sung to the words preserved by Dr. Young in *Transactions of the Royal Irish Academy* (1787), 88.
20. Hugh Shields, *Narrative Singing in Ireland: Lays, Ballads, Come-All-Yes and Other Songs* (Dublin: Irish University Press, 1993), 19–21.
21. Shields, *Narrative Singing*, 16. Ralph Ousley (b. 1839) was a noted antiquarian, a member of the Royal Irish Academy, who contributed papers on the discovery of three Bronze Age horns in Ireland in 1787.
22. See Marjory Kennedy-Fraser, *A Life of Song* (London: Oxford University Press, 1929; reprint Corte Madera: Anro Publications, 1987), 149. The story of Aillte is described in a prefatory note in vol. 2 of *Songs of the Hebrides* (London, 1917), 80: "A love tale of the flight of the Queen of Lochlann with Aillte, a young hero of the Fayne—the descent on Fionn (the leader of the Fayne) of the King of Lochlann with nine other Kings—the total destruction of the invading hosts. Sung by Ossian to Patrick."
23. In vol. 2, the critic Ernest Newman described Kennedy-Fraser as holding "the highest place among British folk-song collectors . . . the songs themselves have a strange beauty that grows on us the better we know them. . . . Schubert and Hugo Wolf would have knelt and kissed the hands of the men who conceived them."
24. "Aillte" was printed earlier in Marjory Kennedy-Fraser and Kenneth Macleod, eds., *Sea Tangle* (London: Boosey, 1913), 13–15.
25. A note by Kenneth MacLeod relates the story of how Cuchullan went to war in Erin mindless of the wife and child he had left behind. Angered, his wife, Aife, put their son under a spell that ensured he would kill at a fateful meeting someone he did not recognize as his son. Discovering whom he had slain, Cuchullan lamented his son's death under a tree on which for days no bird would perch.
26. Marjory Kennedy-Fraser, *A Life of Song*, 148–49.
27. J. F. Campbell, *Leabhar na Feinne*, 218.
28. See, for instance, Helen Creighton and Calum MacLeod, *Gaelic Songs in Nova Scotia* (Ottawa: National Museum of Canada, 1964); Donald A. Fergusson, *From the Farthest Hebrides* (Toronto: Macmillan of Canada, 1978); Margaret MacDonell, *The Emigrant Experience: Songs of Highland Emigrants in North America* (Toronto: University of Toronto Press, 1982); John L. Campbell, ed., *Songs Remembered in Exile: Traditional Gaelic Songs from Nova Scotia recorded in Cape Breton and Antigonish County in 1937 with an account of the causes of Hebridean Emigration, 1790–1835* (Aberdeen: Aberdeen University Press, 1990).

29. See John MacInnes, "Twentieth-Century Recordings of Scottish Gaelic Heroic Ballads," in *Béaloideas* 54/55 (1986), 101–30. Further the CD, *Music from the Western Isles* (Scottish Tradition Series, vol. 2), Greentrax 9002, January 1992; and also the website "Tobar an Dualchais," http://www.tobarandualchais.co.uk, accessed January 30, 2019.
30. Shields, *Narrative Singing*, 27.
31. J. L. Campbell, *Songs Remembered in Exile*, 219–22.
32. J. F. Campbell, *Leabhar na Feinne*, 95–103.
33. Carmichael, *Carmina Gadelica*, passim.
34. For example, the influential French writer and traveler Charles Nodier (1780–1844), whose *Promenade de Dieppe aux Montagnes de l'Écosse* (Paris: J. N. Barba au Palais-Royal, no. 51, 1821) expressed similar opinions. A translation of this popular work into English in the following year was published in Edinburgh (W. Blackwood) and London (T. Cadell); see the segment on Loch Katrine, 164–70, which discusses Ossian in the context of Highland topography.
35. See n. 9. But also see Wilson McLeod, *Divided Gaels: Gaelic Cultural Traditions in Scotland and Ireland, c. 1200–c. 1650* (Oxford: Oxford University Press, 2003). The author argues (pp. 4–5) that despite connections based on social custom, kinship, and shared cultural traditions, Gaelic Ireland and Scotland did not form a single "culture province." The Irish perceived the Scottish Gaels as peripheral.
36. John Derricke, *The Image of Irelande, with a Discoverie of Woodkarne* (1581); the woodcut is illustrated in, for example, Hugh Cheape, *Bagpipes: A National Collection of a National Instrument* (Edinburgh: National Museums of Scotland, 2008), 48.
37. See Donal O'Sullivan, *Carolan: The Life, Times and Music of an Irish Harper* (London: Routledge & Kegan Paul, 1958; new ed. Louth, Lincolnshire: Celtic Music, 1983).
38. See Colm Ó Baoill, "Two Irish Harpers in Scotland," in *Defining Strains: The Musical Life of Scots in the Seventeenth Century*, ed. James Porter (Oxford: Peter Lang, 2007), 227–43.
39. See John Lorne Campbell, "An Account of Some Irish Harpers as Given by Echlin O'Kean, Harper, Anno 1779," *Eigse: A Journal of Irish Studies* 6 (1948–52): 146–48.
40. Henry George Farmer, *History of Music in Scotland* (London: Hinrichsen, 1947), 280.
41. See *Bardachd Shilis na Ceapaich: Poems and Songs by Sileas MacDonald*, ed. Colm O Baoill (Edinburgh: Scottish Gaelic Texts Society, 1972).
42. Rosalind K. Marshall, *The Days of Duchess Anne: Life in the Household of the Duchess of Hamilton, 1656–1716* (London: Collins, 1973), 73.
43. Keith Sanger, "John Elouis," *WireStrungharp.com*, May 7, 2014, www.wirestrungharp.com/harps/harpers/elouis/elouis_john.html.
44. See Luke Gibbons, "From Ossian to O'Carolan: The Bard as Separatist Symbol," in *From Gaelic to Romantic*, 226–51; here, 246–48; also Mary Helen Thuente, *The Harp Re-strung: The United Irishmen and the Rise of Irish Literary Nationalism* (Syracuse, NY: Syracuse University Press, 1994).
45. Arthur O'Neill, "Memoirs," in Charlotte Millington Fox, *Annals of the Irish Harpers* (London: Smith, Elder & Co, 1911).
46. Joan Rimmer, *The Irish Harp* (Cork: Mercier Press, 1969; 3rd ed., Dublin: Mercier Press, 1984).
47. John Egan had business premises in Dublin from 1815 to 1835, constructing more than 2,000 harps. These harps, three feet high, were considered ideal for society ladies to play.

Often elaborately hand-painted with gold shamrocks, they had brass plates with the royal warrant and the coat of arms of George IV.
48. Shields, *Narrative Singing*, 17; see also Julie Henigan, *Literacy and Orality in Eighteenth-Century Irish Song* (London: Pickering & Chatto, 2012), 1–28.
49. "Her lyre, her chosen instrument, greatly resembled a harp but was, however, older in shape and simpler as regards the notes." Germaine de Staël, *Corinne, ou l'Italie*, preface by Simone Balayé (Paris, 1985). Between 1798 and around 1820, instrument makers produced various hybrid forms, such as the "harp-guitar," "harp-lute," "harp-lyre" and "Apollo lyre." A representation of Comala by Jean Baptiste Aubry (1821) has her playing a bowed lyre.
50. David Charlton, "Ossian, Le Sueur and Grand Opera," *Studies in Music* 11 (1977), 37–52. The composer Louis Spohr tells how his wife visited Érard's showroom in London to look at the improved harps but found the new harp difficult to play because of the tight stringing and double action. She finally gave up the harp and performed only as piano accompanist to her husband. See *Pleasures of Music: An Anthology*, ed. Jacques Barzun (London: M. Joseph, 1952), 168.
51. Sanger, "John Elouis," *WireStrungharp.com*. Compositions by two other harpists of the time, Robert-Nicolas-Charles Bochsa (1789–1856) and François Joseph Naderman (1781–1835), are mainly operas (by the former) or suites for the instrument.
52. See also Hans Joachim Zingel, *Harfenmusik im 19. Jahrhundert: Versuch einer historischen Darstellung* (Wilhelmshaven: Heinrichshofen Verlag, 1976); Mark Pelkovic, trans. and ed., *Harp Music in the Nineteenth Century* (Bloomington: Indiana University Press, 1992).

Chapter Three

1. See Hugh M. Milne, ed., *Boswell's Edinburgh Journal, 1767–1786* (Edinburgh: John Donald, 2013), conversation of March 6, 1775.
2. Hume's comments are from Mackenzie's *Report of the Highland Society of Scotland* (1805), 6–7; see also Micheál Mac Craith, "'We Know All These Poems': The Irish Response to Ossian," in *The Reception of Ossian in Europe*, ed. Howard Gaskill, 91–108.
3. See Fiona Stafford, *The Sublime Savage: James Macpherson and the Poems of Ossian* (Edinburgh: Edinburgh University Press, 1988), 13–16.
4. The terms of Alexander Fraser Tytler (1747–1813), the first to theorize on the nature of translation as "tonal" rather than "lexical," in his *Essay on the Principles of Translation* (1791); see Susan Manning, "Henry Mackenzie and *Ossian*, or, the Emotional Value of Asterisks," in *From Gaelic to Romantic*, 144–45. Renatus Gotthelf Loebel (1767–1799) translated Tytler's *Essay* into German in 1793.
5. Barthelemon gradually dispensed with the acute accents in his name.
6. OITHÓNA:/A DRAMATIC POEM,/TAKEN FROM/The PROSE TRANSLATION of/THE CELEBRATED OSSIAN./AS PERFORMED/At the THEATRE ROYAL/In the HAY MARKET./SET TO MUSICK/By MR. BARTHELEMON./LONDON:/ Printed for T. BECKET and P. and A. DE HONDT,/in the Strand. MDCCLXVIII./ [Price Six Pence].

7. See *Public Advertiser*, February 20, 1768.
8. See Lisa Kozlowski, "Terrible Women and Tender Men: A Study of Gender in Macpherson's Ossian," in *From Gaelic to Romantic*, 119–35; here, 128.
9. This is a reference to Giovanni Battista Gervasio (1725–1785), who published a tutor for the instrument, *La moderna scuola del mandolino*, in 1767.
10. The original reads, "He took me in my grief; amidst my tears he raised the sail. He feared the returning Lathmon, the brother of unhappy Oithóna!"
11. See the "Englished" version, Burney's *The Cunning Man*, ed. Kerry S. Grant (Madison, WI: A-R Editions, 1998).
12. On the earl of Kellie, see David Johnson, *Music and Society in Lowland Scotland in the Eighteenth Century*, 2nd ed. (Edinburgh: Mercat Press, 2003), 68–84. Kellie had studied in Mannheim with Carl Stamitz; his String Quartet in A major in the Kilravock Manuscript "provides a compelling example of the *Sturm und Drang* style": see Meredith MacFarlane and Simon McVeigh, "The String Quartet in London Concert Life, 1789–1799," in *Concert Life in Eighteenth-Century Britain*, ed. Susan Wollenberg and Simon McVeigh (Aldershot: Ashgate, 2004), 161–96; here, 179.
13. See Mac Craith, "The Irish Response," 103.
14. See Jenny Burchill, "'The First Talents of Europe': British Music Printers and Publishers and Imported Instrumental Music in the Eighteenth Century," in Susan Wollenberg, ed., *Concert Life in Eighteenth-Century Britain*, 93–113; here, 104. Napier was also to publish the first Ossianic opera by a British composer, Harriet Wainewright, in 1803; see chapter 4.
15. Preston's collection of 1786 was entitled *A Second Sett of Twelve Ballads, the Music by Sigr. Giuseppe Haydn, of Vienna. Adapted to English Words with an Accompaniment for the Harpsichord, or Piano Forte* (Hob. XXVIa.Anh.a: 3 = RISM H4053). See also Gretchen Wheelock, "Marriage à la Mode: Haydn's Instrumental Works 'Englished' for Voice and Piano," *The Journal of Musicology* 8, no. 3 (1990), 357–97.
16. See the summary in Nancy A. Mace, "Haydn and the London Music Sellers: Forster *v.* Longman & Broderip," *Music and Letters* 77, no. 4 (1996), 527–41.
17. See chapter 4. "Sensational," of course, in that it was composed by a woman in an age when such a thing was still an object of male condescension.
18. Four later operas were built around "Oithóna": Pietro Generali's *Gaulo ed Oitona* (1813); two by Greek composers, both entitled *Oitona*: by Dionisio Rodoteato (1876) and by Dionisio Carradi, whose *Oitona* was staged at the Teatro Cavour, Porto Maurizio, Liguria, in 1891; and Edgar Bainton's *Oithóna* (1915), which is discussed in chapter 15.
19. A portrait of William Bach (ca. 1844), attributed to Eduard Magnus, is in the Bach-Museum, Leipzig.
20. The full title is: COLMA./Eine/Episode/aus/den Gedichten Ossians/dramatisirt,/und/in Musik gesetzt/von/William Bach/Königlichen Kammermusikus./Aufgeführt im Konzert der Musikliebhaber/zu Berlin/1791. Its call number in the State Library, Berlin, is Mus. Tb 105.
21. See Paul Barnaby, "Timeline: European Reception of Ossian," in *The Reception of Ossian in Europe*, xxii–xxiii.
22. In Macpherson's original, the name of Minona's brother is Morar. The change by Bach is probably because of the two *r*'s, which the composer perhaps felt would be difficult for the singer of the role to pronounce.

23. *Morning Post and Daily Advertiser*, London, October 20, 1791.
24. The plot was outlined in detail in *The European Magazine and London Review*, vol. 20, October 1791.
25. Such as, for example, Giovanni Pergolesi's popular *La serva padrona*, which had been performed at the King's Theatre, Haymarket, in 1750. An English-language version, by Stephen Storace the Elder and James Oswald, was performed at the Marylebone Gardens in 1759.
26. See Fiske, *Scotland in Music*, 52.
27. The fifth edition appeared in 1795: SONGS, /DUETS, CHORUSES, AND ARGUMENT/OF THE/NEW BALLET PANTOMIME,/(TAKEN FROM OSSIAN)/CALLED/OSCAR AND MALVINA;/OR,/THE HALL OF FINGAL,/PERFORMED AT THE/THEATRE ROYAL,/COVENT GARDEN. For nine examples of the music, see Aloys Fleischmann et al., *Sources of Irish Traditional Music, 1600–1855*, 2 vols. (New York: Garland, 1998), nos. 3053–61. The ballet was performed in provincial theaters such as the Theatre Royal, Newcastle-upon-Tyne, where in 1800 it was staged as a benefit for a Madame Frederick, known for her performances of the Highland strathspey dance in Edinburgh's Theatre Royal (poster, National Library of Scotland, AP.el.24.03).
28. It was staged, for instance, in Boston on October 10, 1796; by this time, it was usually an "afterpiece." See George O. Seilhammer, *History of the American Theater: New Foundations* (New York: Haskell House, 1969), 309.
29. Weippert became quite famous in London society. He later played at a soiree given by Jane Austen's brother Henry and his wife, Eliza, at their house on Sloane Square, April 25, 1811. See Jeffrey A. Nigro, "Favourable to Tenderness and Sentiment: The Many Meanings of Mary Crawford's Harp," *Persuasions Online* 35, no. 1 (2014).
30. See Hugh Cheape, *Bagpipes: A National Collection of a National Instrument* (Edinburgh: National Museums of Scotland, 2008), 104.
31. See Philip H. Highfill et al., *A Biographical Dictionary of Actors, Actresses, Musicians, Dancers, Managers and Stage Personnel in London, 1660–1800* (Carbondale, IL: Southern Illinois University Press, 1973), vol. 10, 391.
32. Nicholas Carolan, "Courtney's 'Union Pipes' and the Terminology of Irish Bellows-Blown Bagpipes," essay online, Irish Traditional Music Archive (May 14, 2012), 1–115, esp. 30–45.
33. "Battle" pieces for violin were known from the works of the Austrian-Bohemian composer Heinrich Biber (1644–1704), and in Scotland, from a programmatic piece by James Oswald (1711–69); see David Johnson, *Scottish Fiddle Music in the Eighteenth Century*, 3rd ed. (Edinburgh: Mercat Press, 2005; orig. ed. Edinburgh: John Donald, 1978), 138–40.
34. Mary Julia Young, *Memoirs of Mrs Crouch*, 2 vols. (London: Printed for James Asperne, 1806), 546–47. Mrs. Crouch (born Anna Maria Phillips, 1763–1805) had an acting career that involved a partnership (and affair) with Michael Kelly.
35. According to Boswell, the English were "exceedingly fond" of *Fingal* until they learned it was Scotch, whereupon "they became jealous and silent." See Ernest Campbell Mossner, *The Forgotten Hume: Le bon David* (New York: Columbia University Press, 1943), 89.
36. On this occasion the ballet appears to have been staged along with, or as part of, the musical drama *Merope*, by Sebastiano Nasolini. With a libretto by Mattia Botturini, it was first performed in Venice in 1796.

37. Scott's poem sold 25,000 copies in the first eight months of publication and, like Ossian, was influential throughout Europe. Simon Mayr's opera *Ginevra di Scozia*, first staged at the Teatro Nuovo in Trieste in 1801, is an example of the growing taste for Scottish (if not specifically Ossianic) operatic scenarios. The songs by Schubert based on a translation of Scott's poem are discussed by Roger Fiske, *Scotland in Music: A European Enthusiasm* (Cambridge: Cambridge University Press, 1983), 88–95; see also John Reed, *The Schubert Song Companion* (Manchester: Manchester University Press, 1985), 214–17.
38. See chapter 6.
39. Ferdinand (1769–1824), a member of the Tuscan branch of the Habsburg dynasty, was grand duke of Tuscany from 1790 to 1801 and again from 1814 to 1824.
40. This is scene 10 in the Milan libretto.
41. The plangent phrase "O (sacro) albergo della morte" had been used by Francesco Moretti in act 2, scene 13, of Francesco Bianchi's opera *La vendetta di Nino, o sia Semiramide*, first performed in three acts at San Carlo, Naples, November 12, 1790, and later, in a two-act version, at the King's Theatre, Haymarket, on April 26, 1794 (the libretto is in Italian and English, with some alterations by Da Ponte). Bianchi had moved from Venice to London in 1793, mainly because of the success of *Semiramide* in Naples. The plot was adapted from Voltaire's tragedy, like Rossini's opera of the same name (1823) with a libretto by Gaetano Rossi.
42. The composer Louis Spohr, who witnessed a performance, had some acid comments to make about this work; see chapter 7. On Rossini's opera, see Stefano Castelvecchi, "Walter Scott, Rossini e la *couleur ossianique*: Il contesto culturale della *Donna del lago*," *Bollettino del Centro Rossiniano do Studi* 33 (Pesaro, 1993).
43. See chapter 7.
44. See chapter 11 for discussion of the Umlauft cantata. Krug's work was performed, for example, in New York (1895) and Chicago (1897), as well as at the 20th Dutch National Song Festival in 1895; Joep Leersen, ed., *National Cultivation of Culture*, vol. 9: *Choral Societies and Nationalism in Europe*, ed. Krysztina Lajosi and Andreas Stynen (Leiden, Netherlands: Brill, 2015), 13.

Chapter Four

1. A version of this chapter was published as "An English Composer and Her Opera: Harriet Wainewright's *Comàla* (1792)" in *Journal of Musicological Research*, vol. 40, no. 2 (2021), 126–44. Wainewright always insisted on spelling her name with an "e," possibly to distinguish it from the more common "Wainwright." The spelling of the name varies in biographical accounts of the family. On the importance of the Hanover Square Rooms as a concert venue, see Michael Forsyth, *Buildings for Music: The Architect, the Musicians, and the Listener from the Seventeenth Century to the Present* (Cambridge, MA: MIT Press, 1985), 35–40.
2. Caracul is taken by Macpherson to be Caracalla, son of the emperor Severus, defeated by Fingal in 211 AD. Further, Macpherson adds, "the variety of the measure shows that the poem was originally set to music, and perhaps presented before the chiefs upon solemn occasions."

3. Hydallan, returning home later in disgrace, dies at the hand of his father, Lamor, in the poem "The War of Caros."
4. The siege of the fortress of Seringapatam in April–May 1799 marked the conclusion of the Fourth Mysore War, between the British East India Company and the Kingdom of Mysore. General David Baird was the leader of the British forces on that occasion. Wainewright later composed her "Chorus on the taking of Seringapatam" (London, [1805?]) to words by William Mason (1724–97).
5. Reproduced as an insert in the three-volume presentation copy in the British Library. The original performing manuscript of the opera is in the Library of Santa Cecilia in Rome (A-MS-3693). It probably arrived there as part of the library ("Fondo Mario") owned by Giovanni De Candia (1810–83), the famous tenor who sang the roles of Ernesto in Donizetti's *Don Pasquale* and first tenor in Rossini's *Stabat Mater*. An avid collector of books and manuscripts, he was a close friend of Antonio Panizzi, head of the British Library, who may have assisted him in finding items of interest. See Annalisa Bini, "La Bibliothèque musicale de Mario, chanteur et collectionneur," in *Collectionner la musique: Au cœur de l'interpretation [actes du colloque de Royaumont, 24–26 octobre 2010]* ed. Denis Herlin (Turnhout, Belgium: Brepols, 2012), 227–65.
6. Presumably because of its performance location, Simon McVeigh, in his *Concert Life in London from Mozart to Haydn* (New York: Cambridge University Press, 1993), 93, terms the work "an oratorio." But Wainewright always referred to it as an opera; she was simply unable to get it staged at any of the theaters in London.
7. Mrs. Col. Stewart, *Critical Remarks on the Art of Singing* (London: [G. Ellerton], 1836), 10. Sophia Corri (1775–1831), daughter of Domenico Corri, married the composer and virtuoso Jan Ladislav Dussek (1760–1812) in September 1792.
8. Ibid., 11.
9. Ibid., 11–12.
10. Ibid., 12.
11. In fact, 248 subscriptions were advanced.
12. The "Home Intelligence" column in *The Asiatic Journal and Monthly Register for British India and Dependencies*, vol. 29, 77, noted the return of Colonel and Mrs. Stewart, Miss Stewart, and a Mrs. J. Stewart as passengers "from the Cape."
13. Gertrud Elisabeth Mara (1749–1833), born in Kassel, was famed for her operatic voice. She visited London and sang there beginning in 1784.
14. Stewart, *Critical Remarks*, 18.
15. *The Musical World: A Magazine of Essays, Critical and Practical, and Weekly Record of Musical Science, Literature, and Intelligence*, no. 217; New Series, no. 124 (May 14, 1840), 311.
16. David Baptie, *Handbook of Musical Biography*, 2nd ed. (London: W. Morley, 1887), 240–41.
17. Ibid., 5. Wainewright's life is sketched briefly in Paula Gillett, "Entrepreneurial Women Musicians in Britain: From the 1790s to the Early 1900s," in *The Musician as Entrepreneur, 1700–1914: Managers, Charlatans, and Idealists*, ed. William Weber (Bloomington: Indiana University Press, 2004), 201–3. See also James D. Brown and Stephen S. Stratton, *British Musical Biography: A Dictionary of Musical Artists, Authors*

and *Composers Born in Britain and Its Colonies* (London: S. S. Stratton, 1897; reprint New York: Da Capo Press, 1971).

18. See Robert J. Bruce, "Worgan, John," *Oxford Dictionary of National Biography* (Oxford: Oxford University Press, 2004), online version, 2005. Worgan's son by his second marriage, Thomas Danvers Worgan (d. 1832), published a polemical work, *The Musical Reformer* (1829), that attacked the reliance on "incessant repetitions of the same operas" in London's King's Theatre.

19. Thomas Busby, in his *Concert Room and Orchestra Anecdotes of Music and Musicians* (London: Clementi; Knight & Lacey, 1825), vol. 1, 221–22, refers to Marchesi as "a model of ignorance and rudeness.... This Venetian vocalist, strange to say, had the power to inspire with feelings of tender attachment, the Princess Albani, Mrs Conway, Annetta Brignole, Chiaretta Contarini, Grassini, and many other distinguished females, with whom his face, his figure, and sweetness and flexibility of voice, seem to have apologized for his want of education, and extreme coarseness of manners."

20. Stewart, *Critical Remarks*, 7–8.

21. Ibid., 9.

22. A "Col. Stewart" is mentioned in Ananda Bhattacharya, "Sannyasi and Fakir Rebellion in Bihar (1767–1800)," *Islam and Muslim Studies: A Social Science Journal* 6, no. 2 (2013), 28–44. The colonel's first name, however, is not given. See appendix 1. British Army records report, however, that a John Stewart was promoted to the rank of colonel on January 8, 1796.

23. India Marriages 1792–1848 (FHL microfilm 498609). *The Edinburgh Magazine, or Literary Miscellany*, vol. 17 (1801), 489, describes the event thus: "At Monghyr, in the East Indies, in October last, Captain Stewart, of the Bengal army, to Miss Harriet Wainwright [sic]"; the city of Monghyr (now Munger) is situated forty-three miles west of the city of Bhagalpur on the River Ganges. *The Asiatic Annual Register*, vol. 3 (1801), 102, while agreeing that the marriage took place, reports that it occurred at "Bhaughulpore." Wherever it took place, it may well have been a civil ceremony conducted by a local registrar. The *Alphabetical List* of officers in the Bengal army (1838) records that "John Stewart, Lieutenant Colonel in the retired Service of the Honorable [sic] East India Company, died, aged 59, on February 18, 1820, at Perth (Scotland)."

24. Stewart, *Remarks*, 12. This is a reference to Sarno, chieftain of Inistore, or the Orkney islands.

25. See the insertion in the copy of her "Chorus on the Taking of Seringapatam," British Library, I.345.

26. *A Collection of Songs, Duets, Trios and Chorus's, Printed for the Author and Sold by Mr Cianchettini* (London, 1811–12). A rare copy is in the library of the Royal College of Music, London (D1439/1). The final piece is a lengthy setting of "The Water King," the Danish ballad used by Matthew Lewis (1775–1818) in his gothic novel *The Monk* (1796). Lewis translated the text from Herder's *Volkslieder*, where it is entitled "Der Wasserman." John Wall Callcott (1766–1821), the leading composer of glees, set ten stanzas of the poem for three voices, with piano accompaniment added later by William Horsley (1774–1858). On the composition of glees at this time, see Christopher Smith, "Ossian in Music," in *The Reception of Ossian*, 375–78.

27. Add. MS 42895.

28. The watermark is "J Whatman 1794" with a lily within arms and the initials GR; various copyists' hands are evident.
29. The libretto is based on the 1773 edition of *The Poems of Ossian*; see the British Library copy of the libretto, 11777.f.67. Copies are also held at the Huntington Library, San Marino, California, and in Oxford.
30. The designation "Italian hand" is uncertain, and may be simply a guess on the part of the writer.
31. This is probably because the famous Cecilia Davies (1756–1836, "detta Inglesina") was contracted to sing in Italian opera houses. According to Burney's *Memoirs*, she was unable to sing in London for "private parties."
32. In his notes to the poem, Macpherson says the name Comala means "maid of the pleasant brow"; Dersagrena, "the brightness of a sun-beam"; Melilcoma, "soft-rolling eye"; and Carun, "winding river" (the modern Carron empties into the Firth of Forth "some miles to the north of Falkirk").
33. This passage is quoted in Matthias Wessel, *Die Ossian-Dichtung in der musikalischen Komposition* (Laaber, Germany: Laaber-Verlag, 1994), 30–32.
34. Mrs. Barthelemon (Polly Young) sang at the premiere of *Comàla*; she was herself a gifted composer and harpsichordist. She was also the niece of another noted singer, Cecilia Young, wife of Thomas Arne. See chapter 3.
35. See, for example, Curtis Price, Judith Milhous, and Robert D. Hume, *Italian Opera in Late Eighteenth-Century London*, vol. 1: *The King's Theatre, Haymarket, 1778–1791* (Oxford: Clarendon Press, 1995).
36. *Belle Assemblée; Or, Court and Fashionable Magazine* (September 1823), 133.
37. See Elaine Sisman, "Haydn's Career and the Idea of the Multiple Audience," in *The Cambridge Companion to Haydn*, ed. Caryl Clark (Cambridge: Cambridge University Press, 2005), 1–16. Not everyone in Europe liked the newer style. Even before Haydn's fame reached Britain, local critics found fault with works of the Mannheim School, influential in the Viennese development of orchestral technique: Dr John Gregory, in his *State and Faculties of Man* (London: J. Dodsley, 1765; reprint of 1774 edition, London: Routledge/Thoemmes, 1994), wrote: "The present mode is to admire a new noisy stile of composition, lately cultivated in Germany . . . [that] sometimes pleases by its spirit and a wild luxuriancy, which makes an agreeable variety in a concert, but possesses too little of the elegance and pathetic expression of music to remain long the public taste."

Chapter Five

1. Tovey's copy of the score is in Edinburgh University Library, Tov. 851. A facsimile edition of the opera is Charles Rosen, ed., *Uthal. Libretto by Jacques Benjamin Saint-Victor. Music by Étienne Nicolas Méhul First Performance: Paris, Théatre Feydeau, May 17, 1806* (New York and London, 1978). The most detailed study of the opera's genesis, autograph, and published scores is by M. Elizabeth C. Bartlet, *Étienne-Nicholas Méhul and Opera: Source and Archival Studies of Lyric Theatre during the French Revolution, Consulate and Empire*, 2 vols. (Chicago: University of Chicago Press, 1982), esp. vol. 2, 545–54.

2. For Grétry, see David Charlton, *Grétry and the Growth of Opéra Comique* (Cambridge: Cambridge University Press, 1986); R. J. Arnold, *Grétry's Operas and the French Public: From the Old Regime to the Restoration* (London: Routledge, 2016).
3. Paul Van Tieghem, *Ossian en France*, 136. But Berlioz later defended the timbre of the viola in his *Grand Traité d'Instrumentation et d'Orchestration*, and used the instrument prominently in his *Harold en Italie: Symphonie en 4 parties avec un alto principal* (1834).
4. Donald Francis Tovey, *Essays in Musical Analysis*, vol. 1: *Symphonies* (London: Oxford University Press, 1935), 132–33. See also Gérard Condé, "Entre *Stratonice* et *Joseph*: Le redécouverte d'*Uthal*," *Lélio* 37 (July 2017), 3–14.
5. David Charlton, "Ossian, Le Sueur and Opera," *Studies in Music* (1977), 37–48; Christopher Smith, "*Ossian, ou les Bardes*: An Opera by Jean-François Le Sueur," in *From Gaelic to Romantic*, ed. Fiona Stafford and Howard Gaskill, 153–62. In London, James Harvey D'Egeville staged a ballet with the same title as the opera at the King's Theatre, in 1805. For Russia, see chapter 7.
6. For a brief description, see Aubrey S. Garlington Jr., "Lesueur, 'Ossian,' and Berlioz," *Journal of the American Musicological Society* 17, no. 2 (1964), 206–8.
7. Le Sueur's attacks on the conservatoire during the Consulate had led to a rift between the two composers.
8. Charlton, "Ossian, Le Sueur and Opera," 37. Further, Jean Mongrédien, *Jean-François Le Sueur: Contribution à l'étude d'un demi-siècle de musique française 1780–1830* (Berne, Switzerland: Peter Lang, 1980).
9. "Chant imité d'Ossian./Par M. J. Chenier./Colma," Bibliothèque nationale de France, "Gallica" catalogue, MS 12542. Méhul had collaborated with Arnault on the famous "Chant du depart," and later, on the occasion of the baptism of the king of Rome (June 9, 1811), he provided the music for Arnault's "Chant d'Ossian."
10. Van Tieghem, *Ossian en France*, 52, notes that Baour-Lormian's *Ossian, Poésies Galliques en vers français* went into five editions: 1801, 1804, 1809, 1818, and 1827.
11. Eventually, Julie-Angélique Scio-Messié (1768–1807) sang the role of Malvina at the premiere in Paris on May 17, 1806. The libretto was translated into German in 1808 as *Arien und Gesänge aus dem heroischen Singspiele Uthal: In einem Akt*, by Karl Alexander Herklots, and it was performed in Berlin seven times, until 1818 (and in other German theaters until 1875, when Otto Devrient produced a new translation). Admired by Napoleon, who heard her in 1809, Pauline Anna Milder-Hauptmann (1785–1838) had sung the title role in Beethoven's *Leonore* in Vienna in 1805, and would sing the equivalent role in *Fidelio* in 1814. She assumed the part of Malvina for *Uthal* when it was premiered at the court theater on January 15, 1810, and it is as Malvina that she is portrayed in this painting (fig. 5.1) attributed to the German Romantic artist Friedrich Wilhelm von Schadow (1789–1862). The date of the painting is probably 1808, when Milder-Hauptmann sang the role of Malvina in Berlin.
12. The original title, apparently, was *Malvina*. Van Tieghem, ibid., 136, suggests that in the father-daughter relationship there is a parallel with Shakespeare's Cordelia and King Lear.
13. Van Tieghem, ibid., 134. The letters on the Ossian-Uthal controversy are reproduced in Bartlet, vol. 2, 804–9.

14. In the printed score, Malvina's cry is written not as "Larmor" but as "L'Armor," which might suggest a Breton connection, "Armorica" being the ancient name for Brittany, with its Celtic legends. On the other hand, it may just have been a printer's error.
15. The MS libretto, "Uthal et Malvina, sujet tiré d'Ossian, en un acte et en vers," is F-Pan AJ 1103 (Archives Nationales, Paris); the printed libretto is entitled *Uthal, opera en un acte et en vers, imité d'Ossian, paroles de M. de Saint-Victor, musique de M. Méhul, représenté pour la première fois sur le theater de l'Opéra-Comique, le 17 Mai 1806*. See Bartlet, *Méhul and Opera*, 546. Saint-Victor dedicated his libretto to the artist Girodet (see chapter 2, figure 2.1).
16. One commentator claims that the opera contains "an important recognition scene for father and daughter." But the recognition scene of central dramatic importance is that between Malvina and Uthal in the forest when she does not immediately recognize him because he is wearing armor; see Winton Dean, "French Opera," in Th*e Age of Beethoven, 1790–1830: The New Oxford History of Music*, vol. 8, ed. Gerald Abraham (London: Oxford University Press, 1982), 47. Recognition scenes for the Parisian audience might recall the recognition of Odysseus by Penelope after his return home, or even of Jesus by Mary Magdalene after the Resurrection.
17. The printed score is headed *Uthal, opera en un acte et en vers, imité d'Ossian, paroles de Mr. St. Victor, musique de Méhul, membre de la Légion d'honneur, de l'institut des sciences et des arts, associé correspondant de l'Académie de Lucques et l'un des inspecteurs du Conservatoire Impérial de Musique*. The *Magasin de musique* issued the printed orchestral parts at the same time.
18. The incorporation of descriptive storm music in the overture to an opera is credited to Salieri in his prologue to *Tarare* (1787), with a later example in Ferdinando Paer's *Camilla* (1801). But the first storms in French opera were in Pierre-Alexandre Monsigny's *Le Roi et le fermier* (1762) and his *La belle Arsène* (1773), as well as François-Joseph Gossec's *Toinon et Toinette* (1767). See also Clive McClelland, *Tempesta: Stormy Music in the Eighteenth Century* (Lanham, MD: Lexington Books, 2017).
19. In the German-language MS score, three bars have been crossed out before bar 77 (of the published version): *Uthal, Singspiel in 1. Aufzuge, nach Ossian und dem Französischen von St Victor, musick von Mehul* (Bibliothèque nationale de France, "Gallica" catalogue, ark:/12148, oblong quarto, 315 pp.).
20. A note in Edward J. Dent's study *The Rise of Romantic Opera*, ed. Winton Dean (Cambridge: Cambridge University Press, 1976), 89, states that other operas such as Grétry's *Le Jugement de Midas* (1778) and Dalayrac's *Azémia* (1786) have "some sort of *tableau vivant* during the overture."
21. Méhul uses a descending figure, rhythmically and tonally similar, in his earlier and most successful opera, *Ariodant* (1799). See Adélaïde de Place, *Étienne-Nicolas Méhul* (Paris: Bleu nuit éditeur, 2005), 120.
22. It is possible that the composer and librettist were acquainted with the journal of Faujas de Saint-Fond (1741–1819) and his visit to the Hebrides, *Voyage en Angleterre, en Écosse et aux Îles Hébrides, ayant pour objet les scienecs, les arts, l'histoire naturelle et les mœurs*, 2 vols. (Paris, 1797), in which the author describes the rowers singing: ". . . le voyageur observe que les rameurs 'semblaient faire le voyage avec plaisir, car ils aiment tout ce qui leur rappelle Ossian.' Il écoute leurs chansons, des chants d'Ossian, 'car il n'y a personne dans ces îles depuis le vieillard jusqu'au jeune enfant qui ne sache par cœur de longues

tirades ou des hymnes de cet antique et célèbre Barde.'" Margaret I. Bain, *Les Voyageurs Français en Écosse, 1770–1830, et leurs curiosités intellectuelles* (Paris: Champion, 1931), 37.

23. Méhul places the stress on the second syllable of "Selma" (Macpherson's uncorrected version of "Seláma"). In some commentaries on the opera this chorus seems to be misconstrued as "Hymne au Soleil" (Hymn to the sun), which is the title of a poem by Lamartine and an organ piece by Louis Vierne. The confusion may also stem from the famous address to the sun at the end of Macpherson's poem "Carthon."

24. The reference to the lily appears in Baour-Lormian's version of *Uthal*, in the lines, "Mon père me voyoit fleurir / Comme le lis de nos montagnes" (ll. 43–44), and perhaps also marks Méhul's love of flowers from his student days, referred to by Cherubini in a notice on the composer in *Revista Musicale Italiana* 16 (1909), 750–51; cited in la Place, Méhul, 11.

25. See n. 22 above; also the cases of Brahms, chapter 12, and of Jongen, chapter 13.

26. Tovey comments in a penciled annotation, "This ought to be a tenor." But he ignores the fact that Larmor, as a baritone, sings up to F above middle C. Méhul has a bard sing, accompanied by a harp, in act 2 of *Ariodant* (1799), which is set at the court of the Scottish King Edgard (with a text derived from Ariosto).

27. Macpherson adds in a note that "this is perhaps that small stream still retaining the name of Balva which runs through the romantic valley of Glentivar in Stirlingshire. Balva signifies *a silent stream*; and Glentivar *the sequestered vale*" (italics in original).

28. *The Harmonicon*, vol. 4 (1826), 3, mentions Méhul's admiration of the actors F.-J. Talma and Mlle. Mars and his visits to the Théâtre Français to hear their declamatory style.

29. For example, the MS score and parts of both extracts in Munich (D-Mb), Mus.Hs.78; the two-stave MS reduction, for voice and keyboard (French and Danish texts) of the *romance* and the three-stave reduction (from bar 35) of the "Hymne au sommeil": Danish National Library (DK-kk), Mf.281; and the reduction for voice and piano of the *romance*, Conservatoire royal de Bruxelles (B-Bc), 8334/5; the Morgan Library, New York, has a manuscript score of nos. 1, 4, and 7 from the opera (Cary 0522).

30. Hector Berlioz, *Evenings with the Orchestra*, trans. Jacques Barzun (Chicago: University of Chicago Press, 1973), 354.

31. Rainer Cadenbach, "Die 'Leonore' des Pierre Gaveaux: Ein Modell für Beethovens 'Fidelio'?," *Collegium Musicologicum: Festschrift Emil Platen*, ed. Martella Guttiérez-Denham (Bonn: Rheinische Friedrich-Wilhelms Universität, 1985), 100–121.

32. The tam-tam was introduced into the orchestra by François-Joseph Gossec in his *Marche lugubre* (1790) and was later used, notably, by Le Sueur in *Ossian, ou les Bardes*, by Kozlowski in his incidental music for Vladislav Ozerov's *Fingal* (1805), and by Spontini in *Fernand Cortez* (1809). For Ozerov, see chapter 7.

33. Performances took place in Stuttgart in 1806; Berlin 1808, 1813; Vienna 1810; Frankfurt 1812; Prague 1813; Königsberg 1814; Copenhagen 1846 (in Danish); Munich 1875, 1894; Karlsruhe 1891; Elberfeld 1900; and Dessau 1904, 1906. Hermann Levi conducted the first performance in Munich, in 1875, which was attended by Joachim, who wrote to Brahms about it beforehand; see Andreas Moser ed., *Johannes Brahms im Briefwechsel mit Joseph Joachim* (Berlin, 1974), 106.

34. Méhul had written no fewer than eleven one-act operas before *Uthal*.

35. The parody of *Uthal* was *Brutal, ou il vaut mieux tard que jamais, vaudeville, en un acte et un prose, parodie d'Uthal . . . par M. M. J. Pain e Vieillard* (Paris, 1806), with the main characters renamed Fringal, Malvienta, Sanremor, and Nullin.
36. See Van Tieghem, *Ossian en France*, 137, for citation of these reviews.
37. From *L'histoire du romantisme* (Paris, 1829); cited in *Music and Aesthetics in the Eighteenth and Early Nineteenth Centuries*, ed. Peter le Huray and James Day (Cambridge: Cambridge University Press, 1981), 418.
38. "Cet hymne, entendu pendant le silence de la nuit, en serenade, est d'un effet ravissant . . . son ensemble mélodieux est agréablement varié par la disposition de l'harmonie et l'étrangeté d'une succession d'accords parfaits adroitement ajustés." *Revue de Paris*, vol. 11 (Paris, 1834), 103.
39. Dent, *The Rise of Romantic Opera*, 94.
40. W. S. Rockstro, *A General History of Music* . . . (London, 1886), 299. On the following page Rockstro notes that he was "fortunate enough to hear a large selection from it [*Uthal*], played, and sung, under the direction of Mendelssohn, in 1846."

Chapter Six

1. The arson of 1996 was the third disastrous fire, following those of 1774 and 1836. At the opening of 1792, servants were allowed to witness the opera by peering through grilles set into the back wall of their masters' boxes, but when the theater was rebuilt in 1837 the grilles were omitted. See John Rosselli, *Music & Musicians in Nineteenth Century Italy* (London: Batsford, 1991), 58. The first opera to be performed since the modern restoration was Verdi's *La traviata* (November 2004).
2. Notable figures in the history of stage design and lighting in Italy include Sebastiano Serlio (1475–ca. 1554), Nicola Sabbatini (1574–1654), and, later, Ferdinando Galli-Bibiena (1657–1743).
3. *Teatro La Fenice di Venezia: The History* (1828). The earlier use of candles for lighting was not only labor intensive (wick-trimmers and snuffers adding to the number of stage-hands) but also dangerous. Oil lamps, therefore, would have been in use in the early eighteenth century, although even with the improvements made to the lamp of Amié Argand (1750–1803) by Antoine Quinquet (1745–1803), constant use would have contributed to pollution.
4. A recent study of the composer is Aldo Salvagno, *La Vita e l'Opera di Stefano Pavesi* (Lucca: Libreria musicale italiana, 2016). Salvagno includes discussion of *Fingallo e Comala*, 18–22, 253–65, and *Ardano e Dartula*, 360–62, citing contemporary reviews of both operas. Details of performances and manuscripts are included, 404–79 (*Fingallo e Comala*) and 477 (*Ardano e Dartula*).
5. The story was taken over by Donizetti for his masterpiece *Don Pasquale* (1843); see Charles P. D. Cronin, "Stefano Pavesi's *Ser Marcantonio* and Donizetti's *Don Pasquale*," *Opera Quarterly* 11, no. 2 (1995), 39–53.
6. The libretto is entitled FINGALLO, E COMALA/DRAMMA SERIO PER MUSICA/ DA RAPPRESENTARSI NEL NOBILISSIMO TEATRO/LA FENICE/NEL CARNOVALE/1805./*Poesia* del Sig. Leopoldo Fidanza ./*Musica* del Sig. Stefano Pavesi.

In Venezia, Nella Stamperia di Vincenzo Rizzi, n.d., pp. 48 +16. The autograph score of the opera is in Milan (I-Mr), and a copy in two volumes is in Florence (I-Fc). Differences exist between the published libretti for the opera, in that some scenes are deleted or compressed, and these differences are reflected in the scores that survive. The copy (incorporating acts 1 and 2) in Florence (F.P.T.381), of 195 and 153 pages, respectively, also shows variation in the structure of the scenes.

7. See Stephen Meyer, "Terror and Transcendence in the Operatic Prison, 1790–1815," *Journal of the American Musicological Society* 55, no. 3 (2002), 477–523. Meyer discusses the cavern scene in Le Sueur's opera (pp. 494–98) but does not mention Pavesi's *Fingallo e Comala*, which was a success in northern Italian opera houses, in the years from its premiere in Venice (1805) to its Milan performance (1814), primarily because of the grotto scene.

8. The original score of Morandi's *Comala* is in the Bibliothèque nationale de France, 2 vols., no. FRBNF43163874. Another score, commissioned later the same year by Calzabigi, is in the Biblioteca del R[eale] Conservatorio, Naples (20.8.B). There are substantial differences between the two scores: in the later version, vocal parts are transposed or rewritten and the orchestra is enlarged with the addition of two flutes, two trumpets, and two trombones, an extra bassoon, a harp, and timpani. For a detailed description of the differences, see Magnus Tessing Schneider, "A Song of Other Times: The Transformation of Ossian in Calzabigi and Morandi's *Comala* (1774/1780)," in *LIR journal* 11(2018), forthcoming.

9. Calzabigi's "Comala" appeared in the first volume of his *Poesie* (Livorno, 1774), where it is described as "Componimento drammatico per Musica. Imitato da quello d'Ossian antico Poeta Celtico, che va sotto lo stesso nome."

10. Calzabigi worked on dramatizing *Comala* from 1774. Banished from Vienna in 1775, he lived in Pisa for the rest of his life. See Lucio Tufano, "Orfeo in Caledonia: Primitivismo e intensità delle passioni nella *Comala* di Calzabigi e Morandi," in *Le arti della scena e l'esotismo in età moderna (The Performing Arts and Exoticism in the Modern Age)*, ed. Francesco Cotticelli and Paologiovanni Maione (Naples: Turchini, 2006), 597–622. Morandi's daughter-in-law, the mezzo-soprano Rosa Morandi, sang in Pavesi's opera *Ser Marcantonio*, at the Theatre-Italien in Paris (1813–17); see Rita Stark, *Rosa Morandi: The Swan of the Paris Opera* (Chapel Hill, NC: Professional Press, 1998). A performance of Morandi's *Comala* was staged at Vadstena, Sweden, on July 22, 2016, along with Paisiello's *Nina* (1789), with eleven later performances, the last on 10 August. The performance of the opera on August 5 was part of a symposium, the proceedings of which are in *Sjuttonhundratal/Nordic Yearbook for Eighteenth-Century Studies*, ed. Magnus Tessing Schneider (2018, forthcoming).

11. See appendix 4.

12. See chapter 7.

13. The main editions of *Canti di Ossian* are: Padua, 1763, 1772; Pisa, 1801; Nice, 1780–81; Bassano, 1789–1805.

14. Niccolò Piccinni, born in Bari, Italy was grandfather of the prolific Parisian composer Louis Alexandre Piccinni (1779–1850), who studied with Le Sueur and made a piano arrangement of the latter's *Ossian, ou les bardes*.

15. See Maria Chiara Bertieri, "Pavesi, Stefano," in *Dizionario Biografico degli italiani*, vol. 81 (Roma: Istituto della Enciclopedia italiana, 2014); also Paolo Fabbri, "Gli esordì

teatrali di Pavesi a Venezia," in *L'aere è fosco, il ciel s'imbruna: Arti e musica a Venezia dalla fine della Repubblica al Congresso di Vienna: Atti del convegno internazionale di studi, Venezia 10–12 aprile 1997* (Venice: Fondazione Levi, 2000), 541–56.

16. On Foppa, see Marco Marica, "La Produzione Librettistica di Giuseppe Maria Foppa a Venezia tra la fine della Repubblica e la Restaurazione," in *L'aere è fosco*, 351–410.

17. On this work, see Fabbri, "Gli esordì teatrali," *L'aere è fosco*, 550–51.

18. Quoted in Fabbri, "Gli esordì teatrali," 545; the original letter from Carpani is in [Giuseppe Carpani], *Lettere di un viaggiatore ad un amico sopra i teatri di Venezia* [1804], in Giuseppe Carpani, *Le Rossiniane, ossia Lettere musico-teatrali* (Padua, 1824); Letter H, December 12, 1804, 29: "[Pavesi] ha ... imparata la lingua che parla, cerca d'esprimere la parola, e dove lussureggi un po' meno nello strumentale, in cui peraltro e valentissimo, e più cerchi di limare e ammorbidire il canto, egli toccherà ben presto la perfezione." See also Salvagno, *La Vita e l'Opera di Stefano Pavesi*, 254–61, where the author quotes another lengthy letter of Carpani; "Lettera III" from *Le Haydine, ovvero lettere sulla vita e le opere del célèbre Maestro Giuseppe Haydn* (Milan, 1812), 38–59.

19. Carpani knew Haydn, Beethoven, Salieri, and Rossini. See Helmut C. Jacobs, *Literatur, Musik und Gesellschaft in Italien und Oesterreich in der Epoche Napoleons und der Restauration: Studien zu Giuseppe Carpani (1751–1825)* (Frankfurt: P. Lang, 1988).

20. See John A. Rice, *Empress Marie Therese and Music at the Viennese Court, 1792–1807* (Cambridge: Cambridge University Press, 2003), 24.

21. "Questo Poema è molto pregevole per la luce, che sparge sopra l'antichità delle composizioni d'Ossian, e al dire dell' immortale Cesarotti è uno dei migliori soggetti per un Dramma serio. Si è dovuta in parte tradire l'istoria per addattarsi al gusto giornaliero del Drammi Italiani, e alla necessaria decenza prescritta alle sceniche rappresentanze."

22. Balsamini's status as a singer was already high. Her fee as prima donna at La Fenice in 1807 was 9,360 francs; by comparison, Pavesi was to receive only 2,088 francs for the two-act comic opera *La donna bianca di Avenello* (1830, written for a minor theater in Milan) from the impresario Bartolomeo Merelli; see *Storia dell'opera italiana*, vol. 4, ed. Lorenzo Bianconi and Giorgio Pestelli (Turin: Edizioni di Torino, 1987), 137 (letter from Pavesi to Count Gaetano Melzi, July 1, 4, and 6, 1830; MTS CA 4793–4795, A1830).

23. "Oscura grotto" in Venice and Milan, "oscuro sotterraneo" in Reggio Emilia.

24. See Manuela Jahrmärker, *Ossian—Eine Figur und eine Idee des europäischen Musiktheaters um 1800* (Köln: Studio U. Tank, 1993), 13. For a discussion of *Ossian, ou Les Bardes*, see Edward J. Dent, *The Rise of Romantic Opera* (Cambridge: Cambridge University Press, 1976), 87–88. A comprehensive discussion of such "prison" scenes, including that in Pavesi's Ossianic opera, can be found in Paolo Mechelli, *La scena di prigione nell'opera italiana fra Settecento e Ottocento* (Munich: GRIN, 2011).

25. Reinhard Strohm, *Dramma per musica: Italian Opera Seria in the Eighteenth Century* (New Haven: Yale University Press, 1997), 29; Marita P. McClymonds, "The Venetian Role in the Transformation of Opera Seria," in *I vicini di Mozart I. Il teatro musicale tra Sette e Ottocento*, ed. Maria Teresa Muraro (Florence: Olschki, 1989), 221–40.

26. The title of the opera in the original Venetian libretto print has a comma (*Fingallo, e Comala*), but this is dispensed with in libretti published later. The history of the comma before "e" and "che" in Italian is complicated. I am indebted to Enrico Mattioda for this point.

27. In scenes 4–5, for example, with Lamor and Fingallo, there is the direction in the score "Siegue con stromenti e Borasca"—that is, the storm proceeds in the orchestra (scenes 6–7 in the Venice and Reggio libretti, 5–6 in the Milan version). In scenes 4–5, for example, again with "Lamor e Fingallo" there is the direction in the score, "Siegue con stromenti e Borasca," that is, the storm proceeds in the orchestra (scenes 6–7 in the Venice and Reggio libretti, 5–6 in the Milan version).

28. The *Zeitung für die elegante Welt*, no. 18 (February 9, 1805), praised the performance that took place on February 2 in Venice; cited by Salvagno, *La Vita e l'Opera di Stefano Pavesi*, 261–62. The Italian version of the review is dated "Venezia, 2 febbraio 1805."

29. The performance, notwithstanding, received favorable reviews in the *Theater-Zeitung* (February 1) and *Der Sammler*, no. 16 (February 1812), 64; both are cited in Salvagno, *La Vita e l'Opera di Stefano Pavesi*, 263–64.

30. Carpani, moving between Venice and Vienna, may have been responsible for encouraging this performance. See Heidelinde Rudy, "Studien zum Opernschaffen Stefano Pavesis" (PhD diss., University of Vienna, 1983), 38, 45.

31. Also scene 9 in the Reggio version, but scene 7 in the Milan libretto. The copy of the *scena* in the Sächsische- und Landesbibliothek (Mus. 1-F-49), ff. 16–20, has "In Firenze: Stamperia di Musica di Giuseppe Lorenzi" inscribed on the title page.

32. In the Yale University Library microfilm copy of the aria (Reel 2610; early eighteenth century), the upper string accompaniment is marked pizzicato; in other copies it is bowed.

33. Omitted from the Milan libretto, and a new text substituted for act 2, scene 4, to accommodate a trio for Morval, Fingal, and Comala, "Fiero nell' anima." In one manuscript copy (Badische Landesbibliothek, MS. Don 1533) the phrase "qual smanie nel petto" (what yearning in my breast) replaces the "qual palpito in petto" of the libretto. "Smanie" is a prominent emotion in the corresponding duet between the protagonist and Dunromath in *Gaulo ed Oitona*, act 2, scene 2.

34. But it is in scene 14 in the Reggio version and in scene 13 in the Milan libretto.

35. In scene 10 of the Venice libretto, scene 9 of the Reggio libretto, and scene 11 of the Milan version. The copy of "Dono del ciel clemente sonno" in the Biblioteca Capitolare, Vicenza (I-Vld), S. 8, has the key transposed from F to E major.

36. This scene was recomposed (as a "scene italienne") by the Swiss composer Joseph Hartmann Stuntz (1793–1859), at that time a pupil of Peter von Winter in Munich. Winter's *Singspiel, Colmal* (1809), may have been an influence. The recomposition was perhaps also conceived from reports of the opera or the libretto, or both; Stuntz's manuscript is dated February 18, 1811. Performances of Pavesi's operas in Munich did not take place until 1816, with *L'avvertimento ai gelosi*, at the Isartortheater, August 31, 1816.

37. Venice had capitulated to Napoleon in May 1797, but as a condition of the Treaty of Campo Formio in October of that year, it was returned to Austria.

38. Despite the warm praise for the overture from Carpani, who did not share the composer's pro-French enthusiasm, a reviewer in Turin, Giuseppe Grassi, writing in the *Courrier de Turin* for January 2, 1809, following a repeat concert there on December 26, 1808, criticized Pavesi for not bringing forward the conventional "cavatina d'entrée," an omission of which Metastasio would not have approved, and accused Pavesi of writing

music that was far too instrumental and "scientific" ("troppo strumentale e 'scientifica'"). Quoted by Fabbri, "Gli esordi di Pavesi," in *L'aere è fosco*, 552n.

39. Such as the quartet for King Darius and three suitors in act 2 of Salieri's *Palmira, regina di Persia*, first staged at the Kärntnertortheater in Vienna on October 14, 1795. See Norbert Dubowy, "Templi, Vergine e Sacerdoti: Aspekte des sakralen in der venezianischen Opera Seria um 1800," in *L'aere è fosco*, 315–49.

40. The libretto is in I-Vnm Misc. B 11545. See also Pier Giuseppe Gillio, "La cantata politico-encomiastica veneziana (1797–1815)," in *L'aere è fosco*, 119–48.

41. Metastasio's libretto was originally set to music by the Neapolitan composer Nicola Conforto (1718–93) and first performed in Madrid in 1756.

42. ARDANO E DARTULA/DRAMMA PER MUSICA/DEL CAVALIERE PAOLO POLA/DA RAPPRESENTARSI/NEL GRAN TEATRO LA FENICE/NEL CAROVALE 1825./LA MUSICA E DEL MAESTRO/SIGNOR STEFANO PAVESI (VENICE, 1825). Dated 1825, the score is "Partiture 11" at the Archivio Storico of La Fenice. A catalogue description details the pagination, performers, and orchestration.

43. Not as much a mystery, perhaps, as J. S. Mayr's *Werter* (1802), with its story based on Goethe's celebrated novel (1774) to a libretto by Sografi. See John Stewart Allitt, *Johann Simon Mayr, Father of 19th Century Italian Music* (Shaftesbury: Element, 1989), and also the afterword.

44. *AMZ*, No. 15 (April 1825), 251. It is difficult to assess how accurate this comment is, and whether it applies to one performance, the premiere, or the entire run of seven productions.

45. Bagnara's design is reproduced in Manuela Jahrmärker, *Themen, Motive und Bilder des Romantischen*, 15. He later designed the set for Rossini's *Barber* at La Fenice in 1825.

46. The role of Cairba was sung by the noted tenor Giovanni David (1790–1864), who performed in two other Ossianic operas: Carlo Saccenti's *Aganadeca* (1817) and Pietro Raimondi's *Clato* (1832). He had roles in operas by Bellini, Donizetti, and, particularly, Rossini (such as Uberto and James V of Scotland, in *La donna del lago*, 1819).

47. The reviewer for *I Teatri, arti e letteratura*, no. 50 (April 7, 1825), while praising [Giovanni] David (as Cairba) and [Antonio] Tamburini (as Carilo), added that on the first evening almost all the pieces were noisily applauded ("la prima sera quasi tutti le pezzi del primo atto vennero rumorosamente applauditi"). But the very positive attitude of the audience and critics could not save the opera from disaster ("Tutta la buona disposizione del pubblico, e de' suoi amici ed estimatori non lo avrebbero salvato da un precipizio"). Cited by Salvagno, *La Vita e l'Opera di Stefano Pavesi*, 361–62.

48. Metternich, visiting in 1815, famously referred to the city as a ruin, a condition brought on by French rule. By 1825 Venice had suffered so much from poor harvests and dwindling resources that the new Austrian-appointed Patriarch Giovanni Ladislao Pyrker (governed 1820–27), a Hungarian, petitioned Emperor Francis to address the economic woes and wrote to both the London *Times* and the *Journal de débats* about the situation; see Bruno Bertoli and Silvio Tramontin, eds., *La Visita Pastorale di Giovanni Ladislao Pyrker nella Diocesi di Venezia* (1821) (Rome: Edizione di storia e letteratura, 1971), liii. This contrasts with the picture conveyed by the visiting English traveler Mariana Starke, about 1824, when she remarked, in *Travels in Europe Between the Years 1824 and 1828* (London, 1828), on "how amply and conveniently this Town is supplied, not only with the necessaries but the luxuries of life" (416).

49. The pairing of harp and flute is also a striking aspect of Ines's cavatina in Pavesi's *Ines di Almeida* (1822), "Perchê non vieni a me" (quoted by Salvagno, *La Vita e l'Opera di Stefano Pavesi*, 154–57).
50. See Marina Marino, "Rossini e Pavesi: A proposito di un' aria dell' *Eduardo e Cristina*," *Bollettino del Centro Rossiniana di Studi* 1–3 (1986), 5–14.
51. See Jahrmärker, *Ossian—Eine Figur*, 22–23.

Chapter Seven

1. CALTO/Dramma per musica/da rappresentarsi/nei nobilissimo teatro/Venier/insane Benedetto/il carnovale dell' anno/1788. A note observes that "L'azione e tratta dai Poemi d'*Ossian*, ed in parte immaginata." Modesto Fenza published the libretto in Venice; the autograph score is in the Biblioteca de Ajuda, Lisbon. Bianchi is described as "Cremonese Maestro d'Organo nella Ducal Capella di S. Marco ed Accademico Filarmonico."
2. According to the libretto, acts 2 and 3 at the Venice premiere included the ballets "Le Ninfe di Diana" and "Il Cavalier Benefico."
3. DUNTALMO/Dramma per musica/da rappresentarsi/nel nobil teatro/Di Torre Argentina/Il Carnevale dell' Anno 1789/Dedicato/All' Inclito Popolo/Romano. The Roman publisher Giaocchino Puccinelli produced the libretto. Copies of extracts from the original score, dated 1789, are in the Conservatorio Giuseppe Verdi, Milan (Mus. Tr. mss. 223, 224, and 226). Caruso was born in Naples and completed some sixty-four operas in a conservative style. His dramma per musica, *Artaserse*, to a libretto by Metastasio, was performed in London in 1774. In 1788 he was named *maestro di cappella* in Perugia, a position he held until his death.
4. Inscribed on a rock there is the legend (not in the scenario of *Calto*): SIRMO DAL FIGLIO ASPETTA/LA GIUSTA SUA VENDETTA (Sirmo awaits the justice of his son's vengeance).
5. See Enrico Mattioda, "Ossian in Italy: From Cesarotti to the Theatre," in *The Reception of Ossian in Europe*, ed. Howard Gaskill, 294–97; for a discussion of ballets, see 302.
6. The ballet is described as a "ballo eroico pantomimo" with choreography by Maria Del Caro Narducci, with Maria De Caro (presumably her stage name) interpreting the role of Malvina.
7. *Clato* is described as a "ballo eroico tragico pantomimo in cinque atti." Monticini (1792–1854) was active as a choreographer in various Italian theaters in the first half of the nineteenth century.
8. Schira is not to be confused with his better-known brother, Francesco (1809–83), who worked in London as a conductor at the Princess and Drury Lane Theatres and Covent Garden.
9. GAULO ED OITONA/Dramma serio per musica,/da rappresentarsi/nel Real Teatro di S. Carlo, nel Carnevale Dell' Anno 1813. In Fidanza's "argomento" he refers to "Il Sig. Makspherson [sic], preteso traduttore degle antichi poemi d'Ossian" (purported translator of the ancient poems of Ossian).
10. CLATO/Dramma serio in Musica con cori/da rappresentarsi/in Bologna/Nel Gran teatro della Commune/nel Carnevale dell' anno MDCCCXVII /Dedicato /all'eminentissimo

e reverendissimo principe/Il Signor Cardinale/Alessandro Lante/Degnissimo Legato di Questa Citta. Lorenzoni announced in a footnote that "il bravo Maestro Generali sa con la musica servire del pari forza del sentimento, ed alla verita della parola" (the excellent Maestro Generali knows how, with his music, to serve both the strength of feeling as well as the accuracy of the text).

11. Tommasso Locatelli, commenting on Generali's *Francesca* in the *Gazzetta di Venezia*, 1828.
12. See John Rosselli, *Music & Musicians in Nineteenth-Century Italy* (London: Batsford, 1973), 76–77.
13. The interpolated ballet ("ballo spettacoloso pantomimico") following act 1 was *Niobe, ossia La Vendetta di Latona*. Latona, the mistress of Jupiter and mother of Apollo and Diana, is forced to flee because of the jealousy of Juno.
14. CLATO/Tragedia Lirica/in/Due Atti/da rappresentarsi/Nel Real Teatro di S. Carlo/Nell' Inverno del' anno 1832. Born in Rome, Raimondi (1786–1843) had a reputation as a skilled contrapuntist. After recognizing the superior dramatic talent of Rossini, he turned to sacred music: his three oratorios, *Putifar–Giuseppe–Giacobbe* (1848), were devised to be staged both separately and simultaneously.
15. The extensive bibliography on Rossini is noted in Richard Osborne, *Rossini: His Life and Works* (Oxford: Oxford University Press, 2007).
16. AGANADECA/tentativo drammatico/da rappresentarsi/nel Real Teatro di S. Carlo (Napoli, 1817).
17. FINGAL:/dramma lirico/ in tre atti/da rappresentarsi/nel R. Teatro Carolino/per nona opera/dell'anno teatrale 1846–47 (Palermo: Presso Francesco Abate, 1847); a reduction of the score, for piano and voice, was made by the composer and published by Ricordi (185?). Raimondi is listed in Gaetano Solito's published libretto of *Fingal* as "Maestro di Cappella Compositore e Direttore," and thus most likely had a hand in approving and promoting Coppola's opera.
18. The origins of the tale are discussed in Derick S. Thomson, *The Gaelic Sources of Macpherson's Ossian*, 29–30.
19. *Louis Spohr's Selbstbiographie*, vol. 2 (Cassel u. Göttingen, 1861), 14–16: "Eine andere Oper, ebenfalls von einem Dilettanten, Herrn Carlo Saccenti, wurde vor acht Tagen gegeben, nachdem man länger also drei Monate daran studirt und probirt hatte . . . der ein unbefragenes Urtheil hemmt, wurde die Oper in optima forma ausgepfiffen. Mit dieser zweiten Vorstellung, der auch ich beiwohnte, wurde die Oper auf ewige Zeiten begraben. Sie heißt 'Aganadeca' der Dichter Signore Vincenzio de Ritis. Die Dichtung nach Ossian soll nicht ohne Verdienst sein, und man bedauert, daß sie keinem besseren Componisten in die Hände defallen sei. Dieser ist übrigens noch nicht zur Erkenntniß gelangt; er gibt der wenigen musikalischen Bildung des neapolitanischen Publikums die Schuld und will sein Werk nach Deutschland schicken. Apollo und die Musen mögen ihren Segen dazu geben!" Spohr also complained about the presence of three parallel fifths, one after the other, in the overture; but this may have been an attempt by Saccenti to capture a musical characteristic he saw as "exotic."
20. Gallenberg, who had studied with Albrechtsberger, married Beethoven's pupil Countess Giulietta Giucciardi, dedicatee of the "Moonlight" Sonata.
21. At least five theatrical tragedies around the story of Agandecca appeared in Italy between 1828 and 1886; see Mattioda, "Ossian in Italy," 300.

22. See Gerald Bär, "Ossian in Portugal," in *The Reception of Ossian in Europe*, 351–74; here, 370. The British soprano Clara Novello sang the role of Agandeca [*sic*]; see her *Reminiscences, Compiled by Her Daughter Contessa Valeria Gigliucci* (London: Edward Arnold, 1910), 138–46.
23. FINGAL: Drama lyrico em 3 actos. Para se representar no R. T. de S. Carlos, Lisboa: Typ. De Solero Antonio Borges, 1851. Costa Sanchez published another edition in Lisbon in 1864. The composer made a piano reduction that was published by Ricordi (Milan, 1844).
24. The phrase occurs in plays and operas such as Gaetano Andreozzi's *Virginia* (1786) and Sebastiano Nasolini's *La Morte di Semiramide* (1819–20), and in the last scene of Rossini's *Ricciardo e Zoraide* (1818), where it is the cavatina for Ricciardo, "Ah ricevi in un amplesso / Di quest' alma amica un pegno." Giovanni David sang the role at the premiere in Naples, and Isabella Colbran was Zoraide.
25. Joseph Kerman draws attention to Verdi's "ironic" fanfares in *Opera as Drama* (New York: Knopf, 1959), 152.
26. The best source for information on the composer is A. M. Sokolova, *Kompozitor Osip Antonovich Kozlovskii* (Moscow: Kotran, 1997). The 1808 subscription edition of the play ends with Kozlowski's score. *Fingal* had first appeared without Ozerov's name on the title page: *Fingal: Tragediia v trekh deistviiakh s khorami i pantomimnymi baletami* (St. Petersburg, 1807). The 1808 edition has a French text as well as the Russian: *Fingal: Tragédie en Trois Actes, traduit du russe, en vers français par Hre. Jn. Dalmas: Partition complète des chœurs, ballets et combats de la tragédie de Fingal, composée par M. Kozlowsky* (St. Petersburg: Au magasin de musique et de pièces de theater, 1808).
27. See Peter France, "Fingal in Russia," in *The Reception of Ossian in Europe*, 259–73; Julie A. Cassiday, "Northern Poetry for a Northern People: Text and Context in Ozerov's *Fingal*," *The Slavonic and East European Review* 78, no. 2 (2000): 240–66.
28. See especially Iurii D. Levin, *Ossian v russkoi literature: Konets XVIII—pervaia tret' XIX veka* (Leningrad: Nauka, 1980). Le Tourneur's two-volume translation is entitled *Ossian, Fils de Fingal, Barde du Troisième Siècle: Poésies Galliques, Traduites sur l'Anglois de M. Macpherson* (Paris: Musier, 1777). Kostrov's translation of Le Tourneur, also in two volumes, is *Ossian, syn Fingalov, bard tret'iago veka: Gal'skiia stikhotvoreniia* (Moscow: Universitetskaia Tipografiia, 1792).
29. The writer A. A. Nikitin presented his translation of three songs from Ossian to Empress Elizabeth, wife of Czar Alexander I, in 1816. A copy of this manuscript is in the Houghton Library of Harvard University, fMS Russ 52.
30. Pushkin's quotation is "A tale of the times of old! The deeds of days of other years!" (Dela davno minuvshikh dnei, / Predan'ia stariny glubokoi). See Mark Altshuller, "Pushkin's 'Ruslan and Liudmila' and the Traditions of the Mock-Epic Poem," in *The Golden Age of Russian Literature and Thought: Selected Papers from the Fourth World Congress for Soviet and East European Studies*, Harrogate, 1990, ed. Derek Offord (Basinstoke: Macmillan, 1992), 7–24; here, 18.
31. Iurii D. Levin, trans., *Dzheims Makferson: Poemy Ossiana* (Leningrad: Nauka, 1983), 451–55; cited by Peter France, "Fingal in Russia," in *The Reception of Ossian in Europe*, 261.
32. Levin, *Ossian v russkoi literature* 93.

33. See Richard Stites, *Serfdom, Society, and the Arts in Imperial Russia: The Pleasure and the Power* (New Haven: Yale University Press, 2005), 184; see also the critical comments by Simon Karlinsky, *Russian Drama from Its Beginnings to the Age of Pushkin* (Berkeley: University of California Press, 1985), 199–200, 207.
34. See France, "Fingal in Russia," 266.
35. A. S. Pushkin, "Moi zamechaniia ob russkom teatre," in Pushkin, *Polnoe sobranie sochinenii*, 17 vols. (Moscow: Voskresen'ie, 1937–59), vol. 11, 9–13; and *Evgenii Onegin: Roman v stikhakh*, chapter 1, stanza XVIII. Both extracts quoted by Julie A. Cassiday, "Northern Poetry," 263.
36. See n. 26 above.
37. See Cassiday, "Northern Poetry," 258.
38. "Umolkni vse v strane podlunni, / Chtob glasy arfy zlatostrunnoi / Po kholmam dal'nim pronesliś, / V pustyniakh gulom razdalis'."
39. "Poiu Fingala divny boi, / Ego zabavy iunykh dnei, / A vy, pochivshie geroi, / Pokrytye syroi zemlei, / Vosstan'te ot mogil bezmolvnykh, / Na vysotakh iavites' kholmnykh" (Ozerov 1960, 195; translation by Peter France, in "Fingal in Russia," 268).
40. See Cassiday, "Northern Poetry," 260.
41. His son Albert Cavos (1800–1863) achieved fame as the architect of the Mariinsky Theatre in St. Petersburg (1859–60) and the Bolshoi in Moscow (1853–56).
42. A. A. Shakhovskoi's *Fingal i Rozkrana, ili kaledonskie obychai, dramaticheskaya poema* was entitled, in its musical form, *Fingal e Roscrana, poema drammatico in tre atti tratto da un canto di Ossian, con musiche di Cavos e Catel*.
43. See Anna Giust, *Ivan Susanin di Catterino Cavos: Un' opera russa prima dell'opera russa* (Turin, 2011), 102. Giust cites P. N. Arapov, *Letopis' russkogo teatra* (St. Petersburg, 1861), 353, where the cast of *Fingal i Rozkrana* is listed.
44. Catel had a success with his three-act opera *Wallace, ou Le Ménestrel écossais*, perfomed at the Opéra-Comique in 1817. The Scottish connection with Ossian may have suggested incorporating elements of Catel's score into the work.

Chapter Eight

1. *Briefe und Gedichte aus dem Album Robert und Clara Schumanns*, ed. Wolfgang Boetticher (Leipzig: Deutscher Verlag für Musik, 1979), 178. Cited by John Daverio, "Schumann's Ossianic Manner," *19th-Century Music*, vol. 21, no. 3 (1998), 247–73; here, 251 (italics in the original). Daverio was perhaps the first musicologist to take the influence of Ossian seriously. See also Matthew Gelbart, *The Invention of "Folk Music" and "Art Music": Emerging Categories from Ossian to Wagner* (New York: Cambridge University Press, 2007), 60–66.
2. See Maynard Solomon, *Beethoven* (New York: Schirmer, 1977); for a summary account of the composer's sketchbooks, see Lewis Lockwood, *Beethoven's Symphonies: An Artistic Vision* (New York: W. W. Norton, 2015); for interpretations of the "Eroica" Symphony, see Scott Burnham, *Beethoven Hero* (Princeton, NJ: Princeton University Press, 1995); Thomas Sipe, *Beethoven*: Eroica *Symphony* (Cambridge: Cambridge University Press, 1998).

3. Henry Edward Krehbiel, *Music & Manners from Pergolesi to Beethoven: Essays* (Westminster: Constable, 1898), 195–96: "I give the following extracts from Mr. Thayer's notebook (kindly placed at my disposal by Mrs. Fox, a niece of the biographer and his heir) without further change than a translation into English." The anecdote about Beethoven's conversation with Hofrath Küffner concerning his favorite symphony is reprinted in *Beethoven: The Man and the Artist, as Revealed in His Own Words*, ed. Friedrich Kerst and Henry Edward Krehbiel (New York: Gay and Bird, 1905; reprinted New York: Dover, 1964), 45.
4. Howard Gaskill, "'Genuine poetry . . . like gold,'" introduction to *The Reception of Ossian in Europe*, ed. Gaskill, 1–20; here, 19. See also Wolf Gerhardt Schmidt, *"Homer des Nordens" und "Mutter der Romantik."* Mme. de Staël coined the phrase "L'Homère du nord" in 1800, and Jean Paul Richter the German phrase of Schmidt's title.
5. See Alan Tyson, "Beethoven's Heroic Phase," *Musical Times* 110 (1969), 139–41; also K. M. Knittel, "Imitation, Individuality and Illness: Behind Beethoven's 'Three Styles,'" in *Beethoven Forum* 4, ed. Lewis Lockwood & James Webster (Lincoln: University of Nebraska Press, 1995), 17–36.
6. Carl Dahlhaus, *Ludwig van Beethoven: Approaches to his Music*, trans. Mary Whittall (Oxford: Clarendon Press, 1991), 25. But Hölderlin turned away from Bonaparte as early as 1799, when the latter appointed himself first consul.
7. The poet Johann Heinrich Voss (1751–1826) made the classic translation of Homer's *Odyssey* (1781, rev. 1793) and *Iliad* (1793) into German.
8. "Vieleicht könnten Sie mir eine Ausgabe von Göthe's und Schillers vollständigen Werken zukommen lassen . . . die zwei Dichter sind meine lieblingsdichter so wie Ossian, Homer welchen letztern ich leider nur in übersetzungen lesen kann." See *Beethovens Sämtliche Briefe: Kritische Ausgabe mit Erläterungen von Dr. Alfr. Chr. Kalischer*, vol. 1, 287–88 (letter 198); English version in *Beethoven's Letters: With Explanatory Notes*, trans. A. C. Kalischer, preface by J. S. Shedlock (Cambridge, 1972; original ed. London: Dent, 1926), 92 (letter 95). See also *Beethoven: The Letters*, ed. Emily Anderson, 3 vols. (London: Macmillan, 1961), 1: 241–42; see also the edition of this work by Alan Tyson (London: Macmillan, 1967).
9. Martin Cooper, *Beethoven: The Last Decade, 1817–1827*, with a medical appendix by Edward Larkin (London: Oxford University Press, 1970), 86–87.
10. William Kinderman, *Beethoven*, 2d ed. (New York: Oxford University Press, 2009), 157. See also Rita Steblin, *A History of Key Characteristics in the Eighteenth and Early Nineteenth Centuries*, 2nd ed. (Rochester, NY: University of Rochester Press, 2002).
11. See Barry Cooper, *Beethoven's Folksong Settings: Chronology, Sources, Style* (Oxford: Clarendon Press, 1994).
12. Ibid., 72–73. These sonatas were never written.
13. Sandro Jung, "The Reception and Reworking of *Ossian* in Klopstock's *Hermanns Schlacht*," in *The Reception of Ossian in Europe*, 143–55; see also Schmidt, *"Homer des Nordens"* 1: 502–26. In 1905 Richard Strauss composed a *Bardengesang* based on Klopstock's *Hermanns Schlacht* for three male four-part choruses and orchestra. In an artistic parallel, the artist Philipp Otto Runge (1777–1810) Germanicized Ossian in a set of twelve line drawings for an edition of the poems that did not, in the end, include them. See afterword.

14. Michael Denis, *Die Gedichte Ossians, eines alten celtischen Dichters*, 3 vols (Vienna, 1768–69). Christian Wilhelm Ahlwardt's bestselling translation *Die Gedichte Ossian's*, 3 vols. (Leipzig, 1811) had not yet appeared.
15. *Oden von Klopstock, mit Melodien von Christian Gottlob Neefe* (Flensburg, 1776). The first two pieces are written on two staves, in C major/minor and E-flat/C minor, respectively; the third in B-flat on three staves, the upper two being in the treble clef. For the third setting, see *German Settings of Ossianic Texts 1770–1815*, ed. Sarah Clemmens Waltz (Madison: A-R Editions, 2016), xxxv–xxxvi, 3–10, 153.
16. *Thayer's Life of Beethoven*, rev. and ed. Elliot Forbes (Princeton, NJ: Princeton University Press, 1967), vol. 1, 246.
17. Beethoven, letter to the Gesellschaft der Musikfreunde, Vienna, January 1824.
18. Goethe was not the only poet to be captivated by the term: see the articles by Howard Gaskill, "Hölderlin and Ossian," *Hölderlin-Jahrbuch* 27 (1990/91), 100–130; "'The Joy of Grief': Moritz and Ossian," *Colloquia Germanica* 28 (1995), 101–25; and "J. M. R. Lenz and Ossian," *From Gaelic to Romantic*, 107–18. More than twenty composers besides Beethoven set Goethe's poem to music.
19. See Kinderman, *Beethoven*, 163–67. The poem was set by at least twenty composers, including Schubert (D260). It was first printed by Willy Hess in 1962; the other autograph is in Paris (BN, MS 21). The sketches for the song can be dated to October 1810 because they follow on directly from the MS of the String Quartet, op. 95.
20. Ibid., 168. Mendelssohn made a transcription that is now housed with the Beethoven autograph in the Goethe-Schiller Archive in Weimar.
21. See Scott Burnham, "On the Programmatic Reception of Beethoven's *Eroica* Symphony," *Beethoven Forum* 1 (Lincoln: University of Nebraska Press, 1992), 1–24.
22. Quoted in O. G. Sonneck, *Beethoven: Impressions By His Contemporaries* (New York: Schirmer, 1926), 161.
23. In Alessandra Comini, *The Changing Image of Beethoven: A Study in Mythmaking* (New York: Rizzoli, 1987), 39. The author believes that "even Goethe was taken in by this great literary hoax [Ossian]." She refers, rather, to the composer's "Promethean scowl."
24. The Padua-born translator of Ossian, Melchiorre Cesarotti (1730–1808), had translated the *Prometheus Bound* of Aeschylus in 1754 as well as a version of Homer's *Iliad*. He was made a Knight of the Iron Crown by Napoleon; see Enrico Mattioda, "Ossian in Italy," in *The Reception of Ossian in Europe*, 274–302.
25. See Maynard Solomon, *Beethoven*, 73–74.
26. Alexander Thayer's biography mentions Beethoven's preoccupation with Napoleon when conversing with Baron de Trémont; see *Life of Beethoven*, 251.
27. The instrument features, for instance, in *Colma* (1780), a monodrama for soprano and small orchestra by Friedrich Wilhelm Rust (1739–96). His son, Wilhelm Karl Rust (1787–1855), moved to Vienna in 1807 and met Beethoven, who praised his playing of Bach; see Thayer, *Life of Beethoven*, 235. Without advancing any evidence, Arnold Schering associated "Colmas Klage" with Beethoven's Piano Sonata, op. 2, no. 1 in F-minor; see *Beethoven und die Dichtung: Mit einer Einleitung zur Geschichte und Aesthetik der Beethovendeutung* (Berlin: Neue deutsche Forschungen, 1936), 547, 560.
28. Especially Constantin Floros, *Beethoven's* Eroica: *Thematic Studies*, trans. Ernest Bernhardt-Kabisch (Frankfurt-am-Main: Lang, 2013), expanded edition of *Beethovens Eroica und Prometheus-Musik: Sujet-Studien* (Wilhelmshaven: Heinrichshofen, 2008).

29. See Kinderman, *Beethoven*, 94–96; also Paul A. Bertagnolli, *Prometheus in Music: Representations of the Myth in the Romantic Era* (Aldershot: Routledge, 2007).
30. Ibid., 287–88. This remark seems more likely, however, to be a rationalization by Beethoven, or one of his ironic jokes.
31. Adolf Bernhard Marx, *Ludwig van Beethoven: Leben und Schaffen* (Berlin, 1859; 6th ed. 1911).
32. Rita Steblin, "Who Died? The Funeral March in Beethoven's 'Eroica' Symphony," *The Musical Quarterly* 89, no. 1 (2006), 62–79.
33. Arnold Schering, "Die Eroica: Eine Homer-Symphonie Beeethovens?," in *Neues Beethoven-Jahrbuch, Fünfter Jahrgang* (Braunschweig, 1934); see n. 55 below. Also Sipe, *Beethoven: Eroica Symphony*, 30–53.
34. Hans Pfitzner, *Die neue Aesthetik der musikalischen Impotenz: ein Verwesungssymptom?* (The New Aesthetic of Musical Impotence: A Sign of Decay?) (Munich: Süddeutsche Monatshefte, 1920); Paul Bekker, *Beethoven* (Berlin and Leipzig, 1911; Eng. trans. Mildred Mary Bozman (London: Dent, 1925). See discussion of the controversy in Leon Botstein, "The Search for Meaning in Beethoven: Popularity, Intimacy, and Politics in Historical Perspective," in *Beethoven and His World*, ed. Scott Burnham and Michael P. Steinberg (Princeton, NJ: Princeton University Press, 2000), 332–66.
35. Ferdinand Ries refers, in his impression of Beethoven, to the composer having some special object in mind in writing his compositions: see Sonneck, *Beethoven*, 53. An "object" could presumably mean a person, a name, a work of literature, or even an event.
36. This narrative is widespread internationally: see Antti Aarne and Stith Thompson, *The Types of the Folktale: A Classification and Bibliography* (Folklore Fellows Communications 3) (Helsinki: Folklore Fellows, 1961), no. 766.
37. Bekker (1911) was one of the first to suggest the link to Prometheus. The syllables of "Prometheus" have their own resonance in the first four notes of the final movement's theme.
38. See Lewis Lockwood, *Beethoven: Studies in the Creative Process* (Cambridge, MA: Harvard University Press, 1992), 166.
39. See Howard Gaskill, "J. M. R. Lenz and Ossian," in *From Gaelic to Romantic*, 109.
40. See also Gaskill, "Introduction: The Translator's Ossian," *Translation and Literature* 22 (2013), 293–301. Arnold Schering drew a detailed comparison between the "Ossian passage" from the novel and elements in the finale of Beethoven's Violin Sonata in C Minor, op. 30, no. 2 (from bars 267–75). See *Beethoven und die Dichtung. Mit einer Einleitung zur Geschichte und Aesthetik der Beethovendeutung* (Berlin: Neue deutsche Forschungen, 1936), 474–82.
41. Mendelssohn set the verses "Charlotte to Werter," written by Frederick William Collard (1772–1860), probably during the composer's visit to London in 1829. The Bavarian Johann Simon Mayr (1763–1845) completed his opera *Verter* with a libretto by Antonio Simeone Sografi, about 1795; see John Stewart Allitt, *J. S. Mayr: Father of 19th Century Italian Music* (Shaftesbury: Element, 1989). See also afterword.
42. Johann Wolfgang von Goethe, *The Sorrows of Young Werther*, trans. David Constantine (Oxford: Oxford University Press, 2012), 73.
43. Margaret Stoljar, "The Sturm und Drang in Music," in *The Literature of the Sturm und Drang*, ed. David Hill (Rochester, NY: Camden House, 2003), 283–308; here, 302.

44. Fiona Stafford, *The Sublime Savage, James Macpherson and the Poems of Ossian* (Edinburgh: Edinburgh University Press, 1988), 2.
45. Goethe was also much affected by the suicide of an army officer's daughter, Christel von Lassberg, who had a copy of *Werther* in her pocket when she threw herself into the River Ilm on January 17, 1778.
46. F. J. Lamport, "Goethe, Ossian and Werther," in *From Gaelic to Romantic*, 97–106.
47. Quoted by Solomon, *Beethoven*, 118–19.
48. Claus Canisius, *Beethoven: Sehnsucht und Unruhe in der Musik: Aspekte zu Leben und Werk* (Mainz: Schott, 1992), 158–64.
49. "Ossians Gedichte bezeichnen den Herbst seines Volkes. Die Blätter färben und krümmen sich; sie fallen und fallen. Der Lusthauch, der sie ablöset, hat keine Erquickung des Frühlinges in sich; sein Spiel indessen ist traurig-angenehm mit den sinkenden Blättern" (Ossian's poetry denotes the autumn of his people. The leaves turn colours and crumple; they fall, and fall. The breeze that loosens them has none of the vigour of spring in it; but as it plays with the falling leaves, it is sadly pleasing); see Herder, *Früchte aus den sogennant goldenen Zeiten des achtzehnten Jahrhunderts*, ed. Johann George Müller (Tübingen, 1809), 406.
50. Alan Tyson, "The 1803 Version of Beethoven's Christus am Oelberge," *The Musical Quarterly* 56 (1970), 551–84; also Barry Cooper, *Beethoven and the Creative Process* (Oxford: Clarendon, 1990), 48.
51. See Joseph Campbell, *The Hero with a Thousand Faces* (New York: Pantheon, 1949); also Heidi Rockwood, "Jung's Psychological Types and Goethe's 'Die Leiden des jungen Werthers,'" *The Germanic Review* 55 (1980), 118–23.
52. There is also Ossian's Minona, not a warrior but a singer of laments in "The Songs of Selma." Minona was the name of the daughter of Josephine Brunsvik, countess Deym, with whom Beethoven is alleged to have had an intimate relationship in 1812.
53. The gendered conception of heroism recalls Zelter's famous letter to Goethe of September 14, 1812, concerning Beethoven's music: "His works seem to me like children, whose father might be a woman, or whose mother, a man."
54. See Glenn Stanley, "Arnold Schering: 'Die Eroica, eine Homer-Symphonie Beethovens?' Translated with an Introduction and Commentary," *Current Musicology* 69 (2000), 68–96; also Burnham, *Beethoven Hero*, 3–28.
55. Stanley, "Arnold Schering," 76; also Sipe, *Beethoven: Eroica Symphony*, 66.
56. See Maynard Solomon, "Beethoven's Tagebuch of 1812–1818," *Beethoven Studies* 3, ed. Alan Tyson (New York: Cambridge University Press, 1982), 193–288.
57. Johann Gottfried Herder, in *Von deutscher Art und Kunst: Einige fliegende Blätter*, ed. Hans Dietrich Irmscher (Stuttgart: Reclam, 1995), 7–62.
58. Printed with the English-language apostrophe, a form that lasted until the twentieth century. See also chapter 12.
59. The ode is discussed in Gail K. Hart, "Schiller's 'An die Freude' and the Question of Freedom," *German Studies Review* 32, no. 3 (2004), 479–93.
60. Wolf Gerhard Schmidt, "'*Menschlichschön*' and '*kolossalisch*': The Discursive Function of Ossian in Schiller's Poetry and Aesthetics," trans. Howard Gaskill, in *The Reception of Ossian in Europe*, 176–97.

61. "Cathmors Seele war wie der Stral des Himmels . . . Aber Cathmor verbarg sich tief in den Wald die Stimme des Lobs nicht zu hören." Cited by Schmidt, "The Discursive Function of *Ossian*," 177.
62. Schmidt, "The Discursive Function of Ossian," 186–87. Merck and Goethe were only responsible for the first two volumes. The edition was then taken over by Fleischer in Leipzig and ceased to be anonymous. I am grateful to Howard Gaskill for this information.
63. Quoted in Peter Le Huray and James Day, *Music and Aesthetics in the Eighteenth and Early-Nineteenth Centuries* (Cambridge: Cambridge University Press, 1981), 138.
64. See Maynard Solomon, "Beethoven and Schiller," chapter 14 in his *Beethoven Essays* (Cambridge, MA: Harvard University Press, 1988), 205–6.
65. "Es ist interessant, zu sehen, mit welchem glücklichen Instinkt alles, was dem sentimentalischen Charakter Nahrung gibt, im 'Werther' zusammengedrängt ist; schwärmerische unglückliche Liebe, Empfindsamkeit für Natur, Religionsgefühle, philosophischer Kontemplationsgeist, endlich, um nichts zu vergessen, die düstre, gestaltlose, schwermütige Ossianische Welt." Friedrich Schiller, *Sämtliche Werke* (Munich, 1960), vol. 5, 738; trans. in William Witte, *Schiller and Burns, and Other Essays* (Oxford: Oxford University Press, 1959), 31.
66. Beethoven was deeply affected by Christian Sturm's *Betrachtungen über die Werke Gottes im Reiche der Natur und der Vorsehung auf alle Tage des Jahres*, 2 parts (Halle, 1772–76) (Observations on the Works of God in Nature and Providence for Every Day of the Year; Eng. trans. 1791), his copy of which he had heavily annotated; see Gerhard von Breuning, *Memories of Beethoven*, ed. Maynard Solomon (Cambridge: Cambridge University Press, 1992), 56.
67. Friedrich Schiller, "On Naïve and Sentimental Poetry," trans. Julius A. Elias, in *German Aesthetics and Literary Criticism: Winckelmann, Lessing, Hamann, Herder, Schiller and Goethe*, ed. Hugh Barr Nisbet (Cambridge: Cambridge University Press, 1985), 180–232; here, 201.
68. Matthisson penned a poem he entitled "An Ossian" (To Ossian); see *Friedrich Matthisson: Gedichte*, vol. 1 (Tübingen, 1912), 11.
69. Friedrich Schiller, "Über Matthissons Gedichte," in *Werke und Briefe* (Frankfurt-am-Main: Deutscher Klassiker-Verlag, 1992), 8: 1023–26, remarks on music. See Charles Rosen, *The Romantic Generation* (Cambridge, MA: Harvard University Press, 1995), 126–31; also Kristina Muxfeldt, "The Romantic Preoccupation with Musical Meaning," in *The Literature of German Romanticism*, ed. Dennis F. Mahoney (Rochester, NY: Camden House, 2004), 253.
70. For example, Glenn Stanley, "Beethoven at Work: Musical Activist and Thinker," in *The Cambridge Companion to Beethoven*, ed. Glenn Stanley (Cambridge: Cambridge University Press, 2000), 14–31; here, 25.
71. It also inspired Schumann's suite of piano pieces *Papillons*, op. 2 (1831). Schering believed that *Die Flegeljahre* was intimately connected with Beethoven's String Quartet No. 2 in E minor; see *Beethoven und die Dichtung*, 270.
72. Alexander Gillies, *A Hebridean in Goethe's Weimar: The Rev. James Macdonald and Cultural Relations between Scotland and Germany* (Oxford: Blackwell, 1969), 13. Macdonald also met Klopstock in Hamburg in 1798, 76–77. See Schmidt, *"Homer des Nordens"* 1, 881.

73. Alexander Gillies, *Herder und Ossian* (Berlin: Juncker und Dunnhaupt, 1933).
74. In the second edition of his *Vorschule*, Jean Paul inserted a notice of the translation of Ossian (1808) by Hölderlin's friend Franz Wilhelm Jung (1757–1833).
75. *Neue Zeitschrift für Musik* 2 (1835), 42.
76. Muxfeldt, "The Romantic Preoccupation," 257, trans. from Amadeus Wendt, *Über die Hauptperioden der Schönen Kunst, oder die Kunst im Laufe der Weltgeschichte dargestellt* (Leipzig, 1831), 308. See also Elisabeth E. Bauer, "Beethoven—unser musikalischer Jean Paul: Anmerkungen zu einer Analogie," in *Beethoven: Analecta varia*, ed. Heinz-Klaus Metzger and Rainier Riehn (Munich: Text + kritik, 1987).
77. Thomas Sipe, "Beethoven, Shakespeare, and the 'Appassionata,'" *Beethoven Forum* 4: 73–96.
78. Martin Geck and Peter Schleuning, *"Geschrieben auf Bonaparte." Beethovens Eroica: Revolution, Reaktion, Rezeption* (Reinbek bei Hamburg: Rowohlt, 1989), 233.
79. Translated by Arthur Ware Lock, in "Beethoven's Instrumental Music: From E. T. A. Hoffman's 'Kreisleriana,'" *The Musical Quarterly* 3, no. 1 (1917), 123–33; here, 128.
80. "Die Musik schließt dem Menschen ein unbekanntes Reich auf; eine Welt, die nichts gemein hat mit der äußern Sinnenwelt, die ihn umgibt, und in der er alle bestimmten Gefühle zurückläßt, um sich einer unaussprechlichen Sehnsucht hinzugeben." Translated in Ruth Solie, ed., *Strunk's Source Readings in Music History*, rev. ed., vol. 6 (New York, 1998: Norton, 151–55. Beethoven made four settings of Goethe's poem "Sehnsucht" (WoO 134) and one of another by that title by Christian Ludwig Reissig (WoO 146).
81. See his analysis of the "Eroica" in *Beethoven: The Philosophy of Music*, ed. Rolf Tiedemann, trans. Edmund Jephcott (Stanford: Stanford University Press, 2002), 101–2.
82. Beethoven's description of the meeting is contained in letters to Breitkopf & Härtel (August 9) and a disputed one to Bettina von Arnim (August 15).

Excursus

1. The small island of Staffa in the Inner Hebrides lies some eight miles (ten kilometers) west of the much larger Isle of Mull. The naturalist Joseph Banks made the island known to the early modern world in 1772, giving the main sea cavern the English name of "Fingal's Cave" in the wake of Macpherson's Ossian poems. The nama "Staffa" (Gaelic "Stafa") was originally given to the island by Vikings because the basalt pillars of the cave reminded them of the vertical wooden supports of their own houses. Recent archaeological digs have shown that there was Bronze Age activity on the island, well before the arrival of the Gaels (from Ireland) or centuries later, the Norsemen.
2. Quoted in Roger Fiske, *Scotland in Music: A European Enthusiasm* (Cambridge: Cambridge University Press, 1983), 134.
3. "Um zu verdeutlichen, wie seltsam mir auf den Hebriden zu Muthe geworden ist, fiel mir eben folgendes bey," in *Felix Mendelssohn Bartholdy: Sämtliche Briefe*, vol. 1, *1816 bis Juni 1830*, ed. Juliette Appold and Regina Back (Kassel: Bärenreiter, 2008), 370–71.
4. In the spring of 1832, the artist J. M. W. Turner (1775–1851) exhibited his painting *Staffa*, to critical acclaim.

5. The memorable opening motif that the composer jotted down is not, as one scholar alleges in a recent study, "usually understood as a musical depiction of a basalt cave on the isle of Staffa," but instead suggests the undulating waves of the seascape around Mull as first experienced by Mendelssohn on August 7, 1829, when he headed the note, "on one of the Hebrides." See Steven Vande Moortele, *The Romantic Overture and Musical Form from Rossini to Wagner* (New York: Cambridge University Press, 2017), 151n16.
6. This subtle effect, often lost in the orchestral texture, is especially difficult to bring off in the composer's four-hand arrangement for piano. W. Gillies Whittaker, in his foreword to the Eulenberg edition of the score (no. 637, n.d.), makes several picturesque references to visual aspects of the score such as this one, but not to the climax of the exposition, bars 77–95, which could be interpreted as the composer's real or imagined sighting of the cave as it came into view. As Mendelssohn completed the work later, this is evidently a case of "sensation recollected in tranquillity," to parody Wordsworth's phrase.
7. For example, Robert S. Hatten, in *Musical Meaning in Beethoven: Markedness, Correlation, and Interpretation* (Bloomington: Indiana University Press, 1994), 254–57, 325.
8. The reception of the symphonies is discussed in Wulf Konold, *Die Sinfonien Menselssohn Bartholdys: Untersuchungen zu Werkgestalt und Formstruktur* (Laaber: Laaber-Verlag, 1992), esp. 229–35.
9. Fiske argues that the title "The Hebrides" (or even "Die einsame Insel" [The lonely island]) is to be preferred for the overture (*Scotland in Music*, 137); but in fact, the turbulence and fresco-like episodes in the music's freely devised sonata structure suggest a much more specific, or deictic (to use a semiotic term), set of synchronic experiences for the composer on his visit to the cave. The alternative title, *Die Fingals-Höhle*, is then more accurate in relation to Mendelssohn's dramatic passages, as the publisher no doubt realized, quite apart from commercial considerations. The geologist Joseph Banks described the cave in 1772: "There is a cave in this island [Staffa] which the natives call the Cave of Fingal. . . . The Giant's Causeway in Ireland, or Stonehenge in England, are but trifles when compared to this island" (*The Gentleman's Magazine*, November 1772, 540). See also his account in Thomas Pennant, *A Tour in Scotland and Voyage to the Hebrides 1772* (Chester, 1774), 262–63.
10. See, for instance, Andreas Eichhorn, *Felix Mendelssohn Bartholdy: Die Hebriden, Ouvertüre für Orchester, op. 26*. Meisterwerke der Musik 66 (Munich, 1998); R. Larry Todd, *Mendelssohn: "The Hebrides" and Other Overtures* (Cambridge: Cambridge University Press, 1993).
11. *Part Second/of the/Complete Repository/of/Original Scots Tunes/Strathspeys Jigs and Dances/ The Dances arranged as Medleys in their respective Keys/for the/HARP,/OR/Piano-forte Violin and Violoncello &c./Humbly Dedicated to Her Grace the /Duchess of Buccleugh/by/ NIEL GOW & SONS . . . Edinburgh* [1802], 6.
12. On the visual aspect of both Mendelssohn's and Gade's overtures, see Thomas S. Grey, "Fingal's Cave and Ossian's Dream: Music, Image, and Phantasmagoric Audition," in *The Arts Entwined: Music and Painting in the Nineteenth Century*, ed. Marsha L. Morton and Peter L. Schmunk (New York and London: Garland, 2000), 63–99.
13. See Max Paddison, "Mimesis and the Aesthetics of Musical Expression," *Music Analysis* 29, nos. 1–3 (2010), 126–48.

14. This was dedicated to the Horsley sisters; the score is in the Bodleian Library, Oxford, with the shelf mark MS Horsley B.1, fols. 1–10.
15. See Ralf Wehner, *Felix Mendelssohn-Bartholdy: Thematisch-systematisches Verzeichnis der musikalischen Werke* (Wiesbaden: Breitkopf & Härtel, 2009), specifically, P 7, Konzert—Ouvertüre Nr. 2: *Die Hebriden/The Isles of Fingal (Zur einsamen Insel)*, h-Moll, op. 26 ("Fingals Höhle"), 244.
16. See, for example, Carl Dahlhaus, ed., *Das Problem Mendelssohn* (Regensburg: Gustav Bosse Verlag, 1974).
17. Thomas S. Grey, "*Tableaux vivants*: Landscape, History Painting, and the Visual Imagination in Mendelssohn's Orchestral Music," *19th-Century Music* 21 (1997), 38–76; R. Larry Todd, "On the Visual in Mendelssohn's Music," in *Cari amici: Festschrift 25 Jahre Carus-Verlag*, ed. Barbara Mohn and Hans Ryschawy (Stuttgart: Caraus, 1997), 115–24.
18. The composer himself seems to have felt some dissatisfaction, as he wrote to his family on January 21, 1832, in a much-quoted letter that refers to the central passage in D major: "Der Mittelsatz im forte d dur ist sehr dumm, und die ganze sogenannte Durchführung schmeckt mehr nach Contrapunct als nach Thran und Möven und Laberdan, und es sollte doch umgekehrt sein." Letter of January 21, 1832, from Paris; *Felix Mendelssohn: Sämtliche Briefe*, vol. 2, 467. The quotation is cited in Todd, *"The Hebrides" and Other Overtures*, 31, 33; the author introduces the term *synesthesia*, 88. On music and synesthesia, see B. M. Galeyev, "The Nature and Factors of Synesthesia in Music," *Leonardo*, vol. 40, no. 3 (2007): 285–88.
19. Peter Mercer-Taylor, "Mendelssohn as Border-Dweller," introduction to *The Companion to Mendelssohn*, ed. Mercer-Taylor (Cambridge: Cambridge University Press, 2004), 7; also Douglass Seaton, "Symphony and Overture," ibid., 102.
20. The pun here is on the line in James Thomson's poem "Rule, Britannia" (set to music by Thomas Arne ca. 1740), "Britannia, rule the waves." Mendelssohn may have known the setting from its use by Handel and Beethoven. The pun is not grammatically correct, since the verb in the poem is an injunction, not a statement.
21. Todd, *"The Hebrides" and Other Overtures*, 64. But see Paul Wingfield and Julian Horton, "Norm and Deformation in Mendelssohn's Sonata Forms," in *Mendelssohn Perspectives*, ed. Nicole Grimes and Angela R. Mace (Farnham: Routledge, 2012), 83–112.
22. Hans Keller, *Of German Music: A Symposium*, ed. Hans-Hubert Schönzeler (London: O. Wolff, 1976), 207.
23. Charles Rosen, *The Romantic Generation*, 571, notes that "Mendelssohn rounds off his phrases, his paragraphs, and eventually his sections with a certain comfortable sweetness."
24. Jerrold Levinson, "Hope in the Hebrides," in his *Music, Art, and Metaphysics: Essays in Philosophical Aesthetics* (Oxford: Oxford University Press, 1990), 336–75.
25. See Rosen, *The Romantic Generation*, 569.
26. James Garrett, "Mendelssohn and the Rise of Musical Historicism," in *The Cambridge Companion to Mendelssohn* (Cambridge: Cambridge University Press, 2004), 55.
27. See n14 above. Mori & Lavenu published the arrangement in London on October 15, 1833, and Breitkopf & Härtel published it in Leipzig in the same year. A later edition appeared as *The overture, to the Isles of Fingal, as a duett, for two performers on the piano forte, composed and dedicated to the Philharmonic Society by F. Mendelssohn Bartholdy* (London: Addison & Hodson [ca. 1845]). Breitkopf & Härtel published a new edition, edited by Christian Martin Schmidt (Wiesbaden, 2010). See also the summary

account in John Michael Cooper, "Knowing Mendelssohn," *Notes*, vol. 61, no. 1 (2004): 35–95, esp. 63–67. The dates on the manuscripts are misleading, as Mendelssohn began composing each new version within the existing autograph *after* applying the dates; see especially Cooper, "Philological and Textual Issues in Mendelssohn's Hebrides Overture, Op. 26," Philomusica Online 3 (2004) (*Revista del Dipartimento di Musicologia e Beni Culturali dell' Università degli Studi di Pavia*).

28. The autograph score is now in the Bodleian Library, Oxford, with the shelfmark MS. M. Deneke Mendelssohn d.71.
29. Balázs Mikusi, "Mendelssohn's 'Scottish' Tonality," *19th-Century Music*, vol. 29, no. 3 (2006), 240–60; Matthew Gelbart, "Once More to Mendelssohn's Scotland: The Laws of Music, the Double Tonic, and the Sublimation of Modality," *19th-Century Music*, vol. 37, no. 1 (2013), 3–36.
30. BL Add. MS 48597. See R. Larry Todd, "Mendelssohn's Ossianic Manner, with a New Source—'On Lena's Gloomy Heath,'" in *Mendelssohn and Schumann: Essays on Their Music and Its Context*, ed. Jon W. Finson and R. Larry Todd (Durham, NC: Duke University Press, 1984), 139–60; reprinted in R. Larry Todd, *Mendelssohn Essays* (New York: Routledge, 2007), 51–72.
31. "Das was mir eine Musik ausspricht, die ich liebe, sind mir [nicht] zu *unbestimmte* Gedanken, um sie in Worte zu fassen, sondern zu *bestimmte*." See also John Michael Cooper, "Words without Songs? Of Texts, Titles, and Mendelssohn's Lieder ohne Worte," in *Musik als Text: Bericht über den internationalen Kongreß der Gesellschaft für Musikforschung, Freiburg im Breisgau 1993*, ed. Hermann Danuser and Tobias Plebuch, 2 vols. (Kassel: Bärenreiter, 1998), vol. 2, 341–46.
32. Cooper, ibid., 341.
33. Liszt, "Berlioz und seine Haroldsinfonie," *Neue Zeitschrift für Musik* 4 (1855), 39. Liszt nevertheless went on to compose his *Großes Konzertstück über Mendelssohns Lieder ohne Worte* for two pianos (1834).
34. Breitkopf & Härtel published the full score in 1854; the autograph score is untraced. Gade himself made a four-hand piano version shortly after the first performance, in 1841.
35. Daverio, "Schumann's Ossianic Manner," 247–73; for the account of Gade's opus 1 and *Comala*, see 254–59.
36. Heinrich Heine, *Die Romantische Schule* (Hamburg, 1836), 347.
37. Ibid., 260–61.
38. Mendelssohn's Piano Quartet in B minor, op. 3, composed in 1824 and published a year later, was arguably his first fully mature work; it was dedicated to Goethe. The approval of Cherubini, when the composer had it performed at the Paris Conservatoire, may have been a factor in his choice of key. See Todd, "The Chamber Music of Mendelsssohn," in Stephen E. Hefling, ed., *Nineteenth-Century Chamber Music* (New York: Routledge, 2004), 178.
39. John Reed, *The Schubert Song Companion*, 492.
40. Mendelssohn's companion on the trip to the island, Karl Klingemann wrote, "Staffa mit seinen närrischen Basaltpfeifern und Höhlen steht in allen Bildenbüchern . . ." (Staffa with its peculiar basalt pillars and caves is in all the picture books), in *Mendelssohn Bartholdy: Sämtliche Briefe*, vol. 1, 366.

41. Coleridge's poem "Kubla Khan," with its images of a cavern "measureless to man," was published in 1816. The poem is supposed to have resulted from an opium-induced dream. Coleridge contemplated an opera based on "Carthon." See John J. Dunn, "Coleridge's Debt to Macpherson's Ossian," *Studies in Scottish Literature*, vol. 7, no. 1 (1969), 76–89.
42. See Rita Steblin, *A History of Key Characteristics* (cited in chapter 8). C. F. D. Schubart listed the characteristics of each of the keys in his *Ideen zu einer Aesthetik der Tonkunst* (Vienna, 1806; reprint Hildesheim: Olms, 1996, 2002).
43. In a letter of March 12, 1842, Mendelssohn wrote to Ferdinand David that the *maestoso* finale should be "Ordentlich deutlich und stark, wie ein Männerchor"; quoted in Martin Witte, "Zur Programmgebundenheit der Sinfonien Mendelssohns," in *Das Problem Mendelssohn*, ed. Carl Dahlhaus (Regensburg: G. Bosse, 1974), 119–27; here, 123.
44. See also Peter Mercer-Taylor, "Mendelssohn's 'Scottish' Symphony and the Music of German Memory," *19th-Century Music* 19, no. 1 (1995), 68–82. The reception of Mendelssohn's works in Germany is discussed by Albrecht Riethmüller, "Das 'Problem Mendelssohn,'" *Archiv für Musikwissenschaft* 59, 3 (2002), 210–21.

Chapter Nine

1. Salgar, spelled thus in "The Songs of Selma," although pronounced "Shalgar."
2. See Ulrike Küster, *Das Melodrama: Zum ästhetikgeschichtlichen Zusammenhang von Dichtung und Musik im 18. Jahrhundert* (Frankfurt-am-Main: Lang, 1994).
3. On the *mélodrame* in France, see Emilio Sala, "Mélodrame: Définitions et métamorphoses d'un genre quasi-opératique," *Revue de Musicologie* 84, no. 2 (1998), 235–46.
4. The autograph score of Rust's *Colma* is Mus. Ms. no. 19106, State Library, Berlin. Another little-known work with Ossianic associations, the *Werther* of Gaetano Pugnani (1731–1798), composed in 1791–92, exemplifies the Italian counterpart of the monodrama, namely the *melólogo*.
5. Rust's text may have been derived from Christian Himburg's edition of Goethe's *Werther*, first issued in Berlin in 1775 and in subsequent editions in 1777 and 1779. These editions show some unauthorized if minor changes by the publisher; on this see Siegfried Unseld, *Goethe and His Publishers*, trans. Kenneth J. Northcott (Chicago: University of Chicago Press, 1996), 67. The edition entitled *German Settings of Ossianic Texts 1770–1815*, ed. Sarah Clemmens Waltz (Madison: A-R Editions, 2016), does not include Rust's setting of 1780. The editor apparently believes that "the story was set as a monodrama with a spoken text" (n.38). There are in fact two prominent arias as well as spoken commentary.
6. At the end of the manuscript are three and one half pages, with one page crossed out; these appear to be a discarded version of the *larghetto* passage.
7. The only extant duodramas on related texts were Franz von Stubenvoll's *Selmar und Selma* (ca. 1800) from Klopstock's poem (later set by Schubert, D286) and *Sulmalle* (1802), for soloists and chorus, by Bernhard Anselm Weber (1764–1821), teacher of Meyerbeer.

8. Rust also contributed incidental music for the dramas *Fingal in Lochlin* (1782) and *Inamorulla oder Ossians Grosmuth* (1783), by Karl Heinrich Wachsmuth (1760–1836).
9. See Gunter Maier, *Die Lieder Johann Rudolf Zumsteegs und ihr Verhältnis zu Schubert* (Göppingen: Kummerle, 1971); Walther Dürr, "'Kolmas Klage': Schuberts Auseinandersetzung mit Reichardts Liedästhetik," *Schubert Jahrbuch 2006–2009*, ed. Volkmar Hansen and Silke Hoffmann (Duisburg: Schubert-Gesellschaft, 2008), 109–26.
10. The song went into seven editions, until 1828. See Matthias Wessel, *Die Ossian-Dichtung*, 101–2. For a modern edition, see Waltz, ed., *German Settings of Ossianic Texts, 1770–1815*, xxi–xxiii, 55–91, 155.
11. See Otto Erich Deutsch, ed., *Schubert: Die Erinnerungen seiner Freunde* (Leipzig: Breitkopf & Härtel Musik-Verlag, 1966), 149.
12. Goethe made two translations of "The Songs of Selma," one for Friederike Brion in 1771 (unpublished in his lifetime), the other for his novel *Die Leiden des jungen Werthers* (1774).
13. Goethe met with Zumsteeg in 1797 and praised the latter's setting as a cantata with piano accompaniment only ("als Cantate, doch nur mit Begleitung des Claviers gesetzt"); see Gunter Maier, *Die Lieder Johann Rudolf Zumsteegs*, 35.
14. Fanny Mendelssohn wrote to Felix mocking Zelter's inability to conduct Bach's *St. Matthew Passion* following Felix's own brilliant concert version, saying that Zelter did not understand the music; see R. Larry Todd, *Mendelssohn: A Life in Music*, 211.
15. See chapter 8, n. 54.
16. Ludwig Gottlieb Crome's iambic translation is in *Unterhaltungen*, vol. 4, no. 1 (1767), "Episode aus dem altschottischen Gedichte Fingal," 617–20. It was reprinted in C. H. Schmid, *Zusätze zur Theorie der Poesie und Nachrichten von den besten Dichtern* (Leipzig, 1767–69); A. F. Ursinus, ed., *Balladen und Lieder altenglischer und altschottischer Dichtart* (Berlin, 1777); and Crome's *Gedichte* (Leipzig, 1795).
17. For a modern edition, see Waltz, ed., *German Settings of Ossianic Texts, 1770–1815*, xlvii–xlviii, 124–49, 156.
18. This is notably similar to Schubert's opening of his "Kolmas Klage," with slow triplet chords in C minor (bars 3–4).
19. On Zelter's drive for the institutionalization of "serious" music, see Celia Applegate, "How German Is It? Nationalism and the Idea of Serious Music in the Early Nineteenth Century," *19th-Century Music* 21, no. 3 (1998), 274–96.
20. The author is unnamed, but may have been Reichardt himself. The first line echoes a line in stanza 4 of Herder's poem "Morgengesang" (Morning Song) in his *Werke: Erster Theil: Gedichte* (Berlin, 1879): "Rund um mich her zur Nacht."
21. The other two songs are "Armins Klage um seine Kinder" and "Kolnadona." The element of lament (*Klage*) is present in several of Reichardt's songs in this collection. For a modern edition of these songs, see *German Settings of Ossianic Texts 1770–1815*, xli–xlv, 92–103, 155.
22. Christian Friedrich Daniel Schubart, *Ideen zu einer Ästhetik der Tonkunst* (Vienna, 1806; new ed. Hildesheim: Olms, 1990), 378.
23. *Goethe Mélanges (Annales de 1749 à 1822)* (Paris, 1863), 30–79.
24. Reichardt's *Lieder aus dem Liederspiel Lieb' und Treu* was published in Berlin by Johann Friedrich Unger in 1800; the first song in the collection is a setting of Goethe's

"Heidenröslein." Reichardt's letter-essay, "Etwas über das Liederspiel," appeared in the Leipzig *Allgemeine Musikalische Zeitung* 43 (July 22, 1801), 709–17. See Susan Youens, *Schubert, Müller and Die Schöne Mullerin* (New York: Cambridge University Press, 1997), 205n8.

25. See *Johann Friedrich Reichardt: Autobiographische Schriften*, ed. Günter Hartung (Halle: Mitteldeutscher Verlag, 2002); *Johann Friedrich Reichardt, Der Lustige Passagier: Errinerungen eines Musikers und Literaten*, ed. Walter Salmen (Freiburg: Atlantis, 1963; Hildesheim: Olms, 2002).

26. Schubert made both major and minor changes to the text, omitting vv. 6 and 9 and, for instance, substituting "entblösst" (bared [sword]) for Reichardt's "gezückt" (drawn) in v. 5.

27. See Raymond Monelle, "Word Setting in the Strophic Lied," *Music & Letters* 65, no. 3 (1984), 229: "The meaning of the word 'Lied' embraced, among other things, a strophic arrangement, for the Lied was meant to reflect the emotions and techniques of oral tradition. This strophic arrangement can be seen, either in fact or echo, through the literature of German song, but Schubert's songs show a resolute departure from it in the direction of *durchkomponieren*."

28. In the manuscript, Schubert noted about the strophes, "Die zweyte Strophe wird durchgehends leiser gesungen, doch die dritte desto stürmischer" (The second strophe should be sung throughout more softly, but the third much more impetuously). Schubert appears at one point to have changed the harmony in the RH part in bar 2, at the word "Nacht," but then crossed it out to maintain triplet eighth notes on the lower C minor chord (second inversion), making the harmonic change above the pedal C only in bars 3–4, at "[ich] irr allein."

Chapter Ten

1. See Rita Benton, "Jean-Frédéric Edelmann, A Musical Victim of the French Revolution," *The Musical Quarterly* 50, no. 2 (1964): 165–87.

2. Even now, a critic could claim with justification that "trop sérieux pour les français, pas assez profond pour les allemands, Gouvy souffre aujourd'hui d'une méconnaissance profonde" (too serious for the French, not deep enough for the Germans, Gouvy suffers today from a profound misunderstanding). See Benjamin Ballifh, Classiquenews.com (31.12.2013); and Martin Kaltenecker's thesis, "Théodore Gouvy" (PhD diss., Paris-Sorbonne, 1986; English version, Lille: M. Kaltenecker, 1987); also Herbert Schneider, ed., *Bericht über den Internationalen Kongreß—Actes du Colloque International Saarbrücken/Homburg-Haut* (Hildesheim: Olms, 2008).

3. It is often listed as a "choral work" but is in fact for baritone or bass ("voix de basse") solo and orchestra.

4. In his diary, Tchaikovsky refers to meeting Gouvy at Reinecke's house in Leipzig in 1888 and says he was surprised to encounter a Frenchman who praised the musical life in Germany to the detriment of his own nation. See Rosa Newmarch, *Tchaikovsky: His Life and Works* (St. Clair Shores, MI: Scholarly Press, 1969), 202.

5. Libraries that hold the score give various dates of publication, sometimes only "1860s," but the Catalogue of the Bibliothèque Nationale lists the work as published by the firm of S. [Simon] Richault in 1858; it was engraved in Leipzig by C. G. Röder.
6. On this point, see Paul Van Tieghem, *Ossian en France* (Paris: Rieder, 1917), vol. 2, 38. I am grateful to Howard Gaskill for this reference.
7. Baour-Lormian seems to have made his version of the passage from "Berrathon" by paraphrasing Le Tourneur's translation. For the original English of Macpherson, see *The Works of James Macpherson* (London, 1765), vol. 1, 370. Gouvy himself may have made the parallel German text. Some minor variations from the French and German texts printed separately are apparent in the music score realization. See appendix 2.
8. From l.14 the text differs from the 1822 edition, and again from l.17. The line "quand ta fureur est apaisée" is now "quand ta colère est apaisée," and the original "Ô le plus grand des rois" has been changed to "Ô mon père, ô mon roi."
9. "Je l'intends . . . il m'appelle . . . ô Fingal, ô mon roi! / Ô mon père adoré, me voici près de toi!"
10. Gouvy does not set the final couplet of the French text that is printed separately.
11. Among the competitors setting the Darcours text at the Académie des Beaux-Arts was Alfred Bruneau (1857–1934), later to influence the direction of French opera, and Raymond Bonheur (1861–1939), friend of Debussy. The judges included Ambroise Thomas, Gounod, Massenet, and Delibes.
12. The idea of "frontiers" or "boundaries" in the title of this chapter is not only geographical. Another borderland composer, the Alsace-born Marie Jaëll (b. Marie Trautmann, 1846–1925), is best known for her theories on piano pedagogy; her most famous pupil was Albert Schweitzer. After marrying the Austrian pianist Alfred Jaëll in 1866, she was for a while part-time secretary to Liszt in Weimar. Liszt so admired her stupendous pianistic ability that he dedicated his *Third Mephisto Waltz* to her. In 1879, the year that saw her admitted to the Société nationale des compositeurs de musique, Marie Jaëll completed an ambitious symphonic poem, *Ossiane*. In this work, the bard Ossian is changed from narrator to protagonist, and from man to woman, as she ascends to the usually unattainable summits inhabited by the god of harmony, Bélès. As an unusual contribution to a form originating with Franck and Liszt, *Ossiane* is laid out for impressive forces: soprano solo, mixed chorus, and a large orchestra that includes triple woodwinds, four horns, three trumpets, four trombones and tuba, four saxhorns, two harps, percussion, and strings. The three-part work, Wagnerian in scale and harmonic richness, had only one airing, when the Orchestre Colonne performed two large extracts on May 13, 1879, in the Salle Érard, Paris. For this premiere, Charles Grandmougin (1850–1930) translated Jaëll's original German text into French. See Sébastien Troester, "A Passion for Composing," in the booklet for the 3-CD set *Marie Jaëll: Portraits*, vol. 3, 73–88 (issued by the Palazzetto Bru Zane for the Centre de musique romantique française). Further, Sébastien Troester, "*Ossiane* ou les *Götterlieder* de Marie Jaëll: Une œuvre musicale hors du commun—Première partie," *Association Marie Jaëll–Alsace: Lettre d'information* 9 (May 2014): 1–3, and "Seconde partie," *Lettre d'information* 10 (November 2014): 3–5. I am grateful to Ralph Locke for drawing Jaëll's work to my attention.
13. The autograph score of *Fingal* is noted in the Catalogue of the Bibliothèque nationale de France as MS-6959 (3).

14. "Lucien Hillemacher/FINGAL/Scène lyrique/Poème de Charles Darcours/Partition, Chant et Piano/Premier Grand Prix de Composition Musicale/Académie des Beaux-Arts/Paris/Alphonse Leduc [1880]." In this regard, compare the "semi-staged" cantatas of Jongen (1897) and Malling (1902).
15. The notion that the sustained E-flat chords echo the opening of Wagner's *Das Rheingold* is speculative, but it is likely that Hillemacher would have been familiar with Wagner's score even though the opera was not performed in Paris until 1901. Schott Söhne Mainz had issued the first printing in 1873.
16. *La Fantaisie artistique et littéraire: Journal hebdomadaire*, November 13, 1880: 13.
17. Victorin Joncières, *Les Annales de Theatre et de la musique* (Paris, 1881), 737.
18. Massenet, in an interview for *Le Figaro*, January 19, 1884, admitted that some of his students at the conservatoire were even more Wagnerian than he; one of these students may well have been Hillemacher. See Steven Huebner, "Massenet and Wagner: Bridling the Influence," *Cambridge Opera Journal* 5, no. 3 (1993): 223–38; here, 226.
19. The quotation is culled from Goethe's novel; the short passage from "Berrathon" there supplies the text of the aria. For a study of Massenet's *Werther*, see Jean-Christophe Branger, "*Werther* de Jules Massenet: Un 'drame lyrique' français ou germanique? Sources et analyse des motifs récurrents," *Revue de musicologie* 87, no. 2 (2001): 419–83.
20. See Jean-Christophe Branger and Alban Ramaut, eds., *Le naturalisme sur la scène lyrique* (St. Etienne: Publications de l'Université de Saint-Étienne, 2004); also, by the same authors, *Le livret d'opéra au temps de Massenet: Actes du colloque des 9–10 novembre 2001, Festival Massenet* (St. Etienne, 2002).

Chapter Eleven

1. Bismarck's younger sister (1827–1904) was named Malwine (i.e., Malvina), a female name in the Bismarck family. Their elder brother Bernhard (1810–93) married Malwine Heloise von Lettow-Vorbeck in 1848. Malwine (or Malwina) as a female forename is still found in Germany, Poland, Finland, and Sweden.
2. See Barbara Eichner, *History in Mighty Sounds: Musical Construction of German National Identity 1848–1914* (Woodbridge: Boydell, 2012), 36; also Daniel Beller-McKenna, *Brahms and the German Spirit* (Cambridge, MA: Harvard University Press, 2004).
3. Max Bruch based his popular cantata *Frithjof* (1864) for soloists, male chorus, and orchestra on an epic poem by the Swedish writer Esaias Tegnér (1782–1846), an admirer of Ossian; Tegnér presented in it an idealized picture of Viking heroism. The popularity of Bruch's work may well have influenced the staging of Hopffer's opera in 1871. See Eichner, *History in Mighty Sounds*, 213–14.
4. Emil provided Max Bruch with the libretto for the opera *Hermione*, op. 40 (1872), and Carl Reinthaler with that for his opera *Edda* (1875). On Bruch's opera, see Christopher Fifield, *Max Bruch: His Life and Work* (Woodbridge: Boydell Press, 1988; new ed. 2005), 127–29.
5. The story of Sakuntala was also the subject of a substantial opera sketch by Schubert (1820), to a text by his friend Johann Philipp Neumann.

6. The lodge is not far from the Niederwalddenkmal, the huge monument to German reunification begun on September 16, 1871, when Wilhelm I laid the first stone. Brahms, who visited Rüdesheim frequently between 1874 and 1895, was present at the event.
7. [Wilhelm] Röstell, "Hopffer, Bernhard," in *Allgemeine Deutsche Biographie* 13 (1881): 105–6.
8. The title page reads: "Louis Ehlert/freundschaflichst zugeeignet./Darthula's Grabesgesang/(Aus Ossian übersetzt von Goethe)/für/Frauenchor und Sopran-Solo/mit Orchester/componirt/von/Bernhard Hopffer/op. 23 . . . Berlin,/Verlag und Eigenthum der Schlesinger'schen Buch & Musikhandlung (Rob. Lienau)." The error of identifying the poet as Goethe rather than Herder was common in the nineteenth century.
9. *Gedichte Ossians, eines alten celtischen Dichters* (Vienna, 1768–69). In 1784 Denis recast his version to accord with Macpherson's English version of 1773.
10. See Wolf Gerhard Schmidt, "The Discursive Function of *Ossian*," 189–90.
11. In the MS, Herder had the correct "Seláma's" (Seláma is in Ulster), but seems to have misremembered it by the time the translation was published.
12. "Maiden of Colla, you are asleep! Around you the blue streams of Selma are silent! They mourn for you, the last of Truthil's line! When will you rise again in your beauty, the most beautiful of Erin's maidens? You are sleeping in your grave a long sleep, and your dawn is distant! Never, Oh never more will the sun come to wake you from your rest: awake, awake Darthula! Spring is out there, the breezes sough, and on the green hills, lovely maiden, flowers wave! In the grove leaves are growing! Withdraw forever, Oh sun, from the maiden of Colla, she is asleep. Never shall she rise again in her beauty! Never more will you see her move in her loveliness." The opening address to the moon in the original poem, "Daughter of Heav'n," has produced one notable response in the cantata (ca. 1775) by Thomas Linley the Younger (see chapter 12). The "wenn" in line 5 is not a printer's error for "wann" but an interrogative usage common in Herder's time.
13. See chapter 12.
14. Sabina Teller Ratner, *Camille Saint-Saëns, 1875–1921: A Thematic Catalogue of his Complete Works, vol. 1: The Instrumental Works* (Oxford: Oxford University Press, 2002), 514. Saint-Saëns set Baour-Lormian's poem "Invocation à la lune" for voice and piano (1855), with a flowing accompaniment that influenced Debussy's more famous piano piece (ca. 1890) from his *Suite Bergamasque*, itself an evocation of Verlaine's poem "Clair de lune" (1869).
15. Yannick Simon, *L'Association artistique d'Angers: Histoire d'une société de concerts populaires, suivie du repertoire des programmes des concerts* (Paris: Société de musicologie française, 2008).
16. The full title is *Un RÊVE d'OSSIAN/Scène lyrique/pour Soli, Chœur et Orchestre/Imitée des Poëmes Gaëliques/Paroles de/Henry Moreau. Musique de JULES BORDIER*. Paris: Durand, Schoenewerk & Co., 1885. The short score for voice and piano is by the composer.
17. Antonin-Guillot-Valeton de Sainbris (1820–87), born in Bordeaux, was a singing teacher who settled in Versailles, where in 1866 he founded the Société chorale d'amateurs, a body he directed for twenty years.
18. The painting was removed at the fall of the empire, and twenty years later Ingres bought the painting back from a Roman art dealer. The artist had it restored and modified in 1835. It is held at the Musée Ingres, Montauban.

19. The significance of the lyre, which unlike the triangular harp is square in construction, was perhaps the result of the influence of Mme. de Staël and her famous novel *Corinne, ou l'Italie* (Paris, 1807); the two instruments are often interchangeable in literary accounts.
20. Macpherson himself remarked on this aspect of the poems. One more recent commentator, Herbert Schöffler, has argued that the absence of religion in the Ossianic world was attractive for a modern reading public at a time when traditional Christian belief was coming under strain, especially in Germany in the mid-nineteenth century: see his *Deutscher Geist im 18. Jahrhundert: Essays zur Geistes- und Religionsgeschichte, hrsg. von Gøtz von Sell* (Göttingen: Vandenhoeck & Ruprecht, 1956), 135–54.
21. See Robert Tombs, *The War Against Paris, 1871* (Cambridge, 1981); also "How Bloody Was the *Semaine sanglante*? A revision," *The Historical Journal* 55, no. 3 (2012): 619–704. The Commune was a key element in the thinking of Karl Marx about revolution: see Marx, *The Civil War in France: The Paris Commune* (New York, 1984).
22. Some of this violence may have been inspired by the poetry of Auguste Lacaussade (1815–97), born in Saint-Denis de l'Île Bourbon, who translated Ossian in 1842 but also, in *Le Siège de Paris* (1871), penned a savage denunciation of the Prussian seizure of the city in 1870; see Christine Raguet, "Lacaussade's Translation of Macpherson—A Literalist Perspective in 1842," in *Through Other Eyes: The Distribution of Anglophone Literature in Europe*, ed. Richard Trim and Sophie Alatorre (Newcastle-upon-Tyne: Cambridge Scholars Publishing, 2007), 99–112. "Tura" (*Fingal*) is a castle in Ulster.
23. Enrico Mattioda, "Ossian in Italy," 274–302; here, 300.
24. The literature on this phenomenon includes Otto Elben's classic, *Der volkstümliche deutsche Männergesang: Geschichte und Stellung im Leben der Nation; der deutsche Sängerbund und seine Glieder* (Tübingen: H. Laupp, 1887). More recent studies are: Dietmar Klenke, *Der singende "deutsche Mann": Gesangvereine und deutsche Nationalbewußtsein von Napoleon bis Hitler* (Münster: Waxmann, 1998); Joep Leersen, "German Influence: Choirs, Repertoires, Nationalities," in Krisztina Lajosi and Andreas Stynen, eds., *Choral Societies and Nationalism in Europe* (Leiden: Brill, 2015), 14–32.
25. His opera *Evanthia* won second prize in the competition, in which 124 composers participated. Published by Verlag Martin Oberdörffer, Leipzig (1893), it was accepted for performance at the Dresden Court Theatre. First prize in the competition was awarded to the Austrian composer Josef Forster for his *Die Rose von Pontevedra*. See Walter Frisch, *German Modernism: Music and the Arts* (Berkeley: University of California Press, 2005), 66–67.
26. AGANDECCA/Dramatisches Gedicht/nach Ossian/für/Soli, Männerchor und Orchester/in Musik gesetzt/und dem/Männergesangverein Liederkranz/zu Frankfurt a/M/gewidmet/von/PAUL UMLAUFT./Op. 40/Leipzig: Verlag von Hans Licht/Hof-Musikalienhandlung, 1884. Several other editions were issued: Leipzig: Licht & Meyer, ca. 1890; Leipzig & Dresden: Klemm, ca. 1890; and Chemnitz: Schmidt, ca. 1890. The original autograph score is housed at the Westfälisches Musikarchiv Hagen, no. 936, boxes 572–73 and boxes 578–79.
27. The piece is the third of four in Reinecke's *Durstige Lieder von Jul. Meyer für 4stimmigen Männerchor*, op. 140: "Der Morgen bestrahlte mit röthlichem Glanz."

28. The Frankfurt Liederkranz was one of the oldest male groups in Germany, founded on February 15, 1828. The chorus parts in the full score are placed between the violas and cellos.
29. It might also have reminded Umlauft of Beethoven's *Trinklied* (WoO 109), "Erhebt das Glas mit froher Hand," with its line in stanza 2, "Nur trinkt, erhebt den Becher hoch / Ihr Brüder, hoch!" (Now drink, brothers, lift high the cup!)"
30. At this point, the composer indicates that a cut may be made, to the *maestoso* section beginning "Heil ihm, dem König tapfer und stark" (p. 37 in the piano reduction).
31. The composer adapted the lines from Herder's "Darthula's Grabesgesang," and inserted the rest of the poem toward the end of scene 3.
32. The *Neue Zeitschrift für Musik* 72, no. 5 (January 25, 1905), for instance, reported a performance of the "valuable" (wertvolle) *Agandecca* in a "brilliant" (glanzvoll) performance at Frankenthal in the Rhineland-Palatinate.
33. *Musikalisches Wochenblatt* 26, no. 23 (May 30, 1895).
34. *The Musical Times* 34, no. 607 (September 1, 1893): 553.

Chapter Twelve

1. The name is usually printed without the hyphen in musical settings, and as "Dartula" in Italian. German settings before 1900, as in Herder's poem, often use the apostrophe in the title name.
2. The story has appeared in a recent retelling in German as *Darthula, Tochter der Nebel: Ein ossianischer Roman*, by Petra Hartmann (Dortmund: Arcanum-Fantasy-Verlag, 2010).
3. See Derick S. Thomson, *The Gaelic Sources of Macpherson's Ossian*, 53–55; also Joseph Falaky Nagy, "Observations on the Ossianesque in Medieval Irish Literature and Modern Irish Folklore," *Journal of American Folklore* 114, no. 454: 436–46.
4. For the Seckendorf setting, see Matthias Wessel, *Die Ossian-Dichtung*, 92–94; also Sarah Clemmens Waltz, ed., *German Settings of Ossian*.
5. Leipzig: In der Breitkopfischen Musikhandlung, 1795.
6. Published in the third volume of his *Volks- und andere Lieder* (Dessau, 1782), 26–31. The manuscript copy in the Staatsbibliothek, Berlin (Mus.ms 30159) is in a leather book with the owner's initials "EHVB" and the date "1774." The caption for the song includes the phrase "Volkslied v. Fr. v. Seckend." It is likely that Seckendorff, as a member of the stellar circle around Duchess Anna Amalia in Weimar, obtained the manuscript of Herder's translation before it was published in 1778–79. The two misprints in the published song—"Blumen" (flowers) instead of "blauen" (blue), and "Winde" (winds) for "Lüfte" (breezes)—are corrected at the end of the song. For the first line of stanza 2, Seckendorff has "erscheinst" (appear) instead of "erstehst" (arise) and in line 16 he substitutes "weichst du dann" (will you soften, then?) for "weiche denn" (withdraw).
7. See Carl von Dittersdorf, *Lebensbeschreibung* (Munich, 1999); trans. A. D. Coleridge, *The Autobiography of Karl von Dittersdorf* (London: Bentley & Son, 1896).
8. Zumsteeg's setting was published in *Kleine Lieder und Balladen* (1782), the text by von Harold; Christmann's copy appeared in *Blumenleser für Klavierliebhaber* (1785).

9. In their settings of the poem "Colma," Rust, Zelter, and Zumsteeg all gravitate toward the tonality of E-flat or its relative minor (C minor). The key of E-flat has often been associated with ideas of nobility and heroism, as in Beethoven's "Eroica" Symphony, the "Emperor" Piano Concerto, and Piano Sonata No. 4, op. 7. For C minor, see chapter 4 of Charles Rosen, *Music and Sentiment* (New Haven: Yale University Press, 2011).
10. Macpherson does not indicate what the usual or idiomatic pronunciation might be, although the presence of the hyphen suggests that it is the second syllable that is stressed; Comala, Crimora, Malvina, and Oithóna are analogous female names normally pronounced with the emphasis on the penultimate syllable.
11. On glees, see Brian Robins, *Catch and Glee Culture in Eighteenth Century England* (Woodbridge: Boydell Press, 2006). Also, *Recollections of R. J. S. Stevens: An Organist in Georgian London*, ed. Mark Argent (London: Macmillan, 1992).
12. See *The Posthumous Works of Mr Linley and Mr T Linley (published by Mrs Linley)* (London, 1800?), 24–39; also Gwilym Beechey, "Thomas Linley, 1756–78, and his Vocal Music," *The Musical Times* 119, no. 1626 (1978): 669–71.
13. There is only a brief reference to *Darthula* in the study by Peter Overbeck, *Die Chorwerke von Thomas Linley dem Jüngeren: Analyse, Vergleich, kompositorisches und biographisches Umfeld* (Hildesheim, 2000), 70.
14. See the list of Schubert's twelve Ossian settings in Wessel, *Die Ossian-Dichtung*, 243–44. On Harold, see Diarmaid ó Catháin, "General Baron Edmund Harold (1737–1808), A 'Celtic' Writer in Germany," *Studia Hibernica* 30 (1998–99): 119–53.
15. Otto Erich Deutsch, *Schubert, a Documentary Biography* (1946); also Roger Fiske, *Scotland in Music*, 84–87, 200–206; further, Alan Crawford Howie, "Schubert and the 'Exotic'—the Macpherson ('Ossian') and Walter Scott Settings," *The Schubertian: Journal of the Schubert Institute*, nos. 39 (April 2003): 12–21, and 40 (July 2003): 15–21.
16. See chapter 9.
17. Lindner's setting is closest to Schubert's homophonic style in its simplicity of treatment—that is, chords moving together with the voice.
18. The manuscript in Berlin (Mus. Ms. autogr. K. G. P. Grädener 1 N [2]) notes of this setting that it is op. 63, no. 2, and that it is dedicated to Karl Hill (1831–1893), the German operatic baritone who sang the role of Alberich at the first performance of Wagner's *Ring* at Bayreuth on August 23, 1876, and that of Klingsor in *Parsifal* at the premiere, on July 26, 1882.
19. Edward F. Kravitt, *The Lied: Mirror of Late Romanticism* (New Haven: Yale University Press, 1996), 166. Adolf Jensen also composed a duet for Frithjof and Ingeborg in 1858, an orchestrated fragment of ten pages (Mus. MS 10132, Bayerische Nationalbibliothek).
20. MS 4442 (Bibliotecamedia di Santa Cecilia, Rome). The composer's name at the top of the page has been erased. He is described in an obituary as "one of the most gifted of the younger generation of Italian composers." See *The Musical Times and Singing Circular* 3, no. 571 (1890): 551.
21. The princess came from a large family prominent in Moscow's cultural life. One of her relatives was Aleksandr Aleksandrovich Shakhovskoi (1777–1846), whose *Fingal i Rozkrana*, a dramatic poem "taken from the poems of Ossian," with music by the Venetian composer Caterino Cavos (1775–1840), was performed in 1824. Cavos was a pupil of Francesco Bianchi, and moved to St. Petersburg in 1797.

22. The title page of the manuscript reads, "Poesia e musica di ——" (the name of Leonardi has been obliterated).
23. The text used by Brahms for "Gesang aus Fingal" was not, as is often asserted, by Herder or an anonymous hand, but by Eduard Brinckmeier, whose translation *Ossians Gedichte* was published in Braunschweig in 1839; see Andreas Zurbriggen, "Eduard Brinckmeier als Übersetzer des 'Gesang aus Fingal': Eine Richtigstellung," *Brahms-Studien*, vol. 17, ed. Beatrix Borchard and Kerstin Schüssler-Bach (Tutzing: Johannes-Brahms-Gesellschaft, 2014), 113–34.
24. See chapter 11.
25. The orchestration includes two horns and harp. The fact of its length is not included in the library description of the piece, "Darthulas Grabgesang aus Ossian" (Mus NL145: Aba 5). See Heinrich Aerni, *Zwischen USA und Deutschem Reich: Hermann Hans Wetzler (1870–1943): Dirigent und Komponist* (Kassel: Bärenreiter, 2015). The MS is dated "5.V. [18] 88."
26. Had Brahms used the translation as printed in Herder's later publication *Stimmen der Völker in Liedern* (Tübingen, 1807), he would have found the grammatically more accurate "Schönstes der Schönen."
27. Brahms was not the only composer to mispronounce an Ossianic name: Méhul does it with "Malvin-AH" in *Uthal*, and Niels Gade, in his cantata, opus 12, consistently stresses "Comala" on the first syllable: CO-mala. The tendency, even for some native English speakers, to mispronounce names in the poems of Ossian had pushed Harriet Wainewright earlier to ensure that in her published score of *Comàla*, a mark resembling the French *accent grave* was placed above the second syllable. See also the case of Jongen, chapter 13.
28. Karl Geiringer, *Brahms: His Life and Work* (London: Allen & Unwin, 1956), 124.
29. Geiringer, *Brahms*, 336. While averse to writing for the stage, Brahms toyed with the idea of an opera: in April 1870 he wrote his friend Julius Allgeyer asking for a copy of Méhul's libretto for his Ossianic opera *Uthal*, performed in Paris in 1806. Brahms's Serenade No. 2, like Méhul's opera, omits violins from the orchestral texture.
30. He would surely have known settings of this poem by Seckendorff [Dittersdorf], Lindner, Bürgel, Reinthaler, Hill, and Taubert, since his setting of 1861 was published only in 1872.
31. No musicologist appears to have noticed this disparity in the placement of musical and verbal accentuation. In his adulatory study of the composer, Hans Gál, commenting on the stylistic differences in this piece, claims merely that "because the musical construction flows so naturally from the words and their expression, one never has any sense of discrepancy." See Hans Gál, *Johannes Brahms: His Work and Personality*, trans. Joseph Stein (London: Weidenfeld & Nicolson, 1963), 126.
32. The autograph score is dated October 19, 1899. The libretto was published by De Erven H. van Munster & Zoon (Amsterdam, 1902).
33. *Annalen van de operagezelschappen in Nederland, 1886–1995*. See also *Stieger Opern-Katalog, Titel-Lexicon*, vol. 1, 299; Matthias Wessel, *Die Ossian-Dichtung*, 246, claims the premiere was in The Hague in 1900; Jahrmärker, *Ossian*, 324, adds Amsterdam, 1901, as a performance location.

34. I am grateful to Simon Groot, University of Amsterdam, for providing scans of both the manuscript piano reduction and full score by the composer (Ms-Mil-5/TNK 2520, Ms-Mil-6/TNK 2521, 2522).
35. See Leo Samama, "Willem Mengelberg: De woelige jaren, 1895–1920," March 18, 1987, https://www.opusklassiek.nl/dirigenten/opusklassiek_lsmengelberg_1895_1920.pdf, accessed January 30, 2019.
36. I thank Nathalie Vanballenberghe for her translation of the composer's spidery annotations in the score.
37. Ithorna, introduced here, appears to be an invention borrowed from Denis's translation of Ossian, where the name refers to an island: "I-thorno" becomes "Ithorna" in Denis. Macpherson's note in "Sul-malla of Lumon" reads: "'I-thorno,' says tradition, was an island of Scandinavia." Van Milligen most likely introduced Ithorna as a counterbalance to the male voices of Darthula's brothers.
38. See Tadeusz Okuljar and Martina Sichardt, eds., *Arnold Schoenberg: Sämtliche Werke, Abteilung V: Fragmente von Chorwerke und Kanons: Skizzen* (Mainz: Schott, 1991), 22–63. In the preface the editors describe the setting of *Darthulas Grabgesang* as "by far the most important" of Schoenberg's sketches. See also Jan Maegaard, "Schoenberg's Incomplete Works and Fragments," in *Constructive Dissonance: Arnold Schoenberg and the Transformations of Twentieth Century Culture*, ed. Juliane Brand and Christopher Hailey (Berkeley: University of California Press, 1997), 131–44. Maegaard cites a length of only thirty-eight bars, but this is only part of the first draft, where the orchestration is written out and where the chorus begins.
39. A list of the composer's works is available in Séamas de Barra, *Aloys Fleischmann (1880–1964)* (Dublin, 2006). See also Joseph P. Cunningham and Ruth Fleischmann, *Aloys Fleischmann: An Immigrant Musician in Ireland* (Cork: Cork University Press, 2010).
40. See Andreas Pernpeintner, *Verzeichnis der musikalischen Werke von Aloys Georg Fleischmann (1880–1964)*, 2013, https://doi.org/10.5282/ubm/epub.17560.
41. This strategy parallels to some extent the archaizing tendency of Schubert, using sparse harmonies, in his Ossian songs such as "Die Nacht" (D534).
42. See chapter 14 on the similar patriotic cast of C. V. Stanford's Ossianic tone poem.
43. I am grateful to Dr. Jürgen Schaarwaechter, Max-Reger-Institut, for providing me with a microfilm copy of Busch's manuscript score (film no. 0512).
44. The fair copy of the MS, with corrections and insertions, has forty-seven pages and bears the dedication "Meiner lieben Frieda [Busch's wife]." The same dedication prefaces Busch's opus 3a, *Drei Lieder* (for voice, viola, piano), published by Simrock in 1922. The second of the three songs is a setting of Goethe's 1775 poem "Wonne der Wehmuth" (Joy of Grief), an iconic phrase coined by Michael Denis in his translation of Macpherson's "Carric-thura." See also Tully Potter, *Adolf Busch: The Life of an Honest Musician*, 2 vols. (London: Toccata, 2007–10).
45. See Peter Graves, "Ossian in Sweden and Swedish-Speaking Finland," in *The Reception of Ossian in Europe*, 207. In his rendering of the title, Runeberg mistranslates Herder's phrase "Mädchen von Kola" (daughter of Colla) as "Flicka från Kola" (maiden from Kola), as if "Kola" were a place name.
46. Published by Gehrmans Kvartett-Bibliotek, 102.
47. Austrian National Library, Vienna, MS F108 Neumann.45: "5 Lieder für eine Singstimme mit Klavier" (undated).

48. Universal Edition published the song as no. 7 of Knab's *Naturlieder* (1929).
49. See Kravitt, *The Lied*, 121–22.
50. In both the MS and the published song, the direction is *Aber nicht schleppen*, which makes it sound more like an imperative than an infinitive.

Chapter Thirteen

1. Rasse's cantata *Comala* exists only in autograph score, but an extract for mezzo soprano and orchestra or piano was published, without date: "Scène dramatique: La nuit entend son voile sombre sur la plaine."
2. *Comala (d'après Ossian). Poème dramatique en 3 Parties*: autograph MS 1897, identified by the inscription "J'ai été laborieux (Bach)" top right, and by the number 5 (top left), with the heading "Grand Concours de Composition Musicale de 1897," 196 pp. The work was never published.
3. Paul Raspé, *Joseph Jongen (1873–1953): Un vie de musicien* (Brussels: Bibliothèque royale de Belgique, 2003), 7.
4. The autograph score in the library of the Conservatoire royal de musique in Brussels has the identification "Litt. F, no. 11.491."
5. This remark (English: I had to be diligent) was attributed to Bach by his biographer, Johann Nikolaus Forkel, in his *Über Johann Sebastian Bachs Leben, Kunst und Kunstwerke. Für patriotische Verehrer echter musikalischer Kunst* (Leipzig, 1802). Perhaps Jongen was also remembering the continuation by Bach: "Wer eben so fleißig ist, der wird es ebenso weit bringen können" (whoever works hard will go far).
6. Gilson won the Prix de Rome in 1889 with his cantata *Sinaï*.
7. Also like Méhul with "Malvin-AH"; see chapters 5 and 12.
8. François Rasse, "Scène dramatique: pour mezzo soprano dramatique et orchestre ou piano: extraite de la cantate Comala" (Brusssels, n.d.).
9. "M.K." [Maurice Kufferath], *Le Guide Musical*, November 7, 1897, 707.
10. KYVALA/DRAMATISK DIGT AF OSSIAN,/FRIT BEARBEJDET OG SAT I MUSIK/FOR/SOLI, KOR OG ORKESTER/AF/JØRGEN MALLING/DEN DANSKE OVER SAETTELSE AF SEV. SØRENSEN. KJØBENHAVN & LEIPZIG: WILHELM HANSEN, MUSIK-FORLAG [1902]. The penciled catalogue number in the Royal Library is: [mu 6406.2301] mu 7005.3061.
11. But "Hidallan," "Malwine," "Fingal," and "Culma" are accented on the first syllable. Malling's source is very probably the Swedish translation of N. Arfvidsson (1846–48), which was from the pseudo-Gaelic version of 1807. This is *The Poems of Ossian, in the original Gaelic, with a literal translation into Latin by the late Robert Macfarlan, A.M* . . . , published under the sanction of the Highland Society of London, 3 vols. London: G. & W. Nicol, 1807. The publication reproduces the version of Ossian concocted in synthetic Gaelic, probably mainly by Macpherson himself, and left in a fragmentary state on his death in 1796.
12. That is, the Empress Maria Feodorovna (1847–1928), wife of Alexander III, emperor of Russia, and mother of Nicholas II, the last czar. She was born in Copenhagen as Marie

Sophie Frederikke Dagmar, the second daughter of King Christian IX of Denmark and Louise of Hesse-Cassel.
13. The composer Carl Nielsen was a later beneficiary of the foundation.
14. *The Musical Times* 31 (1890), 107. *Dozent* in Germany denotes someone qualified to teach at the middle level of tertiary education, below the rank of professor.
15. At two points in the score (pp. 40, 84) corrections are marked: the first (rehearsal no. 4) involves eighteen bars crossed out; the second (rehearsal no. 10) has a correction pasted on that omits two lines in Kyvala's aria ("dass ich fühle die Kraft deines Arms/Du stärkster, du liebster der Männer!"). Markings in blue pencil appear from time to time, possibly by the conductor (e.g., the changed marking of ℃ to ℃ at bar 25), and the composer has underlined the stage directions in red ink. The barring is unnumbered.
16. Like Paul Umlauft in his cantata, *Agandecca*, Malling draws on the well-known poem "Darthula's Grabesgesang" by Herder, written about 1770; see chapters 11 and 12.
17. Danish and German texts are on facing pages in the front matter; throughout the rest, the Danish text is printed below the German. Sørensen, who is otherwise obscure, apparently delivered a eulogy at Malling's funeral.
18. The "Vorspiel" (Prelude) in the vocal score is arranged for four hands.
19. At this point in the autograph score (IV), seventeen bars are crossed out, and a revision of the *larghetto* follows, all in the composer's hand.
20. LEAVES FROM OSSIAN/Fragments from the Poems of the/Ancient Gaelic Bard/ (Macpherson's Translation)./Compiled, Arranged and Set to Music/For Soli Soprano, Contralto, Tenor and Baritone,/Chorus and Orchestra/by/LIZA LEHMANN. London: Chappell & Co., Ltd., 1909. The only other works in which the text is taken from different poems of Ossian (and sometimes from elsewhere) are glees; see chapter 3.
21. Liza Lehmann, *The Life of Liza Lehmann, by Herself* (London: T. Fisher Unwin, 1919; reprint New York: Da Capo, 1980), 165.
22. Walt Whitman's *Leaves of Grass* (1855) may have influenced the choice of title.
23. Lehmann's grandmother was well known in Edinburgh as an amateur singer and harpist, and her mother was a composer of vocal music. Charles Dickens praised her mother's singing: see *Dickens, Interviews and Recollections*, vol. 1, ed. Philip Collins (London, 1981), 149. On Lehmann's lessons with MacCunn in London, see *Life of Liza Lehmann, by Herself*, 61.
24. On the difficulties placed in the way of women, see Derek B. Scott, "The Sexual Politics of Victorian Musical Aesthetics," *Journal of the Royal Musical Association* 119, no. 1 (1994), 91–114; further, Stephen Banfield, *Sensibility and English Song: Critical Studies of the Early Twentieth Century* (Cambridge: Cambridge University Press, 1985). Even in the 1960s the onetime music critic for *The Times*, in chronicling music after the turn of the twentieth century, excluded mention of women composers: see Frank Howes, "Music," in *Edwardian England, 1901–1914*, ed. Simon Nowell-Smith (Oxford: Oxford University Press, 1964), 413–45.
25. Lehmann, *Life*, 115.
26. "Liza Lehmann—To the Young Musician Who Would Compose," *The Musical Standard* 33, no. 857 (1903), 373 (reproduced with extensions in *The Etude* magazine, April 1910).

27. Favorable reviews appeared in, for instance, *The Boston Evening Transcript, Detroit Free Press, Washington Post, New York Evening Mail, Denver Republican, San Francisco Chronicle*, and *Toronto World*.
28. See *Pacific Coast Musical Review* 20, no. 1 (April 1, 1911); *Los Angeles Herald*, no. 211 (April 30, 1911). A more recent English critic, Geoffrey Bush, writing in *Romantic Age, 1800–1914, The Athlone History of Music in England*, vol. 5, ed. Nicholas Temperley (London: Athlone Press, 1981), 282, considers Liza Lehmann to be "woefully undervalued."
29. On Harley Hamilton, see Catherine Parsons Smith, *Making Music in Los Angeles: Transforming the Popular* (Berkeley: University of California Press, 2007), 56–62.
30. The *Deseret News*, May 27, 1919, reported of this performance that "the chorus was well trained, well balanced, and produced agreeable tonal effects. They were watchful and had to be. For Liza Lehmann's score is characterized by uneven passages and abrupt cadence endings. The music is on a par with good opera."
31. Heber J. Grant (1856–1945), president of the Church of Jesus Christ of Latter-Day Saints, was among those dignitaries invited to the performance.
32. Lyneer Charles Smith, "Brigham Cecil Gates: Composer, Conductor, Teacher of Music" (MA thesis, Brigham Young University, 1952), 34. *The Journal* (Logan, Utah) for Friday, May 27, reported that the "oratorio" was enthusiastically received.
33. *Salt Lake Tribune*, April 1, 1934, 16. The performance was with piano accompaniment. The *"Y" News* for April 13 reported that "'The Leaves of Ossian' [sic], a musical cantata, was presented by the double mixed quartet under the direction of Miss Margaret Summerhays last Monday night [April 9] in College hall. . . . The music is not descriptive . . . but it brings out the atmosphere in an artistic and beautiful way."
34. Lehmann has changed the original: "He beholds a dim ghost standing there" to "He beholds the ghost that guards it."
35. Coincidentally, Ravel composed his famous depiction of "sunrise" from the Suite No. 2 of the ballet *Daphnis et Chloé* at just about this time (1909). A commission from Diaghilev, the ballet premiered in Paris in 1912.
36. The conservative taste of some in London, however, is evident in the remark of George du Maurier to Lehmann's mother (after a performance of *In a Persian Garden*): "I have no doubt it is very clever—but I confess it is too *modern* for me—I cannot follow it!" See Lehmann, *Life*, 61.
37. See also M. Patricia McLaughlin, "Liza Lehmann: An Early Twentieth-Century English Woman Composer" (MA thesis, University of Western Ontario, 1987); Susan Kane, "Liza Lehmann (1862–1918): Her Times, Roles, and Songs" (DMA thesis, University of Cincinnati, 2000).

Chapter Fourteen

1. A full score of sixty-five pages and 148+406 bars was published by Banco de Partituras de Música Brasileira in 2002. The University of Akron, Ohio, holds photocopies of a two-piano reduction made by the composer himself in 1892, and a full score of 113 pages copied by Eduardo Dohmen in 1937: M215.L683.C63 1892 and M1002.L27.

C63 1937. The composer's two-piano version is in a neat, practiced hand; the copyist's name, inscribed at the end of the score, is "Leoluca Aloi" (a disembarkation certificate [Certidão de Desembarque 01792], issued at São Paulo, for a thirty-two-year-old Italian with that name is dated November 16, 1888, and this may be the same person). The Fundação Biblioteca Nacional also has a photocopy of 113 pages like that in Akron, possibly of the same version made by Dohmen. It is uncertain whether the copies in Akron came from the collection made by the composer, conductor, and pianist Walter Burle Marx (1902–90), who was a significant advocate of Brazilian music in the US and whose family donated musical scores by Brazilian composers to the University of Akron. The expression markings in the scores are often inconsistent, oscillating between Italian and Portuguese.
2. Her name sometimes appears in sources as "Anne Marie Teodorette Laurette Chassot."
3. See Zosa Szajkowski, *Jews and the French Revolutions of 1798, 1830 and 1848* (New York: Ktav Publishing House, 1970), 98–99; Daniel Stauben [Auguste Vidal], *Scènes de la vie juive en Alsace* (Paris: Salomon, 1860; repr. Malibu, CA: Joseph Simon, 1991).
4. Eduardo Dohmen was a close friend of Alexandre's father, known as Louis (Luiz); after Luiz died, he took over the administration of the Casa Levy. A composer himself, he promoted concerts in São Paulo and presented a radio program in the 1930s.
5. Giraudon, a pupil of Thalberg, also taught another musical child of European immigrants in São Paulo, Henrique Oswald (1852–1931).
6. See Vasco Mariz, *História da Música no Brasil* (Rio de Janeiro: Editors Nova Fronteira, 2005), 116–18; Olga Gudolle Cacciatore, *Dicionário biográfico de música erudita brasileira* (Rio de Janeiro: Forense Universitària, 2005); Camila Dura Segala, "Alexandre Levy: Uma revisão" (MA thesis, Instituto de Artes, Unesp. 2003); Said Tuma, "O Nacional e o Popular na Música de Alexandre Levy: Bases de um Projeto de Modernidade" (MA thesis, Escola de Comunicações e Artes, Universidade de São Paulo, 2008); *Enciclopédia Itaú Cultural*, continuously updated.
7. *Ossian, barde du troisième siècle; poëmes gaëliques recueillis par James Mac-Pherson . . . Traduction . . . par P. Christian* (Paris, 1842).
8. See Gerald Bär, "Ossian in Portugal," 351–74.
9. See chapter 7.
10. The published score renumbers the bars from the *allegro molto tempestuoso* marking. For errors and differences among the scores, see table 14.1.
11. The two-piano reduction by the composer and copied by Leoluca Aloi is entitled "Comala/Poema Symphonico per/Grande Orchestra/per/Alex: Levy/Reduzione per 2 pianos pelo Auctor." It was written in "S. Paulo" and dated "11 Marzo 1892." The markings are in Italian. The copy of the full score by Eduardo Dohmen is entitled "Comala/Poema Symphonico/para grande Orchestra/por/M. Alex. Levy" with the composer's name in capitals below, and "Brasil" in parenthesis. The expressive markings are in Italian as well as Portuguese.
12. The published score (2002) has an erroneous G in the second trombone part (at KK), where it is an F in the scribal copy of the full score made by Eduardo Dohmen in 1937; that is, it is the fifth in a chord of B-flat major. The marking of the chords appears to be *sforzando* in the first trombone for each chord and *piano* for the others; the two-piano score shows only *sforzando* markings.

13. Levy's sense of trombone sonority here is likely to have come from Berlioz and the French orchestras to which the young student would have been exposed in Paris. For Berlioz's use of trombones, see D. Kern Holoman, "Performing Berlioz," in *The Cambridge Companion to Berlioz*, ed. Peter Bloom (Cambridge: Cambridge University Press, 2000), 177.
14. The annotation reads: "Estes 4 compassos devem ser executados por 2 trompetes e 2 trombones ao longe (fora da orquestra)."
15. Studies of Stanford include: John F. Porte, *Sir Charles V. Stanford* (New York: Dutton, 1921; repr. New York, 1976); Jeremy Dibble, *Charles Villiers Stanford: Man and Musician* (Oxford: Oxford University Press, 2002); and Paul Rodmell, *Charles Villiers Stanford* (Aldershot: Ashgate, 2002).
16. J. A. Fuller Maitland, a college friend of Stanford and music critic for *The Times* from 1889 to 1911, termed it "one of the composer's most happily inspired works" (June 9, 1903); see Rodmell, *Charles Villiers Stanford*, 237–38.
17. See Dibble, *Charles Villiers Stanford*, 345. A recorded performance is by the Ulster Orchestra conducted by Vernon Handley: Chandos CD 9049 (1992).
18. GB-Lcm MS 4831.
19. Stanford went on to dedicate his *Irish Rhapsody No. 5* in G minor, completed on February 11, 1917, to the Irish Guards and the memory of their colonel-in-chief, Earl Roberts; see Dibble, *Stanford*, appendix, 475–76. The Irish Guards were formed in 1900 by order of Queen Victoria, to honor the Irish soldiers who fought in the Boer War. The Royal Irish Regiment's history goes back to 1684; it was disbanded with the partition of Ireland in 1922.
20. On these melodies, see Aloys Fleischmann, *Sources of Irish Traditional Music*, 2 vols. (New York: Garland, 1998), vol. 1: "Lament for Owen Roe O'Neill" (3377); vol. 2 "Awake Fianna (Monks of the Screw)" (6769) and "Lay his Sword by his Side" (5739). On the point of death in *Temora* Book I, Oscar asks, "place my sword by my side." The melody was formerly that known as "If the sea were ink," printed in Alfred Moffat, ed., *The Minstrelsy of Ireland* (London: Augener, 1897), 130, and in *O'Neill's Music of Ireland* (Chicago: Lyon & Healy, 1903), 552.
21. See Barry Cooper, "Beethoven's Folksong Settings as Sources of Irish Folk Music," *Irish Music Studies* V (Dublin, 1996); also Alice Anderson Hufstader, "Beethoven's *Irische Lieder*: Sources and Problems," *The Musical Quarterly* 45, no. 3 (1959): 343–60.
22. Sources of the tune include Bunting, *General Collection of Ancient Irish Music* (Dublin: Clementi, 1796), 26; James Hardiman, *Irish Minstrelsy* (London: JH, 1831); John Clinton, *Gems of Ireland* (London: Henry Shade, 1841); Francis O'Neill, *Waifs and Strays of Gaelic Melody* (Chicago: Lyon & Healy, 1922). See also Donal O'Sullivan, *Carolan: The Life, Times and Music of an Irish Harper* (London: Routledge & Kegan Paul, 1958), 222–23.
23. Thomas Davis (1814–45), chief organizer of the "Young Ireland" movement, wrote a ballad commemorating Owen Roe O'Neill. The poem is in eight quatrains with rhyming couplets and begins: "Did they dare? Did they dare, to slay Eoghan Ruadh O'Neill?"
24. In Petrie's collection of 1855 the tune is entitled "Lament for Eoghan Rua" (anglicized as "Owen Roe").

25. George Bernard Shaw was critical of the "fearful conflict between the Celt and the Professor" in Stanford's use of folk tunes. See Dan H. Laurence, ed., *Shaw's Music* (London: Bodley Head, 1984), 876–83.
26. On keening, see Patricia Lysaght, "'Caoineadh os Cionn Coirp': The Lament for the Dead in Ireland," *Folklore* 108 (1997): 65–82.
27. The marking *allegretto moderato* appears to have been changed by Stanford from *allegro moderato*. The title of the melody, "The Monks of the Screw," comes from a song by John Philpot Curran (1750–1817), master of the rolls in Ireland, who began a drinking club with the name The Monks of the Screw because of the members' love of wine and corkscrews.
28. Stanford's 1895 edition of *The Irish Melodies* by Thomas Moore contains "Lay His Sword by his Side" (p. 238), with the subtitle, "Air, If the sea were ink." The marking for the song (presumably Stanford's own) is "*In modo d'una Marcia solenne.*"

Chapter Fifteen

1. The subtitle reads: "A dramatic cantata for soprano, tenor and bass soli, chorus, and orchestra. The libretto written and arranged from Ossian's 'Death of Cuthullin' by W. A. Barratt and 'Hugh Meredyth,' op. 5."
2. See 13 and 14.
3. Eugene Goossens, *Overture and Beginners: A Musical Autobiography* (London, 1951), 115. It is uncertain which "fragment" of Ossian Goossens was referring to, but it may have been a passage from *Fingal*, Book III, or one from *Temora*, Book II, on which Macpherson provides a note (about earthquakes) in the 1773 edition. The composer later withdrew the work. Isidore de Lara (born Isidore Cohen, 1858–1935), composer and singer, established a fund for distressed musicians at the time of World War I.
4. See the collection of studies *Romanticism, Sincerity and Authenticity*, ed. Tim Milnes and Kerry Sinanan (Basingstoke: Palgrave Macmillan, 2010).
5. This composition is often missing from a list of the composer's works. The British Library holds a copy of the score, Music Collections E.862./1091.
6. See, for instance, the CD *Music from the Western Isles* (Scottish Tradition 2), Greentrax Records 9002.
7. John Blackwood McEwen's manuscripts of both the symphonic poem and the projected opera are in Glasgow University Library, Special Collections, McEwen, 542–44.
8. Whyte's manuscripts of the overture and planned opera are housed in the Scottish Music Centre, Glasgow, catalogue no. 3 (5.1.1). He later contributed the music for the romanticized film *Bonnie Prince Charlie* (1948), with David Niven in the title role.
9. His appointment as BBC head of music in Scotland in 1931 may have pushed his enthusiasm for the opera into the background as other duties crowded upon him. See also Elizabeth Clarke, "Ian Whyte, a Scottish Composer's Life in Music," in Elizabeth Alley, John Purser, Elizabeth Clarke, eds., *The Music of Scotland* (Hamilton, New Zealand: University of Waikato, 1994). At the time of Whyte's composition of *Comala*, Erik Chisholm praised his Quintet in "An Outstanding Work by a Native Composer," *The Scottish Musical Magazine* 11 (August 1930): 184–85.

10. The opus 4 is preceded by a quotation from P. Christian's *Ossian, Barde du Troisième Siècle* (Paris 1842), in its various editions by far the most popular French translation of Macpherson's poems.
11. See chapter 13.
12. The composer's scores and papers are housed in the L. Tom Perry Special Collections of the Harold B. Lee Library at Brigham Young University, MSS 922. Seymour also donated a voluminous collection of scores and libretti to the Special Collections Department of the Claremont Colleges, California, and to the Sherratt Library, Southern Utah University.
13. On Thoreau and Ossian, see Ernest E. Leisy, "Thoreau and Ossian," *New England Quarterly* 18, no. 1 (1945): 96–98. On Whitman and Ossian, see Maurice O. Johnson, *Walt Whitman as a Critic of Literature* (Lincoln: University of Nebraska Press, 1970), 23.
14. The vocal score of the opera was published by Harms, New York, 1934. Glen Nelson discusses the relative failure of the work (in which Lawrence Tibbett sang the title role) in "Digging up the Pasha's Garden," *Glimpses*, https://www.mormonartistsgroup.com/new-blog/2017/10/2/digging-up-the-pashas-garden, October 3, 2017 (first published February 2012).
15. David Scull Bispham (1857–1921) was an American baritone strongly in favor of singing opera in English. After his death, the award was intended for composers writing operas with an English-language libretto.
16. The copyright entry for "Shilric's Song" is dated April 27, 1936, and that for "A Dirge for Ryno" January–June 1964, even though it too was published in 1936. The publisher was J. Fischer & Bros. of New York; asterisks next to nos. 4–6 on the title page state "to appear later." The title page, with its ornate engraving of a harp, oak trees with anthropomorphic trunks, and a border of thistles, proclaims the Scottish origin of the odes.
17. This first ode is dedicated to the composer's mother.
18. The third ode is dedicated to the singer Marsden Argall.
19. Glen Nelson, "Digging up the Pasha's Garden."
20. See chapter 13.
21. See Jürgen Schaarwächter, *Two Centuries of British Symphonism, from the Beginnings to 1945: A Preliminary Survey* (Hildesheim: Georg Olms Verlag, 2015), 508–9. The BBC Concert Orchestra conducted by Martin Yates has recorded the symphony, Dutton Digital CDLX 7196 (2007).
22. The autograph score of the *Elegy* is deposited in Special Collections Archive, University of St. Andrews, MS 37754. It is dated November 15, 1932.
23. Thorpe Davie papers, Special Collections Archive, University of St. Andrews, MS 37754–37759. The full score of the *Dirge*, MS37754/9, is dated 1935. Bruce Clements & Co., Edinburgh, published the work in 1937.
24. The title page reads, "DIRGE FOR CUTHULLIN/from/'The Death of Cuthullin' in Macpherson's Ossian/for/Chorus (S.C.T.B.) and Orchestra." The composer also made an arrangement of the accompaniment, for strings, pianoforte, and timpani. The Scottish Music Centre, Glasgow, possesses a photocopy of the full score and autograph copies of the complete set of parts, as well as those for the arrangement for chorus, string orchestra, piano, and timpani made for the 1937 performance.
25. Temora is the royal palace of the Irish kings (Temair = Tara). Macpherson intended the epic poem *Fingal* to be the Celtic counterpart of Homer's *Iliad*, *Temora* to be the

equivalent of the *Odyssey*. *Temora* is built round a genealogical scheme involving two royal lines, that of the Gaels, represented by Fingal, and that of the Firbolg, represented by Cairbar and Cathmor. The founding father of the Gaels was Trenmor, great-great-grandfather of Fingal by way of his elder son Trathal, his grandson Colgar, and his great-grandson Comhal. Fingal was king of Morven in Scotland, Ossian was his son, Oscar his grandson. Cormac, king of Ireland, was slain by Cairbar of the Firbolg tribe, and the epic tells how Fingal restored the royal family of Ireland. Sorglan was the father of Bragéla; Dunscaith is a castle in the Isle of Skye, Tura (the present-day Carrickfergus) a castle in Ulster. For the sources that Macpherson used in manipulating the evidence see John MacQueen, "*Temora* and Legendary History," in *From Gaelic to Romantic: Ossianic Translations*, ed. Fiona Stafford and Howard Gaskill (Amsterdam: Rodopi, 1998), 69–78.

26. Cedric Thorpe Davie, letter to his parents from 44 Belsize Park, London NW3, June 21, 1935.
27. Thorpe Davie, letter to his parents, June 14, 1935.
28. We can compare this remark with the ambivalence Goethe felt about Ossian by the time he completed his famous novel *Die Leiden des jungen Werthers* (1774, rev. ed. 1787). Goethe, through the young character Werther, appears to suggest that his passion for Ossian is a phase of his life he wants to regard as over because of its "formlessness" and dangerous emotional tendencies; see F. J. Lamport, "Goethe, *Ossian*, and Werther," in *From Gaelic to Romantic*, 97–106.
29. Thorpe Davie, typewritten letter to his parents, October 23, 1935.
30. Thorpe Davie, typewritten letter to his parents, November 13, 1935.
31. Howard Ferguson to Thorpe Davie, December 1, 1935. It is unclear just what strictures Kodály was making and to which Ferguson was referring; they are not specified in the correspondence.
32. Vaughan Williams, letter to Thorpe Davie in Helsingfors, 1936 [undated]. Yrjö Kilpinen (1892–1959) was for a time the best-known Finnish composer internationally, after Sibelius.
33. Vaughan Williams, letter to Thorpe Davie, December 31, 1937.
34. The vocal score was published by Bruce, Clements & Co., Edinburgh, in 1937 and taken over by Oxford University Press in 1946. See n. 24 above.
35. In a letter of May 24, 1935, to his parents, Thorpe Davie had described Vaughan Williams's *Sea Symphony* as "a thrilling early work of his."
36. See Fiona Stafford, "Fingal and the Fallen Angels: Macpherson, Milton and Romantic Titanism," in *From Gaelic to Romantic*, ed. Fiona Stafford and Howard Gaskill, 163–82.
37. In a letter to his parents dated December 18, 1935, Thorpe Davie confided, "I wrote a delightful letter to Alban Berg a day or two ago, expressing desire to meet him in Vienna if convenient. Perhaps he'll ignore it, like Bartók."
38. Thorpe Davie wrote the music for seventeen feature films, including Disney's *Rob Roy* (1953), *Kidnapped* (1960), and eight documentaries. He also contributed the music for Tyrone Guthrie's production of Sir David Lyndsay's play *Ane Satire of the Thrie Estatis* (first performed in 1552 and published in 1602) at the 1948 Edinburgh International Festival and repeated at the 1949, 1951, and 1959 festivals.

39. According to an autograph note by Chisholm, Thorpe Davie and others accompanied him on a visit to Riga, in Soviet Latvia, in September 1962; cited in Purser, *Erik Chisholm, Scottish Modernist*, 178.

Chapter Sixteen

1. See Daniel Albright, *Modernism and Music: An Anthology of Sources* (Chicago: University of Chicago Press, 2004).
2. J. Peter Burkholder, "Brahms and Twentieth-Century Classical Music," *19th-Century Music* 8, no. 1 (1984), 75–83; see also Juliet Koss, *Modernism after Wagner* (Minneapolis: University of Minnesota Press, 2010).
3. See Vasilis Kallis, "Principles of Pitch Organization in Scriabin's Early Post-Tonal Period: The Piano Miniatures," *Music Theory Online*, vol. 14, no. 3 (September 2008).
4. His famous essay "Brahms the Progressive" was written in 1947. He would certainly have known Brahms's two works based on Ossian.
5. See chapter 12. The *Gurre* poems took over from Frithjof as a fashionable "northern" subject for continental composers at the turn of the century. Jean Guillou also completed two sets of *Sagas*, op. 20 and op. 38.
6. See James Porter, "Bartók and Janáček: Ideological Convergence and Critical Value," *The Musical Quarterly* 84, no. 3 (2000): 426–51; David E. Schneider, "Bartók and Stravinsky: Respect, Competition, Influence, and the Hungarian Reaction to Modernism in the 1920a," *Bartók and His World*, ed. Peter Laki (Princeton, NJ: Princeton University Press, 1995), 172–202.
7. The notorious criticism of Sibelius, for example, by Theodor W. Adorno appeared, significantly, in a journal devoted not to music but to sociology; his attack was in essence an argument for the supremacy of Austro-German musical modernism. See T. W. Adorno, review of Bengt de Törne, *Sibelius Close Up* (1937), in *Zeitschrift für Sozialforschung* 7 (1938): 460–63.
8. We might compare this to James Macpherson's attempt to rescue his threatened Gaelic-language culture, including Ossian, from the forces of "modernity" by deliberately distancing his poetry from the conventions of the time. Compare the remark by Denis about the poems being "un-modern," quoted at the end of chapter 1.
9. It was also a rejection of the organicist and systematizing obsessions of the German modernists: see Judit Frigyesi, *Béla Bartók and Turn-of-the-Century Budapest* (London: University of California Press, 1998); also Derek Katz, *Janáček Beyond the Borders* (Rochester, NY: University of Rochester Press, 2009).
10. On "modernism" and "modernity" in the British context, see Matthew Riley, ed., *British Music and Modernism, 1895–1960* (Farnham: Ashgate, 2010), 2: "Before the First World War, London heard Elektra, Prometheus, Petrushka, Jeux and Sacre de Printemps."
11. See chapter 15.
12. They also rejected to a large extent the "pastoralism" that was then in vogue in England. Chisholm's use of folk music, for example, was very different from that of the Vaughan Williams–Finzi–Howells group; see John Purser, *Erik Chisholm: Scottish Modernist, 1904–1965: Chasing a Restless Muse* (Woodbridge: Boydell Press, 2009), 93.

13. The work was dedicated to the concert pianist and human rights activist Harold Rubens (1918–2010), born in Cardiff, who spent time in Cape Town, South Africa, teaching at the university and opposing the apartheid regime.
14. See chapter 16; also Purser, *Erik Chisholm*, 111–21.
15. The opera's libretto is by the composer, after a short story by the US-born Irish writer Mary Lavin, "The Black Grave and the Green Grave"; the first performance took place in Cape Town on October 21, 1953.
16. The performance in the King's Theatre, Glasgow, took place before a sparse audience. I vividly remember the staging, with Chisholm conducting a chamber-sized orchestra from the pit. Shortly afterward I wrote him asking about the origin of this orchestration, and he generously sent me his annotated version of the Universal Edition vocal score he had made for his Cape Town University orchestra. This annotated score is now in the Scottish Music Centre in Glasgow.
17. In his *Celtic Song Book* (Moscow, 1964), 42–44, Chisholm also set "Oiséan's Song" from the sixteenth-century Book of the Dean of Lismore, a key Gaelic text recovered by James Macpherson as one of his sources for *The Poems of Ossian*. See chapter 15, n. 20.
18. Ibid., 57–58.
19. See Elliott Antokoletz, "Organic Development and Interval Cycles in Bartók's Three Studies, Op. 18," *Studia Musicologica Akademiai Scientiarum Hungaricae* 36, no. 3–4 (1995): 249–61; also Edward Gollin, "Transformational Techniques in Bartók's Etude Opus 18, no. 2," *Theory and Practice* 20 (1995): 13–30.
20. Antokoletz, "Organic Development," 251–52.
21. Bartók, "Harvard Lectures," in *Béla Bartók Essays*, ed. Benjamin Suchoff (Lincoln: University of Nebraska Press, 1976), 379–81; cited in Antokoletz, ibid., 252.
22. A. H. Fox-Strangways, *The Music of Hindostan* (Oxford: Oxford University Press, 1914); see Purser, *Erik Chisholm*, 115–21.
23. On a visit to the United States in 1958, Chisholm met in Boston the American composer Henry Cowell, who told him about Bartók's asking permission to use Cowell's technique of "tone-clusters." See n. 1 above.
24. Compare the arpeggio octaves in bar 9 of Chisholm's "Third Bard" with a similar effect in Bartók's Study no. 2, op. 18, bar 42.
25. Apart from the Ossian pieces by Gottschalk and the untraced *Bilder aus Ossian* (1866) by Wilhelm Fritze (a pupil of Sobolewski in Bremen), Chisholm's work is one of a very few Ossian compositions for solo piano.
26. Denève (b. 1971) was principal conductor of the Royal Scottish National Orchestra (2005–12) and the Stuttgart Radio Symphony Orchestra (2011–15), and is presently chief conductor of the Brussels Philharmonic (2015–).
27. Stoddart (b. 1959), the queen's sculptor in ordinary since 2008, is best known for his statues of David Hume and Adam Smith on the Royal Mile, Edinburgh.
28. The duration of the work is not officially marked, but it lasts between ten and thirteen minutes. The Stuttgart Radio Symphony Orchestra gave the premiere in July 2013. Further performances were given by the Seattle Symphony, the Royal Scottish Symphony Orchestra, and the Cabrillo Festival Orchestra at the Cabrillo Festival of Contemporary Music in Santa Cruz, California (August 5, 2016).
29. At bar 25 there emerges, in the first violins, a figure reminiscent of Stanford's third theme in his *Lament for the Son of Ossian*.

30. For example, *The Keening* (for large orchestra), written between 1984 and 1986 and premiered only in 2014, is more successful in paraphrasing Gaelic lament and the pain with which such lamenting is imbued.
31. See Richard McGregor, "'A Metaphor for the Deeper Wintriness': Exploring James MacMillan's Musical Identity," *Tempo* 65, no. 257 (2011): 22–39.
32. Prefatory note in the score published by Schott ED9797 (trans. Jeremy Drake). The work is dedicated to the American organist Cherry Rhodes, who was Guillou's assistant for two years at Saint-Eustache in Paris. The composer has recorded the piece on *Jean Guillou joue Guillou* (Phillips 456 511–2).
33. Jules Bordier, also a native of Angers, composed his *Un rêve d'Ossian* there. See chapter 11.
34. In March 2015 he had completed fifty-two years as organist at Saint-Eustache.
35. See his remarks in the preface. Guillou has composed a set of *Six Sagas*, op. 20 (completed 1970, published by Schott, Mainz in 2005) and a *Saga No. 7*, op. 38 (1983; published by Universal Edition, Vienna, in 1984).
36. The literature on music and postmodernism is extensive: basic concepts are summarized in Kenneth Gloag, *Music and Postmodernism* (Cambridge: Cambridge University Press, 2012); see also Jonathan Kramer, "The Nature and Origins of Musical Postmodernism," *Current Musicology* 66 (1999): 7–20; reprinted in *Postmodern Music/Postmodern Thought*, ed. Judy Lochhead and Joseph Aunder (New York: Garland, 2002), 13–26. Recently, hypermodernism has been viewed as marking the end of postmodernism in music: see Louis J. Goldford, Janne E. Irvine, and Robert E. Kohn, "Berio's Sinfonia: From Modernism to Hypermodernism," *Interdisciplinary Literary Studies* 13, nos. 1/2 (2011): 19–44.

Afterword

1. For instance, see the settings of Colma's lament by Ferdinand Hiller (soprano/piano, 1873) and Vinzenz Lachner (mezzo-soprano/orchestra, 1874).
2. See n. 18 below.
3. See, for example, *The Oxford Handbook of Topic Theory*, ed. Danuta Mirka (Oxford: Oxford University Press, 2014), a compendium of twenty-five essays exploring the notion of musical topics. See also chapter 1, n. 16.
4. On this topic, see Ralph P. Locke, *Musical Exoticism: Images and Reflections* (Cambridge: Cambridge University Press, 2009).
5. See, for instance, Jonathan Bellman, "*Aus alten Märchen*: The Chivalric Style of Schumann and Brahms," *Journal of Musicology* 13, no. 1 (1995): 117–35.
6. For the complementary aspect of Leoni's version of Ossian (Smith) to Cesarotti's, and the influence of both on Leopardi, see Francesca Bruggi-Wüthrich, "From Smith's Antiquities to Leoni's *Nuovi Canti*: The Making of the Italian Ossianic Tradition Revisited," in *The Reception of Ossian in Europe*, ed. Howard Gaskill, 303–34; also Bruggi-Wüthrich, "Alle origini del canto lirico: Ossian, Cesarotti e Leopardi," in *Rassegna europaea di letteratura Italiana* 17 (2001): 115–34.

7. See *Lord Byron: The Complete Poetical Works*, ed. Jerome J. McGann, 7 vols. (Oxford: Oxford University Press, 1993), vol. 1, 112–15.
8. As remarked in the preface, names from Ossian have carried their resonance into the modern world, Oscar and Selma being only the best known. Seagoing vessels built in the nineteenth century were given Ossianic names, as with the *Balclutha* (presently moored as a tourist attraction in San Francisco) and the *Fingal* (a Northern Lighthouse ship now converted to a luxury hotel in Edinburgh's port of Leith).
9. See Howard Gaskill, "'Ossian hat in meinen Herzen den Humor verdrångt': Goethe and Ossian Reconsidered," in *Goethe and the English-speaking World: Essays from the Cambridge Symposium for the 250th Anniversary of His Birth*, ed. Nicholas Boyle and John Guthrie (Rochester, NY: University of Rochester Press, 2001), 47–59; here, 48.
10. For the impact of Goethe's novel, see Stuart Pratt Atkins, *The Testament of Werther in Poetry and Drama* (Cambridge, MA: Harvard University Press, 1949). A discussion of the relationship between Werther and Ossian appears in Kathryn Edmunds, "'Der Gesang soll deinen Namen erhalten': Ossian, Werther and Texts of/for Mourning," *Goethe Yearbook*, vol. 8, ed. Thomas P. Saine and Ellis Dye (Columbia, SC: Camden House, 1997), 45–65.
11. The libretto is entitled *Werther, drame lyrique en quatre actes et cinq tableaux (d'après Goethe). Poème, par Ed. Blau, Paul Milliet et Georges Hartmann, musique de J. Massenet* (Paris: Heugel & Cie, 1893); English version by Elizabeth Beall Ginty (New York: Rullman, 1894). Mayr's most famous pupil was Gaetano Donizetti.
12. *Werther. Ein Roman in Musik gesetzt von Pugnani, Musikaufseher des Königs von Sardinien.* A new edition is *Werter, melólogo in due parti da Goethe* (Monumenti musicali italiani, vol. 11) (Milan: Suvini Zerboni, 1985). In his otherwise useful bibliography, S. P. Atkins refers to it as a "tone-poem."
13. The work is catalogued in the Biblioteca del Conservatorio, Milan, under the title *Werter e Carlotta*, but has been confused with *Labino e Carlotta*, a two-act *farsa* quite different from Mayr's version of Goethe's novel.
14. The first performance of Sografi's *Verter* was at the Teatro San Chrisostomo, Venice, on October 30, 1794. See also Luca Bianchini and Anna Trombetta, *Goethe, Mozart e Mayr: Fratelli illuminati* (Milan: Arche, 2001).
15. See chapter 3.
16. The setting is in volume 24 of Thomas Warren's series of annual publications entitled *Catches Canons and Glees for three four and five voices 'most humbly inscribed to the Noblemen and Gentlemen of the Catch Club'* (London: 1762–1793), 44–48.
17. "At thy lone tomb ill fated Youth" and "The conflicts o'er, my love adieu."
18. John Daverio, "Schumann's Ossianic Manner," 247–73; for the account of Gade's opus 1 and *Comala*, see 254–59.
19. Heinrich Heine, *Die Romantische Schule* (Hamburg: Hoffman und Campe, 1836), 347.
20. Daverio, "Schumann's Ossianic Manner," 260.
21. Polish travelers, however, furnished accounts such as Krystyn Lach-Szyrma's *Anglia i Szkocja. Przypomnienia z podrózy roku 1820–1824* (England and Scotland: Recollections of a journey in 1820–24), published in 1828. In the second decade of the nineteenth century, moreover, Ossian was invoked as a major criterion in literary discussions of the day. Chopin would surely have been aware of contemporary interest in the poems; see Nina Taylor-Terlecka, "Ossian in Poland," in *The Reception of Ossian in Europe*, 248–51.

22. James Parakilas, *Ballads Without Words: Chopin and the Tradition of the Instrumental "Ballade"* (Portland, OR: Amadeus Press, 1992); also Jonathan D. Bellman, *Chopin's Polish Ballade: Op. 38 as Narrative of Polish Martyrdom* (Oxford: Oxford University Press, 2010), especially 50–53, where the author refers to Ossian.
23. Jonathan Bellman, "Towards a Well-Tempered Chopin," in *Chopin in Performance: History, Theory, Practice*, ed. Artur Szklenar (Warsaw: Narodowy Instytut Fryderyka Chopina, 2005), 25–38.
24. See Taylor-Terlecka, "Ossian in Poland," 255. Sulzer's influential work was first published in Leipzig in 1794, with a later edition in Vienna, 1806.
25. Roger Fiske, *Scotland in Music: A European Enthusiasm* (Cambridge: Cambridge University Press, 1983), 149–55.
26. According to Schumann, the ballade was inspired by Mickiewicz's poem *The Three Brothers Budrys*, which tells of brothers, ordered by their father to seek treasure, who returned home with three brides. See also Michael Klein, "Chopin's Fourth Ballade as Musical Narrative," *Music Theory Spectrum* 26, no. 1 (2004): 23–56.
27. C. F. D. Schubart, *Ideen zur Aesthetik der Tonkunst* (Vienna, 1806).
28. *Hexaméron: Morceau de concert* (Vienna: Haslinger, 1839).
29. Scott, while skeptical on the "authenticity" issue, had paid tribute to Ossian by referring to the poems as having the power "to interest the admirers of poetry through all Europe," *Edinburgh Review* (July 1805), 429. In *The Bel Canto Operas* (London: Methuen, 1994), 94, Charles Osborne notes that by 1840 there were at least twenty-five Italian operas based on Scott, as well as operas by non-Italians such as Friedrich von Flotow, Heinrich Marschner, Otto Nicolai, Daniel Auber, Adolphe Adam, and Henry Bishop; see also Jerome Mitchell, *The Walter Scott Operas* (Tuscaloosa: University of Alabama Press, 1977).
30. Fiske, in *Scotland in Music* (111–13), comments on later reaction to Donizetti's opera, citing descriptions by Gustave Flaubert (*Madame Bovary*, 1856) and E. M. Forster (*Where Angels Fear to Tread*, 1905). Donizetti later composed a *romanza*, "Malvina la bella" (with a counterpart in French), to words by Andrea de Leone (1843).
31. See chapters 6 and 7.
32. "Par une de ces journées sombres qui attristent la fin de l'année, et que rend encore plus mélancoliques le soufflé glacé du vent du Nord, écoutez, en lisant Ossian, la fantastique harmonie d'un harpe éolienne balancée au sommet d'un arbre dépouillé de verdure, et vous purrez éprouver un sentiment profond de tristesse, un désir vague et infini d'une autre existence, un dégoût immense de celle-ci" (One gloomy autumn day, when the dreary north wind is blowing, read Ossian to the accompaniment of an Aeolian harp hung in the leafless branch of a tree, and you will experience a feeling of intense sadness, an infinite yearning for another state of existence, a disgust with the present). See *Memoirs of Hector Berlioz from 1803 to 1865*, trans. Eleanor Holmes, Rachel Holmes, and Ernest Newman (New York: Dover, 1966; orig. ed. New York: Knopf, 1932), 156–57.
33. There is, however, another mention of Ossian by Berlioz in his monodrama, *Lélio, ou Le Retour à la vie* (1831): "O Shakespeare, Shakespeare! Toi dont les premières années passèrent inaperçues, dont l'histoire est presque aussi incertaines que celles d'Ossian et d'Homère" (O Shakespeare, Shakespeare! Thou whose earliest years passed almost

unnoticed and whose history is nearly as uncertain as that of Ossian and Homer). See *Hector Berlioz, Complete Works*, vol. 7, ed. Peter Bloom (Kassel: Bärenreiter, 1992), 235.
34. See James Porter, "Literary, Artistic and Political Resonances of *Ossian* in the Czech National Revival," in *The Reception of Ossian in Europe*, 209–21.
35. *Bedrich Smetana: Letters and Reminiscences*, ed. František Bartoš, trans. Daphne Rusbridge (Prague: Artia, 1955), 263–64.
36. It appears that Smetana may well have met Berlioz, Le Sueur's pupil, when he gave a series of concerts in Prague in 1846; see John Clapham, *Smetana* (London: Dent, 1972), 19.
37. See Balázs Trencsényi et al., eds., *A History of Modern Political Thought in East Central Europe*, vol. 1: *Negotiating Modernity in the "Long Nineteenth Century"* (Oxford: Oxford University Press, 2016), 107–9.
38. Emil Haraszti, *Béla Bartók: His Life and Works*, trans. Dorothy Swainson (Paris: Lyrebird Press, 1938), 511; see also Jonathan Kregor, *Program Music* (New York: Cambridge University Press, 2015), 229.
39. It is also possible that Wagner found the name in Goethe's novel *Werther*.
40. *Die Kunst und die Revolution* (Art and revolution) and *Das Kunstwerk der Zukunft* (The artwork of the future), were both published in Leipzig (1849), and *Oper und Drama* appeared there shortly afterward (1851). Wagner experienced the Dresden Revolution in 1849, encountering at the barricades the Russian anarchist Mikhail Bakunin, and fled to Switzerland for fear of arrest.
41. Albert Boime discusses the set of Ossian drawings at length in the context of Runge's ideas and his other works in *Art in an Age of Bonapartism, 1800–1815* (Chicago: University of Chicago Press, 1990), 411–510.
42. Goethe, despite his anti-Romantic stance, had Runge's painting *Die Zeiten* (The times of the day) hanging in his piano room after Runge's death, presumably as a symbolic act bringing music and painting together; see Beate Allert, "Goethe, Runge, Friedrich: On Painting," in *The Enlightened Eye: Goethe and Visual Culture*, ed. Evelyn K. Moore and Patricia Anne Simpson (Amsterdam: Rodopi, 2007), 80–83.
43. Wagner never used the term, preferring simply *Motiv* or *Grundthema*, but it has stuck through constant use by commentators. In any case, he intended the idea to be not only a unifying element in the drama, but also flexible in association, not fixed and immutable.
44. In 1856 Jakob Grimm published an essay, *Über Ossian*, in which he defended Macpherson, while his brother Wilhelm made a comparison between Ossian and Parzival, *Gleichnisse im Ossian und Parzival*, that was published posthumously, in *W. Grimm, Kleinere Schriften*, vol. 1 (Berlin: Dümmler, 1881), 48–57. *Parzival* is the medieval romance by Wolfram von Eschenbach, dated to the first quarter of the thirteenth century. It has some features in common with the poems of Ossian, including an emphasis on compassion and humility.
45. On this topic see David Trippett, *Wagner's Melodies: Aesthetics and Materialism in Germany's Musical Identity* (Cambridge: Cambridge University Press, 2013), 311–16.
46. See chapter 11.
47. See chapter 12. Much more could be said about Schoenberg's use of E-flat minor tonality, which appears in his Chamber Symphony No. 2 (begun 1906), the "Litanei" movement of his String Quartet No. 2 (1907–8), and the third movement of *Gurrelieder*

(1901–11); see Ethan Haimo, *Schoenberg's Transformation of Musical Language* (Cambridge: Cambridge University Press, 2006), 59–60, passim.

48. The *Kalevala* was stitched together by Elias Lönnrot (1802–1884) through his field collecting. The example of Macpherson had persuaded him that an assiduous editor could recover a lost national epic.
49. See chapter 9.
50. Sibelius himself related the title to a bard "in the ancient Scandinavian sense and milieu." For an analysis of *Barden*, see Ralph W. Wood, "The Miscellaneous Orchestral and Theatre Music," in *The Music of Sibelius*, ed. Gerald Abraham (London: Lindsay Drummond, 1947), 38–90; here, 56.
51. See the discussion of Sibelius's relationship to Finnish folklore and how the *Kalevala* was to be represented, in Tomi Mäkelä, *Jean Sibelius* (Wiesbaden: Bretkopf & Härtel, 2007); Eng. ed. trans. Steven Lindberg (Woodbridge, Suffolk: Boydell Press, 2011), 179–97.
52. In 1921 Sibelius was entertained in London by the newly appointed Finnish ambassador to the Court of St. James's, Ossian Donner (1866–1957). Ossian was a relatively common given name for males in mid-century Finland.
53. Arnold Mendelssohn, *Gott, Welt und Kunst: Aufzeichnungen* (Darmstadt: Insel-Verl, 1949), 8.
54. Debussy's consciousness of Scottish climate and landscape may have been triggered to some extent by an early poem of Lamartine ("Jocelyn") that apostrophizes the bard: "Ossian! Ossian! lorsque plus jeune encore / Je rêvais des brouillards et des monts d'Inistore; / Quand, tes vers dans le cœur et ta harpe à la main, / Je m'enfonçais l'hiver dans des bois sans chemin, / Que j'écoutais siffler dans la bruyère grise." (Ossian! Ossian! when still younger, / I dreamed of fogs and the mountains of Inistore; / When, your verses in my heart and your harp in my hand, / I ventured into winter in woods without a path, / I listened to a whistling in the gray heather.") Debussy obviously knew his Lamartine well, since he composed his "Invocation" (1883) for male chorus and orchestra on a stanza of Lamartine's poem of that name ("Élevez-vous, voix de mon âme").
55. See Special Edition, "Locating Celtic Music (and Song)," *Western Folklore* 57, no. 4 (1998), ed. James Porter.
56. See Gabriella Hartvig, "Ossian in Hungary," in *The Reception of Ossian in Europe*, 222–39; Peter Bartók et al., *Duke Bluebeard's Castle: Opera in one act to the libretto by Béla Balász* (vocal score) (Homosassa, Florida, 2005).
57. Elliot Antokoletz and Juana Canabal Antokoletz, *Musical Symbolism in the Operas of Debussy and Bartók: Trauma, Gender, and the Unfolding of the Unconscious* (Oxford: Oxford University Press, 2008).
58. See the discussion in Mats Sigvard Johansson, "Making Sense of Genre and Style in the Age of Transcultural Reproduction," *International Review of the Aesthetics and Sociology of Music* 47, no. 1 (2016): 45–62.
59. For example, the annual Festival interceltique de Lorient, Brittany (formerly called Festival interceltique des cornemuses).
60. In 2017 the Celtic Connections Festival in Glasgow, founded in 1997, saw 2,375 musicians from 50 countries perform for more than 110,000 people in over 200 events. The BBC Scottish Symphony Orchestra also played at the festival that year for the first time, thus entering voluntarily into the role of cultural intermediary between the concertgoing public and followers of the vernacular tradition(s). The "Afro Celtic" sound and

"Rock celtique" are further signs of the hybrid forms that "world music" crossovers have inspired.

Appendix Three

1. Indicates the use of sheepskin or deerskin coverings for window apertures, still used in some remote shealings and *bothain* [Macpherson].
2. Shed [Macpherson].
3. Here, probably the "byre" [Macpherson]—that is, the cattle shed.

Selected Bibliography

A number of the following works already appear in the endnotes as occasional points of reference; their presence here (marked with an asterisk) is a further indication of their relevance, both to the study of music and the topic of Ossian in general. Other publications of a broader scope in the listing are useful secondary sources consulted during the writing of this book.

Brown, Terence, ed. *Celticism*. Amsterdam: Rodopi, 1996.
Carruthers, Gerard, and Alan Rawes, eds. *English Romanticism and the Celtic World*. Cambridge: Cambridge University Press, 2002.
Charlton, David. "Ossian, Le Sueur and Grand Opera." *Studies in Music* 10 (1977): 37–52.
*Gaskill, Howard. "'Genuine Poetry . . . like Gold.'" Introduction to *The Reception of Ossian in Europe*, edited by Howard Gaskill, 1–20. London: Thoemmes Continuum, 2004.
*———. "Ossian in Europe." *Canadian Review of Comparative Literature* 21 (1994): 643–78.
———. "'Ossian' Macpherson: Towards a Rehabilitation." *Comparative Criticism* 8 (1986): 113–46.
———, ed. *Ossian Revisited*. Edinburgh: Edinburgh University Press, 1991.
*———. "Ossian, Herder, and the Idea of Folk-Song." In *Literature of the Sturm und Drang*, edited by David Hill, 95–116. Rochester, NY: Camden House, 2003.
*———, ed. *The Poems of Ossian and Related Works*. Edinburgh: Edinburgh University Press, 1996.
*———, ed. "Versions of Ossian: Receptions, Responses, Translation." *Translation & Literature* 22, no. 3 (2013): 293–435.
*Gelbart, Matthew. *The Invention of "Folk Music" and "Art Music": Emerging Categories from Ossian to Wagner*. Cambridge: Cambridge University Press, 2007.
*Jahrmärker, Manuela. *Ossian: Eine Figur und eine Idee des europäischen Musiktheaters um 1800*. Cologne: Studio U. Tank, 1993.
Lamport, Francis. "Goethe, Ossian and Werther." In *From Gaelic to Romantic: Ossianic Translations*, edited by Fiona Stafford and Howard Gaskill, 97–106. Atlanta: Rodopi, 1998.
Leask, Nigel. "Fingalian Topographies: Ossian and the Highland Tour, 1768–1805." *Journal of Eighteenth-Century Studies* 39, no. 2 (2016): 183–96.
Moore, Dafydd, ed. *The International Companion to James Macpherson and the Poems of Ossian*. London: Association for Scottish Literary Studies, 2017.
Moulton, Paul F. "Of Bards and Harps: A Controversy Discarded and Ossian Revealed: An Argument for a Renewed Consideration of The Poems of Ossian." *College Music Symposium* 49/50 (2009–10): 392–401.

Porter, James. "'Bring Me the Head of James Macpherson': The Execution of Ossian and the Wellsprings of Folkloristic Discourse." *Journal of American Folklore* 144 (Special Ossian Edition) (2001): 1–40.

———. "Literary, Artistic and Political Resonances of Ossian in the Czech National Revival." In *The Reception of Ossian in Europe*, edited by Howard Gaskill, 209–21. London: Thoemmes Continuum, 2004.

Rosen, Charles. *The Romantic Generation*. London: Fontana Press, 1999.

Schmidt, Wolf Gerhard. *"Mutter der Romantik" und "Homer des Nordens": James Macphersons Ossian und seine Rezeption in der deutschsprachigen Literatur*. 4 vols. Berlin: Walter de Gruyter, 2003–4.

*Smith, Christopher. "'Ossian, ou Les Bardes': An Opera by Jean-François Le Sueur." In *From Gaelic to Romantic: Ossianic Translations*, edited by Fiona Stafford and Howard Gaskill, 153–63. Atlanta: Rodopi, 1998.

*———. "Ossian in Music." In *The Reception of Ossian in Europe*, edited by Howard Gaskill, 375–92. London: Thoemmes Continuum, 2004.

*Thomson, Derick S. *The Gaelic Sources of Macpherson's Ossian*. Edinburgh: Oliver & Boyd for Aberdeen University Press, 1952.

*Tombo, Rudolf. *Ossian in Germany: Bibliography, General Survey, Ossian's Influence on Klopstock and the Bards*. New York: Columbia University Germanic Studies, 1901; reprint, New York: AMS Press, 1966.

*Trumpener, Katie. *Bardic Nationalism: The Romantic Novel and the British Empire*. Princeton, NJ: Princeton University Press, 1997.

Vande Moortele, Steven. *The Romantic Overture and Musical Form from Rossini to Wagner*. New York: Cambridge University Press, 2017.

*Van Tieghem, Paul. *Ossian en France*. Paris: Rieder, 1917.

*Wessel, Matthias. *Die Ossian-Dichtung in der musikalischen Komposition*. Laaber: Laaber-Verlag, 1994.

Index

For reasons of length this index refers mainly to names, places, and topics in the main body of the text and does not include citation of these from the endnotes. For the same reason, it offers page references only for those composers in appendix 4 who are also named in the text.

Aberdeen (University), 1
Abrams, Harriet, 56
Adam, Adolphe, 147
Adelaide, Queen, 47
Adorno, Theodor Wiesengrund, 112
Agandecca, 5, 7, 38, 44, 93, 95–96
Aganadeca (Saccenti), xi, 44, 87, 93, 317
Agandecca (Umlauft), 14, 44, 171, 186–93, 319
Ahlwardt, Christian Wilhelm, 299
Ailte (Gaelic lay), 24–25, 320
Albéniz, Isaac, 250
Albin, 288
Aldo, 72
Amellér, André, 17, 320
America, xv, 11, 15, 40, 210, 232, 259. *See also* United States
Amsterdam, 15, 143, 205, 249–50
Ancker, Carl Amadeus, 223
Anelli, Angelo, 72
Angers, 177–78, 183, 289
Anon, "I sit by the mossy fount," 36–37, 297
Antigonish, Nova Scotia, 27
Ardano e Dartula (Pavesi), 13, 72, 82–86, 196, 299, 317
Argyll (Argyle), 18, 20
Arne, Thomas, 55–56
Arnold, Matthew, 2
Arnold, Samuel, 11

atonal, 275, 291
Auber, Daniel, 86
Austerlitz, Battle of (1805), 95, 98, 101
Australia, 186
Austria-Hungary, 13. *See also* Budapest; Klagenfurt; Vienna

Bach, Carl Philipp Emmanuel, 38, 124
Bach, Johann Christian, 38
Bach, Johann Christoph Friedrich, 38
Bach, Johann Sebastian, 38, 217
Bach, Wilhelm Friedemann, 134
Bach, William (Wilhelm Friedrich Ernst), 38, 314; *Colma: eine Episode aus den Gedichten Ossians*, 38–39
Bagnara, Francesco, 83, 85
Bainton, Edgar, 257, 320
Baird, Major-General David, 46
Baker, David Erskine, 10
Balclutha, 83
ballade, 298, 317, 319–20
ballet, 5, 10, 12, 40, 73, 87, 90, 96, 106–8, 146, 257, 263, 303
Balsamini, Camilla, 74, 82
Banks, Joseph, 267
Bantock, Granville, 16, 258–59, 271, 320
Baour-Lormian, Pierre, 58, 147, 178
Barratt, William Augustus, 257, 319

Barthélémon, François-Hippolyte, 10, 33–8; *Oithóna* (op), 33–35
Bartleman, James, 45, 48, 50
Bartók, Béla, 263, 273, 275–76, 280, 285, 287, 291, 303
Beethoven, Ludwig van, 8, 11–12, 69, 251; Symphony no. 3 ("Eroica"), 8–9, 102, 106–9, 112; *Wonne der Wehmut*, 104–5
Beethovenhalle (Bonn), 210
Bekker, Paul, 107
Belfast (Harp Festival), 12, 23, 28–29
Belgium, Belgian, 14, 16, 147, 222, 302. *See also* Brussels; Liège
Bellini, Vincenzo, 298, 301
Belorussia, Belorussian, 95
Benburb, Battle of (1646), 251
Benda, Franz, 124, 143
Benda, Georg, 124, 128
Benedict, Julius, 106
Bengal, 49
Berg, Alban, 273
Berlin, 129, 134, 139–40, 147, 171, 289, 301
Berlioz, Hector, 57–58, 68, 117, 146, 288, 299, 302
"Berrathon," 5, 7, 15, 37, 58, 60, 68, 108, 147 231, 236, 251, 260, 293, 296, 302
Berton, Henri-Montan, 124
Bhagalpur, India, 49
Bianchi, Francesco, 87, 90, 101, 301; *Calto* (op), 8, 12, 73, 88, 294, 299
Biarent, Adolphe, 16
Bishop, Henry, 257
Bismarck, Otto, 171
Blackwell, Thomas, 1
Blair, Hugh, 1, 111
Boer War, 16, 251
Boghen, Felice, 259
Bohemia, Bohemian, 3, 299
Boieldieu, François-Adrien, 85
Bologna, Bolognese, 42, 90, 93
Bonaparte, Joseph, 93
Bonaparte, Napoleon, 1–2, 7, 9, 12–13, 57, 73, 79, 82–83, 93, 95, 100–101, 103, 106, 141, 178, 206–8, 302

Bonheur, Raymond, 14
Bonn City Choral Society, 210
Bordeaux, 35
Bordier, Jules-Auguste, 171, 294, 319; *Un rêve d'Ossian* (scène lyrique), 14–15, 177–86
Borodin, Alexander, 302
Borodino, Battle of (1812), 96
Boswell, James, 32, 41
"Bough, Golden," 303
Bouilly, Jean-Nicolas, 69
Bournemouth, 250
Bowie, John, 18, 321; *A Collection of Strathspey Reels & Country Dances* (1789), 18–20
Brahms, Johannes, xiii, 5, 14–15, 110, 147, 171, 177, 201, 217, 232, 250, 253, 274–75, 293, 318; "Darthulas Grabgesang," xiv-xv, 204–5
Brazil, 238–39. *See also* Campinas; São Paulo
Breitkopf & Härtel, 103, 106, 119, 210
Brescia, 77
Breton, 289, 302
Brooke, Charlotte, 22
Bruch, Max, 187, 250
Brussels, 216, 223
Buchanan, Dugald, 32
Buckley, Reginald, 16
Budapest, 265
Bunting, Edward, 23; *The Ancient Music of Ireland* (1840), 28
Bürgel, Constantin, 191, 200; "Das Mädchen von Kola," 203
Burke, Edmund, xvi, 32, 114; *A Philosophical Enquiry into our Ideas of the Sublime and the Beautiful* (essay), 4
Burney, Charles, 48–49
Burns, Robert, 18–19, 31, 120, 297; *The Scots Musical Museum*, 18
Busch, Adolf, 210; *Darthula's Grabgesang nach Ossian*, 210–11
Busoni, Ferruccio, 250
Byrne, James, 40–41
Byron, George Gordon, Lord, xiii, 295–96, 299

Cairbar, 41, 83, 90, 194, 247
Calcutta, 46, 49, 306
Caledonia, Caledonian, 4, 43, 46, 74, 79–80, 91, 100, 159, 314
Callcott, John Wall, 297
"Calthon and Colmal" 78, 87, 100
Calto (Bianchi), 87–88
Calzabigi, Ranieri de' 73
Cambridge (University), 205, 250
Cammarano, Salvatore, 13
Campbell, John Francis, 21, 27
Campinas (Brazil), 238
Caracul, 45, 51, 224–25, 239
Carmichael, Alexander, 27
Caro, Maria de, 41, 90
"Caros, The War of," 231
Caroso, 43
Carpani, Giuseppe, 74, 78–80
Carradi, Dionisio, 15
Caruso, Luigi, 90, 299, 314; *La disfatta di Duntalmo* (op), 8, 89–90
Casa Levy, 238
Catherine the Great, 96
Cavos, Catterino Albertovich, 101
ceilidh, 19
Celega, Niccolò, 16
Celts, Celtic, 97, 101, 107, 164, 187, 260, 263, 265, 267, 275, 298, 302–3
Center, Ronald, 263
Cesarotti, Melchiorre, 44, 73–74, 104
Chambers, Amelia, 230
Chambers, Robert, 232
Chastenay, Victorine de, 12
Chateaubriand, François-Renè, 12
"Chieftains, The," 303
Chemnitz, 191
Chisholm, Erik, 17, 263, 271, 273–74, 285, 290–91; *Night Song of the Bards*, 17, 275–81, 310–12
Chopin, Frédéric [Fryderyk], 297–98
Christian, 27, 284
Christmann, Johann Friedrich, 195
Churchill, Charles, 10
Clessamore, 83–85, 90
Clive, Major General Robert, 46

Clube Haydn, 238
Coenders, Emil, 205
Coignet, Horace, 124
coloratura, 233. *See also* decoration; melisma; ornament
Coleridge, Samuel Taylor, 2
"Colma," 7, 19, 38, 58
Colma (William Bach), 38–39
Colma (Rust), 11–12
Colmal (Winter), 11, 294
Comala (Jongen), 16, 216, 217–23
Comala (Levy), 238–49
Comàla (Wainewright), 45–46, 49–56, 232, 294
Common, Cormac, 23
Concertgebouw Orchestra, 249–50
Cooke, Benjamin, 48
Cooke, Thomas Simpson, 257
Copenhagen, 151
Coppola, Pietro Antonio, 239, 294; *Fingal* (op), 15, 49, 93–95
Coquard, Arthur, 16
cor anglais (English horn), 9, 217, 219, 221–22, 243, 245–46, 248–49, 281, 283–84, 300–302
Corder, Frederick, 257–59
Cork, 207
Corri, Sophia Giustina, 46, 48
Cortesi, Antonio, 90
Cottin, Sophie, 296
Courtney [Courtenay], Denis, 40–41
Cowen, Frederic, 250
Cramer, Franz Seraph, 11
Cramer, William, 37, 45–46
Crimora, 33
"Croma," 275
Crouch, Mrs., 41
Cuchulann (Cu Chulainn, Cuchullan, Cuthullin), 17, 133, 257
Cuchullan's Lament (Bantock), 259
Cuchullan's lament for his son (Gaelic lay), 25–26
Cuthullin, Dirge for (Thorpe Davie), 263–73
Culloden, Battle of (1746), 1
Czech, 3, 299. *See also* Bohemian

Dagmar, Princess of Denmark, Tsarina of Russia, 223, 230
D'Agoult, Marie, 300
Darcours, Charles, 158
"Dar-thula," xiv, 194–215, 260. See also chapter 12
David, Giovanni, 92–93
Davies, Cecilia ("Inglesina"), 50
De Quincy, Thomas Penson, 299
De Ritis, Vincenzo, 44
Debussy, Claude, 14, 146, 238–39, 274, 302
Deirdre, 194
Denève, Stéphane, 281
Denis, Michael, 3, 13, 17, 299; *Die Gedichte Ossians* (trans, 1768–69), 38–39, 172
Denmark, Danish, 13, 120, 223–24, 230, 232. See also Copenhagen
Derricke, John, 27
Derzhavin, Gavrila, 96
Diarmid (Dermid), 22, 26, 58
d'Indy, Vincent, 15, 205
Dittersdorf, Karl Ditters von, 195
Dohnányi, Ernst von, 265
Donizetti, Gaetano, 13, 290
Donn, Rob (Robert MacKay), 32
Dow, Daniel, 303
Dresden, 15, 300
duan (Gaelic narrative verse), 2, 25–26
Duanaire Finn, 22
Dublin, 31, 47, 250–51
duodrama, 128
Dupuis, Sylvain, 16
Durand, Emile, 239

Edda (Poetic), 301
Edelmann, Jean-Frédéric, 146
Edinburgh, 1, 10, 18, 21, 30–33, 103, 111, 179, 297
Edwardian, 26
Eigg, Isle of, 24
Elouis, Jean, 28, 31
Elouis, Mrs., 31
England, 28, 47–48, 197, 216, 222, 230, 232, 258. See also Bournemouth; Brighton; Glastonbury; Liverpool; London
epic, 2, 7, 13–14, 17, 29, 41, 58, 68, 103, 120, 186, 194, 293, 297, 301
episode, episodic, 1–2, 5, 7, 12, 14, 19, 38, 48–49, 51, 93, 95, 98, 108, 112, 118, 135, 186, 230–31, 233, 248, 260, 275, 282, 285, 287, 291–92, 301, 305
Érard, Pierre, 30
Érard, Sebastien, 30
Erin (Ireland), 4, 39, 164, 167–68, 172–73, 204, 209, 264, 269
Erskine, Thomas, Earl of Kellie, 35
esprit celtique, 302. See also Celts
ethnology, ethnomusicology, 26, 259

Fenaroli, Fedele, 73
Fenian Cycle, 22
Ferdinand III, Grand Duke of Tuscany, 42
Ferguson, Howard, 265, 269
Ferroni, Vincenzo, 239
Fidanza, Leopoldo, 74, 90–91, 196
Fingal, 22, 33, 41, 45, 48, 51–53, 55, 60, 62, 74, 77–78, 82–83, 91–93, 95–99, 101, 106–7, 113–15, 117, 119–21, 123, 154, 158–60, 165, 168–70, 178, 183–84, 187, 189–94, 190–94, 197, 204, 217–19, 221–22, 224–25, 229, 231, 233, 239, 243, 245–46, 248–49, 251, 267, 284, 287, 293, 300, 303, 307–8
"Fingal's Cave" (Mendelssohn), 113–15, 117, 119–21, 164, 267, 303
Fingallo (Coppola), 15, 44, 93–95, 234, 239
Fingallo e Comala (Pavesi), 74–83, 85, 87–88, 90–91, 294, 299
Finland, Finnish, 13, 16, 295, 265, 301. See also Helsinki
Fionn, xv, 22, 27, 107, 284
Flachsland, Caroline, 172
Fleischmann, Aloys, 209, 214; *Darthula aus Ossian*, 206, 209
Flemming, Paul, 205
Florence, 42–43, 75, 82, 91, 197, 295

Florida, xv
folklore, 258, 302
Foppa, Giuseppe, 8, 87, 90
forgery, 2–3, 27. *See also* fraud; plagiarism
Forkel, Johann Nikolaus, 217
Fouquet, Mlle. (Jeanne Agnès), 159
fragment, 3, 9, 134–35, 194–95, 201, 107, 224, 231, 256, 258–59, 277, 282–83, 287, 292, 296
Fragments of Ancient Poetry, 38, 123
France, French, 1–5, 7, 10–12, 13–17, 30–33, 35, 40, 57–58, 65, 69–70, 73–74, 82, 95–96, 98, 100–101, 103–4, 109, 123, 133, 140–41, 146–47, 158–59, 178, 186, 197, 238–39, 274, 291, 296, 298. *See also* Angers; Bordeaux; Dijon; Lorient; Marseilles; Paris; Strasbourg
Francis II, Emperor of Austria, 82
Franck, César, 205, 216
Franco-Prussian War, 14, 16, 178
Frankfurt, 108, 187
Fraser, Capt. Simon, 19
fraud, fraudulent, 2–3
French Revolution, 69, 103, 141, 274
Fribourg, 238
Friends of the People, 12
Freudenberg, Wilhelm, 232
Fritze, Wilhelm, 17

Gabetti, Giuseppe, 50
Gade, Nils Wilhelm, 13, 120, 223, 297
Gael, Gaelic, 2–3, 16, 22, 25–27, 32–33, 40–41, 194, 223, 230, 258, 285, 302–3
Gallenberg, Robert, Graf von, 93
Galuppi, Baldassare, 96
Garden, Mary, 258
Garrick, David, 32, 35
Gates, Brigham Cecil, 232
Gaulo, 31, 43, 83, 85
Gaveaux, Pierre, 69
Gazzaniga, Giuseppe, 73
Geibel, Emil, 120, 297
Geminiani, Francesco, 27

gender, xvi, 4, 56
Generali, Pietro, 92–93, 294; *Clato* (op), 8, 91; *Gaulo ed Oitona* (op), 43, 91–92
German, Germanic, 3, 5, 12–13, 15–16, 33, 40, 102–3, 10, 117, 123–24, 128–29, 140–41, 145, 147, 172, 177–78, 186–87, 195, 198, 200, 205, 207, 209, 223–24, 230, 239, 251, 275, 296, 298–99, 300–301
Germany, 3, 7, 10–11, 13–15, 38, 40, 93, 120, 122, 147, 171, 186–87, 210, 216, 232, 257. *See also* Berlin; Chemnitz; Dresden; Hamburg; Königsberg; Leipzig; Munich; Rüdesheim; Schleswig; Stuttgart; Weimar; Wiesbaden
Gervasio, Giovanni Battista, 34
Gesamtkunstwerk, 300
ghost, 1, 39, 51, 87, 107, 113, 124, 127, 133, 150, 164, 189, 225, 230, 246, 248–49, 263, 277, 293
Giardini, Felice de, 35
Gibraltar, 299
Gilson, Paul, 217, 222
Giraudon, Gabriel, 238
Glasgow, 276
Glastonbury, 257
glee, 7, 195, 197, 231–33
Glencolumcille (Co. Donegal), 26
Gluck, Christoph Willibald, 69, 73–74, 133, 274
godless, 182, 284
Goethe, Johann Wolfgang von xiii, 3, 11, 39, 108, 111–12, 121, 128–29, 134, 140, 142, 195; *Die Leiden des jungen Werthers*, 37, 102–7, 108–11, 214, 239
"Golden Bough" (music group), 303
Goldsmith, Oliver, 29
Gomes, Carlos, 238
Goodman, James, 22
Goossens, Eugene, 258
Gottschalk, Louis Moreau, 15, 17, 259
Gounod, Charles, 147, 178, 232

Gouvy, Louis Théodore, 146–48, 154, 158–59, 210; *Le dernier Hymne d'Ossian (scène lyrique)*, 14, 147–58, 170, 194, 307–9
Gow, John, 17, 303
Grädener, Carl Georg Peter, 159; "Darthula's Grabgesang," 200
Grassi, Gaetano, 297
Grétry, André, 57, 69
Grüters, Hugo, 210
Guillou, Jean, 17, 289, 291; *Ballade ossianique no. 2: Les Chants de Selma*, 274, 285–90
Gunn, John, 28

Hagley, Miss, 50
Hague, The, 205
"half-viewless harp," 293
Halkirk, Caithness, 23
Hamann, Johann Georg, 11
Hamburg, 12
Hamilton, Harley, 232
Handel, George Frederick, 27, 35, 47–48, 50, 55–56, 197
Hanover Square Rooms (London), 11, 37, 45–46, 305
Hanoverian, 1
Harold, Edmund de (von), xiii, 7, 196, 198, 297
harp, harper, 2, 4, 9, 12–13, 15, 17–18, 21–23, 26–28, 30–31, 34, 41–42, 51–52, 57, 60, 62, 66, 68–70, 84–85, 92, 95, 97–98, 103, 106, 120, 118, 124, 126–28, 148, 150, 152, 154, 158–59, 164, 172–74, 177–78, 181–82, 187, 189, 207, 217, 219–20, 224–24, 229, 231, 233, 235, 243–46, 249, 251, 253, 255, 257, 259, 266, 268, 270–71, 276, 281–84
Haydn, Franz Joseph, 10–22, 31–32, 36–37, 46, 55–56, 69, 104, 112, 238–39, 297, 314
Hebrides, xiv, xix, 8, 13, 24–25, 113, 117–19, 259, 285, 300–301. *See also* Eigg; Mull; Skye; Staffa; Tiree
Heine, Heinrich, 120, 297

Helbig, Nadine Shakhovskoi, 203
Helbig, Wolfgang, 203
Helsinki, 210, 301–2
Hempson (Ó Hampsey), Denis, 29
Herder, Johann Gottfried, 3, 7, 11, 13–14, 16, 27, 39, 103, 108–9, 111, 118, 172, 174, 177, 189, 191, 195, 199, 204, 207, 210, 212, 214, 223, 229, 275, 297; "Darthula's Grabesgesang" (poem, ca. 1770), 14, 172; *Auszug einer Briefwechsel über Oβian und die Lieder alter Völker* (essay, 1773), 110
Hermann-Leon, M., 159
hero, heroic, heroine, 2, 4, 7–9 14, 17, 20–22, 24–27, 29, 38, 43–44, 46, 55, 68, 70, 74, 78–79, 98–101, 106–11, 117, 122, 126, 146, 17, 182, 184, 186–87, 189, 193–97, 199, 211, 217, 219, 222, 224, 230, 248, 251, 259–60, 263, 274, 287, 300–302, 311
Heward, Leslie, 265
Hidallan (Hydallan), 7, 65, 74, 159–60, 163–65, 168, 170, 217, 222–25, 229, 239, 243, 245, 248
Highlanders, Highlands, 1–2, 8, 10, 16, 18–20, 23–24, 26, 28, 32, 38, 40–41, 83, 109, 117, 259, 276, 281, 298
Hill, Wilhelm, 202–3; "Das Mädchen von Kola," 203
Hillemacher, Lucien, 170; *Fingal (scène lyrique)*, 158–70
Hillemacher, Paul, 158–59
Hohenzollern dynasty, 171
Hölderlin, Friedrich, 103
Holst, Gustav, 250
Homer, xvi, 2–3, 29, 33, 103–4, 106, 108, 103–10, 112
Honegger, Arthur, 265
Hopffer, Bernhard, 171; *Darthula's Grabgesang*, 172–77, 201
Hopffer, Emil, 171
Hopkinson, Francis, 11
horn(s), 4, 53, 55, 60, 62, 69–70, 88, 95, 97–98, 106, 124, 126, 148, 150, 154, 156, 159, 172, 177–78, 182, 184, 187,

197, 209–10, 217–18, 222, 225, 243, 245–46, 248, 253–54, 256, 266–67, 271, 276, 281–83, 300
Hubertusburg, Treaty of (1763), 1
Hume, David, 2, 19, 32, 41
Humperdinck, Engelbert, 187
Hungary, Hungarian, 3, 13, 299–300, 303. *See also* Budapest

"I sit by the mossy fount" (fountain), 37, 207, 260
Iceland, 301. *See also Edda; Völsunga Saga*
incidental music, 12, 15–16, 186
India, Indian, 46–47, 49, 56, 276. *See also* Bhagalpur; Calcutta
Ingres, Jean-Auguste-Dominique, 12, 178–79
Inibaca, 33, 44
Inistore, 5, 45, 143, 218, 224
Ippolitov-Ivanov, Mikhail, 17, 294
Ireland, Irish, 12, 21–22, 26–29, 40, 194, 207, 209, 238, 250–57. *See also* Belfast; Dublin; Limerick; Ulster
Italy, Italian, 3, 5, 8, 12–13, 18, 33, 35, 43–44, 48, 50, 55, 73–74, 77, 85, 87, 91, 93, 95–96, 104, 117, 122, 133, 146, 194, 197, 202, 219, 295–96. *See also* Bergamo; Biella; Bologna; Brescia; Florence; Milan; Naples; Novara; Piacenza; Palermo; Reggio Emilia; Rome; Sicily; Trieste; Turin; Venice

Jacobite, 1, 10
Jaëll, Marie, xvi
James VI, King of Scotland, 32
Janáček, Leoš, 250, 275–76, 294
Jefferson, Thomas, 11
Jensen, Adolf, 199, 202, 214, 294; "Darthulas Grabgesang," 202
Jerusalem, Karl Wilhelm, 108
Joachim, Joseph, 147
Johnson, James, 18
Johnson, Samuel, 2–3, 13, 25, 37
Jongen, Joseph, 222–23; *Comala*, 217–23, 230, 294

"joy of grief," 4, 104, 121. *See also Wonne der Wehmut*

Karamzin, Nikolai Mikhailovich, 96
Karl Eugen, Duke of Swabia, 119
Keane, Frank, 251
Keats, John, 267
Kennedy-Fraser, Marjory, 16, 24–26; *Cuchullan's lament for his son* (lay), 25
Kikta, Valery, 17
Kilpinen, Yrjö, 265
Kiuk'hel'becker, Vilgel'm, 96
Klagenfurt, 223
Klöber, August Karl Friedrich von, 106
Klopstock, Friedrich Gottlieb, 11, 103–4, 297–99, 301
Knab, Armin, 213–14, 294; "Darthulas Grabgesang," 213
Kodály, Zoltán, 265, 269
Koehler-Wümbach, Wilhelm, 205–6
Königsberg, 15, 129
Kostrov, Ermil Ivanovich, 95
Kozlowski, Osip [Jósef], 12, 97–98; incidental music for *Fingal* (Ozerov), 95–101
Kreuzer, Rodolphe, 296
Krug, Arnold, 14, 44, 187
Kunzen, Ludwig Friedrich Aemilius, 12
Kutaisov, Alexander Ivanovich, 96

Lamartine, Alphonse de, 12
Lamb, Lady Caroline, 296
Landini, Antonio, 12, 41, 90
laoidh (lay), 20–22, 26
Lara, Isidore de, 258
Larthmor (Larmor), 58, 60, 62, 65, 67–69, 148
Le Sueur, Jean-François, xiv, 12–13, 36, 43, 57–58, 67–68, 70, 73–74, 91, 98, 100–101
Le Tourneur, Pierre, 17, 58, 95 147, 239
Learmonth family, 96. *See also* Lermontov
Lehmann, Liza, 5, 216; *Leaves from Ossian*, 230–37
Lehmann, Rudolf, 230

396 • INDEX

Leipzig, 111, 117, 121, 124, 140, 186, 250
Lena, 119, 122, 231, 233
Lengefeld, Charlotte von, 110
Leoni, Michele, 295
Leonardi, Antonio, 202–3; "Dartula," 204
Leopardi, Giacomo, 295
Lermontov, Mikhail, 96
Levy, Alexandre, 256, 294; *Comala*, 239–49
Levy, Henrique Louis, 238
Levy, Luiz, 238
lied, lieder, 14, 100, 118–20, 124, 129, 134–35, 140, 143, 171, 186, 190, 195, 198–99, 204, 213
Liège, 216
Lienau, Robert, 171
Lind, Jenny, 232
Lindner, Otto Ernst, 200–202; "Ossian's Mädchen von Kola," 200–201
Linley the Younger, Thomas, 195; *Darthula*, 197–98, 214, 294
Lisbon, 87, 93, 239, 289
Liszt, Franz, 15, 120, 203, 232, 238, 298–99
Livini, Ferdinando, 92
Lochaber, 18
Lochlin, 93, 96–98, 186–87, 190
London, 7, 10–11, 30–31, 33, 35, 38, 40–41, 45, 48–49, 55–56, 90, 117, 119, 230, 232, 250, 257–59, 263, 265, 271, 273, 276, 305
Lönnrot, Elias, 13, 301
Lorenzoni, Adriano, 90, 93
Los Angeles, 232, 259
Louis Ferdinand, Prince, 107
Lowlands, Lowlanders, 19, 32
Lully, Jean-Baptiste, 146

MacCunn, Hamish, 232
MacDonald, Alexander, 32
MacDonald, Rev. James, 111
MacDonald, Sìleas, 28
MacGregor, Dean, 32
MacIntyre, Duncan Ban, 32

MacIsaac, Angus, 27
MacKay, Robert (Rob Donn), 32
MacLeod, Duncan, 26
MacLeod, Kenneth, 24
MacMillan, Calum, 24, 26
MacMillan, James, 274; *The Death of Oscar*, 281–85
Macpherson, James (life): education, xv, 1–2; reputation, 7, 13, 22, 27, 33, 35, 37, 96, 104, 107, 111, 120, 232, 256, 259, 271, 276, 285, 293–97, 304
Macpherson, James (works): "Berrathon," 7, 58, 60 68, 108 147, 251, 302; "Calthon and Colmal," 7, 87, 100, 110, 124–28; "Caros, The War of," 10; "Carric-Thura," 7; "Cath-Loda," 106, 108; "Colma," 5, 7, 11–12, 19, 38–39, 58, 129–45, 124–28; "Comala," 7, 10, 159, 223–24, 230; "Croma," 275; "Dar-thula," 5, 7, 83, 110, 194; *Fingal*, 41, 44, 58, 95, 100–101, 104, 186, 263–64; *Fragments of Ancient Poetry*, 38, 123, 260; "Oina-Morul," 15, 18; "Oithóna," 33–34; "The Songs of Selma," 108, 291; *Temora*, 2, 17, 110, 264, 268, 285, 289, 293
Mahler, Gustav, 207, 301
Malling, Jørgen, 16, 230; *Kyvala*, 216, 223–30
Malling, Otto, 223
Malvina, 5, 7, 17, 30, 38, 40–41, 43, 58–9, 60, 62, 64–65, 67–70, 90, 151, 233, 236, 260, 296
manuscripts, 22, 35, 49, 73, 299
Mann, Thomas, 108
Mara, Madame (Gertrude Elisabeth), 47
Marengo, Battle of (1800), 33
Marchesi, Luigi, 48, 51, 55
Marschner, Wolfgang, 296
Martini, Padre, 73
Matthisson, Friedrich von, 111
Marx, Adolf Bernard, 107
Massenet, Jules, xix, 5, 15, 158, 169–70, 178, 239, 296, 302
Max Franz, Elector, 107

Mayr, Simon, 296
McDonald, Rev. Patrick, 20, 23, 28; *A Collection of Highland Vocal Airs* (1784), 20, 23, 28
McEwen, John Blackwood, 259, 265
McFlahertie, Jago, 28
Méhul, Étienne-Nicholas, 12, 123, 146, 148, 159; *Uthal*, 12, 30, 57–71, 148, 160, 294
melancholy, 4, 51, 70, 104, 111, 118, 121, 168, 223
melisma, 139, 148
Melartin, Erkki, 16, 195, 206, 210
Membrée, Edmond, 14
Mendelssohn, Arnold, 302
Mendelssohn, Fanny, 134
Mendelssohn-Bartholdy, Felix, xix, 5, 8, 13–14, 105, 111, 117–18; Overture, *The Hebrides* (*Fingal's Cave*), 113–19
Mengelberg, Willem, 249–51
Merck, Johann Heinrich, 110
Mertz, Johann Kaspar, 17
Messaien, Olivier, 285, 289, 291
Metastasio (Pietro Armando Dominico Trapassi), 82
Meyer, Charles, 40
Meyerbeer, Giacomo, 134
Mickiewicz, Adam, 298
Milan, 86, 90–91, 239, 297
Milligen, Simon van, 205; *Darthula* (op), 15, 207, 209
Minona, 38–39 123, 131 133, 267–68
modal, modality, 13, 26, 120, 230, 260, 263, 267, 271, 276, 282
mode ossianique, 12, 302
modernism, 274–75, 291–92
Moidart, 27
Moina, 16, 97–98, 100
monodrama, 5, 11–12, 124–28
Monticini, Antonio, 90
Morandi, Pietro, 73; *Comala* (op), 12–13, 294
Moreau, Henry, 178, 182, 186
Morison, Roderick, 28
Morna, 33, 74–77
Morval, 72–75, 77–79, 81

Morven, 45, 52, 58, 60, 62, 74–76, 96, 159, 164, 181, 184, 187, 189, 218, 221–22, 224, 236
Moscheles, Ignaz, 117
Mozart, Leopold, 197
Mozart, Wolfgang Amadeus, 7, 10–11, 31, 35, 38, 69, 178, 187, 299
Mull, Isle of, 26
Munich, 223
Murphy, Gerard, 22. *See also Duanaire Finn*
Murphy, John, 40

Nägeli, Hans-Georg, 195–97
Napier, William, 36, 45, 47, 49–50, 56
Naples, 35, 73, 82, 90, 92–93, 95
Napoleon Bonaparte, 11–12, 7, 9, 12–13, 57, 73, 79, 82–83, 93, 95, 100–101, 103, 106, 141, 178, 206–8, 302
Napoleon III, 182
Nardini, Pietro, 197
nationalism, 15, 275
Nathos, 83, 194, 196–99, 207, 214
nature, xvi, 4, 9, 33, 62, 73; character, xvi, 8, 32, 50
Neefe, Christian Gottlob, 11, 104, 108
Nerval, Gérard de, 299
Netherlands, The, 159, 186, 251. *See also* Amsterdam; Hague, The
Neumann, Friedrich, 135, 206, 212–13; "Darthulas Grabgesang," 212
New Orleans, 15
New York, 260
Newman, Ernest, 258
Nicholl, Joseph Weston, 16–17
Nibelungenlied, 300
nocturne, xvi, 275, 280, 298
Nucci, Giuseppe, 41, 44

Ó Beirn, Pádraig, 28
Ó Catháin, Echlin, 27–28
Ó highne, Micheál, 27
Ó highne, Seámas, 26
O'Brien, John (Bishop), 35
O'Carolan, Turlough, 29, 251
O'Catháin, Ruari Dall, 28

O'Conor, Charles, of Belanagare, 25
O'Farrell, Patrick, 40
Offenbach, Jacques, 238
Oisín, xiii, 24, 27
"Oithóna," 35, 38, 91, 109, 235, 258
Oithóna (Bainton), 297
Oithóna (Barthelemon), 33–35, 41, 45
O'Neill, Arthur, 28
O'Neill, Owen Roe, 251–53, 256
opera: Britain, 10–11, 16, 37–38, 45–56, 257, 259, 276; France, 7, 12, 15, 30, 35, 57–71, 147, 159, 170, 178; Germany, 7, 14–15, 38–39, 171, 187; Italy, 8, 12–13, 15, 41–44, 71–86; Russia, 97–98, 101, 230; other (Brazil; Denmark; Hungary; Mexico; The Netherlands; United States), 15, 205–7, 209, 223, 238, 259–60, 263
oral tradition, 2, 13, 16, 19–20, 22, 26, 33, 83, 258–59. *See also* ethnology, ethnomusicology
orchestration, 12–13, 57, 60, 69, 92, 97–98, 113, 119–20, 124, 159, 169, 193, 210, 258
ornamentation, 73, 81; (artwork), 30. *See also* coloratura; melisma
Orkney Islands, 43, 45, 74, 80, 91
Orpheus, Orphic, 9, 35, 232
Oscar, 5, 40–41, 43, 58, 107, 236, 251, 274, 281, 284, 293, 300
Oscar, The Death of (MacMillan), 221–25
"Ossian" (group), 303
Ossianism, 15–16
Oswald, James, 18–19; "The Maid of Selma," 21
Otto-Peters, Louise, 14
Ozerov, Vladislav, 12, 95–101
overture, xiv, xix, 8, 13, 40–41, 50, 61–62, 68–70, 73, 77, 97. *See also* prelude

Pachierotti, Gaspare, 48, 51
Pacini, Giovanni, 13
Padua, 77, 296
Palermo, 15, 93
Palmgren, Selim, 16, 206, 210, 214; "Darthulas Gravsång," 212, 294

Paris, 1, 9–10, 12, 14–15, 23, 30, 35, 69–70, 74, 82, 95, 100, 146–47, 159, 178, 182–83, 186, 205, 223, 239, 259, 289, 296, 298
pastoral, 146
Patrick, St., 284
Pavesi, Stefano, 90–91, 294, 299; *Ardano e Dartula* (op), 82–86; *Fingallo e Comala* (op), 74–82
Paxton, Stephen, 297
periodicity, 9, 215
Perth, Perthshire, 18, 28
Petrie, George, 251
Philadelphia, 11
Piacenza, 74, 77, 82
Piccinni, Nicolò, 73
Pitois, Christian, 178, 239
Pizzetti, Ildebrando, 259
plagiarism, 37, 195. *See also* fraud; forgery
"Planxty" (group), 303
Pleyel, Camille, 123
Pleyel, Ignaz, 37, 47
Pola, Paolo, 83
Poland, Polish, 3, 12, 15, 298
Polidori, William August, 296
Pope, Rev. Alexander, 25
Portugal, Portuguese, xviii, 95, 239. *See also* Lisbon
Poschiavo (Switzerland), 297
Potemkin, Grigory, Prince, 95
prelude, 223–24, 258, 300. *See also* overture
pre-Romantic (proto-Romantic), xv, 10, 195
Pressburg, Peace of (1805), 82
Prix de Rome, 14, 146, 155, 216–17, 222
Prometheus, 106–8
Provo (Utah), 263
psalms, psalm-singing, 285
Pucitta, Vincenzo, 296
Pugnani, Gaetano, 301
Purcell, Henry, 48
Pushkin, Aleksandr Sergeyevich, xiii, 96–97

"Queen Mary" harp, 28
Queen's Hall, London, 258
Quincy, Thomas de, 299

Radoux, Jean-Théodore, 216
Raimondi, Pietro, 92–93
Rameau, Jean-Philippe, 146
Rasse, François, 216–17, 222
Ratmor, 90
Ravel, Maurice, 17, 158
Ravnkilde, Niels, 232
Reeve, William, 40; *Oscar and Malvina* (ballet-pantomime), 40–42
Reger, Max, 210
Reggio Emilia, 75–77
Reichardt, Johann Friedrich, 11, 13, 129, 139, 143, 145, 294, 301; "Kolma's Klage," 140–42, 144
Reinecke, Carl, 14, 147, 187, 250
Reinthaler, Carl Martin, 204
Rhode, Johann Gottlieb, 299
Richter, Jean-Paul, 111
Riddell, Robert, 18–20
Rimsky-Korsakov, Nikolai, 342
Ritter, Heinrich Ludwig, 296
Robertson family of Lude (Perthshire), 28
Rochlitz, Johann Friedrich, 104–5
Rodoteato, Dionisio, 15
Romagnoli, Ettore, 12
Roman, 298
Romani, Carlo, 12
Romani, Felice, 298
Romani, Pietro, 90
Rome, 8, 29, 50, 90, 203, 232, 259
Rossi, Aldo, 72
Rossini, Gioachino, 41–44, 95, 297; *La donna del lago* (op), 85, 93, 298
Rousseau, Jean-Jacques, 33, 35, 103, 124, 140, 146
Rüdesheim, 171
Runeberg, Johan Ludvig, 208, 210
Runge, Philipp Otto, 300–301
Russia, Russian, 17, 57, 95–98, 100–101, 203, 230. *See also* St. Petersburg

Rust, Friedrich Wilhelm, 129, 133, 135, 145, 301; *Colma: Ein Monodrama mit Prolog nach Ossian*, 124–28, 135, 294
Ryno, 123, 231, 260, 288

Saccenti, Carlo, 186
Sacchini, Antonio, 35
Sainbris, A. Guillot de, 178, 182
Saint-Saëns, Camille, 5, 178, 302
Saint-Victor, Jacques Maximilien Benjamin Bins de, 58, 60, 68
Salieri, Antonio, 85
Salt Lake City, 232
Samoilova, S. V., 57
Sampieri, Francesco, 42–43; *Oscar e Malvina* (op), 41, 44
San Carlo, Naples, 238–39
São Paulo, 238–39
Sarti, Giuseppe, 96
Scandinavia, 4, 35–36
Schering, Arnold, 107, 109
Schiller, Friedrich, 3, 102–4, 106, 109–12, 172, 197–98
Schira, Vincenzo, 90
Schoenberg, Arnold, 2, 5, 16, 110, 194–95, 205, 209–10, 274–75, 285; *Darthulas Grabgesang*, 207–8
Schubart, Christian Friedrich Daniel, 122, 141, 143, 298
Schubert, Franz, 143, 145, 168, 214, 253, 293, 297–99; "Kolma's Klage," 143–45; "Ossians Lied nach dem Falle Nathos," 198–99
Schumann, Clara, 203, 232
Schumann, Robert, 102, 111, 120–21, 147, 191, 201, 235, 239, 244–50, 263, 294, 297–98
Scotland, Scottish, xv, 17–19, 22–23, 25, 27–30, 32, 38, 40–41, 46, 50, 95–97, 103, 111, 117–18, 121–22, 152, 159, 179, 224, 230, 232, 251, 259, 275, 296, 298, 302–3. *See also* Argyll; Culloden; Edinburgh; Eigg; Glasgow; Halkirk; Lochaber; Moidart; Morven; Mull; Orkney Islands; Skye; South Uist; Staffa; Tiree

Scott, Sir Walter, 31, 41, 298
Scriabin, Aleksandr, 274
Seckendorff, Karl Siegmund von, 195–96, 200, 205
Selma (Seláma), 39, 60, 62, 69, 74, 104, 165, 172, 174, 251
Semenova, Ekaterina, 97
sensibility, xvi, 3, 103, 177, 193, 215
sentiment, 34, 46, 78–79, 100, 110, 135, 140, 186, 274
sentimental, 26, 112, 213
Seringapatam, 46, 49
Servières, Georges, 168
Seymour, John Laurence, 17; "Shilric's Song" (*Six Ossianic Odes*), 260–63
Shakespeare, William, 112
Shakhovskoi, Aleksandr Alexandrovich, 101, 203
Sheridan, Richard Brinsley, 56
Shield, William, 10, 40–41
Sibelius, Jean, 210, 263, 265, 275, 283, 285, 301–2
Siboni, Giuseppe, 90
Silcher, Friedrich, 102, 105
Simpson Auditorium, Los Angeles, 232
Simrock, Karl, 300
Sinclair, Donald, 26
Sinclair, Sir John, 23
Skye, Isle of, 26–27
Smetana, Bedrich, 299, 301
Smith, Charlotte, 297
Smith, Rev. John, 295
Smith, Thomas, 29
Sobolewski, (Johann Friedrich) Eduard, 15
Sografi, Antonio Simon, 296
Solito, Gaetano, 239
sonata, 103, 118–20, 158, 250, 273, 276
South Uist, Isle of, 26
Soviet Revolution, 17, 275
Sørensen, Severin, 224
Spohr, Ludwig, 93
St. Patrick, 27, 284
St. Petersburg, 87, 95–97, 101
Staël, Anne Louise Germaine de, 3, 29
Staffa, 113

Stanford, Charles Villiers, 256, 265, 294; *Irish Rhapsody no. 2: Lament for the Son of Ossian*, 249–57
Starno, 5, 93, 95–96, 101, 186–87, 190
Stevens, R. J. S., 197
Stewart, Col John, 47, 49
Stirling, Jane, 298
Stivell, Alan, 303
Stoddart, Alexander, 281
Stollberg, Friedrich Leopold, Graf zu, 300
Storck, Adam, 296
Strauss, Richard, 250, 275
Stravinsky, Igor, 274, 285
Sturm und Drang, 109
Stuttgart, 110
suite, 17, 276, 302
Sulmalla, 11
Sulzer, Johann Georg, 110, 298
Sunset Festival, Utah, 232
Sweden, Swedish, 4, 16, 95, 210–11
Swedenborg, Emanuel, 383
Switzerland, 3, 28, 171, 197, 238. See also Fribourg; Geneva; Poschiavo; Zürich
symphony, symphonic, 8, 15, 34, 36, 69, 102–3, 105–7, 109–11, 121–22, 233, 249–50, 258–59, 263, 267, 276, 301, 303
synesthesia, 117–18
Szymanowski, Karol, 291

Talazac, M., 159
Tartini, Giuseppe, 197
Taubert, Wilhelm, 199–200
Tchaikovsky, Pyotr Ilich, 95, 301
Temora, xii, 2, 17, 110, 264, 266, 268, 285, 289, 293
Temple Auditorium, Los Angeles, 232
Teodoreth, Anne Marie, 238
Thomson, George, 103
Thoreau, Henry David, 259
Thorpe Davie, Cedric, 257, 294; *Dirge for Cuchullin*, 263–73
Tiree, Isle of, 26
Tolmie, Frances, 21–22, 27

tonal, tonality, 7, 50, 53, 55, 57, 60, 62, 65, 67, 69, 85, 98, 109, 113, 118–21, 126–28, 133, 135, 137, 140, 145, 150, 154, 160, 172, 174, 182, 184, 187, 195, 200, 207, 209–10, 214, 222, 225, 229, 233, 235, 246, 248, 254, 256, 259, 263, 268, 271, 275, 277–78, 282, 284–85, 291, 301–2
topic, 3, 7, 14–15, 58, 104, 230, 258, 265, 298, 300
topic (musical), 295
Tovey, Donald Francis, 21, 57, 118
tragedy, 12, 15–16, 34, 95, 97–98, 101, 186, 298
transmediation, xiv, 7–8, 43, 55, 58, 68, 85, 8, 109, 117, 158, 186, 193, 215, 222, 224, 243, 249, 256, 271, 280, 291, 293, 295, 304
Trenmor, 16, 159, 161–62
Trieste, 77
Turin, 41, 82, 90, 296

Uhland, Ludwig, 120, 297
Ullin, 58, 60, 62, 65, 67–68, 97, 99, 101, 104, 123, 187, 189–90, 293
Ulster, 83, 250
Umlauft, Paul, 14, 171; *Agandecca*, 44, 186–93
United Irishmen, 28
United States of America, 15, 40, 210, 232, 259. *See also* Los Angeles; Milwaukee; New Orleans; New York; Philadelphia; St Louis; Salt Lake City
Urbani, Pietro, 297

Väinämöinen, 301
variation, 23, 27, 29, 75, 107–8, 217, 230, 289
Vaughan Williams, Ralph, 250, 263–65, 267, 271, 275
Venice, Venetian, 13, 41, 37–39, 72–75, 82–83, 87, 90, 101, 195–96
Verdi, Giuseppe, 13, 95, 232
Vestris, Armando, 12
Victoria, Queen, 26

Vienna, Viennese, 3, 9, 12–13, 15, 38, 73–74, 77, 85, 103–4, 129, 143, 172, 178, 223, 296
Villa Lante (Rome), 203
Völsunga Saga, 300

Waddington, Sidney Peirce, 265
Wagner, Richard, 14–15, 164, 170, 189, 191, 193, 205, 207, 257
Wainewright, Harriet (Mrs. Col. Stewart), 305; *Comàla* (op), 49–56, 232, 294
Wainwright, Robert, 47
Wales, 29
Walker, Joseph, 23
Waterloo, 7, 12–13, 147, 199
Weber, Bernhard Anselm, 11
Weber, Carl Maria von, 11, 15, 296
Weber, Max Maria von, 106
Weimar, 15, 111, 300
Weippert, John Erhardt, 40
Wellesley, Richard Colley, Marquis of, 45–46, 56, 305
Wetzler, Hermann Hans, 204
Whitman, Walt, 2, 259
Whyte, Ian, 259, 265
Wilkes, John, 10
Winter, Peter (von), 11, 294
Wohlbrück, Wilhelm August, 296
women (female) warriors, 33, 109
Wonne der Wehmut, 121, 164. *See also joy of grief*
Woodward, Richard, 47
Worgan, John, 48, 55

Yermolov, Aleksey Petrovich, 96

Zelter, Carl Friedrich, 15, 102–3, 117, 129; *Kolma: ein altschottische Lied*, 134–39
Zhukovsky Vasili, 96
Zucchinetti, Giovanni Domenico, 73
Zumsteeg, Johann Rudolf, 13, 110; *Colma: ein Gesang Ossians, von Goethe*, 129–34
Zürich, 223